THE

WHOLE WORKS

OF

JOSEPH BUTLER, LL.D.

LATE LORD BISHOP OF DURHAM.

NEW EDITION,

COMPLETE IN ONE VOLUME.

LONDON:

1 INTED FOR THOMAS TEGG, No. 73, CHEAPSIDE;

R. GRIFFIN AND CO., GLASGOW;

AND TEGG AND CO., DUBLIN.

MDCCCXXXIX.

Printing Statement:

Due to the very old age and scarcity of this book, many of the pages may be hard to read due to the blurring of the original text, possible missing pages, missing text, dark backgrounds and other issues beyond our control.

Because this is such an important and rare work, we believe it is best to reproduce this book regardless of its original condition.

Thank you for your understanding.

CONTENTS.

PART II.

OF REVEALED RELIGION.

TWO DISSERTATIONS.

ADVERTISEMENT.

———

I<small>F</small> the reader should meet here with anything which he had not before attended to, it will not be in the observations upon the constitution and course of nature, these being all obvious; but in the application of them: in which, though there is nothing but what appears to me of some real weight, and therefore of great importance; yet he will observe several things which will appear to him of very little, if he can think things to be of little importance, which are of any real weight at all, upon such a subject as religion. However, the proper force of the following Treatise lies in the whole general analogy considered together.

It is come, I know not how, to be taken for granted by many persons, that Christianity is not so much as a subject of inquiry; but that it is now, at length, discovered to be fictitious. And accordingly they treat it as if, in the present age, this were an agreed point among all people of discernment; and nothing remained but to set it up as a principal subject of mirth and ridicule, as it were by way of reprisals, for its having so long interrupted the pleasures of the world. On the contrary, thus much, at least, will be here found, not taken for granted, but proved, that any reasonable man, who will thoroughly consider the matter, may be as much assured as he is of his own being, that it is not, however, so clear a case, that there is nothing in it.] There is, I think, strong evidence of its truth; but it is certain no one can, upon principles of reason, be satisfied of the contrary. And the practical consequence to be drawn from this is not attended to by every one who is concerned in it.

May, 1736.

PREFACE

BY

SAMUEL HALIFAX, D.D.

LORD BISHOP OF GLOUCESTER.

THE religious system of Bishop BUTLER is chiefly to be collected from the following Treatise, entitled, " The Analogy of Religion, Natural and Revealed, to the Constitution and Course of Nature."

" All things are double one against another, and God hath made nothing imperfect;" Eccl'us. xlii. 24. On this single observation of the Son of Sirach, the whole fabric of our Prelate's defence of religion, in his " Analogy," is raised. Instead of indulging to idle speculations, how the world might possibly have been better than it is; or, forgetful of the difference between hypothesis and fact, attempting to explain the divine economy with respect to intelligent creatures from preconceived notions of his own, he first inquires, what the constitution of nature, as made known to us in the way of experiment, actually is? and from this, now seen and acknowledged, he endeavours to form a judgment of that larger constitution which religion discovers to us. If the dispensation of Providence we are now under, considered as inhabitants of this world, and having a temporal interest to secure in it, be found, on examination, to be analogous to, and of a piece with, that further dispensation which relates to us as designed for another world, in which we have an eternal interest, depending on our behaviour here; if both may be traced up to the same general laws, and appear to be carried on according to the same plan of administration; the fair presumption is, that both proceed from one and the same Author. And if the principal parts objected to in this latter dispensation be similar to, and of the same kind with, what we certainly experience under the former; the objections, being clearly inconclusive in one case, because contradicted by plain fact, must, in all reason, be allowed to be inconclusive also in the other.

This way of arguing from what is acknowledged to what is disputed, from things known to other things that resemble them, from that part of the divine establishment which is exposed to our view to that more important one which lies beyond it, is on all hands confessed to be just. By this method, Sir Isaac Newton has unfolded the system of nature; by the same method Bishop Butler has explained the system of grace; and thus, to use the words of a writer whom I quote with pleasure, " has formed and concluded a happy alliance between faith and philosophy."*

And although the argument from analogy be allowed to be imperfect, and by no means sufficient to solve all difficulties respecting the government of God, and the designs of his providence with regard to mankind, (a degree of knowledge which we are not furnished with faculties for attaining, at least in the present state;) yet surely it is of importance to learn from it, that the natural and moral world are intimately connected, and parts of one stupendous whole or system; and that the chief objections which are brought against religion, may be urged with equal force against the constitution and course of nature, where they are certainly false in fact. And this information we may derive from the work before us; the proper design of which, it may be of use to observe, is not to prove the truth of religion, either natural or revealed, but to confirm that proof, already known, by considerations from analogy.

Mr. Mainwaring's Dissertation, prefixed to his volume of Sermons.

After this account of the method of reasoning employed by our author, let us now advert to his manner of applying it; first, to the subject of natural religion; and, secondly, to that of revealed.

I. The foundation of all our hopes and fears is a future life; and with this the Treatise begins. Neither the reason of the thing, nor the analogy of nature, according to Bishop Butler, give ground for imagining, that the unknown event, death, will be our destruction. The states in which we have formerly existed, in the womb and in infancy, are not more different from each other than from that of mature age in which we now exist: therefore, that we shall continue to exist hereafter, in a state as different from the present as the present is from those through which we have passed already, is a presumption favoured by the analogy of nature. All that we know from reason, concerning death, is the effects it has upon animal bodies: and the frequent instances among men, of the intellectual powers continuing in high health and vigour, at the very time when a mortal disease is on the point of putting an end to all the powers of sensation, induce us to hope that it may have no effect at all on the human soul, not even so much as to suspend the exercise of its faculties; though, if it have, the suspension of a power by no means implies its extinction, as sleep or a swoon may convince us.*

The probability of a future state once granted, an important question arises, How best to secure our interest in that state? We find, from what passes daily before us, that the constitution of nature admits of misery as well as happiness; that both of these are the consequences of our own actions; and these consequences we are enabled to foresee: therefore, that our happiness or misery in a future world may depend on our own actions also, and that rewards or punishments hereafter may follow our

* Part i. chap. 1.

a 3

good or ill behaviour here, is but an appointment of the same sort with what we experience under the divine government, according to the regular course of nature.*

This supposition is confirmed from another circumstance, that the natural government of God, under which we now live, is also moral; in which rewards and punishments are the consequences of actions, considered as virtuous and vicious. Not that every man is rewarded or punished here in exact proportion to his desert; for the essential tendencies of virtue and vice, to produce happiness and the contrary, are often hindered from taking effect from accidental causes. However, there are plainly the rudiments and beginnings of a righteous administration to be discerned in the constitution of nature; from whence we are led to expect, that these accidental hinderances will one day be removed, and the rule of distributive justice obtain completely in a more perfect state.†

The moral government of God, thus established, implies in the notion of it some sort of trial, or a moral possibility of acting wrong as well as right, in those who are the subjects of it. And the doctrine of religion, that the present life is in fact a state of probation for a future one, is rendered credible, from its being analogous throughout to the general conduct of Providence towards us with respect to this world; in which prudence is necessary to secure our temporal interest, just as we are taught that virtue is necessary to secure our eternal interest; and both are trusted to ourselves.‡

But the present life is not merely a state of probation, implying in it difficulties and danger; it is also a state of discipline and improvement; and that both in our temporal and religious capacity. Thus childhood is a state of discipline for youth; youth for manhood; and that for old age. Strength of body and maturity of understanding are acquired by degrees; and neither of them without con-

* Chap. 2.   † Chap. 3.   ‡ Chap. 4.

tinual exercise and attention on our part, not only in the beginning of life, but through the whole course of it. So, again, with respect to our religious concerns, the present world is fitted to be, and to good men is, in event, a state of discipline and improvement for a future one. The several passions and propensions implanted in our hearts, incline us, in a multitude of instances, to forbidden pleasures: this inward infirmity is increased by various snares and temptations, perpetually occurring from without: hence arises the necessity of recollection and self-government, of withstanding the calls of appetite, and forming our minds to habits of piety and virtue; habits, of which we are capable, and which to creatures in a state of moral imperfection, and fallen from their original integrity, must be of the greatest use, as an additional security, over and above the principle of conscience, from the dangers to which we are exposed.*

Nor is the credibility here given, by the analogy of nature, to the general doctrine of religion, destroyed or weakened by any notions concerning necessity. Of itself it is a mere word, the sign of an abstract idea; and as much requires an agent, that is, a necessary agent, in order to effect anything, as freedom requires a free agent. Admitting it to be speculatively true, if considered as influencing practice, it is the same as false: for it is matter of experience, that, with regard to our present interest, and as inhabitants of this world, we are treated as if we were free; and therefore the analogy of nature leads us to conclude, that, with regard to our future interest, and as designed for another world, we shall be treated as free also. Nor does the opinion of necessity, supposing it possible, at all affect either the general proof of religion, or its external evidence.†

Still objections may be made against the wisdom and goodness of the divine government, to which analogy,

* Part i. chap. 5.   † Chap. 6.

which can only show the truth or credibility of facts,
affords no answer. Yet even here analogy is of use, if it
suggest that the divine government is a scheme or system,
and not a number of unconnected acts, and that this
system is also above our comprehension. Now the government of the natural world appears to be a system of this
kind; with parts related to each other, and together com-
posing a whole; in which system ends are brought about
by the use of means, many of which means, before experience, would have been suspected to have had a quite
contrary tendency; which is carried on by general laws,
similar causes uniformly producing similar effects: the
utility of which general laws, and the inconveniences which
would probably arise from the occasional or even secret
suspension of them, we are in some sort enabled to discern;* but of the whole we are incompetent judges, because of the small part which comes within our view.
Reasoning, then, from what we know, it is highly credible
that the government of the moral world is a system also,
carried on by general laws, and in which ends are accomplished by the intervention of means; and that both constitutions, the natural and the moral, are so connected, as to
form together but one scheme: but of this scheme, as of
that of the natural world taken alone, we are not qualified
to judge, on account of the mutual respect of the several
parts to each other, and to the whole, and our own incapacity to survey the whole, or, with accuracy, any single
part. All objections, therefore, to the wisdom and goodness of the divine government may be founded merely on
our ignorance; and to such objections our ignorance is the
proper, and a satisfactory answer.†

II. The chief difficulties concerning natural religion being
now removed, our author proceeds, in the next place, to

---

* See a Treatise on *Divine Benevolence,* by Dr. Thomas Balguy,
Part ii.

† Part i. chap. 7.

that which is revealed; and, as an introduction to an inquiry into the credibility of Christianity, begins with the
consideration of its importance.

The importance of Christianity appears in two respects.
First, in its being a republication of natural religion, in its
native simplicity, with authority, and with circumstances
of advantage; ascertaining, in many instances of moment,
what before was only probable, and particularly confirming
the doctrine of a future state of rewards and punishments.
Secondly, as revealing a new dispensation of Providence,
originating from the pure love and mercy of God, and
conducted by the mediation of his Son, and the guidance
of his Spirit, for the recovery and salvation of mankind,
represented in a state of apostacy and ruin.   This account
of Christianity being admitted to be just, and the distinct
offices of these three divine Persons being once discovered
to us, we are as much obliged, in point of duty, to acknowledge the relations we stand in to the Son and Holy Ghost,
as our mediator and sanctifier, as we are obliged in point
of duty to acknowledge the relations we stand in to God
the Father; although the two former of these relations be
learnt from revelation only, and in the last we are instructed
by the light of nature; the obligation in either case arising
from the offices themselves, and not at all depending on the
manner in which they are made known to us.*

The presumptions against revelation in general are, that
it is not discoverable by reason, that it is unlike to what is
so discovered, and that it was introduced and supported by
miracles.   But in a scheme so large as that of the universe,
unbounded in extent and everlasting in duration, there
must of necessity be numberless circumstances which are
beyond the reach of our faculties to discern, and which
can only be known by divine illumination.   And both in
the natural and moral government of the world, under
which we live, we find many things unlike one to another,

* Part ii. chap. 1.

and therefore ought not to wonder if the same unlikeness
obtain between things visible and invisible; although it
be far from true, that revealed religion is entirely unlike
the constitution of nature, as analogy may teach us.   Nor
is there anything incredible in revelation, considered as
miraculous; whether miracles be supposed to have been
performed at the beginning of the world, or after a course
of nature has been established.   Not *at the beginning of
the world;* for then there was either no course of nature
at all, or a power must have been exerted totally different
from what that course is at present.   All men and animals
cannot have been born as they are now; but a pair of each
sort must have been produced at first, in a way altogether
unlike to that in which they have been since produced;
unless we affirm, that men and animals have existed from
eternity in an endless succession.   One miracle, therefore,
at least there must have been, at the beginning of the
world, or the time of man's creation.   Not *after the
settlement of a course of nature,* on account of miracles
being contrary to that course, or, in other words, contrary
to experience; for in order to know whether miracles,
worked in attestation of a divine religion, be contrary to
experience or not, we ought to be acquainted with other
cases, similar or parallel to those in which miracles are
alleged to have been wrought.   But where shall we find
such similar or parallel cases?   The world which we inhabit
affords none: we know of no extraordinary revelations
from God to man, but those recorded in the Old and New
Testament; all of which were established by miracles.   It
cannot therefore be said that miracles are incredible, because contrary to experience, when all the experience we
have is in favour of miracles, and on the side of religion.
Besides, in reasoning concerning miracles, they ought not
to be compared with common natural events, but with
uncommon appearances, such as comets, magnetism, electricity; which, to one acquainted only with the usual pheno-

mena of nature, and the common powers of matter, must, before proof of their actual existence, be thought incredible.*

The presumptions against revelation in general being
despatched, objections against the Christian revelation, in
particular against the scheme of it, as distinguished from
objections against its evidence, are considered next.   Now,
supposing a revelation to be really given, it is highly probable
beforehand, that it must contain many things appearing to
us liable to objections.   The acknowledged dispensation of
nature is very different from what we should have expected:
reasoning then from analogy, the revealed dispensation, it is
credible, would be also different.   Nor are we in any sort
judges, at what time, or in what degree or manner, it is fit
or expedient for God to instruct us, in things confessedly of
the greatest use, either by natural reason or by supernatural
information.   Thus arguing on speculation only, and without
experience, it would seem very unlikely that so important a
remedy as that provided by Christianity for the recovery of
mankind from a state of ruin, should have been for so many
ages withheld; and, when at last vouchsafed, should be
imparted to so few; and after it has been imparted, should
be attended with obscurity and doubt.   And just so we might
have argued, before experience, concerning the remedies
provided in nature for bodily diseases, to which by nature
we are exposed: for many of these were unknown to mankind for a number of ages; are known but to few now; some
important ones probably not discovered yet; and those
which are, neither certain in their application, nor universal
in their use.   And the same mode of reasoning that would
lead us to expect they should have been so, would lead us
to expect that the necessity of them should have been superseded, by there being no diseases; as the necessity of the
Christian scheme, it may be thought, might also have been
superseded, by preventing the fall of man, so that he should
not have stood in need of a redeemer at all.†

* Chap. 2.   † Chap. 3.

As to objections against the wisdom and goodness of Christianity, the same answer may be applied to them as was to the like objections against the constitution of nature. For here also Christianity is a scheme, or economy, composed of various parts, forming a whole; in which scheme means are used for the accomplishing of ends; and which is conducted by general laws: of all of which we know as little as we do of the constitution of nature. And the seeming want of wisdom or goodness in this system, is to be ascribed to the same cause as the like appearances of defects in the natural system—our inability to discern the whole scheme, and our ignorance of the relation of those parts which are discernible to others beyond our view.

The objections against Christianity, as a matter of fact, and against the wisdom and goodness of it, having been obviated together, the chief of them are now to be considered distinctly. One of these, which is levelled against the entire system itself, is of this sort: the restoration of mankind, represented in Scripture as the great design of the gospel, is described as requiring a long series of means, and persons, and dispensations, before it can be brought to its completion; whereas, the whole ought to have been effected at once. Now, everything we see in the course of nature shows the folly of this objection: for, in the natural course of Providence, ends are brought about by means, not operating immediately and at once, but deliberately and in a way of progression; one thing being subservient to another, this to somewhat farther. The change of seasons, the ripening of fruits, the growth of vegetable and animal bodies, are instances of this. And, therefore, that the same progressive method should be followed in the dispensation of Christianity, as is observed in the common dispensation of Providence, is a reasonable expectation, justified by the analogy of nature.*

Another circumstance objected to in the Christian scheme,

* Chap. 4.

is the appointment of a mediator, and the saving of the world through him. But the visible government of God being actually administered in this way, or by the mediation and instrumentality of others, there can be no general presumption against an appointment of this kind, against his invisible government being exercised in the same manner. We have seen already, that with regard to ourselves, this visible government is carried on by rewards and punishments: for happiness and misery are the consequences of our own actions, considered as virtuous and vicious; and these consequences we are enabled to foresee. It might have been imagined, before consulting experience, that after we had rendered ourselves liable to misery by our own ill conduct, sorrow for what was past, and behaving well for the future, would alone and of themselves, have exempted us from deserved punishment, and restored us to the divine favour. But the fact is otherwise; and real reformation is often found to be of no avail, so as to secure the criminal from poverty, sickness, infamy, and death, the never-failing attendants on vice and extravagance, exceeding a certain degree. By the course of nature, then, it appears, God does not always pardon a sinner on his repentance. Yet there is provision made, even in nature, that the miseries which men bring on themselves by unlawful indulgences may, in many cases, be mitigated, and in some removed; partly by extraordinary exertions of the offender himself, but more especially and frequently by the intervention of others, who voluntarily, and from motives of compassion, submit to labour and sorrow, such as produce long and lasting inconveniences to themselves, as the means of rescuing another from the wretched effects of former imprudences. Vicarious punishment, therefore, or one person's sufferings contributing to the relief of another, is a providential disposition in the economy of nature: and it ought not to be matter of surprise, if by a method analogous to this we be redeemed from sin and misery, in the economy of grace. That mankind at present are in a state of degradation, different from that in which they were originally created, is the very ground of the Christian revelation as contained in the Scriptures. Whether we acquiesce in the account, that our being placed in such a state is owing to the crime of our first parents, or choose to ascribe it to any other cause, it makes no difference as to our condition; the vice and unhappiness of the world are still there, notwithstanding all our suppositions; nor is it Christianity that hath put us into this state. We learn also from the same Scriptures, what experience and the use of expiatory sacrifices from the most early times might have taught us, that repentance alone is not sufficient to prevent the fatal consequences of past transgressions; but that there is still room for mercy, and that repentance shall be available, though not of itself, yet through the mediation of a divine person, the Messiah; who from the sublimest principles of compassion, when we were " dead in trespasses and sins," Ephes. ii. 1, suffered and died, the innocent for the guilty, " the just for the unjust," 1 Pet. iii. 18, that we " might have redemption through his blood, even the forgiveness of sins," Col. i. 14. In what way the death of Christ was of that efficacy it is said to be, in procuring the reconciliation of sinners, the Scriptures have not explained: it is enough that the doctrine is revealed; that it is not contrary to any truths which reason and experience teach us; and that it accords in perfect harmony with the usual method of the divine conduct in the government of the world.*

Again, it hath been said, that if the Christian revelation were true, it must have been universal, and could not have been left upon doubtful evidence. But God, in his natural providence, dispenses his gifts in great variety, not only among creatures of the same species, but to the same individuals also at different times. Had the Christian revelation been universal at first, yet from the diversity of

* Chap. 5.

men's abilities, both of mind and body, their various means of improvement, and other external advantages, some persons must soon have been in a situation, with respect to religious knowledge, much superior to that of others, as much perhaps as they are at present: and all men will be equitably dealt with at last; and to whom little is given, of him little will be required. Then, as to the evidence of religion being left doubtful, difficulties of this sort, like difficulties in practice, afford scope and opportunity for a virtuous exercise of the understanding, and dispose the mind to acquiesce and rest satisfied with any evidence that is real. In the daily commerce of life men are obliged to act upon great uncertainties with regard to success in their temporal pursuits; and the case with regard to religion is parallel. However, though religion be not intuitively true, the proofs of it which we have are amply sufficient in reason to induce us to embrace it; and dissatisfaction with those proofs may possibly be men's own fault.*

Nothing remains but to attend to the positive evidence there is for the truth of Christianity. Now, besides its direct and fundamental proofs, which are miracles and prophecies, there are many collateral circumstances, which may be united into one view, and all together may be considered as making up one argument. In this way of treating the subject, the revelation, whether real or otherwise, may be supposed to be wholly historical: the general design of which appears to be, to give an account of the condition of religion, and its professors, with a concise narration of the political state of things, as far as religion is affected by it, during a great length of time, near six thousand years of which are already past. More particularly, it comprehends an account of God's entering into covenant with one nation, the Jews, that he would be their God, and that they should be his people; of his often interposing in their affairs; giving them the promise, and afterwards the possession,

* Chap. 6.

of a flourishing country; assuring them of the greatest
national prosperity, in case of their obedience, and threatening the severest national punishment, in case they forsook
him, and joined in the idolatry of their pagan neighbours.
It contains also a prediction of a particular person, to appear
in the fulness of time, in whom all the promises of God to
the Jews were to be fulfilled: and it relates, that at the time
expected, a person did actually appear, assuming to be the
Saviour foretold; that he worked various miracles among
them in confirmation of his divine authority; and, as was
foretold also, was rejected and put to death by the very
people who had long desired and waited for his coming:
but that his religion, in spite of all opposition, was established in the world by his disciples, invested with supernatural powers for that purpose; of the fate and fortunes
of which religion there is a prophetical description, carried
down to the end of time.   Let any one now, after reading
the above history, and not knowing whether the whole
were not a fiction, be supposed to ask, whether all that is
here related be true? and, instead of a direct answer, let
him be informed of the several acknowledged facts which
are found to correspond to it in real life, and then let him
compare the history and facts together, and observe the
astonishing coincidence of both; such a joint review must
appear to him of very great weight, and to amount to
evidence somewhat more than human.   And unless the
whole series, and every particular circumstance contained
in it can be thought to have arisen from accident, the truth
of Christianity is proved.*

* Chap. 7.   To the Analogy are subjoined two Dissertations, both
originally inserted in the body of the work.   One on *Personal Identity*, in which are contained some strictures on Mr. Locke, who asserts
that consciousness makes or constitutes personal identity; whereas, as
our author observes, consciousness makes only personality, or is necessary to the idea of a person, *i. e.* a thinking intelligent being, but
presupposes, and therefore cannot constitute, personal identity; just as
knowledge presupposes truth, but does not constitute it.   Consciousness of past actions does indeed show us the identity of ourselves, or

The view here given of the moral and religious systems of Bishop Butler, it will immediately be perceived, is chiefly intended for younger students, especially for students in divinity; to whom it is hoped it may be of use, so as to encourage them to peruse, with proper diligence, the original works of the author himself. For it may be necessary to observe, that neither of the volumes of this excellent Prelate are addressed to those who read for amusement, or curiosity, or to get rid of time. All subjects are not to be comprehended with the same ease; and morality and religion, when treated as sciences, each accompanied with difficulties of its own, can neither of them be understood as they ought, without a very peculiar attention. But morality and religion are not merely to be studied as sciences, or as being speculatively true; they are to be regarded in another and higher light, as the rule of life and manners, as containing authoritative directions by which to regulate our faith and practice. And in this view, the infinite importance of them considered, it can never be an indifferent matter whether they be received or rejected: for both claim to be the voice of God; and whether they be so or not, cannot be known till their claims be impartially examined. If they indeed come from him, we are bound to conform to them at our peril: nor is it left to our choice, whether we will submit to the obligations they impose upon us or not; for submit to them we must, in such a sense, as to incur the punishments denounced by both against wilful disobedience to their injunctions.

gives us a certain assurance that we are the same persons or living agents now, which we were at the time to which our remembrance can look back; but still we should be the same persons as we were, though this consciousness of what is past were wanting, though all that had been done by us formerly were forgotten; unless it be true that no person has existed a single moment beyond what he can remember. The other dissertation is *On the Nature of Virtue*, which properly belongs to the moral system of our author, already explained.

The following lines, by way of epitaph, were written soon after the Bishop's decease, and inserted in Webb's Collection of Epitaphs, vol. i. p. 97.

> BENEATH this marble BUTLER lies entomb'd;
> Who, with a soul inflamed by love divine,
> His life in presence of his God consumed,
> Like the bright lamps before the holy shrine.
> His aspect pleasing, mind with learning fraught;
> His eloquence was like a chain of gold,
> That the wild passions of mankind controll'd.
> Merit, wherever to be found he sought:
> Desire of transient riches he had none;
> These he with bounteous hand did well dispense,
> Bent to fulfil the ends of Providence,
> His heart still fix'd on an immortal crown.
> His heart a mirror was of purest kind,
> Where the bright image of his Maker shined;
> Reflecting faithful to the throne above
> The irradiant glories of the Mystic Dove.

N.B.—Bishop Butler was born at Wantage in Berkshire, A. D. 1692; died July 16, 1752, *ætatis* 60. On a flat marble stone, in Bristol Cathedral, where his remains were interred, is the following inscription:

H. S.
Reverendus admodum in Christo Pater
JOSEPHUS BUTLER, LL. D.
Hujusce primo Diœceseos
Deinde Dunelmensis Episcopus.
Qualis quantusq.; Vir erat
Sua libentissimè agnovit ætas:
Et si quid Præsuli aut Scriptori ad famam valent
Mens altissima,
Ingenii perspicacis et subacti Vis,
Animusq.; pius, simplex, candidus, liberalis,
Mortui haud facile evanescet memoria.
Obiit Bathoniæ 16 Kalend. Julii,
A. D. 1752.
Annos natus 60.

INTRODUCTION.

PROBABLE evidence is essentially distinguished from demonstrative by this, that it admits of degrees, and of all variety of them, from the highest moral certainty to the very lowest presumption. We cannot indeed say a thing is probably true upon one very slight presumption for it; because, as there may be probabilities on both sides of a question, there may be some against it: and though there be not, yet a slight presumption does not beget that degree of conviction, which is implied in saying a thing is probably true. But that the slightest possible presumption is of the nature of a probability, appears from hence, that such low presumption, often repeated, will amount even to moral certainty. Thus, a man's having observed the ebb and flow of the tide to-day, affords some sort of presumption, though the lowest imaginable, that it may happen again to-morrow; but the observation of this event for so many days, and months, and ages together, as it has been observed by mankind, gives us a full assurance that it will.

That which chiefly constitutes *probability* is expressed in the word *likely*, *i. e.* like some truth* or true event; like it, in itself, in its evidence, in some more or fewer of its circumstances. For when we determine a thing to be probably true, suppose that an event has or will come to pass, it is from the mind's remarking in it a likeness to some other event, which we have observed has come to pass. And this observation forms, in numberless daily instances,

---

* Verisimile.

a presumption, opinion, or full conviction, that such event has or will come to pass; according as the observation is, that the like event has sometimes, most commonly, or always, so far as our observation reaches, come to pass at like distances of time, or place, or upon like occasions. Hence arises the belief, that a child, if it lives twenty years, will grow up to the stature and strength of a man; that food will contribute to the preservation of its life, and the want of it for such a number of days be its certain destruction. So, likewise, the rule and measure of our hopes and fears concerning the success of our pursuits; our expectations that others will act so and so in such circumstances; and our judgment that such actions proceed from such principles;—all these rely upon our having observed the like to what we hope, fear, expect, judge; I say, upon our having observed the like, either with respect to others or ourselves. And thus, whereas the prince,* who had always lived in a warm climate, naturally concluded, in the way of analogy, that there was no such thing as water becoming hard, because he had always observed it to be fluid and yielding; we, on the contrary, from analogy, conclude, that there is no presumption at all against this; that it is supposable there may be frost in England any given day in January next; probable, that there will on some day of the month; and that there is a moral certainty, *i. e.* ground for an expectation, without any doubt of it, in some part or other of the winter.

Probable evidence, in its very nature, affords but an imperfect kind of information, and is to be considered as relative only to beings of limited capacities. For nothing which is the possible object of knowledge, whether past, present, or future, can be probable to an infinite Intelligence; since it cannot but be discerned absolutely as it is in itself, certainly true, or certainly false. But to us, probability is the very guide of life.

* The story is told by Mr. Locke, in the chapter of Probability.

From these things it follows, that in questions of difficulty, or such as are thought so, where more satisfactory
evidence cannot be had, or is not seen, if the result of
examination be, that there appears, upon the whole, any
the lowest presumption on one side, and none on the other,
or a greater presumption on one side, though in the lowest
degree greater, this determines the question, even in matters
of speculation; and in matters of practice will lay us under
an absolute and formal obligation, in point of prudence and
of interest, to act upon that presumption, or low probability,
though it be so low as to leave the mind in very great
doubt which is the truth. For surely a man is as really
bound in prudence to do what upon the whole appears,
according to the best of his judgment, to be for his happiness,
as what he certainly knows to be so. Nay, further, in
questions of great consequence, a reasonable man will think
it concerns him to remark lower probabilities and presumptions than these; such as amount to no more than showing
one side of a question to be as supposable and credible as
the other; nay, such as but amount to much less even than
this. For numberless instances might be mentioned, respecting the common pursuits of life, where a man would be
thought, in a literal sense, distracted, who would not act,
and with great application too, not only upon an even
chance, but upon much less, and where the probability or
chance was greatly against his succeeding.*

It is not my design to inquire further into the nature,
the foundation, and measure of probability; or whence it
proceeds, that *likeness* should beget that presumption,
opinion, and full conviction, which the human mind is
formed to receive from it, and which it does necessarily
produce in every one; or to guard against the errors to
which reasoning from analogy is liable. This belongs to
the subject of logic, and is a part of that subject which has

* See Chap. 6. Part ii.

not yet been thoroughly considered. Indeed, I shall not take upon me to say, how far the extent, compass, and force of analogical reasoning, can be reduced to general heads and rules, and the whole be formed into a system. But though so little in this way has been attempted by those who have treated of our intellectual powers, and the exercise of them, this does not hinder but that we may be, as we unquestionably are, assured, that analogy is of weight, in various degrees, towards determining our judgment, and our practice. Nor does it in any way cease to be of weight in those cases, because persons, either given to dispute, or who require things to be stated with greater exactness than our faculties appear to admit of in practical matters, may find other cases, in which it is not easy to say, whether it be, or be not, of any weight; or instances of seeming analogies, which are really of none. It is enough to the present purpose to observe, that this general way of arguing is evidently natural, just, and conclusive. For there is no man can make a question but that the sun will rise to-morrow, and be seen, where it is seen at all, in the figure of a circle, and not in that of a square.

Hence, namely, from analogical reasoning, Origen * has with singular sagacity observed, that " he who believes the Scripture to have proceeded from him who is the Author of nature, may well expect to find the same sort of difficulties in it as are found in the constitution of nature." And, in a like way of reflection, it may be added, that he who denies the Scripture to have been from God, upon account of these difficulties, may, for the very same reason, deny the world to have been formed by him. On the other hand, if there be an analogy, or likeness, between that system of things and dispensation of Providence which

---

* Χρη μεν τοι γε τον απαξ παραδεξαμενον του πτισαντος του κοσμον ειναι ταυτας τας γραφας πεπεισθαι, οτι οσα περι της κτισεως απαντα τοις ζητουσι τον περι αυτης λογον, ταυτα και περι των γραφων. Philocal. p. 23. ed. Cant.

revelation informs us of, and that system of things and dispensation of Providence which experience, together with reason, informs us of, *i. e.* the known course of nature; this is a presumption, that they have both the same author and cause; at least so far as to answer objections against the former's being from God, drawn from anything which is analogical or similar to what is in the latter, which is acknowledged to be from him; for an Author of nature is here supposed.

Forming our notions of the constitution and government of the world upon reasoning, without foundation for the principles which we assume, whether from the attributes of God or anything else, is building a world upon hypothesis, like Descartes. Forming our notions upon reasoning from principles which are certain, but applied to cases to which we have no ground to apply them, (like those who explain the structure of the human body, and the nature of diseases and medicines, from mere mathematics, without sufficient *data*,) is an error much akin to the former; since what is assumed, in order to make the reasoning applicable, is *hypothesis*. But it must be allowed just, to join abstract reasonings with the observation of facts, and argue from such facts as are known, to others that are like them; from that part of the divine government over intelligent creatures which comes under our view, to that larger and more general government over them which is beyond it; and, from what is present, to collect what is likely, credible, or not incredible, will be hereafter.

This method, then, of concluding and determining being practical, and what, if we will act at all, we cannot but act upon in the common pursuits of life; being evidently conclusive, in various degrees, proportionable to the degree and exactness of the whole analogy or likeness; and having so great authority for its introduction into the subject of religion, even revealed religion—my design is to apply it to that subject in general, both natural and revealed; taking for proved, that there is an intelligent Author of nature, and natural Governor of the world. For as there is no presumption against this prior to the proof of it, so it has been often proved with accumulated evidence—from this argument of analogy and final causes; from abstract reasonings; from the most ancient tradition and testimony; and from the general consent of mankind. Nor does it appear, so far as I can find, to be denied by the generality of those who profess themselves dissatisfied with the evidence of religion.

As there are some who, instead of thus attending to what is in fact the constitution of nature, form their notions of God's government upon hypothesis; so there are others who indulge themselves in vain and idle speculations, how the world might possibly have been framed otherwise than it is; and upon supposition that things might, in imagining that they should, have been disposed and carried on after a better model than what appears in the present disposition and conduct of them. Suppose, now, a person of such a turn of mind to go on with his reveries, till he had at length fixed upon some particular plan of nature, as appearing to him the best—one shall scarce be thought guilty of detraction against human understanding, if one should say, even beforehand, that the plan which this speculative person would fix upon, though he were the wisest of the sons of men, probably would not be the very best, even according to his own notions of *best;* whether he thought that to be so, which afforded occasions and motives for the exercise of the greatest virtue, or which was productive of the greatest happiness, or that these two were necessarily connected, and run up into one and the same plan. However, it may not be amiss, once for all, to see what would be the amount of these emendations and imaginary improvements upon the system of nature, or how far they would mislead us. And it seems there could be no stopping, till we came to some such conclusions as these:—That all creatures should at first be made as perfect and as happy as they were capable of ever being: that nothing, to be sure, of hazard or danger should be put upon them to do; some indolent persons would perhaps think, nothing at all; or, certainly, that effectual care should be taken, that they should, whether necessarily or not, yet eventually and in fact, always do what was right and most conducive to happiness—which would be thought easy for infinite power to effect, either by not giving them any principles which would endanger their going wrong, or by laying the right motive of action, in every instance, before their minds continually, in so strong a manner as would never fail of inducing them to act conformably to it: and that the whole method of government by punishments should be rejected as absurd; as an awkward round-about method of carrying things on; nay, as contrary to a principal purpose for which it would be supposed creatures were made, namely, happiness.

Now, without considering what is to be said in particular to the several parts of this train of folly and extravagance, what has been above intimated is a full, direct, general answer to it, namely, that we may see beforehand that we have not faculties for this kind of speculation. For though it be admitted that, from the first principles of our nature, we unavoidably judge or determine some ends to be absolutely in themselves preferable to others, and that the ends now mentioned, or, if they run up into one, that this one is absolutely the best, and consequently that we must conclude the ultimate end designed, in the constitution of nature and conduct of Providence, is the most virtue and happiness possible; yet we are far from being able to judge what particular disposition of things would be most friendly and assistant to virtue, or what means might be absolutely necessary to produce the most happiness in a system of such extent as our own world may be, taking in all that is past

and to come, though we should suppose it detached from
the whole of things. Indeed, we are so far from being
able to judge of this, that we are not judges what may
be the necessary means of raising and conducting one person to the highest perfection and happiness of his nature.
Nay, even in the little affairs of the present life, we find
men of different educations and ranks are not competent
judges of the conduct of each other. Our whole nature
leads us to ascribe all moral perfection to God, and to deny
all imperfection of him. And this will for ever be a practical proof of his moral character, to such as will consider
what a practical proof is, because it is the voice of God
speaking in us. And from hence we conclude, that virtue
must be the happiness, and vice the misery, of every creature; and that regularity, and order, and right, cannot but
prevail finally, in a universe under his government. But
we are in no sort judges what are the necessary means of
accomplishing this end.

Let us then, instead of that idle and not very innocent
employment of forming imaginary models of a world, and
schemes of governing it, turn our thoughts to what we experience to be the conduct of nature with respect to intelligent creatures; which may be resolved into general laws
or rules of administration, in the same way as many of the
laws of nature, respecting inanimate matter, may be collected from experiments. And let us compare the known
constitution and course of things with what is said to be the
moral system of nature; the acknowledged dispensations of
Providence, or that government which we find ourselves
under, with what religion teaches us to believe and expect;
and see whether they are not analogous, and of a piece.
And upon such a comparison it will, I think, be found
that they are very much so; that both may be traced up to
the same general laws, and resolved into the same principles of divine conduct.

The analogy here proposed to be considered is of pretty

large extent, and consists of several parts ; in some more, in others less exact. In some few instances, perhaps, it may amount to a real practical proof, in others not so; yet in these it is a confirmation of what is proved otherways. It will undeniably show, what too many want to have shown them, that the system of religion, both natural and revealed, considered only as a system, and prior to the proof of it, is not a subject of ridicule, unless that of nature be so too. And it will afford an answer to almost all objections to the system both of natural and of revealed religion, though not perhaps an answer in so great a degree, yet in a very considerable degree an answer, to the objections against the evidence of it; for, objections against a proof, and objections against what is said to be proved, the reader will observe, are different things.

Now, the Divine government of the world, implied in the notion of religion in general, and of Christianity, contains in it, that mankind is appointed to live in a future state;[*] that there every one shall be rewarded or punished[†]— rewarded or punished, respectively, for all that behaviour here which we comprehend under the words virtuous or vicious, morally good or evil;[‡] that our present life is a probation, a state of trial,[§] and of discipline,[||] for that future one, notwithstanding the objections which men may fancy they have, from notions of necessity, against there being any such moral plan as this at all;[¶] and whatever objections may appear to lie against the wisdom and goodness of it, as it stands so imperfectly made known to us at present:[**] that this world being in a state of apostacy and wickedness, and consequently of ruin, and the sense both of their condition and duty being greatly corrupted amongst men, this gave occasion for an additional dispensation of Providence, of the utmost importance,[††] proved by miracles,[‡‡] but

[*] Chap. 1.	[†] Chap. 2.	[‡] Chap. 3.
[§] Chap. 4.	[||] Chap. 5.	[¶] Chap. 6.
[**] Chap. 7.	[††] Part ii. chap. 1.	[‡‡] Chap. 2.

containing in it many things appearing to us strange, and not to have been expected;* a dispensation of Providence, which is a scheme or system of things,† carried on by the mediation of a divine person, the Messiah, in order to the recovery of the world;‡ yet not revealed to all men, nor proved with the strongest possible evidence to all those to whom it is revealed; but only to such a part of mankind, and with such particular evidence, as the wisdom of God thought fit.§ The design, then, of the following Treatise will be to show, that the several parts principally objected against in this moral and Christian dispensation, including its scheme, its publication, and the proof which God has afforded us of its truth—that the particular parts principally objected against in this whole dispensation—are analogous to what is experienced in the constitution and course of nature, or providence: that the chief objections themselves, which are alleged against the former, are no other than what may be alleged with like justness against the latter, where they are found in fact to be inconclusive; and that this argument, from analogy, is in general unanswerable, and undoubtedly of weight on the side of religion,‖ not-withstanding the objections which may seem to lie against it, and the real ground which there may be for difference of opinion as to the particular degree of weight which is to be laid upon it. This is a general account of what may be looked for in the following Treatise. And I shall begin it with that which is the foundation of all our hopes and of all our fears—all our hopes and fears which are of any con-sideration—I mean, a future life.

---

* Part ii. chap. 3.   † Chap. 4.   ‡ Chap. 5.
§ Chap. 6, 7.   ‖ Chap. 8.

ANALOGY OF RELIGION.

PART I.

OF NATURAL RELIGION.

CHAPTER I.

Of a Future Life.

STRANGE difficulties have been raised by some concerning personal identity, or the sameness of living agents, implied in the notion of our existing now and hereafter, or in any two successive moments; which whoever thinks it worth while may see considered in the first Dissertation at the end of this Treatise. But, without regard to any of them here, let us consider what the analogy of nature, and the several changes which we have undergone, and those which we know we may undergo without being destroyed, suggest, as to the effect which death may, or may not, have upon us; and whether it be not from thence probable, that we may survive this change, and exist in a future state of life and perception.

I. From our being born into the present world in the helpless imperfect state of infancy, and having arrived from thence to mature age, we find it to be a general law of nature in our own species, that the same creatures, the same individuals, should exist in degrees of life and perception, with capacities of action, of enjoyment, and suffering, in one period of their being, greatly different from

B

those appointed them in another period of it. And in other creatures the same law holds: for the difference of their capacities and states of life at their birth (to go no higher) and in maturity; the change of worms into flies, and the vast enlargement of their locomotive powers by such change; and birds and insects bursting the shell, their habitation, and by this means entering into a new world, furnished with new accommodations for them, and finding a new sphere of action assigned them; these are instances of this general law of nature. Thus all the various and wonderful transformations of animals are to be taken into consideration here. But the states of life in which we ourselves existed formerly, in the womb and in our infancy, are almost as different from our present, in mature age, as it is possible to conceive any two states or degrees of life can be. Therefore, that we are to exist hereafter in a state as different (suppose) from our present, as this is from our former, is but according to the analogy of nature; according to a natural order or appointment of the very same kind with what we have already experienced.

II. We know we are endued with capacities of action, of happiness, and misery; for we are conscious of acting, of enjoying pleasure, and suffering pain. Now, that we have these powers and capacities before death, is a presumption that we shall retain them through and after death; indeed, a probability of it abundantly sufficient to act upon, unless there be some positive reason to think that death is the destruction of those living powers; because there is in every case a probability, that all things will continue as we experience they are, in all respects, except those in which we have some reason to think they will be altered. This is that *kind** of presumption or probability from analogy, expressed in the very word *continuance*, which seems our only natural reason for believing the course of the world

---

* I say *kind* of presumption or probability; for I do not mean to affirm, that there is the same degree of conviction that our living powers will continue after death, as there is, that our substances will.

will continue to-morrow, as it has done so far as our experience or knowledge of history can carry us back. Nay, it seems our only reason for believing, that any one substance now existing will continue to exist a moment longer —the Self-existent substance only excepted. Thus, if men were assured that the unknown event, death, was not the destruction of our faculties of perception and of action, there would be no apprehension that any other power or event, unconnected with this of death, would destroy these faculties just at the instant of each creature's death; and therefore no doubt but that they would remain after it: which shows the high probability that our living powers will continue after death, unless there be some ground to think that death is their destruction.* For if it would be in a manner certain that we should survive death, provided it were certain that death would not be our destruction, it must be highly probable we shall survive it, if there be no ground to think death will be our destruction.

Now, though I think it must be acknowledged, that, prior to the natural and moral proofs of a future life, commonly insisted upon, there would arise a general confused suspicion, that in the great shock and alteration which we shall undergo by death, we, i. e. our living powers, might be wholly destroyed; yet even prior to those proofs, there is really no particular distinct ground or reason for this apprehension at all, so far as I can find. If there be, it

---

* *Destruction of living powers*, is a manner of expression unavoidably ambiguous; and may signify either *the destruction of a living being, so as that the same living being shall be incapable of ever perceiving or acting again at all; or, the destruction of those means and instruments by which it is capable of its present life, of its present state of perception and of action.* It is here used in the former sense. When it is used in the latter, the epithet *present* is added. The loss of a man's eye is a destruction of living powers in the latter sense; but we have no reason to think the destruction of living powers in the former sense to be possible. We have no more reason to think a being endued with living powers ever loses them during its whole existence, than to believe that a stone ever acquires them.

must arise either from *the reason of the thing*, or from *the analogy of nature*.

But we cannot argue from *the reason of the thing*, that death is the destruction of living agents, because we know not at all what death is in itself; but only some of its effects, such as the dissolution of flesh, skin, and bones; and these effects do in no wise appear to imply the destruction of a living agent. And besides, as we are greatly in the dark upon what the exercise of our living powers depends, so we are wholly ignorant what the powers themselves depend upon;—the powers themselves, as distinguished, not only from their actual exercise, but also from the present capacity of exercising them; and as opposed to their destruction: for sleep, or however a swoon, shows us, not only that these powers exist when they are not exercised, as the passive power of motion does in inanimate matter; but shows also that they exist when there is no present capacity of exercising them; or that the capacities of exercising them for the present, as well as the actual exercise of them, may be suspended, and yet the powers themselves remain undestroyed. Since, then, we know not at all upon what the existence of our living powers depends, this shows further, there can be no probability collected, from the reason of the thing, that death will be their destruction; because their existence may depend upon somewhat in no degree affected by death; upon somewhat quite out of the reach of this king of terrors. So that there is nothing more certain, than that *the reason of the thing* shows us no connexion between death and the destruction of living agents. Nor can we find anything throughout the whole *analogy of nature*, to afford us even the slightest presumption that animals ever lose their living powers; much less, if it were possible, that they lose them by death; for we have no faculties wherewith to trace any beyond or through it, so as to see what becomes of them. This event removes them from our view. It destroys the *sensible* proof, which we had before their death, of their being possessed of living powers, but does not appear to afford the least reason to believe that they are then, or by that event, deprived of them.

And our knowing that they were possessed of these powers, up to the very period to which we have faculties capable of tracing them, is itself a probability of their retaining them beyond it. And this is confirmed, and a sensible credibility is given to it, by observing the very great and astonishing changes which we have experienced; so great, that our existence in another state of life, of perception and of action, will be but according to a method of providential conduct, the like to which has been already exercised even with regard to ourselves; according to a course of nature, the like to which we have already gone through.

However, as one cannot but be greatly sensible how difficult it is to silence imagination enough to make the voice of reason even distinctly heard in this case; as we are accustomed, from our youth up, to indulge that forward delusive faculty, ever obtruding beyond its sphere; of some assistance, indeed, to apprehension, but the author of all error—as we plainly lose ourselves in gross and crude conceptions of things, taking for granted that we are acquainted with what indeed we are wholly ignorant of; it may be proper to consider the imaginary presumptions, that death will be our destruction, arising from these kinds of early and lasting prejudices; and to show how little they can really amount to, even though we cannot wholly divest ourselves of them.   And,

I. All presumption of death's being the destruction of living beings, must go upon supposition that they are compounded, and so discerptible.   But since consciousness is a single and indivisible power, it should seem that the subject in which it resides must be so too.   For, were the motion of any particle of matter absolutely one and indivisible, so as that it should imply a contradiction to suppose part of this motion to exist, and part not to exist, *i. e.* part of this matter to move, and part to be at rest; then its power of motion would be indivisible; and so also would the subject in which the power inheres, namely, the particle of matter: for, if this could be divided into two, one part might be moved and the other at rest, which is contrary to the supposition. In like manner it has been argued,* and for anything appearing to the contrary, justly, that since the perception, or consciousness, which we have of our own existence is indivisible, so as that it is a contradiction to suppose one part of it should be here, and the other there; the perceptive power, or the power of consciousness, is indivisible too; and, consequently, the subject in which it resides, *i. e.* the conscious being. Now, upon supposition that the living agent each man calls himself is thus a single being, which there is at least no more difficulty in conceiving, than in conceiving it to be a compound, and of which there is the proof now mentioned, it follows, that our organized bodies are no more ourselves, or part of ourselves, than any other matter around us. And it is as easy to conceive how matter, which is no part of ourselves, may be appropriated to us in the manner which our present bodies are, as how we can receive impressions from, and have power over, any matter. It is as easy to conceive that we may exist out of bodies as in them; that we might have animated bodies of any other organs and senses wholly different from those now given us, and that we may hereafter animate these same or new bodies variously modified and organized, as to conceive how we can animate such bodies as our present. And, lastly, the dissolution of all these several organized bodies, supposing ourselves to have successively animated them, would have no more conceivable tendency to destroy the living beings, ourselves, or deprive us of living faculties, the faculties of perception and of action, than the dissolution of any foreign matter, which we are capable of

---

* See Dr. Clarke's Letter to Mr. Dodwell, and the Defences of it.

receiving impressions from, and making use of for the common occasions of life.

II. The simplicity and absolute oneness of a living agent cannot, indeed, from the nature of the thing, be properly proved by experimental observations. But as these *fall in* with the supposition of its unity, so they plainly lead us to *conclude* certainly, that our gross organized bodies with which we perceive the objects of sense, and with which we act, are no part of ourselves, and therefore show us, that we have no reason to believe their destruction to be ours; even without determining whether our living substances be material or immaterial. For we see by experience, that men may lose their limbs, their organs of sense, and even the greatest part of these bodies, and yet remain the same living agents. And persons can trace up the existence of themselves to a time when the bulk of their bodies was extremely small, in comparison of what it is in mature age; and we cannot but think, that they might then have lost a considerable part of that small body, and yet have remained the same living agents, as they may now lose great part of their present body, and remain so. And it is certain that the bodies of all animals are in a constant flux, from that never-ceasing attrition which there is in every part of them. Now, things of this kind unavoidably teach us to distinguish between these living agents, ourselves, and large quantities of matter, in which we are very nearly interested: since these may be alienated, and actually are in a daily course of succession, and changing their owners; whilst we are assured that each living agent remains one and the same permanent being.* And this general observation leads us on to the following ones.

First, That we have no way of determining by experience, what is the certain bulk of the living being each man calls himself; and yet, till it be determined that it is larger in bulk than the solid elementary particles of matter,

* See Dissertation I.

which there is no ground to think any natural power can dissolve, there is no sort of reason to think death to be the dissolution of it, of the living being, even though it should not be absolutely indiscerptible.

Secondly, From our being so nearly related to, and interested in, certain systems of matter, suppose our flesh and bones, and afterwards ceasing to be at all related to them, the living agents, ourselves, remaining all this while undestroyed, notwithstanding such alienation; and consequently these systems of matter not being ourselves; it follows further, that we have no ground to conclude any other, suppose *internal systems* of matter, to be the living agents ourselves, because we can have no ground to conclude this, but from our relation to, and interest in, such other systems of matter; and therefore we can have no reason to conclude what befalls those systems of matter at death, to be the destruction of the living agents. We have already, several times over, lost a great part or perhaps the whole of our body, according to certain common established laws of nature; yet we remain the same living agents: when we shall lose as great a part, or the whole, by another common established law of nature, death, why may we not also remain the same? That the alienation has been gradual in one case, and in the other will be more at once, does not prove anything to the contrary. We have passed undestroyed through those many and great revolutions of matter, so peculiarly appropriated to ourselves; why should we imagine death will be so fatal to us? Nor can it be objected, that what is thus alienated, or lost, is no part of our original solid body, but only adventitious matter; because we may lose entire limbs, which must have contained many solid parts and vessels of the original body: or if this be not admitted, we have no proof that any of these solid parts are dissolved or alienated by death; though, by the way, we are very nearly related to that extraneous or adventitious matter, whilst it continues united to and distending the several parts of our solid body. But, after all, the relation a person bears to those parts of his body to which he is the most nearly related, what does it appear to amount to but this, that the living agent and those parts of the body mutually affect each other? And the same thing—the same thing in kind though not in degree—may be said of all *foreign* matter which gives us ideas, and which we have any power over. From these observations, the whole ground of the imagination is removed, that the dissolution of any matter is the destruction of a living agent, from the interest he once had in such matter.

Thirdly, If we consider our body somewhat more distinctly, as made up of organs and instruments of perception and of motion, it will bring us to the same conclusion. Thus, the common optical experiments show, and even the observation how sight is assisted by glasses shows, that we see with our eyes in the same sense as we see with glasses. Nor is there any reason to believe, that we see with them in any other sense; any other, I mean, which would lead us to think the eye itself a percipient. The like is to be said of hearing; and our feeling distant solid matter by means of somewhat in our hand, seems an instance of the like kind, as to the subject we are considering. All these are instances of foreign matter, or such as is no part of our body, being instrumental in preparing objects for, and conveying them to, the perceiving power, in a manner similar, or like to the manner in which our organs of sense prepare and convey them. Both are, in a like way, instruments of our receiving such ideas from external objects, as the Author of nature appointed those external objects to be the occasions of exciting in us. However, glasses are evidently instances of this, namely of matter which is no part of our body, preparing objects for, and conveying them towards, the perceiving power, in like manner as our bodily organs do. And if we see with our eyes only in the same manner as we do with glasses, the like may justly be concluded, from analogy, of all our other senses. It is not

intended by anything here said to affirm, that the whole
apparatus of vision, or of perception by any other of our
senses, can be traced, through all its steps, quite up to the
living power of seeing, or perceiving; but that, so far as it
can be traced by experimental observations, so far it appears
that our organs of sense prepare and convey on objects, in
order to their being perceived, in like manner as foreign
matter does, without affording any shadow of appearance
that they themselves perceive.   And, that we have no
reason to think our organs of sense percipients, is confirmed by instances of persons losing some of them, the
living beings themselves, their former occupiers, remaining
unimpaired.   It is confirmed also by the experience of
dreams; by which we find we are at present possessed of
a latent, and what would otherwise be an unimagined
unknown power of perceiving sensible objects, in as strong
and lively a manner without our external organs of sense,
as with them.

So also with regard to our power of moving, or directing
motion by will and choice: upon the destruction of a limb,
this active power remains, as it evidently seems, unles-
sened; so as that the living being, who has suffered this loss,
would be capable of moving as before, if it had another
limb to move with.   It can walk by the help of an artificial leg, just as it can make use of a pole or a lever, to
reach towards itself and to move things beyond the length
and the power of its natural arm: and this last it does in
the same manner as it reaches and moves, with its natural
arm, things nearer and of less weight.   Nor is there so
much as any appearance of our limbs being endued with
a power of moving or directing themselves: though they
are adapted, like the several parts of a machine, to be
the instruments of motion to each other; and some parts
of the same limb, to be instruments of motion to other
parts of it.

Thus, a man determines that he will look at such an
object through a microscope; or, being lame, suppose, that

he will walk to such a place with a staff, a week hence. His eyes and his feet no more determine in these cases than the microscope and the staff. Nor is there any ground to think they any more put the determination in practice, or that his eyes are the seers, or his feet the movers, in any other sense than as the microscope and the staff are. Upon the whole, then, our organs of sense and our limbs are certainly instruments, which the living persons, ourselves, make use of to perceive and move with: there is not any probability that they are any more; nor, consequently, that we have any other kind of relation to them, than what we may have to any other foreign matter formed into instruments of perception and motion, suppose into a microscope or a staff (I say, any other kind of relation, for I am not speaking of the degree of it;) nor, consequently, is there any probability that the alienation or dissolution of these instruments is the destruction of the perceiving and moving agent.

And thus our finding, that the dissolution of matter in which living beings were most nearly interested, is not their dissolution; and that the destruction of several of the organs and instruments of perception and of motion belonging to them is not their destruction; shows, demonstratively, that there is no ground to think that the dissolution of any other matter, or destruction of any other organs and instruments, will be the dissolution or destruction of living agents, from the like kind of relation. And we have no reason to think we stand in any other kind of relation to anything which we find dissolved by death.

But it is said, these observations are equally applicable to brutes; and it is thought an insuperable difficulty, that they should be immortal, and, by consequence, capable of everlasting happiness. Now, this manner of expression is both invidious and weak; but the thing intended by it is really no difficulty at all, either in the way of natural or moral consideration. For, 1st, Suppose the invidious thing designed in such a manner of expression were really

implied, as it is not in the least, in the natural immortality
of brutes; namely, that they must arrive at great attain-
ments, and become rational and moral agents; even this
would be no difficulty, since we know not what latent
powers and capacities they may be endued with.   There
was once, prior to experience, as great presumption against
human creatures, as there is against the brute creatures,
arriving at that degree of understanding which we have in
mature age; for we can trace up our own existence to the
same original with theirs.   And we find it to be a general
law of nature, that creatures endued with capacities of
virtue and religion, should be placed in a condition of being
in which they are altogether without the use of them for a
considerable length of their duration, as in infancy and
childhood; and great part of the human species go out of
the present world before they come to the exercise of these
capacities in any degree at all.   But then, 2ndly, The
natural immortality of brutes does not in the least imply,
that they are endued with any latent capacities of a rational
or moral nature.   And the economy of the universe might
require that there should be living creatures without any
capacities of this kind.   And all difficulties, as to the
manner how they are to be disposed of, are so apparently
and wholly founded in our ignorance, that it is wonderful
they should be insisted upon by any, but such as are weak
enough to think they are acquainted with the whole system
of things.   There is, then, absolutely nothing at all in this
objection, which is so rhetorically urged against the greatest
part of the natural proofs or presumptions of the immortality of human minds: I say the greatest part; for it is
less applicable to the following observation, which is more
peculiar to mankind:—

III. That as it is evident our *present* powers and capacities, of reason, memory, and affection, do not depend
upon our gross body, in the manner in which perception
by our organs of sense does; so they do not appear to
depend upon it at all in any such manner as to give ground

to think, that the dissolution of this body will be the destruction of these our *present* powers of reflection, as it will of our powers of sensation; or to give ground to conclude even, that it will be so much as a suspension of the former.

Human creatures exist at present in two states of life and perception, greatly different from each other; each of which has its own peculiar laws, and its own peculiar enjoyments and sufferings. When any of our senses are affected, or appetites gratified with the objects of them, we may be said to exist, or live, in a state of sensation. When none of our senses are affected, or appetites gratified, and yet we perceive, and reason, and act, we may be said to exist, or live, in a state of reflection. Now it is by no means certain, that anything which is dissolved by death is any way necessary to the living being, in this its state of reflection, after ideas are gained. For though, from our present constitution and condition of being, our external organs of sense are necessary for conveying in ideas to our reflecting powers, as carriages, and levers, and scaffolds are in architecture; yet, when these ideas are brought in, we are capable of reflecting in the most intense degree, and of enjoying the greatest pleasure, and feeling the greatest pain, by means of that reflection, without any assistance from our senses; and without any at all, which we know of, from that body which will be dissolved by death.

It does not appear, then, that the relation of this gross body to the reflecting being is, in any degree, necessary to thinking; to our intellectual enjoyments or sufferings; nor, consequently, that the dissolution, or alienation, of the former by death, will be the destruction of those present powers, which render us capable of this state of reflection. Further, there are instances of mortal diseases which do not at all affect our present intellectual powers; and this affords a presumption, that those diseases will not destroy these present powers. Indeed, from the observations made

above,* it appears that there is no presumption, from their
mutually affecting each other, that the dissolution of the
body is the destruction of the living agent. And by the
same reasoning it must appear, too, that there is no presumption, from their mutually affecting each other, that
the dissolution of the body is the destruction of our present
reflecting powers; but instances of their not affecting each
other afford a presumption of the contrary. Instances of
mortal diseases not impairing our present reflecting powers,
evidently turn our thoughts even from imagining such
diseases to be the destruction of them. Several things,
indeed, greatly affect all our living powers, and at length
suspend the exercise of them; as, for instance, drowsiness,
increasing till it ends in sound sleep: and from hence we
might have imagined it would destroy them, till we found
by experience the weakness of this way of judging. But,
in the diseases now mentioned, there is not so much as this
shadow of probability, to lead us to any such conclusion as
to the reflecting powers which we have at present; for in
those diseases, persons the moment before death appear to
be in the highest vigour of life. They discover apprehension, memory, reason, all entire; with the utmost force
of affection; sense of a character, of shame and honour;
and the highest mental enjoyments and sufferings, even to
the last gasp: and these surely prove even greater vigour
of life than bodily strength does. Now, what pretence is
there for thinking, that a progressive disease, when arrived
to such a degree, I mean that degree which is mortal, will
destroy those powers which were not impaired, which were
not affected by it, during its whole progress, quite up to
that degree? And if death, by diseases of this kind, is not
the destruction of our present reflecting powers, it will
scarce be thought that death by any other means is.

It is obvious that this general observation may be carried

* Pages 8, 9, 10.

on further. And there appears so little connexion between
our bodily powers of sensation, and our present powers of
reflection, that there is no reason to conclude that death,
which destroys the former, does so much as suspend the
exercise of the latter, or interrupt our *continuing* to exist
in the like state of reflection which we do now. For, suspension of reason, memory, and the affections which they
excite, is no part of the idea of death, nor is implied in our
notion of it. And our daily experiencing these powers to
be exercised, without any assistance, that we know of, from
those bodies which will be dissolved by death; and our
finding often, that the exercise of them is so lively to the
last;—these things afford a sensible apprehension, that
death may not perhaps be so much as a discontinuance of
the exercise of these powers, nor of the enjoyments and
sufferings which it implies;* so that our posthumous life,
whatever there may be in it additional to our present, yet
may not be entirely beginning anew, but going on. Death
may, in some sort, and in some respects, answer to our
birth, which is not a suspension of the faculties which we
had before it, or a total change of the state of life in which
we existed when in the womb, but a continuation of both,
with such and such great alterations.

Nay, for aught we know of ourselves, of our present life,
and of death, death may immediately, in the natural course
of things, put us into a higher and more enlarged state of
life, as our birth does;† a state in which our capacities and

* There are three distinct questions, relating to a future life, here
considered:—Whether death be the destruction of living agents? if
not, whether it be the destruction of their *present* powers of reflection,
as it certainly is the destruction of their present powers of sensation?
and, if not, whether it be the suspension, or discontinuance of the
exercise of these present reflecting powers? Now, if there be no
reason to believe the last, there will be, if that were possible, less for
the next, and less still for the first.

† This, according to Strabo, was the opinion of the Brahmans;
νομιζειν μεν γαρ δη τον μεν ενθαδε βιον, ως αν ακμην κυομενων ειναι τον
δε θανατον, γενεσιν εις τον οντως βιον, και τον ευδαιμονα τοις φιλοσο-

sphere of perception, and of action, may be much greater
than at present.   For, as our relation to our external
organs of sense renders us capable of existing in our present
state of sensation, so it may be the only natural hinderance
to our existing, immediately and of course, in a higher
state of reflection.   The truth is, reason does not at all
show us in what state death naturally leaves us.   But were
we sure that it would suspend all our perceptive and active
powers, yet the suspension of a power, and the destruction
of it, are effects so totally different in kind, as we experience
from sleep and a swoon, that we cannot in any wise argue
from one to the other; or conclude, even to the lowest
degree of probability, that the same kind of force which is
sufficient to suspend our faculties, though it be increased
ever so much, will be sufficient to destroy them.

These observations together may be sufficient to show,
how little presumption there is that death is the destruction
of human creatures.   However, there is the shadow of an
analogy, which may lead us to imagine it is—the supposed
likeness which is observed between the decay of vegetables
and of living creatures.   And this likeness is indeed sufficient to afford the poets very apt allusions to the flowers of
the field, in their pictures of the frailty of our present life.
But, in reason, the analogy is so far from holding, that
there appears no ground even for the comparison, as to the
present question ; because one of the two subjects compared
is wholly void of that, which is the principal and chief
thing in the other, the power of perception and of action;
and which is the only thing we are inquiring about the
continuance of.   So that the destruction of a vegetable is
an event not similar, or analogous, to the destruction of a
living agent.

But if, as was above intimated, leaving off the delusive

φησασι.′ Lib. xv. p. 1039, edit. Amst. 1707. To which opinion, perhaps, Antoninus may allude in these words, ὡς νυν περιμενεις, ποτε
ευβρυον εκ της γαστρος της γυναικος σου εξελθη, ουτως εκδεχεσθαι την
ὡραν εν ητο ψυχαριον σου του ελυτρου τουτου εκπεσειται.   Lib. ix. c. 3.

custom of substituting imagination in the room of experience, we would confine ourselves to what we do know
and understand; if we would argue only from that, and
from that form our expectations—it would appear, at first
sight, that as no probability of living beings ever ceasing to
be so, can be concluded from the reason of the thing; so
none can be collected from the analogy of nature; because
we cannot trace any living beings beyond death.   But as
we are conscious that we are endued with capacities of
perception and of action, and are living persons, what we
are to go upon is, that we shall continue so till we foresee
some accident, or event, which will endanger those capacities, or be likely to destroy us; which death does in no
wise appear to be.

And thus, when we got out of this world, we may pass
into new scenes, and a new state of life and action, just as
naturally as we came into the present.   And this new state
may naturally be a social one; and the advantages of it,
advantages of every kind, may naturally be bestowed,
according to some fixed general laws of wisdom, upon every
one in proportion to the degrees of his virtue.   And though
the advantages of that future natural state should not be
bestowed, as those of the present in some measure are, by
the will of the society, but entirely by His more immediate
action upon whom the whole frame of nature depends, yet
this distribution may be just as natural, as their being distributed here by the instrumentality of men.   And, indeed,
though one were to allow any confused undetermined
sense, which people please to put upon the word *natural*,
it would be a shortness of thought scarce credible to
imagine, that no system or course of things can be so, but
only what we see at present;* especially whilst the probability of a future life, or the natural immortality of the
soul, is admitted upon the evidence of reason; because this
is really both admitting and denying at once, a state of

* See Part ii. chap. 2, and Part ii. chap 3.

being different from the present to be natural. But the only distinct meaning of that word is *stated, fixed*, or *settled ;* since what is natural as much requires and presupposes an intelligent agent to render it so, *i. e.* to effect it continually, or at stated times, as what is supernatural or miraculous does to effect it for once. And from hence it must follow, that persons' notions of what is natural will be enlarged, in proportion to their greater knowledge of the works of God, and the dispensations of his Providence. Nor is there any absurdity in supposing, that there may be beings in the universe, whose capacities, and knowledge, and views, may be so extensive, as that the whole Christian dispensation may to them appear natural, *i. e.* analogous or conformable to God's dealings with other parts of his creation; as natural as the visible known course of things appears to us. For there seems scarce any other possible sense to be put upon the word, but that only in which it is here used— similar, stated, or uniform.

This credibility of a future life, which has been here insisted upon, how little soever it may satisfy our curiosity, seems to answer all the purposes of religion, in like manner as a demonstrative proof would.   Indeed a proof, even a demonstrative one, of a future life, would not be a proof of religion.   For, that we are to live hereafter, is just as recon- cilable with the scheme of atheism, and as well to be accounted for by it, as that we are now alive is; and there- fore nothing can be more absurd than to argue, from that scheme, that there can be no future state. · But as religion implies a future state, any presumption against such a state is a presumption against religion.   And the foregoing observations remove all presumptions of that sort, and prove, to a very considerable degree of probability, one fundamental doctrine of religion; which, if believed, would greatly open and dispose the mind seriously to attend to the general evidence of the whole.

CHAPTER II.

Of the Government of God by Rewards and Punishments;
and particularly of the latter.

THAT which makes the question concerning a future life
to be of so great importance to us, is our capacity of happiness and misery. And that which makes the consideration of it to be of so great importance to us, is the
supposition of our happiness and misery hereafter, depending upon our actions here.   Without this, indeed, curiosity
could not but sometimes bring a subject, in which we may
be so highly interested, to our thoughts; especially upon
the mortality of others, or the near prospect of our own.
But reasonable men would not take any farther thought
about hereafter, than what should happen thus occasionally
to rise in their minds, if it were certain that our future
interest in no way depended upon our present behaviour;
whereas, on the contrary, if there be ground, either from
analogy or anything else, to think it does, then there is
reason also for the most active thought and solicitude, to
secure that interest; to behave so as that we may escape
that misery, and obtain that happiness in another life,
which we not only suppose ourselves capable of, but which
we apprehend also is put in our own power.   And whether
there be ground for this last apprehension, certainly would
deserve to be most seriously considered, were there no other
proof of a future life and interest, than that presumptive
one which the foregoing observations amount to.

Now, in the present state, all which we enjoy, and a
great part of what we suffer, *is put in our own power*.   For
pleasure and pain are the consequences of our actions; and
we are endued by the Author of our nature with capacities
of foreseeing these consequences.   We find by experience,
he does not so much as preserve our lives, exclusively of

our own care and attention to provide ourselves with and to make use of that sustenance, by which he has appointed our lives shall be preserved; and without which, he has appointed, they shall not be preserved at all. And in general we foresee, that the external things which are the objects of our various passions, can neither be obtained nor enjoyed, without exerting ourselves in such and such manners; but by thus exerting ourselves, we obtain and enjoy those objects in which our natural good consists; or by this means God gives us the possession and enjoyment of them. I know not that we have any one kind or degree of enjoyment, but by the means of our own actions. And by prudence and care we may, for the most part, pass our days in tolerable ease and quiet; or, on the contrary, we may, by rashness, ungoverned passion, wilfulness, or even by negligence, make ourselves as miserable as ever we please. And many do please to make themselves extremely miserable, *i. e.* to do what they know beforehand will render them so. They follow those ways, the fruit of which they know, by instruction, example, experience, will be disgrace, and poverty, and sickness, and untimely death. This every one observes to be the general course of things; though it is to be allowed, we cannot find by experience, that all our sufferings are owing to our own follies.

Why the Author of nature does not give his creatures promiscuously such and such perceptions, without regard to their behaviour; why he does not make them happy without the instrumentality of their own actions, and prevent their bringing any sufferings upon themselves—is another matter. Perhaps there may be some impossibilities in the nature of things which we are unacquainted with.* Or less happiness, it may be, would upon the whole be produced by such a method of conduct than is by the present. Or perhaps Divine Goodness, with which, if I mistake not, we make very free in our speculations, may

* Part i. chap. 7.

not be a bare single disposition to produce happiness; but a disposition to make the good, the faithful, the honest man, happy. Perhaps an infinitely perfect Mind may be pleased with seeing his creatures behave suitably to the nature which he has given them; to the relations which he has placed them in to each other; and to that which they stand in to himself—that relation to himself, which, during their existence, is even necessary, and which is the most important one of all;—perhaps, I say, an infinitely perfect Mind may be pleased with this moral piety of moral agents, in and for itself; as well as upon account of its being essentially conducive to the happiness of his creation. Or, the whole end for which God made and thus governs the world, may be utterly beyond the reach of our faculties: there may be somewhat in it as impossible for us to have any conception of, as for a blind man to have any conception of colours. But, however this be, it is certain matter of universal experience, that the general method of divine administration is, forewarning us, or giving us capacities to foresee, with more or less clearness, that if we act so and so, we shall have such enjoyments, if so and so, such sufferings; and giving us those enjoyments, and making us feel those sufferings, in consequence of our actions.

" But all this is to be ascribed to the general course of nature." True. This is the very thing which I am observing. It is to be ascribed to the general course of nature; *i. e.* not surely to the words or ideas, *course of nature*, but to Him who appointed it, and put things into it; or to a course of operation, from its uniformity or constancy, called natural, and which necessarily implies an operating agent. For when men find themselves necessitated to confess an author of nature, or that God is the natural governor of the world, they must not deny this again, because his government is uniform: they must not deny that he does things at all, because he does them constantly; because the effects of his acting are permanent,

whether his acting be so or not; though there is no reason
to think there is not.   In short, every man, in every thing
he does, naturally acts upon the forethought and apprehension of avoiding evil, or obtaining good ; and if the
natural course of things be the appointment of God, and
our natural faculties of knowledge and experience are given
us by him, then the good and bad consequences which
follow our actions are his appointment, and our foresight
of those consequences is a warning given us by him how
we are to act.

" Is the pleasure, then, naturally accompanying every
particular gratification of passion, intended to put us upon
gratifying ourselves in every such particular instance, and
as a reward to us for so doing ?"   No, certainly.   Nor is it
to be said that our eyes were naturally intended to give us
the sight of each particular object to which they do or can
extend ; objects which are destructive of them, or which,
for any other reason, it may become us to turn our eyes
from.   Yet there is no doubt, but that our eyes were
intended for us to see with.   So neither is there any doubt,
but that the foreseen pleasures and pains belonging to the
passions, were intended, in general, to induce mankind to
act in such and such manners.

Now, from this general observation, obvious to every
one, that God has given us to understand he has appointed
satisfaction and delight to be the consequences of our acting
in one manner, and pain and uneasiness of our acting in
another, and of our not acting at all ; and that we find the
consequences, which we were beforehand informed of,
uniformly to follow ; we may learn that we are at present
actually under his government, in the strictest and most
proper sense—in such a sense, as that he rewards and
punishes us for our actions.   An Author of nature being
supposed, it is not so much a deduction of reason as a
matter of experience, that we are thus under his government ; under his government, in the same sense as we are
under the government of civil magistrates ; because the

annexing pleasure to some actions, and pain to others, in our power to do or forbear, and giving notice of this appointment beforehand to those whom it concerns, is the proper formal notion of government.   Whether the pleasure or pain, which thus follows upon our behaviour, be owing to the Author of nature's acting upon us every moment which we feel it, or to his having at once contrived and executed his own part in the plan of the world, makes no alteration as to the matter before us : for, if civil magistrates could make the sanctions of their laws take place, without interposing at all, after they had passed them ; without a trial, and the formalities of an execution : if they were able to make their laws execute themselves, or every offender to execute them upon himself—we should be just in the same sense under their government then, as we are now ; but in a much higher degree, and more perfect manner.   Vain is the ridicule with which one foresees some persons will divert themselves, upon finding lesser pains considered as instances of divine punishment.   There is no possibility of answering or evading the general thing here intended, without denying all final causes.   For, final causes being admitted, the pleasures and pains now mentioned must be admitted too as instances of them.   And if they are ; if God annexes delight to some actions and uneasiness to others, with an apparent design to induce us to act so and so, then he not only dispenses happiness and misery, but also rewards and punishes actions.   If, for example, the pain which we feel upon doing what tends to the destruction of our bodies, suppose upon too near approaches to fire, or upon wounding ourselves, be appointed by the Author of nature, to prevent our doing what thus tends to our destruction ; this is altogether as much an instance of his punishing our actions, and consequently of our being under his government, as declaring, by a voice from heaven, that if we acted so, he would inflict such pain upon us, and inflicting it whether it be greater or less.

Thus we find, that the true notion or conception of the Author of nature is that of a master or governor, prior to the consideration of his moral attributes. The fact of our case, which we find by experience is, that he actually exercises dominion or government over us at present, by rewarding and punishing us for our actions, in as strict and proper a sense of these words, and even in the same sense, as children, servants, subjects, are rewarded and punished by those who govern them.

And thus the whole analogy of nature, the whole present course of things, most fully shows, that there is nothing incredible in the general doctrine of religion, that God will reward and punish men for their actions hereafter;— nothing incredible, I mean, arising out of the notion of rewarding and punishing, for the whole course of nature is a present instance of his exercising that government over us, which implies in it rewarding and punishing.

But, as divine punishment is what men chiefly object against, and are most unwilling to allow, it may be proper to mention some circumstances in the natural course of punishments at present, which are analogous to what religion teaches us concerning a future state of punishment; indeed so analogous, that as they add a farther credibility to it, so they cannot but raise a most serious apprehension of it in those who will attend to them.

It has been now observed, that such and such miseries naturally follow such and such actions of imprudence and wilfulness, as well as actions more commonly and more distinctly considered as vicious; and that these consequences, when they may be foreseen, are properly natural punishments annexed to such actions. For the general thing here insisted upon is, not that we see a great deal of misery in the world, but a great deal which men bring upon themselves by their own behaviour, which they might have foreseen and avoided. Now, the circumstances of these natural punishments, particularly deserving our attention, are such as these :—That oftentimes they follow, or are inflicted, in consequence of actions which procure many present advantages, and are accompanied with much present pleasure : for instance, sickness and untimely death is the consequence of intemperance, though accompanied with the highest mirth and jollity : That these punishments are often much greater than the advantages or pleasures obtained by the actions, of which they are the punishments or consequences : That though we may imagine a constitution of nature, in which those natural punishments, which are, in fact, to follow, would follow immediately upon such actions being done, or very soon after ; we find, on the contrary, in our world, that they are often delayed a great while, sometimes even till long after the actions occasioning them are forgot ; so that the constitution of nature is such, that delay of punishment is no sort or degree of presumption of final impunity : That, after such delay, these natural punishments or miseries often come, not by degrees, but suddenly, with violence, and at once ; however, the chief misery often does : That as certainty of such distant misery following such actions is never afforded persons, so, perhaps, during the actions, they have seldom a distinct full expectation of its following ;* and many times the case is only thus, that they see in general, or may see, the credibility, that intemperance, suppose, will bring after it diseases ; civil crimes, civil punishments ; when yet the real probability often is, that they shall escape : but things, notwithstanding, take their destined course, and the misery inevitably follows at its appointed time, in very many of these cases. Thus, also, though youth may be alleged as an excuse for rashness and folly, as being naturally

* See Part ii. chap. 6.

c

thoughtless, and not clearly foreseeing all the consequences of being untractable and profligate; this does not hinder but that these consequences follow, and are grievously felt, throughout the whole course of mature life. Habits contracted, even in that age, are often utter ruin; and men's success in the world, not only in the common sense of worldly success, but their real happiness and misery, depends in a great degree, and in various ways, upon the manner in which they pass their youth; which consequences they, for the most part, neglect to consider, and perhaps seldom can properly be said to believe beforehand. It requires also to be mentioned, that, in numberless cases, the natural course of things affords us opportunities for procuring advantages to ourselves at certain times, which we cannot procure when we will; · nor ever recall the opportunities, if we have neglected them. Indeed, the general course of nature is an example of this. If, during the opportunity of youth, persons are indocile and self-willed, they inevitably suffer in their future life, for want of those acquirements which they neglected the natural season of attaining. If the husbandman lets his seed-time pass without sowing, the whole year is lost to him beyond recovery. In like manner, though, after men have been guilty of folly and extravagance, *up to a certain degree*, it is often in their power, for instance, to retrieve their affairs, to recover their health and character, at least in good measure; yet real reformation is, in many cases, of no avail at all towards preventing the miseries, poverty, sickness, infamy, naturally annexed to folly and extravagance, *exceeding that degree*. There is a certain bound to imprudence and misbehaviour, which being transgressed, there remains no place for repentance in the natural course of things. It is, further, very much to be remarked, that neglects from inconsiderateness, want of attention,* not looking

* Part ii. chap. 6.

about us to see what we have to do, are often attended
with consequences altogether as dreadful as any active
misbehaviour, from the most extravagant passion.   And,
lastly, civil government being natural, the punishments
of it are so too ; and some of these punishments are capital, as the effects of a dissolute course of pleasure are
often mortal.   So that many natural punishments are
final* to him who incurs them, if considered only in his
temporal capacity; and seem inflicted by natural appointment, either to remove the offender out of the way of
being further mischievous, or as an example, though frequently a disregarded one, to those who are left behind.

These things are not what we call accidental, or to be
met with only now and then ; but they are things of every
day's experience: they proceed from general laws, very
general ones, by which God governs the world, in the

* The general consideration of a future state of punishment most
evidently belongs to the subject of natural religion.   But if any of these
reflections should be thought to relate more peculiarly to this doctrine
as taught in Scripture, the reader is desired to observe, that Gentile
writers, both moralists and poets, speak of the future punishment of
the wicked, both as to the duration and degree of it, in a like manner
of expression and of description as the Scripture does.   So that all
which can positively be asserted to be matter of mere revelation, with
regard to this doctrine, seems to be, that the great distinction between
the righteous and the wicked shall be made at the end of this world;
that each shall *then* receive according to his deserts.   Reason did, as
well it might, conclude that it should finally, and upon the whole, be
well with the righteous, and ill with the wicked ; but it could not be
determined, upon any principles of reason, whether human creatures
might not have been appointed to pass through other states of life and
being, before that distributive justice should, finally and effectually,
take place.   Revelation teaches us, that the next state of things after
the present, is appointed for the execution of this justice; that it shall
not be longer delayed; but *the mystery of God*, the great mystery of
his suffering vice and confusion to prevail, *shall then be finished;* and
he will *take to him his great power and will reign*, by rendering to
every one according to his works.

natural course of his providence. And they are so analogous to what religion teaches us concerning the future
punishment of the wicked, so much of a piece with it,
that both would naturally be expressed in the very same
words and manner of description. In the book of Pro-
verbs,* for instance, Wisdom is introduced as frequenting
the most public places of resort, and as rejected when
she offers herself as the natural appointed guide of human
life. " How long," speaking to those who are passing
through it, " how long, ye simple ones, will ye love
folly, and the scorners delight in their scorning, and fools
hate knowledge? Turn ye at my reproof. Behold, I
will pour out my spirit upon you, I will make known my
words unto you." But upon being neglected, " Because
I have called, and ye refused, I have stretched out my
hand, and no man regarded; but ye have set at nought
all my counsel, and would none of my reproof; I also
will laugh at your calamity, I will mock when your fear
cometh; when your fear cometh as desolation, and your
destruction cometh as a whirlwind; when distress and
anguish cometh upon you. Then shall they call upon
me, but I will not answer; they shall seek me early, but
they shall not find me." This passage, every one sees,
is poetical, and some parts of it are highly figurative; but
their meaning is obvious. And the thing intended is expressed more literally in the following words: " For that
they hated knowledge, and did not choose the fear of the
Lord; therefore shall they eat of the fruit of their own
way, and be filled with their own devices. For the security of the simple shall slay them, and the prosperity
of fools shall destroy them." And the whole passage is
so equally applicable to what we experience in the present world concerning the consequences of men's actions, and to what religion teaches us is to be expected

* Chap. i.

in another, that it may be questioned which of the two was principally intended.

Indeed, when one has been recollecting the proper proofs of a future state of rewards and punishments, nothing, methinks, can give one so sensible an apprehension of the latter, or representation of it to the mind, as observing, that after the many disregarded checks, admonitions, and warnings, which people meet with in the ways of vice, and folly, and extravagance; warnings from their very nature; from the examples of others; from the lesser inconveniences which they bring upon themselves; from the instructions of wise and virtuous men: after these have been long despised, scorned, ridiculed; after the chief bad consequences, temporal consequences, of their follies, have been delayed for a great while; at length they break in irresistibly, like an armed force; repentance is too late to relieve, and can serve only to aggravate their distress: the case is become desperate; and poverty and sickness, remorse and anguish, infamy and death, the effects of their own doings, overwhelm them, beyond possibility of remedy or escape. This is an account of what is in fact the general constitution of nature.

It is not in any sort meant, that according to what appears at present of the natural course of things, men are always uniformly punished in proportion to their misbehaviour; but that there are very many instances of misbehaviour punished in the several ways now mentioned, and very dreadful instances too, sufficient to show what the laws of the universe may admit; and, if thoroughly considered, sufficient fully to answer all objections against the credibility of a future state of punishments, from any imaginations, that the frailty of our nature and external temptations almost annihilate the guilt of human vices; as well as objections of another sort—from necessity; from suppositions that the will of an infinite Being cannot be contradicted ; or that he must be incapable of offence and provocation.*

Reflections of this kind are not without their terrors to serious persons the most free from enthusiasm, and of the greatest strength of mind ; but it is fit things be stated and considered as they really are. And there is, in the present age, a certain fearlessness with regard to what may be hereafter under the government of God, which nothing but an universally acknowledged demonstration on the side of atheism can justify, and which makes it quite necessary that men be reminded, and, if possible, made to feel, that there is no sort of ground for being thus presumptuous, even upon the most sceptical principles. For, may it not be said of any person, upon his being born into the world, he may behave so as to be of no service to it, but by being made an example of the woful effects of vice and folly; that he may, as any one may, if he will, incur an infamous execution from the hands of civil justice; or in some other course of extravagance shorten his days ; or bring upon himself infamy and diseases worse than death ; so that it had been better for him, even with regard to the present world, that he had never been born ? And is there any pretence of reason for people to think themselves secure, and talk as if they had certain proof, that, let them act as licentiously as they will, there can be nothing analogous to this, with regard to a future and more general interest, under the providence and government of the same God!

* See Chap. 4, and 6.

CHAPTER III.

Of the Moral Government of God.

As the manifold appearances of design and of final causes in the constitution of the world, prove it to be the work of an intelligent Mind, so the particular final causes of pleasure and pain, distributed amongst his creatures, prove that they are under his government—what may be called his natural government of creatures endued with sense and reason. This, however, implies somewhat more than seems usually attended to, when we speak of God's natural government of the world. It implies government of the very same kind with that which a master exercises over his servants, or a civil magistrate over his subjects. These latter instances of final causes as really prove an intelligent *Governor* of the world, in the sense now mentioned, and before* distinctly treated of, as any other instances of final causes prove an intelligent *Maker* of it.

But this alone does not appear, at first sight, to determine any thing certainly concerning the moral character of the Author of nature, considered in this relation of governor; does not ascertain his government to be moral, or prove that he is the righteous Judge of the world. Moral government consists, not barely in rewarding and punishing men for their actions, which the most tyrannical person may do; but in rewarding the righteous and punishing the wicked; in rendering to men according to their actions, considered as good or evil.` And the perfection of moral government consists in doing this, with regard to all intelligent creatures, in an exact proportion to their personal merits or demerits.

Some men seem to think the only character of the Author of nature to be that of simple absolute benevolence.

* Chap. 2.

This, considered as a principle of action, and infinite in
degree, is a disposition to produce the greatest possible
happiness, without regard to persons' behaviour, otherwise
than as such regard would produce higher degrees of it.
And supposing this to be the only character of God, veracity
and justice in him would be nothing but benevolence
conducted by wisdom.   Now, surely, this ought not to be
asserted, unless it can be proved; for we should speak
with cautious reverence upon such a subject.   And whether
it can be proved or no, is not the thing here to be inquired
into; but whether, in the constitution and conduct of the
world, a righteous government be not discernibly planned
out; which necessarily implies a righteous governor.   There
may possibly be in the creation, beings to whom the Author
of nature manifests himself under this most amiable of all
characters, this, of infinite absolute benevolence; for it is
the most amiable, supposing it not, as perhaps it is not,
incompatible with justice : but he manifests himself to us
under the character of a righteous governor.   He may,
consistently with this, be simply and absolutely benevolent,
in the sense now explained; but he is, for he has given us
a proof in the constitution and conduct of the world that he
is, a governor over servants, as he rewards and punishes us
for our actions.   And in the constitution and conduct of it
he may also have given, besides the reason of the thing,
and the natural presages of conscience, clear and distinct
intimations that his government is righteous or moral :
clear to such as think the nature of it deserving their
attention; and yet not to every careless person who casts
a transient reflection upon the subject.*

---

* The objections against religion, from the evidence of it not being
universal, nor so strong as might possibly have been, may be urged
against natural religion, as well as against revealed.   And therefore
the consideration of them belongs to the first part of this Treatise, as
well as the second.   But as these objections are chiefly urged against
revealed religion, I chose to consider them in the Second Part.   And
the answer to them there, chap. vi., as urged against Christianity, being

But it is particularly to be observed, that the divine government which we experience ourselves under in the present state, taken alone, is allowed not to be the perfection of moral government. And yet this by no means hinders, but that there may be somewhat, be it more or less, truly moral in it. A righteous government may plainly appear to be carried on to some degree; enough to give us the apprehension that it shall be completed, or carried on to that degree of perfection which religion teaches us it shall; but which cannot appear, till much more of the divine administration be seen, than can in the present life. And the design of this chapter is to inquire, how far this is the case; how far, over and above the moral nature* which God has given us, and our natural notion of him as righteous governor of those his creatures to whom he has given this nature;† I say how far, besides this, the principles and beginnings of a moral government over the world may be discerned, notwithstanding and amidst all the confusion and disorder of it.

Now one might mention here, what has been often urged with great force, that, in general, less uneasiness, and more satisfaction, are the natural consequences‡ of a virtuous than of a vicious course of life, in the present state, as an instance of a moral government established in nature; an instance of it, collected from experience and present matter of fact. But it must be owned a thing of difficulty to weigh and balance pleasures and uneasinesses each amongst themselves, and also against each other, so as to make an estimate, with any exactness, of the overplus of happiness on the side of virtue. And it is not impossible, that, amidst the infinite disorders of the world, there may be exceptions to the happiness of virtue, even with regard to those persons whose course of life, from

almost equally applicable to them as urged against the religion of nature, to avoid repetition, the reader is referred to that chapter.

* Dissertation II.   † Chap. 6.

‡ See Lord Shaftesbury's Inquiry concerning Virtue, Part ii.

their youth up, has been blameless; and more with regard
to those who have gone on for some time in the ways of
vice, and have afterwards reformed.   For suppose an
instance of the latter case; a person with his passions
inflamed, his natural faculty of self-government impaired
by habits of indulgence, and with all his vices about him,
like so many harpies, craving for their accustomed gratification: who can say how long it might be before such a
person would find more satisfaction in the reasonableness
and present good consequences of virtue, than difficulties
and self-denial in the restraints of it? Experience also
shows, that men can, to a great degree, get over their
sense of shame, so as that, by professing themselves to
be without principle, and avowing even direct villany,
they can support themselves against the infamy of it.
But as the ill actions of any one will probably be more
talked of, and oftener thrown in his way, upon his reformation; so the infamy of them will be much more felt,
after the natural sense of virtue and of honour is recovered.
Uneasiness of this kind ought indeed to be put to the
account of former vices; yet it will be said, they are, in
part, the consequences of reformation. Still I am far
from allowing it doubtful, whether virtue, upon the whole,
be happier than vice in the present world; but if it were,
yet the beginnings of a righteous administration may,
beyond all question, be found in nature, if we will attentively inquire after them.   And,

I. In whatever manner the notion of God's moral government over the world might be treated; if it did not
appear whether he were, in a proper sense, our governor
at all, yet when it is certain matter of experience, that
he does manifest himself to us under the character of a
governor, in the sense explained,* it must deserve to be
considered, whether there be not reason to apprehend
that he may be a righteous or moral governor: since it

* Chap. 2.

appears to be fact, that God does govern mankind by the method of rewards and punishments, according to some settled rules of distribution, it is surely a question to be asked, What presumption is there against his finally rewarding and punishing them according to this particular rule, namely, as they act reasonably or unreasonably, virtuously or viciously? since rendering man happy or miserable by this rule, certainly falls in, much more falls in, with our natural apprehensions and sense of things, than doing so by any other rule whatever; since rewarding and punishing actions by any other rule, would appear much harder to be accounted for by minds formed as he has formed ours. Be the evidence of religion, then, more or less clear, the expectation which it raises in us, that the righteous shall, upon the whole, be happy, and the wicked miserable, cannot, however, possibly be considered as absurd or chimerical; because it is no more than an expectation, that a method of government, already begun, shall be carried on—the method of rewarding and punishing actions; and shall be carried on by a particular rule, which unavoidably appears to us, at first sight, more natural than any other, the rule which we call distributive justice. Nor,

II. Ought it to be entirely passed over, that tranquillity, satisfaction, and external advantages, being the natural consequences of prudent management of ourselves and our affairs; and rashness, profligate negligence, and wilful folly, bringing after them many inconveniences and sufferings; these afford instances of a right constitution of nature: as the correction of children, for their own sakes, and by way of example, when they run into danger or hurt themselves, is a part of right education. And thus, that God governs the world by general fixed laws; that he has endued us with capacities of reflecting upon this constitution of things, and foreseeing the good and bad consequences of our behaviour, plainly implies some sort of moral government; since from such a constitution of things

it cannot but follow, that prudence and imprudence, which
are of the nature of virtue and vice,* must be, as they are,
respectively rewarded and punished.

III. From the natural course of things, vicious actions
are, to a great degree, actually punished as mischievous
to society; and besides punishment actually inflicted upon
this account, there is also the fear and apprehension of it in
those persons whose crimes have rendered them obnoxious
to it, in case of a discovery; this state of fear being itself
often a very considerable punishment. The natural fear
and apprehension of it, too, which restrains from such
crimes, is a declaration of nature against them. It is·
necessary to the very being of society, that vices destructive of it should be punished *as being so;* the vices of
falsehood, injustice, cruelty: which punishment, therefore,
is as natural as society; and so is an instance of a kind
of moral government, naturally established, and actually
taking place. And, since the certain natural course of
things is the conduct of Providence or the government
of God, though carried on by the instrumentality of men,
the observation here made amounts to this, that mankind
find themselves placed by him in such circumstances, as
that they are unavoidably accountable for their behaviour,
and are often punished, and sometimes rewarded, under
his government, in the view of their being mischievous or
eminently beneficial to society.

If it be objected, that good actions, and such as are
beneficial to society, are often punished, as in the case of
persecution, and in other cases, and that ill and mischievous actions are often rewarded; it may be answered
distinctly, first, that this is in no sort necessary, and consequently not natural, in the sense in which it is necessary,
and therefore natural, that ill or mischievous actions should
be punished; and, in the next place, that good actions are
never punished, considered as beneficial to society, nor ill

* See Dissertation II.

actions rewarded, under the view of their being hurtful
to it. So that it stands good, without anything on the
side of vice to be set over against it, that the Author
of nature has as truly directed that vicious actions, considered as mischievous to society, should be punished, and
put mankind under a necessity of thus punishing them, as
he has directed and necessitated us to preserve our lives by
food.

IV. In the natural course of things, virtue, *as such*, is
actually rewarded, and vice, *as such*, punished; which
seems to afford an instance, or example, not only of
government, but of moral government, begun and established; moral in the strictest sense, though not in that
perfection of degree which religion teaches us to expect.
In order to see this more clearly, we must distinguish
between actions themselves, and that quality ascribed to
them, which we call virtuous or vicious. The gratification
itself of every natural passion must be attended with
delight; and acquisitions of fortune, however made, are
acquisitions of the means or materials of enjoyment. An
action, then, by which any natural passion is gratified, or
fortune acquired, procures delight or advantage, abstracted
from all consideration of the morality of such action.
Consequently, the pleasure or advantage in this case is
gained by the action itself, not by the morality, the vir-
tuousness, or viciousness of it, though it be, perhaps,
virtuous or vicious. Thus, to say such an action or course
of behaviour procured such pleasure or advantage, or
brought on such inconvenience and pain, is quite a different thing from saying that such good or bad effect was
owing to the virtue or vice of such action or behaviour.
In one case, an action, abstracted from all moral consideration, produced its effect; in the other case, for it will
appear that there are such cases, the morality of the action,
the action under a moral consideration, *i. e.* the virtuous-
ness or viciousness of it, produced the effect. Now, I say,
virtue, as such, naturally procures considerable advantages

to the virtuous, and vice, as such, naturally occasions great inconvenience, and even misery, to the vicious, in very many instances.   The immediate effects of virtue and vice upon the mind and temper are to be mentioned as instances of it.   Vice, as such, is naturally attended with some sort of uneasiness, and not uncommonly with great disturbance and apprehension.   That inward feeling, which, respecting lesser matters and in familiar speech, we call being vexed with one's self, and, in matters of importance and in more serious language, remorse, is an uneasiness naturally arising from an action of a man's own, reflected upon by himself as wrong, unreasonable, faulty, *i. e.* vicious in greater or less degrees; and this manifestly is a different feeling from that uneasiness which arises from a sense of mere loss or harm.   What is more common than to hear a man lamenting an accident or event, and adding—But, however, he has the satisfaction that he cannot blame himself for it; or, on the contrary, that he has the uneasiness of being sensible it was his own doing?   Thus, also, the disturbance and fear which often follow upon a man's having done an injury, arise from a sense of his being blameworthy; otherwise there would, in many cases, be no ground of disturbance, nor any reason to fear resentment or shame.   On the other hand, inward security and peace, and a mind open to the several gratifications of life, are the natural attendants of innocence and virtue; to which must be added, the complacency, satisfaction, and even joy of heart, which accompany the exercise, the real exercise, of gratitude, friendship, benevolence.

And here, I think, ought to be mentioned, the fears of future punishment, and peaceful hopes of a better life, in those who fully believe or have any serious apprehension of religion; because these hopes and fears are present uneasiness and satisfaction to the mind, and cannot be got rid of by great part of the world, even by men who have thought most thoroughly upon that subject of religion.

And no one can say how considerable this uneasiness and satisfaction may be, or what, upon the whole, it may amount to.

In the next place comes in the consideration, that all honest and good men are disposed to befriend honest and good men, as such, and to discountenance the vicious, as such, and do so in some degree, indeed in a considerable degree; from which favour and discouragement cannot but arise considerable advantage and inconvenience. And though the generality of the world have little regard to the morality of their own actions, and may be supposed to have less to that of others, when they themselves are not concerned; yet, let any one be known to be a man of virtue, somehow or other he will be favoured, and good offices will be done him from regard to his character, without remote views, occasionally, and in some low degree, I think, by the generality of the world, as it happens to come in their way. Public honours, too, and advantages, are the natural consequences, are sometimes at least the consequences in fact, of virtuous actions, of eminent justice, fidelity, charity, love to our country, considered in the view of being virtuous. And sometimes even death itself, often infamy and external inconveniences, are the public consequences of vice, as vice. For instance, the sense which mankind have of tyranny, injustice, oppression, additional to the mere feeling or fear of misery, has doubtless been instrumental in bringing about revolutions, which make a figure even in the history of the world. For it is plain, men resent injuries as implying faultiness, and retaliate, not merely under the notion of having received harm, but of having received wrong; and they have this resentment in behalf of others, as well as of themselves. So, likewise, even the generality are, in some degree, grateful and disposed to return good offices, not merely because such a one has been the occasion of good to them, but under the view that such good offices implied kind intention and good desert

in the doer. To all this may be added two or three particular things, which many persons will think frivolous;
but to me nothing appears so, which at all comes in
towards determining a question of such importance, as
whether there be or be not a moral institution of government, in the strictest sense moral, *visibly* established and
begun in nature. The particular things are these: That
in domestic government, which is doubtless natural, children, and others also, are very generally punished for
falsehood, and injustice, and ill behaviour, as such, and
rewarded for the contrary; which are instances where
veracity, and justice, and right behaviour, as such, are
naturally enforced by rewards and punishments, whether
more or less considerable in degree: That though civil
government be supposed to take cognizance of actions in
no other view than as prejudicial to society, without respect to the immorality of them; yet as such actions are
immoral, so the sense which men have of the immorality
of them very greatly contributes, in different ways, to
bring offenders to justice: and that entire absence of all
crime and guilt, in the moral sense, when plainly appearing, will almost of course procure, and circumstances of
aggravated guilt prevent, a remission of the penalties
annexed to civil crimes, in many cases, though by no
means in all.

Upon the whole, then, besides the good and bad effects
of virtue and vice upon men's own minds, the course of
the world does, in some measure, turn upon the approbation and disapprobation of them, as such, in others. The
sense of well and ill-doing, the presages of conscience,
the love of good characters, and dislike of bad ones,
honour, shame, resentment, gratitude; all these, considered in themselves, and in their effects, do afford manifest
real instances of virtue, as such, naturally favoured, and of
vice, as such, discountenanced, more or less, in the daily
course of human life; in every age, in every relation, in
every general circumstance of it. That God has given

us a moral nature,* may most justly be urged as a proof of our being under his moral government; but that he has placed us in a condition which gives this nature, as one may speak, scope to operate, and in which it does unavoidably operate, *i. e.* influence mankind to act so as thus to favour and reward virtue, and discountenance and punish vice; this is not the same, but a further additional proof of his moral government; for it is an instance of it. The first is a proof, that he will finally favour and support virtue effectually; the second is an example of his favouring and supporting it at present, in some degree.

✓ If a more distinct inquiry be made, whence it arises that virtue, as such, is often rewarded, and vice, as such, is punished, and this rule never inverted; it will be found to proceed, in part, immediately from the moral nature itself which God has given us; and also, in part, from his having given us, together with this nature, so great a power over each other's happiness and misery. For, *first*, it is certain, that peace and delight, in some degree and upon some occasions, is the necessary and present effect of virtuous practice; an effect arising immediately from that constitution of our nature. We are so made, that well-doing, as such, gives us satisfaction, at least in some instances; ill-doing, as such, in none. And, *secondly*, From our moral nature, joined with God's having put our happiness and misery, in many respects, in each other's power, it cannot but be that vice, as such, some kinds and instances of it at least, will be infamous, and men will be disposed to punish it as in itself detestable; and the villain will by no means be able always to avoid feeling that infamy, any more than he will be able to escape this further punishment which mankind will be disposed to inflict upon him, under the notion of his deserving it. But there can be nothing on the side of vice to answer this; because there is nothing in the human mind con-

* See Dissertation II.

tradictory, as the logicians speak, to virtue. For virtue consists in a regard to what is right and reasonable, as being so; in a regard to veracity, justice, charity, in themselves; and there is surely no such thing as a like natural regard to falsehood, injustice, cruelty. If it be thought, that there are instances of an approbation of vice, as such, in itself, and for its own sake, (though it does not appear to me that there is any such thing at all; but, supposing there be,) it is evidently monstrous; as much so as the most acknowledged perversion of any passion whatever. Such instances of perversion, then, being left out as merely imaginary, or, however, unnatural; it must follow, from the frame of our nature, and from our condition, in the respects now described, that vice cannot at all be, and virtue cannot but be, favoured, as such, by others, upon some occasions, and happy in itself in some degree. For what is here insisted upon is, not the degree in which virtue and vice are thus distinguished, but only the thing itself, that they are so in some degree; though the whole good and bad effect of virtue and vice, as such, is not inconsiderable in degree. But that they must be thus distinguished, in some degree, is in a manner necessary; it is matter of fact, of daily experience, even in the greatest confusion of human affairs.

It is not pretended but that, in the natural course of things, happiness and misery appear to be distributed by other rules, than only the personal merit and demerit of characters. They may sometimes be distributed by way of mere discipline. There may be the wisest and best reasons why the world should be governed by general laws, from whence such promiscuous distribution perhaps must follow; and also why our happiness and misery should be put in each other's power, in the degree which they are. And these things, as in general they contribute to the rewarding virtue and punishing vice, as such; so they often contribute also, not to the inversion of this, which is impossible, but to the rendering persons prosperous though wicked, afflicted though righteous; and, which is worse, to the *rewarding some actions*, though vicious, and *punishing other actions*, though virtuous. But all this cannot drown the voice of nature in the conduct of Providence, plainly declaring itself for virtue, by way of distinction from vice, and preference to it. For, our being so constituted as that virtue and vice are thus naturally favoured and discountenanced, rewarded and punished respectively as such, is an intuitive proof of the intent of nature that it should be so; otherwise the con- stitution of our mind, from which it thus immediately and directly proceeds, would be absurd. But it cannot be said, because virtuous actions are sometimes punished, and vicious actions rewarded, that nature intended it: for, though this great disorder is brought about, as all actions are done, by means of some natural passion, yet *this may* be, as it undoubtedly is, brought about by the perversion of such passion, implanted in us for other, and those very good purposes. And indeed these other and good purposes, even of every passion, may be clearly seen.

We have then a declaration, in some degree, of present effect, from Him who is supreme in nature, which side he is of, or what part he takes; a declaration for virtue, and against vice. So far, therefore, as a man is true to virtue, to veracity and justice, to equity and charity, and the right of the case, in whatever he is concerned, so far he is on the side of the divine administration, and co-operates with it; and from hence, to such a man, arises naturally a secret satisfaction and sense of security, and implicit hope of somewhat further. And,

V. This hope is confirmed by the necessary tendencies of virtue, which, though not of present effect, yet are at present discernible in nature; and so afford an instance of somewhat moral in the essential constitution of it. There is, in the nature of things, a tendency in virtue and vice to produce the good and bad effects now men-

tioned, in a greater degree than they do in fact produce
them. For instance, good and bad men would be much
more rewarded and punished as such, were it not that
justice is often artificially eluded, that characters are not
known, and many who would thus favour virtue and discourage vice, are hindered from doing so by accidental
causes. These tendencies of virtue and vice are obvious
with regard to *individuals*. But it may require more particularly to be considered, that power in a *society*, by
being under the direction of virtue, naturally increases,
and has a necessary tendency to prevail over opposite
power, not under the direction of it; in like manner as
power, by being under the direction of reason, increases,
and has a tendency to prevail over brute force. There
are several brute creatures of equal, and several of superior
strength, to that of men; and possibly the sum of the
whole strength of brutes may be greater than that of mankind; but reason gives us the advantage and superiority
over them, and thus man is the acknowledged governing
animal upon the earth. Nor is this superiority considered
by any as accidental; but as what reason has a tendency,
in the nature of the thing, to obtain. And yet, perhaps, difficulties may be raised about the meaning, as
well as the truth of the assertion, that virtue has the like
tendency.

To obviate these difficulties, let us see more distinctly
how the case stands with regard to reason, which is so
readily acknowledged to have this advantageous tendency. Suppose, then, two or three men, of the best
and most improved understanding, in a desolate open
plain, attacked by ten times the number of beasts of prey;
would their reason secure them the victory in this unequal
combat? Power, then, though joined with reason, and
under its direction, cannot be expected to prevail over
opposite power, though merely brutal, unless the one
bears some proportion to the other. Again, Put the
imaginary case, that rational and irrational creatures were

of like external shape and manner: it is certain, before there were opportunities for the first to distinguish each other, to separate from their adversaries, and to form an union among themselves, they might be upon a level, or, in several respects, upon great disadvantage, though, united, they might be vastly superior; since union is of such efficacy, that ten men, united, might be able to accomplish what ten thousand of the same natural strength and understanding, wholly ununited, could not. In this case, then, brute force might more than maintain its ground against reason, for want of union among the rational creatures. Or suppose a number of men to land upon an island inhabited only by wild beasts; a number of men who, by the regulations of civil government, the inventions of art, and the experience of some years, could they be preserved so long, would be really sufficient to subdue the wild beasts, and to preserve themselves in security from them; yet a conjunction of accidents might give such advantage to the irrational animals, as that they might at once overpower, and even extirpate, the whole species of rational ones. Length of time, then, proper scope and opportunities for reason to exert itself, may be absolutely necessary to its prevailing over brute force. Further still: There are many instances of brutes succeeding in attempts, which they could not have undertaken, had not their irrational nature rendered them incapable of foreseeing the danger of such attempts, or the fury of passion hindered their attending to it; and there are instances of reason and real prudence preventing men's undertaking what, it hath appeared afterwards, they might have succeeded in by a lucky rashness. And in certain conjunctures, ignorance and folly, weakness and discord, may have their advantages. So that rational animals have not necessarily the superiority over irrational ones; but, how improbable soever it may be, it is evidently possible, that, in some globes, the latter may be superior. And were the former wholly at variance and

disunited, by false self-interest and envy, by treachery
and injustice, and consequent rage and malice against
each other, whilst the latter were firmly united among
themselves by instinct, this might greatly contribute to
the introducing such an inverted order of things. For
every one would consider it as inverted, since reason has,
in the nature of it, a tendency to prevail over brute force,
notwithstanding the possibility it may not prevail, and the
necessity which there is for many concurring circumstances
to render it prevalent.

Now, I say, virtue in a society has a like tendency to
procure superiority and additional power, whether this
power be considered as the means of security from
opposite power, or of obtaining other advantages. And it
has this tendency, by rendering public good an object
and end to every member of the society; by putting
every one upon consideration and diligence, recollection
and self-government, both in order to see what is the
most effectual method, and also in order to perform their
proper part for obtaining and preserving it; by uniting
a society within itself, and so increasing its strength,
and, which is particularly to be mentioned, uniting
it by means of veracity and justice. For as these last
are principal bonds of union, so benevolence, or public
spirit, undirected, unrestrained by them, is—nobody knows
what.

And suppose the invisible world, and the invisible
dispensations of Providence, to be in any sort analogous to
what appears; or that both together make up one uniform
scheme, the two parts of which, the part which we see,
and that which is beyond our observation, are analogous
to each other; then there must be a like natural
tendency in the derived power, throughout the universe,
under the direction of virtue, to prevail in general over
that which is not under its direction; as there is in reason,
derived reason, in the universe, to prevail over brute
force. But then, in order to the prevalence of virtue, or

that it may actually produce what it has a tendency to produce, the like concurrences are necessary as are to the prevalence of reason. There must be some proportion between the natural power of force which is, and that which is not, under the direction of virtue : there must be sufficient length of time; for the complete success of virtue, as of reason, cannot, from the nature of the thing, be otherwise than gradual : there must be, as one may speak, a fair field of trial, a stage large and extensive enough, proper occasions and opportunities for the virtuous to join together, to exert themselves against lawless force, and to reap the fruit of their united labours. Now, indeed, it is to be hoped, that the disproportion between the good and the bad, even here on earth, is not so great, but that the former have natural power sufficient to their prevailing to a considerable degree, if circumstances would permit this power to be united. For, much less, very much less power, under the direction of virtue, would prevail over much greater, not under the direction of it. However, good men over the face of the earth cannot unite; as for other reasons, so because they cannot be sufficiently ascertained of each other's characters. And the known course of human things, the scene we are now passing through, particularly the shortness of life, denies to virtue its full scope in several other respects. The natural tendency which we have been considering, though real, is *hindered* from being carried into effect in the present state; but these hinderances may be removed in a future one. Virtue, to borrow the Christian allusion, is militant here, and various untoward accidents contribute to its being often overborne; but it may combat with greater advantage hereafter, and prevail completely, and enjoy its consequent rewards in some future states. Neglected as it is, perhaps unknown, perhaps despised and oppressed here, there may be scenes in eternity, lasting enough, and in every other way adapted, to afford it a sufficient sphere of action,

and a sufficient sphere for the natural consequences of it
to follow in fact. If the soul be naturally immortal, and
this state be a progress towards a future one, as childhood is towards mature age, good men may naturally
unite, not only amongst themselves, but also with other
orders of virtuous creatures, in that future state. For
virtue, from the very nature of it, is a principle and bond
of union, in some degree, amongst all who are endued
with it, and known to each other; so as that by it a good
man cannot but recommend himself to the favour and
protection of all virtuous beings, throughout the whole
universe, who can be acquainted with his character, and
can any way interpose in his behalf in any part of his
duration. And one might add, that suppose all this
advantageous tendency of virtue to become effect amongst
one or more orders of creatures, in any distant scenes
and periods, and to be seen by any orders of vicious
creatures throughout the universal kingdom of God; this
happy effect of virtue would have a tendency, by way of
example, and possibly in other ways, to amend those of
them who are capable of amendment, and being recovered
to a just sense of virtue. If our notions of the plan of
Providence were enlarged, in any sort proportionable to
what late discoveries have enlarged our views with respect
to the material world, representations of this kind would
not appear absurd or extravagant. However, they are
not to be taken, as intended, for a literal delineation of
what is, in fact, the particular scheme of the universe,
which cannot be known without revelation; for suppositions are not to be looked on as true, because not
incredible; but they are mentioned to show, that our
finding virtue to be hindered from procuring to itself such
superiority and advantages, is no objection against its
having, in the essential nature of the thing, a tendency to
procure them. And the suppositions now mentioned do
plainly show this; for they show, that these hinderances
are so far from being necessary, that we ourselves can

easily conceive how they may be removed in future states, and full scope be granted to virtue. And all these advantageous tendencies of it are to be considered as declarations of God in its favour. This, however, is taking a pretty large compass; though it is certain, that as the material world appears to be, in a manner, boundless and immense, there must be *some* scheme of Providence vast in proportion to it.

But let us return to the earth, our habitation, and we shall see this happy tendency of virtue, by imagining an instance not so vast and remote—by supposing a kingdom, or society of men, upon it, perfectly virtuous, for a succession of many ages; to which, if you please, may be given a situation advantageous for universal monarchy. In such a state there would be no such thing as faction; but men of the greatest capacity would, of course, all along, have the chief direction of affairs willingly yielded to them, and they would share it among themselves without envy. Each of these would have the part assigned him to which his genius was peculiarly adapted; and others, who had not any distinguished genius, would be safe, and think themselves very happy, by being under the protection and guidance of those who had. Public determinations would really be the result of the united wisdom of the community, and they would faithfully be executed by the united strength of it. Some would in a higher way contribute, but all would in some way contribute, to the public prosperity; and in it each would enjoy the fruits of his own virtue. And as injustice, whether by fraud or force, would be unknown among themselves, so they would be sufficiently secured from it in their neighbours. For cunning and false self-interest, confederacies in injustice, ever slight, and accompanied with faction and intestine treachery: these, on one hand, would be found mere childish folly and weakness, when set in opposition against wisdom, public spirit, union inviolable, and fidelity on the other, allowing both a

D

sufficient length of years to try their force. Add the
general influence which such a kingdom would have over
the face of the earth, by way of example particularly, and
the reverence which would be paid it. It would plainly be
superior to all others, and the world must gradually come
under its empire; not by means of lawless violence, but
partly by what must be allowed to be just conquest, and
partly by other kingdoms submitting themselves voluntarily to it throughout a course of ages, and claiming its
protection one after another, in successive exigencies.
The head of it would be an universal monarch, in another
sense than any mortal has yet been, and the eastern style
would be literally applicable to him, that *all people,
nations, and languages, should serve him.* And though
indeed our knowledge of human nature, and the whole
history of mankind, show the impossibility, without some
miraculous interposition, that a number of men here on
earth should unite in one society or government, in the
fear of God and universal practice of virtue, and that
such a government should continue so united for a
succession of ages; yet, admitting or supposing this,
the effect would be as now drawn out. And thus, for
instance, the wonderful power and prosperity promised to
the Jewish nation in the Scripture, would be, in a great
measure, the consequence of what is predicted of them;
that the " people should be all righteous, and inherit the
land for ever," Isaiah lx. 21.; were we to understand
the latter phrase of a long continuance only, sufficient to
give things time to work. The predictions of this kind,
for there are many of them, cannot come to pass in the
present known course of nature; but suppose them come
to pass, and then the dominion and pre-eminence promised must naturally follow, to a very considerable
degree.

Consider, now, the general system of religion: that
the government of the world is uniform, and one, and
moral; that virtue and right shall finally have the

advantage, and prevail over fraud and lawless force, over
the deceits as well as the violence of wickedness, under the
conduct of one supreme Governor; and from the observations above made it will appear, that God has, by our
reason, given us to see a peculiar connexion in the several
parts of this scheme, and a tendency towards the completion
of it, arising out of the very nature of virtue; which
tendency is to be considered as somewhat moral in the
essential constitution of things. If any one should think all
this to be of little importance, I desire him to consider what
he would think, if vice had, essentially and in its nature,
these advantageous tendencies, or if virtue had essentially
the direct contrary ones.

But it may be objected, that notwithstanding all these
natural effects, and these natural tendencies of virtue, yet
things may be now going on throughout the universe, and
may go on hereafter, in the same mixed way as here at
present upon earth; virtue sometimes prosperous, sometimes depressed; vice sometimes punished, sometimes
successful. The answer to which is, that it is not the
purpose of this chapter, nor of this treatise, properly to
prove God's perfect moral government over the world, or
the truth of religion, but to observe what there is in the
constitution and course of nature to confirm the proper
proof of it, supposed to be known, and that the weight of the
foregoing observations to this purpose may be thus distinctly
proved. Pleasure and pain are indeed, to a certain degree,
say to a very high degree, distributed amongst us, without
any apparent regard to the merit or demerit of characters.
And, were there nothing else, concerning this matter,
discernible in the constitution and course of nature,
there would be no ground, from the constitution and
course of nature, to hope or to fear, that men would be
rewarded or punished hereafter according to their deserts;
which, however, it is to be remarked, implies, that even
then there would be no ground, from appearances, to think
that vice, upon the whole, would have the advantage,

rather than that virtue would. And thus the proof of a
future state of retribution would rest upon the usual known
arguments for it; which are, I think, plainly unanswerable,
and would be so, though there were no additional
confirmation of them from the things above insisted
on. But these things are a very strong confirmation of
them. For,

First, They show that the Author of nature is not
indifferent to virtue and vice. They amount to a declaration from him, determinate, and not to be evaded, in
favour of one, and against the other: such a declaration
as there is nothing to be set over against, or answered, on
the part of vice. So that, were a man, laying aside the
proper proof of religion, to determine from the course of
nature only, whether it were most probable that the
righteous or the wicked would have the advantage in a
future life, there can be no doubt but that he would
determine the probability to be, that the former would.
The course of nature, then, in the view of it now given,
furnishes us with a real practical proof of the obligations of
religion.

Secondly, When, conformably to what religion teaches
us, God shall reward and punish virtue and vice, as such,
so as that every one shall, upon the whole, have his deserts,
this distributive justice will not be a thing different in *kind*,
but only in *degree*, from what we experience in his present
government. It will be that in *effect*, toward which we now
see a *tendency*. It will be no more than the *completion* of
that moral government, the *principles and beginning* of
which have been shown, beyond all dispute, discernible in
the present constitution and course of nature. And from
hence it follows,

Thirdly, That as, under the natural government of
God, our experience of those kinds and degrees of happiness and misery, which we do experience at present,
gives just ground to hope for and to fear higher degrees
and other kinds of both in a future state, supposing a

future state admitted; so, under his moral government, our experience that virtue and vice are, in the manners above mentioned, actually rewarded and punished at present, in a certain degree, gives just ground to hope and to fear, that they *may be* rewarded and punished in a higher degree hereafter. It is acknowledged, indeed, that this alone is not sufficient ground to think that they *actually will be* rewarded and punished in a higher degree, rather than in a lower: But then,

Lastly, There is sufficient ground to think so, from the good and bad tendencies of virtue and vice. For these tendencies are essential, and founded in the nature of things; whereas, the hinderances to their becoming effect are, in numberless cases, not necessary, but artificial only. Now, it may be much more strongly argued, that these tendencies, as well as the actual rewards and punishments of virtue and vice which arise directly out of the nature of things, will remain hereafter, than that the accidental hinderances of them will. And if these hinderances do not remain, those rewards and punishments cannot but be carried on much further towards the perfection of moral government; *i. e.* the tendencies of virtue and vice will become effect; but when, or where, or in what particular way, cannot be known at all but by revelation.

Upon the whole, there is a kind of moral government implied in God's natural government;* virtue and vice are naturally rewarded and punished as beneficial and mischievous to society,† and rewarded and punished directly as virtue and vice.‡ The notion, then, of a moral scheme of government is not fictitious, but natural; for it is suggested to our thoughts by the constitution and course of nature, and the execution of this scheme is actually begun, in the instances here mentioned. And these things are to be considered as a declaration of the

* Page 35.   † Page 36.   ‡ Page 37, &c.

Author of nature, for virtue, and against vice; they give
a credibility to the supposition of their being rewarded
and punished hereafter, and also ground to hope and
to fear, that they may be rewarded and punished in
higher degrees than they are here. And as all this is
confirmed, so the argument for religion, from the constitution and course of nature, is carried on farther,
by observing, that there are natural tendencies, and,
in innumerable cases, only artificial hinderances, to this
moral scheme being carried on much farther towards
perfection than it is at present.* The notion, then, of a
moral scheme of government, much more perfect than
what is seen, is not a fictitious, but a natural notion;
for it is suggested to our thoughts · by the essential
tendencies of virtue and vice. And these tendencies
are to be considered as intimations, as implicit promises and threatenings, from the Author of nature, of
much greater rewards and punishments to follow virtue
and vice, than do at present. And, indeed, every *natural*
tendency, which is to continue, but which is hindered
from becoming effect by only *accidental* causes, affords a
presumption, that such tendency will, some time or other,
become effect: a presumption in degree proportionable
to the length of the duration through which such
tendency will continue. And from these things together
arises a real presumption, that the moral scheme of government established in nature shall be carried on much farther
towards perfection hereafter, and, I think, a presumption
that it will be absolutely completed. But from these things,
joined with the moral nature which God has given us,
considered as given us by him, arises a practical proof†
that it will be completed; a proof from fact, and therefore
a distinct one from that which is deduced from the
eternal and unalterable relations, the fitness and unfitness
of actions.

* Page 43, &c.   † See this proof drawn out briefly, Chap. 6

CHAPTER IV.

*Of a State of Probation, as implying Trial, Difficulties,
and Danger.*

THE general doctrine of religion, that our present life
is a state of probation for a future one, comprehends
under it several particular things, distinct from each
other. But the first and most common meaning of it
seems to be, that our future interest is now depending,
and depending upon ourselves; that we have scope and
opportunities here for that good and bad behaviour,
which God will reward and punish hereafter; together
with temptations to one, as well as inducements of reason
to the other. And this is, in great measure, the same
with saying, that we are under the moral government of
God, and to give an account of our actions to him. For
the notion of a future account, and general righteous
judgment, implies some sort of temptations to what is
wrong, otherwise there would be no moral possibility of
doing wrong, nor ground for judgment or discrimination.
But there is this difference, that the word *probation* is
more distinctly and particularly expressive of allurements
to wrong, or difficulties in adhering uniformly to what is
right, and of the danger of miscarrying by such temptations,
than the words *moral government*. A state of probation,
then, as thus particularly implying in it trial, difficulties,
and danger, may require to be considered distinctly by
itself.

And as the moral government of God, which religion
teaches us, implies, that we are in a state of trial with
regard to a future world; so also his natural government
over us implies, that we are in a state of trial, in the like
sense, with regard to the present world. Natural government, by rewards and punishments, as much implies

natural trial, as moral government does moral trial. The
natural government of God here meant,[*] consists in his
annexing pleasure to some actions, and pain to others,
which are in our power to do or forbear, and in giving us
notice of such appointment beforehand. This necessarily
implies that he has made our happiness and misery, or
our interest, to depend in part upon ourselves. And, so
far as men have temptations to any course of action,
which will probably occasion them greater temporal
inconvenience and uneasiness than satisfaction, so far their
temporal interest is in danger from themselves, or they
are in a state of trial with respect to it. Now, people
often blame others, and even themselves, for their misconduct in their temporal concerns. And we find many
are greatly wanting to themselves, and miss of that
natural happiness which they might have obtained in the
present life; perhaps every one does in some degree.
But many run themselves into great inconvenience, and
into extreme distress and misery, not through incapacity
of knowing better, and doing better for themselves, which
would be nothing to the present purpose, but through
their own fault. And these things necessarily imply
temptation, and danger of miscarrying, in a greater or
less degree, with respect to our worldly interest or
happiness. Every one, too, without having religion in his
thoughts, speaks of the hazards which young people run
upon their setting out in the world; hazards from other
causes than merely their ignorance and unavoidable
accidents. And some courses of vice, at least, being
contrary to men's worldly interest or good, temptations to
these must, at the same time, be temptations to forego our
present and our future interest. Thus, in our natural
or temporal capacity, we are in a state of trial, *i. e.* of
difficulty and danger, analogous or like to our moral and
religious trial.

* Chap. 2.

This will more distinctly appear to any one, who thinks it worth while more distinctly to consider what it is which constitutes our trial in both capacities, and to observe how mankind behave under it.

And that which constitutes this our trial, in both these capacities, must be somewhat either in our external circumstances, or in our nature. For, on the one hand, persons may be betrayed into wrong behaviour upon surprise, or overcome upon any other very singular and extraordinary external occasions, who would otherwise have preserved their character of prudence and of virtue: in which cases, every one, in speaking of the wrong behaviour of these persons, would impute it to such particular external circumstances. And, on the other hand, men who have contracted habits of vice and folly of any kind, or have some particular passions in excess, will seek opportunities, and, as it were, go out of their way, to gratify themselves in these respects, at the expense of their wisdom and their virtue; led to it, as every one would say, not by external temptations, but by such habits and passions. And the account of this last case is, that particular passions are no more coincident with prudence, or that reasonable self-love, the end of which is our worldly interest, than they are with the principle of virtue and religion, but often draw contrary ways to one as well as to the other; and so such particular passions are as much temptations to act imprudently with regard to our worldly interest, as to act viciously.* However, as when we say, men are misled by external circumstances of temptation, it cannot but be understood that there is somewhat within themselves to render those circumstances temptations, or to render them susceptible of impressions from them; so, when we say they are misled by passions, it is always supposed that there are occasions, circumstances, and objects, exciting these passions and affording means

* See Sermons preached at the Rolls, 1726, 2nd Edit. p. 205, &c. Pref. p. 25, &c. Serm. p. 21, &c.

for gratifying them : and therefore temptations from within
and from without coincide, and mutually imply each other.
Now the several external objects of the appetites, passions,
and affections, being present to the senses, or offering
themselves to the mind, and so exciting emotions suitable
to their nature, not only in cases where they can be gratified
consistently with innocence and prudence, but also in cases
where they cannot, and yet can be gratified imprudently
and viciously ; this as really puts them in danger of voluntarily foregoing their present interest or good as their
future, and as really renders self-denial necessary to secure
one as the other; *i. e.* we are in a like state of trial with
respect to both, by the very same passions, excited by the
very same means.   Thus mankind having a temporal
interest depending upon themselves, and a prudent course
of behaviour being necessary to secure it, passions inor-
dinately excited, whether by means of example or by
any other external circumstance, towards such objects,
at such times, or in such degrees, as that they cannot be
gratified consistently with worldly prudence, are temptations, dangerous, and too often successful temptations,
to forego a greater temporal good for a less ; *i. e.* to forego
what is, upon the whole, our temporal interest, for the
sake of a present gratification.   This is a description of
our state of trial in our temporal capacity.   Substitute now
the word *future* for *temporal*, and *virtue* for *prudence*, and
it will be just as proper a description of our state of trial
in our religious capacity; so analogous are they to each
other.

   If, from consideration of this our like state of trial in
both capacities, we go on to observe farther, how mankind
behave under it, we shall find there are some who have
so little sense of it, that they scarce look beyond the
passing day; they are so taken up with present gratifications, as to have, in a manner, no feeling of consequences, no regard to their future ease or fortune in this
life, any more than to their happiness in another.   Some

appear to be blinded and deceived by inordinate passion in their worldly concerns, as much as in religion. Others are not deceived, but, as it were, forcibly carried away by the like passions, against their better judgment, and feeble resolutions, too, of acting better. And there are men, and truly they are not a few, who shamelessly avow, not their interest, but their mere will and pleasure, to be their law of life; and who, in open defiance of everything that is reasonable, will go on in a course of vicious extravagance, foreseeing, with no remorse and little fear, that it will be their temporal ruin; and some of them, under the apprehension of the consequences of wickedness in another state. And, to speak in the most moderate way, human creatures are not only continually liable to go wrong voluntarily, but we see likewise that they often actually do so, with respect to their temporal interests, as well as with respect to religion.

Thus, our difficulties and dangers, or our trials in our temporal and our religious capacity, as they proceed from the same causes, and have the same effect upon men's behaviour, are evidently analogous, and of the same kind.

It may be added, that as the difficulties and dangers of miscarrying in our religious state of trial are greatly increased, and, one is ready to think, in a manner wholly *made*, by the ill behaviour of others; by a wrong education, wrong in a moral sense, sometimes positively vicious; by a general bad example; by the dishonest artifices which are got into business of all kinds; and, in very many parts of the world, by religions being corrupted into superstitions which indulge men in their vices; so, in like manner, the difficulties of conducting ourselves prudently in respect to our present interest, and our danger of being led aside from pursuing it, are greatly increased by a foolish education, and, after we come to mature age, by the extravagance and carelessness of others whom we have intercourse with; and by mistaken notions, very generally prevalent, and taken up from common opinion, concerning temporal happiness, and wherein it consists. And persons, by their own negligence and folly in their temporal affairs, no less than by a course of vice, bring themselves into new difficulties, and, by habits of indulgence, become less qualified to go through them; and one irregularity after another embarrasses things to such a degree that they know not whereabout they are, and often makes the path of conduct so intricate and perplexed, that it is difficult to trace it out; difficult even to determine what is the prudent or the moral part. Thus, for instance, wrong behaviour in one stage of life, youth; wrong, I mean, considering ourselves only in our temporal capacity, without taking in religion; this, in several ways, increases the difficulties of right behaviour in mature age; *i. e.* puts us into a more disadvantageous state of trial in our temporal capacity.

We are an inferior part of the creation of God: there are natural appearances of our being in a state of degradation;* and we certainly are in a condition which *does not seem*, by any means, the most advantageous we could imagine or desire, either in our natural or moral capacity, for securing either our present or future interest. However, this condition, low, and careful, and uncertain as it is, does not afford any just ground of complaint. For, as men may manage their temporal affairs with prudence, and so pass their days here on earth in tolerable ease and satisfaction, by a moderate degree of care; so, likewise, with regard to religion, there is no more required than what they are well able to do, and what they must be greatly wanting to themselves if they neglect. And for persons to have that put upon them which they are well able to go through, and no more, we naturally consider as an equitable thing, supposing it done by proper authority. Nor have we any more reason to complain of it, with regard to the Author of nature, than of his not

* Part ii. chap. 5.

having given us other advantages, belonging to other orders
of creatures.

But the thing here insisted upon is, that the state of
trial which religion teaches us we are in, is rendered
credible, by its being throughout uniform and of a piece
with the general conduct of Providence towards us, in
all other respects within the compass of our knowledge.
Indeed, if mankind, considered in their natural capacity
as inhabitants of this world only, found themselves, from
their birth to their death, in a settled state of security
and happiness, without any solicitude or thought of their
own; or, if they were in no danger of being brought into
inconveniences and distress by carelessness, or the folly
of passion, through bad example, the treachery of others,
or the deceitful appearances of things; were this our natural
condition, then it might seem strange, and be some presumption against the truth of religion, that it represents
our future and more general interest as not secure of course,
but as depending upon our behaviour, and requiring recollection and self-government to obtain it. For it might
be alleged, " What you say is our condition in one respect,
is not in any wise of a sort with what we find, by experience, our condition is in another. Our whole present
interest is secured in our hands, without any solicitude
of ours, and why should not our future interest, if we
have any such, be so too?" But since, on the contrary,
thought and consideration, the voluntary denying ourselves
many things which we desire, and a course of behaviour
far from being always agreeable to us, are absolutely
necessary to our acting even a common decent and common prudent part, so as to pass with any satisfaction
through the present world, and be received upon any
tolerable good terms in it; since this is the case, all
presumption against self-denial and attention being necessary to secure our higher interest is removed. Had we
not experience, it might perhaps speciously be urged,
that it is impossible anything of hazard and danger should

be put upon us by an infinite Being, when everything
which is hazard and danger in our manner of conception,
and will end in error, confusion, and misery, is now
already certain in his foreknowledge. And, indeed, why
anything of hazard and danger should be put upon such
frail creatures as we are, may well be thought a difficulty
in speculation; and cannot but be so, till we know the
whole, or, however, much more of the case. But still, the
constitution of nature is as it is. Our happiness and
misery are trusted to our conduct, and made to depend
upon it. Somewhat, and, in many circumstances, a great
deal too, is put upon us, either to do, or to suffer, as we
choose. And all the various miseries of life, which people
bring upon themselves by negligence and folly, and might
have avoided by proper care, are instances of this; which
miseries are, beforehand, just as contingent and undetermined as their conduct, and left to be determined by it.

These observations are an answer to the objections
against the credibility of a state of trial, as implying temptations, and real danger of miscarrying with regard to our
general interest, under the moral government of God; and
they show, that, if we are at all to be considered in such
a capacity, and as having such an interest, the general
analogy of Providence must lead us to apprehend ourselves
in danger of miscarrying, in different degrees, as to this
interest, by our neglecting to act the proper part belonging
to us in that capacity. For we have a present interest,
under the government of God, which we experience here
upon earth. And this interest, as it is not forced upon us,
so neither is it offered to our acceptance, but to our acquisition; in such sort, as that we are in danger of missing it,
by means of temptations to neglect or act contrary to it;
and without attention and self-denial, must and do miss of
it. It is then perfectly credible, that this may be our case
with respect to that chief and final good which religion
proposes to us.

CHAPTER V.

Of a State of Probation, as intended for moral Discipline and Improvement.

From the consideration of our being in a probation-state of so much difficulty and hazard, naturally arises the question, how we came to be placed in it? But such a general inquiry as this would be found involved in insuperable difficulties: for, though some of these difficulties would be lessened by observing, that all wickedness is voluntary, as is implied in its very notion, and that many of the miseries of life have apparent good effects, yet when we consider other circumstances belonging to both, and what must be the consequence of the former in a life to come, it cannot but be acknowledged plain folly and presumption, to pretend to give an account of the whole reasons of this matter; the whole reasons of our being allotted a condition, out of which so much wickedness and misery, so circumstanced, would, in fact, arise. Whether it be not beyond our faculties, not only to find out, but even to understand, the whole account of this; or, though we should be supposed capable of understanding it, yet, whether it would be of service or prejudice to us to be informed of it, is impossible to say. But as our present condition can in no wise be shown inconsistent with the perfect moral government of God; so religion teaches us we were placed in it, that we might qualify ourselves, by the practice of virtue, for another state, which is to follow it. And this, though but a partial answer, a very partial one indeed, to the inquiry now mentioned, yet is a more satisfactory answer to another, which is of real, and of the utmost importance to us to have answered—the inquiry, What is our business here? The known end, then, why we are placed in a state of so much affliction, hazard, and difficulty, is, our improvement in virtue and piety, as the requisite qualification for a future state of security and happiness.

Now, the beginning of life, considered as an education for mature age in the present world, appears plainly, at first sight, analogous to this our trial for a future one; the former being, in our temporal capacity, what the latter is in our religious capacity. But some observations, common to both of them, and a more distinct consideration of each, will more distinctly show the extent and force of the analogy between them; and the credibility which arises from hence, as well as from the nature of the thing, that the present life was intended to be a state of discipline for a future one.

I. Every species of creatures is, we see, designed for a particular way of life, to which the nature, the capacities, temper, and qualifications, of each species, are as necessary as their external circumstances. Both come into the notion of such state, or particular way of life, and are constituent parts of it. Change a man's capacities or character to the degree in which it is conceivable they may be changed, and he would be altogether incapable of a human course of life and human happiness; as incapable as if, his nature continuing unchanged, he were placed in a world where he had no sphere of action, nor any objects to answer his appetites, passions, and affections of any sort. One thing is set over against another, as an ancient writer expresses it. Our nature corresponds to our external condition. Without this correspondence, there would be no possibility of any such thing as human life and human happiness; which life and happiness are, therefore, a *result* from our nature and condition jointly; meaning, by human life, not *living*, in the literal sense, but the whole complex notion commonly understood by those words. So that, without determining what will be the employment and happiness, the particular life of good men hereafter, there must be some determinate capacities, some necessary character and qualifications, without which per-

sons cannot but be utterly incapable of it; in like manner
as there must be some, without which men would be incapable of their present state of life. Now,

II. The constitution of human creatures, and indeed
of all creatures which come under our notice, is such, as
that they are capable of naturally becoming qualified for
states of life, for which they were once wholly unqualified.
In imagination we may indeed conceive of creatures, as
incapable of having any of their faculties naturally enlarged, or as being unable naturally to acquire any new
qualifications; but the faculties of every species known
to us are made for enlargement, for acquirements of
experience and habits. We find ourselves, in particular,
endued with capacities, not only of perceiving ideas, and
of knowledge or perceiving truth, but also of storing up
our ideas and knowledge by memory. We are capable,
not only of acting, and of having different momentary
impressions made upon us, but of getting a new facility
in any kind of action, and of settled alterations in our
temper or character. The power of the two last is the
power of habits. But neither the perception of ideas,
nor knowledge of any sort, are habits, though absolutely
necessary to the forming of them. However, apprehension, reason, memory, which are the capacities of acquiring
knowledge, are greatly improved by exercise. Whether
the word *habit* is applicable to all these improvements,
and, in particular, how far the powers of memory and
of habits may be powers of the same nature, I shall not
inquire. But that perceptions come into our minds readily
and of course, by means of their having been there before,
seems a thing of the same sort as readiness in any particular kind of action, proceeding from being accustomed
to it. And aptness to recollect practical observations of
service in our conduct, is plainly habit in many cases.
There are habits of perception, and habits of action. An
instance of the former, is our constant and even involuntary
readiness in correcting the impressions of our sight con-

cerning magnitudes and distances, so as to substitute judgment in the room of sensation, imperceptibly to ourselves. And it seems as if all other associations of ideas, not naturally connected, might be called passive habits, as properly as our readiness in understanding languages upon sight, or hearing of words. And our readiness in speaking and writing them is an instance of the latter, of active habits. For distinctness, we may consider habits as belonging to the body or the mind; and the latter will be explained by the former. Under the former are comprehended all bodily activities or motions, whether graceful or unbecoming, which are owing to use: under the latter, general habits of life and conduct, such as those of obedience and submission to authority, or to any particular person; those of veracity, justice, and charity; those of attention, industry, self-government, envy, revenge. And habits of this latter kind seem produced by repeated acts, as well as the former. And in like manner as habits belonging to the body are produced by external acts, so habits of the mind are produced by the exertion of inward practical purposes; *i. e.* by carrying them into act, or acting upon them—the principles of obedience, of veracity, justice, and charity. Nor can those habits be formed by any external course of action, otherwise than as it proceeds from these principles; because it is only these inward principles exerted, which are strictly acts of obedience, of veracity, of justice, and of charity. So, likewise, habits of attention, industry, self-government, are, in the same manner, acquired by exercise; and habits of envy and revenge by indulgence, whether in outward act or in thought and intention, *i. e.* inward act; for such intention is an act. Resolutions also to do well are properly acts; and endeavouring to force upon our own minds a practical sense of virtue, or to beget in others that practical sense of it which a man really has himself, is a virtuous act. All these, therefore, may and will contribute towards forming good habits.

But, going over the theory of virtue in one's thoughts, talking well, and drawing fine pictures of it, this is so far from necessarily or certainly conducing to form a habit of it in him who thus employs himself, that it may harden the mind in a contrary course, and render it gradually more insensible, *i. e.* form a habit of insensibility to all moral considerations. For, from our very faculties of habits, passive impressions, by being repeated, grow weaker. Thoughts, by often passing through the mind, are felt less sensibly: being accustomed to danger, begets intrepidity; *i. e.* lessens fear; to distress, lessens the passion of pity; to instances of other's mortality, lessens the sensible apprehension of our own. And from these two observations together, that practical habits are formed and strengthened by repeated acts, and that passive impressions grow weaker by being repeated upon us, it must follow, that active habits may be gradually forming and strengthening, by a course of acting upon such and such motives and excitements, whilst these motives and excitements themselves are, by proportionable degrees, growing less sensible, *i. e.* are continually less and less sensibly felt, even as the active habits strengthen. And experience confirms this; for active principles, at the very time that they are less lively in perception than they were, are found to be somehow wrought more thoroughly into the temper and character, and become more effectual in influencing our practice. The three things just mentioned may afford instances of it. Perception of danger is a natural excitement of passive fear and active caution; and, by being inured to danger, habits of the latter are gradually wrought, at the same time that the former gradually lessens. Perception of distress in others is a natural excitement, passively to pity, and actively to relieve it; but let a man set himself to attend to, inquire out, and relieve distressed persons, and he cannot but grow less and less sensibly affected with the various miseries of life with which he must become acquainted;

when yet, at the same time, benevolence, considered not
as a passion, but as a practical principle of action, will
strengthen; and, whilst he passively compassionates the
distressed less, he will acquire a greater aptitude actively
to assist and befriend them. So also, at the same time
that the daily instances of men's dying around us give
us daily a less sensible passive feeling or apprehension of
our own mortality, such instances greatly contribute to the
strengthening a practical regard to it in serious men, *i. e.*
to forming a habit of acting with a constant view to it.
And this seems again further to show, that passive impressions made upon our minds by admonition, experience,
example, though they may have a remote efficacy, and a
very great one, towards forming active habits, yet can have
this efficacy no otherwise than by inducing us to such a
course of action; and that it is, not being affected so and
so, but acting, which forms those habits; only it must be
always remembered, that real endeavours to enforce good
impressions upon ourselves, are a species of virtuous action.
Nor do we know how far it is possible, in the nature
of things, that effects should be wrought in us at once
equivalent to habits, *i. e.* what is wrought by use and
exercise. However, the thing insisted upon is, not what
may be possible, but what is in fact the appointment of
nature, which is, that active habits are to be formed by
exercise. Their progress may be so gradual as to be
imperceptible in its steps; it may be hard to explain
the faculty by which we are capable of habits, throughout
its several parts, and to trace it up to its original, so as to
distinguish it from all others in our mind; and it seems as
if contrary effects were to be ascribed to it. But the thing
in general, that our nature is formed to yield, in some
such manner as this, to use and exercise, is matter of
certain experience.

Thus, by accustoming ourselves to any course of action,
we get an aptness to go on, a facility, readiness, and
often pleasure in it. The inclinations which rendered us

averse to it grow weaker; the difficulties in it, not only the imaginary, but the real ones, lessen; the reasons for it offer themselves of course to our thoughts upon all occasions; and the least glimpse of them is sufficient to make us go on in a course of action to which we have been accustomed. And practical principles appear to grow stronger, absolutely in themselves, by exercise, as well as relatively, with regard to contrary principles; which, by being accustomed to submit, do so habitually, and of course. And thus a new character, in several respects, may be formed; and many habitudes of life, not given by nature, but which nature directs us to acquire.

III. Indeed we may be assured, that we should never have had these capacities of improving by experience, acquired knowledge and habits, had they not been necessary, and intended to be made use of. And, accordingly, we find them so necessary, and so much intended, that without them we should be utterly incapable of that which was the end for which we were made, considered in our temporal capacity only—the employments and satisfactions of our mature state of life.

Nature does in no wise qualify us wholly, much less at once, for this mature state of life. Even maturity of understanding and bodily strength are not only arrived to gradually, but are also very much owing to the continued exercise of our powers of body and mind from infancy. But if we suppose a person brought into the world with both these in maturity, as far as this is conceivable, he would plainly at first be as unqualified for the human life of mature age as an idiot. He would be in a manner distracted with astonishment, and apprehension, and curiosity, and suspense; nor can one guess how long it would be before he would be familiarized to himself, and the objects about him, enough even to set himself to any thing. It may be questioned, too, whether the natural information of his sight and hearing would be of any manner of use at all to him in acting, before experience.

And it seems that men would be strangely headstrong and self-willed, and disposed to exert themselves with an impetuosity which would render society insupportable, and the living in it impracticable, were it not for some acquired moderation and self-government, some aptitude and readiness in restraining themselves, and concealing their sense of things. Want of everything of this kind which is learned, would render a man as incapable of society as want of language would; or as his natural ignorance of any of the particular employments of life would render him incapable of providing himself with the common conveniences, or supplying the necessary wants of it. In these respects, and probably in many more, of which we have no particular notion, mankind is left by nature an unformed, unfinished creature, utterly deficient and unqualified, before the acquirement of knowledge, experience, and habits, for that mature state of life which was the end of his creation, considering him as related only to this world.

But then, as nature has endued us with a power of supplying these deficiencies, by acquired knowledge, experience, and habits; so, likewise, we are placed in a condition, in infancy, childhood, and youth, fitted for it; fitted for our acquiring those qualifications of all sorts, which we stand in need of in mature age. Hence children, from their very birth, are daily growing acquainted with the objects about them, with the scene in which they are placed, and to have a future part; and learning somewhat or other necessary to the performance of it. The subordinations to which they are accustomed in domestic life teach them self-government in common behaviour abroad, and prepare them for subjection and obedience to civil authority. What passes before their eyes, and daily happens to them, gives them experience, caution against treachery and deceit, together with numberless little rules of action and conduct, which we could not live without, and which are learnt so insensibly and so perfectly, as to be mistaken, perhaps, for instinct; though they are the effect of long experience and exercise—as much so as language, or knowledge in particular business, or the qualifications and behaviour belonging to the several ranks and professions. Thus, the beginning of our days is adapted to be, and is, a state of education in the theory and practice of mature life. We are much assisted in it by example, instruction, and the care of others; but a great deal is left to ourselves to do. And of this, as part is done easily, and of course, so part requires diligence and care, the voluntary foregoing many things which we desire, and setting ourselves to what we should have no inclination to, but for the necessity or expedience of it. For, that labour and industry which the station of so many absolutely requires, they would be greatly unqualified for in maturity, as those in other stations would be for any other sorts of application, if both were not accustomed to them in their youth. And according as persons behave themselves, in the general education which all go through, and in the particular ones adapted to particular employments, their character is formed, and made appear; they recommend themselves more or less; and are capable of, and placed in, different stations in the society of mankind.

The former part of life, then, is to be considered as an important opportunity, which nature puts into our hands, and which, when lost, is not to be recovered. And our being placed in a state of discipline throughout this life for another world, is a providential disposition of things, exactly of the same kind as our being placed in a state of discipline during childhood, for mature age. Our condition, in both respects, is uniform and of a piece, and comprehended under one and the same general law of nature.

And if we were not able at all to discern, how or in what way the present life could be our preparation for another, this would be no objection against the credibility

of its being so. For we do not discern how food and
sleep contribute to the growth of the body, nor could
have any thought that they would, before we had
experience. Nor do children at all think, on the one hand,
that the sports and exercises, to which they are so much
addicted, contribute to their health and growth; nor, on
the other, of the necessity which there is for their being
restrained in them; nor are they capable of understanding
the use of many parts of discipline, which, nevertheless,
they must be made to go through, in order to qualify them
for the business of mature age. Were we not able, then,
to discover in what respects the present life could form us
for a future one, yet nothing would be more supposable
than that it might, in some respects or other, from the
general analogy of Providence. And this, for aught I see,
might reasonably be said, even though we should not take
in the consideration of God's moral government over the
world. But,

IV. Take in this consideration, and consequently, that
the character of virtue and piety is a necessary qualification
for the future state, and then we may distinctly see how, and
in what respects, the present life may be a preparation for
it; since we *want, and are capable of, improvement in that
character, by moral and religious habits;* and *the present
life is fit to be a state of discipline for such improvement;*
in like manner, as we have already observed, how and in
what respects infancy, childhood, and youth, are a necessary preparation, and a natural state of discipline, for
mature age.

Nothing which we at present see would lead us to the
thought of a solitary inactive state hereafter; but, if we
judge at all from the analogy of nature, we must suppose,
according to the Scripture account of it, that it will be
a community. And there is no shadow of any thing
unreasonable in conceiving, though there be no analogy for
it, that this community will be, as the Scripture represents
it, under the more immediate, or, if such an expression may

be used, the more sensible government of God. Nor is our ignorance, what will be the employments of this happy community, nor our consequent ignorance, what particular scope or occasion there will be for the exercise of veracity, justice, and charity, amongst the members of it with regard to each other, any proof that there will be no sphere of exercise for those virtues. Much less, if that were possible, is our ignorance any proof that there will be no occasion for that frame of mind, or character, which is formed by the daily practice of those particular virtues here, and which is a result from it. This at least must be owned in general, that as the government established in the universe is moral, the character of virtue and piety must, in some way or other, be the condition of our happiness, or the qualification for it.

Now, from what is above observed concerning our natural power of habits, it is easy to see, that we are *capable* of moral improvement by discipline. And how greatly we *want* it, need not be proved to any one who is acquainted with the great wickedness of mankind, or even with those imperfections which the best are conscious of. But it is not perhaps distinctly attended to by every one, that the occasion which human creatures have for discipline, to improve in them this character of virtue and piety, is to be traced up higher than to excess in the passions by indulgence and habits of vice. Mankind, and perhaps all finite creatures, from the very constitution of their nature, before habits of virtue, are deficient, and in danger of deviating from what is right, and therefore stand in need of virtuous habits for a security against this danger. For, together with the general principle of moral understanding, we have in our inward frame various affections towards particular external objects. These affections are naturally, and of right, subject to the government of the moral principle, as to the occasions upon which they may be gratified, as to the times, degrees, and manner, in which the objects of them may be pursued; but then the principle of virtue can neither excite them, nor

E

prevent their being excited. On the contrary, they are
naturally felt, when the objects of them are present to the
mind, not only before all consideration whether they can be
obtained by lawful means, but after it is found they cannot.
For the natural objects of affection continue so; the necessaries, conveniences, and pleasures of life, remain naturally
desirable, though they cannot be obtained innocently; nay,
though they cannot possibly be obtained at all: and when
the objects of any affection whatever cannot be obtained
without unlawful means, but may be obtained by them, such
affection, though its being excited, and its continuing some
time in the mind, be as innocent as it is natural and necessary, yet cannot but be conceived to have a tendency to
incline persons to venture upon such unlawful means, and
therefore must be conceived as putting them in some danger
of it. Now, what is the general security against this danger,
against their actually deviating from right? As the danger
is, so also must the security be, from within, from the
practical principle of virtue.* And the strengthening or
improving this principle, considered as practical, or as a
principle of action, will lessen the danger or increase the

* It may be thought, that a sense of interest would as effectually
restrain creatures from doing wrong. But if by a *sense of interest* is
meant, a speculative conviction or belief that such and such indulgence
would occasion them greater uneasiness, upon the whole, than satisfaction, it is contrary to present experience to say, that this sense of
interest is sufficient to restrain them from thus indulging themselves.
And if by a *sense of interest* is meant, a practical regard to what is
upon the whole our happiness, this is not only coincident with the
principle of virtue or moral rectitude, but is a part of the idea itself.
And it is evident this reasonable self-love wants to be improved, as
really as any principle in our nature: for we daily see it overmatched,
not only by the more boisterous passions, but by curiosity, shame, love
of imitation, by anything, even indolence: especially if the interest,
the temporal interest, suppose, which is the end of such self-love, be
at a distance. So greatly are profligate men mistaken, when they
affirm they are wholly governed by interestedness and self-love; and
so little cause is there for moralists to disclaim this principle. See
p. 57, &c.

security against it.   And this moral principle is capable of
improvement, by proper discipline and exercise; by recollecting the practical impressions which example and experience have made upon us; and, instead of following humour
and mere inclination, by continually attending to the equity
and right of the case, in whatever we are engaged, be it in
greater or less matters, and accustoming ourselves always
to act upon it; as being itself the just and natural motive of
action; and as this moral course of behaviour must necessarily, under divine government, be our final interest.
*Thus the principle of virtue, improved into a habit, of
which improvement we are thus capable, will plainly be, in
proportion to the strength of it, a security against the
danger which finite creatures are in, from the very nature
of propension or particular affections.*   This way of
putting the matter supposes particular affections to remain
in a future state, which it is scarce possible to avoid supposing.   And if they do, we clearly see, that acquired habits
of virtue and self-government may be necessary for the
regulation of them.   However, though we were not distinctly
to take in this supposition, but to speak only in general, the
thing really comes to the same.   For habits of virtue, thus
acquired by discipline, are improvement in virtue; and
improvement in virtue must be advancement in happiness,
if the government of the universe be moral.

From these things we may observe, and it will farther
show this our natural and original need of being improved
by discipline, how it comes to pass, that creatures made
upright, fall; and that those who preserve their uprightness, by so doing raise themselves to a more secure state
of virtue.   To say that the former is accounted for by
the nature of liberty, is to say no more than that an
event's actually happening is accounted for by a mere
possibility of its happening.   But it seems distinctly conceivable from the very nature of particular affections or
propensions.   For, suppose creatures intended for such
a particular state of life, for which such propensions were

necessary; suppose them endued with such propensions, together with moral understanding, as well including a practical sense of virtue as a speculative perception of it; and that all these several principles, both natural and moral, forming an inward constitution of mind, were in the most exact proportion possible, *i. e.* in a proportion the ·most exactly adapted to their intended state of life; such creatures would be made upright, or finitely perfect. Now, particular propensions, from their very nature, must be felt, the objects of them being present, though they cannot be gratified at all, or not with the allowance of the moral principle. But if they can be gratified without its allowance, or by contradicting it, then they must be conceived to have some tendency, in how low a degree soever, yet some tendency, to induce persons to such forbidden gratification. This tendency, in some one particular propension, may be increased by the greater frequency of occasions naturally exciting it, than of occasions exciting others. The least voluntary indulgence in forbidden circumstances, though but in thought, will increase this wrong tendency, and may increase it further, till, peculiar conjunctures perhaps conspiring, it becomes effect; and danger of deviating from right, ends in actual deviation from it: a danger necessarily arising from the very nature of propension, and which, therefore, could not have been prevented, though it might have been escaped, or got innocently through. The case would be, as if we were to suppose a strait path marked out for a person, in which such a degree of attention would keep him steady; but if he would not attend in this degree, any one of a thousand objects catching his eye might lead him out of it. Now it is impossible to say, how much even the first full overt act of irregularity might disorder the inward constitution, unsettle the adjustments, and alter the proportions which formed it, and in which the uprightness of its make consisted. But repetition of irregularities would produce habits. And thus the constitution would be spoiled, and creatures, made upright, become corrupt and depraved in their settled character, proportionably to their repeated irregularities in occasional acts. But, on the contrary, these creatures might have improved and raised themselves to a higher and more secure state of virtue, by the contrary behaviour, by steadily following the moral principle, supposed to be one part of their nature, and thus withstanding that unavoidable danger of defection, which necessarily arose from propension, the other part of it. For, by thus preserving their integrity for some time, their danger would lessen, since propensions, by being inured to submit, would do it more easily and of course; and their security against this lessening danger would increase, since the moral principle would gain additional strength by exercise;—both which things are implied in the notion of virtuous habits. Thus, then, vicious indulgence is not only criminal in itself, but also depraves the inward constitution and character. And virtuous self-government is not only right in itself, but also improves the inward constitution or character; and may improve it to such a degree, that though we should suppose it impossible for particular affections to be absolutely coincident with the moral principle, and consequently should allow, that such creatures as have been above supposed would for ever remain defectible; yet their danger of actually deviating from right may be almost infinitely lessened, and they fully fortified against what remains of it—if that may be called danger against which there is an adequate effectual security. But still this their higher perfection may continue to consist in habits of virtue formed in a state of discipline, and this their more complete security remain to proceed from them. And thus it is plainly conceivable, that creatures without blemish, as they came out of the hands of God, may be in danger of going wrong, and so may stand in need of the security of virtuous habits additional to the moral principle

wrought into their natures by him. That which is the
ground of their danger, or their want of security, may be
considered as a deficiency in them, to which virtuous habits
are the natural supply. And as they are naturally capable
of being raised and improved by discipline, it may be a
thing fit and requisite, that they should be placed in circumstances with an eye to it; in circumstances peculiarly fitted
to be, to them, a state of discipline for their improvement in
virtue.

But how much more strongly must this hold with
respect to those who have corrupted their natures, are
fallen from their original rectitude, and whose passions
are become excessive by repeated violations of their
inward constitution? Upright creatures may want to be
improved; depraved creatures want to be renewed. Education and discipline, which may be in all degrees and
sorts of gentleness and of severity, is expedient for those,
but must be absolutely necessary for these. For these,
discipline, of the severer sort too, and in the higher
degrees of it, must be necessary, in order to wear out
vicious habits; to recover their primitive strength of
self-government, which indulgence must have weakened;
to repair, as well as raise into a habit, the moral principle,
in order to their arriving at a secure state of virtuous
happiness.

Now, whoever will consider the thing may clearly see,
that the present world is *peculiarly fit* to be a state of
discipline for this purpose, to such as will set themselves
to amend and improve. For, the various temptations
with which we are surrounded; our experience of the
deceits of wickedness, having been in many instances
led wrong ourselves; the great viciousness of the world;
the infinite disorders consequent upon it; our being made
acquainted with pain and sorrow, either from our own
feeling of it, or from the sight of it in others; these things,
though some of them may indeed produce wrong effect
upon our minds, yet, when duly reflected upon, have all

of them a direct tendency to bring us to a settled moderation and reasonableness of temper; the contrary both to
thoughtless levity, and also to that unrestrained self-will,
and violent bent to follow present inclination, which may
be observed in undisciplined minds. Such experience as
the present state affords of the frailty of our nature, of
the boundless extravagance of ungoverned passion, of the
power which an infinite Being has over us, by the various
capacities of misery which he has given us; in short, that
kind and degree of experience which the present state
affords us, that the constitution of nature is such as to
admit the possibility, the danger, and the actual event of
creatures losing their innocence and happiness, and becoming vicious and wretched; hath a tendency to give us
a practical sense of things very different from a mere speculative knowledge that we are liable to vice, are capable
of misery. And who knows, whether the security of creatures in the highest and most settled state of perfection,
may not, in part, arise from their having had such a sense
of things as this formed, and habitually fixed, within
them, in some state of probation? And passing through
the present world with that moral attention which is
necessary to the acting a right part in it, may leave everlasting impressions of this sort upon our minds. But to be
a little more distinct: allurements to what is wrong; difficulties in the discharge of our duty; our not being able
to act an uniform right part without some thought and
care; and the opportunities which we have, or imagine we
have, of avoiding what we dislike, or obtaining what we
desire, by unlawful means, when we either cannot do it at
all, or at least not so easily, by lawful ones; these things,
i. e. the snares and temptations of vice, are what render
the present world peculiarly fit to be a state of discipline
to those who will preserve their integrity; because they
render being upon our guard, resolution, and the denial
of our passions, necessary in order to that end. And the
exercise of such particular recollection, intention of

mind, and self-government, in the practice of virtue, has, from the make of our nature, a peculiar tendency to form habits of virtue, as implying not only a real, but also a more continued, and a more intense, exercise of the virtuous principle; or a more constant and a stronger effort of virtue exerted into act. Thus, suppose a person to know himself to be in particular danger, for some time, of doing anything wrong, which yet he fully resolves not to do; continued recollection, and keeping upon his guard in order to make good his resolution, is a *continued* exerting of that act of virtue in a *high degree*, which need have been, and perhaps would have been, only *instantaneous* and *weak*, had the temptation been so. It is indeed ridiculous to assert, that self-denial is essential to virtue and piety; but it would have been nearer the truth, though not strictly the truth itself, to have said, that it is essential to discipline and improvement. For, though actions materially virtuous, which have no sort of difficulty, but are perfectly agreeable to our particular inclinations, may possibly be done only from these particular inclinations, and so may not be any exercise of the principle of virtue, *i. e.* not be virtuous actions at all; yet, on the contrary, they may be an exercise of that principle, and, when they are, they have a tendency to form and fix the habit of virtue. But when the exercise of the virtuous principle is more continued, oftener repeated, and more intense, as it must be in circumstances of danger, temptation, and difficulty, of any kind and in any degree, this tendency is increased proportionably, and a more confirmed habit is the consequence.

This undoubtedly holds to a certain length, but how far it may hold, I know not. Neither our intellectual powers, nor our bodily strength, can be improved beyond such a degree, and both may be over-wrought. Possibly there may be somewhat analogous to this with respect to the moral character; which is scarce worth considering; and I mention it only, lest it should come into some persons' thoughts, not as an exception to the foregoing observations, which perhaps it is, but as a confutation of them, which it is not.   And there may be several other exceptions.   Observations of this kind cannot be supposed to hold minutely, and in every case.   It is enough that they hold in general.   And these plainly hold so far, as that from them may be seen distinctly, which is all that is intended by them, that *the present world is peculiarly fit to be a state of discipline for our improvement in virtue and piety;* in the same sense as some sciences, by requiring and engaging the attention, not, to be sure, of such persons as will not, but of such as will set themselves to them, are fit to form the mind to habits of attention.

Indeed, the present state is so far from proving, in event, a discipline of virtue to the generality of men, that, on the contrary, they seem to make it a discipline of vice. And the viciousness of the world is, in different ways, the great temptation which renders it a state of virtuous discipline, in the degree it is, to good men.   The whole end, and the whole occasion, of mankind being placed in such a state as the present, is not pretended to be accounted for. That which appears amidst the general corruption is, that there are some persons, who, having within them the principle of amendment and recovery, attend to and follow the notices of virtue and religion, be they more clear or more obscure, which are afforded them ; and that the present world is not only an exercise of virtue in these persons, but an exercise of it in ways and degrees peculiarly apt to improve it ; apt to improve it, in some respects, even beyond what would be, by the exercise of it, required in a perfectly virtuous society, or in a society of equally imperfect virtue with themselves.   But that the present world does not actually become a state of moral discipline to many, even to the generality, *i. e.* that they do not improve or grow better in it, cannot be urged as a proof that it was not intended for moral discipline, by any who at all observe the analogy of nature. For, of the numerous seeds of vegetables and bodies of animals, which are adapted and put in the way to improve to such a point or state of natural maturity and perfection, we do not see perhaps that one in a million actually does. Far the greatest part of them decay before they are improved to it, and appear to be absolutely destroyed. Yet no one, who does not deny all final causes, will deny, that those seeds and bodies which do attain to that point of maturity and perfection, answer the end for which they were really designed by nature; and therefore that nature designed them for such perfection. And I cannot forbear adding, though it is not to the present purpose, that the *appearance* of such an amazing *waste* in nature, with respect to these seeds and bodies, by foreign causes, is to us as unaccountable as, what is much more terrible, the present and future ruin of so many moral agents by themselves, *i. e.* by vice.

Against this whole notion of moral discipline it may be objected, in another way, that so far as a course of behaviour, materially virtuous, proceeds from hope and fear, so far it is only a discipline and strengthening of self-love. But doing what God commands, because he commands it, is obedience, though it proceeds from hope or fear: and a course of such obedience will form habits of it; and a constant regard to veracity, justice, and charity, may form distinct habits of these particular virtues, and will certainly form habits of self-government, and of denying our inclinations, whenever veracity, justice, or charity requires it. Nor is there any foundation for this great nicety, with which some affect to distinguish in this case, in order to depreciate all religion proceeding from hope or fear. For, veracity, justice, and charity, regard to God's authority, and to our own chief interest, are not only all three coincident, but each of them is, in itself, a just and natural motive or principle of action. And he who begins a good life from any one of them, and perseveres in it, as

he is already in some degree, so he cannot fail of becoming
more and more of that character, which is correspondent to
the constitution of nature as moral, and to the relation
which God stands in to us as moral governor of it; nor,
consequently, can he fail of obtaining that happiness,
which this constitution and relation necessarily suppose
connected with that character.

These several observations concerning the active principle of virtue and obedience to God's commands, are
applicable to passive submission or resignation to his will;
which is another essential part of a right character, connected with the former, and very much in our power to
form ourselves to.   It may be imagined, that nothing but
afflictions can give occasion for or require this virtue; that
it can have no respect to, nor be any way necessary to
qualify for, a state of perfect happiness ; but it is not experience which can make us think thus.   Prosperity itself,
whilst anything supposed desirable is not ours, begets
extravagant and unbounded thoughts.   Imagination is
altogether as much a source of discontent as anything in
our external condition.   It is indeed true, that there can
be no scope for patience, when sorrow shall be no more;
but there may be need of a temper of mind, which shall
have been formed by patience.   For, though self-love,
considered merely as an active principle leading us to
pursue our chief interest, cannot but be uniformly coincident with the principle of obedience to God's commands,
our interest being rightly understood; because this obedience, and the pursuit of our own chief interest, must be
in every case one and the same thing; yet it may be questioned, whether self-love, considered merely as the desire
of our own interest or happiness, can, from its nature, be
thus absolutely and uniformly coincident with the will of
God, any more than particular affections can;* coincident
in such sort, as not to be liable to be excited upon occa-

* Page 61.

sions and in degrees, impossible to be gratified consistently
with the constitution of things, or the divine appointments.
So that *habits* of resignation may, upon this account, be
requisite for all creatures; habits, I say, which signify
what is formed by use.   However, in general, it is obvious,
that both self-love and particular affections in human
creatures, considered only as passive feelings, distort and
rend the mind, and therefore stand in need of discipline.   Now, denial of those particular affections, in a
course of active virtue and obedience to God's will, has
a tendency to moderate them, and seems also to have
a tendency to habituate the mind to be easy and satisfied
with that degree of happiness which is allotted us, *i. e.*
to moderate self-love.   But the proper discipline for
resignation is affliction.   For a right behaviour under
that trial, recollecting ourselves so as to consider it, in
the view in which religion teaches us to consider it, as
from the hand of God; receiving it as what he appoints
or thinks proper to permit in this world, and under his
government, this will habituate the mind to a dutiful
submission; and such submission, together with the active
principle of obedience, make up the temper and character
in us which answers to his sovereignty, and which absolutely belongs to the condition of our being, as dependent
creatures.   Nor can it be said, that this is only breaking the mind to a submission to mere power, for mere
power may be accidental, and precarious, and usurped;
but it is forming within ourselves the temper of resignation to his rightful authority, who is, by nature, supreme
over all.

Upon the whole, such a character, and such qualifications, are necessary for a mature state of life in the present world, as nature alone does in no wise bestow, but
has put it upon us in great part to acquire, in our progress from one stage of life to another, from childhood
to mature age—put it upon us to acquire them, by giving
us capacities of doing it, and by placing us, in the begin-

ning of life, in a condition fit for it. And this is a general
analogy to our condition in the present world, as in a
state of moral discipline for another. It is in vain, then,
to object against the credibility of the present life being
intended for this purpose, that all the trouble and the
danger unavoidably accompanying such discipline might
have been saved us, by our being made at once the creatures and the characters *which we were to be:* for we
experience, that *what we were to be,* was to the effect
of *what we would do;* and that the general conduct of
nature is, not to save us trouble or danger, but to make
us capable of going through them, and to put it upon us
to do so. Acquirements of our own experience and habits
are the *natural* supply to our deficiencies, and security
against our dangers; since it is as plainly natural to set
ourselves to acquire the qualifications as the external things
which we stand in need of. In particular, it is as plainly
a general law of nature, that we should, with regard to
our temporal interest, form and cultivate practical principles within us, by attention, use, and discipline, as anything whatever is a natural law; chiefly in the beginning
of life, but also throughout the whole course of it. And
the alternative is left to our choice, either to improve
ourselves, and better our condition, or, in default of such
improvement, to remain deficient and wretched. It is
therefore perfectly credible, from the analogy of nature,
that the same may be our case with respect to the happiness of a future state, and the qualifications necessary
for it.

There is a third thing, which may seem implied in the
present world being in a state of probation, that it is a
theatre of action for the manifestation of persons' characters with respect to a future one; not, to be sure, to an
all-knowing Being, but to his creation, or part of it. This
may perhaps be only a consequence of our being in a state
of probation in the other senses. However, it is not impossible that men's showing and making manifest what is

in their heart, what their real character is, may have respect to a future life, in ways and manners which we are
not acquainted with; particularly it may be a means (for
the Author of nature does not appear to do anything
without means) of their being disposed of suitably to their
characters, and of its being known to the creation, by way
of example, that they are thus disposed of. But not to
enter upon any conjectural account of this, one may just
mention, that the manifestation of persons' characters contributes very much, in various ways, to the carrying on a
great part of that general course of nature respecting mankind, which comes under our observation at present. I
shall only add, that probation, in both these senses, as well
as in that treated of in the foregoing chapter, is implied in
moral government; since by persons' behaviour under it,
their characters cannot but be manifested, and, if they
behave well, improved.

CHAPTER VI.

Of the Opinion of Necessity, considered as influencing Practice.

Throughout the foregoing Treatise it appears, that the
condition of mankind, considered as inhabitants of the
world only, and under the government of God which we
experience, is greatly analogous to our condition as designed for another world, or under that farther government
which religion teaches us. If therefore any assert, as a
fatalist must, that the opinion of universal necessity is
reconcileable with the former, there immediately arises a
question in the way of analogy—whether he must not also
own it to be reconcileable with the latter; i. e. with the
system of religion itself, and the proof of it. The reader,
then, will observe, that the question now before us is not
absolute, whether the opinion of fate be reconcileable with

religion; but hypothetical, whether, upon supposition of its being reconcileable with the constitution of nature, it be not reconcileable with religion also? or, what pretence a fatalist—not other persons, but a fatalist—has to conclude, from his opinion, that there can be no such thing as religion? And as the puzzle and obscurity, which must unavoidably arise from arguing upon so absurd a supposition as that of universal necessity, will, I fear, easily be seen, it will, I hope, as easily be excused.

But since it has been all along taken for granted, as a thing proved, that there is an intelligent Author of nature, or natural Governor of the world; and since an objection may be made against the proof of this, from the opinion of universal necessity, as it may be supposed that such necessity will itself account for the origin and preservation of all things; it is requisite that this objection be distinctly answered, or that it be shown that a fatality, supposed consistent with what we certainly experience, does not destroy the proof of an intelligent Author and Governor of nature, before we proceed to consider, whether it destroys the proof of a moral Governor of it, or of our being in a state of religion.

Now, when it is said by a fatalist, that the whole constitution of nature, and the actions of men, that everything, and every mode and circumstance of everything, is necessary, and could not possibly have been otherwise, it is to be observed, that this necessity does not exclude deliberation, choice, preference, and acting from certain principles, and to certain ends; because all this is matter of undoubted experience, acknowledged by all, and what every man may, every moment, be conscious of. And from hence it follows, that necessity, alone and of itself, is in no sort an account of the constitution of nature, and how things came *to be* and *continue* as they are; but only an account of this *circumstance* relating to their origin and continuance, that they could not have been otherwise than they are and have been. The assertion, that everything is by necessity of nature, is not an answer to the question, Whether the world came into being as it is, by an intelligent Agent forming it thus, or not, but to quite another question—Whether it came into being as it is, in that way and manner which we call *necessarily*, or in that way and manner which we call *freely*. For, suppose further, that one who was a fatalist, and one who kept to his natural sense of things, and believed himself a free agent, were disputing together, and vindicating their respective opinions, and they should happen to instance in a house, they would agree that it was built by an architect: their difference concerning necessity and freedom would occasion no difference of judgment concerning this, but only concerning another matter, whether the architect built it necessarily or freely. Suppose, then, they should proceed to inquire concerning the constitution of nature; in a lax way of speaking, one of them might say, it was by necessity, and the other, by freedom; but, if they had any meaning to their words, as the latter must mean a free agent, so the former must at length be reduced to mean an agent, whether he would say one or more, acting by necessity; for abstract notions can do nothing. Indeed, we ascribe to God a necessary existence, uncaused by any agent. For we find within ourselves the idea of infinity, *i. e.* immensity and eternity, impossible, even in imagination, to be removed out of being. We seem to discern intuitively, that there must, and cannot but be, somewhat external to ourselves, answering this idea, or the archetype of it. And from hence (*for this abstract,* as much as any other, implies a *concrete*) we conclude, that there is, and cannot but be, an infinite and immense eternal Being existing, prior to all design contributing to his existence, and exclusive of it. And from the scantiness of language a manner of speaking has been introduced, that necessity is the foundation, the reason, the account of the existence of God. But it is not alleged, nor can it be at all intended, that *everything* exists as it does by this kind of necessity, a necessity antecedent in nature to design; it cannot, I say, be meant, that everything exists as it does by this kind of necessity, upon several accounts; and particularly, because it is admitted that design, in the actions of men, contributes to many alterations in nature.   For, if any deny this, I shall not pretend to reason with them.

From these things it follows, *first*, that when a fatalist asserts that everything is by *necessity*, he must mean, *by an agent acting necessarily:* he must, I say, mean this; for I am very sensible he would not choose to mean it. And, *secondly*, That the necessity, by which such an agent is supposed to act, does not exclude intelligence and design. So that, were the system of fatality admitted, it would just as much account for the formation of the world as for the structure of a house, and no more.   Necessity as much requires and supposes a necessary agent, as freedom requires and supposes a free agent to be the former of the world.   And the appearances of *design* and of *final causes* in the constitution of nature, as really prove this acting agent to be an *intelligent designer*, or to act from choice, upon the scheme of necessity, supposed possible; as upon that of freedom.

It appearing thus that the notion of necessity does not destroy the proof that there is an intelligent Author of nature and natural Governor of the world, the present question, which the analogy before mentioned* suggests, and which, I think, it will answer, is this: Whether the opinion of necessity, supposed consistent with possibility, with the constitution of the world, and the natural government which we experience exercised over it, destroys all reasonable ground of belief that we are in a state of religion; or whether that opinion be reconcileable with religion, with the system and the proof of it?

Suppose, then, a fatalist to educate any one, from his youth up, in his own principles; that the child should

* Page 86.

reason upon them, and conclude, that since he cannot possibly behave otherwise than he does, he is not a subject of
blame or commendation, nor can deserve to be rewarded or
punished; imagine him to eradicate the very perceptions of
blame and commendation out of his mind, by means of this
system; to form his temper and character, and behaviour
to it; and from it to judge of the treatment he was to
expect, say, from reasonable men, upon his coming abroad
into the world—as the fatalist judges from this system,
what he is to expect from the Author of nature, and with
regard to a future state; I cannot forbear stopping here to
ask, whether any one of common sense would think fit
that a child should be put upon these speculations, and be
left to apply them to practice? And a man has little pretence to reason, who is not sensible that we are all children
in speculations of this kind. However, the child would
doubtless be highly delighted to find himself freed from the
restraints of fear and shame with which his play-fellows
were fettered and embarrassed, and highly conceited in his
superior knowledge, so far beyond his years. But·conceit
and vanity would be the least bad part of the influence
which these principles must have, when thus reasoned and
acted upon, during the course of his education. He must
either be allowed to go on, and be the plague of all about
him, and himself too, even to his own destruction, or else
correction must be continually made use of, to supply the
want of those natural perceptions of blame and commendation which we have supposed to be removed, and to give
him a practical impression of what he had reasoned himself
out of the belief of, that he was, in fact, an accountable
child, and to be punished for doing what he was forbid.
It is therefore in reality impossible, but that the correction
which he must meet with in the course of his education
must convince him, that if the scheme he was instructed
in were not false, yet that he reasoned inconclusively
upon it, and, somehow or other, misapplied it to practice
and common life: as what the fatalist experiences of the

conduct of Providence at present ought, in all reason, to convince him, that this scheme is misapplied, when applied to the subject of religion.*   But, supposing the child's temper could remain still formed to the system, and his expectation of the treatment he was to have in the world be regulated by it, so as to expect that no reasonable man would blame or punish him for anything which he should do, because he could not help doing it; upon this supposition, it is manifest he would, upon his coming abroad into the world, be insupportable to society, and the treatment which he would receive from it, would render it so to him; and he could not fail of doing somewhat very soon, for which he would be delivered over into the hands of civil justice: and thus, in the end, he would be convinced of the obligations he was under to his wise instructor.   Or suppose this scheme of fatality, in any other way, applied to practice, such practical application of it will be found equally absurd, equally fallacious in a practical sense: for instance, that if a man be destined to live such a time, he shall live to it, though he take no care of his own preservation; or, if he be destined to die before that time, no care can prevent it; therefore all care about preserving one's life is to be neglected: which is the fallacy instanced in by the ancients.   But now, on the contrary, none of these practical absurdities can be drawn, from reasoning upon the supposition that we are free; but all such reasoning, with regard to the common affairs of life, is justified by experience.   And, therefore, though it were admitted that this opinion of necessity were speculatively true, yet, with regard to practice, it is as if it were false, so far as our experience reaches; that is, to the whole of our present life.   For, the constitution of the present world, and the condition in which we are actually placed, is as if we were free.   And it may perhaps justly be concluded, that since the whole

* Page 101.

process of action, through every step of it—suspense, deliberation, inclining one way, determining, and at last
doing as we determine—is as if we were free, therefore
we are so.   But the thing here insisted upon is, that under
the present natural government of the world, we find
we are treated and dealt with as if we were free, prior
to all consideration whether we are or not.   Were this
opinion, therefore, of necessity admitted to be ever so true,
yet such is, in fact, our condition and the natural course
of things, that, whenever we apply it to life and practice,
this application of it always misleads us, and cannot but
mislead us, in a most dreadful manner, with regard to
our present interest.   And how can people think themselves so very secure, then, that the same application of
the same opinion may not mislead them also, in some
analogous manner, with respect to a future, a more general, and more important interest?   For, religion being a
practical subject, and the analogy of nature showing us,
that we have not faculties to apply this opinion, were it
a true one, to practical subjects; whenever we do apply
it to the subject of religion, and thence conclude that
we are free from its obligations, it is plain this conclusion
cannot be depended upon.   There will still remain just
reason to think, whatever appearances are, that we deceive
ourselves; in somewhat of a like manner as when people
fancy they can draw contradictory conclusions from the
idea of infinity.

From these things together, the attentive reader will
see it follows, that if, upon supposition of freedom, the
evidence of religion be conclusive, it remains so, upon
supposition of necessity; because the notion of necessity
is not applicable to practical subjects; *i. e.* with respect to
them is as if it were not true.   Nor does this contain any
reflection upon reason, but only upon what is unreasonable.   For, to pretend to act upon reason, in opposition to
practical principles, which the Author of our nature gave
us to act upon, and to pretend to apply our reason to

subjects, with regard to which our own short views, and even our experience, will show us it cannot be depended upon— and such, at best, the subject of necessity must be—this is vanity, conceit, and unreasonableness.

But this is not all. For we find within ourselves a will, and are conscious of a character. Now, if this, in us, be reconcileable with fate, it is reconcileable with it in the Author of nature. And, besides, natural government and final causes imply a character and a will in the Governor and Designer;* a will concerning the creatures whom he governs. The Author of nature, then, being certainly of some cha- racter or other, notwithstanding necessity, it is evident this necessity is as reconcileable with the particular character of benevolence, veracity, and justice in him, which attributes are the foundation of religion, as with any other character; since we find this necessity no more hinders *men* from being benevolent, than cruel; true, than faithless; just, than un- just; or, if the fatalist pleases, what we call unjust. For it is said, indeed, that what upon supposition of freedom, would be just punishment, upon supposition of necessity, becomes manifestly unjust; because it is punishment in- flicted for doing that which persons could not avoid doing: as if the necessity, which is supposed to destroy the injustice of murder, for instance, would not also destroy the injustice of punishing it. However, as little to the purpose as this objection is in itself, it is very much to the purpose to observe from it, how the notions of justice and injustice remain, even whilst we endeavour to suppose them removed; how they force themselves upon the mind, even whilst we are making suppositions destructive of them: for there is not, perhaps, a man in the world, but would be ready to make this ob- jection at first thought.

---

* By *will* and *character* is meant that which, in speaking of men, we should express, not only by these words, but also by the words *temper, taste, dispositions, practical principles; that whole frame of mind from whence we act in one manner rather than in another.*

But though it is most evident, that universal necessity, if it be reconcileable with anything, is reconcileable with that character in the Author of nature which is the foundation of religion; " yet, does it not plainly destroy the proof that he is of that character, and consequently the proof of religion?" By no means.   For we find that happiness and misery are not our fate, in any such sense as not to be the consequences of our behaviour, but that they are the consequences of it.* We find God exercises the same kind of government over us, with that which a father exercises over his children, and a civil magistrate over his subjects.   Now, whatever becomes of abstract questions concerning liberty and necessity, it evidently appears to us, that veracity and justice must be the natural rule and measure of exercising this authority, or government, to a Being, who can have no competitions, or interfering of interests, with his creatures and his subjects.

But as the doctrine of liberty, though we experience its truth, may be perplexed with difficulties which run up into the most abstruse of all speculations, and as the opinion of necessity seems to be the very basis upon which infidelity grounds itself, it may be of some use to offer a more particular proof of the obligations of religion, which may distinctly be shown not to be destroyed by this opinion.

The proof, from final causes, of an intelligent Author of nature, is not affected by the opinion of necessity; supposing necessity a thing possible in itself, and reconcileable with the constitution of things.† And it is a matter of fact, independent on this or any other speculation, that he governs the world by the method of rewards and punishments;‡ and also that he hath given us a moral faculty, by which we distinguish between actions, and approve some as virtuous and of good desert, and disapprove others as vicious and of ill desert.§   Now

---

* Chap. ii.   † Page 107, &c.   ‡ Chap. ii.   § Dissertation II.

this moral discernment implies, in the notion of it, a rule
of action, and a rule of a very peculiar kind; for it carries
in it authority and a right of direction; authority in such a
sense, as that we cannot depart from it without being self-
condemned.* And, that the dictates of this moral faculty,
which are by nature a rule to us, are moreover the laws of
God—laws in a sense including sanctions—may be thus
proved. Consciousness of a rule or guide of action, in
creatures who are capable of considering it as given them
by their Maker, not only raises immediately a sense of
duty, but also a sense of security in following it, and of
danger in deviating from it. A direction of the Author of
nature, given to creatures capable of looking upon it as
such, is plainly a command from him; and a command from
him necessarily includes in it, at least, an implicit promise
in case of obedience, or threatening in case of disobedience.
But then the sense or perception of good and ill desert,†
which is contained in the moral discernment, renders the
sanction explicit, and makes it appear, as one may say,
expressed. For, since his method of government is to
reward and punish actions, his having annexed to some
actions an inseparable sense of good desert, and to others of
ill, this surely amounts to declaring upon whom his punishments shall be inflicted, and his rewards be bestowed. For
he must have given us this discernment and sense of things,
as a presentiment of what is to be hereafter; that is, by way
of information beforehand, what we are finally to expect in
this world. There is, then, most evident ground to think,
that the government of God, upon the whole, will be found
to correspond to the nature which he has given us, and that
in the upshot and issue of things, happiness and misery
shall, in fact and event, be made to follow virtue and vice
respectively; as he has already, in so peculiar a manner,
associated the ideas of them in our minds. And from hence
might easily be deduced the obligations of religious worship,

* Sermon 2d at the Rolls.   † Dissertation II.

were it only to be considered as a means of preserving upon our minds a sense of this moral government of God, and securing our obedience to it; which yet is an extremely imperfect view of that most important duty.

Now, I say, no objection from necessity can lie against this general proof of religion: none against the proposition reasoned upon, that we have such a moral faculty and discernment; because this is a mere matter of fact, a thing of experience, that human kind is thus constituted: none against the conclusion, because it is immediate, and wholly from this fact. For the conclusion, that God will finally reward the righteous and punish the wicked, is not here drawn from its appearing to us fit* that *he should*, but from its appearing that he has told us *he will*. And this he hath certainly told us, in the promise and threatening which, it hath been observed, the notion of a command implies, and the sense of good and ill desert, which he has given us, more distinctly expresses. And this reasoning from fact is confirmed, and in some degree even verified, by other facts; by the natural tendencies of virtue and of vice;† and by this, that God, in the natural course of his providence, punishes

---

* However, I am far from intending to deny, that the will of God is determined by what is fit, by the right and reason of the case; though one chooses to decline matters of such abstract speculation, and to speak with caution when one does speak of them. But if it be intelligible to say, that *it is fit and reasonable for every one to consult his own happiness*, then, *fitness of action, or the right and reason of the case*, is an intelligible manner of speaking. And it seems as inconceivable, to suppose God to approve one course of action, or one end, preferably to another, which yet his acting at all from design implies that he does, without supposing somewhat prior in that end to be the ground of the preference; as to suppose him to discern an abstract proposition to be true, without supposing somewhat prior in it to be the ground of the discernment. It does not, therefore, appear that moral right is any more relative to perception than abstract truth is; or that it is any more improper to speak of the fitness and rightness of actions and ends, as founded in the nature of things, than to speak of abstract truth as thus founded.

† Page 43.

vicious actions as mischievous to society; and also vicious actions, as such, in the strictest sense.*   So that the general proof of religion is unanswerably real, even upon the wild supposition which we are arguing upon.

It must likewise be observed farther, that natural religion hath, besides this, an external evidence, which the doctrine of necessity, if it could be true, would not affect.   For, suppose a person, by the observations and reasoning above, or by any other, convinced of the truth of religion—that there is a God, who made the world, who is the moral Governor and Judge of mankind, and will, upon the whole, deal with every one according to his works; I say, suppose a person convinced of this by reason, but to know nothing at all of antiquity, or the present state of mankind, it would be natural for such a one to be inquisitive, what was the history of this system of doctrine; at what time, and in what manner, it came first into the world; and whether it were believed by any considerable part of it.   And were he upon inquiry to find, that a particular person, in a late age, first of all proposed it as a deduction of reason, and that mankind were before wholly ignorant of it; then, though its evidence from reason would remain, there would be no additional probability of its truth from the account of its discovery.   But instead of this being the fact of the case, on the contrary, he would find what could not but afford him a very strong confirmation of its truth; *First*, That somewhat of this system, with more or fewer additions and alterations, hath been professed in all ages and countries of which we have any certain information relating to this matter.   *Secondly*, That it is certain historical fact, so far as we can trace things up, that this whole system of belief, that there is one God, the Creator and moral Governor of the world, and that mankind is in a state of religion, was received in the first ages.   And, *thirdly*, That as there is no hint or intimation in history, that this system was

* Page 43, &c.

F

first reasoned out; so there is express historical or traditional evidence, as ancient as history, that it was taugh
first by revelation.   Now, these things must be allowed to
be of great weight.   The first of them, general consent
shows this system to be conformable to the common sense
of mankind.   The second, namely, that religion was believed in the first ages of the world, especially as it does not
appear that there were then any superstitious or false additions to it, cannot but be a farther confirmation of its truth.
For it is a proof of this alternative—either that it came into
the world by revelation, or that it is natural, obvious, and
forces itself upon the mind.   The former of these is the conclusion of learned men.   And whoever will consider, how
unapt for speculation rude and uncultivated minds are, will,
perhaps from hence alone, be strongly inclined to believe it
the truth.   And as it is shown in the second part* of this
Treatise, that there is nothing of such peculiar presumption
against a revelation in the beginning of the world, as there
is supposed to be against subsequent ones; a sceptic could
not, I think, give any account, which would appear more
probable even to himself, of the early pretences to revelation, than by supposing some real original one, from
whence they were copied.   And the third thing above
mentioned, that there is express historical or traditional
evidence, as ancient as history, of the system of religion
being taught mankind by revelation; this must be admitted as some degree of real proof that it was so taught.
For why should not the most ancient tradition be admitted
as some additional proof of a fact, against which there
is no presumption?   And this proof is mentioned here,
because it has its weight to show that religion came into
the world by revelation, prior to all consideration of the
proper authority of any book supposed to contain it; and
even prior to all consideration, whether the revelation
itself be uncorruptly handed down and related, or mixed

* Chap. ii.

and darkened with fables. Thus the historical account
which we have of the origin of religion, taking in all circumstances, is a real confirmation of its truth, no way
affected by the opinion of necessity. And the *external*
evidence, even of natural religion, is by no means inconsiderable.

But it is carefully to be observed, and ought to be recollected after all proofs of virtue and religion, which are only
general, that as speculative reason may be neglected, prejudiced, and deceived, so also may our moral understanding
be impaired and perverted, and the dictates of it not impartially attended to. This, indeed, proves nothing against
the reality of our speculative or practical faculties of perception; against their being intended by nature to inform
us in the theory of things, and instruct us how we are to
behave, and what we are to expect in consequence of our
behaviour. Yet our liableness, in the degree we are liable,
to prejudice and perversion, is a most serious admonition to
us to be upon our guard, with respect to what is of such
consequence as our determinations concerning virtue and
religion; and particularly, not to take custom, and fashion,
and slight notions of honour, or imaginations of present
ease, use, and convenience to mankind, for the only moral
rule.*

The foregoing observations, drawn from the nature of
the thing, and the history of religion, amount, when taken
together, to a real practical proof of it, not to be confuted;
such a proof as, considering the infinite importance of the
thing, I apprehend, would be admitted fully sufficient, in
reason, to influence the actions of men who act upon thought
and reflection; if it were admitted that there is no proof of
the contrary. But it may be said, " There are many probabilities, which cannot indeed be confuted, *i. e.* shown to
be no probabilities, and yet may be overbalanced by greater
probabilities on the other side; much more by demonstration.

* Dissertation II.

And there is no occasion to object against particular arguments alleged for an opinion, when the opinion itself may be clearly shown to be false, without meddling with such arguments at all, but leaving them just as they are.   Now, the method of government by rewards and punishments, and especially rewarding and punishing good and ill desert, as such, respectively, must go upon supposition that we are free, and not necessary agents.   And it is incredible, that the Author of nature should govern us upon a supposition as true, which he knows to be false: and therefore absurd to think, he will reward or punish us for our actions hereafter; especially that he will do it under the notion that they are of good or ill desert."   Here, then, the matter is brought to a point.   And the answer to all this is full, and not to be evaded—that the whole constitution and course of things, the whole analogy of Providence, shows, beyond possibility of doubt, that the conclusion from this reasoning is false, wherever the fallacy lies.   The doctrine of freedom, indeed, clearly shows where—in supposing ourselves necessary, when in truth we are free agents.   But, upon the supposition of necessity, the fallacy lies in taking for granted, that it is incredible necessary agents should be rewarded and punished.   But that, somehow or other, the conclusion now mentioned is false, is most certain.   For it is fact that God does govern even brute creatures by the method of rewards and punishments, in the natural course of things. And men are rewarded and punished for their actions— punished for actions mischievous to society as being so, punished for vicious actions, as such, by the natural instrumentality of each other, under the present conduct of Providence.   Nay, even the affection of gratitude, and the passion of resentment, and the rewards and punishments following from them, which in general are to be considered as natural, *i. e.* from the Author of nature; these rewards and punishments, being naturally* annexed

* Sermon 8th, at the Rolls.

to actions considered as implying good intention and good
desert, ill intention and ill desert; these natural rewards
and punishments, I say, are as much a contradiction to the
conclusion above, and show its falsehood, as a more exact
and complete rewarding and punishing of good and ill
desert, as such.   So that, if it be incredible that necessary
agents should be thus rewarded and punished, then men
are not necessary, but free; since it is matter of fact that
they are thus rewarded and punished.   But if, on the contrary, which is the supposition we have been arguing upon.
it be insisted that men are necessary agents, then there is
nothing incredible in the farther supposition of necessary
agents being thus rewarded and punished; since we ourselves are thus dealt with.

From the whole, therefore, it must follow, that a necessity supposed possible, and reconcileable with the constitution of things, does in no sort prove that the Author of
nature will not, nor destroy the proof that he will, finally,
and upon the whole, in his eternal government, render his
creatures happy or miserable, by some means or other, as
they behave well or ill.   Or, to express this conclusion in
words conformable to the title of the chapter, the analogy
of nature shows us, that the opinion of necessity, considered
as practical, is false.   And if necessity, upon the supposition above mentioned, doth not destroy the· proof of
natural religion, it evidently makes no alteration in the
proof of revealed.

From these things likewise we may learn, in what sense
to understand that general assertion, that the opinion of
necessity is essentially destructive of all religion.   *First*,
In a practical sense; that by this notion atheistical men
pretend to satisfy and encourage themselves in vice, and
justify to others their disregard to all religion.   And.
secondly, In the strictest sense; that it is a contradiction
to the whole constitution of nature, and to what we may
every moment experience in ourselves, and so overturns
everything.   But by no means is this assertion to be

understood, as if necessity, supposing it could possibly be reconciled with the constitution of things, and with what we experience, were not also reconcileable with religion; for upon this supposition it demonstrably is so.

CHAPTER VII.

Of the Government of God, considered as a Scheme, or Constitution, imperfectly comprehended.

Though it be, as it cannot but be, acknowledged, that the analogy of nature gives a strong credibility to the general doctrine of religion, and to the several particular things contained in it, considered as so many matters of fact; and likewise that it shows this credibility not to be destroyed by any notions of necessity; yet still, objections may be insisted upon against the wisdom, equity, and goodness of the divine government, implied in the notion of religion, and against the method by which this government is conducted; to which objections analogy can be no direct answer. For the credibility, or the certain truth, of a matter of fact, does not immediately prove anything concerning the wisdom or goodness of it; and analogy can do no more, immediately or directly, than show such and such things to be true or credible, considered only as matters of fact. But still, if, upon supposition of a moral constitution of nature, and a moral government over it, analogy suggests and makes it credible that this government must be a scheme, system, or constitution of government, as distinguished from a number of single unconnected acts of distributive justice and goodness; and likewise that it must be a scheme, so imperfectly comprehended, and of such a sort in other respects, as to afford a direct general answer to all objections against the justice and goodness of it; then analogy is, remotely, of great service in answering those objections, both by suggesting the answer, and showing it to be a credible one.

Now this, upon inquiry, will be found to be the case. For, *first*, upon supposition that God exercises a moral government over the world, the analogy of his natural government suggests, and makes it credible, that his moral government must be a scheme quite beyond our comprehension; and this affords a general answer to all objections against the justice and goodness of it. And, *secondly*, a more distinct observation of some particular things contained in God's scheme of natural government, the like things being supposed, by analogy, to be contained in his moral government, will farther show how little weight is to be laid upon these objections.

I. Upon supposition that God exercises a moral government over the world, the analogy of his natural government suggests and makes it credible, that his moral government must be a scheme quite beyond our comprehension: and this affords a general answer to all objections against the justice and goodness of it. It is most obvious, analogy renders it highly credible, that upon supposition of a moral government it must be a scheme—for the world, and the whole natural government of it, appears to be so—to be a scheme, system, or constitution, whose parts correspond to each other, and to a whole, as really as any work of art, or as any particular model of a civil constitution and government. In this great scheme of the natural world, individuals have various peculiar relations to other individuals of their own species. And whole species are, we find, variously related to other species, upon this earth. Nor do we know how much farther these kinds of relations may extend. And as there is not any action, or natural event, which we are acquainted with, so single and unconnected as not to have a respect to some other actions and events; so, possibly, each of them, when it has not an immediate, may yet have a remote, natural relation to other actions and events, much beyond the compass of this present world. There seems, indeed, nothing from whence we can so much as make a conjecture, whether all creatures, actions, and events, throughout the whole of nature, have relations to each other. But, as it is obvious that all events have future unknown consequences, so, if we trace any, as far as we can go, into what is connected with it, we shall find, that if such event were not connected with somewhat farther in nature unknown to us, somewhat both past and present, such event could not possibly have been at all. Nor can we give the whole account of any one thing whatever; of all its causes, ends, and necessary adjuncts; those adjuncts, I mean, without which it could not have been. By this most astonishing connexion, these reciprocal correspondences and mutual relations, everything which we see in the course of nature is actually brought about: and things, seemingly the most insignificant imaginable, are perpetually observed to be necessary conditions to other things of the greatest importance; so that any one thing whatever may, for aught we know to the contrary, be a necessary condition to any other. The natural world, then, and natural government of it, being such an incomprehensible scheme; so incomprehensible, that a man must really, in the literal sense, know nothing at all, who is not sensible of his ignorance in it; this immediately suggests, and strongly shows the credibility, that the moral world and government of it may be so too. Indeed, the natural and moral constitution and government of the world are so connected, as to make up together but one scheme: and it is highly probable, that the first is formed and carried on merely in subserviency to the latter, as the vegetable world is for the animal, and organized bodies for minds. But the thing intended here is, without inquiring how far the administration of the natural world is subordinate to that of the moral, only to observe the credibility, that one should be analogous or similar to the other: that, therefore, every act of divine justice and goodness may be supposed to look much beyond itself and its immediate object; may have some reference to other parts of God's moral administration, and to a general moral plan: and that every circumstance of this his moral government may be adjusted beforehand with a view to the whole of it. Thus, for example; the determined length of time, and the degrees and ways in which virtue is to remain in a state of warfare and discipline, and in which wickedness is permitted to have its progress; the times appointed for the execution of justice; the appointed instruments of it; the kinds of rewards and punishments, and the manners of their distribution; all particular instances of divine justice and goodness, and every circumstance of them—may have such respects to each other, as to make up all together a whole, connected and related in all its parts; a scheme, or system, which is as properly one as the natural world is, and of the like kind. And supposing this to be the case, it is most evident, that we are not competent judges of this scheme, from the small parts of it which come within our view in the present life; and therefore no objections against any of these parts can be insisted upon by reasonable men.

This our ignorance, and the consequence here drawn from it, are universally acknowledged upon other occasions; and, though scarce denied, yet are universally forgot, when persons come to argue against religion. And it is not perhaps easy, even for the most reasonable men, always to bear in mind the degree of our ignorance, and make due allowances for it. Upon these accounts, it may not be useless to go on a little farther, in order to show more distinctly, how just an answer our ignorance is, to objections against the scheme of Providence. Suppose, then, a person boldly to assert, that the things complained of, the origin and continuance of evil, might easily have been prevented by repeated interpositions;* interpositions

* Pages 109, 110, &c.

so guarded and circumstanced, as would preclude all mischief arising from them: or, if this were impracticable, that a *scheme* of government is itself an imperfection; since more good might have been produced without any scheme, system, or constitution at all, by continued single unrelated acts of distributive justice and goodness; because these would have occasioned no irregularities. And farther than this, it is presumed, the objections will not be carried. Yet the answer is obvious; that were these assertions true, still the observations above, concerning our ignorance in the scheme of divine government, and the consequence drawn from it, would hold in great measure, enough to vindicate religion against all objections from the disorders of the present state. Were these assertions true, yet the government of the world might be just and good notwithstanding; for, at the most, they would infer nothing more than that it might have been better. But, indeed, they are mere arbitrary assertions; no man being sufficiently acquainted with the possibilities of things, to bring any proof of them to the lowest degree of probability. For, however possible what is asserted may seem, yet many instances may be alleged, in things much less out of our reach, of suppositions absolutely impossible, and reducible to the most palpable self-contradictions, which not every one by any means would perceive to be such, nor perhaps any one at first sight suspect. From these things it is easy to see distinctly, how our ignorance, as it is the common, is ·really a satisfactory answer to all objections against the justice and goodness of Providence. If a man, contemplating any one providential dispensation, which had no relation to any others, should object, that he discerned in it a disregard to justice or a deficiency of goodness, nothing would be less an answer to such objection, than our ignorance in other parts of Providence, or in the possibilities of things, no way related to what he was contemplating. But when we know not but the parts objected against may be relative to other parts unknown to us, and

when we are unacquainted with what is, in the nature of the
thing, practicable in the case before us, then our ignorance
is a satisfactory answer; because some unknown relation,
or some unknown impossibility, may render what is objected against just and good; nay, good in the highest
practicable degree.

II. And how little weight is to be laid upon such objections will farther appear, by a more distinct observation
of some particular things contained in the natural government of God, the like to which may be supposed, from
analogy, to be contained in his moral government.

First, As, in the scheme of the natural world, no ends
appear to be accomplished without means, so we find that
means very undesirable often conduce to bring about ends,
in such a measure desirable, as greatly to overbalance the
disagreeableness of the means.   And in cases where such
means are conducive to such ends, it is not reason, but
experience, which shows us that they are thus conducive.
Experience also shows many means to be conducive and
necessary to accomplish ends, which means, before experience, we should have thought would have had even a contrary tendency.   Now, from these observations relating to
the natural scheme of the world, the moral being supposed
to be analogous to it, arises a great credibility, that the
putting our misery in each other's power to the degree it is,
and making men liable to vice to the degree we are ; and,
in general, that those things which are objected against the
moral scheme of Providence may be, upon the whole,
friendly and assistant to virtue, and productive of an overbalance of happiness; *i. e.* the things objected against may
be means by which an over-balance of good will, in the end,
be found produced.   And, from the same observations, it
appears to be no presumption against this, that we do not,
if indeed we do not, see those means to have any such tendency, or that they seem to us to have a contrary one.
Thus, those things which we call irregularities, may not be
so at all; because they may be means of accomplishing

wise and good ends more considerable. And it may be added, as above,* that they may also be the only means by which these wise and good ends are capable of being accomplished.

After these observations it may be proper to add, in order to obviate an absurd and wicked conclusion from any of them, that though the constitution of our nature, from whence we are capable of vice and misery, may, as it undoubtedly does, contribute to the perfection and happiness of the world; and though the actual permission of evil may be beneficial to it, (*i. e.* it would have been more mischievous, not that a wicked person had himself abstained from his own wickedness, but that any one had forcibly prevented it, than that it was permitted;) yet, notwithstanding, it might have been much better for the world if this very evil had never been done. Nay, it is most clearly conceivable, that the very commission of wickedness may be beneficial to the world, and yet that it would be infinitely more beneficial for men to refrain from it. For thus, in the wise and good constitution of the natural world, there are disorders which bring their own cures; diseases, which are themselves remedies. Many a man would have died, had it not been for the gout or a fever; yet it would be thought madness to assert, that sickness is a better or more perfect state than health; though the like, with regard to the moral world, has been asserted. But,

Secondly, The natural government of the world is carried on by general laws. For this there may be wise and good reasons; the wisest and best, for aught we know to the contrary. And that there are such reasons, is suggested to our thoughts by the analogy of nature; by our being made to experience good ends to be accomplished, as indeed all the good which we enjoy is accomplished, by this means, that the laws, by which the world is go-

* Page 107.

verned, are general.   For we have scarce any kind of
enjoyments, but what we are, in some way or other, instrumental in procuring ourselves, by acting in a manner
which we foresee likely to procure them: now this foresight could not be at all, were not the government of the
world carried on by general laws.   And though, for aught
we know to the contrary, every single case may be, at
length, found to have been provided for even by these;
yet, to prevent all irregularities, or remedy them as they
arise, by the wisest and best general laws, may be impossible in the nature of things, as we see it is absolutely
impossible in civil government.   But then we are ready
to think that the constitution of nature remaining as it
is, and the course of things being permitted to go on in
other respects as it does, there might be interpositions to
prevent irregularities, though they could not have been
prevented or remedied by any general laws.   And there
would indeed be reason to wish—which, by the way, is
very different from a right claim—that all irregularities
were prevented or remedied by present interpositions, if
those interpositions would have no other effect than this.
But it is plain they would have some visible and immediate bad effects; for instance, they would encourage
idleness and negligence, and they would render doubtful
the natural rule of life, which is ascertained by this very
thing, that the course of the world is carried on by general
laws.   And farther, it is certain they would have distant
effects, and very great ones too, by means of the wonderful
connexions before mentioned.*   So that we cannot so
much as guess what would be the whole result of the
interpositions desired.   It may be said, any bad result
might be prevented by farther interpositions whenever
there was occasion for them; but this again is talking
quite at random, and in the dark.†   Upon the whole,
then, we see wise reasons why the course of the world

* Page 104, &c.   † Pages 105, 106.

should be carried on by general laws, and good ends accomplished by this means; and, for aught we know, there may be the wisest reasons for it, and the best ends accomplished by it. We have no ground to believe, that all irregularities could be remedied as they arise, or could have been precluded by general laws. We find that interpositions would produce evil, and prevent good; and, for aught we know, they would produce greater evil than they would prevent, and prevent greater good than they would produce. And if this be the case, then the not interposing is so far from being a ground of complaint, that it is an instance of goodness. This is intelligible and sufficient; and going farther seems beyond the utmost reach of our faculties.

But it may be said, that, "after all, these supposed impossibilities and relations are what we are unacquainted with; and we must judge of religion, as of other things, by what we do know, and look upon the rest as nothing: or, however, that the answers here given to what is objected against religion, may equally be made use of to invalidate the proof of it, since their stress lies so very much upon our ignorance." But,

First, Though total ignorance, in any matter, does indeed equally destroy, or rather preclude, all proof concerning it, and objections against it, yet partial ignorance does not. For we may in any degree be convinced, that a person is of such a character, and consequently will pursue such ends, though we are greatly ignorant what is the proper way of acting in order the most effectually to obtain those ends: and in this case, objections against his manner of acting as seemingly not conducive to obtain them, might be answered by our ignorance, though the proof that such ends were intended might not at all be invalidated by it. Thus the proof of religion is a proof of the moral character of God, and, consequently, that his government is moral, and that every one, upon the whole, shall receive according to his deserts; a proof that this is the designed end of his government.   But we are not competent judges what is the proper way of acting, in order the most effectually to accomplish this end.   Therefore our ignorance is an answer to objections against the con-duct of Providence, in permitting irregularities, as seeming contradictory to this end.   Now, since it is so obvious that our ignorance may be a satisfactory answer to objections against a thing, and yet not affect the proof of it; till it can be shown, it is frivolous to assert, that our ignorance invalidates the proof of religion, as it does the objections against it.

Secondly, Suppose unknown impossibilities, and unknown relations, might justly be urged to invalidate the proof of religion, as well as to answer objections against it, and that, in consequence of this, the proof of it were doubtful; yet still, let the assertion be despised, or let it be ridiculed, it is undeniably true, that moral obligations would remain certain, though it were not certain what would, upon the whole, be the consequences of observing or violating them. For these obligations arise immediately and necessarily from the judgment of our own mind, unless perverted, which we cannot violate without being self-condemned.   And they would be certain, too, from considerations of interest. For, though it were doubtful what will be the future conse-quences of virtue and vice, yet it is however credible, that they may have those consequences which religion teaches us they will: and this credibility is a certain* obligation, in point of prudence, to abstain from all wickedness, and to live in the conscientious practice of all that is good.   But,

Thirdly, The answer above given to the objections against religion, cannot equally be made use of to invali-date the proof of it.   For, upon supposition that God exercises a moral government over the world, analogy does most strongly lead us to conclude, that this moral govern-ment must be a scheme, or constitution, beyond our

* Part. ii. chap. 6.

comprehension.   And a thousand particular analogies show us, that parts of such a scheme, from their relation to other parts, may conduce to accomplish ends, which we should have thought they had no tendency at all to accomplish; nay, ends which, before experience, we should have thought such parts were contradictory to, and had a tendency to prevent.   And, therefore, all these analogies show, that the way of arguing made use of in objecting against religion is delusive; because they show it is not at all incredible, that, could we comprehend the whole, we should find the permission of the disorders objected against, to be consistent with justice and goodness, and even to be instances of them.   Now this is not applicable to the proof of religion, as it is to the objections against it;* and therefore cannot invalidate that proof, as it does these objections.

Lastly, From the observation now made it is easy to see, that the answers above given to the objections against Providence, though, in a general way of speaking, they may be said to be taken from our ignorance, yet are by no means taken merely from that, but from somewhat which analogy shows us concerning it.   For analogy shows us positively, that our ignorance in the possibilities of things, and the various relations in nature, renders us incompetent judges, and leads us to false conclusions, in cases similar to this, in which we pretend to judge and to object.   So that the things above insisted upon are not mere suppositions of unknown impossibilities and relations; but they are suggested to our thoughts, and even forced upon the observation of serious men, and rendered credible too, by the analogy of nature.   And, therefore, to take these things into the account, is to judge by experience, and what we do know; and it is not judging so to take no notice of them.

* Sermon at the Rolls, p. 312. 2d Edit.

CONCLUSION.

THE observations of the last chapter lead us to consider this little scene of human life, in which we are so busily engaged, as having a reference, of some sort or other, to a much larger plan of things. Whether we are any way related to the more distant parts of the boundless universe into which we are brought, is altogether uncertain. But it is evident that the course of things, which comes within our view, is connected with somewhat past, present, and future, beyond it.* So that we are placed, as one may speak, in the middle of a scheme, not a fixed, but a progressive one, every way incomprehensible; incomprehensible, in a manner, equally with respect to what has been, what now is, and what shall be hereafter. And this scheme cannot but contain in it somewhat as wonderful, and as much beyond our thought and conception,† as anything in that of religion. For, will any man in his senses say, that it is less difficult to conceive how the world came to be, and to continue as it is, without, than with, an intelligent Author and Governor of it? or, admitting an intelligent Governor of it, that there is some other rule of government more natural, and of easier conception, than that which we call moral? Indeed, without an intelligent Author and Governor of nature, no account at all can be given, how this universe, or the part of it particularly in which we are concerned, came to be, and the course of it to be carried on, as it is; nor any of its general end and design, without a moral Governor of it. That there is an intelligent Author of nature, and natural Governor of the world, is a principle gone upon in the foregoing Treatise as proved, and generally known and confessed to be proved. And the very notion of an intelligent Author of nature, proved by particular final causes, implies a will and a character.‡

* Page 103, &c.   † See Part ii. chap. 2.   ‡ Page 94.

Now, as our whole nature, the nature which he has given us, leads us to conclude his will and character to be moral, just, and good; so we can scarce in imagination conceive that it can be otherwise. However, in consequence of this his will and character, whatever it be, he formed the universe as it is, and carries on the course of it as he does, rather than in any other manner; and has assigned to us, and to all living creatures, a part and a lot in it. Irrational creatures act this their part, and enjoy and undergo the pleasures and the pains allotted them, without any reflection. But one would think it impossible, that creatures endued with reason could avoid reflecting sometimes upon all this;—reflecting, if not from whence we came, yet, at least, whither we are going, and what the mysterious scheme, in the midst of which we find ourselves, will at length come out and produce; a scheme in which it is certain we are highly interested, and in which we may be interested even beyond conception. For many things prove it palpably absurd to conclude, that we shall cease to be at death. Particular analogies do most sensibly show us, that there is nothing to be thought strange in our being to exist in another state of life. And, that we are now living beings, affords a strong probability that we shall *continue* so; unless there be some positive ground—and there is none from reason or analogy—to think death will destroy us. Were a persuasion of this kind ever so well grounded, there would, surely, be little reason to take pleasure in it. But, indeed, it can have no other ground than some such imagination as that of our gross bodies being ourselves; which is contrary to experience. Experience, too, most clearly shows us the folly of concluding, from the body and the living agent affecting each other mutually, that the dissolution of the former is the destruction of the latter. And there are remarkable instances of their not affecting each other, which lead us to a contrary conclusion. The supposition, then, which in all reason we are to go upon, is, that our living nature will *continue* after death. And it is infinitely unreasonable to form an institution of life, or to act, upon any other supposition. Now all expectation of immortality, whether more or less certain, opens an unbounded prospect to our hopes and our fears; since we see the constitution of nature is such as to admit of misery, as well as to be productive of happiness, and experience ourselves to partake of both in some degree; and since we cannot but know what higher degrees of both we are capable of. And there is no presumption against believing farther, that our future interest depends upon our present behaviour; for we see our present interest doth; and that the happiness and misery, which are naturally annexed to our actions, very frequently do not follow till long after the actions are done to which they are respectively annexed. So that, were speculation to leave us uncertain, whether it were likely that the Author of nature, in giving happiness and misery to his creatures, hath regard to their actions or not; yet, since we find by experience that he hath such regard, the whole sense of things which he has given us plainly leads us, at once, and without any elaborate inquiries, to think, that it may, indeed must, be to good actions chiefly that he hath annexed happiness, and to bad actions misery; or, that he will, upon the whole, reward those who do well, and punish those who do evil. To confirm this from the constitution of the world, it has been observed, that some sort of moral government is necessarily implied in that natural government of God which we experience ourselves under; that good and bad actions, at present, are naturally rewarded and punished, not only as beneficial and mischievous to society, but also as virtuous and vicious; and that there is, in the very nature of the thing, a tendency to their being rewarded and punished in a much higher degree than they are at present. And though this higher degree of distributive justice, which nature thus points out and leads towards, is prevented for a time from taking place, it is by obstacles which the state of this world unhappily throws in its way, and which, therefore, are in their nature temporary. Now, as these things, in the natural conduct of Providence, are observable on the side of virtue, so there is nothing to be set against them on the side of vice. A moral scheme of government, then, is visibly established, and, in some degree, carried into execution; and this, together with the essential tendencies of virtue and vice duly considered, naturally raise in us an apprehension that it will be carried on farther towards perfection in a future state, and that every one shall there receive according to his deserts. And if this be so, then our future and general interest, under the moral government of God, is appointed to depend upon our behaviour, notwithstanding the difficulty which this may occasion of securing it, and the danger of losing it; just in the same manner as our temporal interest, under his natural government, is appointed to depend upon our behaviour, notwithstanding the like difficulty and danger. For, from our original constitution, and that of the world which we inhabit, we are naturally trusted with ourselves, with our own conduct and our own interest. And from the same constitution of nature, especially joined with that course of things which is owing to men, we have temptations to be unfaithful in this trust, to forfeit this interest, to neglect it, and run ourselves into misery and ruin. From these temptations arise the difficulties of behaving so as to secure our temporal interest, and the hazard of behaving so as to miscarry in it. There is, therefore, nothing incredible in supposing, there may be the like difficulty and hazard with regard to that chief and final good which religion lays before us. Indeed, the whole account, how it came to pass that we were placed in such a condition as this, must be beyond our comprehension. But it is in part accounted for by what religion teaches us, that the character of virtue and piety must be a necessary qualification for a future state of security and happiness, under the moral government of God; in like manner as some certain qualifications or other are necessary for every particular condition of life, under his natural government; and that the present state was intended to be a school of discipline, for improving in ourselves that character. Now, this intention of nature is rendered highly credible by observing, that we are plainly made for improvement of all kinds; that it is a general appointment of Providence, that we cultivate practical principles, and form within ourselves habits of action, in order to become fit for what we were wholly unfit for before; that, in particular, childhood and youth is naturally appointed to be a state of discipline for mature age; and that the present world is peculiarly fitted for a state of moral discipline. And, whereas, objections are urged against the whole notion of moral government and a probation-state, from the opinion of necessity, it has been shown, that God hath given us the evidence, as it were, of experience, that all objections against religion on this head, are vain and delusive. He has, also, in his natural government, suggested an answer to all our short-sighted objections against the equity and goodness of his moral government; and, in general, he has exemplified to us the latter by the former.

These things, which it is to be remembered, are matters of fact, ought in all common sense to awaken mankind, to induce them to consider, in earnest, their condition, and what they have to do. It is absurd—absurd to the degree of being ridiculous, if the subject were not of so serious a kind, for men to think themselves secure in a vicious life, or even in that immoral thoughtlessness which far the greatest part of them are fallen into. And the credibility of religion, arising from experience and facts here considered, is fully sufficient, in reason, to engage them to live in the general practice of all virtue and piety; under the serious apprehension, though it should be mixed with some doubt,* of a righteous administration established in nature, and a future judgment in consequence of it; especially when we consider how very questionable it is whether any thing at all can be gained by vice;† how unquestionably little, as well as precarious, the pleasures and profits of it are at the best; and how soon they must be parted with at the longest. For, in the deliberations of reason, concerning what we are to pursue, and what to avoid, as temptations to anything from mere passion are supposed out of the case; so inducements to vice, from cool expectations of pleasure and interest, so small, and uncertain, and short, are really so insignificant, as, in the view of reason, to be almost nothing in themselves, and in comparison with the import- ance of religion, they quite disappear and are lost. Mere passion, indeed, may be alleged, though not as a reason, yet as an excuse, for a vicious course of life. And how sorry an excuse it is will be manifest by observing, that we are placed in a condition in which we are unavoidably inured to govern our passions, by being necessitated to govern them, and to lay ourselves under the same kind of restraints, and as great ones, too, from temporal regards, as virtue and piety, in the ordinary course of things, require. The plea of ungovernable passion, then, on the side of vice, is the poorest of all things, for it is no reason, and but a poor excuse. But the proper motives to religion, are the proper proofs of it, from our moral nature, from the presages of conscience, and our natural apprehension of God, under the character of a righteous Governor and Judge; a nature, and conscience, and apprehension given us by him; and from the confirmation of the dictates of reason, by *life and im- mortality brought to light by the gospel; and the wrath of God revealed from heaven, against all ungodliness and unrighteousness of men.*

* Part ii. chap. 6.   † Page 33.

THE

ANALOGY OF RELIGION.

PART II.

OF REVEALED RELIGION.

CHAPTER I.

Of the Importance of Christianity.

SOME persons, upon pretence of the sufficiency of the light
of nature, avowedly reject all revelation, as, in its very
notion, incredible, and what must be fictitious.   And indeed
it is certain no revelation would have been given, had the
light of nature been sufficient in such a sense, as to render
one not wanting and useless.   But no man, in seriousness
and simplicity of mind, can possibly think it so, who considers the state of religion in the heathen world before
revelation, and its present state in those places which have
borrowed no light from it; particularly, the doubtfulness of
some of the greatest men concerning things of the utmost
importance, as well as the natural inattention and ignorance
of mankind in general.   It is impossible to say who would
have been able to have reasoned out that whole system,
which we call natural religion, in its genuine simplicity, clear
of superstition; but there is certainly no ground to affirm
that the generality could; if they could, there is no sort of
probability that they would.   Admitting there were, they
would highly want a standing admonition, to remind them
of it, and inculcate it upon them.   And farther still, were

they as much disposed to attend to religion as the better
sort of men are, yet, even upon this supposition, there would
be various occasions for supernatural instruction and assistance, and the greatest advantages might be afforded by
them: so that to say revelation is a thing superfluous, what
there was no need of, and what can be of no service, is, I
think, to talk quite wildly and at random. Nor would it be
more extravagant to affirm, that mankind is so entirely at
ease in the present state, and life so completely happy, that
it is a contradiction to suppose our condition capable of
being in any respect better.

There are other persons not to be ranked with these, who
seem to be getting into a way of neglecting, and, as it were,
overlooking revelation, as of small importance, provided
natural religion be kept to. With little regard, either to the
evidence of the former, or to the objections against it, and
even upon supposition of its truth, " The only design
of it," say they, " must be to establish a belief of the moral
system of nature, and to enforce the practice of natural piety
and virtue. The belief and practice of these things were,
perhaps, much promoted by the first publication of Christianity; but whether they are believed and practised upon the
evidence and motives of nature, or of revelation, is no great
matter."* This way of considering revelation, though it is
not the same with the former, yet borders nearly upon it,
and very much, at length, runs upon it, and requires to be
particularly considered, with regard to the persons who seem
to be getting into this way. The consideration of it will,
likewise, farther show the extravagance of the former opinion,
and the truth of the observations in answer to it, just men-

---

* Invenis multos——propterea nolle fieri Christianos, quia quasi
sufficiunt sibi de bona vita sua. Bene vivere opus est, ait. Quid mihi
præceptures est Christus? Ut bene vivam? Jam bene vivo. Quid
mihi necessarius est Christus? Nullum homicidium, nullum furtum,
nullam rapinam facio, res alienas non concupisco, nullo adulterio con-
taminor. Nam inveniatur in vita mea aliquid quod reprehendatur, et
qui reprehenderit faciat Christianum.   *Aug. in Psal.* xxxi.

tioned. And an inquiry into the importance of Christianity, cannot be an improper introduction to a treatise concerning the credibility of it.

Now, if God has given a revelation to mankind, and commanded those things which are commanded in Christianity, it is evident, at first sight, that it cannot in any wise be an indifferent matter, whether we obey or disobey those commands, unless we are certainly assured that we know all the reasons for them, and that all those reasons are now ceased, with regard to mankind in general, or to ourselves in particular. And it is absolutely impossible we can be assured of this; for our ignorance of these reasons proves nothing in the case, since the whole analogy of nature shows, what is indeed in itself evident, that there may be infinite reasons for things with which we are not acquainted.

But the importance of Christianity will more distinctly appear, by considering it more distinctly: *First*, As a republication, and external institution, of natural or essential religion, adapted to the present circumstances of mankind, and intended to promote natural piety and virtue; and, *secondly*, As containing an account of a dispensation of things not discoverable by reason, in consequence of which several distinct precepts are enjoined us. For, though natural religion is the foundation and principal part of Christianity, it is not in any sense the whole of it.

I. Christianity is a republication of natural religion. It instructs mankind in the moral system of the world; that it is the work of an infinitely perfect Being, and under his government; that virtue is his law; and that he will finally judge mankind in righteousness, and render to all according to their works, in a future state. And, which is very material, it teaches natural religion in its genuine simplicity, free from those superstitions with which it was totally corrupted, and under which it was in a manner lost.

Revelation is, farther, an authoritative publication of

natural religion, and so affords the evidence of testimony
for the truth of it. Indeed, the miracles and prophecies
recorded in Scripture were intended to prove a particular dispensation of Providence—the redemption of the
world by the Messiah; but this does not hinder but that
they may also prove God's general providence over the
world, as our moral Governor and Judge. And they
evidently do prove it; because this character of the Author
of nature is necessarily connected with, and implied in,
that particular revealed dispensation of things: it is likewise
continually taught expressly, and insisted upon, by those
persons who wrought the miracles and delivered the
prophecies. So that, indeed, natural religion seems as
much proved by the Scripture revelation, as it would have
been had the design of revelation been nothing else than to
prove it.

But it may possibly be ·disputed, how far miracles can
prove natural religion; and notable objections may be
urged against this proof of it, considered as a matter of
speculation; but, considered as a practical thing, there
can be none. For, suppose a person to teach natural
religion to a nation who had lived in total ignorance or
forgetfulness of it, and to declare he was commissioned
by God so to do: suppose him, in proof of his commission, to foretell things future, which no human foresight
could have guessed at; to divide the sea with a word;
feed great multitudes with bread from heaven; cure all
manner of diseases; and raise the dead, even himself, to
life: would not this give additional credibility to his
teaching, a credibility beyond what that of a common
man would have, and be an authoritative publication of
the law of nature, *i. e.* a new proof of it? It would be
a practical one, of the strongest kind, perhaps, which
human creatures are capable of having given them. The
law of Moses, then, and the gospel of Christ, are authoritative publications of the religion of nature; they afford
a proof of God's general providence, as moral Governor

of the world, as well as of his particular dispensations of providence towards sinful creatures, revealed in the law and the gospel. As they are the only evidence of the latter, so they are an additional evidence of the former.

To show this further, let us suppose a man of the greatest and most improved capacity, who had never heard of revelation, convinced upon the whole, notwithstanding the disorders of the world, that it was under the direction and moral government of an infinitely perfect Being, but ready to question, whether he were not got beyond the reach of his faculties; suppose him brought, by this suspicion, into great danger of being carried away by the universal bad example of almost every one around him, who appeared to have no sense, no practical sense at least, of these things; and this, perhaps, would be as advantageous a situation, with respect to religion, as nature alone ever placed any man in: what a confirmation now must it be to such a person, all at once to find that this moral system of things was revealed to mankind, in the name of that infinite Being whom he had, from principles of reason, believed in; and that the publishers of the revelation proved their commission from him, by making it appear that he had intrusted them with a power of suspending and changing the general laws of nature!

Nor must it, by any means, be omitted, for it is a thing of the utmost importance, that life and immortality are eminently brought to light by the gospel. The great doctrines of a future state, the danger of a course of wickedness, and the efficacy of repentance, are not only confirmed in the gospel, but are taught, especially the last is, with a degree of light to which that of nature is but darkness.

Farther; As Christianity served these ends and purposes, when it was first published, by the miraculous publication itself; so it was intended to serve the same purposes in future ages, by means of the settlement of a visible church—of a society, distinguished from common ones, and from the rest of the world, by peculiar religious institutions; by an instituted method of instruction, and an instituted form of external religion. Miraculous powers were given to the first preachers of Christianity, in order to their introducing it into the world: a visible church was established, in order to continue it, and carry it on successively throughout all ages. Had Moses and the prophets, Christ and his apostles, only taught, and by miracles proved, religion to their contemporaries, the bene-fits of their instructions would have reached but to a small part of mankind. Christianity must have been, in a great degree, sunk and forgot in a very few ages. To prevent this, appears to have been one reason why a visible church was instituted; to be, like a city upon a hill, a standing memorial to the world of the duty which we owe our Maker; to call men continually, both by example and instruction, to attend to it, and, by the form of religion ever before their eyes, remind them of the reality; to be the repository of the oracles of God; to hold up the light of revelation in aid to that of nature, and propagate it throughout all generations to the end of the world— the light of revelation, considered here in no other view than as designed to enforce natural religion. And, in proportion as Christianity is professed and taught in the world, religion, natural or essential religion, is thus dis-tinctly and advantageously laid before mankind, and brought again and again to their thoughts as a matter of infinite importance. A visible church has also a farther tendency to promote natural religion, as being an insti-tuted method of education, originally intended to be of more peculiar advantage to those who would conform to it. For one end of the institution was, that, by admo-nition and reproof, as well as instruction; by a general regular discipline, and public exercises of religion, *the body of Christ*, as the Scripture speaks, should be *edified;* *i. e.* trained up in piety and virtue, for a higher and better state. This settlement, then, appearing thus beneficial;

tending, in the nature of the thing, to answer, and, in some degree, actually answering those ends; it is to be remembered, that the very notion of it implies positive institutions; for the visibility of the church consists in them. Take away everything of this kind, and you lose the very notion itself. So that, if the things now mentioned are advantages, the reason and importance of positive institutions in general is most obvious; since, without them, these advantages could not be secured to the world. And it is mere idle wantonness to insist upon knowing the reasons why such particular ones were fixed upon, rather than others.

The benefit arising from this supernatural assistance which Christianity affords to natural religion, is what some persons are very slow in apprehending; and yet it is a thing distinct in itself, and a very plain obvious one. For will any, in good earnest, really say, that the bulk of mankind in the heathen world were in as advantageous a situation, with regard to natural religion, as they are now amongst us? that it was laid before them, and enforced upon them, in a manner as distinct, and as much tending to influence their practice?

The objections against all this, from the perversion of Christianity, and from the supposition of its having had but little good influence, however innocently they may be proposed, yet cannot be insisted upon as conclusive, upon any principles but such as lead to downright atheism; because the manifestation of the law of nature by reason, which, upon all principles of theism, must have been from God, has been perverted and rendered ineffectual in the same manner. It may indeed, I think, truly be said, that the good effects of Christianity have not been small; nor its supposed ill effects, any effects at all of it, properly speaking. Perhaps, too, the things themselves done have been aggravated; and if not, Christianity hath been often only a pretence; and the same evils, in the main, would have been done upon some other pretence. However, great and shocking as the corruptions and abuses of it have really been, they cannot be insisted upon as arguments against it, upon principles of theism; for one cannot proceed one step in reasoning upon natural religion, any more than upon Christianity, without laying it down as a first principle, that the dispensations of Providence are not to be judged of by their perversions, but by their genuine tendencies; not by what they do actually seem to effect, but by what they would effect if mankind did their part—that part which is justly put and left upon them. It is altogether as much the language of one as of the other: *He that is unjust, let him be unjust still; and he that is holy, let him be holy still.* Rev. xxii. 11. The light of reason does not, any more than that of revelation, force men to submit to its authority: both admonish them of what they ought to do and avoid, together with the consequences of each; and, after this, leave them at full liberty to act just as they please, till the appointed time of judgment. Every moment's experience shows, that this is God's general rule of government.

To return, then: Christianity being a promulgation of the law of nature; being, moreover, an authoritative promulgation of it, with new light, and other circumstances of peculiar advantage, adapted to the wants of mankind; these things fully show its importance. And it is to be observed farther, that as the nature of the case requires, so all Christians are commanded to contribute, by their profession of Christianity, to preserve it in the world, and render it such a promulgation and enforcement of religion. For it is the very scheme of the gospel, that each Christian should, in his degree, contribute towards continuing and carrying it on; all by uniting in the public profession, and external practice of Christianity; some by instructing, by having the oversight, and taking care of this religious community, the church of God. Now this farther shows the importance of Christianity, and, which is what I chiefly intend, its importance in a practical sense, or the high obligations we are under to take it into our most serious consideration; and the danger there must necessarily be, not only in treating it despitefully which I am not now speaking of, but in disregarding and neglecting it. For this is neglecting to do what is expressly enjoined us, for continuing those benefits to the world, and transmitting them down to future times. And all this holds, even though the only thing to be considered in Christianity were its subserviency to natural religion. But,

II. Christianity is to be considered in a further view, as containing an account of a dispensation of things not at all discoverable by reason, in consequence of which several distinct precepts are enjoined us. Christianity is not only an external institution of natural religion, and a new promulgation of God's general Providence, as righteous Governor and Judge of the world; but it contains also a revelation of a particular dispensation of providence, carrying on by his Son and Spirit, for the recovery and salvation of mankind, who are represented, in Scripture, to be in a state of ruin. And, in consequence of this, revelation being made, we are commanded *to be baptized*, not only *in the name of the Father*, but also *of the Son, and of the Holy Ghost;* and other obligations of duty, unknown before, to the Son and the Holy Ghost, are revealed. Now, the importance of these duties may be judged of by observing, that they arise, not from positive command merely, but also from the offices which appear, from Scripture, to belong to those divine persons in the gospel dispensation, or from the relations which, we are there informed, they stand in to us. By reason is revealed the relation which God the Father stands in to us: hence arises the obligation of duty which we are under to him. In Scripture are revealed the relations which the Son and Holy Spirit stand in to us: hence arise the obligations of duty which we are under to them. The truth of the case, as one may speak, in each of these

three respects, being admitted, that God is the Governor
of the world, upon the evidence of reason; that Christ is
the Mediator between God and man; and the Holy Ghost
our Guide and Sanctifier, upon the evidence of revelation—
the truth of the case, I say, in each of these respects, being
admitted, it is no more a question, why it should be commanded that we be baptized in the name of the Son and of
the Holy Ghost, than that we be baptized in the name of
the Father.   This matter seems to require to be more fully
stated.*

Let it be remembered, then, that religion comes under
the twofold consideration of internal and external; for
the latter is as real a part of religion, of true religion, as
the former.   Now, when religion is considered under the
first notion, as an inward principle, to be exerted in such
and such inward acts of the mind and heart, the essence
of natural religion may be said to consist in religious
regards to *God the Father Almighty;* and the essence
of revealed religion, as distinguished from natural, to consist in religious regards to *the Son* and to *the Holy Ghost.*
And the obligation we are under, of paying these religious
regards to each of these divine persons respectively, arises
from the respective relations which they each stand in to us.
How these relations are made known, whether by reason or
revelation, makes no alteration in the case; because the
duties arise out of the relations themselves, not out of the
manner in which we are informed of them.   The Son and
Spirit have each his proper office in that great dispensation of Providence, the redemption of the world: the one
our Mediator, the other our Sanctifier.   Does not, then,
the duty of religious regards to both these divine persons,
as immediately arise, to the view of reason, out of the very
nature of these offices and relations, as the inward good-
will and kind attention, which we owe to our fellow-

* See the Nature, Obligation, and Efficacy, of the Christian Sacra-
ments, &c. and *Colliber* of Revealed Religion, as there quoted.

creatures, arises out of the common relations between us
and them? But it will be asked, " What are the inward
religious regards appearing thus obviously due to the Son
and Holy Spirit, as arising, not merely from command in
Scripture, but from the very nature of the revealed relations
which they stand in to us?" I answer, the religious
regards of reverence, honour, love, trust, gratitude, fear,
hope. In what external manner this inward worship is to
be expressed, is a matter of pure revealed command; as,
perhaps, the external manner in which God the Father is to
be worshipped may be more so than we are ready to think :
but the worship, the internal worship itself, to the Son and
Holy Ghost, is no farther matter of pure revealed command, than as the relations they stand in to us are matter
of pure revelation; for the relations being known, the
obligations to such internal worship are obligations of
reason, arising out of those relations themselves. In short,
the history of the gospel as immediately shows us the reason of these obligations, as it shows us the meaning of the
words, Son and Holy Ghost.

If this account of the Christian religion be just, those
persons who can speak lightly of it, as of little consequence,
provided natural religion be kept to, plainly forget, that
Christianity, even what is peculiarly so called, as distinguished from natural religion, has yet somewhat very
important, even of a moral nature. For, the office of our
Lord being made known, and the relation he stands in to
us, the obligation of religious regards to him is plainly
moral, as much as charity to mankind is; since this obligation arises, before external command, immediately out of
that office and relation itself. Those persons appear to
forget what revelation is to be considered as informing us
of—somewhat new in the state of mankind, and in the
government of the world; as acquainting us with some
relations we stand in, which could not otherwise have been
known. And these relations being real, (though before
revelation we could be under no obligations from them, yet,

upon their being revealed,) there is no reason to think, but that neglect of behaving suitably to them will be attended with the same kind of consequences under God's government, as neglecting to behave suitably to any other relations made known to us by reason. And ignorance, whether unavoidable or voluntary, so far as we can possibly see, will, just as much, and just as little, excuse in one case as in the other, the ignorance being supposed equally unavoidable, or equally voluntary, in both cases.

If, therefore, Christ be indeed the Mediator between God and man, *i. e.* if Christianity be true; if he be indeed our Lord, our Saviour, and our God, no one can say what may follow, not only the obstinate, but the careless disregard to him in those high relations. Nay, no one can say, what may follow such disregard, even in the way of natural consequence.* For, as the natural consequences of vice in this life are doubtless to be considered as judicial punishments inflicted by God; so likewise, for aught we know, the judicial punishments of the future life may be, in a like way, or a like sense, the natural consequence of vice; † of men's violating or disregarding the relations which God has placed them in here, and made known to them.

Again, If mankind are corrupted and depraved in their moral character, and so are unfit for that state which Christ is gone to prepare for his disciples; and if the assistance of God's Spirit be necessary to renew their nature, in the degree requisite to their being qualified for that state; all which is implied in the express, though figurative declaration, *Except a man be born of the Spirit, he cannot enter into the kingdom of God*, John iii. 5: supposing this, is it possible any serious person can think it a slight matter, whether or no he makes use of the means expressly commanded by God for obtaining this divine assistance? especially since the whole analogy of nature shows, that we are not to expect any benefits, without making use of

* Pages 17, 18.   † Chap. 5.

the appointed means for obtaining or enjoying them. Now, reason shows us nothing of the particular immediate means of obtaining either temporal or spiritual benefits. This, therefore, we must learn, either from experience or revelation. And experience, the present case does not admit of.

The conclusion from all this evidently is, that Christianity being supposed either true or credible, it is unspeakable irreverence, and really the most presumptuous rashness, to treat it as a light matter. It can never justly be esteemed of little consequence, till it be positively supposed false. Nor do I know a higher or more important obligation which we are under, than that of examining most seriously into the evidence of it, supposing its credibility; and of embracing it upon supposition of its truth.

The two following deductions may be proper to be added, in order to illustrate the foregoing observations, and to prevent their being mistaken.

First, Hence we may clearly see, where lies the distinction between what is positive and what is moral in religion. Moral *precepts* are precepts, the reasons of which we see; positive *precepts* are precepts, the reasons of which we do not see.* Moral *duties* arise out of the nature of the case itself, prior to external command: positive *duties* do not arise out of the nature of the case, but from external command; nor would they be duties at all, were it not for such command received from Him whose creatures and subjects we are. But the manner in which the nature of the case, or the fact of the relation, is made known, this doth not denominate any duty, either positive or moral. That we be baptized in the

* This is the distinction between moral and positive precepts, considered respectively as such. But yet, since the latter have somewhat of a moral nature, we may see the reason of them considered in this view. Moral and positive precepts are in some respects alike, in other respects different. So far as they are alike, we discern the reasons of both: so far as they are different, we discern the reasons of the former, but not of the latter. See p. 126, &c. and p. 133.

name of the Father, is as much a positive duty as that
we be baptized in the name of the Son; because both
arise equally from revealed command: though the relation
which we stand in to God the Father, is made known
to us by reason; the relation we stand in to Christ, by
revelation only. On the other hand, the dispensation of
the gospel admitted, gratitude as immediately becomes
due to Christ, from his being the voluntary minister of
this dispensation, as it is due to God the Father, from
his being the fountain of all good; though the first is
made known to us by revelation only, the second by
reason.   Hence also we may see, and, for distinctness'
sake, it may be worth mentioning, that positive institutions come under a two-fold consideration.   They are
either institutions founded on natural religion, as baptism
in the name of the Father—though this has also a particular reference to the gospel dispensation, for it is in
the name of God, as the Father of our Lord Jesus Christ;
or they are external institutions founded on revealed
religion, as baptism in the name of the Son, and of the
Holy Ghost.

Secondly, From the distinction between what is moral
and what is positive in religion, appears the ground of that
peculiar preference which the Scripture teaches us to be
due to the former.

The reason of positive institutions in general is very
obvious, though we should not see the reason why such
particular ones are pitched upon, rather than others.
Whoever, therefore, instead of cavilling at words, will
attend to the thing itself, may clearly see, that positive
institutions in general, as distinguished from this or that
particular one, have the nature of moral commands;
since the reasons of them appear. Thus, for instance,
the *external* worship of God is a moral duty, though no
particular mode of it be so. Care, then, is to be taken,
when a comparison is made between positive and moral
duties, that they be compared no farther than as they

are different; no farther than as the former are positive, or arise out of mere external command, the reasons of which we are not acquainted with; and as the latter are moral, or arise out of the apparent reason of the case, without such external command. Unless this caution be observed, we shall run into endless confusion.

Now, this being premised, suppose two standing precepts enjoined by the same authority; that, in certain conjunctures, it is impossible to obey both; that the former is moral, *i. e.* a precept of which we see the reasons, and that they hold in the particular case before us; but that the latter is positive, *i. e.* a precept of which we do not see the reasons:—it is indisputable that our obligations are to obey the former, because there is an apparent reason for this preference, and none against it. Farther, positive institutions, I suppose all those which Christianity enjoins, are means to a moral end; and the end must be acknowledged more excellent than the means. Nor is observance of these institutions any religious obedience at all, or of any value, otherwise than as it proceeds from a moral principle. This seems to be the strict logical way of stating and determining this matter; but will, perhaps, be found less applicable to practice, than may be thought at first sight.

And therefore, in a more practical, though more lax way of consideration, and taking the words *moral law* and *positive institutions* in the popular sense, I add, that the whole moral law is as much matter of revealed command as positive institutions are; for the Scripture enjoins every moral virtue. In this respect, then, they are both upon a level. But the moral law is, moreover, written upon our hearts, interwoven into our very nature. And this is a plain intimation of the Author of it, which is to be preferred, when they interfere.

But there is not altogether so much necessity for the determination of this question as some persons seem to think. Nor are we left to reason alone to determine it.

For, *first*, Though mankind have, in all ages, been greatly
prone to place their religion in peculiar positive rites, by
way of equivalent for obedience to moral precepts; yet,
without making any comparison at all between them,
and consequently without determining which is to have
the preference, the nature of the thing abundantly shows
all notions of that kind to be utterly subversive of true
religion; as they are, moreover, contrary to the whole
general tenor of Scripture, and likewise to the most express particular declarations of it, that nothing can render us accepted of God, without moral virtue. *Secondly,*
Upon the occasion of mentioning together positive and
moral duties, the Scripture always puts the stress of religion upon the latter, and never upon the former; which,
though no sort of allowance to neglect the former, when
they do not interfere with the latter, yet is plain intimation, that when they do, the latter are to be preferred.
And, farther, as mankind are for placing the stress of
their religion anywhere, rather than upon virtue, lest
both the reason of the thing, and the general spirit of
Christianity, appearing in the intimation now mentioned,
should be ineffectual against this prevalent folly; our
Lord himself, from whose command alone the obligation
of positive institutions arises, has taken occasion to make
the comparison between them and moral precepts, when
the Pharisees censured him for *eating with publicans and
sinners;* and also when they censured his disciples for
plucking the ears of corn on the Sabbath-day. Upon this
comparison he has determined expressly, and in form,
which shall have the preference when they interfere.
And by delivering his authoritative determination in a
proverbial manner of expression, he has made it general:
I will have mercy, and not sacrifice, Matth. ix. 13, and
xii. 7. The propriety of the word *proverbial* is not the
thing insisted upon, though, I think, the manner of speaking is to be called so. But that the manner of speaking
very remarkably renders the determination general, is

surely indisputable. For, had it, in the latter case, been said only that God preferred mercy to the rigid observance of the Sabbath, even then, by parity of reason, most justly might we have argued, that he preferred mercy, likewise, to the observance of other ritual institutions, and, in general, moral duties to positive ones. And thus the determination would have been general, though its being so were inferred, and not expressed. But as the passage really stands in the gospel, it is much stronger; for the sense, and the very literal words of our Lord's answer, are as applicable to any other instance of a comparison between positive and moral duties, as to this upon which they were spoken. And if, in case of competition, mercy is to be preferred to positive institutions, it will scarcely be thought that justice is to give place to them. It is remarkable, too, that as the words are a quotation from the Old Testament, they are introduced, on both the forementioned occasions, with a declaration, that the Pharisees did not understand the meaning of them. This, I say, is very remarkable; for, since it is scarcely possible for the most ignorant person not to understand the literal sense of the passage in the Prophet, Hos. vi., and since understanding the literal sense would not have prevented their *condemning the guiltless,* (see Matt. xii. 7,) it can hardly be doubted, that the thing which our Lord really intended in that declaration was, that the Pharisees had not learnt from it, as they might, wherein the *general* spirit of religion consists; that it consists in moral piety and virtue, as distinguished from forms and ritual observances. However, it is certain we may learn this from his divine application of the passage in the gospel.

But, as it is one of the peculiar weaknesses of human nature, when, upon a comparison of two things, one is found to be of greater importance than the other, to consider this other as of scarcely any importance at all; it is highly necessary that we remind ourselves, how great presumption it is to make light of any institutions of divine appointment; that our obligations to obey all God's commands whatever, are absolute and indispensable; and that commands merely positive, admitted to be from him, lay us under a moral obligation to obey them—an obligation moral in the strictest and most proper sense.

To these things I cannot forbear adding, that the account now given of Christianity most strongly shows and enforces upon us the obligation of searching the Scriptures, in order to see what the scheme of revelation really is, instead of determining beforehand, from reason, what the scheme of it must be.*   Indeed, if in revelation there be found any passages, the seeming meaning of which is contrary to natural religion, we may most certainly conclude such seeming meaning not to be the real one.   But it is not any degree of a presumption against an interpretation of Scripture, that such interpretation contains a doctrine, which the light of nature cannot discover,† or a precept, which the law of nature does not oblige to.

CHAPTER II.

Of the supposed Presumption against a Revelation considered as miraculous.

HAVING shown the importance of the Christian revelation, and the obligations which we are under seriously to attend to it, upon supposition of its truth or its credibility; the next thing in order is, to consider the supposed presumptions against revelation in general; which shall be the subject of this chapter; and the objections against the Christian in particular, which shall be the subject of some following ones.‡   For it seems the most natural method to remove the prejudices against Christianity, before we proceed to the consideration of the positive evidence for it, and the objections against that evidence.§

---

* See Chap. 3.   † Pages 139, 140.
‡ Chap. 3, 4, 5, 6.   § Chap. 7.

It is, I think, commonly supposed, that there is some peculiar presumption, from the analogy of nature, against the Christian scheme of things, at least against miracles; so as that stronger evidence is necessary to prove the truth and reality of them, than would be sufficient to convince us of other events or matters of fact. Indeed, the consideration of this supposed presumption cannot but be thought very insignificant by many persons; yet, as it belongs to the subject of this treatise, so it may tend to open the mind, and remove some prejudices; however needless the consideration of it be, upon its own account.

I. I find no appearance of a presumption, from the analogy of nature, against the general scheme of Christianity, that God created and invisibly governs the world by Jesus Christ, and by him also will hereafter judge it in righteousness, *i. e.* render to every one according to his works; and that good men are under the secret influence of his Spirit. Whether these things are, or are not, to be called miraculous, is, perhaps, only a question about words; or, however, is of no moment in the case. If the analogy of nature raises any presumption against this general scheme of Christianity, it must be, either because it is not discoverable by reason or experience, or else because it is unlike that course of nature which is. But analogy raises no presumption against the truth of this scheme, upon either of these accounts.

First, There is no presumption, from analogy, against the truth of it, upon account of its not being discoverable by reason or experience. For, suppose one who never heard of revelation, of the most improved understanding, and acquainted with our whole system of natural philosophy and natural religion—such a one could not but be sensible, that it was but a very small part of the natural and moral system of the universe which he was acquainted with. He could not but be sensible, that there must be innumerable things, in the dispensations of Providence past, in the invisible government over the world at present carrying on, and in what is to come, of which he was wholly ignorant,* and which could not be discovered without revelation. Whether the scheme of nature be, in the strictest sense, infinite or not, it is evidently vast, even beyond all possible imagination. And, doubtless, that part of it which is opened to our view, is but as a point, in comparison of the whole plan of Providence, reaching throughout eternity, past and future; in comparison of what is even now going on in the remote parts of the boundless universe; nay, in comparison of the whole scheme of this world. And, therefore, that things lie beyond the natural reach of our faculties, is no sort of presumption against the truth and reality of them; because it is certain, there are innumerable things, in the constitution and government of the universe, which are thus beyond the natural reach of our faculties. *Secondly,* Analogy raises no presumption against any of the things contained in this general doctrine of Scripture now mentioned, upon account of their being unlike the known course of nature. For there is no presumption at all, from analogy, that the *whole* course of things, or divine government, naturally unknown to us, and *everything* in it, is like to anything in that which is known; and therefore no peculiar presumption against anything in the former, upon account of its being unlike to anything in the latter. And in the constitution and natural government of the world, as well as in the moral government of it, we see things, in a great degree. unlike one another; and therefore ought not to wonder at such unlikeness between things visible and invisible. However, the scheme of Christianity is by no means entirely unlike the scheme of nature; as will appear in the following part of this treatise.

The notion of a miracle, considered as a proof of a divine mission, has been stated with great exactness by divines; and is, I think, sufficiently understood by every one. There are also invisible miracles; the incarnation

* Page 105.

of Christ, for instance, which, being secret, cannot be alleged as a proof of such a mission; but require themselves to be proved by visible miracles. Revelation itself, too, is miraculous, and miracles are the proof of it; and the supposed presumption against these shall presently be considered. All which I have been observing here is, that, whether we choose to call everything in the dispensations of Providence, not discoverable without revelation, nor like the known course of things, miraculous; and whether the general Christian dispensation now mentioned is to be called so, or not; the foregoing observations seem certainly to show, that there is no presumption against it from the analogy of nature.

II. There is no presumption, from analogy, against some operations which we should now call miraculous; particularly, none against a revelation at the beginning of the world; nothing of such presumption against it, as is supposed to be implied or expressed in the word *miraculous*. For a miracle, in its very notion, is relative to a course of nature; and implies somewhat different from it, considered as being so.   Now, either there was no course of nature at the time which we are speaking of; or, if there were, we are not acquainted what the course of nature is upon the first peopling of worlds.   And therefore the question, whether mankind had a revelation made to them at that time, is to be considered, not as a question concerning a miracle, but as a common question of fact.   And we have the like reason, be it more or less, to admit the report of tradition concerning this question, and concerning common matters of fact of the same antiquity; for instance, what part of the earth was first peopled?

Or thus: When mankind was first placed in this state, there was a power exerted, totally different from the present course of nature. Now, whether this power, thus wholly different from the present course of nature, for we cannot properly apply to it the word *miraculous;* whether this power stopped immediately after it had made man, or went on, and exerted itself farther in giving him a revelation, is a question of the same kind, as whether an ordinary power exerted itself in such a particular degree and manner, or not.

Or suppose the power exerted in the formation of the world be considered as miraculous, or rather, be called by that name, the case will not be different : since it must be acknowledged that such a power was exerted. For, supposing it acknowledged that our Saviour spent some years in a course of working miracles; there is no more presumption, worth mentioning, against his having exerted this miraculous power in a certain degree greater, than in a certain degree less; in one or two more instances, than in one or two fewer; in this, than in another manner.

It is evident, then, that there can be no peculiar presumption, from the analogy of nature, against supposing a revelation when man was first placed upon the earth.

Add, that there does not appear the least intimation, in history or tradition, that religion was first reasoned out; but the whole of history and tradition makes for the other side, that it came into the world by revelation.   Indeed, the state ·of religion in the first ages of which we have any account, seems to suppose and imply that this was the original of it amongst mankind.   And these reflections together, without taking in the peculiar authority of Scripture, amount to real and a very material degree of evidence, that there was a revelation at the beginning of the world.   Now this, as it is a confirmation of natural religion, and therefore mentioned in the former part of this treatise ;* so, likewise, it has a tendency to remove any prejudices against a subsequent revelation.

III. But still it may be objected, that there is .some peculiar presumption, from analogy, against miracles; particularly against revelation, after a settlement, and during the continuance, of a course of nature.

* Page 97, &c.

Now, with regard to this supposed presumption, it is to be observed in general, that before we can have ground for raising what can, with any propriety, be called an *argument* from analogy for or against revelation, considered as some-what miraculous, we must be acquainted with a similar or parallel case. But the history of some other world, seemingly in like circumstances with our own, is no more than a parallel case; and therefore nothing short of this can be so. Yet, could we come at a presumptive proof, for or against a revelation, from being informed whether such world had one, or not; such a proof, being drawn from one single instance only, must be infinitely precarious. More particularly: *First* of all, There is a very strong presumption against common speculative truths, and against the most ordinary facts, before the proof of them; which yet is overcome by almost any proof. There is a presumption of millions to one against the story of *Cæsar*, or of any other man. For suppose a number of common facts, so and so circumstanced, of which one had no kind of proof, should happen to come into one's thoughts; every one would, without any possible doubt, conclude them to be false. And the like may be said of a single common fact. And from hence it appears, that the question of importance, as to the matter before us, is concerning the degree of the peculiar presumption supposed against miracles; not whether there be any peculiar presumption at all against them. For, if there be the presumption of millions to one against the most common facts, what can a small presumption, additional to this, amount to, though it be peculiar? It cannot be estimated, and is as nothing. The only material question is, whether there be any such presumption against miracles, as to render them in any sort incredible? *Secondly*, If we leave out the consideration of religion, we are in such total darkness, upon what causes, occasions, reasons, or circumstances, the present course of nature depends, that there does not appear any improbability for or against supposing, that five or six thousand years may have given scope for causes, occasions,

reasons, or circumstances, from whence miraculous interpositions may have arisen. And from this, joined with the
foregoing observations, it will follow, that there must be a
presumption, beyond all comparison greater, against the
particular common fact just now instanced in, than against
miracles *in general;* before any evidence of either. But,
thirdly, Take into the consideration religion, or the moral
system of the world, and then we see distinct particular
reasons for miracles—to afford mankind instruction additional to that of nature, and to attest the truth of it. And
this gives a real credibility to the supposition, that it
might be part of the original plan of things, that there
should be miraculous interpositions. Then, *lastly,* Miracles must not be compared to common natural events;
or to events, which though uncommon, are similar to what
we daily experience; but to the extraordinary phenomena
of nature. And then the comparison will be between the
presumption against miracles, and the presumption against
such uncommon appearances, suppose, as comets, and
against there being any such powers in nature as magnetism and electricity, so contrary to the properties of
other bodies not endued with these powers. And before
any one can determine, whether there be any peculiar
presumption against miracles, more than against other
extraordinary things, he must consider what, upon first
hearing, would be the presumption against the last mentioned
appearances and powers, to a person acquainted only with
the daily, monthly, and annual course of nature respecting
this earth, and with those common powers of matter which
we every day see.

Upon all this I conclude, that there certainly is no such
presumption against miracles, as to render them in any
way incredible; that, on the contrary, our being able to
discern reasons for them, gives a positive credibility to the
history of them, in cases where those reasons hold; and that
it is by no means certain that there is any peculiar presumption at all, from analogy, even in the lowest degree, against

miracles, as distinguished from other extraordinary phenomena; though it is not worth while to perplex the reader
with inquiries into the abstract nature of evidence, in order
to determine a question, which, without such inquiries, we
see* is of no importance.

CHAPTER III.

*Of our Incapacity of judging what were to be expected in a
Revelation: and the Credibility, from analogy, that it
must contain Things appearing liable to Objections.*

BESIDES the objections against the evidence for Christianity, many are alleged against the scheme of it; against
the whole manner in which it is put and left with the
world; as well as against several particular relations in
Scripture;—objections drawn from the deficiencies of
revelation; from things in it appearing to men *foolishness*,
1 Cor. i. 28; from its containing matters of offence, which
have led, and it must have been foreseen would lead, into
strange enthusiasm and superstition, and be made to serve
the purposes of tyranny and wickedness; from its not
being universal; and, which is a thing of the same kind,
from its evidence not being so convincing and satisfactory
as it might have been—for this last is sometimes turned
into a positive argument against its truth.† It would be
tedious, indeed impossible, to enumerate the several particulars comprehended under the objections here referred
to, they being so various, according to the different
fancies of men. There are persons who think it a strong
objection against the authority of Scripture, that it is not
composed by rules of art, agreed upon by critics, for
polite and correct writing. And the scorn is inexpressible with which some of the prophetic parts of Scripture

* Page 142, &c.   † See Chap. 6.

are treated; partly through the rashness of interpreters, but very much also on account of the hieroglyphical and figurative language in which they are left us. Some of the principal things of this sort shall be particularly considered in the following chapters. But my design at present is to observe, in general, with respect to this whole way of arguing, that, upon supposition of a revelation, it is highly credible beforehand we should be incompetent judges of it, to a great degree; and that it would contain many things appearing to us liable to great objections, in case we judge of it otherwise than by the analogy of nature. And, therefore, though objections against the evidence of Christianity are most seriously to be considered, yet objections against Christianity itself are, in a great measure, frivolous—almost all objections against it, excepting those which are alleged against the particular proofs of its coming from God. I express myself with caution, lest I should be mistaken to vilify reason, which is indeed the only faculty we have wherewith to judge concerning anything, even revelation itself; or be misunderstood to assert, that a supposed revelation cannot be proved false from internal characters. For, it may contain clear immoralities or contradictions; and either of these would prove it false. Nor will I take upon me to affirm, that nothing else can possibly render any supposed revelation incredible. Yet still the observation above is, I think, true beyond doubt, that objections against Christianity, as distinguished from objections against its evidence, are frivolous. To make out this, is the general design of the present chapter. And, with regard to the whole of it, I cannot but particularly wish, that the proofs might be attended to, rather than the assertions cavilled at, upon account of any unacceptable consequences, whether real or supposed, which may be drawn from them. For, after all, that which is true must be admitted; though it should show us the shortness of our faculties, and that we are in nowise judges of

many things, of which we are apt to think ourselves very
competent ones. Nor will this be any objection with reasonable men; at least, upon second thought, it will not be
any objection, with such, against the justness of the following observations.

As God governs the world, and instructs his creatures,
according to certain laws or rules, in the known course
of nature, known by reason together with experience;
so the Scripture informs us of a scheme of divine Providence additional to this. It relates that God has, by
revelation, instructed men in things concerning his government, which they could not otherwise have known,
and reminded them of things which they might otherwise
know; and attested the truth of the whole by miracles.
Now, if the natural and the revealed dispensation of
things are both from God, if they coincide with each
other, and together make up one scheme of Providence,
our being incompetent judges of one, must render it credible that we may be incompetent judges also of the
other. Since, upon experience, the acknowledged constitution and course of nature is found to be greatly different from what, before experience, would have been
expected; and such as, men fancy, there lie great objections against; this renders it beforehand highly credible,
that they may find the revealed dispensation likewise, if
they judge of it as they do of the constitution of nature,
very different from expectations formed beforehand, and
liable, in appearance, to great objections—objections
against the scheme itself, and against the degrees and
manners of the miraculous interpositions by which it was
attested and carried on. Thus, suppose a prince to
govern his dominions in the wisest manner possible, by
common laws; and that upon some exigencies he should
suspend these laws, and govern, in several instances, in a
different manner: if one of his subjects were not a competent judge, beforehand, by what common rules the
government should or would be carried on, it could not

be expected that the same person would be a competent judge, in what exigencies, or in what manner, or to what degree, those laws commonly observed would be suspended or deviated from. If he were not a judge of the wisdom of the ordinary administration, there is no reason to think he would be a judge of the wisdom of the extraordinary. If he thought he had objections against the former, doubtless, it is highly supposable, he might think also that he had objections against the latter. And thus, as we fall into infinite follies and mistakes, whenever we pretend, otherwise than from experience and analogy, to judge of the constitution and course of nature, it is evidently supposable beforehand, that we should fall into as great, in pretending to judge, in like manner, concerning revelation. Nor is there any more ground to expect that this latter should appear to us clear of objections, than that the former should.

These observations, relating to the whole of Christianity, are applicable to inspiration in particular. As we are in no sort judges beforehand, by what laws or rules, in what degree, or by what means, it were to have been expected that God would naturally instruct us; so, upon supposition of his affording us light and instruction, by revelation, additional to what he has afforded us by reason and experience, we are in no sort judges, by what methods, and in what proportion, it were to be expected that this supernatural light and instruction would be afforded us. We know not beforehand, what degree or kind of natural information it were to be expected God would afford men, each by his own reason and experience; nor how far he would enable, and effectually dispose them to communicate it, whatever it should be, to each other; nor whether the evidence of it would be certain, highly probable, or doubtful; nor whether it would be given with equal clearness and conviction to all. Nor could we guess, upon any good ground I mean, whether natural knowledge, or even the faculty itself by which we are capable of attaining it, reason would be given us at once, or gradually. In like manner, we are wholly ignorant what degree of new knowledge it were to be expected God would give mankind by revelation, upon supposition of his affording one; or how far, or in what way, he would interpose miraculously to qualify them, to whom he should originally make the revelation, for communicating the knowledge given by it; and to secure their doing it to the age in which they should live; and to secure its being transmitted to posterity. We are equally ignorant, whether the evidence of it would be certain, or highly probable, or doubtful;* or whether all who should have any degree of instruction from it, and any degree of evidence of its truth, would have the same; or whether the scheme would be revealed at once, or unfolded gradually. Nay, we are not in any sort able to judge, whether it were to have been expected that the revelation should have been committed to writing; or left to be handed down, and consequently corrupted, by verbal tradition; and at length sunk under it, if mankind so pleased, and during such time as they are permitted, in the degree they evidently are, to act as they will.

But it may be said, " that a revelation in some of the above-mentioned circumstances, one, for instance, which was not committed to writing, and thus secured against danger of corruption, would not have answered its purpose." I ask, what purpose? It would not have answered all the purposes which it has now answered, and in the same degree; but it would have answered others, or the same in different degrees. And which of these were the purposes of God, and best fell in with his general government, we could not at all have determined beforehand.

Now, since it has been shown that we have no principles of reason upon which to judge, beforehand, how it were to be expected revelation should have been left, or what was most suitable to the divine plan of government in any of

---

* See Chap. 6.

the fore-mentioned respects; it must be quite frivolous to object afterwards as to any of them, against its being left in one way rather than another; for this would be to object against things, upon account of their being different from expectations which have been shown to be without reason. And thus we see, that the only question concerning the truth of Christianity is, whether it be a real revelation; not whether it be attended with every circumstance which we should have looked for: and concerning the authority of Scripture, whether it be what it claims to be; not whether it be a book of such sort, and so promulgated, as weak men are apt to fancy a book containing a divine revelation should.   And therefore, neither obscurity, nor seeming inaccuracy of style, nor various readings, nor early disputes about the authors of particular parts, nor any other things of the like kind, though they had been much more considerable in degree than they are, could overthrow the authority of the Scripture; unless the Prophets, Apostles, or our Lord, had promised, that the book containing the divine revelation should be secure from those things.   Nor indeed can any objections overthrow such a kind of revelation as the Christian claims to be, since there are no objections against the morality of it,* but such as can show, that there is no proof of miracles wrought originally in attestation of it; no appearance of anything miraculous in its obtaining in the world; nor any of prophecy, that is, of events foretold, which human sagacity could not foresee.   If it can be shown, that the proof alleged for all these is absolutely none at all, then is revelation overturned.   But were it allowed, that the proof of any one, or all of them, is lower than is allowed; yet, whilst any proof of them remains, revelation will stand upon much the same foot it does at present, as to all the purposes of life and practice, and ought to have the like influence upon our behaviour.

From the foregoing observations, too, it will follow, and

---

* Page 156.

those who will thoroughly examine into revelation will find
it worth remarking, that there are several ways of arguing,
which, though just with regard to other writings, are not
applicable to Scripture; at least, not to the prophetic parts
of it. We cannot argue, for instance, that this cannot be
the sense or intent of such a passage of Scripture; for if it
had, it would have been expressed more plainly, or have
been represented under a more apt figure or hieroglyphic:
yet we may justly argue thus with respect to common
books. And the reason of this difference is very evident——
that in Scripture we are not competent judges, as we are
in common books, how plainly it were to have been expected what is the true sense should have been expressed,
or under how apt an image figured. The only question is,
what appearance there is that this is the sense? and scarce
at all, how much more determinately or accurately it might
have been expressed or figured.

" But is it not self-evident, that internal improbabilities
of all kinds weaken external probable proof?" Doubtless.

But to what practical purpose can this be alleged here,
when it has been proved before,* that real internal improbabilities, which rise even to moral certainty, are overcome
by the most ordinary testimony? and when it now has been
made appear, that we scarce know what are improbabilities
as to the matter we are here considering? as it will farther
appear from what follows.

For though, from the observations above made, it is
manifest, that we are not in any sort competent judges
what supernatural instruction were to have been expected;
and though it is self-evident that the objections of an
incompetent judgment must be frivolous; yet it may be
proper to go one step farther, and observe, that if men
will be regardless of these things, and pretend to judge of
the Scripture by preconceived expectations, the analogy
of nature shows beforehand, not only that it is highly

* Page 142.

credible they may, but also probable that they will, imagine they have strong objections against it, however really
unexceptionable: for so, prior to experience, they would
think they had, against the circumstances, and degrees,
and the whole manner of that instruction which is afforded
by the ordinary course of nature. Were the instruction
which God affords, the brute creatures by instincts and
mere propensions, and to mankind by these together with
reason, matter of probable proof, and not of certain observation, it would be rejected as incredible, in many
instances of it, only upon account of the means by which
this instruction is given, the seeming disproportions, the
limitations, necessary conditions, and circumstances of it.
For instance: would it not have been thought highly
improbable, that men should have been so much more
capable of discovering, even to certainty, the general laws
of matter, and the magnitudes, paths, and revolutions of
the heavenly bodies; than the occasions and cures of
distempers, and many other things, in which human life
seems so much more nearly concerned than in astronomy?
How capricious and irregular a way of information, would
it be said, is that of *invention*, by means of which nature
instructs us in matters of science, and in many things
upon which the affairs of the world greatly depend; that
a man should, by this faculty, be made acquainted with
a thing in an instant, when, perhaps, he is thinking of
somewhat else, which he has in vain been searching after,
it may be for years. So, likewise, the imperfections
attending the only method by which nature enables and
directs us to communicate our thoughts to each other,
are innumerable. Language is, in its very nature, inadequate, ambiguous, liable to infinite abuse, even from negligence; and so liable to it from design, that every man
can deceive and betray by it. And, to mention but one
instance more, that brutes, without reason, should act, in
many respects, with a sagacity and foresight vastly greater
than what men have in those respects, would be thought

impossible: yet it is certain they do act with such superior
foresight: whether it be their own, indeed, is another question.   From these things it is highly credible beforehand,
that upon supposition God should afford men some additional instruction by revelation, it would be with circumstances, in manners, degrees, and respects, which we should
be apt to fancy we had great objections against the credibility of.   Nor are the objections against the Scripture,
nor against Christianity in general, at all more or greater
than the analogy of nature would beforehand—not perhaps
give grounds to expect; for this analogy may not be sufficient, in some cases, to ground an expectation upon;—but
no more nor greater than analogy would show it, beforehand, to be supposable and credible that there might seem
to lie against revelation.

By applying these general observations to a particular
objection, it will be more distinctly seen, how·they are
applicable to others of the like kind; and indeed to almost
all objections against Christianity, as distinguished from
objections against its evidence.   It appears from Scripture, that as it was not unusual, in the apostolic age, for
persons, upon their conversion to Christianity, to be endued with miraculous gifts; so some of those persons
exercised these gifts in a strangely irregular and disorderly manner: and this is made an objection against
their being really miraculous.   Now the foregoing observations quite remove this objection, how considerable
soever it may appear at first sight.   For, consider a person endued with any of these gifts, for instance, that of
tongues: it is to be supposed that he had the same power
over this miraculous gift, as he would have had over it
had it been the effect of habit, of study, and use, as it
ordinarily is; or the same power over it, as he had over
any other natural endowment.   Consequently, he would
use it in the same manner he did any other; either regularly and upon proper occasions only, or irregularly
and upon improper ones; according to his sense of

decency and his character of prudence. Where, then, is the objection? Why, if this miraculous power was indeed given to the world, to propagate Christianity and attest the truth of it, we might, it seems, have expected, that other sort of persons should have been chosen to be invested with it; or that these should, at the same time, have been endued with prudence; or that they should have been continually restrained and directed in the exercise of it; *i. e.* that God should have miraculously interposed, if at all, in a different manner or higher degree. But, from the observations made above, it is undeniably evident, that we are not judges in what degrees and manners it were to have been expected he should miraculously interpose; upon supposition of his doing it in some degree and manner. Nor, in the natural course of Providence, are superior gifts of memory, eloquence, knowledge, and other talents of great influence, conferred only on persons of prudence and decency, or such as are disposed to make the properest use of them. Nor is the instruction and admonition naturally afforded us for the conduct of life, particularly in our education, commonly given in a manner the most suited to recommend it; but often with circumstances apt to prejudice us against such instruction.

One might go on to add, that there is a great resemblance between the light of nature and of revelation, in several other respects. Practical Christianity, or that faith and behaviour which renders a man a Christian, is a plain and obvious thing; like the common rules of conduct, with respect to our ordinary temporal affairs. The more distinct and particular knowledge of those things, the study of which the apostle calls *going on unto perfection*, Heb. vi. 1, and of the prophetic parts of revelation, like many parts of natural and even civil knowledge, may require very exact thought and careful consideration. The hinderances, too, of natural and of supernatural light and knowledge, have been of the same kind. And as it is owned the whole scheme of Scripture is not yet understood, so, if it ever comes to be understood before the *restitution of all things*, Acts iii. 21, and without miraculous interpositions, it must be in the same way as natural knowledge is come at—by the continuance and progress of learning and of liberty, and by particular persons attending to, comparing, and pursuing, intimations scattered up and down it, which are overlooked and disregarded by the generality of the world. For this is the way in which all improvements are made; by thoughtful men tracing on obscure hints, as it were, dropped us by nature accidentally, or which seem to come into our minds by chance. Nor is it at all incredible, that a book, which has been so long in the possession of mankind, should contain many truths as yet undiscovered. For, all the same phenomena, and the same faculties of investigation, from which such great discoveries in natural knowledge have been made in the present and last age, were equally in the possession of mankind several thousand years before. And possibly it might be intended, that events, as they come to pass, should open and ascertain the meaning of several parts of Scripture.

It may be objected, that this analogy fails in a material respect; for that natural knowledge is of little or no consequence. But I have been speaking of the general instruction which nature does or does not afford us. And, besides, some parts of natural knowledge, in the more common restrained sense of the words, are of the greatest consequence to the ease and convenience of life. But suppose the analogy did, as it does not, fail in this respect, yet it might be abundantly supplied from the whole constitution and course of nature; which shows, that God does not dispense his gifts according to our notions of the advantage and consequence they would be of to us. And this in general, with his method of dispensing knowledge in particular, would together make out an analogy full to the point before us.

But it may be objected still farther and more generally; " The Scripture represents the world as in a state of ruin, and Christianity as an expedient to recover it, to help in those respects where nature fails; in particular, to supply the deficiencies of natural light. Is it credible, then, that so many ages should have been let pass, before a matter of such a sort, of so great and so general importance, was made known to mankind: and then that it should be made known to so small a part of them? Is it conceivable, that this supply should be so very deficient, should have the like obscurity and doubtfulness, be liable to the like perversions, in short; lie open to all the like objections, as the light of nature itself?"* Without determining how far this in fact is so, I answer, It is by no means incredible that it might be so, if the light of nature and of revelation be from the same hand. Men are naturally liable to diseases; for which God, in his good providence, has provided natural remedies.† But remedies existing in nature have been unknown to mankind for many ages; are known but to few now; probably many valuable ones are not known yet. Great has been, and is, the obscurity and difficulty in the nature and application of them. Circumstances seem often to make them very improper, where they are absolutely necessary. It is after long labour and study, and many unsuccessful endeavours, that they are brought to be as useful as they are; after high contempt and absolute rejection of the most useful we have; and after disputes and doubts, which have seemed to be endless. The best remedies, too, when unskilfully, much more if dishonestly applied, may produce new diseases; and, with the rightest application, the success of them is often doubtful. In many cases they are not at all effectual; where they are, it is often very slowly: and the application of them, and the necessary regimen accompanying it, is, not uncommonly,

* Chap. 6.   † See Chap. 5.

so disagreeable, that some will not submit to them; and satisfy themselves with the excuse, that if they would, it is not certain whether it would be successful. And many persons, who labour under diseases, for which there are known natural remedies, are not so happy as to be always, if ever, in the way of them. In a word, the remedies which nature has provided for diseases are neither certain, perfect, nor universal. And indeed the same principles of arguing which would lead us to conclude, that they must be so, would lead us likewise to conclude, that there could be no occasion for them; *i. e.* that there could be no diseases at all. And, therefore, our experience that there are diseases shows, that it is credible beforehand, upon supposition nature has provided remedies for them, that these remedies may be, as by experience we find they are, not certain, nor perfect, nor universal; because it shows that the principles upon which we should expect the contrary are fallacious.

And now, what is the just consequence from all these things? Not that reason is no judge of what is offered to us as being of divine revelation: for this would be to infer, that we are unable to judge of anything, because we are unable to judge of all things. Reason can, and it ought to judge, not only of the meaning, but also of the morality and the evidence, of revelation. *First,* It is the province of reason to judge of the morality of the Scripture; *i. e.* not whether it contains things different from what we should have expected from a wise, just, and good Being; for objections from hence have been now obviated; but whether it contains things plainly contradictory to wisdom, justice, or goodness; to what the light of nature teaches us of God. And I know nothing of this sort objected against Scripture, excepting such objections as are formed upon suppositions which would equally conclude that the constitution of nature is contradictory to wisdom, justice, or goodness; which most certainly it is not. Indeed, there are some particular precepts in Scripture given to particular persons, requiring actions which would be immoral and vicious, were it not for such precepts. But it is easy to see, that all these are of such a kind as that the precept changes the whole nature of the case and of the action; and both constitutes and shows that not to be unjust or immoral, which, prior to the precept, must have appeared and really have been so: which may well be, since none of these precepts are contrary to immutable morality. If it were commanded to cultivate the principles, and act from the spirit of treachery, ingratitude, cruelty; the command would not alter the nature of the case, or of the action, in any of these instances. But it is quite otherwise in precepts which require only the doing an external action; for instance, taking away the property or life of any. For men have no right to either life or property, but what arises solely from the grant of God: when this grant is revoked, they cease to have any right at all in either; and when this revocation is made known, as surely it is possible it may be, it must cease to be unjust to deprive them of either. And though a course of external acts, which without command would be immoral, must make an immoral habit, yet a few detached commands have no such natural tendency. I thought proper to say thus much of the few Scripture precepts which require, not vicious actions, but actions which would have been vicious had it not been for such precepts; because they are sometimes weakly urged as immoral, and great weight is laid upon objections drawn from them. But to me there seems no difficulty at all in these precepts, but what arises from their being offences; *i. e.* from their being liable to be perverted, as indeed they are, by wicked designing men, to serve the most horrid purposes, and, perhaps, to mislead the weak and enthusiastic. And objections from this head are not objections against revelation, but against the whole notion of religion, as a trial; and against the general constitution of nature. *Secondly*, Reason is able to

judge, and must, of the evidence of revelation, and of the
objections urged against the evidence; which shall be the
subject of a following chapter.*

But the consequence of the foregoing observations is,
that the question upon which the truth of Christianity
depends, is scarce at all, what objections there are against
its scheme, since there are none against the morality of it;
but *what objections there are against its evidence?* or, *what
proof there remains of it, after due allowance made for the
objections against that proof?* because it has been shown
that the *objections against Christianity, as distinguished
from objections against its evidence, are frivolous.* For
surely very little weight, if any at all, is to be laid upon a
way of arguing and objecting, which, when applied to the
general constitution of nature, experience shows not to be
conclusive: and such, I think, is the whole way of objecting treated of throughout this chapter.   It is resolvable into
principles, and goes upon suppositions, which mislead us to
think that the Author of nature would not act as we experience he does; or would act, in such and such cases, as
we experience he does not in like cases.   But the unreasonableness of this way of objecting will appear yet more
evidently from hence, that the chief things thus objected
against are justified, as shall be farther shown,† by distinct,
particular, and full analogies, in the constitution and course
of nature.

But it is to be remembered, that as frivolous as objections of the foregoing sort against revelation are, yet, when
a supposed revelation is more consistent with itself, and has
a more general and uniform tendency to promote virtue,
than, all circumstances considered, could have been expected from enthusiasm and political views; this is a presumptive proof of its not proceeding from them, and so of
its truth: because we are competent judges, what might
have been expected from enthusiasm and political views.

* Chap. 7.   † Chap. 4, latter part; and 5, 6.

CHAPTER IV.

*Of Christianity, considered as a Scheme or Constitution
imperfectly comprehended.*

It hath been now shown,[*] that the analogy of nature
renders it highly credible beforehand, that supposing a
revelation to be made, it must contain many things very
different from what we should have expected, and such as
appear open to great objections: and that this observation,
in good measure, takes off the force of these objections, or
rather precludes them.   But it may be alleged, that this is
a very partial answer to such objections, or a very unsatisfactory way of obviating them; because it doth not show
at all, that the things objected against can be wise, just,
and good; much less that it is credible they are so.   It will,
therefore, be proper to show this distinctly, by applying to
these objections against the wisdom, justice, and goodness
of Christianity, the answer above[†] given to the like objections against the constitution of nature, before we consider the particular analogies in the latter to the particular
things objected against in the former.   Now, that which
affords a sufficient answer to objections against the wisdom,
justice, and goodness of the constitution of nature, is its
being a constitution, a system, or scheme, imperfectly
comprehended; a scheme, in which means are made use of
to accomplish ends, and which is carried on by general
laws.   For from these things it has been proved, not
only to be possible, but also to be credible, that those
things which are objected against, may be consistent
with wisdom, justice, and goodness; nay, may be instances of them: and even that the constitution and
government of nature may be perfect in the highest pos-

[*] In the foregoing chapter.
[†] Part i. chap. 7, to which this all along refers.

sible degree. If Christianity, then, be a scheme, and of the like kind, it is evident, the like objections against it must admit of the like answer.   And,

I. Christianity is a scheme quite beyond our comprehension. The moral government of God is exercised, by gradually conducting things so in the course of his providence, that every one, at length and upon the whole, shall receive according to his deserts; and neither fraud nor violence, but truth and right, shall finally prevail. Christianity is a particular scheme under this general plan of providence, and a part of it, conducive to its completion, with regard to mankind: consisting itself also of various parts, and a mysterious economy, which has been carrying on from the time the world came into its present wretched state, and is still carrying on, for its recovery, by a divine person, the Messiah; " who is to gather together in one the children of God that are scattered abroad," John xi. 52; and establish " an everlasting kingdom, wherein dwelleth righteousness," 2 Pet. iii. 13. And in order to it, after various manifestations of things relating to this great and general scheme of providence, through a succession of many ages;—(" For the Spirit of Christ, which was in the prophets, testified beforehand his sufferings, and the glory that should follow: unto whom it was revealed, that not unto themselves, but unto us, they did minister the things which are now reported unto us by them that have preached the gospel; which things the angels desire to look into," 1 Peter i. 11, 12)—after various dispensations, looking forward and preparatory to this final salvation, " In the fulness of time," when Infinite Wisdom thought fit, he, " being in the form of God, made himself of no reputation, and took upon him the form of a servant, and was made in the likeness of men; and being found in fashion as a man, he humbled himself, and became obedient to death, even the death of the cross: wherefore God also hath highly exalted him, and given him a name which is above every name; that at the name of Jesus every knee should bow, of things in heaven, and things in the earth, and things under the earth; and that every tongue should confess that Jesus Christ is Lord, to the glory of God the Father," Phil. ii. Parts likewise of this economy are, the miraculous mission of the Holy Ghost, and his ordinary assistances given to good men; the invisible government which Christ at present exercises over his church; that which he himself refers to in these words, " In my Father's house are many mansions—I go to prepare a place for you," John xiv. 2; and his future return to " judge the world in righteousness," and completely re-establish the kingdom of God. " For the Father judgeth no man, but hath committed all judgment unto the Son; that all men should honour the Son, even as they honour the Father," John v. 22, 23. " All power is given unto him in heaven and in earth," Matt. xxviii. 18. " And he must reign, till he hath put all enemies under his feet. Then cometh the end, when he shall have delivered up the kingdom to God, even the Father; when he shall have put down all rule, and all authority and power. And when all things shall be subdued unto him, then shall the Son also himself be subject unto him that put all things under him, that God may be all in all," 1 Cor. xv. Now little, surely, need be said to show, that this system, or scheme of things, is but imperfectly comprehended by us. The Scripture expressly asserts it to be so. And indeed one cannot read a passage relating to this " great mystery of godliness," 1 Tim. iii. 16, but what immediately runs up into something which shows us our ignorance in it; as everything in nature shows us our ignorance in the constitution of nature. And whoever will seriously consider that part of the Christian scheme which is revealed in Scripture, will find so much more unrevealed, as will convince him, that, to all the purposes of judging and objecting, we know as little of it as of the constitution of nature. Our ignorance, therefore, is as much an answer to our objections against the perfection of one, as against the perfection of the other.*

II. It is obvious, too, that in the Christian dispensation, as much as in the natural scheme of things, means are made use of to accomplish ends. And the observation of this furnishes us with the same answer to objections against the perfection of Christianity, as to objections of the like kind against the constitution of nature. It shows the credibility, that the things objected against, how *foolish* (1 Cor. i.) soever they appear to men, may be the very best means of accomplishing the very best ends. And their appearing *foolishness* is no presumption against this, in a scheme so greatly beyond our comprehension.†

III. The credibility, that the Christian dispensation may have been, all along, carried on by general laws,‡ no less than the course of nature, may require to be more distinctly made out. Consider, then, upon what ground it is we say, that the whole common course of nature is carried on according to general foreordained laws. We know, indeed, several of the general laws of matter; and a great part of the natural behaviour of living agents is reducible to general laws. But we know, in a manner, nothing, by what laws storms and tempests, earthquakes, famine, pestilence, become the instruments of destruction to mankind. And the laws, by which persons born into the world at such a time and place, are of such capacities, geniuses, tempers; the laws, by which thoughts come into our mind, in a multitude of cases; and by which innumerable things happen, of the greatest influence upon the affairs and state of the world—these laws are so wholly unknown to us, that we call the events, which come to pass by them, accidental; though all reasonable men know certainly, that there cannot, in reality, be any such thing as chance; and conclude, that the things which have this appearance are the result of

* Page 99, &c.   † Page 104.   ‡ Pages 105, 106.

general laws, and may be reduced into them. It is then but an exceeding little way, and in but a very few respects, that we can trace up the natural course of things before us to general laws. And it is only from analogy that we conclude the whole of it to be capable of being reduced into them; only from our seeing, that part is so. It is from our finding, that the course of nature, in some respects and so far, goes on by general laws, that we conclude this of the rest. And if that be a just ground for such a conclusion, it is a just ground also, if not to conclude, yet to apprehend, to render it supposable and credible, which is sufficient for answering objections, that God's miraculous interpositions may have been, all along, in like manner, by *general* laws of wisdom. Thus, that miraculous powers should be exerted at such times, upon such occasions, in such degrees and manners, and with regard to such persons, rather than others; that the affairs of the world, being permitted to go on in their natural course so far, should, just at such a point, have a new direction given them by miraculous interpositions; that these interpositions should be exactly in such degrees and respects only; all this may have been by general laws. These laws are unknown, indeed, to us; but no more unknown, than the laws from whence it is that some die as soon as they are born, and others live to extreme old age; that one man is so superior to another in understanding; with innumerable more things, which, as was before observed, we cannot reduce to any laws or rules at all, though it is taken for granted, they are as much reducible to general ones as gravitation. Now, if the revealed dispensations of Providence, and miraculous interpositions, be by general laws, as well as God's ordinary government in the course of nature, made known by reason and experience; there is no more reason to expect, that every exigence, as it arises, should be provided for by these general laws or miraculous interpositions, than that every exigence in nature should, by the general laws of nature:

yet there might be wise and good reasons, that miraculous interposition should be by general laws, and that these laws should not be broken in upon, or deviated from, by other miracles.

Upon the whole, then, the appearance of deficiencies and irregularities in nature, is owing to its being a scheme but in part made known, and of such a certain particular kind in other respects. Now we see no more reason why the frame and course of nature should be such a scheme, than why Christianity should. And, that the former is such a scheme, renders it credible that the latter, upon supposition of its truth, may be so too. And as it is manifest that Christianity is a scheme revealed but in part, and a scheme in which means are made use of to accomplish ends, like to that of nature ; so the credibility, that it may have all along been carried on by general laws, no less than the course of nature, has been distinctly proved. And from all this it is beforehand credible, that there might, I think probable that there would, be the like appearances of deficiencies and irregularities in Christianity as in nature ; *i. e.* that Christianity would be liable to the like objections as the frame of nature. And these objections are answered by these observations concerning Christianity ; as the like objections against the frame of nature, are answered by the like observations concerning the frame of nature.

THE objections against Christianity, considered as a matter of fact,* having, in general, been obviated in the preceding chapter ; and the same, considered as made against the wisdom and goodness of it, having been obviated in this ; the next thing, according to the method proposed, is to show, that the principal objections in particular against Christianity, may be answered by parti-

* Page 103.

cular and full analogies in nature. And as one of them is made against the whole scheme of it together, as just now described, I choose to consider it here, rather than in a distinct chapter by itself. The thing objected against the scheme of the gospel is, " That it seems to suppose God was reduced to the necessity of a long series of intricate means, in order to accomplish his ends, the recovery and salvation of the world; in like sort as men, for want of understanding, or power, not being able to come at their ends directly, are forced to go round-about ways, and make use of many perplexed contrivances to arrive at them." Now, everything which we see shows the folly of this, considered as an objection against the truth of Christianity. For, according to our manner of conception, God makes use of variety of means, what we often think tedious ones, in the natural course of providence, for the accomplishment of all his ends. Indeed it is certain, there is somewhat in this matter quite beyond our comprehension; but the mystery is as great in nature as in Christianity. We know what we ourselves aim at, as final ends; and what courses we take, merely as means conducing to those ends. But we are greatly ignorant, how far things are considered by the Author of nature under the single notion of means and ends: so as that it may be said, this is merely an end, and that merely means, in his regard. And whether there be not some peculiar absurdity, in our very manner of conception, concerning this matter, somewhat contradictory, arising from our extremely imperfect views of things, it is impossible to say. However, this much is manifest, that the whole natural world and government of it, is a scheme, or system; not a fixed, but a progressive one: a scheme in which the operation of various means takes up a great length of time, before the ends they tend to can be attained. The change of seasons, the ripening of the fruits of the earth, the very history of a flower, is an instance of this; and so is human life. Thus vegetable bodies, and those of animals, though possibly formed at once, yet grow up by degrees to a mature state.   And thus rational agents, who animate these latter bodies, are naturally directed to form, each his own manners and character, by the gradual gaining of knowledge and experience, and by a long course of action.   Our existence is not only successive, as it must be of necessity, but one state of our life and being is appointed by God to be a preparation for another; and that, to be the means of attaining to another succeeding one—infancy to childhood; childhood to youth; youth to mature age.   Men are impatient, and for precipitating things; but the Author of nature appears deliberate throughout his operations; accomplishing his natural ends by slow successive steps.   And there is a plan of things beforehand laid out, which, from the nature of it, requires various systems of means, as well as length of time, in order to the carrying on its several parts into execution.   Thus, in the daily course of natural providence, God operates in the very same manner as in the dispensation of Christianity; making one thing subservient to another; this to somewhat farther; and so on, through a progressive series of means, which extend, both backward and forward, beyond our utmost view.   Of this manner of operation, everything we see in the course of nature is as much an instance, as any part of the Christian dispensation.

CHAPTER V.

Of the particular System of Christianity; the Appointment of a Mediator, and the Redemption of the World by him.

THERE is not, I think, anything relating to Christianity which has been more objected against, than the mediation of Christ, in some or other of its parts.   Yet, upon thorough consideration, there seems nothing less justly liable to it.   For,

I. The whole analogy of nature removes all imagined presumption against the general notion of " a mediator between God and man," 1 Tim. ii. 5. For we find, all living creatures are brought into the world, and their life in infancy is preserved, by the instrumentality of others; and every satisfaction of it, some way or other, is bestowed by the like means. So that the visible government which God exercises over the world, is by the instrumentality and mediation of others. And how far his invisible government be, or be not so, it is impossible to determine at all by reason. And the supposition that part of it is so, appears, to say the least, altogether as credible as the contrary. There is then no sort of objection, from the light of nature, against the general notion of a mediator between God and man, considered as a doctrine of Christianity, or as an appointment in this dispensation; since we find by experience, that God does appoint mediators to be the instruments of good and evil to us, the instruments of his justice and his mercy. And the objection here referred to is urged, not against mediation in that high, eminent, and peculiar sense in which Christ is our mediator, but absolutely against the whole notion itself of a mediator at all.

II. As we must suppose that the world is under the proper moral government of God, or in a state of religion, before we can enter into consideration of the revealed doctrine concerning the redemption of it by Christ; so that supposition is here to be distinctly taken notice of. Now, the divine moral government which religion teaches us implies, that the consequence of vice shall be misery, in some future state, by the righteous judgment of God. That such consequent punishment shall take effect by his appointment, is necessarily implied. But as it is not in any sort to be supposed, that we are made acquainted with all the ends or reasons for which it is fit future punishments should be inflicted, or why God has appointed such and such consequent misery should follow vice; and as we are altogether in the dark, how or in what manner it shall follow, by what immediate occasions, or by the instrumentality of what means; there is no absurdity in supposing it may follow in a way analogous to that in which many miseries follow such and such courses of action at present—poverty, sickness, infamy, untimely death by diseases, death from the hands of civil justice.   There is no absurdity in supposing future punishment may follow wickedness of course, as we speak, or in the way of natural consequence, from God's original constitution of the world; from the nature he has given us, and from the condition in which he places us; or, in a like manner, as a person rashly trifling upon a precipice, in the way of natural consequence, falls down; in the way of natural consequence, breaks his limbs, suppose; in the way of natural consequence of this, without help, perishes.

Some good men may, perhaps, be offended with hearing it spoken of as a supposable thing, that the future punishments of wickedness may be in the way of natural consequence; as if this were taking the execution of justice out of the hands of God, and giving it to nature. But they should remember, that when things come to pass according to the course of nature, this does not hinder them from being his doing, who is the God of nature; and that the Scripture ascribes those punishments to divine justice which are known to be natural, and which must be called so, when distinguished from such as are miraculous.   But, after all, this supposition, or rather this way of speaking, is here made use of only by way of illustration of the subject before us: for, since it must be admitted, that the future punishment of wickedness is not a matter of arbitrary appointment, but of reason, equity, and justice; it comes, for aught I see, to the same thing, whether it is supposed to be inflicted in a way analogous to that in which the temporal punishments of vice and folly are inflicted, or in any other way.   And though there were a difference, it is allowable in the present case to make this supposition, plainly not an incredible one, That future punishment may follow wickedness in the way of natural consequence, or according to some general laws of government already established in the universe.

III. Upon this supposition, or even without it, we may observe somewhat, much to the present purpose, in the constitution of nature, or appointments of Providence: the provision which is made, that all the bad natural consequences of men's actions should not always actually follow; or, that such bad consequences as, according to the settled course of things, would inevitably have followed, if not prevented, should, in certain degrees, be prevented. We are apt presumptuously to imagine, that the world might have been so constituted as that there would not have been any such thing as misery or evil. On the contrary, we find the Author of nature permits it. But then, he has provided reliefs, and, in many cases, perfect remedies for it, after some pains and difficulties; reliefs and remedies even for that evil which is the fruit of our own misconduct; and which, in the course of nature, would have continued, and ended in our destruction, but for such remedies. And this is an instance both of severity and of indulgence, in the constitution of nature. Thus, all the bad consequences, now mentioned, of a man's trifling upon a precipice, might be prevented: and, though all were not, yet some of them might, by proper interposition, if not rejected; by another's coming to the rash man's relief, with his own laying hold on that relief, in such sort as the case required. Persons may do a great deal themselves towards preventing the bad consequences of their follies; and more may be done by themselves, together with the assistance of others, their fellow-creatures; which assistance nature requires and prompts us to. This is the general constitution of the world. Now, suppose it had been so constituted, that after such actions were done, as were foreseen naturally to draw after them misery to the doer, it should have been no more in human power to have prevented that naturally consequent misery, in any instance, than it is in all; no one can say, whether such a more severe constitution of things might not yet have been really good: but that, on the contrary, provision is made by nature, that we may and do, to so great degree, prevent the bad natural effects of our follies;—this may be called mercy, or compassion, in the original constitution of the world; compassion, as distinguished from goodness in general.   And, the whole known constitution and course of things affording us instances of such compassion, it would be according to the analogy of nature to hope, that, however ruinous the natural consequences of vice might be, from the general laws of God's government over the universe, yet provision might be made, possibly might have been originally made, for preventing those ruinous consequences from inevitably following; at least from following universally, and in all cases.

Many, I am sensible, will wonder at finding this made a question, or spoken of as in any degree doubtful.   The generality of mankind are so far from having that awful sense of things, which the present state of vice and misery and darkness seems to make but reasonable, that they have scarce any apprehension, or thought at all, about this matter, any way; and some serious persons may have spoken unadvisedly concerning it.   But let us observe, what we experience to be, and what, from the very constitution of nature, cannot but be, the consequences of irregular and disorderly behaviour; even of such rashness, wilfulness, neglects, as we scarce call vicious.   Now, it is natural to apprehend, that the bad consequences of irregularity will be greater, in proportion as the irregularity is so.   And there is no comparison between these irregularities and the greater instances of vice, or a dissolute profligate disregard to all religion; if there be anything at all in religion.   For, consider what it is for creatures,

I

moral agents, presumptuously to introduce that confusion and misery into the kingdom of God, which mankind
have, in fact, introduced; to blaspheme the sovereign
Lord of all; to contemn his authority; to be injurious to
the degree they are to their fellow-creatures, the creatures
of God: add, that the effects of vice, in the present
world, are often extreme misery, irretrievable ruin, and
even death: and, upon putting all this together, it will
appear, that as no one can say in what degree fatal the
unprevented consequences of vice may be, according to the
general rule of divine government; so it is by no means
intuitively certain, how far these consequences could
possibly, in the nature of the thing, be prevented, consistently with the eternal rule of right, or with what
is, in fact, the moral constitution of nature. However,
there would be large ground to hope, that the universal
government was not so severely strict but that there was
room for pardon, or for having those penal consequences
prevented. Yet,

IV. There seems no probability, that anything we
could do would, alone and of itself, prevent them; prevent their following, or being inflicted. But one would
think, at least, it were impossible that the contrary should
be thought certain. For we are not acquainted with the
whole of the case: we are not informed of all the reasons
which render it fit that future punishment should be
inflicted; and therefore cannot know, whether anything
we could do would make such an alteration, as to render
it fit that they should be remitted: we do not know
what the whole natural or appointed consequences of
vice are, nor in what way they would follow, if not prevented; and therefore can in no sort say, whether we
could do anything which would be sufficient to prevent
them. Our ignorance being thus manifest, let us recollect the analogy of nature, or providence. For though
this may be but a slight ground to raise a positive opinion
upon in this matter, yet it is sufficient to answer a mere

arbitrary assertion, without any kind of evidence, urged by
way of objection against a doctrine, the proof of which is
not reason but revelation. Consider, then, people ruin their
fortunes by extravagance; they bring diseases upon themselves by excess; they incur the penalties of civil laws; and
surely civil government is natural: will sorrow for these
follies past, and behaving well for the future, alone and of
itself, prevent the natural consequences of them?   On the
contrary, men's natural abilities of helping themselves are
often impaired; or, if not, yet they are forced to be beholden
to the assistance of others, upon several accounts, and in
different ways: assistance which they would have had no
occasion for, had it not been for their misconduct; but
which, in the disadvantageous condition they have reduced
themselves to, is absolutely necessary to their recovery,
and retrieving their affairs.   Now, since this is our case,
considering ourselves merely as inhabitants of this world,
and as having a temporal interest here, under the natural
government of God, which, however, has a great deal moral
in it; why is it not supposable, that this may be our case
also in our more important capacity, as under his perfect
moral government, and having a more general and future
interest depending?   If we have misbehaved in this higher
capacity, and rendered ourselves obnoxious to the future
punishment which God has annexed to vice; it is plainly
credible, that behaving well for the time to come may be—
not useless, God forbid—but wholly insufficient, alone and
of itself, to prevent that punishment; or to put us in the
condition which we should have been in, had we preserved
our innocence.

 And, though we ought to reason with all reverence,
whenever we reason concerning the divine conduct, yet it
may be added, that it is clearly contrary to all our notions
of government, as well as to what is, in fact, the general
constitution of nature, to suppose that doing well for the
future should, in all cases, prevent all the judicial bad consequences of having done evil, or all the punishment annexed

to disobedience. And we have manifestly nothing from whence to determine, in what degree, and in what cases, reformation would prevent this punishment, even supposing that it would in some. And, though the efficacy of repentance itself alone, to prevent what mankind had rendered themselves obnoxious to, and recover what they had forfeited, is now insisted upon, in opposition to Christianity; yet, by the general prevalence of propitiatory ·sacrifices over the heathen world, this notion, of repentance alone being sufficient to expiate guilt, appears to be contrary to the general sense of mankind.

Upon the whole, then, had the laws, the general laws of God's government, been permitted to operate, without any interposition in our behalf, the future punishment, for aught we know to the contrary, or have any reason to think, must inevitably have followed, notwithstanding anything we could have done to prevent it. Now,

V. In this darkness, or this light of nature, call it which you please, revelation comes in; confirms every doubting fear, which could enter into the heart of man, concerning the future unprevented consequence of wickedness; supposes the world to be in a state of ruin, (a supposition which seems the very ground of the Christian dispensation, and which, if not proveable by reason, yet it is in no wise contrary to it;) teaches us, too, that the rules of divine government are such, as not to admit of pardon immediately and directly upon repentance, or by the sole efficacy of it; but then teaches, at the same time, what nature might justly have hoped, that the moral government of the universe was not so rigid, but that there was room for an interposition to avert the fatal consequences of vice; which, therefore, by this means, does admit of pardon. Revelation teaches us, that the unknown laws of God's moral general government, no less than the particular laws by which we experience he governs us at present, are compassionate,* as well as good, in the more general notion of goodness; and that he hath

* Page 170, &c.

mercifully provided, that there should be an interposition
to prevent the destruction of human kind, whatever that
destruction unprevented would have been. " God so loved
the world, that he gave his only begotten Son, that whosoever believeth," not, to be sure, in a speculative, but in a
practical sense, " that whosoever believeth in him should
not perish," John iii. 16:—gave his Son in the same way
of goodness to the world, as he affords particular persons the
friendly assistance of their fellow-creatures, when, without
it, their temporal ruin would be the certain consequence of
their follies;—in the same way of goodness, I say, though
in a transcendent and infinitely higher degree. And the Son
of God " loved us, and gave himself for us," with a love
which he himself compares to that of human friendship;
though, in this case, all comparisons must fall infinitely
short of the thing intended to be illustrated by them.   He
interposed in such a manner, as was necessary and effectual
to prevent that execution of justice upon sinners, which God
had appointed should otherwise have been executed upon
them; or, in such a manner as to prevent that punishment
from actually following, which, according to the general
laws of divine government, must have followed the sins of
the world, had it not been for such interposition.*

* It cannot, I suppose, be imagined, even by the most cursory
reader, that it is in any sort affirmed, or implied, in anything said
in this chapter, that none can have the benefit of the general redemption, but such as have the advantage of being made acquainted with
it in the present life. But it may be needful to mention, that several
questions, which have been brought into the subject before us, and
determined, are not in the least entered into here; questions which
have been, I fear, rashly determined, and, perhaps, with equal rashness, contrary ways. For instance: Whether God could have saved
the world by other means than the death of Christ, consistently with
the general laws of his government? And, had not Christ come into
the world, what would have been the future condition of the better
sort of men; those just persons over the face of the earth, for whom
Manasses, in his prayer, asserts repentance was not appointed? The

If anything here said should appear, upon first thought, inconsistent with divine goodness, a second, I am persuaded, will entirely remove that appearance. For, were we to suppose the constitution of things to be such, as that the whole creation must have perished had it not been for somewhat which God had appointed should be in order to prevent that ruin; even this supposition would not be inconsistent, in any degree, with the most absolutely perfect goodness. But still it may be thought, that this whole manner of treating the subject before us, supposes mankind to be naturally in a very strange state. And truly so it does. But it is not Christianity which has put us into this state. Whoever will consider the manifold miseries, and the extreme wickedness of the world; that the best have great wrongnesses within themselves, which they complain of, and endeavour to amend; but that the generality grow more profligate and corrupt with age; that heathen moralists thought the present state to be a state of punishment; and, what might be added, that the earth, our habitation, has the appearances of being a ruin;—whoever, I say, will consider all these, and some other obvious things, will think he has little reason to object against the Scripture account, that mankind is in a state of degradation; against this being the fact; how difficult soever he may think it to account for, or even to form a distinct conception of, the occasions and circumstances of it. But that the crime of our first parents was the occasion of our being placed in a more disadvantageous condition, is a thing throughout and particularly analogous to what we see in the daily course of

meaning of the first of these questions is greatly ambiguous; and neither of them can properly be answered, without going upon that infinitely absurd supposition, that we know the whole of the case. And, perhaps, the very inquiry, *what would have followed if God had not done as he has?* may have in it some very great impropriety, and ought not to be carried on any farther than is necessary to help our partial and inadequate conceptions of things.

natural providence; as the recovery of the world, by the interposition of Christ, has been shown to be so in general.

VI. The particular manner in which Christ interposed in the redemption of the world, or his office as Mediator, in the largest sense, *between God and man*, is thus represented to us in the Scripture: "He is the light of the world," John i. viii. 12; the revealer of the will of God in the most eminent sense: He is a propitiatory sacrifice, Rom. iii. 25, v. 11; 1 Cor. v. 7; Eph. v. 2; 1 John ii. 2; Matt. xxvi. 28; the "Lamb of God," John i. 29, 36;* and, as he voluntarily offered himself up, he is styled our High-priest.† And, which seems of peculiar weight, he is described beforehand, in the Old Testament, under the same characters of a priest, and an expiatory victim, Isaiah liii.; Dan. ix. 24; Psalm cx. 4. And whereas it is objected, that all this is merely by way of allusion to the sacrifices of the Mosaic law, the apostle on the contrary affirms, that the law was a shadow of good things to come, and not the very image of the things, Heb. x. 1; and that the priests that offer gifts according to the law, serve unto the example and shadow of heavenly things, as Moses was admonished of God, when he was about to make the tabernacle: " For see," saith he, " that thou make all things according to the pattern showed to thee in the Mount," Heb. viii. 4, 5: *i. e.* the Levitical priesthood was a shadow of the priesthood of Christ, in like manner as the tabernacle made by Moses was according to that showed him in the Mount. The priesthood of Christ, and the tabernacle in the Mount, were the originals: of the former of which, the Levitical priesthood was a type; and of the latter, the tabernacle made by Moses was a copy. The doctrine of the epistle, then, plainly is, that the legal sacrifices were allusions to the great and final atonement to be made by the blood of Christ; and not that this was an allusion to those. Nor

---

* And throughout the book of Revelation.
† Throughout the Epistle to the Hebrews.

can anything be more express and determinate than the
following passage: " It is not possible that the blood of
bulls and of goats should take away sin. Wherefore,
when he cometh into the world, he saith, Sacrifice and
offering," *i. e.* of bulls and of goats, " thou wouldst not,
but a body thou hast prepared me—Lo, I come to do thy
will, O God.—By which will we are sanctified, through
the offering of the body of Jesus Christ once for all,"
Heb. x. 4, 5, 7, 9, 10.   And to add one passage more of
the like kind: " Christ was once offered to bear the sins
of many; and unto them that look for him shall he appear
the second time, without sin;" *i. e.* without bearing sin,
as he did at his first coming, by being an offering for it;
without having our *iniquities* again *laid upon him*, without
being any more a sin offering;—" unto them that look
for him shall he appear the second time, without sin, unto
salvation," Heb. ix. 28.   Nor do the inspired writers at
all confine themselves to this manner of speaking concerning the satisfaction of Christ, but declare an efficacy
in what he did and suffered for us, additional to, and beyond mere instruction, example, and government, in great
variety of expression:—" That Jesus should die for that
nation," the Jews; " and not for that nation only, but
that also," plainly by the efficacy of his death, " he should
gather together in one the children of God that were
scattered abroad," John xi. 51, 52: that " he suffered
for sins, the just for the unjust," 1 Pet. iii. 18: that " he
gave his life, himself, a ransom," Matt. xx. 28; Mark x.
45; 1 Tim. ii. 6: that " we are bought, bought with a
price," 2 Pet. ii. 1; Rev. xiv. 4; 1 Cor. vi. 20: that
" he redeemed us with his blood, redeemed us from the
curse of the law, being made a curse for us," 1 Pet. i. 19;
Rev. v. 9; Gal. iii. 13: that " he is our advocate, inter-
cessor, and propitiation," Heb. vii. 25; 1 John ii. 1, 2:
that " he was made perfect (or consummate) through
sufferings; and being thus made perfect, he became the
author of salvation," Heb. ii. 10, v. 9: that " God was

in Christ, reconciling the world to himself, by the death of
his Son by the cross; not imputing their trespasses unto
them," 2 Cor. v. 19; Rom. v. 10; Eph. ii. 16; and, lastly,
that " through death he destroyed him that had the power
of death," Heb. ii. 14.*   Christ, then, having thus " humbled himself, and become obedient to death, even the death
of the cross, God also hath highly exalted him, and given
him a name which is above every name;" hath given all
things into his hands; hath committed all judgment unto
him; " that all men should honour the Son, even as they
honour the father," Phil. ii. 8, 9; John iii. 25, v. 22, 23.
For, " worthy is the Lamb that was slain, to receive power,
and riches, and wisdom, and strength, and honour, and
glory, and blessing!   And every creature which is in heaven, and on the earth, heard I saying, Blessing, and honour,
and glory, and power, be unto him that sitteth upon the
throne, and unto the Lamb for ever and ever," Rev. v. 12, 13.

These passages of Scripture seem to comprehend and
express the chief parts of Christ's office, as Mediator between God and man; so far, I mean, as the nature of this
his office is revealed; and it is usually treated of by divines
under three heads:—

First, He was, by way of eminence, the Prophet; "that
Prophet that should come into the world," John vi. 14, to
declare the divine will.   He published anew the law of
nature, which men had corrupted; and the very knowledge
of which, to some degree, was lost among them.   He
taught mankind, taught us authoritatively, to " live soberly,
righteously, and godly, in this present world," in expectation of the future judgment of God.   He confirmed the
truth of this moral system of nature, and gave us additional
evidence of it; the evidence of testimony.†   He distinctly
revealed the manner in which God would be worshipped,
the efficacy of repentance, and the rewards and punish-

---

* See also a remarkable passage in the book of Job, xxxiii. 24.
† Page 123, &c.

ments of a future life. Thus he was a prophet in a sense
in which no other ever was. To which is to be added,
that he set us a perfect "example, that we should follow
his steps."

Secondly, He has a "kingdom which is not of this
world." He founded a church, to be to mankind a standing memorial of religion, and invitation to it; which he
promised to be with always, even to the end. He exercises an invisible government over it himself, and by his
Spirit; over that part of it which is militant here on earth,
a government of discipline, " for the perfecting of the saints,
for the edifying his body; till we all come in the unity of
the faith, and of the knowledge of the Son of God, unto a
perfect man, unto the measure of the stature of the fulness
of Christ," Eph. iv. 12, 13. Of this church, all persons
scattered over the world, who live in obedience to his laws,
are members. For these he is " gone to prepare a place,
and will come again to receive them unto himself, that
where he is, there they may be also; and reign with him
for ever and ever," John xiv. 2, 3; Rev. iii. 21, xi. 15;
and likewise " to take vengeance on them that know not
God, and obey not his gospel," 2 Thess. i. 8.

Against these parts of Christ's office, I find no objections but what are fully obviated in the beginning of this
chapter.

Lastly, Christ offered himself a propitiatory sacrifice,
and made atonement for the sins of the world: which is
mentioned last, in regard to what is objected against it.
Sacrifices of expiation were commanded of the Jews, and
obtained amongst most other nations, from tradition,
whose original probably was revelation. And they were
continually repeated, both occasionally and at the returns
of stated times; and made up great part of the external
religion of mankind. " But now once in the end of the
world Christ appeared, to put away sin by the sacrifice
of himself," Heb. ix. 26. And this sacrifice was in the
highest degree, and with the most extensive influence, of

that efficacy for obtaining pardon of sin, which the heathens may be supposed to have thought their sacrifices to have been, and which the Jewish sacrifices really were in some degree, and with regard to some persons.

How, and in what particular way, it had this efficacy, there are not wanting persons who have endeavoured to explain; but I do not find that the Scripture has explained it. We seem to be very much in the dark concerning the manner in which the ancients understood atonement to be made, *i. e.* pardon to be obtained by sacrifices. And if the Scripture has, as surely it has, left this matter of the satisfaction of Christ mysterious, left somewhat in it unrevealed, all conjectures about it must be, if not evidently absurd, yet at least uncertain. Nor has any one reason to complain for want of farther information, unless he can show his claim to it.

Some have endeavoured to explain the efficacy of what Christ has done and suffered for us, beyond what the Scripture has authorized; others, probably because they could not explain it, have been for taking it away, and confining his office, as Redeemer of the world, to his instruction, example, and government of the church: whereas the doctrine of the gospel appears to be, not only that he taught the efficacy of repentance, but rendered it of the efficacy which it is, by what he did and suffered for us: that he obtained for us the benefit of having our repentance accepted unto eternal life: not only that he revealed to sinners that they were in a capacity of salvation, and how they might obtain it; but, moreover, that he put them into this capacity of salvation by what he did and suffered for them; put us into a capacity of escaping future punishment, and obtaining future happiness. And it is our wisdom thankfully to accept the benefit, by performing the conditions upon which it is offered on our part, without disputing how it was procured on his. For,

VII. Since we neither know by what means punishment in a future state would have followed wickedness in this; nor in what manner it would have been inflicted, had it not been prevented; nor all the reasons why its infliction would have been needful; nor the particular nature of that state of happiness which Christ is gone to prepare for his disciples; and since we are ignorant how far anything which we could do would, alone and of itself, have been effectual to prevent that punishment to which we were obnoxious, and recover that happiness which we had forfeited; it is most evident we are not judges, antecedently to revelation, whether a mediator was or was not necessary to obtain those ends—to prevent that future punishment, and bring mankind to the final happiness of their nature. And for the very same reasons, upon supposition of the necessity of a mediator, we are no more judges, antecedently to revelation, of the whole nature of his office, or the several parts of which it consists; of what was fit and requisite to be assigned him, in order to accomplish the ends of divine Providence in the appointment. And from hence it follows, that to object against the expediency or usefulness of particular things revealed to have been done or suffered by him, because we do not see how they were conducive to those ends, is highly absurd. Yet nothing is more common to be met with than this absurdity. But if it be acknowledged beforehand that we are not judges in the case, it is evident that no objection can, with any shadow of reason, be urged against any particular part of Christ's mediatorial office revealed in Scripture, till it can be shown positively not to be requisite, or conducive, to the ends proposed to be accomplished; or that it is in itself unreasonable.

And there is one objection made against the satisfaction of Christ, which looks to be of this positive kind—that the doctrine of his being appointed to suffer for the sins of the world, represents God as being indifferent whether he punished the innocent or the guilty. Now,

from the foregoing observations, we may see the extreme
slightness of all such objections; and (though it is most
certain all who make them do not see the consequence)
that they conclude altogether as much against God's whole
original constitution of nature, and the whole daily course
of divine Providence in the government of the world;
i. e. against the whole scheme of theism and the whole
notion of religion, as against Christianity. For the world
is a constitution, or system, whose parts have a mutual
reference to each other; and there is a scheme of things
gradually carrying on, called the course of nature, to the
carrying on of which God has appointed us, in various
ways, to contribute. And when, in the daily course of
natural providence, it is appointed that innocent people
should suffer for the faults of the guilty, this is liable to
the very same objection as the instance we are now considering. The infinitely greater importance of that appointment of Christianity which is objected against, does
not hinder, but it may be, as it plainly is, an appointment
of the very same kind with what the world affords us daily
examples of. Nay, if there were any force at all in the
objection, it would be stronger, in one respect, against
natural providence, than against Christianity; because,
under the former, we are in many cases commanded, and
even necessitated, whether we will or no, to suffer for the
faults of others; whereas the sufferings of Christ were voluntary. The world's being under the righteous government of God does indeed imply, that finally and upon the
whole every one shall receive according to his personal
deserts; and the general doctrine of the whole Scripture is,
that this shall be the completion of the divine government.
But, during the progress, and, for aught we know, even
in order to the completion of this moral scheme, vicarious
punishments may be fit, and absolutely necessary. Men,
by their follies, run themselves into extreme distress: into
difficulties which would be absolutely fatal to them, were
it not for the interposition and assistance of others. God

commands, by the law of nature, that we afford them this
assistance, in many cases where we cannot do it without
very great pains, and labour, and sufferings to ourselves.
And we see in what variety of ways one person's sufferings contribute to the relief of another; and how, or by
what particular means this comes to pass, or follows, from
the constitution and laws of nature which come under
our notice: and being familiarized to it, men are not
shocked with it. So that the reason of their insisting
upon objections of the foregoing kind, against the satisfaction of Christ, is, either that they do not consider God's
settled and uniform appointments as his appointments at
all, or else they forget that vicarious punishment is a
providential appointment of every day's experience: and
then, from their being unacquainted with the more general
laws of nature, or divine government over the world,
and not seeing how the sufferings of Christ could contribute to the redemption of it, unless by arbitrary and
tyrannical will, they conclude his sufferings could not
contribute to it any other way. And yet, what has been
often alleged in justification of this doctrine, even from
the apparent natural tendency of this method of our redemption—its tendency to vindicate the authority of God's
laws, and deter his creatures from sin; this has never yet
been answered, and is, I think, plainly unanswerable:
though I am far from thinking it an account of the whole
of the case. But without taking this into consideration,
it abundantly appears, from the observations above made,
that this objection is, not an objection against Christianity, but against the whole general constitution of nature. And if it were to be considered as an objection
against Christianity, or considering it as it is, an objection
against the constitution of nature, it amounts to no more
in conclusion than this, that a divine appointment cannot
be necessary, or expedient, because the objector does
not discern it to be so; though he must own that the
nature of the case is such as renders him incapable of

judging whether it be so or not; or of seeing it to be necessary, though it were so.

It is, indeed, a matter of great patience to reasonable men, to find people arguing in this manner, objecting against the credibility of such particular things revealed in Scripture, that they do not see the necessity or expediency of them. For, though it is highly right, and the most pious exercise of our understanding, to inquire with due reverence into the ends and reasons of God's dispensations; yet, when those reasons are concealed, to argue from our ignorance, that such dispensations cannot be from God, is infinitely absurd. The presumption of this kind of objections seems almost lost in the folly of them. And the folly of them is yet greater, when they are urged, as usually they are, against things in Christianity analogous or like to those natural dispensations of Providence which are matter of experience. Let reason be kept to; and, if any part of the Scripture account of the redemption of the world by Christ can be shown to be really contrary to it, let the Scripture, in the name of God, be given up; but let not such poor creatures as we go on objecting against an infinite scheme, that we do not see the necessity or usefulness of all its parts, and call this reasoning; and, which still farther heightens the absurdity in the present case, parts which we are not actively concerned in. For, it may be worth mentioning,

Lastly, That not only the reason of the thing, but the whole analogy of nature, should teach us, not to expect to have the like information concerning the divine conduct, as concerning our own duty. God instructs us by experience, (for it is not reason, but experience, which instructs us,) what good or bad consequences will follow from our acting in such and such manners; and by this he directs us how we are to behave ourselves. But, though we are sufficiently instructed for the common purposes of life, yet it is but an almost infinitely small part of natural providence which we are at all let into. The case is the same with regard to revelation. The doctrine of a mediator between God and man, against which it is objected that the expediency of some things in it is not understood, relates only to what was done on God's part in the appointment, and on the Mediator's in the execution of it. For what is required of us, in consequence of this gracious dispensation, is another subject, in which none can complain for want of information. The constitution of the world, and God's natural government over it, is all mystery, as much as the Christian dispensation. Yet, under the first, he has given men all things pertaining to life; and under the other, all things pertaining unto godliness. And it may be added, that there is nothing hard to be accounted for in any of the common precepts of Christianity; though, if there were, surely a divine command is abundantly sufficient to lay us under the strongest obligations to obedience. But the fact is, that the reasons of all the Christian precepts are evident. Positive institutions are manifestly necessary to keep up and propagate religion amongst mankind. And our duty to Christ, the internal and external worship of him; this part of the religion of the gospel manifestly arises out of what he has done and suffered, his authority and dominion, and the relation which he is revealed to stand in to us.*

CHAPTER VI.

Of the Want of Universality in Revelation; and of the supposed Deficiency in the Proof of it.

It has been thought by some persons, that if the evidence of revelation appears doubtful, this itself turns into a positive argument against it; because it cannot be supposed, that, if it were true, it would be left to subsist upon

* Page 128, &c.

doubtful evidence. And the objection against revelation, from its not being universal, is often insisted upon as of great weight.

Now, the weakness of these opinions may be shown, by observing the suppositions on which they are founded, which are really such as these:—that it cannot be thought God would have bestowed any favour at all upon us, unless in the degree which, we think, he might, and which, we imagine, would be most to our particular advantage; and also, that it cannot be thought he would bestow a favour upon any, unless he bestowed the same upon all: suppositions which we find contradicted, not by a few instances in God's natural government of the world, but by the general analogy of nature together.

Persons who speak of the evidence of religion as doubtful, and of this supposed doubtfulness as a positive argument against it, should be put upon considering, what that evidence indeed is which they act upon with regard to their temporal interests. For, it is not only extremely difficult, but, in many cases, absolutely impossible, to balance pleasure and pain, satisfaction and uneasiness, so as to be able to say on which side the overplus is. There are the like difficulties and impossibilities, in making the due allowances for a change of temper and taste, for satiety, disgusts, ill health; any of which render men incapable of enjoying, after they have obtained, what they most eagerly desired. Numberless, too, are the accidents, besides that one of untimely death, which may even probably disappoint the best concerted schemes; and strong objections are often seen to lie against them, not to be removed or answered, but which seem overbalanced by reasons on the other side; so as that the certain difficulties and dangers of the pursuit are, by every one, thought justly disregarded, upon account of the appearing greater advantages in case of success, though there be but little probability of it. *Lastly*, Every one observes our liableness, if we be not upon our guard, to be deceived by the falsehood of men, and

the false appearances of things; and this danger must
be greatly increased, if there be a strong bias within,
suppose from indulged passion, to favour the deceit.
Hence arises that great uncertainty and doubtfulness
of proof, wherein our temporal interest really consists;
what are the most probable means of attaining it; and
whether those means will eventually be successful. And
numberless instances there are, in the daily course of
life, in which all men think it reasonable to engage in
pursuits, though the probability is greatly against succeeding; and to make such provision for themselves, as it
is supposable they may have occasion for, though the
plain acknowledged probability is, that they never shall.
Then those who think the objection against revelation,
from its light not being universal, to be of weight, should
observe that the Author of nature, in numberless instances,
bestows that upon some, which he does not upon others,
who seem equally to stand in need of it. Indeed, he
appears to bestow all his gifts, with the most promiscuous
variety, among creatures of the same species: health and
strength, capacities of prudence and of knowledge, means
of improvement, riches, and all external advantages. And
as there are not any two men found of exactly like shape
and features, so, it is probable, there are not any two
of an exactly like constitution, temper, and situation,
with regard to the goods and evils of life. Yet, notwithstanding these uncertainties and varieties, God does exercise a natural government over the world; and there is
such a thing as a prudent and imprudent institution of life,
with regard to our health and our affairs, under that his
natural government.

As neither the Jewish nor Christian revelation have
been universal, and as they have been afforded to a greater
or less part of the world at different times, so, likewise,
at different times, both revelations have had different degrees of evidence. The Jews who lived during the succession of Prophets, that is from Moses till after the Cap-

tivity, had higher evidence of the truth of their religion
than those who had lived in the interval between the last
mentioned period and the coming of Christ; and the first
Christians had higher evidence of the miracles wrought
in attestation of Christianity than what we have now. They
had also a strong presumptive proof of the truth of it,
perhaps of much greater force, in way of argument, than
many think, of which we have very little remaining; I
mean, the presumptive proof of its truth, from the influence
which it had upon the lives of the generality of its professors.
And we, or future ages, may possibly have a proof of it,
which they could not have, from the conformity between
the prophetic history, and the state of the world, and of
Christianity. And farther: If we were to suppose the
evidence, which some have of religion, to amount to little
more than seeing that it may be true, but that they remain
in great doubts and uncertainties about both its evidence
and its nature, and great perplexities concerning the rule of
life; others to have a full conviction of the truth of religion,
with a distinct knowledge of their duty; and others severally to have all the intermediate degrees of religious light
and evidence which lie between these two—If we put the
case, that for the present it was intended revelation should
be no more than a small light, in the midst of a world
greatly overspread, notwithstanding it, with ignorance and
darkness; that certain glimmerings of this light should
extend, and be directed, to remote distances, in such a
manner as that those who really partook of it should not
discern from whence it originally came; that some, in a
nearer situation to it, should have its light obscured, and
in different ways and degrees intercepted; and that
others should be placed within its clearer influence, and
be much more enlivened, cheered, and directed by it;
but yet, that even to these it should be no more than " a
light shining in a dark place:" all this would be perfectly
uniform and of a piece with the conduct of Providence,

in the distribution of its other blessings. If the fact of
the case really were, that some have received no light at
all from the Scripture; as many ages and countries in
the heathen world: that others, though they have, by
means of it, had essential or natural religion enforced
upon their consciences, yet have never had the genuine
Scripture revelation, with its real evidence, proposed to
their consideration: and the ancient Persians and modern
Mahometans may possibly be instances of people in a
situation somewhat like to this: that others, though they
have had the Scripture laid before them as of divine
revelation, yet have had it with the system and evidence
of Christianity so interpolated—the system so corrupted,
the evidence so blended with false miracles—as to leave
the mind in the utmost doubtfulness and uncertainty
about the whole; which may be the state of some thoughtful men in most of those nations who call themselves
Christian: and, *lastly*, that others have had Christianity
offered to them in its genuine simplicity, and with its
proper evidence, as persons in countries and churches of
civil and of Christian liberty; but, however, that even
these persons are left in great ignorance in many respects,
and have by no means light afforded them enough to satisfy
their curiosity, but only to regulate their life, to teach them
their duty, and encourage them in the careful discharge
of it:—I say, if we were to suppose this somewhat of a
general true account of the degrees of moral and religious
light and evidence which were intended to be afforded
mankind, and of what has actually been and is their
situation in their moral and religious capacity, there would
be nothing in all this ignorance, doubtfulness, and uncertainty, in all these varieties and supposed disadvantages of
some in comparison of others, respecting religion, but may
be paralleled by manifest analogies in the natural dispensations of Providence at present, and considering ourselves
merely in our temporal capacity.

Nor is there anything shocking in all this, or which would seem to bear hard upon the moral administration in nature, if we would really keep in mind, that every one shall be dealt equitably with; instead of forgetting this, or explaining it away after it is acknowledged in words. All shadow of injustice, and indeed all harsh appearances, in this various economy of Providence, would be lost, if we would keep in mind, that every merciful allowance shall be made, and no more be required of any one, than what might have been equitably expected of him from the circumstances in which he was placed; and not what might have been expected, had he been placed in other circumstances; *i. e.* in Scripture language, that every man shall be " accepted according to what he had, not according to what he had not," 2 Cor. viii. 12.   This, however, doth not by any means imply, that all persons' condition here is equally advantageous with respect to futurity.   And Providence's designing to place some in greater darkness with respect to religious knowledge, is no more a reason why they should not endeavour to get out of that darkness, and others to bring them out of it, than why ignorant and slow people, in matters of other knowledge, should not endeavour to learn, or should not be instructed.

It is not reasonable to suppose, that the same wise and good principle, whatever it was, which disposed the Author of nature to make different kinds and orders of creatures, disposed him also to place creatures of like kinds in different situations; and that the same principle which disposed him to make creatures of different moral capacities, disposed him also to place creatures of like moral capacities in different religious situations; and even the same creatures, in different periods of their being. And the account or reason of this, is also most probably the account, why the constitution of things is such as that creatures of moral natures or capacities, for a considerable part of that duration in which they are living agents, are not at all subjects of morality and religion; but grow up to be so, and grow up to be so more and more, gradually, from childhood to mature age.

What, in particular, is the account or reason of these things, we must be greatly in the dark, were it only that we know so very little of even our own case. Our present state may possibly be the consequence of somewhat past, which we are wholly ignorant of; as it has a reference to somewhat to come, of which we know scarce any more than is necessary for practice. A system, or constitution in its notion, implies variety; and so complicated a one as this world, very great variety. So that were revelation universal, yet from men's different capacities of understanding, from the different lengths of their lives, their different educations, and other external circumstances, and from their difference of temper and bodily constitution—their religious situations would be widely different, and the disadvantage of some, in comparison of others, perhaps altogether as much as at present. And the true. account, whatever it be, why mankind, or such a part of them, are placed in this condition of ignorance, must be supposed also the true account of our further ignorance, in not knowing the reasons why, or whence it is, that they are placed in this condition. But the following practical reflections may deserve the serious consideration of those persons, who think the circumstances of mankind, or their own, in the fore-mentioned respects, a ground of complaint.

First, The evidence of religion not appearing obvious, may constitute one particular part of some men's trial in the religious sense; as it gives scope for a virtuous exercise, or vicious neglect, of their understanding, in examining or not examining into that evidence. There seems no possible reason to be given, why we may not be in a state of moral probation with regard to the exercise of our understanding upon the subject of religion, as we are with regard to our behaviour in common affairs. The

former is as much a thing within our power and choice
as the latter. And I suppose it is to be laid down for
certain, that the same character, the same inward principle
which, after a man is convinced of the truth of religion,
renders him obedient to the precepts of it, would,
were he not thus convinced, set him about an examination
of it, upon its system and evidence being offered to
his thoughts: and that, in the latter state, his examination would be with an impartiality, seriousness, and solicitude proportionable to what his obedience is in the
former. And as inattention, negligence, want of all serious
concern about a matter of such a nature and such importance, when offered to men's consideration, is, before
a distinct conviction of its truth, as real immoral depravity, and dissoluteness, as neglect of religious practice
after such conviction; so active solicitude about it, and
fair impartial consideration of its evidence before such
conviction, is as really an exercise of a morally right
temper, as is religious practice after. Thus, that religion is not intuitively true, but a matter of deduction and
inference; that a conviction of its truth is not forced upon
every one, but left to be, by some, collected with heedful
attention to premises: this as much constitutes religious
probation, as much affords sphere, scope, opportunity,
for right and wrong behaviour, as anything whatever
does: and their manner of treating this subject, when laid
before them, shows what is in their heart, and is an exertion
of it.

Secondly, It appears to be a thing as evident, though
it is not so much attended to, that if, upon consideration
of religion, the evidence of it should seem to any persons
doubtful, in the highest supposable degree, even this
doubtful evidence will, however, put them into a *general
state of probation*, in the moral and religious sense. For
suppose a man to be really in doubt, whether such a person had not done him the greatest favour; or whether
his whole temporal interest did not depend upon that

person; no one, who had any sense of gratitude and of prudence, could possibly consider himself in the same situation, with regard to such person, as if he had no such doubt. In truth, it is as just to say, that certainty and doubt are the same, as to say, the situations now mentioned would leave a man as entirely at liberty, in point of gratitude or prudence, as he would be, were he certain he had received no favour from such person, or that he no way depended upon him. And thus, though the evidence of religion which is afforded to some men should be little more, than that they are given to see the system of Christianity, or religion in general, to be supposable and credible, this ought in all reason to beget a serious practical apprehension that it may be true. And even this will afford matter of exercise for religious suspense and deliberation, for moral resolution and self-government; because the apprehension that religion may be true, does as really lay men under obligations, as a full conviction that it is true. It gives occasion and motives to consider farther the important subject; to preserve attentively upon their minds a general implicit sense that they may be under divine moral government; an awful solicitude about religion, whether natural or revealed. Such apprehension ought to turn men's eyes to every degree of new light which may be had, from whatever side it comes, and induce them to refrain, in the mean time, from all immoralities, and live in the conscientious practice of every common virtue. Especially are they bound to keep at the greatest distance from all dissolute profaneness; for this the very nature of the case forbids; and to treat with highest reverence a matter upon which their own whole interest and being, and the fate of nature, depends. This behaviour, and an active endeavour to maintain within themselves this temper, is the business, the duty, and the wisdom of those persons who complain of the doubtfulness of religion; is what they are under the most proper obligations to: and such behaviour is an exertion of, and has a tendency to improve in them, that character, which the practice of all the several duties of religion, from a full conviction of its truth, is an exertion of, and has a tendency to improve in others—others, I say, to whom God has afforded such conviction. Nay, considering the infinite importance of religion, revealed as well as natural, I think it may be said in general, that whoever will weigh the matter thoroughly, may see there is not near so much difference, as is commonly imagined, between what ought in reason to be the rule of life, to those persons who are fully convinced of its truth, and to those who have only a serious doubting apprehension that it may be true. Their hopes, and fears, and obligations, will be in various degrees; but, as the subject-matter of their hopes and fears is the same, so the subject-matter of their obligations, what they are bound to do and to refrain from, is not so very unlike.

It is to be observed farther, that, from a character of understanding, or a situation of influence in the world, some persons have it in their power to do infinitely more harm or good, by setting an example of profaneness and avowed disregard to all religion, or, on the contrary, of a serious, though perhaps doubting apprehension of its truth, and of a reverend regard to it under this doubtfulness, than they can do by acting well or ill in all the common intercourses amongst mankind; and, consequently, they are most highly accountable for a behaviour which, they may easily foresee, is of such importance, and in which there is most plainly a right and a wrong; even admitting the evidence of religion to be as doubtful as is pretended.

The ground of these observations, and that which renders them just and true, is, that doubting necessarily implies some degree of evidence for that of which we doubt. For no person would be in doubt concerning the truth of a number of facts so and so circumstanced, which should accidentally come into his thoughts, and of which he had no evidence at all. And though in the case of an

K

even chance, and where consequently we were in doubt, we should in common language say, that we had no evidence at all for either side; yet that situation of things which renders it an even chance, and no more, that such an event will happen, renders this case equivalent to all others, where there is such evidence on both sides of a question* as leaves the mind in doubt concerning the truth. Indeed, in all these cases, there is no more evidence on the one side than on the other; but there is (what is equivalent to) much more for either, than for the truth of a number of facts which come into one's thoughts at random. And thus, in all these cases, doubt as much presupposes evidence, lower degrees of evidence, as belief presupposes higher, and certainty higher still. Any one, who will a little attend to the nature of evidence, will easily carry this observation on, and see, that between no evidence at all, and that degree of it which affords ground of doubt, there are as many intermediate degrees, as there are between that degree which is the ground of doubt, and demonstration. And, though we have not faculties to distinguish these degrees of evidence with any sort of exactness, yet, in proportion as they are discerned, they ought to influence our practice; for it is as real an imperfection in the moral character, not to be influenced in practice by a lower degree of evidence when discerned, as it is in the understanding not to discern it. And as, in all subjects which men consider, they discern the lower as well as higher degrees of evidence, proportionably to their capacity of understanding; so, in practicable subjects, they are influenced in practice by the lower as well as higher degrees of it, proportionably to their fairness and honesty. And as, in proportion to defects in the understanding, men are unapt to see lower degrees of evidence, are in danger of overlooking evidence when it is not glaring, and are easily imposed upon in such cases; so, in proportion to the corruption of the

* Introduction.

heart, they seem capable of satisfying themselves with having no regard in practice to evidence acknowledged real, if it be not overbearing. From these things it must follow, that doubting concerning religion implies such a degree of evidence for it, as, joined with the consideration of its importance, unquestionably lays men under the obligations before mentioned, to have a dutiful regard to it in all their behaviour.

Thirdly, The difficulties in which the evidence of religion is involved, which some complain of, is no more a just ground of complaint, than the external circumstances of temptation which others are placed in; or than difficulties in the practice of it, after a full conviction of its truth. Temptations render our state a more improving state of discipline* than it would be otherwise; as they give occasion for a more attentive exercise of the virtuous principle, which confirms and strengthens it more than an easier or less attentive exercise of it could. Now, speculative difficulties are, in this respect, of the very same nature with these external temptations. For, the evidence of religion not appearing obvious, is, to some persons, a temptation to reject it without any consideration at all; and therefore requires such an attentive exercise of the virtuous principle, seriously to consider that evidence, as there would be no occasion for, but for such temptation. And the supposed doubtfulness of its evidence, after it has been in some sort considered, affords opportunity to an unfair mind of explaining away, and deceitfully hiding from itself, that evidence which it might see; and also for men's encouraging themselves in vice from hopes of impunity, though they do clearly see thus much at least, that these hopes are uncertain: in like manner as the common temptation to many instances of folly, which end in temporal infamy and ruin, is the ground for hope of not being detected, and of escaping with impunity; *i. e.* the doubtfulness of the proof

* Part i. chap. 5.

K 2

beforehand, that such foolish behaviour will thus end in infamy and ruin. On the contrary, supposed doubtfulness in the evidence of religion calls for a more careful and attentive exercise of the virtuous principle, in fairly yielding themselves up to the proper influence of any real evidence, though doubtful; and in practising conscientiously all virtue, though under some uncertainty whether the government in the universe may not possibly be such as that vice may escape with impunity. And, in general, temptation, meaning by this word the lesser allurements to wrong, and difficulties in the discharge of our duty, as well as the greater ones—temptation, I say, as such, and of every kind and degree, as it calls forth some virtuous efforts, additional to what would otherwise have been wanting, cannot but be an additional discipline and improvement of virtue, as well as probation of it, in the other senses of that word.* So that the very same account is to be given, why the evidence of religion should be left in such a manner as to require, in some, an attentive, solicitous, perhaps painful exercise of their understanding about it; as why others should be placed in such circumstances, as that the practice of its common duties, after a full conviction of the truth of it, should require attention, solicitude, and pains; or, why appearing doubtfulness should be permitted to afford matter of temptation to some; as why external difficulties and allurements should be permitted to afford matter of temptation to others. The same account also is to be given, why some should be exercised with temptations of both these kinds, as why others should be exercised with the latter in such very high degrees as some have been, particularly as the primitive Christians were.

Nor does there appear any absurdity in supposing, that the speculative difficulties in which the evidence of religion is involved, may make even the principal part of

* Part i. chap. 4, and pages 84, &c.

some persons' trial.   For, as the chief temptations of the
generality of the world are the ordinary motives to injustice or unrestrained pleasure, or to live in the neglect of
religion, from that frame of mind which renders many
persons almost without feeling as to anything distant, or
which is not the object of their senses; so there are other
persons without this shallowness of temper, persons of a
deeper sense as to what is invisible and future, who not
only see, but have a general practicable feeling, that what
is to come will be present, and that things are not less
real for their not being the objects of sense; and who,
from their natural constitution of body and of temper,
and from their external condition, may have small temptations to behave ill, small difficulty in behaving well, in
the common course of life.   Now, when these latter persons
have a distinct full conviction of the truth of religion, without any possible doubts or difficulties, the practice of it is
to them unavoidable, unless they will do a constant violence
to their own minds; and religion is scarce any more a
discipline to them, than it is to creatures in a state of
perfection.   Yet these persons may possibly stand in need
of moral discipline and exercise, in a higher degree than
they would have by such an easy practice of religion.   Or
it may be requisite, for reasons unknown to us, that they
should give some further manifestation * what is their
moral character, to the creation of God, than such a
practice of it would be.   Thus, in the great variety of
religious situations in which men are placed, what constitutes, what chiefly and peculiarly constitutes the probation,
in all senses, of some persons, may be the difficulties in
which the evidence of religion is involved; and their principal and distinguished trial may be, how they will behave
under and with respect to these difficulties.   Circumstances
in men's situation in their temporal capacity, analogous
in good measure to this respecting religion, are to be

* Page 85.

observed. We find some persons are placed in such a situation in the world, as that their chief difficulty, with regard to conduct, is not the doing what is prudent when it is known; for this, in numberless cases, is as easy as the contrary; but to some the principal exercise is recollection, and being upon their guard against deceits—the deceits, suppose, of those about them; against false appearances of reason and prudence. To persons in some situations, the principal exercise, with respect to conduct, is attention, in order to inform themselves what is proper, what is really the reasonable and prudent part to act.

But as I have hitherto gone upon supposition, that men's dissatisfaction with the evidence of religion is not owing to their neglects or prejudices; it must be added, on the other hand, in all common reason, and as what the truth of the case plainly requires should be added, that such dissatisfaction possibly may be owing to those, possibly may be men's own fault. For,

If there are any persons who never set themselves heartily, and in earnest, to be informed in religion; if there are any who secretly wish it may not prove true, and are less attentive to evidence than to difficulties, and more to objections than to what is said in answer to them; these persons will scarce be thought in a likely way of seeing the evidence of religion, though it were most certainly true, and capable of being ever so fully proved. If any accustom themselves to consider this subject usually in the way of mirth and sport; if they attend to forms and representations, and inadequate manners of expression, instead of the real things intended by them, (for signs often can be no more than inadequately expressive of the things signified;) or, if they substitute human errors in the room of divine truth; why may not all, or any of these things, hinder some men from seeing that evidence, which really is seen by others: as a like turn of mind, with respect to matters of common speculation

and practice, does,' we find by experience, hinder them
from attaining that knowledge and right understanding in
matters of common speculation and practice, which more
fair and attentive minds attain to? And the effect will be
the same, whether their neglect of seriously considering the
evidence of religion, and their indirect behaviour with
regard to it, proceed from mere carelessness, or from the
grosser vices; or whether it be owing to this, that forms,
and figurative manners of expression, as well as errors,
administer occasions of ridicule, when the things intended, ·
and the truth itself, would not. Men may indulge a ludicrous turn so far as to lose all sense of conduct and prudence in worldly affairs, and even, as it seems, to impair
their faculty of reason. And in general, levity, carelessness, passion, and prejudice, do hinder us from being
rightly informed with respect to common things; and they
may, in like manner, and perhaps in some farther providential manner, with respect to moral and religious subjects
—may hinder evidence from being laid before us, and from
being seen when it is. The Scripture does declare, " that
every one shall not understand," Dan. xii. 10.* And it
makes no difference by what providential conduct this
comes to pass; whether the evidence of Christianity was
originally, and with design, put and left so as that those,
who are desirous of evading moral obligations, should not
see it, and that honest-minded persons should; or whether
it comes to pass by any other means.

Farther: The general proof of natural religion and of
Christianity does, I think, lie level to common men; even

* See also Isa. xxix. 13, 14; Matt. vi. 23, xi. 25, xiii. 11, 12;
John iii. 19; John v. 44; 1 Cor. ii. 14; 2 Cor. iv. 4; 2 Tim. iii. 13;
and that affectionate, as well as authoritative admonition, so very
many times inculcated, " He that hath ears to hear, let him hear."
Grotius saw so strongly the thing intended in these and other passages
of Scripture of the like sense, as to say that the proof given us of
Christianity was less than it might have been, for this very purpose:
*Ut ita sermo Evangelii tanquam lapis esset Lydius, ad quem ingenia
sanabilia explorarentur.* De Ver. R. C. lib. 2, towards the end.

those, the greatest part of whose time, from childhood to old age, is taken up with providing, for themselves and their families, the common conveniences, perhaps necessaries of life; those, I mean, of this rank, who ever think at all of asking after proof, or attending to it. Common men, were they as much in earnest about religion as about their temporal affairs, are capable of being convinced, upon real evidence, that there is a God who governs the world; and they feel themselves to be of a moral nature, and accountable creatures. And as Christianity entirely falls in with this their natural sense of things; so they are capable, not only of being persuaded, but of being made to see, that there is evidence of miracles wrought in attestation of it, and many appearing completions of prophecy. But though this proof is real and conclusive, yet it is liable to objections, and may be run up into difficulties; which, however, persons who are capable, not only of talking of, but of really seeing, are capable also of seeing through: *i. e.* not of clearing up and answering them, so as to satisfy their curiosity, for of such knowledge we are not capable with respect to any one thing in nature; but capable of seeing that the proof is not lost in these difficulties, or destroyed by these objections. But then a thorough examination into religion, with regard to these objections, which cannot be the business of every man, is a matter of pretty large compass, and, from the nature of it requires some knowledge, as well as time and attention, to see how the evidence comes out upon balancing one thing with another, and what, upon the whole, is the amount of it. Now, if persons who have picked up these objections from others, and take for granted they are of weight, upon the word of those from whom they received them; or, by often retailing of them, come to see, or fancy they see, them to be of weight—will not prepare themselves for such an examination with a competent degree of knowledge; or will not give that time and attention to the subject, which, from the nature of it, is necessary for attaining such information;—in this case, they must remain in doubtfulness, ignorance, or error; in the same way as they must, with regard to common sciences and matters of common life, if they neglect the necessary means of being informed in them.

But still, perhaps, it will be objected, that if a prince or common master were to send directions to a servant, he would take care that they should always bear the certain marks who they came from, and that their sense should be always plain; so as that there should be no possible doubt, if he could help it, concerning the authority or meaning of them.   Now, the proper answer to all this kind of objections is, that, wherever the fallacy lies, it is even certain we cannot argue thus with respect to him who is the Governor of the world; and particularly, that he does not afford us such information with respect to our temporal affairs and interests—as experience abundantly shows.   However, there is a full answer to this objection, from the very nature of religion.   For the reason why a prince would give his directions in this plain manner is, that he absolutely desires such an external action should be done, without concerning himself with the motive or principle upon which it is done; *i. e.* he regards only the external event, or the thing's being done, and not at all, properly speaking, the doing of it, or the action.   Whereas the whole of morality and religion consisting merely in action itself, there is no sort of parallel between the cases.   But if the prince be supposed to regard only the action; *i. e.* only to desire to exercise, or in any sense prove, the understanding or loyalty of a servant, he would not always give his orders in such a plain manner.   It may be proper to add, that the will of God, respecting morality and religion, may be considered either as absolute, or as only conditional. If it be absolute, it can only be thus, that we should act virtuously in such given circumstances; not that we should be brought to act so, by his changing of our circumstances. And if God's will be thus absolute, then it is in our power, in the highest and strictest sense, to do or to contradict his will; which is a most weighty consideration. Or his will may be considered only as conditional—that if we act so and so, we shall be rewarded; if otherwise, punished: of which conditional will of the Author of nature, the whole constitution of it affords most certain instances.

Upon the whole: That we are in a state of religion necessarily implies, that we are in a state of probation; and the credibility of our being at all in such a state being admitted, there seems no peculiar difficulty in supposing our probation to be just as it is, in those respects which are above objected against. There seems no pretence, from *the reason of the thing*, to say that the trial cannot equitably be anything, but whether persons will act suitably to certain information, or such as admits no room for doubt; so as that there can be no danger of miscarriage, but either from their not attending to what they certainly know, or from overbearing passion hurrying them on to act contrary to it. For, since ignorance and doubt afford scope for probation in all senses, as really as intuitive conviction or certainty; and since the two former are to be put to the same account as difficulties in practice; men's moral probation may also be, whether they will take due care to inform themselves by impartial consideration, and afterwards whether they will act as the case requires, upon the evidence which they have, however doubtful. And this, we find by *experience*, is frequently our probation,* in our temporal capacity. For the information which we want, with regard to our worldly interests, is by no means always given us of course, without any care of our own. And we are greatly liable to self-deceit from inward secret prejudices, and

* Pages 25, 197, 198, 199.

also to the deceits of others; so that to be able to judge
what is the prudènt part, often requires much and difficult
consideration.   Then, after we have judged the very best
we can, the evidence upon which we must act, if we will live
and act at all, is perpetually doubtful to a very high degree.
And the constitution and course of the world in fact is
such, as that want of impartial consideration what we
have to do, and venturing upon extravagant courses,
because it is doubtful what will be the consequence, are
often naturally, *i. e.* providentially, altogether as fatal,
as misconduct occasioned by heedless inattention to what
we certainly know, or disregarding it from overbearing
passion.

Several of the observations here made may well seem
strange, perhaps unintelligible, to many good men.   But if
the persons for whose sake they are made think so; persons
who object as above, and throw off all regard to religion
under pretence of want of evidence; I desire them to
consider again, whether their thinking so be owing to
anything unintelligible in these observations, or to their own
not having such a sense of religion, and serious solicitude
about it, as even their state of scepticism does in all reason
require?   It ought to be forced upon the reflection of
these persons, that our nature and condition necessarily
require us, in the daily course of life, to act upon evidence
much lower than what is commonly called probable; to
guard not only against what we fully believe will, but also
against what we think it supposable may happen; and to
engage in pursuits when the probability is greatly against
success, if it be credible that possibly we may succeed in
them.

CHAPTER VII.

Of the particular Evidence for Christianity.

THE presumptions against revelation, and objections against the general scheme of Christianity, and particular things relating to it, being removed, there remains to be considered, what positive evidence we have for the truth of it; chiefly in order to see what the analogy of nature suggests with regard to that evidence, and the objections against it; or to see what is, and is allowed to be, the plain natural rule of judgment and of action, in our temporal concerns, in cases where we have the same kind of evidence, and the same kind of objections against it, that we have in the case before us.

Now, in the evidence of Christianity, there seem to be several things of great weight, not reducible to the head either of miracles or the completion of prophecy, in the common acceptation of the words. But these two are its direct and fundamental proofs; and those other things, however considerable they are, yet ought never to be urged apart from its direct proofs, but always to be joined with them. Thus the evidence of Christianity will be a long series of things, reaching, as it seems, from the beginning of the world to the present time, of great variety and compass, taking in both the direct and also the collateral proofs, and making up, all of them together, one argument; the conviction arising from which kind of proof may be compared to what they call *the effect* in architecture or other works of art; a result from a great number of things so and so disposed, and taken into one view. I shall therefore, *first*, make some observations relating to miracles, and the appearing completions of prophecy; and consider what analogy suggests, in answer to the objections brought against this evidence: And, *secondly*, I shall endeavour to give some account of the general argument now mentioned, consisting both of the direct and

collateral evidence, considered as making up one argument:
this being the kind of proof upon which we determine most
questions of difficulty concerning common facts, alleged to
have happened, or seeming likely to happen; especially
questions relating to conduct.

First, I shall make some observations upon the direct
proof of Christianity from miracles and prophecy, and upon
the objections alleged against it.

I. Now, the following observations, relating to the historical evidence of miracles wrought in attestation of Christianity, appear to be of great weight.

.1. The Old Testament affords us the same historical
evidence of the miracles of Moses and of the prophets,
as of the common civil history of Moses and the kings of
Israel; or, as of the affairs of the Jewish nation. And
the Gospels and the Acts afford us the same historical
evidence of the miracles of Christ and the Apostles, as
of the common matters related in them. This, indeed,
could not have been affirmed by any reasonable man, if
the authors of these books, like many other historians,
had appeared to make an entertaining manner of writing
their aim; though they had interspersed miracles in their
works, at proper distances, and upon proper occasions.
These might have animated a dull relation, amused the
reader, and engaged his attention; and the same account
would naturally have been given of them, as of the speeches
and descriptions of such authors; the same account, in a
manner, as is to be given, why the poets make use of wonders and prodigies. But the facts, both miraculous and
natural, in Scripture, are related in plain unadorned narratives; and both of them appear, in all respects, to stand
upon the same foot of historical evidence. Farther: Some
parts of Scripture, containing an account of miracles fully
sufficient to prove the truth of Christianity, are quoted as
genuine, from the age in which they are said to be written,
down to the present; and no other parts of them, material
in the present question, are omitted to be quoted in such

manner, as to afford any sort of proof of their not being
genuine. And, as common history, when called in question in any instance, may often be greatly confirmed by
contemporary or subsequent events more known and acknowledged; and as the common Scripture history, like
many others, is thus confirmed; so likewise is the miraculous history of it, not only in particular instances, but
in general. For, the establishment of the Jewish and
Christian religions, which were events contemporary with
the miracles related to be wrought in attestation of both,
or subsequent to them—these events are just what we
should have expected, upon supposition such miracles
were really wrought to attest the truth of those religions.
These miracles are a satisfactory account of those events,
of which no other satisfactory account can be given, nor any
account at all, but what is imaginary merely, and invented.
It is to be added, that the most obvious, the most easy and
direct account of this history, how it came to be written,
and to be received in the world as a true history, is, that it
really is so; nor can any other account of it be easy and
direct. Now, though an account, not at all obvious, but
very far-fetched and indirect, may indeed be, and often is,
the true account of a matter; yet it cannot be admitted on
the authority of its being asserted. Mere guess, supposition, and possibility, when opposed to historical evidence,
prove nothing, but that historical evidence is not demonstrative.

Now, the just consequence from all this, I think, is
that the Scripture history, in general, is to be admitted
as an authentic genuine history, till somewhat positive be
alleged sufficient to invalidate it. But no man will deny
the consequence to be, that it cannot be rejected, or
thrown by as of no authority, till it can be proved to be
of none; even though the evidence now mentioned for
its authority were doubtful. This evidence may be con-
fronted by historical evidence on the other side, if there
be any: or general incredibility in the things related, or

inconsistence in the general turn of the history, would prove
it to be of no authority.   But since, upon the face of the
matter, upon a first and general view, the appearance is that
it is an authentic history, it cannot be determined to be
fictitious without some proof that it is so.   And the following observations, in support of these and coincident
with them, will greatly confirm the historical evidence for
the truth of Christianity.

2. The Epistles of St. Paul, from the nature of episto-
lary writing, and, moreover, from several of them being
written, not to particular persons, but to churches, carry
in them evidences of their being genuine, beyond what
can be, in a mere historical narrative, left to the world at
large.   This evidence, joined with that which they have
in common with the rest of the New Testament, seems
not to leave so much as any particular pretence for denying
their genuineness, considered as an ordinary matter of fact,
or of criticism: I say, *particular* pretence for *denying it;*
because any single fact, of such a kind and such antiquity,
may have *general doubts* raised concerning it, from the
very nature of human affairs and human testimony.   There
is also to be mentioned, a distinct and particular evidence
of the genuineness of the epistle chiefly referred to here,
the First to the Corinthians, from the manner in which it
is quoted by *Clemens Romanus* in an epistle of his own
to that church.*   Now these epistles afford a proof of
Christianity, detached from all others, which is, I think, a
thing of weight; and also a proof of a nature and kind
peculiar to itself.   For,

In them the author declares, that he received the gospel in general, and the institution of the communion in
particular, not from the rest of the apostles, or jointly together with them, but alone from Christ himself; whom
he declares, likewise, conformably to the history in the
Acts, that he 'saw after his ascension: Gal. i.; 1 Cor. xi.
23, &c.; 1 Cor. xv. 8.   So that the testimony of St. Paul

* Clem. Rom. Ep. i. c. 47.

is to be considered as detached from that of the rest of
the apostles.

And he declares farther, that he was endued with a
power of working miracles, as what was publicly known to
those very people; speaks of frequent and great variety of
miraculous gifts as then subsisting in those very churches
to which he was writing; which he was reproving for
several irregularities; and where he had personal opposers:
he mentions these gifts incidentally, in the most easy
manner, and without effort; by way of reproof to those
who had them, for their indecent use of them; and by way
of depreciating them, in comparison of moral virtues. In
short, he speaks to these churches, of these miraculous
powers, in the manner any one would speak to another
of a thing which was as familiar, and as much known in
common to them both, as anything in the world. (Rom.
xv. 19; 1 Cor. xii. 8, 9, 10—28, &c.; xiii. 1, 2, 8, and
chap. xiv.; 2 Cor. xii. 12, 13; Gal. iii. 2, 5.) And this,
as hath been observed by several persons, is surely a very
considerable thing.

3. It is an acknowledged historical fact, that Christianity
offered itself to the world, and demanded to be received,
upon the allegation, *i. e.* as unbelievers would speak,
upon the pretence of miracles, publicly wrought to attest
the truth of it in such an age; and that it was actually
received by great numbers in that very age, and upon the
professed belief of the reality of these miracles. And
Christianity, including the dispensation of the Old Testament, seems distinguished by this from all other religions:
I mean, that this does not appear to be the case with
regard to any other: for surely it will not be supposed
to lie upon any person to prove, by positive historical
evidence, that it was not. It does in no sort appear that
Mahometanism was first received in the world upon the
foot of supposed miracles,* *i. e.* public ones; for, as
revelation is itself miraculous, all pretence to it must

* See the Koran, chap. 13, and chap. 17.

necessarily imply some pretence of miracles: and it is
a known fact, that it was immediately, at the very first,
propagated by other means.   And as particular institutions, whether in paganism or popery, said to be confirmed by miracles after those institutions had obtained,
are not to the purpose; so, were there what might be
called historical proof, that any of them were introduced
by a supposed divine command, believed to be attested
by miracles, these would not be in any wise parallel.   For
single things of this sort are easy to be accounted for,
after parties are formed, and have power in their hands;
and the leaders of them are in veneration with the multitude; and political interests are blended with religious
claims and religious. distinctions.   But before anything
of this kind, for a few persons, and those of the lowest
rank, all at once to bring over such great numbers to a new
religion, and get it to be received upon the particular
evidence of miracles—this is quite another thing.   And
I think it will be allowed by any fair adversary, that the
fact now mentioned, taking in all the circumstances of it,
is peculiar to the Christian religion.   However, the fact
itself is allowed, that Christianity obtained, *i. e.* was professed to be received in the world, upon the belief of
miracles, immediately in the age in which it is said those
miracles were wrought: or that this is what its first converts would have alleged as the reason for their embracing
it.   Now, certainly, it is not to be supposed that such
numbers of men, in the most distant parts of the world,
should forsake the religion of their country, in which they
had been educated; separate themselves from their
friends, particularly in their festival shows and solemnities,
to which the common people are so greatly addicted,
and which were of a nature to engage them much more
than anything of that sort amongst us; and embrace a
religion, which could not but expose them to many inconveniences, and indeed must have been a giving up the
world in a great degree, even from the very first, and

before the empire engaged in form against them: it cannot be supposed, that such numbers should make so great, and, to say the least, so inconvenient a change in their whole institution of life, unless they were really convinced of the truth of those miracles, upon the knowledge or belief of which they professed to make it. And it will, I suppose, readily be acknowledged, that the generality of the first converts to Christianity must have believed them; that as, by becoming Christians, they declared to the world they were satisfied of the truth of those miracles, so this declaration was to be credited. And this their testimony is the same kind of evidence for those miracles, as if they had put it in writing, and these writings had come down to us. And it is real evidence, because it is of facts which they had capacity and full opportunity to inform themselves of. It is also distinct from the direct or express historical evidence, though it is of the same kind; and it would be allowed to be distinct in all cases. For, were a fact expressly related by one or more ancient historians, and disputed in after ages; that this fact is acknowledged to have been believed by great numbers of the age in which the historian says it was done, would be allowed an additional proof of such fact, quite distinct from the express testimony of the historian. The credulity of mankind is acknowledged, and the suspicions of mankind ought to be acknowledged too; and their backwardness even to believe, and greater still to practise, what makes against their interest. And it must particularly be remembered, that education, and prejudice, and authority, were against Christianity, in the age I am speaking of. So that the immediate conversion of such numbers, is a real presumption of somewhat more than human in this matter: I say presumption, for it is not alleged as a proof alone and by itself. Nor need any one of the things mentioned in this chapter be considered as a proof by itself; and yet all of them together may be one of the strongest.

Upon the whole; as there is large historical evidence, both direct and circumstantial, of miracles wrought in attestation of Christianity, collected by those who have writ upon the subject; it lies upon unbelievers to show, why this evidence is not to be credited. This way of speaking is, I think, just, and what persons who write in defence of religion naturally fall into. Yet in a matter of such unspeakable importance, the proper question is, not whom it lies upon, according to the rules of argument, to maintain or confute objections; but whether there really are any against this evidence, sufficient in reason, to destroy the credit of it? However, unbelievers seem to take upon them the part of showing that there are.

They allege, that numberless enthusiastic people, in different ages and countries, expose themselves to the same difficulties which the primitive Christians did: and are ready to give up their lives for the most idle follies imaginable. But it is not very clear, to what purpose this objection is brought. For every one, surely, in every case, must distinguish between opinions and facts. And though testimony is no proof of enthusiastic opinions, or of any opinions at all; yet it is allowed, in all other cases, to be a proof of facts. And a person's laying down his life in attestation of facts, or of opinions, is the strongest proof of his believing them. And if the apostles and their contemporaries did believe the facts, in attestation of which they exposed themselves to sufferings and death, this their belief, or rather knowledge, must be a proof of those facts; for they were such that came under the observation of their senses. And though it is not of equal weight, yet it is of weight, that the martyrs of the next age, notwithstanding they were not eye-witnesses of those facts, as were the apostles and their contemporaries, had, however, full opportunity to inform themselves whether they were true or not, and give equal proof of their believing them to be true.

But enthusiasm, it is said, greatly weakens the evi-

dence of testimony even for facts, in matters relating to
religion: some seem to think, it totally and absolutely
destroys the evidence of testimony upon this subject.
And, indeed the powers of enthusiasm, and of diseases,
too, which operate in a like manner, are very wonderful,
in particular instances. But if great numbers of men,
not appearing in any peculiar degree weak, nor under
any peculiar suspicion of negligence, affirm that they saw
and heard such things plainly with their eyes and their
ears, and are admitted to be in earnest; such testimony
is evidence of the strongest kind we can have, for any
matter of fact. Yet possibly it may be overcome, strong
as it is, by incredibility in the things thus attested, or
by contrary testimony. And in an instance where one
thought it was so overcome, it might be just to consider,
how far such evidence could be accounted for by enthusiasm; for it seems as if no other imaginable account
were to be given of it. But till such incredibility be
shown, or contrary testimony produced, it cannot surely
be expected, that so far-fetched, so indirect and wonderful
an account of such testimony, as that of enthusiasm
must be; an account so strange, that the generality of
mankind can scarce be made to understand what is meant
by it; it cannot, I say, be expected, that such account
will be admitted of such evidence, when there is this
direct, easy, and obvious account of it, that people really
saw and heard a thing not incredible, which they affirm
sincerely, and with full assurance, they did see and hear.
Granting, then, that enthusiasm is not (strickly speaking)
an absurd, but a possible account of such testimony, it is
manifest that the very mention of it goes upon the previous
supposition that the things so attested are incredible, and
therefore need not be considered, till they are shown
to be so. Much less need it be considered, after the
contrary has been proved. And I think it has been
proved, to full satisfaction, that there is no incredibility
in a revelation, in general, or in such a one as the Christian,

in particular.   However, as religion is supposed peculiarly
liable to enthusiasm, it may just be observed, that prejudices
almost without number and without name, romance, affectation, humour, a desire to engage attention or to surprise,
the party-spirit, custom, little competitions, unaccountable
likings and dislikings; these influence men strongly in
common matters.   And as these prejudices are often scarce
known or reflected upon by the persons themselves who are
influenced by them, they are to be considered as influences
of a like kind to enthusiasm.   Yet human testimony
in common matters is naturally and justly believed notwithstanding.

It is intimated farther, in a more refined way of observation, that though it should be proved that the apostles
and first Christians could not, in some respects, be deceived themselves, and, in other respects, cannot be
thought to have intended to impose upon the world, yet
it will not follow, that their general testimony is to be
believed, though truly handed down to us; because they
might still in part, i. e. in other respects, be deceived
themselves, and in part also designedly impose upon
others; which, it is added, is a thing very credible, from
that mixture of real enthusiasm and real knavery to be
met with in the same characters.   And, I must confess,
I think the matter of fact contained in this observation
upon mankind is not to be denied; and that somewhat
very much akin to it is often supposed in Scripture as a
very common case, and most severely reproved.   But it
were to have been expected, that persons capable of
applying this observation as applied in the objection, might
also frequently have met with the like mixed character
in instances where religion was quite out of the case.
The thing plainly is, that mankind are naturally endued
with reason, or a capacity of distinguishing between truth
and falsehood; and as naturally they are endued with
veracity, or a regard to truth in what they say; but, from
many occasions, they are liable to be prejudiced, and

biassed, and deceived themselves, and capable of intending to deceive others, in every different degree; insomuch
that, as we are all liable to be deceived by prejudice,
so likewise it seems to be not an uncommon thing
for persons, who, from their regard to truth, would not
invent a lie entirely without any foundation at all, to propagate it with heightening circumstances after it is once
invented and set agoing; and others, though they would
not *propagate* a lie, yet, which is a lower degree of falsehood, will let it pass without contradiction. But, notwithstanding all this, human testimony remains still a natural
ground of assent; and this assent, a natural principle of
action.

It is objected farther, that, however it has happened, the
fact is, that mankind have, in different ages, been strangely
deluded with pretences to miracles and wonders. But it is
by no means to be admitted, that they have been oftener,
or are at all more liable to be deceived by these pretences,
than by others.

It is added, that there is a very considerable degree of
historical evidence for miracles which are, on all hands,
acknowledged to be fabulous. But suppose there were
even *the like* historical evidence for these to what there
is for those alleged in proof of Christianity; which yet is
in no wise allowed, but suppose this; the consequence
would not be, that the evidence of the latter is not to be
admitted. Nor is there a man in the world who, in common cases, would conclude thus. For what would such
a conclusion really amount to but this, that evidence
confuted by contrary evidence, or any way overbalanced,
destroys the credibility of other evidence neither confuted nor overbalanced? To argue, that because there
is, if there were, like evidence from testimony, for
miracles acknowledged false, as for those in attestation
of Christianity, therefore the evidence in the latter case
is not to be credited; this is the same as to argue, that
if two men of equally good reputation had given evidence

in different cases no way connected, and one of them had been convicted of perjury, this confuted the testimony of the other.

Upon the whole, then, the general observation, that human creatures are so liable to be deceived from enthusiasm in religion, and principles equivalent to enthusiasm in common matters, and in both from negligence; and that they are so capable of dishonestly endeavouring to deceive others; this does indeed weaken the evidence of testimony in all cases, but does not destroy it in any. And these things will appear, to different men, to weaken the evidence of testimony in different degrees; in degrees proportionable to the observations they have made, or the notions they have any way taken up, concerning the weakness, and negligence, and dishonesty of mankind; or concerning the powers of enthusiasm, and prejudices equivalent to it. But it seems to me, that people do not know what they say, who affirm these things to destroy the evidence from testimony which we have of the truth of Christianity. Nothing can destroy the evidence of testimony in any case, but a proof or probability that persons are not competent judges of the facts to which they give testimony, or that they are actually under some indirect influence in giving it, in such particular case. Till this be made out, the *natural* laws of human actions require that testimony be admitted. It can never be sufficient to overthrow direct historical evidence, indolently to say, that there are so many principles from whence men are liable to be deceived themselves and disposed to deceive others, especially in matters of religion, that one knows not what to believe. And it is surprising persons can help reflecting, that this very manner of speaking supposes, they are not satisfied that there is nothing in the evidence of which they speak thus; or that they can avoid observing, if they do make this reflection, that it is, on such a subject, a very material one.*

* See the foregoing Chapter.

And over against all these objections is to be set the importance of Christianity, as what must have engaged the attention of its first converts, so as to have rendered them less liable to be deceived from carelessness, than they would in common matters; and likewise the strong obligations to veracity, which their religion laid them under: so that the first and most obvious presumption is, that they could not be deceived themselves, nor would deceive others. And this presumption, in this degree, is peculiar to the testimony we have been considering.

In argument, assertions are nothing in themselves, and have an air of positiveness, which sometimes is not very easy: yet they are necessary, and necessary to be repeated, in order to connect a discourse, and distinctly to lay before the view of the reader, what is proposed to be proved, and what is left as proved. Now, the conclusion from the foregoing observations is, I think, beyond all doubt this: that unbelievers must be forced to admit the external evidence for Christianity, *i. e.* the proof of miracles wrought to attest it, to be of real weight and very considerable; though they cannot allow it to be sufficient to convince them of the reality of those miracles. And as they must, in all reason, admit this, so it seems to me, that, upon consideration, they would, in fact, admit it; those of them, I mean, who know anything at all of the matter: in like manner as persons, in many cases, own, they see strong evidence from testimony for the truth of things, which yet they cannot be convinced are true; cases, suppose, where there is contrary testimony, or things which they think, whether with or without reason, to be incredible. But there is no testimony contrary to that which we have been considering; and it has been fully proved, that there is no incredibility in Christianity in general, or in any part of it.

II. As to the evidence for Christianity from prophecy, I shall only make some few general observations, which are suggested by the analogy of nature; *i. e.* by the acknowledged natural rules of judging of common matters, concerning evidence of a like kind to this from prophecy.

1. The obscurity or unintelligibleness of one part of a prophecy, does not, in any degree, invalidate the proof of foresight, arising from the appearing completion of those other parts which are understood. For the case is evidently the same as if those parts, which are not understood, were lost, or not written at all, or written in an unknown tongue. Whether this observation be commonly attended to or not, it is so evident, that one can scarce bring one's self to set down an instance in common matters to exemplify it. However, suppose a writing, partly in cipher and partly in plain words at length, and that, in the part one understood, there appeared mention of several known facts; it would never come into any man's thoughts to imagine, that, if he understood the whole, perhaps he might find that those facts were not, in reality, known by the writer. Indeed, both in this example, and the thing intended to be exemplified by it, our not understanding the whole (the whole, suppose, of a sentence or a paragraph) might sometimes occasion a doubt, whether one understood the literal meaning of such a part; but this comes under another consideration.

For the same reason, though a man should be incapable, for want of learning, or opportunities of inquiry, or from not having turned his studies this way, even so much as to judge whether particular prophecies have been throughout completely fulfilled; yet he may see, in general, that they have been fulfilled to such a degree, as upon very good ground to be convinced of foresight more than human in such prophecies, and of such events being intended by them. For the same reason also, though, by means of the deficiencies in civil history, and the different accounts of historians, the most learned should not be able to make out to satisfaction, that such parts of the prophetic history have been minutely and throughout fulfilled; yet a very strong proof of foresight may arise from

L

that general completion of them which is made out; as much proof of foresight, perhaps, as the Giver of prophecy intended should ever be afforded by such parts of prophecy.

2. A long series of prophecy being applicable to such and such events, is itself a proof that it was intended of them; as the rules by which we naturally judge and determine in common cases parallel to this will show. This observation I make in answer to the common objection against the application of the prophecies, that, considering each of them distinctly by itself, it does not at all appear that they were intended of those particular events to which they are applied by Christians; and therefore it is to be supposed, that, if they meant anything, they were intended of other events unknown to us, and not of these at all.

Now, there are two kinds of writing which bear a great resemblance to prophecy, with respect to the matter before us—the mythological, and the satirical, where the satire is, to a certain degree, concealed. And a man might be assured that he understood what an author intended by a fable or parable, related without any application or moral, merely from seeing it to be easily capable of such application, and that such a moral might naturally be deduced from it: and he might be fully assured, that such persons and events were intended in a satirical writing, merely from its being applicable to them. And, agreeably to the last observation, he might be in a good measure satisfied of it, though he were not enough informed in affairs, or in the story of such persons, to understand half the satire. For his satisfaction, that he understood the meaning, the intended meaning, of these writings, would be greater or less in proportion as he saw the general turn of them to be capable of such application, and in proportion to the number of particular things capable of it. And thus, if a long series of prophecy is applicable to the present state of the church, and to the political situations of the kingdoms of the world, some thousand years after these prophecies were delivered, and a long series of prophecy delivered before the coming of Christ is applicable to him; these things are in themselves a proof, that the prophetic history was intended of him, and of those events, in proportion as the general turn of it is capable of such application, and to the number and variety of particular prophecies capable of it. And though, in all just way of consideration, the appearing completion of prophecies is to be allowed to be thus explanatory of, and to determine their meaning; yet it is to be remembered farther, that the ancient Jews applied the prophecies to a Messiah before his coming, in much the same manner as Christians do now; and that the primitive Christians interpreted the prophecies respecting the state of the church and of the world, in the last ages, in the sense which the event seems to confirm and verify. And from these things it may be made appear,

3. That the showing, even to a high probability, if that could be, that the prophets thought of some other events in such and such predictions, and not those at all which Christians allege to be completions of those predictions; or that such and such prophecies are capable of being applied to other events than those to which Christians apply them—that this would not confute or destroy the force of the argument from prophecy, even with regard to those, very instances. For, observe how this matter really is. If one knew such a person to be the sole author of such a book, and was certainly assured or satisfied to any degree, that one knew the whole of what he intended in it, one should be assured or satisfied to such degree, that one knew the whole meaning of that book; for the meaning of a book is nothing but the meaning of the author: but if one knew a person to have compiled a book out of memoirs, which he received from another, of vastly superior knowledge in the subject of it, especially if it were a book full of great intricacies and diffi-

culties, it would in no wise follow, that one knew the whole meaning of the book, from knowing the whole meaning of the compiler; for the original memoirs, *i. e.* the author of them, might have, and there would be no degree of presumption, in many cases, against supposing him to have, some farther meaning than the compiler saw. To say, then, that the Scriptures and the things contained in them can have no other or farther meaning than those persons thought or had who first recited or wrote them, is evidently saying, that those persons were the original, proper, and sole authors of those books, *i. e.* that they are not inspired; which is absurd, whilst the authority of these books is under examination, *i. e.* till you have determined they are of no divine authority at all. Till this be determined, it must in all reason be supposed, not indeed that they have, for this is taking for granted that they are inspired, but that they may have some farther meaning than what the compilers saw or understood. And, upon this supposition, it is supposable also that this farther meaning may be fulfilled. Now, events corresponding to prophecies, interpreted in a different meaning from that in which the prophets are supposed to have understood them; this affords, in a manner, the same proof that this different sense was originally intended, as it would have afforded, if the prophets had not understood their predictions in the sense it is supposed they did; because there is no presumption of their sense of them being the whole sense of them. And it has been already shown, that the apparent completions of prophecy must be allowed to be explanatory of its meaning. So that the question is, whether a series of prophecy has been fulfilled in a natural or proper, *i. e.* in any real sense of the words of it. For such completion is equally a proof of foresight more than human, whether the prophets are or are not supposed to have understood it in a different sense. I say, supposed; for though I think it clear, that the prophets did not understand the full meaning of their predictions, it is another question, how far they thought they did, and in what sense they understood them.

Hence may be seen, to how little purpose those persons busy themselves, who endeavour to prove that the prophetic history is applicable to events of the age in which it was written, or of ages before it. Indeed, to have proved this before there was any appearance of a farther completion of it, might have answered some purpose; for it might have prevented the expectation of any such farther completion. Thus, could Porphyry have shown that some principal parts of the book of Daniel, for instance, the seventh verse of the seventh chapter, which the Christians interpreted of the latter ages, was applicable to events which happened before or about the age of Antiochus Epiphanes; this might have prevented them from expecting any farther completion of it. And unless there was then, as I think there must have been, external evidence concerning that book, more than is come down to us, such a discovery might have been a stumbling-block in the way of Christianity itself; considering the authority which our Saviour has given to the book of Daniel, and how much the general scheme of Christianity presupposes the truth of it. But even this discovery, had there been any such,* would be of very little weight with reasonable men now, if this passage, thus applicable to events before the age of Porphyry, appears to be applicable also to events which succeeded the dissolution of the Roman empire. I mention this, not at all as intending to insinuate, that the division of this empire into ten parts (for it plainly was divided into about that number) were, alone and by itself, of any

---

* It appears that Porphyry did nothing worth mentioning in this way. For Jerom on the place says: *Duas posteriores bestias—in uno Macedonum regno ponit.* And as to the ten kings: *Decem reges enumerat, qui fuerunt sævissimi: ipsosque reges non unius ponit regni, verbi gratia Macedoniæ, Syriæ, Asiæ, et Ægypti; sed de diversis regnis unum efficit regum ordinem.* And in this way of interpretation, anything may be made of anything.

moment in verifying the prophetic history; but only as an example of the thing I am speaking of. And thus, upon the whole, the matter of inquiry evidently must be, as above put, whether the prophecies are applicable to Christ, and to the present state of the world and of the church—applicable in such a degree as to imply foresight; not whether they are capable of any other application; though I know no pretence for saying the general turn of them is capable of any other.

These observations are I think just, and the evidence referred to in them real; though there may be people who will not accept of such imperfect information from Scripture. Some, too, have not integrity and regard enough to truth, to attend to evidence, which keeps the mind in doubt, perhaps perplexity, and which is much of a different sort from what they expected. And it plainly requires a degree of modesty and fairness, beyond what every one has, for a man to say, not to the world, but to himself, that there is a real appearance of somewhat of great weight in this matter, though he is not able thoroughly to satisfy himself about it; but it shall have its influence upon him, in proportion to its appearing reality and weight. It is much more easy, and more falls in with the negligence, presumption, and wilfulness of the generality, to determine at once, with a decisive air, there is nothing in it. The prejudices arising from that absolute contempt and scorn with which this evidence is treated in the world, I do not mention. For what indeed can be said to persons who are weak enough in their understandings to think this any presumption against it; or, if they do not, are yet weak enough in their temper to be influenced by such prejudices, upon such a subject?

I shall now, *secondly*, endeavour to give some account of the general argument for the truth of Christianity, consisting both of the direct and circumstantial evidence, considered as making up one argument. Indeed, to state and examine this argument fully, would be a work much beyond the compass of this whole treatise; nor is so much as a proper abridgment of it to be expected here.   Yet the present subject requires to have some brief account of it given; for it is the kind of evidence upon which most questions of difficulty, in common practice, are determined; evidence arising from various coincidences, which support and confirm each other, and in this manner prove, with more or less certainty, the point under consideration. And I choose to do it also, *first*, Because it seems to be of the greatest importance, and not duly attended to by every one, that the proof of revelation is, not some direct and express things only, but a great variety of circumstantial things also; and that though each of these direct and circumstantial things is indeed to be considered separately, yet they are afterwards to be joined together; for that the proper force of the evidence consists in the result of those several things, considered in their respects to each other, and united into one view: and, in the *next* place, Because it seems to me, that the matters of fact here set down, which are acknowledged by unbelievers, must be acknowledged by them also to contain together a degree of evidence of great weight, if they could be brought to lay these several things before themselves distinctly, and then with attention consider them together, instead of that cursory thought of them to which we are familiarized; for being familiarized to the cursory thought of things, as really hinders the weight of them from being seen, as from having its due influence upon practice.

The thing asserted, and the truth of which is to be inquired into, is this: That, over and above our reason and affections, which God has given us for the information of our judgment and the conduct of our lives, he has also, by external revelation, given us an account of himself and his moral government over the world, implying a future state of rewards and punishments; *i. e.* hath revealed the system of natural religion; for natural religion may

be externally* revealed by God, as the ignorant may be
taught it by mankind, their fellow-creatures;—that God, I
say, has given us the evidence of revelation, as well as the
evidence of reason, to ascertain this moral system; together
with an account of a particular dispensation of Providence
which reason could no way have discovered, and a particular institution of religion founded on it, for the recovery
of mankind out of their present wretched condition, and
raising them to the perfection and final happiness of their
nature.

This revelation, whether real or supposed, may be considered as wholly historical. For prophecy is nothing but
the history of events before they come to pass: doctrines
also are matters of fact; and precepts come under the same
notion. And the general design of Scripture, which contains in it this revelation, thus considered as historical, may
be said to be, to give us an account of the world, in this
one single view, as God's world; by which it appears
essentially distinguished from all other books, so far as I
have found, except such as are copied from it. It begins
with an account of God's creation of the world, in order to
ascertain and distinguish from all others, who is the object
of our worship, by what he has done; in order to ascertain
who he is, concerning whose providence, commands, promises, and threatenings, this sacred book all along treats;
the Maker and Proprietor of the world, he whose creatures
we are, the God of nature: in order likewise to distinguish
him from the idols of the nations, which are either imaginary beings, *i. e.* no beings at all; or else part of that
creation, the historical relation of which is here given.
And St. John, not improbably with an eye to this Mosaic
account of the creation, begins his Gospel with an account
of our Saviour's pre-existence, and that " all things were
made by him, and without him was not anything made that
was made," John i. 3; agreeably to the doctrine of St. Paul,

* Pages 122, 123.

that " God created all things by Jesus. Christ," Eph. iii. 9.
This being premised, the Scripture, taken together, seems
to profess to contain a kind of an abridgment of the history of the world, in the view just now mentioned; that is,
a general account of the condition of religion and its professors, during the continuance of that apostacy from God,
and state of wickedness, which it everywhere supposes the
world to lie in. And this account of the state of religion
carries with it some brief account of the political state of
things, as religion is affected by it. Revelation, indeed,
considers the common affairs of this world, and what is
going on in it, as a mere scene of distraction, and cannot be
supposed to concern itself with foretelling, at what time
Rome, or Babylon, or Greece, or any particular place,
should be the most conspicuous seat of that tyranny and
dissoluteness which all places equally aspire to be; cannot,
I say, be supposed to give any account of this wild scene
for its own sake. But it seems to contain some very
general account of the chief governments of the world, as
the general state of religion has been, is, or shall be affected
by them, from the first transgression, and during the whole
interval of the world's continuing in its present state, to a
certain future period, spoken of both in the Old and New
Testament, very distinctly, and in great variety of expression: " The times of the restitution of all things," Acts iii.
21; when " the mystery of God shall be finished, as he
hath declared to his servants the prophets," Rev. x. 7;
when " the God of heaven shall set up a kingdom which
shall never be destroyed; and the kingdom shall not be left
to other people," Dan. ii. 44, as it is represented to be
during this apostacy; but "judgment shall be given to the
saints," Dan. vii. 22, and " they shall reign," Rev. xxii. 5;
" and the kingdom, and dominion, and the greatness of
the kingdom under the whole heaven, shall be given to the
people of the saints of the Most High," Dan. vii. 27.

Upon this general view of the Scripture I would remark,
how great a length of time the whole relation takes up,

near six thousand years of which are past; and how great
a variety of things it treats of—the natural and moral
system or history of the world, including the time when
it was formed, all contained in the very first book, and
evidently written in a rude and unlearned age; and in subsequent books, the various common and prophetic history,
and the particular dispensation of Christianity.   Now all
this together gives the largest scope for criticism, and for
confutation of what is capable of being confuted either
from reason, or from common history, or from any inconsistence in its several parts.   And it is a thing which
deserves, I think, to be mentioned, that whereas some
imagine the supposed doubtfulness of the evidence for
revelation implies a positive argument that it is not true;
it appears, on the contrary, to imply a positive argument
that it is true.   For, could any common relation, of such
antiquity, extent, and variety, (for in these things the stress
of what I am now observing lies,) be proposed to the
examination of the world; that it could not, in an age of
knowledge and liberty, be confuted, or shown to have
nothing in it, to the satisfaction of reasonable men; this
would be thought a strong presumptive proof of its truth.
And indeed it must be a proof of it, just in proportion to
the probability that, if it were false, it might be shown to
be so; and this, I think, is scarce pretended to be shown,
but upon principles and in ways of arguing which have
been clearly obviated.*   Nor does it at all appear, that
any set of men who believe natural religion are of the
opinion that Christianity has been thus confuted.   But to
proceed:—

Together with the moral system of the world, the Old
Testament contains a chronological account of the beginning of it, and from thence an unbroken genealogy of
mankind for many ages before common history begins;
and carried on as much farther, as to make up a continued

* Chap. 2, 3, &c.

thread of history of the length of between three and four
thousand years. It contains an account of God's making
a covenant with a particular nation, that they should be
his people, and he would be their God, in a peculiar sense;
of his often interposing miraculously in their affairs; giving
them the promise, and, long after, the possession, of a
particular country; assuring them of the greatest national
prosperity in it, if they would worship him, in opposition
to the idols which the rest of the world worshipped, and
obey his commands; and threatening them with unex-
ampled punishments, if they disobeyed him, and fell into
the general idolatry; insomuch, that this one nation should
continue to be the observation and the wonder of all the
world. It declares particularly, that " God would scatter
them among all people, from one end of the earth unto the
other;" but that, " when they should return unto the Lord
their God, he would have compassion upon them, and
gather them from all the nations whither he had scattered
them;" that " Israel should be saved in the Lord, with an
everlasting salvation, and not be ashamed or confounded,
world without end." And as some of these promises are
conditional, others are as absolute as anything can be
expressed: that the time should come when " the people
should be all righteous, and inherit the land for ever:" that
" though God would make a full end of all nations whither
he had scattered them, yet would he not make a full end of
them:" that " he would bring again the captivity of his
people Israel, and plant them upon their land, and they
should be no more pulled up out of their land:" that " the
seed of Israel should not cease from being a nation for ever."
Deut. xxviii. 64, xxx. 2, 3; Isa. xlv. 17, lx. 21; Jer.
xxx. 11, xlvi. 28; Amos ix. 15; Jer. xxxi. 36. It
foretells, that God would raise them up a particular person,
in whom all his promises should finally be fulfilled—the
Messiah, who should be, in a high and eminent sense, their
anointed Prince and Saviour. This was foretold in such a
manner as raised a general expectation of such a person in

the nation, as appears from the New Testament, and is an acknowledged fact; an expectation of his coming at such a particular time, before any one appeared claiming to be that person, and when there was no ground for such an expectation but from the prophecies; which expectation, therefore, must in all reason be presumed to be explanatory of those prophecies, if there were any doubt about their meaning. It seems moreover to foretell, that this person should be rejected by that nation to whom he had been so long promised, and though he was so much desired by them. Isa. viii. 14, 15, xlix. 5, and chap. liii.; Mal. i. 10, 11, and chap. iii. And it expressly foretells that he should be the Saviour of the Gentiles; and even that the completion of the scheme contained in this book, and then begun and in its progress, should be somewhat so great, that, in comparison with it, the restoration of the Jews alone would be but of small account. " It is a light thing that thou shouldst be my servant to raise up the tribes of Jacob, and to restore the preserved of Israel: I will also give thee for a light to the Gentiles, that thou mayst be for salvation unto the end of the earth." And, " In the last days the mountain of the Lord's house shall be established in the top of the mountains, and shall be exalted above the hills; and all nations shall flow into it—for out of Zion shall go forth the law, and the word of the Lord from Jerusalem. And he shall judge among the nations—and the Lord alone shall be exalted in that day, and the idols he shall utterly abolish." Isa. xlix. 6, ch. ii. xi. and lvi. 7; Mal. i. 11.* The Scripture further contains an account, that, at the time the Messiah was expected, a person rose up, in this nation, claiming to be that Messiah, to be the person whom all the prophecies referred to, and in whom they should centre: that he spent some years in a continued

---

* To which must be added the other prophecies of the like kind, several in the New Testament, and very many in the Old, which describe what shall be the completion of the revealed plan of Providence.

course of miraculous works, and endued his immediate
disciples and followers with a power of doing the same, as
a proof of the truth of that religion which he commissioned
them to publish: that, invested with this authority and
power, they made numerous converts in the remotest
countries, and settled and established his religion in the
world; to the end of which, the Scripture professes to give
a prophetic account of the state of this religion amongst
mankind.

Let us now suppose a person, utterly ignorant of history,
to have all this related to him out of the Scripture. Or,
suppose such a one, having the Scripture put into his
hands, to remark these things in it, not knowing but that
the whole, even its civil history, as well as the other parts
of it, might be, from beginning to end, an entire invention;
and to ask, what truth was in it, and whether the revelation
here related was real or a fiction? And, instead of a direct
answer, suppose him, all at once, to be told the following
confessed facts; and then to unite them into one view.

Let him first be told, in how great a degree the profession and establishment of natural religion, the belief
that there is one God to be worshipped, that virtue is his
law, and that mankind shall be rewarded and punished
hereafter, as they obey and disobey it here; in how very
great a degree, I say, the profession and establishment of
this moral system in the world is owing to the revelation,
whether real or supposed, contained in this book; the
establishment of this moral system, even in those countries which do not acknowledge the proper authority of
the Scripture.* Let him be told also, what number of
nations do acknowledge its proper authority. Let him
then take in the consideration, of what importance religion is to mankind. And upon these things he might,
I think, truly observe, that this supposed revelation's
obtaining and being received in the world, with all the

* Page 190.

circumstances and effects of it, considered together as
one event, is the most conspicuous and important event in
the history of mankind; that a book of this nature, and
thus promulged and recommended to our consideration,
demands, as if by a voice from heaven, to have its claims
most seriously examined into; and that, before such examination, to treat it with any kind of scoffing and ridicule, is an offence against natural piety. But it is to be
remembered, that how much soever the establishment of
natural religion in the world is owing to the Scripture revelation, this does not destroy the proof of religion from
reason; any more than the proof of *Euclid's Elements* is
destroyed by a man's knowing or thinking, that he should
never have seen the truth of the several propositions contained in it, nor had those propositions come into his
thoughts, but for that mathematician.

Let such a person as we are speaking of be, in the
next place, informed of the acknowledged antiquity of the
first parts of this book; and that its chronology, its account of the time when the earth, and the several parts
of it, were first peopled with human creatures, is no way
contradicted, but is really confirmed, by the natural and
civil history of the world, collected from common historians, from the state of the earth, and from the late
invention of arts and sciences: and, as the Scripture
contains an unbroken thread of common and civil history,
from the creation to the captivity, for between three and
four thousand years; let the person we are speaking of
be told, in the next place, that this general history, as it
is not contradicted, but is confirmed by profane history,
as much as there would be reason to expect upon supposition of its truth; so there is nothing in the whole
history itself, to give any reasonable ground of suspicion
of its not being, in the general, a faithful and literally
true genealogy of men, and series of things. I speak
here only of the common Scripture history, or of the
course of ordinary events related in it, as distinguished

from miracles, and from the prophetic history. In all the
Scripture narrations of this kind, following events arise
out of foregoing ones, as in all other histories. There
appears nothing related as done in any age, not conformable to the manners of that age; nothing in the account
of a succeeding age, which one would say could not be
true, or was improbable, from the account of things in the
preceding one. There is nothing in the characters which
would raise a thought of their being feigned; but all the
internal marks imaginable of their being real. It is to be
added also, that mere genealogies, bare narratives of the
number of years which persons called by such and such
names lived, do not carry the face of fiction—perhaps do
carry some presumption of veracity; and all unadorned
narratives, which have nothing to surprise, may be thought
to carry somewhat of the like presumption too. And the
domestic and the political history is plainly credible.
There may be incidents in Scripture which, taken alone
in the naked way they are told, may appear strange, especially to persons of other manners, temper, education;
but there are also incidents of undoubted truth, in many
or most persons' lives, which, in the same circumstances,
would appear to the full as strange. There may be
mistakes of transcribers, there may be other real or seeming mistakes, not easy to be particularly accounted for;
but there are certainly no more things of this kind in the
Scripture, than what were to have been expected in books
of such antiquity; and nothing, in any wise, sufficient to
discredit the general narrative. Now, that a history,
claiming to commence from the creation, and extending
in one continued series through so great a length of
time and variety of events, should have such appearances
of reality and truth in its whole contexture, is surely a
very remarkable circumstance in its favour. And as all
this is applicable to the common history of the New Testament, so there is a farther credibility, and a very high
one, given to it by profane authors; many of these writing

of the same times, and confirming the truth of customs and
events, which are incidentally as well as more purposely
mentioned in it. And this credibility of the common
Scripture history gives some credibility to its miraculous
history; especially as this is interwoven with the common,
so as that they imply each other, and both together make
up one relation.

Let it then be more particularly observed to this person,
that it is an acknowledged matter of fact, which is indeed
implied in the foregoing observation, that there was such
a nation as the Jews, of the greatest antiquity, whose
government and general polity was founded on the law
here related to be given them. by Moses as from heaven:
that natural religion, though with rites additional, yet no
way contrary to it, was their established religion, which
cannot be said of the Gentile world; and that their very
being, as a nation, depended upon their acknowledgment
of one God, the God of the universe. For suppose, in
their captivity in Babylon, they had gone over to the
religion of their conquerors, there would have remained no
bond of union to keep them a distinct people. And whilst
they were under their own kings, in their own country, a
total apostacy from God would have been the dissolution
of their whole government. They in such a sense nation-
ally acknowledged and worshipped the Maker of heaven
and earth, when the rest of the world were sunk in idolatry,
as rendered them, in fact, the peculiar people of God. And
this so remarkable an establishment and preservation of
natural religion amongst them, seems to add some peculiar
credibility to the historical evidence for the miracles of
Moses and the prophets; because these miracles are a full
satisfactory account of this event, which plainly wants to
be accounted for, and cannot otherwise.

Let this person, supposed wholly ignorant of history, be
acquainted farther, that one claiming to be the Messiah, of
Jewish extraction, rose up at the time when this nation,
from the prophecies above mentioned, expected the Messiah;

that he was rejected, as it seemed to have been foretold he should, by the body of the people, under the direction of their rulers: that in the course of a very few years he was believed on, and acknowledged, as the promised Messiah, by great numbers among the Gentiles, agreeably to the prophecies of Scripture, yet not upon the evidence of prophecy, but of miracles,* of which miracles we also have strong historical evidence; (by which I mean here no more than must be acknowledged by unbelievers; for let pious frauds and follies be admitted to weaken, it is absurd to say they destroy, our evidence of miracles wrought in proof of Christianity :)† that this religion approving itself to the reason of mankind, and carrying its own evidence with it, so far as reason is a judge of its system, and being no way contrary to reason in those parts of it which require to be believed upon the mere authority of its Author; that this religion, I say, gradually spread and supported itself, for some hundred years, not only without any assistance from temporal power, but under constant discouragements, and often the bitterest persecutions from it, and then became the religion of the world: that, in the mean time, the Jewish nation and government were destroyed in a very remarkable manner, and the people carried away captive and dispersed through the most distant countries; in which state of dispersion they have remained fifteen hundred years; and that they remain a numerous people, united amongst themselves, and distinguished from the rest of the world, as they were in the days of Moses, by the profession of his law; and everywhere looked upon in a manner which one scarce knows how distinctly to express, but in the words of the prophetic account of it, given so many ages before it came to pass: " Thou shalt become an astonishment, a proverb, and a by-word, among all nations whither the Lord shall lead thee," Deut. xxviii. 37.

* Page 209, &c.   † Page 216, &c.

The appearance of a standing miracle, in the Jews remaining a distinct people in their dispersion, and the confirmation which this event appears to give to the truth of revelation, may be thought to be answered by their religion forbidding them intermarriages with those of any other, and prescribing them a great many peculiarities in their food, by which they are debarred from the means of incorporating with the people in whose countries they live. This is not, I think, a satisfactory account of that which it pretends to account for. But what does it pretend to account for? The correspondence between this event and the prophecies; or the coincidence of both with a long dispensation of Providence, of a peculiar nature, towards that people formerly? No. It is only the event itself which is offered to be thus accounted for; which single event taken alone, abstracted from all such correspondence and coincidence, perhaps would not have appeared miraculous; but that correspondence and coincidence may be so, though the event itself be supposed not. Thus the concurrence of our Saviour being born at Bethlehem, with a long foregoing series of prophecy and other coincidences, is doubtless miraculous, the series of prophecy, and other coincidences, and the event, being admitted; though the event itself, his birth at that place, appears to have been brought about in a natural way; of which, however, no one can be certain.

And as several of these events seem, in some degree, expressly to have verified the prophetic history already; so likewise they may be considered farther, as having a peculiar aspect towards the full completion of it—as affording some presumption that the whole of it shall, one time or other, be fulfilled. Thus, that the Jews have been so wonderfully preserved in their long and wide dispersion; which is indeed the direct fulfilling of some prophecies, but is now mentioned only as looking forward to somewhat yet to come: that natural religion came forth from Judea, and spread in the degree it has done

over the world, before lost in idolatry; which, together
with some other things, have distinguished that very
place, in like manner as the people of it are distinguished:
that this great change of religion over the earth was
brought about under the profession and acknowledgment
that Jesus was the promised Messiah:—things of this kind
naturally turn the thoughts of serious men towards the
full completion of the prophetic history concerning the
final restoration of that people; concerning the establishment of the everlasting kingdom among them, the kingdom
of the Messiah: and the future state of the world under
this sacred government. Such circumstances and events
compared with these prophecies, though no completions of
them, yet would not, I think, be spoken of as nothing in
the argument, by a person upon his first being informed of
them. They fall in with the prophetic history of things
still future, give it some additional credibility, have the
appearance of being somewhat in order to the full completion of it.

Indeed, it requires a good degree of knowledge, and great
calmness and consideration, to be able to judge thoroughly
of the evidence for the truth of Christianity, from that part
of the prophetic history which relates to the situation of the
kingdoms of the world, and to the state of the church from
the establishment of Christianity to the present time. But
it appears, from a general view of it, to be very material.
And those persons who have thoroughly examined it—and
some of them were men of the coolest tempers, greatest
capacities, and least liable to imputations of prejudice—insist
upon it as determinately conclusive.

Suppose now a person quite ignorant of history, first
to recollect the passages above mentioned out of Scripture, without knowing but that the whole was a late fiction; then to be informed of the correspondent facts now
mentioned, and to unite them all into one view; that the
profession and establishment of natural religion in the
world is greatly owing, in different ways, to this book,

and the supposed revelation which it contains; that it is acknowledged to be of the earliest antiquity; that its chronology and common history are entirely credible; that this ancient nation, the Jews, of whom it chiefly treats, appear to have been, in fact, the people of God, in a distinguished sense; that, as there was a national expectation amongst them, raised from the prophecies, of a Messiah to appear at such a time, so one at this time appeared, claiming to be that Messiah; that he was rejected by this nation, but received by the Gentiles, not upon the evidence of prophecy, but of miracles; that the religion he taught supported itself under the greatest difficulties, gained ground, and at length became the religion of the world; that in the mean time the Jewish polity was utterly destroyed, and the nation dispersed over the face of the earth; that, notwithstanding this, they have remained a distinct numerous people for so many centuries, even to this day; which not only appears to be the express completion of several prophecies concerning them, but also renders it, as one may speak, a visible and easy possibility that the promises made to them as a nation may yet be fulfilled. And to these acknowledged truths, let the person we have been supposing add, as I think he ought, whether every one will allow it or not, the obvious appearances which there are of the state of the world, in other respects besides what relates to the Jews, and of the Christian church, having so long answered, and still answering to the prophetic history. Suppose, I say, these facts set over against the things before mentioned out of the Scripture, and seriously compared with them; the joint view of both together must, I think, appear of very great weight to a considerate reasonable person; of much greater, indeed, upon having been first laid before him, than is easy for us, who are so familiarized to them, to conceive, without some particular attention for that purpose.

All these things, and the several particulars contained

under them, require to be distinctly and most thoroughly
examined into—that the weight of each may be judged of
upon such examination, and such conclusion drawn as results
from their united force.   But this has not been attempted
here.   I have gone no farther than to show, that the general
imperfect view of them now given, the confessed historical
evidence for miracles, and the many obvious appearing
completions of prophecy, together with the collateral
things* here mentioned, and there are several others of the
like sort; that all this together, which, being fact, must be
acknowledged by unbelievers, amounts to real evidence of
somewhat more than human in this matter; evidence much
more important, than careless men, who have been accustomed only to transient and partial views of it, can imagine;
and indeed abundantly sufficient to act upon.   And these
things, I apprehend, must be acknowledged by unbelievers.
For though they may say, that the historical evidence of
miracles, wrought in attestation of Christianity, is not
sufficient to convince them that such miracles were really
wrought, they cannot deny that there is such historical
evidence, it being a known matter of fact that there is.
They may say, the conformity between the prophecies
and events is by accident; but there are many instances
in which such conformity itself cannot be denied.   They
may say, with regard to such kind of collateral things as
those above mentioned, that any odd accidental events,
without meaning, will have a meaning found in them by
fanciful people; and that such as are fanciful in any one
certain way, will make out a thousand coincidences, which
seem to favour their peculiar follies.   Men, I say, may talk
thus; but no one who is serious can possibly think these
things to be nothing, if he considers the importance of
collateral things, and even of lesser circumstances, in the

---

* All the particular things mentioned in this chapter, not reducible
to the head of certain miracles, or determinate completions of prophecy. See pages 205, 206.

evidence of probability, as distinguished in nature from the evidence of demonstration. In many cases, indeed, it seems to require the truest judgment, to determine with exactness the weight of circumstantial evidence; but it is very often altogether as convincing, as that which is the most express and direct.

This general view of the evidence for Christianity, considered as making one argument, may also serve to recommend to serious persons to set down everything, which they think may be of real weight at all in proof of it, and particularly the many seeming completions of prophecy; and they will find, that, judging by the natural rules by which we judge of probable evidence in common matters, they amount to a much higher degree of proof, upon such a joint review, than could be supposed upon considering them separately, at different times, how strong soever the proof might before appear to them upon such separate views of it. For probable proofs, by being added, not only increase the evidence, but multiply it. Nor should I dissuade any one from setting down what he thought made for the contrary side. But then it is to be remembered, not in order to influence his judgment, but his practice, that a mistake on one side may be, in its consequences, much more dangerous than a mistake on the other. And what course is most safe, and what most dangerous, is a consideration thought very material, when we deliberate, not concerning events, but concerning conduct in our temporal affairs. To be influenced by this consideration in our judgment, to believe or disbelieve upon it, is indeed as much prejudice as anything whatever. And, like other prejudices, it operates contrary ways in different men. For some are inclined to believe what they hope, and others what they fear. And it is manifest unreasonableness, to apply to men's passions in order to gain their assent. But, in deliberations concerning conduct, there is nothing which reason more requires to be taken in the account, than the importance of it. For, suppose it doubtful what would be the consequence of acting in this, or in a contrary manner; still, that taking one side could be attended with little or no bad consequence, and taking the other might be attended with the greatest, must appear, to unprejudiced reason, of the highest moment towards determining how we are to act. But the truth of our religion, like the truth of common matters, is to be judged of by all the evidence taken together. And unless the whole series of things which may be alleged in this argument, and every particular thing in it, can reasonably be supposed to have been by accident (for here the stress of the argument for Christianity lies,) then is the truth of it proved; in like manner as if, in any common case, numerous events acknowledged were to be alleged in proof of any other event disputed: the truth of the disputed event would be proved, not only if any one of the acknowledged ones did of itself clearly imply it, but, though no one of them singly did so, if the whole of the acknowledged events, taken together, could not in reason be supposed to have happened unless the disputed one were true.

It is obvious, how much advantage the nature of this evidence gives to those persons who attack Christianity, especially in conversation. For it is easy to show, in a short and lively manner, that such and such things are liable to objection, that this and another thing is of little weight in itself; but impossible to show in like manner, the united force of the whole argument in one view.

However, *lastly*, As it has been made appear that there is no presumption against a revelation as miraculous; that the general scheme of Christianity, and the principal parts of it, are conformable to the experienced constitution of things, and the whole perfectly credible; so the account now given of the positive evidence for it shows, that this evidence is such as, from the nature of it, cannot be destroyed, though it should be lessened.

CHAPTER VIII.

*Of the Objections which may be made against arguing
from the Analogy of Nature to Religion.*

If every one would consider, with such attention as they
are bound, even in point of morality, to consider, what they
judge* and give characters of, the occasion of this chapter
would be, in some good measure at least, superseded.   But
since this is not to be expected; for some, we find, do not
concern themselves to understand even what they write
against; since this treatise, in common with most others,
lies open to objections which may appear very material to
thoughtful men at first sight; and, besides that, seems
peculiarly liable to the objections of such as can judge
without thinking, and of such as can censure without judging; it may not be amiss to set down the chief of these
objections which occur to me, and consider them to their
hands.   And they are such as these :—

" That it is a poor thing to solve difficulties in revelation
by saying, that there are the same in natural religion;
when what is wanting is to clear both of them of these their
common, as well as other their respective difficulties : but
that it is a strange way indeed of convincing men of the
obligations of religion, to show them that they have as
little reason for their worldly pursuits; and a strange way
of vindicating the justice and goodness of the Author of
nature, and of removing the objections against both, to
which the system of religion lies open, to show that the
like objections lie against natural providence; a way of
answering objections against religion, without so much
as pretending to make out, that the system of it, or the
particular things in it objected against, are reasonable :
especially, perhaps some may be inattentive enough to add,
must this be thought strange, when it is confessed that
analogy is no answer to such objections; that when this

sort of reasoning is carried to the utmost length it can be imagined capable of, it will yet leave the mind in a very unsatisfied state; and that it must be unaccountable ignorance of mankind to imagine, they will be prevailed with to forego their present interests and pleasures, from regard to religion, upon doubtful evidence."

Now, as plausible as this way of talking may appear, that appearance will be found in a great measure owing to half views, which show but part of an object, yet show that indistinctly; and to undeterminate language. By these means, weak men are often deceived by others, and ludicrous men by themselves. And even those who are serious and considerate cannot always readily disentangle, and at once clearly see through, the perplexities in which subjects themselves are involved; and which are heightened by the deficiencies and the abuse of words. To this latter sort of persons, the following reply to each part of this objection, severally, may be of some assistance; as it may also tend a little to stop and silence others.

First, The thing wanted, *i. e.* what men require, is to have all difficulties cleared. And this is, or at least, for anything we know to the contrary, it may be the same, as requiring to comprehend the divine nature, and the whole plan of Providence from everlasting to everlasting. But it hath always been allowed to argue from what is acknowledged to what is disputed. And it is in no other sense a poor thing to argue from natural religion to revealed, in the manner found fault with, than it is to argue in numberless other ways of probable deduction and inference, in matters of conduct, which we are continually reduced to the necessity of doing. Indeed the epithet *poor* may be applied, I fear, as properly to great part, or the whole, of human life, as it is to the things mentioned in the objection. Is it not a poor thing for a physician to have so little knowledge in the cure of diseases, as even the most eminent have?—to act upon conjecture and guess, where the life of man is concerned? Undoubtedly it is; but not in comparison of having no skill at all in that useful art, and being obliged to act wholly in the dark.

Further: Since it is as unreasonable as it is common to urge objections against revelation, which are of equal weight against natural religion; and those who do this, if they are not confuted themselves, deal unfairly with others, in making it seem that they are arguing only against revelation, or particular doctrines of it, when in reality they are arguing against moral providence; it is a thing of consequence to show, that such objections are as much levelled against natural religion as against revealed. And objections which are equally applicable to both, are, properly speaking, answered, by its being shown that they are so, provided the former be admitted to be true. And without taking in the consideration how distinctly this is admitted, it is plainly very material to observe, that as the things objected against in natural religion, are of the same kind with what is certain matter of experience in the course of providence, and in the information which God affords us concerning our temporal interest under his government; so the objections against the system of Christianity, and the evidence of it, are of the very same kind with those which are made against the system and evidence of natural religion. However, the reader upon review may see, that most of the analogies insisted upon, even in the latter part of this Treatise, do not necessarily require to have more taken for granted than is in the former—that there is an Author of nature, or natural Governor of the world; and Christianity is vindicated, not from its analogy to natural religion, but chiefly from its analogy to the experienced constitution of nature.

[*Secondly*, Religion is a practical thing, and consists in such a determinate course of life, as being what, there is reason to think, is commanded by the Author of nature, and will, upon the whole, be our happiness under his government. Now, if men can be convinced that they have the like reason to believe this, as to believe that taking care of their temporal affairs will be to their advantage; such conviction cannot but be an argument to them for the practice of religion.   And if there be really any reason for believing one of these, and endeavouring to preserve life, and secure ourselves the necessaries and conveniences of it; then there is reason also for believing the other, and endeavouring to secure the interest it proposes to us.   And if the interest which religion proposes to us be infinitely greater than our whole temporal interest, then there must be proportionably greater reason for endeavouring to secure one than the other; since, by the supposition, the probability of our securing one, is equal to the probability of our securing the other.   This seems plainly unanswerable; and has a tendency to influence fair minds, who consider what our condition really is, or upon what evidence we are naturally appointed to act; and who are disposed to acquiesce in the terms upon which we live, and attend to and follow that practical instruction, whatever it be, which is afforded us.

But the chief and proper force of the argument referred to in the objection, lies in another place: for it is said, that the proof of religion is involved in such inextricable difficulties, as to render it doubtful; and that it cannot be supposed, that, if it were true, it would be left upon doubtful evidence.   Here, then, over and above the force of each particular difficulty or objection, these difficulties and objections taken together, are turned into a positive argument against the truth of religion; which argument would stand thus:—If religion were true, it would not be left doubtful and open to objections to the degree in which it is; therefore, that it is thus left, not only renders the evidence of it weak, and lessens its force, in proportion to the weight of such objections; but also shows it to be false, or is a general presumption of its being so.   Now the observation, that, from the natural constitution and course of things, we must in our temporal concerns almost continually, and in matters of great consequence, act upon evidence of a like

kind and degree to the evidence of religion, is an answer
to this argument; because it shows, that it is according
to the conduct and character of the Author of nature, to
appoint we should act upon evidence like to that which
this argument presumes he cannot be supposed to appoint
we should act upon: it is an instance, a general one made
up of numerous particular ones, of somewhat in his dealing
with us, similar to what is said to be incredible. And as
the force of this answer lies merely in the parallel which
there is between the evidence for religion and for our
temporal conduct, the answer is equally just and conclusive,
whether the parallel be made out by showing the evidence
of the former to be higher, or the evidence of the latter to
be lower.

Thirdly, The design of this Treatise is not to vindicate
the character of God, but to show the obligations of
men: it is not to justify his providence, but to show what
belongs to us to do. These are two subjects, and ought
not to be confounded. And though they may at length
run up into each other, yet observations may immediately
tend to make out the latter, which do not appear, by any
immediate connexion, to the purpose of the former; which
is less our concern than many seem to think. For, 1*st*,
It is not necessary we should justify the dispensations
of Providence against objections, any farther than to
show that the things objected against may, for aught we
know, be consistent with justice and goodness. Suppose,
then, that there are things in the system of this world,
and plan of Providence relating to it, which taken alone
would be unjust; yet it has been shown unanswerably,
that if we could take in the reference which these things
may have to other things present, past, and to come—to
the whole scheme, which the things objected against are
parts of; these very things might, for aught we know,
be found to be, not only consistent with justice, but instances of it. Indeed it has been shown, by the analogy
of what we see, not only possible that this may be the

case, but credible that it is. And thus objections drawn
from such things are answered, and Providence is vindicated, as far as religion makes its vindication necessary.
Hence it appears, *2ndly*, That objections against the
divine justice and goodness are not endeavoured to be
removed, by showing that the like objections, allowed to
be really conclusive, lie against natural providence; but
those objections being supposed, and shown not to be conclusive, the things objected against, considered as matters
of fact, are farther shown to be credible, from their conformity to the constitution of nature: for instance, that
God will reward and punish men for their actions hereafter, from the observation, that he does reward and
punish them for their actions here. And this, I apprehend, is of weight. And I add, *3rdly*, It would be of
weight, even though those objections were not answered.
For, there being the proof of religion above set down,
and religion implying several facts; for instance, again,
the fact last mentioned, that God will reward and punish
men for their actions hereafter; the observation that his
present method of government is by rewards and punishments, shows that future fact not to be incredible; whatever objections men may think they have against it, as
unjust or unmerciful, according to their notions of justice and mercy; or as improbable, from their belief of
necessity. I say, *as improbable;* for it is evident no objection against it, *as unjust,* can be urged from necessity;
since this notion as much destroys injustice, as it does
justice. Then, *4thly,* Though objections against the
reasonableness of the system of religion cannot indeed be
answered without entering into consideration of its reasonableness, yet objections against the credibility or truth of
it may: because the system of it is reducible into what
is properly matter of fact; and the truth, the probable
truth, of facts may be shown, without consideration of
their reasonableness. Nor is it necessary, though in
some cases and respects it is highly useful and proper,

yet it is not necessary, to give a proof of the reasonableness of every precept enjoined us, and of every particular dispensation of Providence which comes into the system of religion. Indeed, the more thoroughly a person
of a right disposition is convinced of the perfection of
the divine nature and conduct, the farther he will ad-
vance towards that perfection of religion which St. John
speaks of, 1 John iv. 18. But the general obligations of
religion are fully made out, by proving the reasonableness of the practice of it. And that the practice of religion *is* reasonable may be shown, though no more could
be proved than that the system of it *may be* so, for aught
we know to the contrary; and even without entering into
the distinct consideration of this. And from hence, 5*thly*,
It is easy to see, that though the analogy of nature is not
an immediate answer to objections against the wisdom,
the justice, or goodness, of any doctrine or precept of
religion, yet it may be, as it is, an immediate and direct
answer to what is really intended by such objections;
which is to show, that the things objected against are
incredible.

Fourthly, It is most readily acknowledged, that the
foregoing Treatise is by no means satisfactory; very far
indeed from it: but so would any natural institution of
life appear, if reduced into a system, together with its
evidence. Leaving religion out of the case, men are
divided in their opinions, whether our pleasures overbalance our pains; and whether it be, or be not, eligible
to live in this world. And were all such controversies
settled, which perhaps, in speculation, would be found
involved in great difficulties; and were it determined,
upon the evidence of reason, as nature has determined it
to our hands, that life is to be preserved; yet still the
rules which God has been pleased to afford us, for escaping the miseries of it, and obtaining its satisfactions—the
rules, for instance, of preserving health, and recovering
it when lost—are not only fallible and precarious, but

very far from being exact.   Nor are we informed by nature
in future contingencies and accidents, so as to render it at
all certain what is the best method of managing our affairs.
What will be the success of our temporal pursuits, in the
common sense of the word *success*, is highly doubtful.   And
what will be the success of them, in the proper sense of the
word, *i. e.* what happiness or enjoyment we shall obtain by
them, is doubtful in a much higher degree.   Indeed, the
unsatisfactory nature of the evidence with which we are
obliged to take up in the daily course of life, is scarce to be
expressed.   Yet men do not throw away life, or disregard
the interests of it upon account of this doubtfulness.   The
evidence of religion, then, being admitted real, those who
object against it as not satisfactory, *i. e.* as not being what
they wish it, plainly forget the very condition of our being;
for satisfaction, in this sense, does not belong to such a
creature as man.   And, which is more material, they forget
also the very nature of religion.   For religion presupposes,
in all those who will embrace it, a certain degree of integrity and honesty; which it was intended to try whether
men have or not, and to exercise, in such as have it, in
order to its improvement.   Religion presupposes this as
much, and in the same sense, as speaking to a man presupposes he understands the language in which you speak;
or as warning a man of any danger, presupposes that he
hath such a regard to himself as that he will endeavour to
avoid it.   And, therefore, the question is not at all, Whether the evidence of religion be satisfactory? but, Whether
it be, in reason, sufficient to prove and discipline that
virtue which it presupposes?   Now, the evidence of it
is fully sufficient for all those purposes of probation; how
far soever it is from being satisfactory as to the purposes of
curiosity, or any other: and indeed it answers the purposes
of the former in several respects, which it would not do, if
it were as overbearing as is required.   One might add
farther, that whether the motives, or the evidence for any
course of action, be satisfactory, meaning here by that word,

what satisfies a man that such a course of action will in
event be for his good; this need never be, and I think,
strictly speaking, never is, the practical question in common matters. But the practical question, in all cases, is,
Whether the evidence for a course of action be such as,
taking in all circumstances, makes the faculty within us,
which is the guide and judge of conduct,* determine that
course of action to be prudent? Indeed, satisfaction that
it will be for our interest or happiness, abundantly determines an action to be prudent; but evidence, almost infinitely lower than this, determines actions to be so too, even
in the conduct of every day.

Fifthly, As to the objection concerning the influence
which this argument, or any part of it, may or may not
be expected to have upon men, I observe, as above, that
religion being intended for a trial and exercise of the
morality of every person's character who is a subject of
it; and there being, as I have shown, such evidence for it,
as is sufficient in reason to influence men to embrace
it; to object, that it is not to be imagined mankind will
be influenced by such evidence, is nothing to the purpose of the foregoing Treatise. For the purpose of it is
not to inquire, What sort of creatures mankind are; but,
What the light and knowledge, which is afforded them,
requires they should be? to show how, in reason, they
ought to behave; not how, in fact, they will behave.
This depends upon themselves, and is their own concern;
the personal concern of each man in particular. And
how little regard the generality have to it, experience,
indeed, does too fully show. But religion, considered as
a probation, has had its end upon all persons, to whom it
has been proposed with evidence sufficient in reason to
influence their practice; for by this means they have
been put into a state of probation; let them behave as
they will in it. And thus, not only revelation, but reason

---

* See Dissertation ii.

also, teaches us, that by the evidence of religion being laid before men, the designs of Providence are carrying on, not only with regard to those who will, but likewise with regard to those who will not, be influenced by it. However, *lastly*, the objection here referred to, allows the things insisted upon in this Treatise to be of some weight; and if so, it may be hoped it will have some 'influence. And if there be a probability that it will have any at all, there is the same reason in kind, though not in degree, to lay it before men, as there would be, if it were likely to have a greater influence.

And farther, I desire it may be considered, with respect to the whole of the foregoing objections, that in this Treatise I have argued upon the principles of others,* not my own; and have omitted what I think true, and of the utmost importance, because by others thought unintelligible, or not true. Thus I have argued upon the principles of the Fatalists, which I do not believe; and have omitted a thing of the utmost importance, which I do believe—the moral fitness and unfitness of actions, prior to all will whatever; which I apprehend as certainly to determine the Divine conduct, as speculative truth and falsehood necessarily determine the Divine judgment. Indeed, the principle of liberty, and that of moral fitness, so force themselves upon the mind, that moralists, the ancients as well as moderns, have formed their language upon it. And probably it may appear in mine, though I have endeavoured to avoid it; and, in order to avoid it, have sometimes been obliged to express myself in a manner which will appear strange to such as do not observe the reason for it: but the general argument here pursued does not at all suppose, or proceed upon, these principles.

* By *arguing upon the principles of others*, the reader will observe is meant, not proving anything *from* those principles, but *notwithstanding* them. Thus religion is proved, not *from* the opinion of necessity, which is absurd, but *notwithstanding*, or *even though*, that opinion were admitted to be true.

Now, these two abstract principles of liberty and moral
fitness being omitted, religion can be considered in no
other view than merely as a question of fact; and in this
view it is here considered.   It is obvious, that Christianity, and the proof of it, are both historical.   And even
natural religion is, properly, a matter of fact: for, that
there is a righteous Governor of the world, is so: and
this proposition contains the general system of natural
religion.   But then, several abstract truths, and in particular those two principles, are usually taken into consideration in the proof of it; whereas it is here treated of
only as a matter of fact.   To explain this: that the three
angles of a triangle are equal to two right ones, is an abstract truth; but that they appear so to our mind, is only
a matter of fact.   And this last must have been admitted,
if anything was, by those ancient sceptics, who would
not have admitted the former; but pretended to doubt,
Whether there were any such thing as truth; or, Whether
we could certainly depend upon our faculties of understanding for the knowledge of it in any case.   So likewise, that there is, in the nature of things, an original
standard of right and wrong in actions, independent upon
all will, but which unalterably determines the will of God
to exercise that moral government over the world which
religion teaches, i. e. finally and upon the whole to reward
and punish men respectively as they act right or wrong;
this assertion contains an abstract truth, as well as matter
of fact.   But suppose, in the present state, every man,
without exception, was rewarded and punished, in exact
proportion as he followed or transgressed that sense of
right and wrong which God has implanted in the nature
of every man; this would not be at all an abstract truth,
but only a matter of fact.   And though this fact were
acknowledged by every one, yet the very same difficulties
might be raised, as are now, concerning the abstract
questions of liberty and moral fitness: and we should
have a proof, even the certain one of experience, that the

government of the world was perfectly moral, without taking in the consideration of those questions: and this proof would remain, in what way soever they were determined. And thus, God having given mankind a moral faculty, the object of which is actions, and which naturally approves some actions as right and of good desert, and condemns others as wrong and of ill desert; that he will, finally and upon the whole, reward the former, and punish the latter, is not an assertion of an abstract truth, but of what is as mere a fact, as his doing so at present would be. This future fact I have not indeed proved with the force with which it might be proved, from the principles of liberty and moral fitness: but without them have given a really conclusive practical proof of it, which is greatly strengthened by the general analogy of nature; a proof easily cavilled at, easily shown not to be demonstrative, for it is not offered as such; but impossible, I think, to be evaded or answered. And thus the obligations of religion are made out, exclusively of the questions concerning liberty and moral fitness; which have been perplexed with difficulties and abstruse reasonings, as everything may.

Hence, therefore, may be observed distinctly, what is the force of this Treatise. It will be, to such as are convinced of religion, upon the proof arising out of the two last-mentioned principles, an additional proof and a confirmation of it: to such as do not admit those principles, an original proof of it,* and a confirmation of that proof. Those who believe, will here find the scheme of Christianity cleared of objections, and the evidence of it in a peculiar manner strengthened: those who do not believe, will at least be shown the absurdity of all attempts to prove Christianity false; the plain undoubted credibility of it; and, I hope, a good deal more.

And thus, though some perhaps may seriously think, that analogy, as here urged, has too great stress laid upon

* Page 94, &c.

it; and ridicule, unanswerable ridicule, may be applied to show the argument from it in a disadvantageous light; yet there can be no question but that it is a real one. For religion, both natural and revealed, implying in it numerous facts; analogy, being a confirmation of all facts to which it can be applied, as it is the only proof of most, cannot but be admitted by every one to be a material thing, and truly of weight on the side of religion, both natural and revealed; and it ought to be particularly regarded by such as profess to follow nature, and to be less satisfied with abstract reasonings.

CONCLUSION.

WHATEVER account may be given of the strange inattention and disregard, in some ages and countries, to a matter of such importance as religion, it would, before experience, be incredible, that there should be the like disregard in those who have had the moral system of the world laid before them, as it is by Christianity, and often inculcated upon them; because this moral system carries in it a good degree of evidence for its truth, upon its being barely proposed to our thoughts. There is no need of abstruse reasonings and distinctions to convince an unprejudiced understanding, that there is a God who made and governs the world, and will judge it in righteousness; though they may be necessary to answer abstruse difficulties when once such are raised; when the very meaning of those words which express most intelligibly the general doctrine of religion, is pretended to be uncertain, and the clear truth of the thing itself is obscured by the intricacies of speculation. But to an unprejudiced mind, ten thousand thousand instances of design cannot but prove a Designer. And it is intuitively manifest, that creatures ought to live under a dutiful sense of their Maker; and that justice and charity must be his laws, to creatures whom he has made social, and placed in society. Indeed, the truth of revealed religion, peculiarly so called, is not self-evident, but requires external proof, in order to its being received. Yet inattention, among us, to revealed religion, will be found to imply the same dissolute immoral temper of mind, as inattention to natural religion; because, when both are laid before us, in the manner they are in Christian countries of liberty, our obligations to inquire into both, and to embrace both upon supposition of their truth, are obligations of the same nature. For revelation claims to be the voice of God; and our obligation to attend to his voice is, surely, moral in all cases. And as it is insisted that its evidence is conclusive, upon thorough consideration of it; so it offers itself to us with manifest obvious appearances of having something more than human in it, and therefore, in all reason, requires to have its claims most seriously examined into. It is to be added, that though light and knowledge, in what manner soever afforded us, is equally from God; yet a miraculous revelation has a peculiar tendency, from the first principles of our nature, to awaken mankind, and inspire them with reverence and awe: and this is a peculiar obligation to attend to what claims to be so, with such appearances of truth. It is therefore most certain, that our obligations to inquire seriously into the evidence of Christianity, and, upon supposition of its truth, to embrace it, are of the utmost importance, and moral in the highest and most proper sense. Let us then suppose, that the evidence of religion in general, and of Christianity, has been seriously inquired into by all reasonable men among us. Yet we find many professedly to reject both, upon speculative principles of infidelity. And all of them do not content themselves with a bare neglect of religion, and enjoying their imaginary freedom from its restraints. Some go much beyond this: they deride God's moral government over the world; they renounce his protection and defy his justice; they ridicule and vilify Christianity, and blaspheme the Author of it; and take all occasions to manifest a scorn and contempt of revelation. This amounts to an active setting themselves against religion; to what may be considered as a positive principle of irreligion: which they cultivate within themselves, and, whether they intend this effect or not, render habitual, as a good man does the contrary principle. And others, who are not chargeable with all this profligateness, yet are in avowed opposition to religion, as if discovered to be groundless. Now admitting, which is the supposition we go upon, that these persons act upon what they think principles of reason, and otherwise they are not to be argued with; it is really inconceivable that they should imagine they clearly see the whole evidence of it, considered in itself, to be nothing at all: nor do they pretend this. They are far indeed from having a just notion of its evidence; but they would not say its evidence was nothing, if they thought the system of it, with all its circumstances, were credible, like other matters of science or history. So that their manner of treating it must proceed, either from such kind of objections against all religion as have been answered or obviated in the former part of this Treatise: or else from objections and difficulties supposed more peculiar to Christianity. Thus they entertain prejudices against the whole notion of a revelation and miraculous interpositions. They find things in Scripture, whether in incidental passages or in the general scheme of it, which appear to them unreasonable. They take for granted, that, if Christianity were true, the light of it must have been more general, and the evidence of it more satisfactory, or rather overbearing; that it must and would have been, in some way, otherwise put and left, than it is. Now, this is not imagining they see the evidence itself to be nothing, or inconsiderable; but quite another thing. It is being fortified against the evidence, in some degree acknowledged, by thinking they see the system of Christianity, or somewhat which appears to them

necessarily connected with it, to be incredible or false:
fortified against that evidence which might, otherwise,
make great impression upon them.   Or, lastly, if any of
these persons are, upon the whole, in doubt concerning the
truth of Christianity, their behaviour seems owing to their
taking for granted, through strange inattention, that such
doubting is in a manner the same thing as being certain
against it.

   To these persons, and to this state of opinion concerning religion, the foregoing Treatise is adapted.   For, all
the general objections against the moral system of nature
having been obviated, it is shown that there is not any
peculiar presumption at all against Christianity, either
considered as not discoverable by reason, or as unlike to
what is so discovered; nor any worth mentioning against
it as miraculous, if any at all; none, certainly, which can
render it in the least incredible.   It is shown, that, upon
supposition of a divine revelation, the analogy of nature
renders it beforehand highly credible, I think probable,
that many things in it must appear liable to great objections; and that we must be incompetent judges of, to
a great degree.   This observation is, I think, unquestionably true, and of the very utmost importance; but it is
urged, as I hope it will be understood, with great caution
of not vilifying the faculty of reason, which is " the candle of the Lord within us," Prov. xx. 27; though it can
afford no light where he does not shine; nor judge, where
it has no principles to judge upon.   The objections here
spoken of, being first answered in the view of objections
against Christianity as a matter of fact, are in the next
place considered as urged, more immediately, against the
wisdom, justice, and goodness of the Christian dispensation.   And it is fully made out, that they admit of exactly
the like answer, in every respect, to what the like objections against the constitution of nature admit of: that, as
partial views give the appearance of wrong to things,
which, upon farther consideration and knowledge of their

relations to other things, are found just and good, so it is perfectly credible, that the things objected against the wisdom and goodness of the Christian dispensation, may be rendered instances of wisdom and goodness by their reference to other things beyond our view; because Christianity is a scheme as much above our comprehension as that of nature; and, like that, a scheme in which means are made use of to accomplish ends, and which, as is most credible, may be carried on by general laws. And it ought to be attended to, that this is not an answer taken merely or chiefly from our ignorance, but from somewhat positive, which our observation shows us. For, to like objections, the like answer is experienced to be just, in numberless parallel cases. The objections against the Christian dispensation, and the method by which it is carried on, having been thus obviated, in general and together; the chief of them are considered distinctly, and the particular things objected to are shown credible, by their perfect analogy, each apart, to the constitution of nature. Thus, if man be fallen from his primitive state, and to be restored, and infinite wisdom and power engages in accomplishing our recovery; it were to have been expected, it is said, that this should have been effected at once, and not by such a long series of means, and such a various economy of person and things; one dispensation preparatory to another, this to a farther one, and so on through an indefinite number of ages, before the end of the scheme proposed can be completely accomplished; a scheme conducted by infinite wisdom, and executed by almighty power. But now, on the contrary, our finding that everything in the constitution and course of nature is thus carried on, shows such expectations concerning revelation to be highly unreasonable; and is a satisfactory answer to them, when urged as objections against the credibility that the great scheme of Providence in the redemption of the world may be of this kind, and to be accomplished in this manner. As to the

particular method of our redemption, the appointment of
a mediator between God and man; this has been shown
to be most obviously analogous to the general conduct of
nature, *i. e.* the God of nature, in appointing others to be
the instruments of his mercy—as we experience in the
daily course of Providence. The condition of this world,
which the doctrine of our redemption by Christ presupposes, so much falls in with natural appearances, that
heathen moralists inferred it from those appearances;
inferred, that human nature was fallen from its original
rectitude, and, in consequence of this, degraded from its
primitive happiness. Or, however this opinion came into
the world, these appearances must have kept up the tradition, and confirmed the belief of it. And as it was the
general opinion, under the light of nature, that repentance
and reformation, alone and by itself, was not sufficient to
do away sin, and procure a full remission of the penalties
annexed to it; and as the reason of the thing does not at
all lead to any such conclusion, so every day's experience
shows us, that reformation is not, in any sort, sufficient
to prevent the present disadvantages and miseries, which,
in the natural course of things, God has annexed to folly
and extravagance. Yet there may be ground to think,
that the punishments which, by the general laws of divine
government, are annexed to vice, may be prevented; that
provision may have been, even originally, made, that they
should be prevented by some means or other, though they
could not by reformation alone. For we have daily instances of such mercy, in the general conduct of nature;
compassion provided for misery,* medicines for diseases,
friends against enemies. There is provision made, in the
original constitution of the world, that much of the natural
bad consequences of our follies, which persons themselves
alone cannot prevent, may be prevented by the assistance
of others; assistance which nature enables, and disposes,

* Sermon 6th, at the Rolls.

and appoints them to afford. By a method of goodness analogous to this, when the world lay in wickedness, and consequently in ruin, " God so loved the world, that he gave his only begotten Son" to save it; and " he, being made perfect by suffering, became the author of eternal salvation to all them that obey him," John iii. 16; Heb. v. 9. Indeed, neither reason nor analogy would lead us to think, in particular, that the interposition of Christ, in the manner in which he did interpose, would be of that efficacy for recovery of the world, which the Scripture teaches us it was; but neither would reason nor analogy lead us to think, that other particular means would be of the efficacy which experience shows they are, in number-less instances. And therefore, as the case before us does not admit of experience; so, that neither reason nor analogy can show how, or in what particular way, the interposition of Christ, as revealed in Scripture, is of that efficacy which it is there represented to be; this is no kind nor degree of presumption against its being really of that efficacy. Farther: the objections against Christianity, from the light of it not being universal, nor its evidence so strong as might possibly be given us, have been an-swered by the general analogy of nature. That God has made such variety of creatures, is indeed an answer to the former; but that he dispenses his gifts in such variety, both of degrees and kinds, amongst creatures of the same species, and even to the same individuals at different times, is a more obvious and full answer to it. And it is so far from being the method of Providence, in other cases, to afford us such overbearing evidence as some require in proof of Christianity, that, on the contrary, the evidence upon which we are naturally appointed to act in common matters, throughout a very great part of life, is doubtful in a high degree. And, admitting the fact, that God has afforded to some no more than doubtful evidence of religion, the same account may be given of it, as of difficulties and temptations with regard to practice.

But as it is not impossible,* surely, that this alleged doubt-fulness may be men's own fault, it deserves their most serious consideration, whether it be not so. However, it is certain that doubting implies a degree of evidence for that of which we doubt; and that this degree of evidence as really lays us under obligations, as demonstrative evidence.

The whole, then, of religion is throughout credible; nor is there, I think, anything relating to the revealed dispen-sation of things more different from the experienced consti-tution and course of nature, than some parts of the consti-tution of nature are from other parts of it. And if so, the only question which remains is, what positive evidence can be alleged for the truth of Christianity? This too, in gene-ral, has been considered, and the objections against it estimated. Deduct, therefore, what is to be deducted from that evidence, upon account of any weight which may be thought to remain in these objections, after what the ana-logy of nature has suggested in answer to them; and then consider, what are the practical consequences from all this, upon the most sceptical principles one can argue upon (for I am writing to persons who entertain these principles:) and upon such consideration it will be obvious, that immo-rality, as little excuse as it admits of in itself, is greatly aggravated in persons who have been made acquainted with Christianity, whether they believe it or not; because the moral system of nature, or natural religion, which Chris-tianity lays before us, approves itself, almost intuitively, to a reasonable mind, upon seeing it proposed. In the next place, with regard to Christianity, it will be observed that there is a middle, between a full satisfaction of the truth of it, and a satisfaction of the contrary. The middle state of mind between these two consists in a serious apprehension that it may be true, joined with doubt whether it be so. And this, upon the best judgment I am able to make, is as far towards speculative infidelity as any sceptic can at all

* Page 202, &c.

be supposed to go, who has had true Christianity, with the proper evidence of it, laid before him, and has in any tolerable measure considered them. For I would not be mistaken to comprehend all who have ever heard of it; because it seems evident, that in many countries called Christian, neither Christianity, nor its evidence, are fairly laid before men. And in places where both are, there appear to be some who have very little attended to either, and who reject Christianity with a scorn proportionate to their inattention; and yet are by no means without understanding in other matters. Now it has been shown, that a serious apprehension that Christianity may be true, lays persons under the strictest obligations of a serious regard to it, throughout the whole of their life; a regard not the same exactly, but in many respects nearly the same, with what a full conviction of its truth would lay them under. *Lastly*, it will appear, that blasphemy and profaneness, I mean with regard to Christianity, are absolutely without excuse. For there is no temptation to it, but from the wantonness of vanity or mirth; and these, considering the infinite importance of the subject, are no such temptations as to afford any excuse for it. If this be a just account of things, and yet men can go on to vilify or disregard Christianity, which is to talk and act as if they had a demonstration of its falsehood; there is no reason to think they would alter their behaviour to any purpose, though there were a demonstration of its truth.

TWO DISSERTATIONS:

OF

PERSONAL IDENTITY;

AND

OF THE NATURE OF VIRTUE.

DISSERTATION I.

OF PERSONAL IDENTITY.

WHETHER we are to live in a future state, as it is the most important question which can possibly be asked, so it is the most intelligible one which can be expressed in language. Yet strange perplexities have been raised about the meaning of that identity, or sameness of person, which is implied in the notion of our living now and hereafter, or in any two successive moments. And the solution of these difficulties hath been stranger than the difficulties themselves. For personal identity has been explained so by some, as to render the inquiry concerning a future life of no consequence at all to us, the persons who are making it. And though few men can be misled by such subtleties, yet it may be proper a little to consider them.

Now, when it is asked wherein personal identity consists, the answer should be the same as if it were asked, wherein consists similitude or equality—that all attempts to define would but perplex it. Yet there is no difficulty at all in ascertaining the idea. For as, upon two triangles being compared or viewed together, there arises to the mind the idea of similitude; or upon twice two and four, the idea of equality; so likewise, upon comparing the consciousness of one's self, or one's own existence in any two moments, there as immediately arises to the mind the idea of personal identity. And as the two former comparisons not only give us the ideas of similitude and equality, but also show

us that two triangles are alike, and twice two and four are
equal; so the latter comparison not only gives us the idea
of personal identity, but also shows us the identity of ourselves in those two moments; the present suppose, and that
immediately past; or the present, and that a month, a year,
or twenty years past. Or, in other words, by reflecting
upon that which is myself now, and that which was myself
twenty years ago, I discern they are not two, but one and
the same self.

But though consciousness of what is past does thus
ascertain our personal identity to ourselves, yet to say that
it makes personal identity, or is necessary to our being the
same persons, is to say, that a person has not existed a
single moment, nor done one action, but what he can remember; indeed none but what he reflects upon. And
one should really think it self-evident, that consciousness of
personal identity presupposes, and therefore cannot constitute personal identity, any more than knowledge, in any
other case, can constitute truth, which it presupposes.

This wonderful mistake may possibly have arisen from
hence, that to be endued with consciousness, is inseparable
from the idea of a person or intelligent being. For this
might be expressed inaccurately thus—that consciousness
makes personality; and from hence it might be concluded
to make personal identity. But though present consciousness of what we at present do and feel, is necessary to our
being the persons we now are; yet present consciousness
of past actions, or feelings, is not necessary to our being
the same persons who performed those actions, or had those
feelings.

The inquiry what makes vegetables the same, in the
common acceptation of the word, does not appear to have
any relation to this of personal identity; because the
word *same*, when applied to them and to person, is not
only applied to different subjects, but it is also used in
different senses. For, when a man swears to the same
tree as having stood fifty years in the same place, he

means only the same as to all the purposes of property
and uses of common life, and not that the tree has been
all that time the same in the strict philosophical sense
of the word.   For he does not know whether any one
particle of the present tree be the same with any one particle of the tree which stood in the same place fifty years
ago.   And if they have not one common particle of
matter, they cannot be the same tree in the proper
philosophic sense of the word *same;* it being evidently a
contradiction in terms to say they are, when no part of their
substance, and no one of their properties, is the same:
no part of their substance by the supposition; no one of
their properties, because it is allowed that the same
property cannot be transferred from one substance to
another.   And therefore, when we say the identity, or
sameness, of a plant consists in a continuation of the
same life, communicated under the same organization, to a
number of particles of matter, whether the same or not,
the word *same,* when applied to life and to organization, ·
cannot possibly be understood to signify what it signifies
in this very sentence, when applied to matter.   In a loose
and popular sense, then, the life, and the organization,
and the plant, are justly said to be the same, notwithstanding the perpetual change of the parts.   But in a strict
and philosophical manner of speech, no man, no being, no
mode of being, no anything, can be the same with that
with which it hath indeed nothing the same.   Now, sameness is used in this latter sense when applied to persons.
The identity of these, therefore, cannot subsist with diversity
of substance.

The thing here considered, and demonstratively, as I
think, determined, is proposed by Mr. Locke in these
words, *Whether it,* i. e. the same self or person, *be the same
identical substance?*   And he has suggested what is a much
better answer to the question than that which he gives it
in form: for he defines person, *a thinking intelligent
being,* &c. and personal identity, *the sameness of a rational*

being.* The question then is, whether the same rational being is the same substance; which needs no answer, because being and substance, in this place, stand for the same idea. The ground of the doubt, whether the same person be the same substance, is said to be this: that the consciousness of our own existence, in youth and in old age, or in any two joint successive moments, is not *the same individual action,*† i. e. not the same consciousness, but different successive consciousnesses. Now, it is strange that this should have occasioned such perplexities. For it is surely conceivable, that a person may have a capacity of knowing some object or other to be the same now which it was when he contemplated it formerly; yet in this case, where, by the supposition, the object is perceived to be the same, the perception of it in any two moments cannot be one and the same perception. And thus, though the successive consciousnesses which we have of our own existence are not the same, yet are they consciousnesses of one and the same thing or object; of the same person, self, or living agent. The person of whose existence the consciousness is felt now, and was felt an hour or a year ago, is discerned to be, not two persons, but one and the same person; and therefore is one and the same.

Mr. Locke's observations upon this subject appear hasty; and he seems to profess himself dissatisfied with suppositions which he has made relating to it.‡ But some of those hasty observations have been carried to a strange length by others; whose notion, when traced and examined to the bottom, amounts, I think, to this :§ " That personality is not a permanent, but a transient thing: that it lives and dies, begins and ends, continually; that no one can any more remain one and the same person two moments together, than two successive moments

---

* Locke's Works, vol. i. p. 146.   † Ibid. pp. 146, 147.
‡ Ibid. p. 152.
§ See an answer to Dr. Clark's third Defence of his Letter to Mr. Dodwell, 2nd edit. pp. 44, 56, &c.

can be one and the same moment: that our substance is indeed continually changing; but whether this be so or not, is, it seems, nothing to the purpose; since it is not substance, but consciousness alone, which constitutes personality; which consciousness, being successive, cannot be the same in any two moments, nor consequently the personality constituted by it." And from hence it must follow, that it is a fallacy upon ourselves, to charge our present selves with anything we did, or to imagine our present selves interested in anything which befell us yesterday, or that our present self will be interested in what will befall us to-morrow; since our present self is not, in reality, the same with the self of yesterday, but another like self or person coming in its room, and mistaken for it; to which another self will succeed to-morrow. This, I say, must follow: for if the self or person of to-day, and that of to-morrow, are not the same, but only like persons, the person of to-day is really no more interested in what will befall the person of to-morrow, than in what will befall any other person. It may be thought, perhaps, that this is not a just representation of the opinion we are speaking of; because those who maintain it allow, that a person is the same as far back as his remembrance reaches. And, indeed, they do use the words *identity* and *same* person. Nor will language permit these words to be laid aside; since, if they were, there must be, I know not what ridiculous periphrasis substituted in the room of them. But they cannot, consistently with themselves, mean that the person is really the same. For it is self-evident, that the personality cannot be really the same, if, as they expressly assert, that in which it consists is not the same. And as, consistently with themselves, they cannot, so I think it appears they do not mean, that the person is *really* the same, but only that he is so in a fictitious sense; in such a sense only as they assert; for this they do assert, that any number of persons whatever may be the same person.

N 2

The bare unfolding this notion, and laying it thus naked and open, seems the best confutation of it. However, since great stress is said to be put upon it, I add the following things:—

First, This notion is absolutely contradictory to that certain conviction which necessarily, and every moment, rises within us, when we turn our thoughts upon ourselves; when we reflect upon what is past, and look forward upon what is to come. All imagination of a daily change of that living agent which each man calls himself, for another, or of any such change throughout our whole present life, is entirely borne down by our natural sense of things. Nor is it possible for a person in his wits to alter his conduct, with regard to his health or affairs, from a suspicion, that though he should live to-morrow, he should not, however, be the same person he is to-day. And yet, if it be reasonable to act, with respect to a future life, upon this notion, that personality is transient, it is reasonable to act upon it, with respect to the present. Here, then, is a notion equally applicable to religion and to our temporal concerns; and every one sees and feels the inexpressible absurdity of it in the latter case. If, therefore, any can take up with it in the former, this cannot proceed from the reason of the thing, but must be owing to an inward unfairness, and secret corruption of heart.

Secondly, It is not an idea, or abstract notion, or quality, but a being only, which is capable of life and action, of happiness and misery. Now, all beings confessedly continue the same during the whole time of their existence. Consider then a living being now existing, and which has existed for any time alive: this living being must have done, and suffered, and enjoyed, what it has done, and suffered, and enjoyed formerly, (this living being, I say, and not another,) as really as it does, and suffers, and enjoys, what it does, and suffers, and enjoys this instant. All these successive actions, enjoyments, and sufferings, are actions, enjoyments, and sufferings of the same living being. And they are so, prior to all consideration of its remembering or forgetting; since remembering or forgetting can make no alteration in the truth of past matter of fact. And, suppose this being endued with limited powers of knowledge and memory, there is no more difficulty in conceiving it to have a power of knowing itself to be the same living being which it was some time ago, of remembering some of its actions, sufferings, and enjoyments, and forgetting others, than in conceiving it to know, or remember, or forget, anything else.

Thirdly, Every person is conscious that he is now the same person or self he was, as far back as his remembrance reaches: since, when any one reflects upon a past action of his own, he is just as certain of the person who did that action, namely himself, the person who now reflects upon it, as he is certain that the action was at all done. Nay, very often a person's assurance of an action having been done, of which he is absolutely assured, arises wholly from the consciousness that he himself did it. And this he, person, or self, must either be a substance, or the property of some substance. If he, in person, be a substance, then consciousness that he is the same person, is consciousness that he is the same substance. If the person, or he, be the property of a substance, still consciousness that he is the same property, is as certain a proof that his substance remains the same, as consciousness that he remains the same substance would be; since the same property cannot be transferred from one substance to another.

But though we are thus certain that we are the same agents, living beings, or substances, now, which we were as far back as our remembrance reaches; yet it is asked, Whether we may not possibly be deceived in it? And this question may be asked at the end of any demonstration whatever; because it is a question concerning the truth of perception by memory. And he who can

doubt, whether perception by memory can in this case
be depended upon, may doubt also, whether perception
by deduction and reasoning, which also includes memory,
or, indeed, whether intuitive perception can. Here, then,
we can go no farther. For it is ridiculous to attempt to
prove the truth of those perceptions, whose truth we can
no otherwise prove than by other perceptions of exactly
the same kind with them, and which there is just the
same ground to suspect; or to attempt to prove the
truth of our faculties, which can no otherwise be proved
than by the use or means of those very suspected faculties themselves.

DISSERTATION II.

OF THE NATURE OF VIRTUE.

That which renders beings capable of moral government,
is their having a moral nature, and moral faculties of
perception and of action. Brute creatures are impressed
and actuated by various instincts and propensions: so also
are we. But, additional to this, we have a capacity of
reflecting upon actions and characters, and making them an
object to our thought: and on our doing this, we naturally
and unavoidably approve some actions, under the peculiar
view of their being virtuous and of good desert; and disapprove others, as vicious and of ill desert. That we have
this moral approving and disapproving* faculty, is certain

---

* This way of speaking is taken from Epictetus, (Arr. Epict. lib. i.
cap. i.), and is made use of, as seeming the most full, and least liable
to cavil. And the moral faculty may be understood to have these
two epithets, δοκιμαστικη and αποδοκιμαστικη, upon a double account;

from our experiencing it in ourselves, and recognizing it in
each other.   It appears from our exercising it unavoidably,
in the approbation and disapprobation even of feigned
characters: from the words, right and wrong, odious and
amiable, base and worthy, with many others of like signi-
fication in all languages, applied to actions and characters:
from the many written systems of morals which suppose
it; since it cannot be imagined, that all these authors,
throughout all these treatises, had absolutely no meaning
at all to their words, or a meaning merely chimerical:
from our natural sense of gratitude, which implies a distinction between merely being the instrument of good,
and intending it: from the like distinction, every one
makes, between injury and mere harm, which, Hobbes
says, is peculiar to mankind; and between injury and
just punishment—a distinction plainly natural prior to the
consideration of human laws.   It is manifest, great part
of common language, and of common behaviour, over the
world, is formed upon supposition of such a moral faculty;
whether called conscience, moral reason, moral sense, or
divine reason; whether considered as a sentiment of the
understanding, or as a perception of the heart, or, which
seems the truth, as including both.   Nor is it at all doubtful, in the general, what course of action this faculty, or
practical discerning power within us approves, and what
it disapproves.   For, as much as it has been disputed
wherein virtue consists, or whatever ground for doubt
there may be about particulars, yet, in general, there is
in reality an universally acknowledged standard of it.   It

because, upon a survey of actions, whether before or after they are
done, it determines them to be good or evil; and also because it
determines itself to be the guide of action and of life, in contradistinction from all other faculties, or natural principles of action: in
the very same manner as speculative reason *directly* and naturally
judges of speculative truth and falsehood; and, at the same time, is
attended with a consciousness upon *reflection*, that the natural right
to judge of them belongs to it.

is that which all ages and all countries have made profession of in public; it is that which every man you meet
puts on the show of; it is that which the primary and
fundamental laws of all civil constitutions, over the face
of the earth, make it their business and endeavour to
enforce the practice of upon mankind; namely, justice,
veracity, and regard to common good. It being manifest
then, in general, that we have such a faculty or discernment as this, it may be of use to remark some things, more
distinctly, concerning it

First, It ought to be observed, that the object of. this
faculty is actions,* comprehending under that name, active
or practical principles; those principles from which men
would act, if occasions and circumstances gave them power;
and which, when fixed and habitual in any person, we call
his character. It does not appear that brutes have the least
reflex sense of actions as distinguished from events; or that
will and design, which constitute the very nature of actions
as such, are at all an object to their perception. But to ours
they are; and they are the object, and the only one, of the
approving and disapproving faculty. Acting, conduct,
behaviour, abstracted from all regard to what is, in fact and
event, the consequence of it, is itself the natural object of
the moral discernment, as speculative truth and falsehood is
of speculative reason. Intention of such and such consequences, indeed, is always included; for it is part of the
action itself; but though the intended good or bad consequences do not follow, we have exactly the same sense of
the action as if they did. In like manner, we think well or
ill of characters, abstracted from all consideration of the
good or the evil, which persons of such characters have
it actually in their power to do. We never, in the moral
way, applaud or blame either ourselves or others, for what
we enjoy or what we suffer, or for having impressions made

* Ουδε η αρετη και κακια—εν πεισει, αλλα ενεργεια. M. Anton.
lib. 9. 16. Virtutis laus omnis in actione consistit. Cic. Off. lib.
i. c. 6.

upon us which we consider as altogether out of our power;
but only for what we do or would have done, had it been in
our power; or for what we leave undone which we might
have done, or would have left undone though we could have
done it.

Secondly, Our sense or discernment of actions, as
morally good or evil, implies in it a sense or discernment
of them as of good or ill desert. It may be difficult to
explain this perception, so as to answer all the questions
which may be asked concerning it; but every one speaks
of such and such actions as deserving punishment; and
it is not, I suppose, pretended, that they have absolutely
no meaning at all to the expression. Now, the meaning
plainly is not, that we conceive it for the good of society
that the doer of such actions should be made to suffer:
for if unhappily it were resolved, that a man who, by
some innocent action, was infected with the plague,
should be left to perish, lest, by other people coming near
him, the infection should spread; no one would say he
deserved this treatment. Innocence and ill desert are
inconsistent ideas. Ill desert always supposes guilt; and
if one be not part of the other, yet they are evidently and
naturally connected in our mind. The sight of a man in
misery raises our compassion towards him; and, if this
misery be inflicted on him by another, our indignation
against the author of it. But when we are informed that
the sufferer is a villain, and is punished only for his
treachery or cruelty, our compassion exceedingly lessens,
and, in many instances, our indignation wholly subsides.
Now, what produces this effect is the conception of
that in the sufferer which we call ill desert. Upon considering, then, or viewing together, our notion of vice and
that of misery, there results a third, that of ill desert.
And thus there is in human creatures an association of
the two ideas, natural and moral evil, wickedness and
punishment. If this association were merely artificial or
accidental, it were nothing; but being most unquestionably

natural, it greatly concerns us to attend to it, instead of endeavouring to explain it away.

It may be observed farther, concerning our perception of good and of ill desert, that the former is very weak with respect to common instances of virtue. One reason of which may be, that it does not appear to a spectator, how far such instances of virtue proceed from a virtuous principle, or in what degree this principle is prevalent; since a very weak regard to virtue may be sufficient to make men act well in many common instances. And, on the other hand, our perception of ill desert in vicious actions lessens in proportion to the temptations men are thought to have had to such vices. For, vice in human creatures consisting chiefly in the absence or want of the virtuous principle, though a man be overcome, suppose, by tortures, it does not from thence appear, to what degree the virtuous principle was wanting: all that appears is, that he had it not in such a degree as to prevail over the temptation; but possibly he had it in a degree which would have rendered him proof against common temptations.

Thirdly, Our perception of vice and ill desert arises from, and is the result of, a comparison of actions with the nature and capacities of the agent. For, the mere neglect of doing what we ought to do, would, in many cases, be determined by all men to be in the highest degree vicious. And this determination must arise from such comparison, and be the result of it; because such neglect would not be vicious in creatures of other natures and capacities, as brutes. And it is the same also with respect to positive vices, or such as consist in doing what we ought not. For every one has a different sense of harm done by an idiot, madman, or child, and by one of mature and common understanding; though the action of both, including the intention, which is part of the action, be the same: as it may be, since idiots and madmen, as well as children, are capable, not only of doing mischief, but also of intending it. Now, this difference must arise from somewhat discerned in the nature or capacities of one, which renders the action vicious; and the want of which in the other renders the same action innocent, or less vicious: and this plainly supposes a comparison, whether reflected upon or not, between the action and capacities of the agent, previous to our determining an action to be vicious.   And hence arises a proper application of the epithets, incongruous, unsuitable, disproportionate, unfit, to actions which our moral faculty determines to be vicious.

Fourthly, It deserves to be considered, whether men are more at liberty, in point of morals, to make themselves miserable without reason, than to make other people so; or dissolutely to neglect their own greater good for the sake of a present lesser gratification, than they are to neglect the good of others whom nature has committed to their care. It should seem, that a due concern about our own interest or happiness, and a reasonable endeavour to secure and promote it, which is, I think, very much the meaning of the word *prudence* in our language—it should seem, that this is virtue, and the contrary behaviour faulty and blameable; since, in the calmest way of reflection, we approve of the first, and condemn the other conduct, both in ourselves and others. This approbation and disapprobation are altogether different from mere desire of our own or of their happiness, and from sorrow upon missing it. For the object or occasion of this last kind of perception is satisfaction or uneasiness; whereas the object of the first is active behaviour. In one case, what our thoughts fix upon is our condition; in the other, our conduct. It is true, indeed, that nature has not given us so sensible a disapprobation of imprudence and folly, either in *ourselves,* or *others,* as of falsehood, injustice, and cruelty: I suppose, because that constant habitual sense of private interest and good, which we always carry about with us, renders such sensible disapprobation less necessary, less wanting, to keep us from imprudently neglecting our own happiness, and foolishly injuring ourselves, than it is necessary and wanting to keep us from injuring others, to whose good we cannot have so strong and constant a regard; and also, because imprudence and folly, appearing to bring its own punishment more immediately and constantly than injurious behaviour, it less needs the additional punishment which would be inflicted upon it by others, had they the same sensible indignation against it as against injustice, and fraud, and cruelty. Besides, unhappiness being in itself the natural object of compassion, the unhappiness which people bring upon themselves, though it be wilfully, excites in us some pity for them; and this, of course, lessens our displeasure against them. But still it is matter of experience, that we are formed so as to reflect very severely upon the greater instances of imprudent neglects and foolish rashness, both in ourselves and others. In instances of this kind, men often say of themselves with remorse, and of others with some indignation, that they deserved to suffer such calamities, because they brought them upon themselves, and would not take warning. Particularly, when persons come to poverty and distress by a long course of extravagance, and after frequent admonitions, though without falsehood or injustice; we plainly do not regard such people as alike objects of compassion with those who are brought into the same condition by unavoidable accidents. From these things it appears, that prudence is a species of virtue, and folly of vice; meaning by *folly*, somewhat quite different from mere incapacity; a thoughtless want of that regard and attention to our own happiness, which we had capacity for. And this the word properly includes, and, as it seems, in its usual acceptation; for we scarce apply it to brute creatures.

However, if any person be disposed to dispute the matter, I shall very willingly give him up the words *virtue* and *vice*, as not applicable to prudence and folly; but must beg leave to insist, that the faculty within us, which is the judge of actions, approves of prudent actions, and disapproves imprudent ones; I say, prudent and imprudent *actions* as such, and considered distinctly from the happiness or misery which they occasion. And, by the way, this observation may help to determine, what justness there is in that objection against religion, that it teaches us to be interested and selfish.

Fifthly, Without inquiring how far, and in what sense, virtue is resolvable into benevolence, and vice into the want of it; it may be proper to observe, that benevolence, and the want of it, singly considered, are in no sort the whole of virtue and vice. For if this were the case, in the review of one's own character, or that of others, our moral understanding and moral sense would be indifferent to everything, but the degrees in which benevolence prevailed, and the degrees in which it was wanting. That is, we should neither approve of benevolence to some persons rather than to others, nor disapprove injustice and falsehood, upon any other account, than merely as an overbalance of happiness was foreseen likely to be produced by the first, and of misery by the second. But now, on the contrary, suppose two men competitors for anything whatever, which would be of equal advantage to each of them; though nothing, indeed, would be more impertinent than for a stranger to busy himself to get one of them preferred to the other, yet such endeavour would be virtue, in behalf of a friend or benefactor, abstracted from all consideration of distant consequences; as that examples of gratitude, and the cultivation of friendship, would be of general good to the world. Again, suppose one man should by fraud or violence, take from another the fruit of his labour, with intent to give it to a third, who, he thought, would have as much pleasure from it as would balance the pleasure which the first possessor would have had in the enjoyment, and his vexation in the loss of it; suppose also, that no bad consequences would follow; yet such an action would surely be vicious. Nay, farther, were treachery, violence, and injustice, no otherwise vicious than as foreseen likely to produce an overbalance of misery to society; then, if in any case a man could procure to himself as great advantage by an act of injustice, as the whole foreseen inconvenience likely to be brought upon others by it would amount to, such a piece of injustice would not be faulty or vicious at all, because it would be no more than, in any other case, for a man to prefer his own satisfaction to another's in equal degrees. The fact, then, appears to be, that we are constituted so as to condemn falsehood, unprovoked violence, injustice, and to approve of benevolence to some preferably to others, abstracted from all consideration which conduct is likeliest to produce an overbalance of happiness or misery. And therefore, were the Author of nature to propose nothing to himself as an end but the production of happiness—were his moral character merely that of benevolence; yet ours is not so. Upon that supposition, indeed, the only reason of his giving us the above-mentioned approbation of benevolence to some persons rather than others, and disapprobation of falsehood, unprovoked violence, and injustice, must be, that he foresaw this constitution of our nature would produce more happiness than forming us with a temper of mere general benevolence. But still, since this is our constitution, falsehood, violence, injustice, must be vice in us, and benevolence to some preferably to others, virtue, abstracted from all consideration of the overbalance of evil or good which they may appear likely to produce.

Now, if human creatures are endued with such a moral nature as we have been explaining, or with a moral faculty, the natural object of which is actions; moral government must consist in rendering them happy and unhappy, in rewarding and punishing them, as they follow, neglect, or depart from the moral rule of action interwoven in their nature, or suggested and enforced by this moral faculty;* in rewarding and punishing them upon account of their so doing.

I am not sensible that I have, in this fifth observation, contradicted what any author designed to assert. But some of great and distinguished merit have, I think, expressed themselves in a manner which may occasion some danger to careless readers, of imagining the whole of virtue to consist in singly aiming, according to the best of their judgment, at promoting the happiness of mankind in the present state; and the whole of vice, in doing what they foresee, or might foresee, is likely to produce an over-balance of unhappiness in it;—than which mistakes none can be conceived more terrible. For it is certain, that some of the most shocking instances of injustice, adultery, mur-der, perjury, and even of persecution, may, in many sup-posable cases, not have the appearance of being likely to produce an overbalance of misery in the present state; perhaps sometimes may have the contrary appearance. For this reflection might easily be carried on; but I forbear——The happiness of the world is the concern of him who is the Lord and the Proprietor of it; nor do we know what we are about, when we endeavour to promote the good of mankind in any ways but those which he has directed; that is, indeed, in all ways not contrary to vera-city and justice. I speak thus upon supposition of persons really endeavouring, in some sort, to do good without regard to these. But the truth seems to be, that such supposed endeavours proceed almost always from ambition, the spirit of party, or some indirect principle, concealed perhaps in great measure from persons themselves. And though it is our business and our duty to endeavour, within the bounds of veracity and justice, to contribute to the ease, convenience, and even cheerfulness and diversion of our fellow-creatures; yet, from our short views, it is greatly uncertain whether this endeavour will, in particular in-

* Part i. chap. 6, p. 99.

stances, produce an overbalance of happiness upon the whole; since so many and distant things must come into the account. And that which makes it our duty is, that there is some appearance that it will, and no positive appearance sufficient to balance this on the contrary side; and also, that such benevolent endeavour is a cultivation of that most excellent of all virtuous principles, the active principle of benevolence.

However, though veracity, as well as justice, is to be our rule of life, it must be added, (otherwise a snare will be laid in the way of some plain men,) that the use of common forms of speech generally understood cannot be falsehood; and, in general, that there can be no designed falsehood without designing to deceive. It must likewise be observed, that, in numberless cases, a man may be under the strictest obligations to what he foresees will deceive, without his intending it. For it is impossible not to foresee, that the words and actions of men in different ranks and employments, and of different educations, will perpetually be mistaken by each other; and it cannot but be so, whilst they will judge with the utmost carelessness, as they daily do, of what they are not, perhaps, enough informed to be competent judges of, even though they considered it with great attention.

THE END.

Baine Brothers, Printers, 38, Gracechurch Street, London.

FIFTEEN SERMONS

PREACHED AT THE ROLLS CHAPEL;

TO WHICH ARE ADDED,

SIX SERMONS

PREACHED ON PUBLIC OCCASIONS, &c. &c.

BY JOSEPH BUTLER, LL.D.

LATE LORD BISHOP OF DURHAM.

A NEW EDITION.

LONDON:

PRINTED FOR THOMAS TEGG, No. 73, CHEAPSIDE;

R. GRIFFIN AND CO. GLASGOW;

AND TEGG AND CO. DUBLIN.

MDCCCXXXIX.

WILLIAM TYLER,
PRINTER,
BOLT COURT, LONDON.

CONTENTS.

SERMONS PREACHED ON PUBLIC OCCASIONS.

PREFACE.

Though it is scarce possible to avoid judging, in some way or other, of almost every thing which offers itself to one's thoughts, yet it is certain that many persons, from different causes, never exercise their judgment upon what comes before them, in the way of determining whether it be conclusive and holds. They are perhaps entertained with some things, not so with others; they like and they dislike: But whether that which is proposed to be made out, be really made out or not; whether a matter be stated according to the real truth of the case, seems to the generality of people merely a circumstance of no consideration at all. Arguments are often wanted for some accidental purpose: But proof, as such, is what they never want for themselves; for their own satisfaction of mind, or conduct in life. Not to mention the multitudes who read merely for the sake of talking, or to qualify themselves for the world, or some such kind of reasons; there are, even of the few who read for their own entertainment, and have a real curiosity to see what is said, several (which is prodigious) who have no sort of curiosity to see what is true: I say, curiosity; because it is too obvious to be mentioned, how much that religious and sacred attention, which is due to truth, and to the important question, What is the rule of life? is lost out of the world.

For the sake of this whole class of readers, for they are of different capacities, different kinds, and get into this way from different occasions, I have often wished that it had been the custom to lay before people nothing in matters of argument but premises, and leave them to draw conclusions themselves; which, though it could not be done in all cases, might in many.

B

The great number of books and papers of amusement, which, of one kind or another, daily come in one's way, have in part occasioned, and most perfectly fall in with and humour, this idle way of reading and considering things. By this means, time, even in solitude, is happily got rid of, without the pain of attention: Neither is any part of it more put to the account of idleness, one can scarce forbear saying, is spent with less thought, than great part of that which is spent in reading.

Thus people habituate themselves to let things pass through their minds, as one may speak, rather than to think of them. Thus, by use, they become satisfied merely with seeing what is said, without going any further. Review and attention, and even forming a judgment, become fatigue; and to lay any thing before them that requires it, is putting them quite out of the way.

There are also persons, and there are at least more of them than have a right to claim such superiority, who take for granted, that they are acquainted with every thing; and that no subject, if treated in the manner it should be, can be treated in any manner but what is familiar and easy to them.

It is true, indeed, that few persons have a right to demand attention; but it is also true, that nothing can be understood without that degree of it, which the very nature of the thing requires. Now morals, considered as a science, concerning which speculative difficulties are daily raised, and treated with regard to those difficulties, plainly require a very peculiar attention. For here ideas never are in themselves determinate, but become so by the train of reasoning and the place they stand in; since it is impossible that words can always stand for the same ideas, even in the same author, much less in different ones. Hence an argument may not readily be apprehended, which is different from its being mistaken; and even caution to avoid being mistaken, may, in some cases, render it less readily apprehended. It is very unallowable for a work of imagination or entertainment not to be of easy comprehension, but may be unavoidable in a work of another kind, where a man is not to form or accommodate, but to state things as he finds them.

It must be acknowledged, that some of the following dis-

8

courses are very abstruse and difficult ; or, if you please, obscure : But I must take leave to add, that those alone are judges, whether or no, and how far this is a fault; who are judges whether or no, and how far it might have been avoided—those only who will be at the trouble to understand what is here said, and to see how far the things here insisted upon, and not other things, might have been put in a plainer manner; which yet I am very far from asserting that they could not.

Thus much however will be allowed, that general criticisms concerning obscurity, considered as a distinct thing from confusion and perplexity of thought, as in some cases there may be ground for them, so, in others, they may be nothing more at the bottom than complaints, that every thing is not to be understood with the same ease that some things are. Confusion and perplexity in writing is indeed without excuse, because any one may, if he pleases, know whether he understands and sees through what he is about ; and it is unpardonable for a man to lay his thoughts before others, when he is conscious that he himself does not know whereabouts he is, or how the matter before him stands. It is coming abroad in a disorder, which he ought to be dissatisfied to find himself in at home.

But even obscurities, arising from other causes than the abstruseness of the argument, may not be always inexcusable. Thus, a subject may be treated in a manner which all along supposes the reader acquainted with what has been said upon it, both by ancient and modern writers ; and with what is the present state of opinion in the world concerning such subject. This will create a difficulty of a very peculiar kind, and even throw an obscurity over the whole, before those who are not thus informed ; but those who are, will be disposed to excuse such a manner, and other things of the like kind, as a saving of their patience.

However, upon the whole, as the title of *Sermons* gives some right to expect what is plain and of easy comprehension, and as the best auditories are mixed, I shall not set about to justify the propriety of preaching, or under that title publishing, discourses so abstruse as some of these are : Neither is it worth while to trouble the reader with the account of my doing either. He must not, however, impute to me, as a repetition of the impropriety, this second edition,* but to the demand for it.

Whether he will think he has any amends made him, by the following illustrations of what seemed most to require them, I myself am by no means a proper judge.

There are two ways in which the subject of morals may be treated. One begins from inquiring into the abstract relations of things; the other, from a matter of fact, namely, what the particular nature of man is, its several parts, their economy or constitution; from whence it proceeds to determine what course of life it is, which is correspondent to this whole nature. In the former method the conclusion is expressed thus, that vice is contrary to the nature and reasons of things; in the latter, that it is a violation or breaking in upon our own nature. Thus they both lead us to the same thing, our obligations to the practice of virtue; and thus they exceedingly strengthen and enforce each other. The first seems the most direct formal proof, and in some respects the least liable to cavil and dispute: The latter is in a peculiar manner adapted to satisfy a fair mind, and is more easily applicable to the several particular relations and circumstances in life.

The following discourses proceed chiefly in this latter method. The three first wholly. They were intended to explain what is meant by the nature of man, when it is said that virtue consists in following, and vice in deviating from it; and, by explaining, to show that the assertion is true. That the ancient moralists had some inward feeling or other, which they chose to express in this manner, that man is born to virtue, that it consists in following nature, and that vice is more contrary to this nature than tortures or death, their works in our hands are instances. Now, a person who found no mystery in this way of speaking of the ancients: who, without being very explicit with himself, kept to his natural feeling, went along with them, and found within himself a full conviction that what they laid down was just and true; such an one would probably wonder to see a point, in which he never perceived any difficulty, so laboured as this is, in the second and third sermons; insomuch, perhaps, as to be at a loss for the occasion,

* The Preface stands exactly as it did before the second edition of the Sermons.

2

scope, and drift of them.   But it need not be thought
strange, that this manner of expression, though familiar
with them, and if not usually carried so far, yet not uncommon amongst ourselves, should want explaining; since
there are several perceptions daily felt and spoken of, which
yet it may not be very easy at first view to explicate, to
distinguish from all others, and ascertain exactly what the
idea or perception is.   The many treatises upon the passions are a proof of this; since so many would never have
undertaken to unfold their several complications, and trace
and resolve them into their principles, if they had thought,
what they were endeavouring to show was obvious to every
one who felt and talked of those passions.   Thus though
there seems no ground to doubt, but that the generality of
mankind have the inward perception expressed so commonly in that manner by the ancient moralists, more than
to doubt whether they have those passions, yet it appeared
of use to unfold that inward conviction, and lay it open in
a more explicit manner than I had seen done; especially
when there were not wanting persons, who manifestly mis-
took the whole thing, and so had great reason to express
themselves dissatisfied with it.   A late author, of great and
deserved reputation, says, that to place virtue in following
nature, is, at best, a loose way of talk.   And he has reason
to say this, if what I think he intends to express, though
with great decency, be true, that scarce any other sense can
be put upon those words, but acting as any of the several
parts, without distinction, of a man's nature, happened most
to incline him.*

Whoever thinks it worth while to consider this matter
thoroughly, should begin with stating to himself exactly
the idea of a system, economy, or constitution, of any particular nature, or particular any thing; and he will, I suppose, find, that it is an one or a whole, made up of several
parts; but yet that the several parts, even considered as a
whole, do not complete the idea, unless in the notion of a
whole, you include the relations and respects which those
parts have to each other.   Every work, both of nature and
of art, is a system: And as every particular thing, both
natural and artificial, is for some use or purpose out of and

* Religion of Nature Delineated.   Ed. 1724. Pages 22, 23.

beyond itself, one may add to what has been already
brought into the idea of a system, its conduciveness to this
one or more ends. Let us instance in a watch: Suppose
the several parts of it taken to pieces, and placed apart
from each other: Let a man have ever so exact a notion of
these several parts, unless he considers the respect and relations which they have to each other, he will not have any
thing like the idea of a watch. Suppose these several
parts brought together and any how united: Neither will
he yet, be the union ever so close, have an idea which will
bear any resemblance to that of a watch. But let him
view those several parts put together, or consider them as
to be put together, in the manner of a watch; let them form
a notion of the relations which those several parts have to
each other—all conducive, in their respective ways, to this
purpose, showing the hour of the day; and then he has the
idea of a watch. Thus it is with regard to the inward
frame of man. Appetites, passions, affections, and the principle of affection, considered merely as the several parts of
our inward nature, do not at all give us an idea of the system or constitution of this nature: because the constitution
is formed by somewhat not yet taken into consideration,
namely, by the relations which these several parts have to
each other; the chief of which is the authority of reflection
or conscience. It is from considering the relations which
the several appetites and passions in the inward frame have
to each other, and, above all, the supremacy of reflection
or conscience, that we get the idea of the system or constitution of human nature. And from the idea itself it will as
fully appear, that this our nature, *i. e.* constitution, is adapted
to virtue, as from the idea of a watch it appears, that its
nature, *i. e.* constitution or system, is adapted to measure
time. What in fact or event commonly happens, is nothing
to this question. Every work of art is apt to be out of
order; but this is so far from being according to its system, that let the disorder increase, and it will totally destroy it. This is merely by way of explanation, what an
economy, system, or constitution is. And thus far the
cases are perfectly parallel. If we go further, there is indeed a difference, nothing to the present purpose, but too
important an one ever to be omitted. A machine is inanimate and passive: But we are agents. Our constitution is

put in our power; we are charged with it, and therefore are accountable for any disorder or violation of it.

Thus nothing can possibly be more contrary to nature than vice; meaning by nature not only the *several parts* of our internal frame, but also the *constitution* of it. Poverty and disgrace, tortures and death, are not so contrary to it. Misery and injustice are indeed equally contrary to some different parts of our nature taken singly: but injustice is moreover contrary to the whole constitution of the nature.

If it be asked, whether this constitution be really what those philosophers meant, and whether they would have explained themselves in this manner, the answer is the same as if it should be asked, whether a person, who had often used the word resentment, and felt the thing, would have explained this passion exactly in the same manner in which it is done in one of these discourses. As I have no doubt but that this is a true account of that passion, which he referred to and intended to express by the word resentment, so I have no doubt, but that this is the true account of the ground of that conviction which they referred to, when they said, vice was contrary to nature. And though it should be thought that they meant no more than that vice was contrary to the higher and better part of our nature, even this implies such a constitution as I have endeavoured to explain. For the very terms, *higher* and *better*, imply a relation or respect of parts to each other; and these relative parts, being in one and the same nature, form a constitution, and are the very idea of it. They had a perception that injustice was contrary to their nature, and that pain was so also. They observed these two perceptions totally different, not in degree, but in kind; and the reflecting upon each of them, as they thus stood in their nature, wrought a full intuitive conviction, that more was due, and of right belonging to one of these inward perceptions, than to the other; that it demanded in all cases to govern such a creature as man. So that, upon the whole, this is a fair and true account of what was the ground of their conviction; of what they intended to refer to when they said, virtue consisted in following nature—a manner of speaking, not loose and undeterminate, but clear and distinct, strictly just and true.

Though I am persuaded the force of this conviction is felt by almost every one, yet since, considered as an argument and put in words, it appears somewhat abstruse, and since the connexion of it is broken in the three first sermons, it may not be amiss to give the reader the whole argument here in one view.

Mankind has various instincts and principles of action, as brute creatures have; some leading most directly and immediately to the good of the community, and some most directly to private good.

Man has several which brutes have not; particularly reflection or conscience, an approbation of some principles or actions, and disapprobation of others.

Brutes obey their instincts or principles of action, according to certain rules; suppose the constitution of their body, and the objects around them.

The generality of mankind also obey their instincts and principles, all of them; those propensions we call good, as well as the bad, according to the same rules—namely, the constitution of their body, and the external circumstances which they are in. [Therefore it is not a true representation of mankind, to affirm that they are wholly governed by self-love, the love of power and sensual appetites: since, as on the one hand, they are often actuated by these, without any regard to right or wrong; so on the other, it is manifest fact, that the same persons, the generality, are frequently influenced by friendship, compassion, gratitude, and even a general abhorrence of what is base, and liking of what is fair and just, takes its turn amongst the other motives of action. This is the partial inadequate notion of human nature treated of in the first discourse: and it is by this nature, if one may speak so, that the world is in fact influenced, and kept in that tolerable order in which it is.]

Brutes, in acting according to the rules before mentioned, their bodily constitution and circumstances, act suitably to their whole nature. [It is however to be distinctly noted, that the reason why we affirm this, is not merely that brutes in fact act so; for this alone, however universal, does not at all determine whether such course of action be correspondent to their whole nature. But the reason of the assertion is, that as, in acting thus, they plainly act conformably to somewhat in their nature, so, from all observations we are able to make upon them, there does not appear the least ground to imagine them to have any thing else in their nature, which requires a different rule or course of action.]

Mankind also, in acting thus, would act suitably to their whole nature, if no more were to be said of man's nature than what has been now said; if that, as it is a true, were also a complete, adequate account of our nature.

But that is not a complete account of man's nature. Somewhat further must be brought in to give us an adequate notion of it—namely, that one of those principles of action, conscience, or reflection, compared with the rest, as they all stand together in the nature of man, plainly bears upon it marks of authority over all the rest, and claims the absolute direction of them all, to allow or forbid their gratification; a disapprobation of reflection being in itself a principle manifestly superior to a mere propension. And the conclusion is, that to allow no more to this superior principle or part of our nature, than to other parts; to let it govern and guide only occasionally in common with the rest, as its turn happens to come, from the temper and circumstances one happens to be in; this is not to act conformably to the constitution of man. Neither can any human creature be said to act conformably to his constitution of nature, unless he allows to that superior principle the absolute authority which is due to it. And this conclusion is abundantly confirmed from hence, that one may determine what course of action the economy of man's nature requires, without so much as knowing in what degrees of *strength* the several principles prevail, or which of them have actually the greatest influence.

The practical reason of insisting so much upon this natural authority of the principle of reflection or conscience is, that it seems in a great measure overlooked by many, who are by no means the worst sort of men. It is thought sufficient to abstain from gross wickedness, and to be humane and kind to such as happen to come in their way. Whereas, in reality, the very constitution of our nature requires, that we bring our whole conduct before this superior faculty; wait its determination; enforce upon ourselves its authority; and make it the business of our lives, as it is absolutely the whole business of a moral agent, to conform ourselves to it. This is the true meaning of that ancient precept, *Reverence thyself*.

The not taking into consideration the authority, which is implied in the idea of reflex approbation or disapprobation, seems a material deficiency or omission in *Lord Shaftesbury's Inquiry concerning Virtue*. He has shown, beyond all contradiction, that virtue is naturally the interest or happiness, and vice the misery of such a creature as man, placed in the circumstances which we are in this world. But suppose there are particular exceptions; a case which this author was unwilling to put, and yet surely it is to be put. Or suppose a case which he has put and determined, that of a sceptic not convinced of this happy tendency of virtue, or being of a contrary opinion: His determination is, that it would be *without remedy*.* One may say more explicitly, that, leaving out the authority of reflex approbation or disapprobation, such an one would be under an obligation to act viciously; since interest, one's own happiness, is a manifest obligation, and there is not supposed to be any other obligation in the case. "But does it much mend the matter, to take in that natural authority of reflection? There indeed would be an obligation to virtue; but would not the obligation from supposed interest on the side of vice remain?" If it should, yet to be under two contrary obligations, *i. e.* under none at all, would not be exactly the same as to be under a formal obligation to be vicious, or to be in circumstances in which the constitution of man's nature plainly required, that vice should be preferred. But the obligation on the side of interest really does not remain. For the natural authority of the principle of reflection, is an obligation the most near and intimate, the most certain and known: whereas the contrary obligation can at the utmost appear no more than probable; since no man can be *certain*, in any circumstances, that vice is his interest in the present world, much less can he be certain against another. And thus the certain obligation would entirely supersede and destroy the uncertain one; which yet would have been of real force without the former.

* Characteristics, vol. ii. p. 69.

In truth, the taking in this consideration totally changes the whole state of the case, and shows, what this author does not seem to have been aware of, that the greatest degree of scepticism which he thought possible, will still leave men under the strictest moral obligations, whatever their opinion be concerning the happiness of virtue. For, that mankind, upon reflection, felt an approbation of what was good, and disapprobation of the contrary, he thought a plain matter of fact, as it undoubtedly is, which none could deny, but from mere affectation. Take in, then, that authority and obligation, which is a constituent part of this reflex approbation, and it will undeniably follow, though a man should doubt of every thing else, yet, that he would still remain under the nearest and most certain obligation to the practice of virtue; an obligation implied in the very idea of virtue, in the very idea of reflex approbation.

And how little influence soever this obligation alone can be expected to have, in fact, upon mankind, yet one may appeal even to interest and self-love, and ask, since from man's nature, condition, and the shortness of life, so little, so very little, indeed, can possibly in any case be gained by vice, whether it be so prodigious a thing to sacrifice that little to the most intimate of all obligations; and which a man cannot transgress without being self-condemned, and, unless he has corrupted his nature, without real self-dislike? This question, I say, may be asked, even upon suspicion that the prospect of a future life were ever so uncertain.

The observation that man is thus, by his very nature, a law to himself, pursued to its just consequences, is of the utmost importance; because from it will follow, that though men should, through stupidity, or speculative scepticism, be ignorant of, or disbelieve, any authority in the universe to punish the violation of this law; yet, if there should be such authority, they would be as really liable to punishment, as though they had been before-hand convinced, that such punishment would follow. For, in whatever sense we understand justice, even supposing, what I think would be very presumptuous to assert, that the end of divine punishment is no other than that of civil punishment—namely, to prevent further mischief; upon this bold supposition, ignorance or disbelief of the sanction would by no means ex-

empt even from this injustice; because it is not foreknowledge of the punishment which renders obnoxious to it, but
merely violating a known obligation.

And here it comes in one's way to take notice of a manifest error, or mistake, in the author now cited, unless,
perhaps, he has incautiously expressed himself so as to be
misunderstood—namely, that "it is malice only, and not
goodness, which can make us afraid."* Whereas, in reality, goodness is the natural and just object of the greatest
fear to an ill man. Malice may be appeased or satiated;
humour may change; but goodness is a fixed, steady, immoveable principle of action. If either of the former holds
the sword of justice, there is plainly ground for the greatest of crimes to hope for impunity: but if it be goodness,
there can be no possible hope, whilst the reason of things,
or the ends of government, call for punishment. Thus,
every one sees how much greater chance of impunity an ill
man has, in a partial administration, than in a just and upright one. It is said, that "the interest, or good of the
whole, must be the interest of the universal Being, and that
He can have no other." Be it so. This author has proved,
that vice is naturally the misery of mankind in this world.
Consequently, it was for the good of the whole, that it
should be so. What shadow of reason, then, is there to
assert, that this may not be the case hereafter? Danger of
future punishment (and if there be danger, there is ground
of fear) no more supposes malice than the present feeling
of punishment does.

The sermon *upon the character of Balaam*, and that
upon self-deceit, both relate to one subject. I am persuaded
that a very great part of the wickedness of the world is,
one way or other, owing to the self-partiality, self-flattery,
and self-deceit endeavoured there to be laid open and explained. It is to be observed amongst persons of the
lowest rank, in proportion to their compass of thought, as
much as amongst men of education and improvement. It
seems, that people are capable of being thus artful with
themselves, in proportion as they are capable of being so
with others. Those who have taken notice that there is
really such a thing—namely, plain falseness and insincerity
in men, with regard to themselves, will readily see the drift

* Characteristics, vol. i. p. 39.

and design of these discourses : And nothing that I can add
will explain the design of them to him, who has not beforehand remarked at least somewhat of the character. And
yet the admonitions they contain may be as much wanted
by such a person as by others ; for it is to be noted, that a
man may be entirely possessed by this unfairness of mind,
without having the least speculative notion what the thing is.

The account given of *resentment,* in the eighth sermon,
is introductory to the following one, *upon forgiveness of
injuries.* It may possibly have appeared to some, at first
sight, a strange assertion, that injury is the only natural
object of settled resentment ; or that men do not, in fact,
resent deliberately any thing but under this appearance of
injury. But I must desire the reader not to take any
assertion alone by itself, but to consider the whole of what
is said upon it : Because this is necessary, not only in order
to judge of the truth of it, but often, such is the nature of
language, to see the very meaning of the assertion. Particularly as to this, injury and injustice is, in the sermon
itself, explained to mean, not only the more gross and
shocking instances of wickedness, but also contempt, scorn,
neglect, any sort of disagreeable behaviour towards a person, which he thinks other than what is due to him. And
the general notion of injury, or wrong, plainly comprehends this, though the words are mostly confined to the
higher degrees of it.

Forgiveness of injuries is one of the very few moral obligations which has been disputed. But the proof that it
is really an obligation, what our nature and condition require, seems very obvious, were it only from the consideration, that revenge is doing harm merely for harm's sake.
And as to the love of our enemies : Resentment cannot
supersede the obligations to universal benevolence, unless
they are in the nature of the thing inconsistent, which they
plainly are not.

This divine precept, to forgive injuries and love our
enemies, though to be met with in Gentile moralists, yet is
in a peculiar sense a precept of Christianity ; as our Saviour has insisted more upon it than upon any other single
virtue. One reason of this, doubtless, is, that it so peculiarly becomes an imperfect, faulty creature. But it may
be observed also, that a virtuous temper of mind, con-

sciousness of innocence, and good meaning towards every body, and a strong feeling of injustice and injury, may, itself, such is the imperfection of our virtue, lead a person to violate this obligation, if he be not upon his guard. And it may be well supposed, that this is another reason why it is so much insisted upon by him, who *knew what was in man.*

(The chief design of the eleventh discourse, is to state the notion of self-love and disinterestedness, in order to show that benevolence is not more unfriendly to self-love than any other particular affection whatever. There is a strange affectation in many people of explaining away all particular affections, and representing the whole of life as nothing but one continued exercise of self-love.) Hence arises that surprising confusion and perplexity in the Epicureans* of old, Hobbs, the author of *Reflections, Sentences, et Maximes Morales,* and this whole set of writers ; the confusion of calling actions interested, which are done in contradiction to the most manifest known interest, merely for the gratification of a present passion. (Now, all this confusion might easily be avoided, by stating to ourselves wherein the idea of self-love in general consists, as distinguished from all particular movements towards particular external objects; the appetites of sense, resentment, compassion, curiosity, ambition, and the rest. When this is done, if the words *selfish* and *interested* cannot be parted with, but must be applied to every thing; yet, to avoid such total confusion of all language, let the distinction be made by epithets ; and the first may be called cool, or settled selfishness, and the other passionate, or sensual selfishness. But the most natural way of speaking plainly is, to call the first only, self-love, and the actions proceeding

---

* One need only look into Torquatus's account of the Epicurean system, in Cicero's first book *De Finibus,* to see in what a surprising manner this was done by them. Thus, the desire of praise, and of being beloved, he explains to be no other than desire of safety : Regard to our country, even in the most virtuous character, to be nothing but regard to ourselves. The author of *Reflections, &c. Morales,* says, " curiosity proceeds from interest, or pride ; which pride also would doubtless have been explained to be self-love ;" (Page 85. *Ed.* 1725) —as if there were no passions in mankind, as desire of esteem, or of being beloved, or of knowledge. Hobbs' account of the affections of good-will and pity, are instances of the same kind.

from it, interested ; and to say of the latter, that they are
not love to ourselves, but movements towards somewhat
external,——honour, power, the harm or good of another :
And that the pursuit of these external objects, so far as it
proceeds from these movements, (for it may proceed from
self-love,) is no otherwise interested, than as every action
of every creature must, from the nature of the thing, be ;
for no one can act but from a desire, or choice, or preference of his own.)

Self-love and any particular passion may be joined together ; and from this complication, it becomes impossible,
in numberless instances, to determine precisely how far an
action, perhaps even of one's own, has for its principle
general self-love, or some particular passion. But this need
create no confusion in the ideas themselves of self love and
particular passions. We distinctly discern what one is, and
what the other are ; though we may be uncertain how far
one or the other influences us. And though, from this uncertainty, it cannot but be, that there will be different
opinions concerning mankind, as more or less governed by
interest ; and some will ascribe actions to self-love, which
others will ascribe to particular passions ; yet it is absurd
to say, that mankind are wholly actuated by either ; since
it is manifest that both have their influence. For as, on
the one hand, men form a general notion of interest, some
placing it in one thing, and some in another, and have a
considerable regard to it throughout the course of their
life, which is owing to self-love ; so, on the other hand,
they are often set on work by the particular passions themselves, and a considerable part of life is spent in the actual
gratification of them ; *i. e.* is employed, not by self-love,
but by the passions.

Besides, the very idea of an interested pursuit, necessarily presupposes particular passions or appetites ; since
the very idea of interest, or happiness, consists in this, that
an appetite, or affection, enjoys its object. It is not because we love ourselves that we find delight in such and
such objects, but because we have particular affections
towards them. Take away these affections, and you leave
self-love absolutely nothing at all to employ itself about ;
no end, or object, for it to pursue, excepting only that of
avoiding pain. Indeed, the Epicureans, who maintained

that absence of pain was the highest happiness, might, consistently with themselves, deny all affection, and, if they
had so pleased, every sensual appetite too: But the very
idea of interest, or happiness, other than absence of pain,
implies particular appetites or passions ; these being necessary to constitute that interest or happiness.

The observation, that benevolence is no more disinterested than any of the common particular passions, seems in
itself worth being taken notice of; but is insisted upon to
obviate that scorn, which one sees rising upon the faces of
people, who are said to know the world, when mention is
made of a disinterested, generous, or public-spirited action.
The truth of that observation might be made appear in a
more formal manner of proof: For, whoever will consider
all the possible respects and relations which any particular
affection can have to self-love and private interest, will, I
think, see demonstrably, that benevolence is not in any
respect more at variance with self-love, than any other particular affection whatever, but that it is, in every respect,
at least as friendly to it.

If the observation be true, it follows, that self-love and
benevolence, virtue and interest, are not to be opposed,
but only to be distinguished from each other ; in the same
way as virtue and any other particular affection, love of
arts, suppose, are to be distinguished. Every thing is what
it is, and not another thing. The goodness, or badness of
actions, does not arise from hence, that the epithet, interested, or disinterested, may be applied to them, any
more than that any other indifferent epithet, suppose inquisitive or jealous, may, or may not, be applied to them ;
not from their being attended with present or future pleasure or pain, but from their being what they are ; namely,
what becomes such creatures as we are, what the state of
the case requires, or the contrary. Or, in other words, we
may judge and determine that an action is morally good or
evil, before we so much as consider, whether it be interested
or disinterested. This consideration no more comes in to
determine, whether an action be virtuous, than to determine whether it be resentful. Self-love, in its due degree,
is as just and morally good as any affection whatever.
Benevolence towards particular persons may be to a degree of weakness, and so be blameable. And disinterested-

ness is so far from being in itself commendable, that the utmost possible depravity, which we can in imagination conceive, is that of disinterested cruelty.

Neither does there appear any reason to wish self-love were weaker in the generality of the world than it is.—The influence which it has, seems plainly owing to its being constant and habitual, which it cannot but be, and not to the degree or strength of it. Every caprice of the imagination, every curiosity of the understanding, every affection of the heart, is perpetually showing its weakness, by prevailing over it. Men daily, hourly, sacrifice the greatest known interest to fancy, inquisitiveness, love or hatred, any vagrant inclination. The thing to be lamented is, not that men have so great regard to their own good or interest in the present world, for they have not enough; but that they have so little to the good of others. And this seems plainly owing to their being so much engaged in the gratification of particular passions unfriendly to benevolence, and which happen to be most prevalent in them, much more than to self-love. As a proof of this may be observed, that there is no character more void of friendship, gratitude, natural affection, love to their country, common justice, or more equally and uniformly hard-hearted, than the *abandoned* in, what is called, the way of pleasure——hard-hearted and totally without feeling in behalf of others; except when they cannot escape the sight of distress, and so are interrupted by it in their pleasures. And yet it is ridiculous to call such an abandoned course of pleasure interested, when the person engaged in it knows beforehand, and goes on under the feeling and apprehension, that it will be as ruinous to himself, as to those who depend upon him.

Upon the whole, if the generality of mankind were to cultivate within themselves the principle of self-love; if they were to accustom themselves often to set down and consider, what was the greatest happiness they were capable of attaining for themselves in this life; and if self-love were so strong and prevalent, as that they would uniformly pursue this their supposed chief temporal good, without being diverted from it by any particular passion, it would manifestly prevent numberless follies and vices. This was in a great measure the *Epicurean* system of philosophy. It is indeed by no means the religious, or even moral institution of life. Yet with all the mistakes men would fall into about interest, it would be less mischievous than the extravagances of mere appetite, will, and pleasure: For certainly self-love, though confined to the interest of this life, is, of the two, a much better guide than passion, which has absolutely no bound nor measure, but what is set to it by this self-love, or moral considerations.

From the distinction above made, between self-love and the several particular principles or affections in our nature, we may see how good ground there was for that assertion, maintained by the several ancient *schools* of philosophy against the *Epicureans*, namely, that virtue is to be pursued as an end, eligible in and for itself. For, if there be any principles or affections in the mind of man distinct from self-love, that the things those principles tend towards, or that the objects of those affections are, each of them, in themselves eligible to be pursued upon its own account, and to be rested in as an end, is implied in the very idea of such principle or affection. They indeed asserted much higher things of virtue, and with very good reason: but to say thus much of it, that it is to be pursued for itself, is to say no more of it than may truly be said of the object of every natural affection whatever.

The question which was a few years ago disputed in France, concerning *the love of God*, which was there called enthusiasm, as it will every where by the generality of the world; this question, I say, answers, in *religion*, to that old one in *morals* now mentioned. And both of them are, I think, fully determined by the same observation, namely, that the very nature of affection, the idea itself, necessarily implies resting in its object as an end.

I shall not here add anything further to what I have said in the two discourses upon that most important subject, but only this, that if we are constituted such sort of creatures, as, from our very nature, to feel certain affections or movements of mind, upon the sight or contemplation of the meanest inanimate part of the creation, for the flowers of the field have their beauty; certainly there must be somewhat due to him himself, who is the Author and Cause of all things; who is more intimately present to us than any thing else can be; and with whom we have a nearer and more constant intercourse, than we can have with any creature : There must be some movements of mind and heart which correspond to his perfections, or of which those perfections are the natural object. And that when we are commanded to *love the Lord our God, with all our heart, and with all our mind, and with all our soul,* somewhat more must be meant than merely that we live in hope of rewards, or fear of punishments from him ; somewhat more than this must be intended ; though these regards themselves are most just and reasonable, and absolutely necessary to be often recollected, in such a world as this.

It may be proper just to advertise the reader, that he is not to look for any particular reason for the choice of the greatest part of these discourses ; their being taken from amongst many others, preached in the same place, through a course of eight years, being in great measure accidental. Neither is he to expect to find any other connexion between them, than that uniformity of thought and design, which will always be found in the writings of the same person, when he writes with simplicity and in earnest.

STANHOPE, *Sept.* 16, 1729.

SERMON I.

UPON HUMAN NATURE.

Romans xii. 4, 5.

For as we have many members in one body, and all members
have not the same office; so we, being many, are one body
in Christ, and every one members one of another.

THE epistles in the New Testament have all of them a
particular reference to the condition and usages of the
Christian world at the time they were written.   Therefore,
as they cannot be thoroughly understood, unless that condition and those usages are known and attended to; so,
further, though they be known, yet, if they be discontinued
or changed, exhortations, precepts, and illustrations of
things, which refer to such circumstances now ceased or
altered, cannot at this time be urged in that manner, and
with that force, which they were to the primitive Christians.
Thus, the text now before us, in its first intent and design,
relates to the decent management of those extraordinary
gifts which were then in the church,* but which are now
totally ceased.   And even as to the allusion, that "we are
one body in Christ," though what the apostle here intends
is equally true of Christians in all circumstances; and the
consideration of it is plainly still an additional motive, over
and above moral considerations, to the discharge of the
several duties and offices of a Christian; yet it is manifest
this allusion must have appeared with much greater force to
those, who, by the many difficulties they went through for

* 1 Cor. xii.

the sake of their religion, were led to keep always in view
the relation they stood in to their Saviour, who had undergone the same ; to those who, from the idolatries of all
around them, and their ill treatment, were taught to consider themselves as not of the world in which they lived,
but as a distinct society of themselves; with laws, and ends,
and principles of life and action, quite contrary to those
which the world professed themselves at that time influenced
by. Hence the relation of a Christian was by them considered as nearer than that of affinity and blood ; and they
almost literally esteemed themselves as members one of
another.

It cannot indeed possibly be denied, that our being God's
creatures, and virtue being the natural law we are born
under, and the whole constitution of man being plainly
adapted to it, are prior obligations to piety and virtue, than
the consideration that God sent his Son into the world to
save it, and the motives which arise from the peculiar relation of Christians, as members one of another, under
Christ our head. However, though all this be allowed, as
it expressly is by the inspired writers, yet it is manifest,
that Christians, at the time of the Revelation, and immediately after, could not but insist mostly upon considerations
of this latter kind.

These observations show the original particular reference
of the text ; and the peculiar force with which the thing
intended by the allusion in it, must have been felt by the
primitive Christian world. They likewise afford a reason
for treating it at this time in a more general way.

The relation which the several parts or members of the
natural body have to each other, and to the whole body, is
here compared to the relation which each particular person
in society has to other particular persons, and to the whole
society ; and the latter is intended to be illustrated by the
former.   And if there be a likeness between these two
relations, the consequence is obvious : That the latter shows
us we were intended to do good to others, as the former
shows us, that the several members of the natural body
were intended to be instruments of good to each other, and
to the whole body. But as there is scarce any ground for
a comparison between society and the mere material body,
this without the mind being a dead unactive thing ; much

less can the comparison be carried to any length. And since the apostle speaks of the several members as having distinct offices, which implies the mind, it cannot be thought an allowable liberty, instead of the *body* and *its members*, to substitute the *whole nature of man, and all the variety of internal principles which belong to it.* And then the comparison will be between the nature of man as respecting self, and tending to private good, his own preservation and happiness; and the nature of man as having respect to society, and tending to promote public good, the happiness of that society. These ends do indeed perfectly coincide; and to aim at public and private good are so far from being inconsistent, that they mutually promote each other; yet, in the following discourse, they must be considered as entirely distinct; otherwise the nature of man, as tending to one, or as tending to the other, cannot be compared. There can no comparison be made, without considering the things compared as distinct and different.

From this review and comparison of the nature of man as respecting self, and as respecting society, it will plainly appear, that *there are as real and the same kind of indications in human nature, that we were made for society and to do good to our fellow-creatures, as that we were intended to take care of our own life, and health, and private good; and that the same objections lie against one of these assertions as against the other.* For,

First, There is a natural principle of *benevolence** in

---

* Suppose a man of learning to be writing a grave book upon human nature, and to show in several parts of it that he had an insight into the subject he was considering; amongst other things, the following one would require to be accounted for; the appearance of benevolence or good-will in men towards each other in the instances of natural relation, and in others.* Cautious of being deceived with outward show, he retires within himself, to see exactly what that is in the mind of man from whence this appearance proceeds; and, upon deep reflection, asserts the principle in the mind to be only the love of power, and delight in the exercise of it. Would not every body think here was a mistake of one word for another? That the philosopher was contemplating and accounting for some other human actions, some other behaviour of man to man? And could any one be thoroughly satisfied, that what is commonly called benevolence or good-will was really the affection meant, but only by being made to understand that this learned person had a general hypothesis, to which the appearance of good-will could no otherwise be reconciled? That what has this appearance, is often nothing but ambition; that delight in

[* Hobbs of Human Nature, c. 2. § 17.]

man, which is in some degree to *society*, what *self-love* is to the *individual*. And if there be in mankind any disposition to friendship; if there be any such thing as compas-

superiority often (suppose always) mixes itself with benevolence, only makes it more specious to call it ambition than hunger, of the two: But in reality that passion does no more account for the whole appearance of good-will than this appetite does. Is there not often the appearance of one man's wishing that good to another, which he knows himself unable to procure him; and rejoicing in it, though bestowed by a third person? And can love of power any way possibly come in to account for this desire or delight? Is there not often the appearance of men's distinguishing between two or more persons, preferring one before another, to do good to, in cases where love of power cannot in the least account for the distinction and preference? For this principle can no otherwise distinguish between objects, than as it is a greater instance and exertion of power to do good to one rather than to another. Again, suppose good-will in the mind of man to be nothing but delight in the exercise of power: Men might indeed be restrained by distant and accidental considerations; but these restraints being removed, they would have a disposition to, and delight in mischief, as an exercise and proof of power: And this disposition and delight would arise from, or be the same principle in the mind, as a disposition to, and delight in charity. Thus cruelty, as distinct from envy and resentment, would be exactly the same in the mind of man as good will: That one tends to the happiness, the other to the misery of our fellow-creatures, is, it seems, merely an accidental circumstance, which the mind has not the least regard to. These are the absurdities which even men of capacity run into, when they have occasion to belie their nature, and will perversely disclaim that image of God which was originally stamped upon it; the traces of which, however faint, are plainly discernible upon the mind of man.

If any person can in earnest doubt, whether there be such a thing as good-will in one man towards another (for the question is not concerning either the degree or extensiveness of it, but concerning the affection itself;) let it be observed, that *whether man be thus, or otherwise constituted, what is the inward frame in this particular*, is a mere question of fact or natural history, not proveable immediately by reason. It is therefore to be judged of and determined in the same way other facts or matters of natural history are: By appealing to the external senses, or inward perceptions, respectively, as the matter under consideration is cognizable by one or the other: By arguing from acknowledged facts and actions; for a great number of actions of the same kind, in different circumstances, and respecting different objects, will prove, to a certainty, what principles they do not, and, to the greatest probability, what principles they do proceed from: And, lastly, by the testimony of mankind. Now, that there is some degree of benevolence amongst men, may be as strongly and plainly proved in all these ways as it could possibly be proved, supposing there was this affection in our nature. And should any one think fit to assert, that resentment in the mind of man was absolutely nothing but reasonable

sion, for compassion is momentary love ; if there be any
such thing as the paternal or filial affections; if there be
any affection in human nature, the object and end of which
is the good of another; this is itself benevolence, or the
love of another.   Be it ever so short, be it n ever so low
a degree, or ever so unhappily confined; it proves the assertion, and points out what we were designed for, as really
as though it were in a higher degree and more extensive. I
must however remind you, that though benevolence and
self-love are different; though the former tends most directly to public good, and the latter to private ; yet they
are so perfectly coincident, that the greatest satisfactions to
ourselves depend upon our having benevolence in a due
degree ; and that self-love is one chief security of our right
behaviour towards society.   It may be added, that their
mutual coinciding, so that we can scarce promote one without the other, is equally a proof that we were made for both.

Secondly, This will further appear from observing, that
the several *passions* and *affections*, which are distinct* both
from benevolence and self-love, do in general contribute

concern for our own safety, the falsity of this, and what is the real
nature of that passion, could be shown in no other ways than those in
which it may be shown, that there is such a thing in *some degree* as
real good-will in man towards man.   It is sufficient that the seeds of
it be implanted in our nature by God.   There is, it is owned, much
left for us to do upon our own heart and temper; to cultivate, to
improve, to call it forth, to exercise it in a steady uniform manner.
This is our work : this is Virtue and Religion.

* Every body makes a distinction between self-love, and the several particular passions, appetites and affections ; and yet they are
often confounded again.   That they are totally different, will be seen
by any one who will distinguish between the passions and appetites
themselves and *endeavouring* after the means of their gratification.
Consider the appetite of hunger, and the desire of esteem ; these
being the occasion both of pleasure and pain, the coolest *self-love*, as
well as the appetites and passions themselves, may put us upon making use of the *proper methods of obtaining* that pleasure, and avoiding
that pain ; but the *feelings themselves*, the pain of hunger and shame,
and the delight from esteem, are no more self-love than they are any
thing in the world.   Though a man hated himself, he would as muc
feel the pain of hunger as he would that of the gout ; and t is plainly
supposable, there may be creatures with self-love in them to the highest degree, who may be quite insensible and indifferent (as men in
some cases are) to the contempt and esteem of those upon whom
their happiness does not in some further respects depend.   And as
self-love and the several particular passions and appetites are in them-

C

and lead us to *public* good as really as to *private*. It might
be thought too minute and particular, and would carry us
too great a length, to distinguish between, and compare together the several passions or appetites, distinct from benevolence, whose primary use and intention is the security
and good of society; and the passions distinct from self-
love, whose primary intention, and design is the security
and good of the individual.* It is enough to the present
argument, that desire of esteem from others, contempt and
esteem of them, love of society as distinct from affection to
the good of it, indignation against successful vice, that
these are public affections or passions, have an immediate
respect to others, naturally lead us to regulate our behaviour in such a manner as will be of service to our fellow-
creatures. If any or all of these may be considered likewise as private affections, as tending to private good, this
does not hinder them from being public affections too, or
destroy the good influence of them upon society, and their

selves totally different; so that some actions proceed from one, and
some from the other, will be manifest to any who will observe the two
following very supposable cases :—One man rushes upon certain ruin
for the gratification of a present desire; nobody will call the principle of this action self-love. Suppose another man to go through
some laborious work, upon promise of a great reward, without any
distinct knowledge what the reward will be; this course of action
cannot be ascribed to any particular passion. The former of these
actions is plainly to be imputed to some particular passion or affection, the latter as plainly to the general affection or principle of self-
love. That there are some particular pursuits or actions concerning
which we cannot determine how far they are owing to one, and how
far to the other, proceeds from this, that the two principles are frequently mixed together, and run into each other. This distinction is
further explained in the eleventh sermon.

* If any desire to see this distinction and comparison made in a
particular instance, the appetite and passion now mentioned may serve
for one. Hunger is to be considered as a private appetite; because
the end for which it was given us, is the preservation of the individual.
Desire of esteem is a public passion; because the end for which
it was given us is to regulate our behaviour towards society. The
respect which this has to private good is as remote as the respect that
has to public good; and the appetite is no more self-love, than the
passion is benevolence. The object and end of the former is merely
food; the object and end of the latter is merely esteem : but the latter
can no more be gratified, without contributing to the good of society,
than the former can be gratified, without contributing to the preservation of the individual.

tendency to public good. It may be added, that as persons
without any conviction from reason of the desirableness of
life, would yet of course preserve it merely from the appetite of hunger ; so, by acting merely from regard (suppose)
to reputation, without any consideration of the good of
others, men often contribute to public good.) In both these
instances they are plainly instruments in the hands of
another, in the hands of Providence, to carry on ends, the
preservation of the individual and good of society, which
they themselves have not in their view or intention. The
sum is, men have various appetites, passions, and particular affections, quite distinct both from self-love and from
benevolence ; all of these have a tendency to promote both
public and private good, and may be considered as respecting others and ourselves equally and in common ; but some
of them seem most immediately to respect others, or tend
to public good ; others of them most immediately to respect self, or tend to private good. As the former are not
benevolence, so the latter are not self-love : neither sort are
instances of our love either to ourselves or others, but only
instances of our Maker's care and love both of the individual and the species, and proofs that he intended we should
be instruments of good to each other, as well as that we
should be so to ourselves.

Thirdly, There is a principle of reflection in men, by
which they distinguish between, approve, and disapprove
their own actions. We are plainly constituted such sort of
creatures as to reflect upon our own nature. The mind
can take a view of what passes within itself, its propensions,
aversions, passions, affections, as respecting such objects,
and in such degrees, and of the several actions consequent
thereupon. In this survey it approves of one, disapproves
of another, and towards a third is affected in neither of
these ways, but is quite indifferent. This principle in man,
by which he approves or disapproves his heart, temper, and
actions, is conscience ; for this is the strict sense of the
word, though sometimes it is used so as to take in more.
And that this faculty tends to restrain men from doing
mischief to each other, and leads them to do good, is too
manifest to need being insisted upon. Thus, a parent has
the affection of love to his children : this leads him to take
care of, to educate, to make due provision for them. The

natural affection leads to this; but the reflection that it is
his proper business, what belongs to him, that it is right
and commendable so to do; this, added to the affection,
becomes a much more settled principle, and carries him on
through more labour and difficulties for the sake of his
children, than he would undergo for that affection alone, if
he thought it, and the course of action it led to, either indifferent or criminal.   This indeed is impossible,—to do
that which is good, and not to approve of it; for which
reason they are frequently not considered as distinct,
though they really are : for men often approve of the actions of others, which they will not imitate, and likewise do
that which they approve not.   It cannot possibly be denied,
that there is this principle of reflection or conscience in
human nature.   Suppose a man to relieve an innocent person in great distress ; suppose the same man afterwards, in
the fury of anger, to do the greatest mischief to a person
who had given no just cause of offence ; to aggravate the
injury, add the circumstances of former friendship, and
obligation from the injured person ; let the man who is supposed to have done these two different actions, coolly reflect upon them afterwards, without regard to their consequences to himself ;—to assert that any common man would
be affected in the same way towards these different actions,
that he would make no distinction between them, but approve or disapprove them equally, is too glaring a falsity to
need being confuted.   There is therefore this principle of
reflection or conscience in mankind.   It is needless to compare the respect it has to private good, with the respect it
has to public ; since it plainly tends as much to the latter
as to the former, and is commonly thought to tend chiefly
to the latter.   This faculty is now mentioned merely as
another part in the inward frame of man, pointing out to
us in some degree what we are intended for, and as what
will naturally and of course have some influence.   The particular place assigned to it by nature, what authority it has,
and how great influence it ought to have, shall be hereafter
·   considered.
     From this comparison of benevolence and self-love, of
our public and private affections, of the courses of life they
lead to, and of the principle of reflection or conscience as
respecting each of them, it is as manifest, that *we were*
                              4

made for society, and to promote the happiness of it ; as
that we were intended to take care of our own life, and health,
and private good.

And from this whole review must be given a different
draught of human nature from what we are often presented
with. Mankind are by nature so closely united, there is
such a correspondence between the inward sensations of
one man and those of another, that disgrace is as much
avoided as bodily pain, and to be the object of esteem and
love as much desired as any external goods : and, in many
particular cases, persons are carried on to do good to others,
as the end their affections tend to, and rest in ; and manifest that they find real satisfaction and enjoyment in this
course of behaviour. There is such a natural principle of
attraction in man towards man, that having trod the same
track of land, having breathed in the same climate, barely
having been born in the same artificial district, or division,
becomes the occasion of contracting acquaintances and
familiarities many years after ; for any thing may serve the
purpose. Thus, relations, merely nominal, are sought and
invented, not by governors, but by the lowest of the people;
which are found sufficient to hold mankind together in
little fraternities and copartnerships : weak ties indeed, and
what may afford fund enough for ridicule, if they are absurdly considered as the real principles of that union ; but
they are, in truth, merely the occasions, as any thing may
be of any thing, upon which our nature carries us on according to its own previous bent and bias ; which occasions,
therefore, would be nothing at all, were there not this prior
disposition and bias of nature. Men are so much one
body, that in a peculiar manner they feel for each other,
shame, sudden danger, resentment, honour, prosperity, distress : one or another, or all of these, from the social nature
in general, from benevolence, upon the occasion of natural
relation, acquaintance, protection, dependence ; each of
these being distinct cements of society. And, therefore,
to have no restraint from, no regard to others in our behaviour, is the speculative absurdity of considering ourselves
as single and independent, as having nothing in our nature
which has respect to our fellow-creatures, reduced to action
and practice. And this is the same absurdity, as to sup-

pose a hand, or any part, to have no natural respect to any other, or to the whole body.

But allowing all this, it may be asked, "Has not man dispositions and principles within, which lead him to do evil to others, as well as to do good? whence come the many miseries else, which men are the authors and instruments of to each other?" These questions, as far as they relate to the foregoing discourse, may be answered by asking, "Has not man also dispositions and principles within, which lead him to do evil to himself, as well as good? whence come the many miseries else, sickness, pain, and death, which men are the instruments and authors of to themselves?"

It may be thought more easy to answer one of these questions than the other, but the answer to both is really the same: that mankind have ungoverned passions which they will gratify at any rate, as well to the injury of others, as in contradiction to known private interest: but that as there is no such thing as self-hatred, so neither is there any such thing as ill-will in one man towards another, emulation and resentment being away; whereas there is plainly benevolence or good-will: there is no such thing as love of injustice, oppression, treachery, ingratitude; but only eager desires after such and such external goods; which, according to a very ancient observation, the most abandoned would choose to obtain by innocent means if they were as easy, and as effectual to their end: that even emulation and resentment, by any one who will consider what these passions really are in nature,* will be found nothing to the purpose of this objection; and that the principles and pas-

* Emulation is merely the desire and hope of equality with, or superiority over others, with whom we compare ourselves. There does not appear to be any *other grief* in the natural passion, but only *that want* which is implied in desire. However, this may be so strong as to be the occasion of great *grief*. To desire the attainment of this equality, or superiority, by the *particular means* of others being brought down to our own level, or below it, is, I think, the distinct notion of envy. From whence it is easy to see, that the real end which the natural passion, emulation, and which the unlawful one, envy, aims at, is exactly the same; namely, that equality or superiority; and, consequently, that to do mischief is not the end of envy, but merely the means it make use of to attain its end. As to resentment, see the eighth sermon.

sions in the mind of man, which are distinct both from self-
love and benevolence, primarily and most directly lead to
right behaviour with regard to others as well as himself,
and only secondarily and accidentally to what is evil. Thus
though men, to avoid the shame of one villany, are sometimes guilty of a greater; yet it is easy to see, that the
original tendency of shame is to prevent the doing of
shameful actions; and its leading men to conceal such actions when done, is only in consequence of their being done,
i. e. of the passion's not having answered its first end.

If it be said, that there are persons in the world, who
are, in great measure, without the natural affections towards
their fellow-creatures; there are likewise instances of persons without the common natural affections to themselves:
but the nature of man is not to be judged of by either of
these, but what appears in the common world, in the bulk
of mankind.

I am afraid it would be thought very strange, if, to confirm the truth of this account of human nature, and make
out the justness of the foregoing comparison, it should be
added, that from what appears, men, in fact, as much and
as often contradict that *part* of their nature which respects
self, and which leads them to their *own private* good and
happiness, as they contradict that *part* of it which respects
society, and tends to *public* good: that there are as few persons, who attain the greatest satisfaction and enjoyment
which they might attain in the present world, as who do the
greatest good to others which they might do; nay, that
there are as few who can be said really and in earnest to
aim at one, as at the other. Take a survey of mankind;
the world in general, the good and bad, almost without exception, equally are agreed, that were religion out of the
case, the happiness of the present life would consist in a
manner wholly in riches, honours, sensual gratifications; insomuch that one scarce hears a reflection made upon prudence, life, conduct, but upon this supposition. Yet, on
the contrary, that persons in the greatest affluence of fortune are no happier than such as have only a competency;
that the cares and disappointments of ambition for the most
part far exceed the satisfactions of it; as also the miserable
intervals of intemperance and excess, and the many untimely

deaths occasioned by a dissolute course of life : these things
are all seen, acknowledged, by every one acknowledged;
but are thought no objections against, though they expressly contradict this universal principle, that the happiness of
the present life consists in one or other of them.   Whence
is all this absurdity and contradiction?   Is not the middle
way obvious?   Can any thing be more manifest, than that
the happiness of life consists in these, possessed and enjoyed
only to a certain degree; that to pursue them beyond this
degree, is always attended with more inconvenience than
advantage to man's self, and often with extreme misery and
unhappiness? Whence then, I say, is all this absurdity and
contradiction?   Is it really the result of consideration in
mankind, how they may become most easy to themselves,
most free from care, and enjoy the chief happiness attainable in this world? or is it not manifestly owing either to
this, that they have not cool and reasonable concern enough
for themselves to consider wherein their chief happiness in
the present life consists; or else, if they do consider it, that
they will not act conformably to what is the result of that
consideration? *i. e.* reasonable concern for themselves, or
cool self-love, is prevailed over by passion and appetite.
So that, from what appears, there is no ground to assert,
that those principles in the nature of man, which most directly lead to promote the good of our fellow-creatures, are
more generally or in a greater degree violated, than those
which most directly lead us to promote our own private
good and happiness.

The sum of the whole is plainly this.   The nature of
man, considered in his single capacity, and with respect
only to the present world, is adapted and leads him to attain
the greatest happiness he can for himself in the present
world.   The nature of man, considered in his public or social capacity, leads him to a right behaviour in society, to
that course of life which we call virtue.   Men follow or
obey their nature in both these capacities and respects to a
certain degree, but not entirely; their actions do not come
up to the whole of what their nature leads them to in either
of these capacities or respects; and they often violate their
nature in both; *i. e.* as they neglect the duties they owe to
their fellow-creatures, to which their nature leads them;

and are injurious, to which their nature is abhorrent: so there is a manifest negligence in men of their real happiness or interest in the present world, when that interest is inconsistent with a present gratification; for the sake of which they negligently, nay, even knowingly, are the authors and instruments of their own misery and ruin. Thus they are as often unjust to themselves as to others, and for the most part are equally so to both by the same actions.

SERMON II, III.

UPON HUMAN NATURE.

―――――――

ROMANS ii. 14.

*For when the Gentiles, which have not the law, do by
nature the things contained in the law, these having not
the law, are a law unto themselves.*

As speculative truth admits of different kinds of proof, so
likewise moral obligations may be shown by different
methods. If the real nature of any creature leads him,
and is adapted to such and such purposes only, or more
than to any other; this is a reason to believe the Author
of that nature intended it for those purposes. Thus there
is no doubt the eye was intended for us to see with. And
the more complex any constitution is, and the greater
variety of parts there are which thus tend to some one end,
the stronger is the proof that such end was designed.
However, when the inward frame of man is considered as
any guide in morals, the utmost caution must be used that
none make peculiarities in their own temper, or any thing
which is the effect of particular customs, though observable
in several, the standard of what is common to the species;
and, above all, that the highest principle be not forgot or
excluded, that to which belongs the adjustment and correction of all other inward movements and affections: which
principle will of course have some influence, but which,
being in nature supreme, as shall now be shown, ought to
preside over and govern all the rest. The difficulty of
rightly observing the two former cautions, the appearance
there is of some small diversity amongst mankind with
respect to this faculty, with respect to their natural sense of
moral good and evil; and the attention necessary to survey

with any exactness what passes within, have occasioned that it is not so much agreed what is the standard of the internal nature of man, as of his external form. Neither is this last exactly settled. Yet we understand one another when we speak of the shape of a human body; so likewise we do when we speak of the heart and inward principles, how far soever the standard is from being exact or precisely fixed. There is, therefore, ground for an attempt of showing men to themselves, of showing them what course of life and behaviour their real nature points out, and would lead them to. Now, obligations of virtue shown, and motives to the practice of it enforced, from a review of the nature of man, are to be considered as an appeal to each particular person's heart and natural conscience; as the external senses are appealed to for the proof of things cognisable by them. Since, then, our inward feelings, and the perceptions we receive from our external senses, are equally real; to argue from the former to life and conduct, is as little liable to exception, as to argue from the latter, to absolute speculative truth. A man can as little doubt whether his eyes were given him to see with, as he can doubt of the truth of the science of *optics*, deduced from ocular experiments. And allowing the inward feeling, shame; a man can as little doubt whether it was given him to prevent his doing shameful actions, as he can doubt whether his eyes were given him to guide his steps. And as to these inward feelings themselves; that they are real— that man has in his nature passions and affections, can no more be questioned, than that he has external senses. Neither can the former be wholly mistaken, though to a certain degree liable to greater mistakes than the latter.

There can be no doubt but that several propensions or instincts, several principles in the heart of man, carry him to society, and to contribute to the happiness of it, in a sense and a manner in which no inward principle leads him to evil. These principles, propensions, or instincts, which lead him to do good, are approved of by a certain faculty within, quite distinct from these propensions themselves. All this hath been fully made out in the foregoing discourse.

But it may be said, " What is all this, though true, to the purpose of virtue and religion? these require, not only

11

that we do good to others when we are led this way, by benevolence or reflection happening to be stronger than other
principles, passions, or appetites; but likewise, that the
whole character be formed upon thought and reflection;
that *every* action be directed by some determinate rule,
some other rule than the strength and prevalency of any
principle or passion. What sign is there in our nature (for
the inquiry is only about what is to be collected from
thence) that this was intended by its Author? or how does
so various and fickle a temper as that of man appear
adapted thereto? It may indeed be absurd and unnatural
for men to act without any reflection; nay, without regard
to that particular kind of reflection which you call conscience;
because this does belong to our nature. For, as there never
was a man but who approved one place, prospect, building,
before another; so it does not appear that there ever was a
man who would not have approved an action of humanity
rather than of cruelty; interest and passion being quite out
of the case. But interest and passion do come in, and are
often too strong for, and prevail over reflection and conscience. Now, as brutes have various instincts, by which
they are carried on to the end, the Author of their nature
intended them for; is not man in the same condition, with
this difference only, that to his instincts (*i. e.* appetites and
passions) is added the principle of reflection or conscience?
And as brutes act agreeably to their nature, in following
that principle or particular instinct which for the present is
strongest in them; does not man likewise act agreeably to
his nature, or obey the law of his creation, by following
that principle, be it passion or conscience, which for the
present happens to be strongest in him? Thus, different
men are by their particular nature hurried on to pursue
honour, or riches, or pleasure: there are also persons
whose temper leads them in an uncommon degree to kindness, compassion, doing good to their fellow-creatures; as
there are others who are given to suspend their judgment,
to weigh and consider things, and to act upon thought and
reflection. Let every one then quietly follow his nature; as
passion, reflection, appetite, the several parts of it, happen
to be the strongest; but let not the man of virtue take upon
him to blame the ambitious, the covetous, the dissolute;
since these, equally with him, obey and follow their nature.

Thus, as in some cases, we follow our nature in doing the works *contained in the law*, so in other cases we follow nature in doing contrary."

Now, all this licentious talk entirely goes upon a supposition, that men follow their nature in the same sense, in violating the known rules of justice and honesty for the sake of a present gratification, as they do in following those rules when they have no temptation to the contrary. And if this were true, that could not be so which St. Paul asserts, that men are " by nature a law to themselves." If by following nature were meant only acting as we please, it would indeed be ridiculous to speak of nature as any guide in morals: nay, the very mention of deviating from nature would be absurd; and the mention of following it, when spoken by way of distinction, would absolutely have no meaning. For, did ever any one act otherwise than as he pleased? And yet the ancients speak of deviating from nature, as vice; and of following nature so much as a distinction, that, according to them, the perfection of virtue consists therein. So that language itself should teach people another sense to the words *following nature*, than barely acting as we please. Let it however be observed, though the words *human nature* are to be explained, yet the real question of this discourse is not concerning the meaning of words, any otherwise than as the explanation of them may be needful to make out and explain the assertion, *that every man is naturally a law to himself, that every one may find within himself the rule of right, and obligations to follow it*. This St. Paul affirms in the words of the text, and this the foregoing objection really denies, by seeming to allow it. And the objection will be fully answered, and the text before us explained, by observing, that *nature* is considered in different views, and the word used in different senses; and by showing in what view it is considered, and in what sense the word is used, when intended to express and signify that which is the guide of life, that by which men are a law to themselves. I say, the explanation of the term will be sufficient, because from thence it will appear, that in some senses of the word, *nature* cannot be, but that in another sense, it manifestly is, a law to us.

I. By nature is often meant no more than some principle

in man, without regard either to the kind or degree of it.
Thus, the passion of anger, and the affection of parents to
their children, would be called equally *natural*. And as
the same person hath often contrary principles, which at
the same time draw contrary ways, he may by the same
action both follow and contradict his nature in this sense
of the word; he may follow one passion, and contradict
another.

II. *Nature* is frequently spoken of as consisting in those
passions which are strongest, and most influence the actions;
which being vicious ones, mankind is in this sense naturally
vicious, or vicious by nature. Thus St. Paul says of the
Gentiles, *who were dead in trespasses and sins, and walked
according to the spirit of disobedience*, that *they were by
nature the children of wrath.** They could be no otherwise
children of wrath by nature, than they were vicious by
nature.

Here then are two different senses of the word *nature*,
in neither of which men can at all be said to be a law to
themselves. They are mentioned only to be excluded; to
prevent their being confounded, as the latter is in the
objection, with another sense of it, which is now to be
inquired after and explained.

III. The apostle asserts, that the Gentiles *do by nature
the things contained in the law*. Nature is indeed here put
by way of distinction from revelation, but yet it is not a
mere negative. He intends to express more than that by
which they *did not*, that by which they *did* the works of
the law; namely, by nature. It is plain the meaning of
the word is not the same in this passage as in the former,
where it is spoken of as evil; for in the latter it is spoken
of as good; as that by which they acted, or might have
acted virtuously. What that is in man by which he is
naturally a law to himself, is explained in the following
words: *which shows the work of the law written in their
hearts, their consciences also bearing witness, and their
thoughts the meanwhile accusing or else excusing one another.*
If there be a distinction to be made between the *works
written in their hearts*, and the *witness of conscience*; by
the former must be meant, the natural disposition to
kindness and compassion, to do what is of good report, to

---

* Ephes. ii. 3.

which this apostle often refers ; that part of the nature of
man, treated of in the foregoing discourse, which, with very
little reflection and of course, leads him to society, and by
means of which he naturally acts a just and good part in it,
unless other passions or interest lead him astray. Yet
since other passions, and regards to private interest, which
lead us (though indirectly, yet they lead us) astray, are
themselves in a degree equally natural, and often most
prevalent ; and since we have no method of seeing the particular degrees in which one or the other is placed in us by
nature, it is plain the former, considered merely as natural,
good and right as they are, can no more be a law to us than
the latter. But there is a superior principle of reflection or
conscience in every man, which distinguishes between the
internal principles of his heart, as well as his external
actions ; which passes judgment upon himself and them ;
pronounces determinately some actions to be in themselves
just, right, good ; others to be in themselves evil, wrong,
unjust ; which, without being consulted, without being
advised with, magisterially exerts itself, and approves or
condemns him, the doer of them, accordingly ; and which,
if not forcibly stopped, naturally and always of course goes
on to anticipate a higher and more effectual sentence,
which shall hereafter second and affirm its own. But this
part of the office of conscience is beyond my present design
explicitly to consider. It is by this faculty natural to man,
that he is a moral agent, that he is a law to himself : by
this faculty, I say, not to be considered merely as a principle in his heart, which is to have some influence as well
as others ; but considered as a faculty, in kind and in
nature, supreme over all others, and which bears its own
authority of being so.

This *prerogative*, this *natural supremacy*, of the faculty
which surveys, approves, or disapproves the several affections of our mind, and actions of our lives, being that by
which men *are a law to themselves*, their conformity, or disobedience to which law of our nature renders their actions,
in the highest and most proper sense, natural or unnatural ;
it is fit it be further explained to you : and I hope it will
be so, if you will attend to the following reflections.

Man may act according to that principle or inclination
which for the present happens to be strongest, and yet act
in a way disproportionate to, and violate his real proper

nature. Suppose a brute creature, by any bait to be allured
into a snare, by which he is destroyed; he plainly followed
the bent of his nature, leading him to gratify his appetite:
there is an entire correspondence between his whole nature
and such an action: such action therefore is natural. But
suppose a man, foreseeing the same danger of certain ruin,
should rush into it for the sake of a present gratification:
he in this instance would follow his strongest desire, as did
the brute creature, but there would be as manifest a disproportion between the nature of man and such an action,
as between the meanest work of art and the skill of the
greatest master in that art; which disproportion arises, not
from considering the action singly in *itself*, or in its *consequences*, but from *comparison* of it with the nature of the
agent. And since such an action is utterly disproportionate
to the nature of man, it is in the strictest and most proper
sense unnatural; this word expressing that disproportion.
Therefore, instead of the words *disproportionate to his
nature*, the word *unnatural* may now be put; this being
more familiar to us: but let it be observed, that it stands
for the same thing precisely.

Now, what is it which renders such a rash action unnatural? Is it that he went against the principle of reasonable and cool self-love, considered *merely* as a part of his
nature? No: for if he had acted the contrary way, he
would equally have gone against a principle, or part of his
nature, namely, passion or appetite. But to deny a present
appetite, from foresight that the gratification of it would end
in immediate ruin or extreme misery, is by no means an
unnatural action: whereas to contradict or go against cool
self-love for the sake of such gratification, is so in the
instance before us. Such an action then being unnatural,
and its being so not arising from a man's going against a
principle or desire barely, nor in going against that principle
or desire which happens for the present to be strongest; it
necessarily follows, that there must be some other difference
or distinction to be made between these two principles,
passion and cool self-love, than what I have yet taken
notice of. And this difference, not being a difference in
strength or degree, I call a difference in *nature* and in *kind*.
And since, in the instance still before us, if passion prevails
over self-love, the consequent action is unnatural; but if
self-love prevails over passion, the action is natural; it is

manifest, that self-love is in human nature a superior principle to passion. This may be contradicted without violating that nature, but the former cannot. So that, if we will act conformably to the economy of man's nature reasonable self-love must govern. Thus, without particular consideration of conscience, we may have a clear conception of the *superior nature* of one inward principle to another; and see that there really is this natural superiority, quite distinct from degrees of strength and prevalency.

Let us now take a view of the nature of man, as consisting partly of various appetites, passions, affections, and partly of the principle of reflection or conscience; leaving quite out all consideration of the different degrees of strength, in which either of them prevail; and it will further appear, that there is this natural superiority of one inward principle to another, or that it is even part of the idea of reflection or conscience.

Passion or appetite implies a direct simple tendency towards such and such objects, without distinction of the means by which they are to be obtained. Consequently, it will often happen there will be a desire of particular objects, in cases where they cannot be obtained without manifest injury to others. Reflection, or conscience, comes in, and disapproves the pursuit of them in these circumstances; but the desire remains. Which is to be obeyed, appetite or reflection? Cannot this question be answered from the economy and constitution of human nature merely, without saying which is strongest? or need this all come into consideration? Would not the question be *intelligibly* and fully answered by saying, that the principle of reflection or conscience being compared with the various appetites, passions, and affections in men, the former is manifestly superior and chief, without regard to strength? And how often soever the latter happens to prevail, it is mere *usurpation*. The former remains in nature and in kind its superior: and every instance of such prevalence of the latter, is an instance of breaking in upon, and violation of the constitution of man.

All this is no more than the distinction which every body is acquainted with, between *mere power* and *authority*: only, instead of being intended to express the difference between what is possible, and what is lawful in civil go-

vernment, here it has been shown applicable to the several
principles in the mind of man. Thus, that principle by
which we survey, and either approve or disapprove our
own heart, temper, and actions, is not only to be considered
as what is in its turn to have some influence ; which may be
said of every passion, of the lowest appetites ; but likewise
as being superior ; as from its very nature manifestly claiming superiority over all others ; insomuch that you cannot
form a notion of this faculty, conscience, without taking in
judgment, direction, superintendency. This is a constituent
part of the idea, that is, of the faculty itself : and to preside
and govern, from the very economy and constitution of man,
belongs to it. Had it strength, as it has right ; had it power,
as it has manifest authority, it would absolutely govern the
world.

This gives us a further view of the nature of man ; shows
us what course of life we were made for ; not only that our
real nature leads us to be influenced in some degree by reflection and conscience, but likewise in what degree we are
to be influenced by it, if we will fall in with, and act agreeably to the constitution of our nature : that this faculty
was placed within to be our proper governor ; to direct and
regulate all under principles, passions, and motives of action. This is its right and office ; thus sacred is its authority. And how often soever men violate and rebelliously
refuse to submit to it, for supposed interest which they cannot otherwise obtain, or for the sake of passion which they
cannot otherwise gratify ; this makes no alteration as to the
natural right and *office* of conscience.

Let us now turn this whole matter another way, and suppose there was no such thing at all as this natural supremacy of conscience ; that there was no distinction to be
made between one inward principle and another, but only
that of strength, and see what would be the consequence.

Consider, then, what is the latitude and compass of
the actions of man with regard to himself, his fellow-creatures, and the Supreme Being ? What are their bonds, besides that of our natural power ? With respect to the two
first, they are plainly no other than these : no man seeks
misery as such for himself : and no one provoked does mischief to another for its own sake. For in every degree
within these bounds, mankind knowingly, from passion or

wantonness, bring ruin and misery upon themselves and others : and impiety and profaneness, I mean what every one would call so who believes the being of God, have absolutely no bounds at all. Men blaspheme the Author of nature, formally and in words renounce their allegiance to their Creator. Put an instance then with respect to any one of these three. Though we should suppose profane swearing, and in general that kind of impiety now mentioned, to mean nothing, yet it implies wanton disregard and irreverence towards an infinite Being, our Creator; and is this as suitable to the nature of man, as reverence and dutiful submission of heart towards that Almighty Being ? Or suppose a man guilty of parricide, with all the circumstances of cruelty which such an action can admit of : this action is done in consequence of its principle being for the present strongest : and if there be no difference between inward principles, but only that of strength ; the strength being given, you have the whole nature of the man given, so far as it relates to this matter. The action plainly corresponds to the principle, the principle being in that degree of strength it was ; it therefore corresponds to the whole nature of the man. Upon comparing the action and the whole nature, there arises no disproportion, there appears no unsuitableness between them. Thus the *murder of a father* and the *nature of man* correspond to each other, as the same nature and an act of filial duty. If there be no difference between inward principles, but only that of strength, we can make no distinction between these two actions, considered as the actions of such a creature, but in our coolest hours must approve or disapprove them equally : than which nothing can be reduced to a greater absurdity.

SERMON III.

The natural supremacy of reflection or conscience being thus established ; we may from it form a distinct notion of what is meant by *human nature*, when virtue is said to consist in following it, and vice in deviating from it.

As the idea of a civil constitution implies in it united strength, various subordinations, under one direction, that

of the supreme authority; the different strength of each particular member of the society not coming into the idea:
whereas, if you leave out the subordination, the union, and
the one direction, you destroy and lose it; so reason, several appetites, passions, and affections, prevailing in different degrees of strength, is not *that* idea or notion of *human nature;* but *that nature* consists in these several principles considered as having a natural respect to each other,
in the several passions being naturally subordinate to the
one superior principle of reflection or conscience. Every
bias, instinct, propension within, is a real part of our nature
but not the whole: add to these the superior faculty, whose
office it is to adjust, manage, and preside over them, and
take in this its natural superiority, and you complete the
idea of human nature. And as in civil government the
constitution is broken in upon and violated, by power and
strength prevailing over authority; so the constitutional
man is broken in upon and violated by the lower faculties or
principles within prevailing over that, which is in its nature
supreme over them all. Thus, when it is said by ancient
writers, that tortures and death are not so contrary to human nature as injustice; by this, to be sure, is not meant,
that the aversion to the former in mankind is less strong
and prevalent than their aversion to the latter; but that the
former is only contrary to our nature, considered in a partial view, and which takes in only the lowest part of it, that
which we have in common with the brutes; whereas the
latter is contrary to our nature, considered in a higher sense,
as a system and constitution, contrary to the whole economy of man.*

* Every man, in his physical nature, is one individual single agent.
He has likewise properties and principles, each of which may be considered separately, and without regard to the respects which they have
to each other. Neither of these are the nature we are taking a view
of. But it is the inward frame of man, considered as a *system or constitution;* whose several parts are united, not by a physical principle
of individuation, but by the respects they have to each other; the chief
of which is the subjection which the appetites, passions, and particular
affections have to the one supreme principle of reflection or conscience. The system, or constitution, is formed by, and consists in these
respects and this subjection. Thus, the body is a *system or constitution;*
so is a tree; so is every machine. Consider all the several parts of a
tree, without the natural respects they have to each other, and you

And from all these things put together, nothing can be more evident, than that, exclusive of revelation, man cannot be considered as a creature left by his Maker to act at random, and live at large up to the extent of his natural power, as passion, humour, wilfulness, happen to carry him; which is the condition brute creatures are in; but that, *from his make, constitution, or nature, he is, in the strictest and most proper sense, a law to himself.* He hath the rule of right within: what is wanting is only that he honestly attend to it.

The inquiries which have been made by men of leisure after some general rule, the conformity to, or disagreement from which, should denominate our actions good or evil, are in many respects of great service. Yet, let any plain, honest man, before he engages in any course of action, ask himself, is this I am going about right, or is it wrong? Is it good, or is it evil? I do not in the least doubt but that this question would be answered agreeably to truth and virtue, by almost any fair man in almost any circumstance. Neither do there appear any cases which look like exceptions to this; but those of superstition and of partiality to

have not at all the idea of a tree; but add these respects, and this gives you the idea. The body may be impaired by sickness, a tree may decay, a machine be out of order, and yet the system and constitution of them not totally dissolved. There is plainly somewhat which answers to all this in the moral constitution of man. Whoever will consider his own nature will see, that the several appetites, passions, and particular affections, have different respects among themselves. They are restraints upon, and are in proportion to, each other. This proportion is just and perfect, when all those under principles are perfectly coincident with conscience, so far as their nature permits, and, in all cases, under its absolute and entire direction. The least excess or defect, the least alteration of the due proportions amongst themselves, or of their coincidence with conscience, though not proceeding into action, is some degree of disorder in the moral constitution. But perfection, though plainly intelligible and supposable, was never attained by any man. If the higher principle of reflection maintains its place, and, as much as it can, corrects that disorder, and hinders it from breaking out into action, that is all that can be expected in such a creature as man. And though the appetites and passions have not their exact due proportion to each other; though they often strive for mastery with judgment or reflection; yet, since the superiority of this principle to all others is the chief respect which forms the constitution, so far as this superiority is maintained, the character, the man, is good, worthy, virtuous.

ourselves. Superstition may, perhaps, be somewhat of an exception ; but partiality to ourselves is not ; this being itself dishonesty. For a man to judge that to be the equitable, the moderate, the right part for him to act, which he would see to be hard, unjust, oppressive in another : this is plain vice, and can proceed only from great unfairness of mind.

But, allowing that mankind hath the rule of right within himself, yet it may be asked, "What obligations are we under to attend and follow it?" I answer : it has been proved that man by his nature is a law to himself, without the particular distinct consideration of the positive sanctions of that law ; the rewards and punishments which we feel, and those which, from the light of reason, we have ground to believe are annexed to it. The question then carries its own answer along with it. Your obligation to obey this law, is its being the law of your nature. That your conscience approves of and attests to such a course of action, is itself alone an obligation. Conscience does not only offer itself to show us the way we should walk in, but it likewise carries its own authority with it, that it is our natural guide, the guide assigned us by the Author of our nature : it therefore belongs to our condition of being ; it is our duty to walk in that path, and follow this guide, without looking about to see whether we may not possibly forsake them with impunity.

However, let us hear what is to be said against obeying this law of our nature. And the sum is no more than this "Why should we be concerned about any thing out of, and beyond ourselves ? If we do find within ourselves regard to others, and restraints of we know not how many different kinds ; yet these being embarrassments, and hindering us from going the nearest way to our own 'good, why should we not endeavour to suppress and get over them ?"

Thus, people go on with words, which, when applied to human nature, and the condition in which it is placed in this world, have really no meaning. For does not all this kind of talk go upon supposition, that our happiness in this world consists in somewhat quite distinct from regard to others, and that it is the privilege of vice to be without restraint or confinement ? Whereas, on the contrary, the enjoyments, in a manner all the common enjoyments of life, even the pleasures of vice, depend upon these regard of one kind or another to our fellow-creatures. Throw of

all regards to others, and we should be quite indifferent to
infamy and to honour: there could be no such thing at all
as ambition, and scarce any such thing as covetousness;
for we should likewise be equally indifferent to the disgrace
of poverty, the several neglects and kinds of contempt
which accompany this state; and to the reputation of riches,
the regard and respect they usually procure.   Neither is
restraint by any means peculiar to one course of life; but
our very nature, exclusive of conscience, and our condition,
lays us under an absolute necessity of it.   We cannot gain
any end whatever without being confined to the proper
means, which is often the most painful and uneasy confinement.   And, in numberless instances, a present appetite
cannot be gratified without such apparent and immediate
ruin and misery, that the most dissolute man in the world
chooses to forego the pleasure, rather than endure the pain.

Is the meaning, then, to indulge those regards to our
fellow-creatures, and submit to those restraints, which,
upon the whole, are attended with more satisfaction than
uneasiness, and get over only those which bring more uneasiness and inconvenience than satisfaction?   "Doubtless
this was our meaning."   You have changed sides, then.—
Keep to this: be consistent with yourselves; and you and
the men of virtue are, in general, perfectly agreed.   But
let us take care, and avoid mistakes.   Let it not be taken
for granted, that the temper of envy, rage, resentment,
yields greater delight than meekness, forgiveness, compassion and good-will: especially when it is acknowledged,
that rage, envy, resentment, are in themselves mere misery;
and the satisfaction arising from the indulgence of them is
little more than relief from that misery; whereas the
temper of compassion and benevolence is itself delightful;
and the indulgence of it, by doing good, affords new positive delight and enjoyment.   Let it not be taken for granted, that the satisfaction arising from the reputation of
riches and power, however obtained, and from the respect
paid to them, is greater than the satisfaction arising from
the reputation of justice, honesty, charity, and the esteem
which is universally acknowledged to be their due.   And if
it be doubtful which of these satisfactions is the greatest,
as there are persons who think neither of them very considerable, yet there can be no doubt concerning ambition

and covetousness, virtue and a good mind, considered in themselves, and as leading to different courses of life ; there can, I say, be no doubt, which temper and which course is attended with most peace and tranquillity of mind ; which, with most perplexity, vexation and inconvenience. And both the virtues and vices which have been now mentioned, do in a manner equally imply in them regards of one kind or another to our fellow-creatures. And with respect to restraint and confinement : whoever will consider the restraints from fear and shame, the dissimulation, mean arts of concealment, servile compliances, one or other of which belong to almost every course of vice, will soon be convinced, that the man of virtue is by no means upon a disadvantage in this respect. How many instances are there in which men feel, and own, and cry aloud under the chains of vice with which they are enthralled, and which yet they will not shake off ? How many instances, in which persons manifestly go through more pain and self-denial to gratify a vicious passion, than would have been necessary to the conquest of it ? To this is to be added, that when virtue is become habitual, when the temper of it is acquired, what was before confinement ceases to be so, by becoming choice and delight. Whatever restraint and guard upon ourselves may be needful to unlearn any unnatural distortion or odd gesture ; yet, in all propriety of speech, natural behaviour must be the most easy and unrestrained. It is manifest, that in the common course of life there is seldom any inconsistency between our duty and what is called interest : it is much seldomer that there is an inconsistency between duty and what is really our present interest : meaning by interest, happiness and satisfaction. Self-love, then, though confined to the interest of the present world, does in general perfectly coincide with virtue, and leads us to one and the same course of life. But, whatever exceptions there are to this, which are much fewer than they are commonly thought, all shall be set right at the final distribution of things. It is a manifest absurdity to suppose evil prevailing finally over good, under the conduct and administration of a perfect mind.

The whole argument which I have been now insisting upon, may be thus summed up and given you in one view. The nature of man is adapted to some course of action or other. Upon comparing some actions with this nature, they appear suitable and correspondent to it : from comparison of other actions with the same nature, there arises to our view some unsuitableness or disproportion. The correspondence of actions to the nature of the agent, renders them natural ; their disproportion to it, unnatural. That an action is correspondent to the nature of the agent, does not arise from its being agreeable to the principle which happens to be the strongest ; for it may be so, and yet be quite disproportionate to the nature of the agent. The correspondence, therefore, or disproportion, arises from somewhat else. This can be nothing but a difference in nature and kind (altogether distinct from strength) between the inward principles. Some, then, are in nature and kind superior to others. And the correspondence arises from the action being conformable to the higher principle ; and the unsuitableness, from its being contrary to it. Reasonable self-love and conscience are the chief or superior principles in the nature of man : because an action may be suitable to this nature, though all other principles be violated ; but becomes unsuitable, if either of those are. Conscience and self-love, if we understand our true happiness, always lead us the same way.—Duty and interest are perfectly coincident ; for the most part in this world, but entirely, and in every instance, if we take in the future, and the whole ; this being implied in the notion of a good and perfect administration of things. Thus, they who have been so wise in their generation, as to regard only their own supposed interest, at the expense and to the injury of others, shall at last find, that he who has given up all the advantages of the present world, rather than violate his conscience and the relations of life, has infinitely better provided for himself, and secured his own interest and happiness.

SERMON IV.

UPON THE GOVERNMENT OF THE TONGUE.

James i. 26.

If any man among you seem to be religious, and bridleth not his tongue, but deceiveth his own heart, this man's religion is vain.

The translation of this text would be more determinate by being more literal, thus: " If any man among you seemeth to be religious, not bridling his tongue, but deceiving his own heart, this man's religion is vain." This determines that the words, " but deceiveth his own heart," are not put in opposition to, " seemeth to be religious," but to, " bridleth not his tongue." The certain determinate meaning of the text then being, that he who seemeth to be religious and bridleth not his tongue, but, in that particular, deceiveth his own heart, this man's religion is vain; we may observe somewhat very forcible and expressive in these words of St. James. As if the apostle had said, No man surely can make any pretences to religion, who does not at least believe that he bridleth his tongue : if he puts on any appearance or face of religion, and yet does not govern his tongue, he must surely deceive himself in that particular, and think he does : and whoever is so unhappy as to deceive himself in this, to imagine he keeps that unruly faculty in due subjection, when, indeed, he does not, whatever the other part of his life be, his religion is vain ; the government of the tongue being a most material restraint which virtue lays us under : without it, no man can be truly religious.

In treating upon this subject, I will consider,—

First, What is the general vice, or fault, here referred to; or, what disposition in men is supposed in moral reflections and precepts concerning "bridling the tongue."

Secondly, When it may be said of any one, that he has a due government over himself in this respect.

I. Now, the fault referred to, and the disposition supposed, in precepts and reflections concerning the government of the tongue, is not evil-speaking from malice, nor lying or bearing false witness from indirect selfish designs. The disposition to these, and the actual vices themselves, all come under other subjects. The tongue may be employed about, and made to serve all the purposes of vice in tempting and deceiving, in perjury and injustice. But the thing here supposed and referred to, is talkativeness; a disposition to be talking, abstract from the consideration of what is to be said; with very little or no regard to, or thought of doing, either good, or harm. And let not any imagine this to be a slight matter, and that it deserves not to have so great weight laid upon it, till he has considered what evil is implied in it, and the bad effects which follow from it. It is, perhaps, true, that they who are addicted to this folly, would choose to confine themselves to trifles and indifferent subjects, and so intend only to be guilty of being impertinent; but as they cannot go on for ever talking of nothing, as common matters will not afford a sufficient fund for perpetual continued discourse, when subjects of this kind are exhausted, they will go on to defamation, scandal, divulging of secrets, their own secrets as well as those of others; any thing rather than be silent. They are plainly hurried on, in the heat of their talk, to say quite different things from what they first intended, and which they afterwards wish unsaid; or improper things, which they had no other end in saying, but only to afford employment to their tongue. And if these people expect to be heard and regarded, for there are some content merely with talking, they will invent to engage your attention; and, when they have heard the least imperfect hint of an affair, they will, out of their own head, add the circumstances of time and place, and other matters, to make out their story, and give the appearance of probability to it; not that they have any concern about being believed, otherwise than as a means of being heard. The thing is to engage your attention; to take you up wholly for the present time; what reflections will be made afterwards, is in truth the least of their thoughts. And further, when persons who indulge themselves in these liberties of the tongue, are in any degree offended with another, as little disgusts and misunderstandings will be, they allow themselves to defame and revile such an one without any moderation or bounds; though the offence is so very slight, that they themselves would not do, nor perhaps wish, him an injury in any other way. And in this case the scandal and revilings are chiefly owing to talkativeness, and not bridling their tongue; and so come under our present subject. The least occasion in the world will make the humour break out in this particular way, or in another. It is like a torrent, which must and will flow; but the least thing imaginable will first of all give it either this or another direction—turn it into this or that channel: or like a fire, the nature of which, when in a heap of combustible matter, is to spread and lay waste all around; but any one of a thousand little accidents will occasion it to break out first either in this or another particular part.

The subject then before us, though it does run up into, and can scarce be treated as entirely distinct from, all others, yet it needs not be so much mixed and blended with them as it often is. Every faculty and power may be used as the instrument of premeditated vice and wickedness, merely as the most proper and effectual means of executing such designs. But if a man, from deep malice and desire of revenge, should meditate a falsehood, with a settled design to ruin his neighbour's reputation, and should, with great coolness and deliberation, spread it, nobody would choose to say of such an one, that he had no government of his tongue. A man may use the faculty of speech as an instrument of false-witness, who yet has so entire a command over that faculty, as never to speak but from forethought and cool design. Here the crime is injustice and perjury; and, strictly speaking, no more belongs to the present subject, than perjury and injustice in any other way. But there is such a thing as a disposition to be talking for its own sake; from which persons often say any thing good or bad, of others, merely as a subject of discourse, according to the particular temper they themselves happen to be in, and to pass away the present time. There is likewise to be observed in persons, such a strong and eager desire of engaging attention to what they say, that they will speak good or evil, truth or otherwise, merely as one or the other seems to be most hearkened to : and this, though it is sometimes joined, is not the same with the desire of being thought important and men of consequence. There is in some such a disposition to be talking, that an offence of the slightest kind, and such as would not raise any other resentment, yet raises, if I may so speak, the resentment of the tongue, puts it into a flame, into the most ungovernable motions. This outrage, when the person it respects is present, we distinguish in the lower rank of people by a peculiar term: and let it be observed, that though the decencies of behaviour are a little kept, the same outrage and virulence, indulged when he is absent, is an offence of the same kind. But, not to distinguish any further in this manner; men run into faults and follies, which cannot so properly be referred to any one general head as this, that they have not a due government over their tongue.

And this unrestrained volubility and wantonness of speech is the occasion of numberless evils and vexations in life. It begets resentment in him who is the subject of it ; sows the seed of strife and dissension amongst others ; and inflames little disgusts and offences, which, if let alone, would wear away of themselves : it is often of as bad effect upon the good name of others, as deep envy or malice : and, to say the least of it in this respect, it destroys and perverts a certain equity, of the utmost importance to society to be observed ; namely, that praise and dispraise, a good or bad character, should always be bestowed according to desert.—— The tongue, used in such a licentious manner, is like a sword in the hand of a madman; it is employed at random, it can scarce possibly do any good, and, for the most part, does a world of mischief; and implies not only great folly, and a trifling spirit, but great viciousness of mind, great indifference to truth and falsity, and to the reputation, welfare, and good of others. So much reason is there for what St. James says of the tongue,* " It is a fire, a world of iniquity ; it defileth the whole body, setteth on fire the

* Chap. iii. 6.

course of nature, and is itself set on fire of hell." This is
the faculty or disposition which we are required to keep a
guard upon ; these are the vices and follies it runs into,
when not kept under due restraint.

II. Wherein the due government of the tongue consists,
or when it may be said of any one, in a moral and religious
sense, that he "bridleth his tongue," I come now to consider.

The due and proper use of any natural faculty or power,
is to be judged of by the end and design for which it was
given us.   The chief purpose for which the faculty of
speech was given to man, is plainly, that we might communicate our thoughts to each other, in order to carry on the
affairs of the world ; for business, and for our improvement
in knowledge and learning.   But the good Author of our
nature designed us not only necessaries, but likewise enjoyment and satisfaction, in that being he hath graciously
given, and in that condition of life he hath placed us in.
There are secondary uses of our faculties : they administer
to delight, as well as to necessity ; and as they are equally
adapted to both, there is no doubt but he intended them for
our gratification, as well as for the support and continuance
of our being.   The secondary use of speech is to please
and be entertaining to each other in conversation.   This is
in every respect allowable and right ; it unites men closer
in alliances and friendships ; gives us a fellow-feeling of the
prosperity and unhappiness of each other ; and is, in several
respects, serviceable to virtue, and to promote good behaviour in the world.   And provided there be not too much
time spent in it, if it were considered only in the way of
gratification and delight, men must have strange notions of
God and of religion, to think that he can be offended with
it, or that it is any way inconsistent with the strictest virtue.
But the truth is, such sort of conversation, though it has no
particular good tendency, yet it has a general good one ; it
is social and friendly, and tends to promote humanity, good-
nature, and civility.

As the end and use, so likewise the abuse of speech,
relates to the one or the other of these ; either to business
or to conversation.   As to the former, deceit in the management of business and affairs does not properly belong
to the subject now before us ; though one may just mention
that multitude, that endless number of words, with which

business is perplexed, when a much fewer would, as it should seem, better serve the purpose; but this must be left to those who understand the matter. The government of the tongue, considered as a subject of itself, relates chiefly to conversation; to that kind of discourse which usually fills up the time spent in friendly meetings, and visits of civility. And the danger is, lest persons entertain themselves and others at the expense of their wisdom and their virtue, and to the injury or offence of their neighbour. If they will observe and keep clear of these, they may be as free, and easy, and unreserved, as they can desire.

The caution to be given for avoiding these dangers, and to render conversation innocent and agreeable, fall under the following particulars: silence; talking of indifferent things; and, which makes up too great a part of conversation, giving of characters, speaking well or evil of others.

The wise man observes, that " there is a time to speak, and a time to keep silence." One meets with people in the world, who seem never to have made the last of these observations. And yet these great talkers do not at all speak from their having any thing to say, as every sentence shows, but only from their inclination to be talking. Their conversation is merely an exercise of the tongue; no other human faculty has any share in it. It is strange these persons can help reflecting, that unless they have in truth a superior capacity, and are in an extraordinary manner furnished for conversation; if they are entertaining, it is at their own expense. Is it possible, that it should never come into people's thoughts to suspect, whether or no it be to their advantage to show so very much of themselves ? " O that ye would altogether hold your peace ! and it should be your wisdom."* Remember likewise, there are persons who love fewer words, an inoffensive sort of people, and who deserve some regard, though of too still and composed tempers for you. Of this number was the Son of Sirach ; for he plainly speaks from experience, when he says, " As hills of sand are to the steps of the aged, so is one of many words to a quiet man." But one would think it should be obvious to every one, that when they are in company with their superiors of any kind, in years, knowledge,

* Job xiii. 5.

and experience; when proper and useful subjects are discoursed of, which they cannot bear a part in; that these
are times for silence; when they should learn to hear, and
be attentive, at least in their turn.   It is indeed a very unhappy way these people are in: they in a manner cut themselves out from all advantage of conversation, except that
of being entertained with their own talk; their business in
coming into company not being at all to be informed, to
hear, to learn, but to display themselves, or rather to exert
their faculty and talk without any design at all.   And if we
consider conversation as an entertainment, as somewhat to
unbend the mind, as a diversion from the cares, the business,
and the sorrows of life; it is of the very nature of it, that
the discourse be mutual.   This, I say, is implied in the
very notion of what we distinguish by conversation, or being
in company.   Attention to the continued discourse of one
alone, grows more painful often, than the cares and business
we come to be diverted from.   He, therefore, who imposes
this upon us, is guilty of a double offence; arbitrarily en-
joining silence upon all the rest, and likewise obliging them
to this painful attention.

I am sensible these things are apt to be passed over, as
too little to come into a serious discourse; but in reality,
men are obliged, even in point of morality and virtue, to
observe all the decencies of behaviour.   The greatest evils
in life have had their rise from somewhat, which was
thought of too little importance to be attended to.   And as
to the matter we are now upon, it is absolutely necessary
to be considered.   For if people will not maintain a due
government over themselves, in regarding proper times and
seasons for silence, but *will* be talking, they certainly,
whether they design it or not at first, will go on to scandal
and evil-speaking, and divulging secrets.

If it were needful to say any thing further, to persuade
men to learn this lesson of silence, one might put them in
mind, how insignificant they render themselves by this excessive talkativeness: insomuch, that if they do chance to
say any thing which deserves to be attended to and regarded,
it is lost in the variety and abundance which they utter of
another sort.

The occasions of silence then are obvious, and one would
think should be easily distinguished by every body; namely,

when a man has nothing to say, or nothing but what is better unsaid; better, either in regard to the particular persons he is present with; or from its being an interruption to conversation itself; or to conversation of a more agreeable kind; or better, lastly, with regard to himself. I will end this particular with two reflections of the wise man; one of which, in the strongest manner, exposes the ridiculous part of this licentiousness of the tongue; and the other the great danger and viciousness of it. "When he that is a fool walketh by the way side, his wisdom faileth him, and he saith to every one that he is a fool."* The other is, "In the multitude of words there wanteth not sin."†

As the government of the tongue, in respect to talking upon indifferent subjects: after what has been said concerning the due government of it in respect to the occasions and times for silence, there is little more necessary, than only to caution men to be fully satisfied, that the subjects are indeed of an indifferent nature; and not to spend too much time in conversation of this kind. But persons must be sure to take heed, that the subject of their discourse be at least of an indifferent nature: that it be no way offensive to virtue, religion, or good manners; that it be not of a licentious dissolute sort, this leaving always ill impressions upon the mind; that it be no way injurious or vexatious to others: and that too much time be not spent this way, to the neglect of those duties and offices of life which belong to their station and condition in the world. However, though there is not any necessity that men should aim at being important and weighty in every sentence they speak: yet, since useful subjects, at least of some kinds, are as entertaining as others, a wise man, even when he desires to unbend his mind from business, would choose that the conversation might turn upon somewhat instructive.

The last thing is, the government of the tongue as relating to discourse of the affairs of others, and giving of characters. These are in a manner the same. And one can scarce call it an indifferent subject, because discourse upon it almost perpetually runs into somewhat criminal.

And first of all, it were very much to be wished that this did not take up so great a part of conversation; because it

* Eccles. x. 3.   † Prov. x. 19.

is indeed a subject of a dangerous nature. Let any one consider the various interests, competitions, and little misunderstandings which arise among men, and he will soon see, that he is not unprejudiced and impartial: that he is not, as I may speak, neutral enough, to trust himself with talking of the character and concerns of his neighbour, in a free, careless, and unreserved manner. There is perpetually, and often it is not attended to, a rivalship amongst people of one kind or another, in respect to wit, beauty, learning, fortune; and that one thing will insensibly influence them to speak to the disadvantage of others, even where there is no formed malice or ill design. Since therefore it is so hard to enter into this subject without offending, the first thing to be observed is, that people should learn to decline it: to get over that strong inclination most have to be talking of the concerns and behaviour of their neighbour.

But since it is impossible that this subject should be wholly excluded conversation, and since it is necessary that the characters of men should be known; the next thing is, that it is a matter of importance what is said; and therefore, that we should be religiously scrupulous and exact, to say nothing, either good or bad, but what is true. I put it thus, because it is in reality of as great importance to the good of society, that the characters of bad men should be known, as that the characters of good men should. People who are given to scandal and detraction, may indeed make an ill use of this observation; but truths, which are of service towards regulating our conduct, are not to be disowned, or even concealed, because a bad use may be made of them. This, however, would be effectually prevented, if these two things were attended to. *First*, That though it is equally of bad consequence to society, that men should have either good or ill characters which they do not deserve; yet, when you say somewhat good of a man which he does not deserve, there is no wrong done him in particular; whereas, when you say evil of a man, which he does not deserve, here is a direct formal injury, a real piece of injustice done him. This therefore makes a wide difference; and gives us, in point of virtue, much greater latitude in speaking well, than ill, of others. *Secondly*, A good man is friendly to his fellow-creatures, and a lover of mankind, and so will, upon every occasion, and often without any, say all the good he

can of every body : but, so far as he is a good man, will
never be disposed to speak evil of any, unless there be some
other reason for it, besides barely that it is true.   If he be
charged with having given an ill character, he will scarce
think it a sufficient justification of himself to say it was a
true one, unless he can also give some farther account how
he came to do so : a just indignation against particular instances of villany, where they are great and scandalous : or
to prevent an innocent man from being deceived and betrayed, when he has great trust and confidence in one who
does not deserve it.   Justice must be done to every part of
a subject when we are considering it. If there be a man who
bears a fair character in the world, whom yet we know to be
without faith or honesty, to be really an ill man ; it must be
allowed in general, that we shall do a piece of service to society, by letting such an one's true character be known.
This is no more than what we have an instance of in our
Saviour himself,* though he was mild and gentle beyond
example.   However, no words can express too strongly the
caution which should be used in such a case as this.

Upon the whole matter : if people would observe the obvious occasions of silence ; if they would subdue the inclination to tale-bearing, and that eager desire to engage
attention, which is an original disease in some minds ; they
would be in little danger of offending with their tongue, and
would in a moral and religious sense, have due government
over it.

I will conclude with some precepts and reflections of the
Son of Sirach upon this subject.   " Be swift to hear ; and,
if thou hast understanding, answer thy neighbour ; if not,
lay thy hand upon thy mouth.   Honour and shame is in
talk.   A man of an ill tongue is dangerous in his city ; and
he that is rash in his talk shall be hated.   A wise man will
hold his tongue, till he see opportunity ; but a babbler and a
fool will regard no time.   He that useth many words shall
be abhorred ; and he that taketh to himself authority therein,
shall be hated. A backbiting tongue hath disquieted many ;
strong cities hath it pulled down, and overthrown the
houses of great men.   The tongue of a man is his fall ; but
if thou love to hear, thou shalt receive understanding."

* Mark xii. 38—40.

SERMON V.

UPON COMPASSION.

ROMANS xii. 15.

*Rejoice with them that do rejoice, and weep with them
that weep.*

EVERY man is to be considered in two capacities, the private and public; as designed to pursue his own interest, and likewise to contribute to the good of others. Whoever will consider may see, that in general there is no contrariety between these; but, that from the original constitution of man, and the circumstances he is placed in, they perfectly coincide, and mutually carry on each other. But amongst the great variety of affections or principles of action in our nature, some in their primary intention and design seem to belong to the single or private, others to the public or social capacity. The affections required in the text are of the latter sort. When we rejoice in the prosperity of others, and compassionate their distresses, we, as it were, substitute them for ourselves, their interest for our own; and have the same kind of pleasure in their prosperity, and sorrow in their distress, as we have from reflection upon our own. Now, there is nothing strange, or unaccountable in our being thus carried out, and affected towards the interests of others. For if there be any appetite, or any inward principle besides self-love; why may there not be an affection to the good of our fellow-creatures, and delight from that affection being gratified, and uneasiness from things going contrary to it?*

Of these two, delight in the prosperity of others and compassion for their distresses, the last is felt much more generally than the former. Though men do not universally rejoice with all whom they see rejoice, yet, accidental obstacles removed, they naturally compassionate all in some degree whom they see in distress; so far as they have any

* There being manifestly this appearance of men's substituting others for themselves, and being carried out and affected towards them as towards themselves; some persons who have a system which excludes every affection of this sort, have taken a pleasant method to solve it; and tell you, it is *not another* you are at all concerned about, but your *self only*, when you feel the affection called compassion: *i. e.* here is a plain matter of fact, which men cannot reconcile with the general account they think fit to give of things; they, therefore, instead of *that* manifest fact, substitute *another*, which is reconcileable to their own scheme. For, does not every body by compassion mean, an affection, the object of which is another in distress? Instead of this, but designing to have it mistaken for this, they speak of an affection, or passion the object of which is ourselves, or danger to ourselves. Hobbs defines pity, *imagination, or fiction, of future calamity to ourselves, proceeding from the sense* (he means sight, or knowledge) *of another man's calamity*. Thus, fear and compassion would be the same idea, and a fearful and a compassionate man the same character, which every one immediately sees are totally different. Further, to those who give any scope to their affections, there is no perception or inward feeling more universal than this; that one who has been merciful and compassionate throughout the course of his behaviour, should himself be treated with kindness, if he happens to fall into circumstances of distress. Is fear then, or cowardice, so great a recommendation to the favour of the bulk of mankind? Or, is it not plain, that mere fearlessness (and, therefore, not the contrary) is one of the most popular qualifications? This shows that mankind are not affected towards compassion as fear, but as somewhat totally different.

Nothing would more expose such accounts as these of the affections which are favourable and friendly to our fellow-creatures, than to substitute the definitions which this author, and others who follow his steps, give of such affections, instead of the words by which they are commonly expressed. Hobbs, after having laid down that pity, or compassion, is only fear for ourselves, goes on to explain the reason why we pity our friends in distress more than others. Now substitute the *definition* instead of the word *pity* in this place, and the inquiry will be, why we fear our friends? &c. which words (since he really does not mean why we are afraid of them) make no question or sentence at all. So that common language, the words to *compassionate*, *to pity*, cannot be accommodated to his account of compassion.

real perception or sense of that distress: insomuch that words expressing this latter, pity, compassion, frequently occur, whereas, we have scarce any single one by which the former is distinctly expressed.   Congratulation, indeed, answers condolence: but both these words are intended to signify certain forms of civility, rather than any inward sensation, or feeling.   This difference or inequality is so remarkable, that we plainly consider compassion as itself an original, distinct, particular affection in human nature ; whereas

The very joining of the words to *pity our friends*, is a direct contradiction to his definition of pity : because those words, so joined, necessarily express that our friends are the objects of the passion ; whereas his definition of it asserts, that ourselves (or danger to ourselves) are the only objects of it.   He might, indeed, have avoided this absurdity, by plainly saying what he is going to account for ; namely, why the sight of the innocent, or of our friends in distress, raises greater fear for ourselves than the sight of other persons in distress. But had he put the thing thus plainly, the fact itself would have been doubted that *the sight of our friends in distress, raises in us greater fear for ourselves, than the sight of others in distress*.   And, in the next place, it would immediately have occurred to every one, that the fact now mentioned, which, at least, is *doubtful*, whether true or false, was not the same with this fact, which nobody ever doubted, that *the sight of our friends in distress raises in us greater compassion than the sight of others in distress ;* every one, I say, would have seen that these are not the *same*, but *two different* inquiries ; and consequently, that fear and compassion are not the same.   Suppose a person to be in real danger, and by some means or other to have forgotten it, any trifling accident, any sound might alarm him, recall the danger to his remembrance, and renew his fear : but it is almost too grossly ridiculous (though it is to show an absurdity) to speak of that sound, or accident, as an object of compassion ; and yet, according to Mr. Hobbs, our greatest friend in distress is no more to us, no more the object of compassion, or of any affection in our heart.   Neither the one nor the other raises any emotion in our mind, but only the thoughts of our liableness to calamity, and the fear of it ; and both equally do this. It is right such sorts of accounts of human nature should be shown to be what they really are, because there is raised upon them a general scheme, which undermines the whole foundation of common justice and honesty.—See Hobbs *of Hum. Nat.* c. 9. sec. 10.

There are often three different perceptions, or inward feelings, upon sight of persons in distress : real sorrow and concern for the misery of our fellow-creatures ; some degree of satisfaction, from a consciousness of our freedom from that misery ; and as the mind passes on from one thing to another, it is not unnatural, from such an occasion, to reflect upon our own liableness to the same or other calamities.   The two last frequenty laccompany the first, but it is the first *only* which is properly compassion, of which the distressed are the objects, and to rejoice in the good of others, is only a consequence of the general affection of love and good will to them. The reason and account of which matter is this: when a man has obtained any particular advantage or felicity, his end is gained; and he does not in that particular want the assistance of another; there was, therefore, no need of a distinct affection towards that felicity of another already obtained; neither would such affection directly carry him on to do good to that person: whereas, men in distress want assistance, and compassion leads us directly to assist them. The object of the former is the present felicity of another; the object of the latter is the present misery of another. It is easy to see that the latter wants a particular affection for its relief, and that the former does not want one, because it does not want assistance. And, upon supposition of a distinct affection in both cases, the one must rest in the exercise of itself, having nothing further to gain; the other does not rest in itself, but carries us on to assist the distressed.

But, supposing these affections natural to the mind, particularly the last, "Has not each man troubles enough of his own? must he indulge an affection which appropriates to himself those of others? which leads him to contract the least desirable of all friendships—friendships with the unfortunate? must we invert the known rule of prudence, and choose to associate ourselves with the distressed? Or, allowing that we ought, so far as it is in our power, to relieve

which directly carries us with calmness and thought to their assistance. Any one of these, from various and complicated reasons, may, in particular cases, prevail over the other two; and there are, I suppose, instances where the bare *sight* of distress, without our feeling any compassion for it, may be the occasion of either or both of the two latter perceptions. One might add, that if there be really any such thing as the fiction or imagination of danger to ourselves, from sight of the miseries of others, which Hobbs speaks of, and which he has absurdly mistaken for the whole of compassion; if there be any thing of this sort common to mankind, distinct from the reflection of reason, it would be a most remarkable instance of what was furthest from his thoughts, namely, of a mutual sympathy between each particular of the species, a fellow-feeling common to mankind. It would not, indeed, be an example of our substituting others for ourselves, but it would be an example of our substituting ourselves for others. And as it would not be an instance of benevolence, so neither would it be any instance of self-love; for this phantom of danger to ourselves, naturally rising to view upon sight of the distresses of others, would be no more an instance of love to ourselves, than the pain of hunger is.

them, yet is it not better to do this from reason and duty ? Does not passion and affection of every kind perpetually mislead us ? Nay, is not passion and affection itself a weakness, and what a perfect being must be entirely free from ?" Perhaps so : but it is mankind I am speaking of ; imperfect creatures, and who naturally, and from the condition we are placed in, necessarily depend upon each other. With respect to such creatures, it would be found of as bad consequence to eradicate all natural affections, as to be entirely governed by them. This would almost sink us to the condition of brutes ; and that would leave us without a sufficient principle of action. Reason alone, whatever any one may wish, is not, in reality, a sufficient motive of virtue in such a creature as man ; but this reason, joined with those affections which God has impressed upon his heart : and when these are allowed scope to exercise themselves, but under strict government and direction of reason ; then it is we act suitably to our nature, and to the circumstances God has placed us in. Neither is affection itself at all a weakness ; nor does it argue defect, any otherwise than as our senses and appetites do ; they belong to our condition of nature, and are what we cannot be without. God Almighty is, to be sure, unmoved by passion or appetite— unchanged by affection ; but then it is to be added, that he neither sees, nor hears, nor perceives things by any senses like ours ; but in a manner infinitely more perfect. Now, as it is an absurdity almost too gross to be mentioned, for a man to endeavour to get rid of his senses, because the Supreme Being discerns things more perfectly without them, it is as real, though not so obvious, an absurdity, to endeavour to eradicate the passions he has given us, because He is without them. For, since our passions are as really a part of our constitution as our senses—since the former as really belong to our condition of nature as the latter—to get rid of either is equally a violation of, and breaking in upon, that nature and constitution he has given us. Both our senses and our passions are a supply to the imperfection of our nature : thus they show, that we are such sort of creatures, as to stand in need of those helps which higher orders of creatures do not. But it is not the supply, but the deficiency ; as it is not a remedy, but a disease, which is the imperfection. However, our appetites, passions, senses, no way imply disease; nor, indeed, do they imply deficiency or imperfection of any sort; but only this, that the constitution of nature, according to which God has made us, is such as to require them. And it is so far from being true, that a wise man must entirely suppress compassion, and all fellow-feeling for others, as a weakness, and trust to reason alone to teach and enforce upon him the practice of the several charities we owe to our kind; that, on the contrary, even the bare exercise of such affections would itself be for the good and happiness of the world; and the imperfections of the higher principles of reason and religion in man, the little influence they have upon our practice, and the strength and prevalency of contrary ones, plainly require those affections to be a restraint upon these latter, and a supply to the deficiencies of the former.

First, The very exercise itself of these affections, in a just and reasonable manner and degree, would, upon the whole, increase the satisfactions, and lessen the miseries of life.

It is the tendency and business of virtue and religion to procure, as much as may be, universal good-will, trust, and friendship, amongst mankind. If this could be brought to obtain; and each man enjoyed the happiness of others, as every one does that of a friend; and looked upon the success and prosperity of his neighbour, as every one does upon that of his children and family; it is too manifest to be insisted upon, how much the enjoyments of life would be increased. There would be so much happiness introduced into the world, without any deduction or inconvenience from it, in proportion as the precept of *rejoicing with those who rejoice,* was universally obeyed. Our Saviour has owned this good affection as belonging to our nature, in the parable of the *lost sheep:* and does not think it to the disadvantage of a perfect state, to represent its happiness as capable of increase, from reflection upon that of others.

But since, in such a creature as man, compassion, or sorrow for the distress of others, seems so far necessarily connected with joy in their prosperity, as that whoever rejoices in one must unavoidably compassionate the other: there cannot be that delight or satisfaction, which appears to be so considerable, without the inconveniences, whatever they are, of compassion.

However, without considering this connexion, there is no doubt but that more good than evil, more delight than sorrow, arises from compassion itself; there being so many things which balance the sorrow of it. There is, first, the relief which the distressed feel from this affection in others towards them. There is likewise the additional misery which they would feel from the reflection that no one commiserated their case. It is indeed true, that any disposition, prevailing beyond a certain degree, becomes somewhat wrong; and we have ways of speaking, which, though they do not directly express that excess, yet always lead our thoughts to it, and give us the notion of it. Thus, when mention is made of delight in being pitied, this always conveys to our mind the notion of somewhat which is really a weakness: the manner of speaking, I say, implies a certain weakness and feebleness of mind, which is and ought to be disapproved. But men of the greatest fortitude would in distress feel uneasiness from knowing that no person in the world had any sort of compassion or real concern for them; and in some cases, especially when the temper is enfeebled by sickness, or any long and great distress, doubtless would feel a kind of relief even from the helpless good-will and ineffectual assistances of those about them. Over against the sorrow of compassion is likewise to be set a peculiar calm kind of satisfaction, which accompanies it, unless in cases where the distress of another is by some means so brought home to ourselves, as to become in a manner our own; or when, from weakness of mind, the affection rises too high, which ought to be corrected. This tranquillity, or calm satisfaction, proceeds partly from consciousness of a right affection and temper of mind, and partly from a sense of our own freedom from the misery we compassionate. This last may possibly appear to some at first sight faulty; but it really is not so. It is the same with that positive enjoyment, which sudden ease from pain for the present affords, arising from a real sense of misery, joined with a sense of our freedom from it; which in all cases must afford some degree of satisfaction.

To these things must be added the observation, which

respects both the affections we are considering, that they
who have got over all fellow-feeling for others, have withal
contracted a certain callousness of heart, which renders
them insensible to most other satisfactions, but those of the
grossest kind.

Secondly, Without the exercise of these affections, men
would certainly be much more wanting in the offices of
charity they owe to each other, and likewise more cruel
and injurious, than they are at present.

The private interest of the individual would not be
sufficiently provided for by reasonable and cool self-love
alone : therefore the appetites and passions are placed
within, as a guard and further security, without which it
would not be taken due care of. It is manifest our life
would be neglected, were it not for the calls of hunger, and
thirst, and weariness : notwithstanding that without them
reason would assure us, that the recruits of food and sleep
are the necessary means of our preservation. It is therefore absurd to imagine, that, without affection, the same
reason alone would be more effectual to engage us to perform the duties we owe to our fellow-creatures. One of
this make would be as defective, as much wanting, considered with respect to society, as one of the former make
would be defective, or wanting, considered as an individual,
or in his private capacity. Is it possible any can in earnest
think that a public spirit, *i. e.* a settled reasonable principle
of benevolence to mankind, is so prevalent and strong in
the species, as that we may venture to throw off the under
affections, which are its assistants, carry it forward, and
mark out particular courses for it ; family, friends, neighbourhood, the distressed, our country ? The common joys
and the common sorrows, which belong to these relations
and circumstances, are as plainly useful to society, as the
pain and pleasure belonging to hunger, thirst, and weariness, are of service to the individual. In defect of that
higher principle of reason, compassion is often the only way
by which the indigent can have access to us : and therefore to eradicate this, though it is not indeed formally to
deny them that assistance which is their due ; yet it is to
cut them off from that which is too frequently their only
way of obtaining it. And as for those who have shut up

this door against the complaints of the miserable, and con-
quered this affection in themselves; even these persons
will be under great restraints from the same affection in
others. Thus, a man who has himself no sense of injustice, cruelty, oppression, will be kept from running the
utmost lengths of wickedness, by fear of that detestation,
and even resentment of inhumanity, in many particular
instances of it, which compassion for the object towards
whom such inhumanity is exercised, excites in the bulk of
mankind. And this is frequently the chief danger, and the
chief restraint, which tyrants and the great oppressors of
the world feel.

In general, experience will show, that as want of natural
appetite to food supposes and proceeds from some bodily
disease; so the apathy the Stoics talk of, as much supposes, or is accompanied with somewhat amiss in the
moral character, in that which is the health of the mind.
Those who formerly aimed at this upon the foot of philosophy, appear to have had better success in eradicating the
affections of tenderness and compassion, than they had
with the passions of envy, pride, and resentment: these
latter, at best, were but concealed, and that imperfectly
too. How far this observation may be extended to such as
endeavour to suppress the natural impulses of their affections, in order to form themselves for business and the
world, I shall not determine. But there does not appear
any capacity or relation to be named, in which men ought
to be entirely deaf to the calls of affection, unless the judicial one is to be excepted.

And as to those who are commonly called the men of
pleasure, it is manifest that the reason they set up for
hardness of heart, is to avoid being interrupted in their
course, by the ruin and misery they are the authors of:
neither are persons of this character always the most free
from the impotencies of envy and resentment. What may
men at last bring themselves to, by suppressing their passions and affections of one kind, and leaving those of the
other in their full strength? But surely it might be expected, that persons who make pleasure their study and their
business, if they understood what they profess, would reflect, how many of the entertainments of life, how many

of those kind of amusements which seem peculiarly to belong to men of leisure and education, they become insensible to by this acquired hardness of heart.

I shall close these reflections with barely mentioning the behaviour of that divine Person, who was the example of all perfection in human nature, as represented in the gospels, mourning, and even, in a literal sense, weeping over the distresses of his creatures.

The observation already made, that, of the two affections mentioned in the text, the latter exerts itself much more than the former; that, from the original constitution of human nature, we much more generally and sensibly compassionate the distressed, than rejoice with the prosperous, requires to be particularly considered. This observation, therefore, with the reflections which arise out of it, and which it leads our thoughts to, shall be the subject of another discourse.

For the conclusion of this, let me just take notice of the danger of over great refinements; of going besides or beyond the plain, obvious, first appearance of things, upon the subject of morals and religion. The least observation will show how little the generality of men are capable of speculations. Therefore morality and religion must be somewhat plain and easy to be understood: it must appeal to what we call plain common sense, as distinguished from superior capacity and improvement, because it appeals to mankind. Persons of superior capacity and improvement have often fallen into errors, which no one of mere common understanding could. Is it possible that one of this latter character could ever of himself have thought, that there was absolutely no such thing in mankind as affection to the good of others: suppose of parents to their children? or, that what he felt upon seeing a friend in distress, was only fear for himself; or, upon supposition of the affections of kindness and compassion, that it was the business of wisdom and virtue to set him about extirpating them as fast as he could: And yet each of these manifest contradictions to nature has been laid down by men of speculation as a discovery in moral philosophy; which they, it seems, have found out through all the specious appearances to the contrary. This reflection may be extended further. The extravagances of enthusiasm and superstition do not at all lie in the road of common sense : and, therefore, so far as they are *original mistakes*, must be owing to going beside or beyond it.   Now, since inquiry and examination can relate only to things so obscure and uncertain as to stand in need of it, and to persons who are capable of it, the proper advice to be given to plain honest men, to secure them from the extremes both of superstition and irreligion, is that of the Son of Sirach : *In every good work trust thy own soul; for this is the keeping of the commandment.**

* Eccles. xxxii. 23.

SERMON VI.

UPON COMPASSION.

PREACHED THE FIRST SUNDAY IN LENT.

ROMANS xii. 15.

Rejoice with them that do rejoice, and weep with them that weep.

THERE is a much more exact correspondence between the natural and moral world, than we are apt to take notice of. The inward frame of man does, in a peculiar manner, answer to the external condition and circumstances of life in which he is placed. This is a particular instance of that general observation of the Son of Sirach, *All things are double one against another, and God hath made nothing imperfect.* The several passions and affections in the heart of man, compared with the circumstances of life in which he is placed, afford, to such as will attend to them, as certain instances of final causes, as any whatever which are more commonly alleged for such: since those affections lead him to a certain determinate course of action suitable to those circumstances; as (for instance) compassion, to relieve the distressed. And as all observations of final causes, drawn from the principles of action in the heart of man, compared with the condition he is placed in, serve all the good uses which instances of final causes in the material world about us do; and both these are equally proofs of wisdom and design in the Author of nature; so the former

* Eccles. xlii. 24.

serve to further good purposes; they show us what course
of life we are made for, what is our duty, and in a peculiar
manner, enforce upon us the practice of it.

Suppose we are capable of happiness and of misery in
degrees equally intense and extreme, yet we are capable
of the latter for a much longer time, beyond all comparison.
We see men in the tortures of pain for hours, days, and
excepting the short suspensions of sleep, for months together, without intermission; to which no enjoyments of
life do, in degree and continuance, bear any sort of proportion. And such is our make, and that of the world about
us, that any thing may become the instrument of pain and
sorrow to us. Thus, almost any one man is capable of
doing mischief to any other, though he may not be capable
of doing him good; and if he be capable of doing him
some good, he is capable of doing him more evil. And it
is, in numberless cases, much more in our power to lessen
the miseries of others, than to promote their positive happiness, any otherwise than as the former often includes the
latter; ease from misery occasioning, for some time, the
greatest positive enjoyment. This constitution of nature,
namely, that it is so much more in our power to occasion,
and likewise to lessen misery, than to promote positive
happiness, plainly required a particular affection, to hinder
us from abusing, and to incline us to make a right use of
the former powers, *i. e.* the powers both to occasion and to
lessen misery; over and above what was necessary to induce us to make a right use of the latter power, that of
promoting positive happiness. The power we have over
the misery of our fellow-creatures, to occasion or lessen it,
being a more important trust than the power we have of
promoting their positive happiness; the former requires,
and has a further, an additional security and guard against
its being violated, beyond, and over and above what the
latter has. The social nature of man, and general good-will
to his species, equally prevent him from doing evil, incline
him to relieve the distressed, and to promote the positive
happiness of his fellow-creatures; but compassion only
restrains from the first, and carries him to the second; it
hath nothing to do with the third.

The final causes then of compassion are, to prevent and
to relieve misery.

As to the former: this affection may plainly be a restraint upon resentment, envy, unreasonable self-love; that is, upon all the principles from which men do evil to one another. Let us instance only in resentment. It seldom happens, in regulated societies, that men have an enemy so entirely in their power, as to be able to satiate their resentment with safety. But if we were to put this case, it is plainly supposable, that a person might bring his enemy into such a condition, as, from being the object of anger or rage, to become an object of compassion, even to himself, though the most malicious man in the world : and in this case compassion would stop him, if he could stop with safety, from pursuing his revenge any farther. But since nature has placed within us more powerful restraints to prevent mischief, and since the final cause of compassion is much more to relieve misery, let us go on to the consideration of it in this view.

As this world was not intended to be a state of any great satisfaction or high enjoyment; so neither was it intended to be a mere scene of unhappiness and sorrow. Mitigations and reliefs are provided, by the merciful Author of nature, for most of the afflictions in human life. There is kind provision made even against our frailties ; as we are so constituted, that time abundantly abates our sorrows, and begets in us that resignment of temper, which ought to have been produced by a better cause ; a due sense of the authority of God, and our state of dependence. This holds in respect to far the greatest part of the evils of life; I suppose, in some degree, as to pain and sickness. Now, this part of the constitution or make of man, considered as some relief to misery, and not as provision for positive happiness, is, if I may so speak, an instance of nature's compassion for us, and every natural remedy or relief to misery, may be considered in the same view.

But since, in many cases, it is very much in our power to alleviate the miseries of each other ; and benevolence, though natural in man to man, yet is, in a very low degree, kept down by interest and competitions ; and men, for the most part, are so engaged in the business and pleasures of the world, as to overlook and turn away from objects of misery, which are plainly considered as interruptions to them in their way, as intruders upon their business, their

E

gaiety and mirth ;—compassion is an advocate within us in
their behalf, to gain the unhappy admittance and access, to
make their case attended to.   If it sometimes serves a contrary purpose, and makes men industriously turn away from
the miserable, these are only instances of abuse and perversion : for the end for which the affection was given us,
most certainly is, not to make us avoid, but to make us attend to the objects of it.   And if men would only resolve
to allow this much to it, let it bring before their view, the
view of their mind, the miseries of their fellow-creatures :
let it gain for them that their case be considered ; I am
persuaded it would not fail of gaining more, and that very
few real objects of charity would pass unrelieved.   Pain,
and sorrow, and misery, have a right to our assistance :
compassion puts us in mind of the debt, and that we owe
it to ourselves, as well as to the distressed.   For to endeavour to get rid of the sorrow of compassion, by turning
from the wretched, when yet it is in our power to relieve
them, is as unnatural as to endeavour to get rid of the pain
of hunger by keeping from the sight of food.   That we can
do one with greater success than we can the other, is no
proof that one is less a violation of nature than the other.
Compassion is a call, a demand of nature, to relieve the unhappy ; as hunger is a natural call for food.   This affection
plainly gives the objects of it an additional claim to relief
and mercy, over and above what our fellow-creatures in
common have to our good-will.   Liberality and bounty are
exceedingly commendable ; and a particular distinction in
such a world as this, where men set themselves to contract
their heart, and close it to all interests but their own.   It is
by no means to be opposed to mercy, but always accompanies it : the distinction between them is only, that the
former leads our thoughts to a more promiscuous and
undistinguished distribution of favours ; to those who are
not, as well as those who are necessitous ; whereas, the
object of compassion is misery.   But in the comparison,
and where there is not a possibility of both, mercy is to
have the preference : the affection of compassion manifestly
leads us to this preference.   Thus, to relieve the indigent
and distressed ; to single out the unhappy, from whom can
be expected no returns, either of present entertainment or
future service, for the objects of our favours ; to esteem a

11

man's being friendless as a recommendation ; dejection, and
incapacity of struggling through the world, as a motive for
assisting him ; in a word, to consider these circumstances of
disadvantage, which are usually thought a sufficient reason
for neglect and overlooking a person, as a motive for helping him forward : this is the course of benevolence, which
compassion marks out and directs us to ; this is that humanity, which is so peculiarly becoming our nature and
circumstances in this world.

To these considerations, drawn from the nature of man,
must be added the reason of the thing itself we are recommending, which accords to and shows the same. For,
since it is so much more in our power to lessen the misery
of our fellow-creatures, than to promote their positive happiness ; in cases where there is an inconsistency, we shall
be likely to do much more good by setting ourselves to mi-
tigate the former, than by endeavouring to promote the
latter. Let the competition be between the poor and the
rich. It is easy, you will say, to see which will have the
preference. True : but the question is, which ought to
have the preference ? What proportion is there between the
happiness produced by doing a favour to the indigent, and
that produced by doing the same favour to one in easy circumstances ? It is manifest, that the addition of a very
large estate to one who before had an affluence, will in
many instances yield him less new enjoyment or satisfaction,
than any ordinary charity would yield to a necessitous person. So that it is not only true that our nature, *i. e.* the
voice of God within us, carries us to the exercise of charity
and benevolence in the way of compassion or mercy, preferably to any other way ; but we also manifestly discern
much more good done by the former ; or, if you will allow
me the expressions, more misery annihilated, and happiness
created. If charity, and benevolence, and endeavouring
to do good to our fellow-creatures be any thing, this observation deserves to be most seriously considered by all who
have to bestow. And it holds with great exactness, when
applied to the several degrees of greater and less indigency
throughout the various ranks in human life : the happiness
or good produced not being in proportion to what is bestowed, but in proportion to this joined with the need there
was of it.

E 2

It may perhaps be expected, that upon this subject notice
should be taken of occasions, circumstances, and characters,
which seem at once to call forth affections of different sorts.
Thus, vice may be thought the object both of pity and
indignation ; folly, of pity and of laughter. How far this is
strictly true, I shall not inquire; but only observe upon the
appearance, how much more humane it is to yield and give
scope to affections, which are most directly in favour of,
and friendly towards our fellow-creatures ; and that there is
plainly much less danger of being led wrong by these, than
by the other.

But, notwithstanding all that has been said in recommendation of compassion, that it is most amiable, most
becoming human nature, and most useful to the world ; yet
it must be owned, that every affection, as distinct from a
principle of reason, may rise too high, and be beyond its
just proportion. And by means of this one carried too far,
a man throughout his life is subject to much more uneasiness than belongs to his share : and in particular instances,
it may be in such a degree, as to incapacitate him from
assisting the very person who is the object of it. But as
there are some who, upon principle, set up for suppressing
this affection itself as weakness, there is also I know not
what of fashion on this side : and, by some means or other,
the whole world almost is run into the extremes of insensibility towards the distresses of their fellow-creatures ; so
that general rules and exhortations must always be on the
other side.

And now, to go on to the uses we should make of the
foregoing reflections, the further views they lead us to, and
the general temper they have a tendency to beget in us.
There being that distinct affection implanted in the nature
of man, tending to lessen the miseries of life, that particular
provision made for abating its sorrows, more than for
increasing its positive happiness, as before explained ; this
may suggest to us, what should be our general aim respecting ourselves, in our passage through this world ; namely,
to endeavour chiefly to escape misery, keep free from uneasiness, pain, and sorrow, or to get relief and mitigation of
them ; to propose to ourselves peace and tranquillity of
mind, rather than pursue after high enjoyments. This is
what the constitution of nature, before explained, marks

out as the course we should follow, and the end we should aim at. To make pleasure, and mirth, and jollity, our business, and be constantly hurrying about after some gay amusement, some new gratification of sense or appetite, to those who will consider the nature of man and our condition in this world, will appear the most romantic scheme of life that ever entered into thought. And yet, how many are there who go on in this course, without learning better from the daily, the hourly disappointments, listlessness, and satiety, which accompany this fashionable method of wasting away their days?

The subject we have been insisting upon would lead us into the same kind of reflections, by a different connexion. The miseries of life brought home to ourselves by compassion, viewed through this affection, considered as the sense by which they are perceived, would beget in us that moderation, humility, and soberness of mind, which has been now recommended; and which peculiarly belongs to a season of recollection, the only purpose of which is to bring us to a just state of things, to recover us out of that forgetfulness of ourselves, and our true state, which, it is manifest, far the greatest part of men pass their whole life in. Upon this account Solomon says, that *it is better to go to the house of mourning, than to go to the house of feasting; i. e.* it is more to a man's advantage to turn his eyes towards objects of distress, to recall sometimes to his remembrance the occasions of sorrow, than to pass all his days in thoughtless mirth and gaiety. And he represents the wise as choosing to frequent the former of these places; to be sure, not for its own sake, but because *by the sadness of the countenance the heart is made better.* Every one observes, how temperate and reasonable men are when humbled and brought low by afflictions, in comparison of what they are in high prosperity. By this voluntary resort to the house of mourning, which is here recommended, we might learn all those useful instructions which calamities teach, without undergoing them ourselves; and grow wiser and better at a more easy rate than men commonly do. The objects themselves, which in that place of sorrow lie before our view, naturally give us a seriousness and attention, check that wantonness which is the growth of prosperity and ease, and lead us to reflect upon the deficiencies of human life itself; that *every man, at his best estate, is altogether vanity*.   This would correct the florid and gaudy prospects and expectations which we are too apt to indulge, teach us to lower our notions of happiness and enjoyment, bring them down to the reality of things, to what is attainable, to what the frailty of our condition will admit of, which for any continuance, is only tranquillity, ease, and moderate satisfactions.   Thus we might at once become proof against the temptations, with which the whole world almost is carried away; since it is plain, that not only what is called a life of pleasure, but also vicious pursuits in general, aim at somewhat besides, and beyond these moderate satisfactions.

And as to that obstinacy and wilfulness, which render men so insensible to the motives of religion; this right sense of ourselves and of the world about us, would bend the stubborn mind, soften the heart, and make it more apt to receive impression : and this is the proper temper in which to call our ways to remembrance, to review and set home upon ourselves the miscarriages of our past life.   In such a compliant state of mind, reason and conscience will have a fair hearing; which is the preparation for, or rather the beginning of that repentance, the outward show of which we all put on at this season.

Lastly, The various miseries of life which lie before us wherever we turn our eyes, the frailty of this mortal state we are passing through, may put us in mind that the present world is not our home; that we are merely strangers and travellers in it, as all our fathers were.   It is therefore to be considered as a foreign country, in which our poverty and wants, and the insufficient supplies of them, were designed to turn our views to that higher and better state we are heirs to ; a state, where will be no follies to be overlooked, no miseries to be pitied, no wants to be relieved; where the affection we have been now treating of, will happily be lost, as there will be no objects to exercise it upon : for *God shall wipe away all tears from their eyes ; and there shall be no more death, neither sorrow, nor crying ; neither shall there be any more pain ; for the former things are passed away.*

SERMON VII.

UPON THE CHARACTER OF BALAAM.

PREACHED THE SECOND SUNDAY AFTER EASTER.

NUMBERS xxiii. 10.

Let me die the death of the righteous, and let my last end be like his.

THESE words taken alone, and without respect to him who spoke them, lead our thoughts immediately to the different ends of good and bad men. For, though the comparison is not expressed, yet it is manifestly implied; as is also the preference of one of these characters to the other in that last circumstance, death. And since dying the death of the righteous, or of the wicked, necessarily implies men's being righteous or wicked, *i. e.* having lived righteously or wickedly; a comparison of them in their lives also might come into consideration from such a single view of the words themselves. But my present design is, to consider them with a particular reference or respect to him who spoke them : which reference, if you please to attend, you will see. And if what shall be offered to your considera-:ion at this time, be thought a discourse upon the whole history of this man, rather than upon the particular words I have read, this is of no consequence ; it is sufficient if it afford reflections of use and service to ourselves.

But in order to avoid cavils respecting this remarkable

relation in Scripture, either that part of it which you have heard in the first lesson for the day, or any other, let me just observe, that as this is not the place for answering them, so they no way affect the following discourse; since the character there given is plainly a real one in life, and such as there are parallels to.

The occasion of Balaam's coming out of his own country into the land of Moab, where he pronounced this solemn prayer or wish, he himself relates in the first parable or prophetic speech, of which it is the conclusion; in which is a custom referred to, proper to be taken notice of—that of devoting enemies to destruction, before the entrance upon a war with them. This custom appears to have prevailed over a great part of the world, for we find it amongst the most distant nations. The Romans had public officers, to whom it belonged as a stated part of their office. But there was somewhat more particular in the case now before us; Balaam being looked upon as an extraordinary person, whose blessing or curse was thought to be always effectual.

In order to engage the reader's attention to this passage, the sacred historian has enumerated the preparatory circumstances, which are these. Balaam requires the king of Moab to build him seven altars, and to prepare him the same number of oxen and of rams. The sacrifice being over, he retires alone to a solitude sacred to these occasions, there to wait the divine inspiration or answer, for which the foregoing rites were the preparation. "And God met Balaam, and put a word in his mouth;"* upon receiving which, he returns back to the altars, where was the king, who had all this while attended the sacrifice, as appointed, he and all the princes of Moab standing, big with expectation of the prophet's reply. "And he took up his parable, and said, Balak the king of Moab hath brought me from Aram, out of the mountains of the east, saying, Come, curse me Jacob, and come, defy Israel. How shall I curse, whom God hath not cursed? Or how shall I defy, whom the Lord hath not defied? For from the top of the rocks I see him, and from the hills I behold him: lo, the people shall dwell alone, and shall not be reckoned among the nations. Who can count the dust of Jacob, and the number

* Ver. 4, 5.

of the fourth part of Israel? Let me die the death of the
righteous, and let my last end be like his."*

It is necessary, as you will see in the progress of this
discourse, particularly to observe what he understood by
righteous. And he himself is introduced in the book of
Micah† explaining it; if by *righteous* is meant *good*, as to
be sure it is. "O my people, remember now what Balak
king of Moab consulted, and what Balaam, the son of Beor,
answered him from Shittim unto Gilgal." From the mention of Shittim, it is manifest that it is this very story
which is here referred to, though another part of it, the
account of which is not now extant; as there are many
quotations in Scripture out of books which are not come
down to us. "Remember what Balaam answered, that ye
may know the righteousness of the Lord," *i. e.* the righteousness which God will accept. Balak demands, "Wherewith
shall I come before the Lord, and bow myself before the
high God? Shall I come before him with burnt-offerings,
with calves of a year old? Will the Lord be pleased with
thousands of rams, or with ten thousands of rivers of oil?
Shall I give my first-born for my transgression, the fruit of
my body for the sin of my soul?" Balaam answers him,
"He hath showed thee, O man, what is good: and what
doth the Lord require of thee, but to do justly, and to love
mercy, and to walk humbly with thy God?" Here is a
good man expressly characterised, as distinct from a dishonest and a superstitious man. No words can more
strongly exclude dishonesty and falseness of heart, than
doing justice and *loving mercy;* and both these, as well as
walking humbly with God, are put in opposition to those
ceremonial methods of recommendation, which Balak hoped
might have served the turn. From hence appears what he
meant by the *righteous,* whose *death* he desires to die.

Whether it was his own character shall now be inquired:
and in order to determine it, we must take a view of his
whole behaviour upon this occasion. When the elders of
Moab came to him, though he appears to have been much
allured with the rewards offered, yet he had such regard to
the authority of God, as to keep the messengers in suspense
until he had consulted his will. "And God said to him,

* Ver. 7—10.   † Micah vi.

E 5

Thou shalt not go with them, thou shalt not curse the
people, for they are blessed."* Upon this he dismisses the
ambassadors, with an absolute refusal of accompanying
them back to their king. Thus far his regard to his duty
prevailed; neither does there any thing appear as yet amiss
in his conduct. His answer being reported to the king of
Moab, a more honourable embassy is immediately dis-
patched, and greater rewards proposed. Then the iniquity
of his heart began to disclose itself. A thorough honest
man would, without hesitation, have repeated his former
answer, that he could not be guilty of so infamous a prosti-
tution of the sacred character with which he was invested,
as, in the name of a prophet, to curse those whom he knew
to be blessed. But instead of this, which was the only
honest part in these circumstances that lay before him, he
desires the princes of Moab to tarry that night with him
also; and, for the sake of the reward, deliberates whether,
by some means or other, he might not be able to obtain
leave to curse Israel: to do that which had been before revealed to him to be contrary to the will of God, which yet
he resolves not to do without that permission. Upon
which, as when this nation afterwards rejected God from
reigning over them, he gave them a king in his anger; in
the same way, as appears from other parts of the narration,
he gives Balaam the permission he desired: for this is the
most natural sense of the words. Arriving in the territories
of Moab, and being received with particular distinction by
the king, and he repeating in person the promise of the rewards he had before made to him by his ambassadors, he
seeks, the text says, by *sacrifices* and *enchantments*, (what
these were is not to our purpose,) to obtain leave of God to
curse the people; keeping still his resolution, not to do it
without that permission; which not being able to obtain,
he had such regard to the command of God, as to keep this
resolution to the last. The supposition of his being under
a supernatural restraint, is a mere fiction of Philo: he is
plainly represented to be under no other force or restraint
than the fear of God. However, he goes on persevering in
that endeavour, after he had declared that "God had not
beheld iniquity in Jacob, neither had he seen perverseness

* Chap. xxii. 12.

UPON THE CHARACTER OF BALAAM.   63

in Israel;"* *i. e.* they were a people of virtue and piety, so
far as not to have drawn down, by their iniquity, that curse
which he was soliciting leave to pronounce upon them. So
that the state of Balaam's mind was this: he wanted to do
what he knew to be very wicked, and contrary to the express command of God; he had inward checks and restraints, which he could not entirely get over; he therefore
casts about for ways to reconcile this wickedness with his
duty.   How great a paradox soever this may appear, as it
is indeed a contradiction in terms, it is the very account
which the Scripture gives us of him.

But there is a more surprising piece of iniquity yet behind.   Not daring in his religious character, as a prophet,
to assist the king of Moab, he considers whether there might
not be found some other means of assisting him against that
very people, whom he himself, by the fear of God, was
restrained from cursing in words.   One would not think it
possible that the weakness, even of religious self-deceit in
its utmost excess, could have so poor a distinction, so fond
an evasion, to serve itself of.   But so it was: and he could
think of no other method, than to betray the children of
Israel to provoke His wrath, who was their only strength
and defence.   The temptation which he pitched upon, was
that concerning which Solomon afterwards observed, that it
had " cast down many wounded; yea, many strong men had
been slain by it."   And of which he himself was a sad example, when " his wives turned away his heart after other
gods."   This succeeded: the people sin against God; and
thus the prophet's counsel brought on that destruction,
which he could by no means be prevailed upon to assist
with the religious ceremony of execration, which the king
of Moab thought would itself have effected it.   Their
crime and punishment are related in Deuteronomy,† and
Numbers.‡   And from the relation repeated in Numbers,§
it appears that Balaam was the contriver of the whole
matter.   It is also ascribed to him in the Revelation,‖
where he is said to have " taught Balak to cast a stumbling-
block before the children of Israel."

This was the man, this Balaam, I say, was the man, who

* Ver. 21.   † Chap. iv.   ‡ Chap. xxv.
    § Chap. xxxi.   ‖ Chap. ii.

desired to " die the death of the righteous," and that his
" last end might be like his :" and this was the state of his
mind when he pronounced these words.

So that the object we have now before us is the most
astonishing in the world : a very wicked man, under a deep
sense of God and religion, persisting still in his wickedness,
and preferring the wages of unrighteousness, even when he
had before him a lively view of death, and that approaching
period of his days, which should deprive him of all those
advantages for which he was prostituting himself; and likewise a prospect, whether certain or uncertain, of a future
state of retribution : all this, joined with an explicit ardent
wish, that when he was to leave this world, he might be in
the condition of a righteous man. Good God! what inconsistency, what perplexity is here ! With what different
views of things, with what contradictory principles of action, must such a mind be torn and distracted ! It was not
unthinking carelessness by which he ran on headlong in vice
and folly, without ever making a stand to ask himself what
he was doing. No; he acted upon the cool motives of interest
and advantage.   Neither was he totally hard and callous to
impressions of religion, what we call abandoned ; for he
absolutely denied to curse Israel. When reason assumes her
place, when convinced of his duty, when he owns and feels,
and is actually under the influence of the Divine authority ;
whilst he is carrying on his views to the grave, the end of
all temporal greatness under the sense of things, with the
better character and more desirable state present——full before him—in his thoughts, in his wishes, voluntarily to choose
the worse—what fatality is here ! Or how otherwise can
such a character be explained ? And yet, strange as it may
appear, it is not altogether an uncommon one : nay, with
some small alterations, and put a little lower, it is applicable to a very considerable part of the world.   For, if the
reasonable choice be seen and acknowledged, and yet men
make the unreasonable one, is not this the same contradiction ; that very inconsistency, which appeared so unaccountable ?

To give some little opening to such characters and behaviour, it is to be observed in general, that there is no account to be given, in the way of reason, of men's so strong
attachments to the present world : our hopes and fears, and

pursuits, are in degrees beyond all proportion to the known value of the things they respect. This may be said, without taking into consideration religion and a future state; and when these are considered, the disproportion is. infinitely heightened. Now, when men go against their reason, and contradict a more important interest at a distance, for one nearer, though of less consideration ; if this be the whole of the case, all that can be said is, that strong passions, some kind of brute force within, prevails over the principle of rationality.   However, if this be with a clear, full, and distinct view of the truth of things, then it is doing the utmost violence to themselves, acting in the most palpable contradiction to their very nature.   But if there be any such thing in mankind, as putting half-deceits upon themselves; which there plainly is, either by avoiding reflection, or (if they do reflect) by religious equivocation, subterfuges, and palliating matters to themselves ; by these means conscience may be laid asleep, and they may go on in a course of wickedness with less disturbance.   All the various turns, doubles, and intricacies in a dishonest heart, cannot be unfolded or laid open ; but that there is somewhat of that kind is manifest, be it to be called self-deceit, or by any other name. Balaam had before his eyes the authority of God, absolutely forbidding him what he, for the sake of a reward, had the strongest inclination to : he was likewise in a state of mind sober enough to consider death and his last end : by these considerations he was restrained, first, from going to the king of Moab, and after he did go, from cursing Israel. But notwithstanding this, there was great wickedness in his heart. He could not forego the rewards of unrighteousness : he therefore first seeks for indulgences ; and, when these could not be obtained, he sins against the whole meaning, end, and design of the prohibition, which no consideration in the world could prevail with him to go against the letter of. And surely that impious counsel he gave to Balak against the children of Israel was, considered in itself, a greater piece of wickedness, than if he had cursed them in words.

If it be inquired, what his situation, his hopes, and fears were, in respect to this his wish, the answer must be, That consciousness of the wickedness of his heart must necessa‧rily have destroyed all settled hopes of dying the death of the righteous ; he could have no calm satisfaction in this

2

view of his last end : yet, on the other hand, it is possible
that those partial regards to his duty, now mentioned, might
keep him from perfect despair.

Upon the whole, it is manifest that Balaam had the most
just and true notions of God and religion ; as appears, partly
from the original story itself, and more plainly from the
passage in Micah ; where he explains religion to consist
in real virtue and real piety, expressly distinguished from
superstition, and in terms which most strongly exclude dishonesty and falseness of heart. Yet you see his behaviour :
he seeks indulgences for plain wickedness ; which not being
able to obtain, he glosses over that same wickedness, dresses
it up in a new form, in order to make it pass off more
easily with himself : that is, he deliberately contrives to deceive and impose upon himself, in a matter which he knew
to be of the utmost importance.

To bring these observations home to ourselves : it is too
evident that many persons allow themselves in very unjustifiable courses, who yet make great pretences to religion ; not to deceive the world, none can be so weak as to
think this will pass in our age ; but from principles, hopes,
and fears respecting God and a future state ; and go on
thus with a sort of tranquillity and quiet of mind. This
cannot be upon a thorough consideration and full resolution that the pleasures and advantages they propose are to
be pursued at all hazards, against reason, against the law
of God, and though everlasting destruction is to be the
consequence. This would be doing too great violence upon
themselves. No : they are for making a composition with
the Almighty. These of his commands they will obey :
but as to others—why they will make all the atonements
in their power ; the ambitious, the covetous, the dissolute
man, each in a way which shall not contradict his respective
pursuit. Indulgences before, which was Balaam's first attempt, though he was not so successful in it as to deceive
himself, or atonements afterwards, are all the same. And
here perhaps come in faint hopes that they may, and half
resolves that they will, one time or other, make a change.

Besides these, there are also persons, who, from a more
just way of considering things, see the infinite absurdity of
this, of substituting sacrifice instead of obedience : there
are persons far enough from superstition, and not with-

out some real sense of God and religion upon their minds, who yet are guilty of most unjustifiable practices, and go on with great coolness and command over themselves. The same dishonesty and unsoundness of heart discovers itself in these another way. In all common ordinary cases, we see intuitively at first view what is our duty, what is the honest part. This is the ground of the observation, that the first thought is often the best. In these cases doubt and deliberation is itself dishonesty; as it was in Balaam upon the second message. That which is called considering what is our duty in a particular case, is very often nothing but endeavouring to explain it away. Thus those courses which, if men would fairly attend to the dictates of their own consciences, they would see to be corruption, excess, oppression, uncharitableness; these are refined upon;— things were so and so circumstanced;—great difficulties are raised about fixing bounds and degrees; and thus every moral obligation whatever may be evaded. Here is scope, I say, for an unfair mind to explain away every moral obligation to itself. Whether men reflect again upon this internal management and artifice, and how explicit they are with themselves, is another question. There are many operations of the mind, many things pass within, which we never reflect upon again, which a by-stander, from having frequent opportunities of observing us and our conduct, may make shrewd guesses at.

That great numbers are in this way of deceiving themselves is certain. There is scarce a man in the world, who has entirely got over all regards, hopes, and fears, concerning God and a future state; and these apprehensions in the generality, bad as we are, prevail in considerable degrees; yet men will and can be wicked, with calmness and thought; we see they are. There must, therefore, be some method of making it sit a little easy upon their minds, which, in the superstitious, is those indulgences and atonements beforementioned, and this self-deceit of another kind in persons of another character. And both these proceed from a certain unfairness of mind, a peculiar inward dishonesty; the direct contrary to that simplicity which our Saviour recommends, under the notion of "becoming little children," as a necessary qualification for our entering into the kingdom of heaven.

But to conclude : how much soever men differ in the
course of life they prefer, and in their ways of palliating
and excusing their vices to themselves ; yet all agree in one
thing, desiring to "die the death of the righteous." This
is surely remarkable. The observation may be extended
further, and put thus : even without determining what
that is, which we call guilt or innocence, there is no m a
but would choose, after having had the pleasure or advantage of a vicious action, to be free of the guilt of it, to be
in the state of an innocent man. This shows at least a
disturbance, and implicit dissatisfaction in vice. If we inquire into the grounds of it, we shall find it proceeds partly
from an immediate sense of having done evil ; and, partly,
from an apprehension, that this inward sense shall one
time or other, be seconded by a higher judgment, upon
which our whole being depends. Now, to suspend and
drown this sense, and these apprehensions, be it by the
hurry of business or of pleasure, or by superstition, or moral
equivocations, this is in a manner one and the same, and
makes no alteration at all in the nature of our case. Things
and actions are what they are, and the consequences of
them will be what they will be : why then should we desire to be deceived ? As we are reasonable creatures, and
have any regard to ourselves, we ought lay these things
plainly and honestly before our mind, and upon this, act
as you please, as you think most fit ; make that choice,
and prefer that course of life, which you can justify to
yourselves, and which sits most easy upon your own
mind. It will immediately appear, that vice cannot be the
happiness, but must, upon the whole, be the misery, of
such a creature as man ; a moral, an accountable agent.
Superstitious observances, self-deceit, though of a more
refined sort, will not, in reality, at all amend matters with
us. And the result of the whole can be nothing else, but
that with simplicity and fairness we "keep innocency, and
take heed unto the thing that is right ; for this alone shall
bring a man peace at the last."

SERMON VIII.

UPON RESENTMENT.

MATTHEW v. 43, 44.

Ye have heard that it hath been said, Thou shalt love thy neighbour, and hate thine enemy: But I say unto you, Love your enemies, bless them that curse you, do good to them that hate you, and pray for them that despitefully use you, and persecute you.

SINCE perfect goodness in the Deity is the principle from whence the universe was brought into being, and by which it is preserved : and since general benevolence is the great law of the whole moral creation; it is a question which immediately occurs, "Why had man implanted in him a principle, which appears the direct contrary to benevolence?" Now, the foot upon which inquiries of this kind should be treated is this; to take human nature as it is, and the circumstances in which it is placed as they are ; and then consider the correspondence between that nature and those circumstances, or what course of action and behaviour, respecting those circumstancees, any particular affection or passion leads us to. This I mention to distinguish the matter now before us from disquisitions of quite another kind ; namely, "Why are we not made more perfect creatures, or placed in better circumstances ?" These being questions which we have not, that I know of, any thing at all to do with. God Almighty undoubtedly foresaw the disorders, both natural and moral, which would happen in this state of things. If upon this we set ourselves to search

and examine why he did not prevent them; we shall, I am
afraid, be in danger of running into somewhat worse than
impertinent curiosity. But upon this to examine how far
the nature which he hath given us hath a respect to those
circumstances, such as they are; how far it leads us to act
a proper part in them; plainly belongs to us: and such
inquiries are in many ways of excellent use. Thus, the
thing to be considered is not, "Why we are not made of
such a nature, and placed in such circumstances, as to have
no need of so harsh and turbulent a passion as resentment;"
but, taking our nature and condition as being what they
are, "Why, or for what end, such a passion was given
us:" and this chiefly in order to show, what are the abuses
of it.

The persons who laid down for a rule, "Thou shalt love
thy neighbour, and hate thine enemy," made short work
with this matter. They did not, it seems, perceive any
thing to be disapproved in hatred more than in good-will:
and, according to their system of morals, our enemy was
the proper natural object of one of those passions, as our
neighbour was of the other of them.

This was all they had to say, and all they thought needful to be said, upon the subject. But this cannot be satisfactory: because hatred, malice, and revenge, are directly
contrary to the religion we profess, and to the nature and
reason of the thing itself. Therefore, since no passion God
hath endued us with can be in itself evil; and yet since
men frequently indulge a passion in such ways and degrees,
that at length it becomes quite another thing from what it
was originally in our nature; and those vices of malice and
revenge, in particular, take their occasion from the natural
passion of resentment: it will be needful to trace this up to
its original, that we may see, "What it is in itself, as placed
in our nature by its Author;" from which it will plainly appear, "For what ends it was placed there." And when we
know what the passion is in itself, and the ends of it, we
shall easily see, "What are the abuses of it, in which malice
and revenge consist;" and which are so strongly forbidden
in the text, by the direct contrary being commanded.

Resentment is of two kinds: *Hasty and sudden*, or *settled and deliberate*. The former is called anger, and often
passion; which, though a general word, is frequently ap-

propriated and confined to the particular feeling, sudden
anger, as distinct from deliberate resentment, malice and
revenge.   In all these words is usually implied somewhat
vicious; somewhat unreasonable as to the occasion of the
passion or immoderate as to the degree or duration of it.
But that the natural passion itself is indifferent, St. Paul has
asserted in that precept, " Be ye angry and sin not ;"* which,
though it is by no means to be understood as an encouragement to indulge ourselves in anger, the sense being certainly
this, "Though ye be angry, sin not ;" yet here is evidently
a distinction made, between anger and sin, between the
natural passion and sinful anger.

Sudden anger, upon certain occasions, is mere instinct ;
as merely so, as the disposition to close our eyes upon the
apprehension of somewhat falling into them ; and no more
necessarily implies any degree of reason. I say *necessarily :*
for, to be sure, *hasty*, as well as *deliberate* anger, may be
occasioned by injury or contempt; in which cases, reason
suggests to our thoughts that injury and contempt, which
is the occasion of the passion: but I am speaking of the
former only so far as it is to be distinguished from the latter.   The only way in which our reason and understanding
can raise anger, is by representing to our mind injustice or
injury of some kind or other.   Now, momentary anger is
frequently raised, not only without any real, but without
any apparent reason ; that is, without any appearance of injury, as distinct from hurt or pain. It cannot, I suppose,
be thought that this passion, in infants, in the lower species
of animals, and, which is often seen, in men towards them ;
it cannot, I say, be imagined, that these instances of this
passion are the effect of reason: no, they are occasioned
by mere sensation and feeling. It is opposition, sudden
hurt, violence, which naturally excites the passion : and the
real demerit or fault of him who offers that violence, or is
the cause of that opposition or hurt, does not, in many
cases, so much as come into thought.

The reason and end for which man was made thus liable
to this passion, is, that he might be better qualified to prevent, and likewise (or perhaps chiefly) to resist and defeat
sudden force, violence, and opposition, considered merely as

* Ephes. iv. 26.

such, and without regard to the fault or demerit of him who is the author of them. Yet, since violence may be considered in this other and further view, as implying fault; and since injury, as distinct from harm, may raise sudden anger, sudden anger may likewise accidently serve to prevent, or remedy, such fault and injury. But considered as distinct from settled anger, it stands in our nature for self-defence, and not for the administration of justice. There are plainly cases, and in the uncultivated parts of the world, and where regular governments are not formed, they frequently happen, in which there is no time for consideration, and yet to be passive is certain destruction; in which sudden resistance is the only security.

But from *this, deliberate anger or resentment* is essentially distinguished, as the latter is not naturally excited by, or intended to prevent mere harm without appearance of wrong or injustice. Now, in order to see, as exactly as we can, what is the natural object and occasion of such resentment, let us reflect upon the manner in which we are touched with reading, suppose, a feigned story of baseness and villany, properly worked up to move our passions. This immediately raises indignation, somewhat of a desire that it should be punished. And though the designed injury be prevented, yet that it was designed is sufficient to raise this inward feeling. Suppose the story true, this inward feeling would be as natural and as just: and one may venture to affirm, that there is scarce a man in the world, but would have it upon some occasions. It seems *in us* plainly connected with a sense of virtue and vice, of moral good and evil. Suppose further, we knew both the person who did and who suffered the injury: neither would this make any alteration, only that it would probably affect us more. The indignation raised by cruelty and injustice, and the desire of having it punished, which persons unconcerned would feel, is by no means malice. No; it is resentment against vice and wickedness: it is one of the common bonds by which society is held together; a fellow-feeling which each individual has in behalf of the whole species, as well as of himself. And it does not appear that this, generally speaking, is at all too high amongst mankind. Suppose now the injury I have been speaking of, to be done against ourselves, or those whom we consider as ourselves: it is

plain, the way in which we should be affected, would be
exactly the same in kind; but it would certainly be in a
higher degree, and less transient: because a sense of our
own happiness and misery is most intimately and always
present to us; and, from the very constitution of our nature,
we cannot but have a greater sensibility to, and be more
deeply interested in, what concerns ourselves. And this
seems to be the whole of this passion which is, properly
speaking, natural to mankind; namely, a resentment against
injury and wickedness in general: and in a higher degree
when towards ourselves, in proportion to the greater regard
which men naturally have for themselves, than for others.
From hence it appears, that it is not natural, but moral
evil; it is not suffering, but injury, which raises that anger
or resentment, which is of any continuance, The natural
object of it is not one, who appears to the suffering person to have been only the innocent occasion of his pain or
loss, but one, who has been in a moral sense injurious either
to ourselves or others. This is abundantly confirmed by
observing, what it is which heightens or lessens resentment;
namely, the same which aggravates or lessens the fault;
friendship and former obligations, on one hand; or inadvertency, strong temptations, and mistake, on the other. All
this is so much understood by mankind, how little soever it
be reflected upon, that a person would be reckoned quite distracted, who should coolly resent a harm, which had not
to himself the appearance of injury or wrong. Men do indeed resent what is occasioned through carelessness; but
then they expect observance as their due, and so that carelessness is considered as faulty. It is likewise true, that
they resent more strongly an injury done, than one which,
though designed, was prevented, in cases where the guilt is
perhaps the same; the reason however is, not that bare pain
or loss raises resentment, but, that it gives a new, and, as I may
speak, additional sense of the injury or injustice. According to the natural course of the passions, the degrees of resentment are in proportion, not only to the degree of design
and deliberation in the injurious person, but in proportion
to this, joined with the degree of the evil designed or premeditated; since this likewise comes in to make the injustice
greater or less. And the evil or harm will appear greater
when they feel it, than when they only reflect upon it: so,

therefore, will the injury : and consequently the resentment will be greater.

The natural object or occasion of settled resentment, then, being injury, as distinct from pain or loss, it is easy to see, that to prevent and to remedy such injury, and the miseries arising from it, is the end for which this passion was implanted in man. It is to be considered as a weapon put into our hands by nature, against injury, injustice, and cruelty : how it may be innocently employed and made use of, shall presently be mentioned.

The account which has been now given of this passion, is in brief, that sudden anger is raised by, and was chiefly intended to prevent or remedy, mere harm, distinct from injury : but that it *may* be raised by injury, and *may* serve to prevent or to remedy it ; and then the occasions and effects of it are the same with the occasions and effects of deliberate anger. But they are essentially distinguished in this, that the latter is never occasioned by harm, distinct from injury ; and its natural proper end, is to remedy or prevent only that harm, which implies, or is supposed to imply, injury or moral wrong. Every one sees, that these observations do not relate to those who have habitually suppressed the course of their passions and affections, out of regard either to interest or virtue ; or who, from habits of vice and folly, have changed their nature. But, I suppose, there can be no doubt but this, now described, is the general course of resentment, considered as a natural passion, neither increased by indulgence, nor corrected by virtue, nor prevailed over by other passions, or particular habits of life.

As to the abuses of anger, which it is to be observed may be in all different degrees, the first which occurs is what is commonly called *passion ;* to which some men are liable, in the same way as others are to the *epilepsy,* or any sudden particular disorder. This distemper of the mind seizes them upon the least occasion in the world, and perpetually without any real reason at all ; and by means of it they are plainly, every day, every waking hour of their lives, liable and in danger of running into the most extravagant outrages. Of a less boisterous, but not of a more innocent kind, is *peevishness ;* which I mention with pity, with real pity to the unhappy creatures, who, from their

inferior station, or other circumstances and relations, are
obliged to be in the way of, and to serve for a supply to it.
Both these, for aught that I can see, are one and the same
principle : but, as it takes root in minds of different makes,
it appears differently, and so is come to be distinguished by
different names. That which, in a more feeble temper,
is peevishness, and languidly discharges itself upon every
thing which comes in its way ; the same principle, in a temper of greater force and stronger passions, becomes rage
and fury. In one, the humour discharges itself at once ; in
the other, it is continually discharging. This is the account
of *passion* and *peevishness*, as distinct from each other, and
appearing in different persons. It is no objection against
the truth of it, that they are both to be seen sometimes in
one and the same person.

With respect to deliberate resentment, the chief instances
of abuse are : when, from partiality to ourselves, we
imagine an injury done us, when there is none : when this
partiality represents it to us greater than it really is : when
we fall into that extravagant and monstrous kind of resentment, towards one who has innocently been the occasion
of evil to us ; that is, resentment upon account of pain or
inconvenience, without injury ; which is the same absurdity,
as settled anger at a thing that is inanimate : when the indignation against injury and injustice rises too high, and is
beyond proportion to the particular ill action it is exercised
upon : or lastly, when pain or harm of any kind is inflicted
merely in consequence of, and to gratify that resentment,
though naturally raised.

It would be endless to descend into and explain all the
peculiarities of perverseness, and wayward humour, which
might be traced up to this passion. But there is one thing,
which so generally belongs to and accompanies all excess
and abuse of it as to require being mentioned : a certain
determination, and resolute bent of mind, not to be convinced or set right ; though it be ever so plain, that there is
no reason for the displeasure, that it was raised merely by
error or misunderstanding. In this there is doubtless a
great mixture of pride ; but there is somewhat more, which
I cannot otherwise express than that resentment has taken
possession of the temper and of the mind, and will not quit
its hold. It would be too minute to inquire, whether this

be any thing more than bare obstinacy ; it is sufficient to
observe, that it, in a very particular manner and degree,
belongs to the abuses of this passion.

But, notwithstanding all these abuses, " Is not just indignation against cruelty and wrong, one of the *instruments of death* which the Author of our nature hath provided ? Are not cruelty, injustice, and wrong, the natural
objects of that indignation ? Surely then it may, one way
or other, be innocently employed against them." True.
Since therefore it is necessary for the very subsistence of
the world, that injury, injustice, and cruelty, should be
punished : and since compassion, which is so natural to
mankind, would render that execution of justice exceedingly difficult and uneasy ; indignation against vice and
wickedness is, and may be allowed to be, a balance to that
weakness of pity, and also to any thing else which would
prevent the necessary methods of severity. Those who
have never thought upon these subjects, may perhaps not
see the weight of this : but let us suppose a person guilty
of murder, or any other action of cruelty, and that mankind had naturally no indignation against such wickedness
and the authors of it ; but that every body was affected towards such a criminal in the same way as towards an innocent man : compassion, amongst other things, would render
the execution of justice exceedingly painful and difficult,
and would often quite prevent it. And notwithstanding
that the principle of benevolence is denied by some, and is
really in a very low degree, that men are in great measure
insensible to the happiness of their fellow-creatures ; yet
they are not insensible to their misery, but are very strongly
moved with it : insomuch that there plainly is occasion for
that feeling which is raised by guilt and demerit, as a
balance to that of compassion. Thus much may, I think,
justly be allowed to resentment, in the strictest way of
moral consideration.

The good influence which this passion has, in fact, upon
the affairs of the world, is obvious to every one's notice.
Men are plainly restrained from injuring their fellow-creatures by fear of their resentment ; and it is very happy
that they are so, when they would not be restrained by a
principle of virtue. And after an injury is done, and there
is a necessity that the offender should be brought to justice ;

the cool consideration of reason, that the security and peace of society require examples of justice should be made, might indeed be sufficient to procure laws to be enacted, and sentence passed : but is it that cool reflection in the injured person, which, for the most part, brings the offender to justice ? Or is it not resentment and indignation against the injury and the author of it ? I am afraid there is no doubt which is commonly the case. This, however, is to be considered as a good effect, notwithstanding it were much to be wished, that men would act from a better principle—reason and cool reflection.

The account now given of the passion of resentment, as distinct from all the abuses of it, may suggest to our thoughts the following reflections.

First, That vice is indeed of ill desert, and must finally be punished. Why should men dispute concerning the reality of virtue, and whether it be founded in the nature of things, which yet surely is not matter of question ; but why should this, I say, be disputed, when every man carries about him this passion, which affords him demonstration that the rules of justice and equity are to be the guide of his actions ? For every man naturally feels an indignation upon seeing instances of villany and baseness, and therefore cannot commit the same without being self-condemned.

Secondly, That we should learn to be cautious, lest we *charge God foolishly*, by ascribing that to him, or the nature he has given us, which is owing wholly to our own abuse of it. Men may speak of the degeneracy and corruption of the world, according to the experience they have had of it ; but human nature, considered as the Divine workmanship, should, methinks, be treated as sacred : for *in the image of God made he man*. That passion, from whence men take occasion to run into the dreadful vices of malice and revenge ; even that passion, as implanted in our nature by God, is not only innocent, but a generous movement of mind. It is in itself, and in its original, no more than indignation against injury and wickedness : that which is the only deformity in the creation, and the only reasonable object of abhorrence and dislike. How manifold evidence have we of the Divine wisdom and goodness, when even pain in the natural world, and the passion we have been now considering in the moral, come out instances of it !

F

SERMON IX.

UPON FORGIVENESS OF INJURIES.

MATTHEW v. 43, 44.

Ye have heard that it hath been said, Thou shalt love thy neighbour, and hate thine enemy: But I say unto you, Love your enemies, bless them that curse you, do good to them that hate you, and pray for them which despitefully use you and persecute you.

As God Almighty foresaw the irregularities and disorders, both natural and moral, which would happen in this state of things, he hath graciously made some provision against them, by giving us several passions and affections, which arise from, or whose objects are, those disorders. Of this sort are fear, resentment, compassion, and others; of which there could be no occasion or use in a perfect state: but in the present we should be exposed to greater inconveniences without them; though there are very considerable ones, which they themselves are the occasions of. They are incumbrances indeed, but such as we are obliged to carry about with us through this various journey of life; some of them as a guard against the violent assaults of others; and, in our own defence, some in behalf of others; and all of them to put us upon and help to carry us through a course of behaviour suitable to our condition, in default of that perfection of wisdom and virtue, which would be, in all respects, our better security.

The passion of anger or resentment hath already been largely treated of. It hath been shown, that mankind naturally feel some emotion of mind against injury and in-

justice, whoever are the sufferers by it, and even though
the injurious design be prevented from taking effect. Let
this be called anger, indignation, resentment, or by whatever name any one shall choose, the thing itself is understood, and is plainly natural.   It has likewise been observed
that this natural indignation is generally moderate and low
enough in mankind, in each particular man, when the injury which excites it doth not affect himself, or one whom
he considers as himself.   Therefore the precepts to *forgive*
and to *love our enemies*, do not relate to that general indignation against injury, and the authors of it, but to this feeling, or resentment, when raised by private or personal injury.   But no man could be thought in earnest who should
assert, that though indignation against injury, when others
are the sufferers, is innocent and just, yet the same indignation against it, when we ourselves are the sufferers, becomes faulty and blameable.   These precepts therefore cannot be understood to forbid this in the latter case, more
than in the former.   Nay, they cannot be understood to
forbid this feeling in the latter case, though raised to a
higher degree than in the former ; because as was also
observed further, from the very constitution of our nature,
we cannot but have a greater sensibility to what concerns
ourselves.   Therefore the precepts in the text, and others of
the like import with them, must be understood to forbid
only the excess and abuse of this natural feeling, in cases of
personal and private injury : the chief instances of which
excess and abuse have likewise been already remarked, and
all of them, excepting that of retaliation, do so plainly, in
the very terms, express somewhat unreasonable, disproportionate, and absurd, as to admit of no pretence or shadow
of justification.

But, since custom and false honour are on the side of
retaliation and revenge, when the resentment is natural and
just ; and reasons are sometimes offered in justification of
revenge in these cases ; and since love of our enemies is
thought *too hard a saying* to be obeyed, I will show *the
absolute unlawfulness of the former—the obligations we are
under to the latter—*and then proceed *to some reflections,
which may have a more direct and immediate tendency
to beget in us a right temper of mind towards those who
have offended us.*

F 2

In showing the unlawfulness of revenge, it is not my present design to examine what is alleged in favour of it, from the tyranny of custom and false honour, but only to consider the nature and reason of the thing itself; which ought now to extirpate every thing of that kind.

First, Let us begin with the supposition of that being innocent which is pleaded for, and which shall be shown to be altogether vicious, the supposition that we were allowed to *render evil for evil*, and see what would be the consequence. Malice or resentment towards any man hath plainly a tendency to beget the same passion in him who is the object of it, and this again increases it in the other. It is of the very nature of this vice to propagate itself, not only by way of example, which it does in common with other vices, but in a peculiar way of its own; for resentment itself, as well as what is done in consequence of it, is the object of resentment. Hence it comes to pass, that the first offence, even when so slight as presently to be dropt and forgotten, becomes the occasion of entering into a long intercourse of ill offices: neither is it at all uncommon to see persons, in this progress of strife and variance, change parts, and him who was at first the injured person become more injurious and blameable than the aggressor. Put the case, then, that the law of retaliation was universally received and allowed as an innocent rule of life by all: and the observance of it thought by many (and then it would soon come to be thought by all) a point of honour: this supposes every man in private cases to pass sentence in his own cause; and likewise that anger or resentment is to be the judge. Thus from the numberless partialities which we all have for ourselves, every one would often think himself injured when he was not, and in most cases would represent an injury as much greater than it really is; the imagined dignity of the person offended would scarce ever fail to magnify the offence. And if bare retaliation, or returning just the mischief received, always begets resentment in the person upon whom we retaliate, what would that excess do? Add to this that he likewise has his partialities.—There is no going on to represent this scene of rage and madness: it is manifest there would be no bounds nor any end. "If the beginning of strife is as when one letteth out water," what would it come to when allowed this free and unre-

strained course? "As coals are to burning coals, or wood
to fire," so would these "contentious men be to kindle
strife." And since the indulgence of revenge hath manifestly this tendency, and does actually produce these effects
in proportion as it is allowed; a passion of so dangerous
a nature ought not to be indulged, were there no other
reason against it.

Secondly, It hath been shown that the passion of resentment was placed in man, upon supposition of, and as a
prevention or remedy to, irregularity and disorder. Now,
whether it be allowed or not, that the passion itself, and the
gratification of it, joined together, are painful to the malicious person; it must however be so with respect to the
person towards whom it is exercised, and upon whom the
revenge is taken. Now, if we consider mankind, according
to that fine allusion of St. Paul, "as one body, and every
one members one of another," it must be allowed that resentment is with respect to society, a painful remedy.
Thus, then, the very notion or idea of this passion, as a remedy or prevention of evil, and as in itself a painful means,
plainly shows that it ought never to be made use of, but
only in order to produce some greater good.

It is to be observed that this argument is not founded
upon an allusion or simile, but that it is drawn from the very
nature of the passion itself, and the end for which it was
given us. We are obliged to make use of words taken from
sensible things, to explain what is most remote from them :
and every one sees from whence the words prevention and
remedy are taken. But, if you please, let these words be
dropped : the thing itself, I suppose, may be expressed
without them.

That mankind is a community, that we all stand in a relation to each other, that there is a public end and interest
of society which each particular is obliged to promote, is
the sum of morals. Consider then the passion of resentment, as given to this one body, as given to society.
Nothing can be more manifest, than that resentment is to
be considered as a secondary passion, placed in us upon
supposition, upon account of, and with regard to injury; not
to be sure, to promote and further it, but to render it, and
the inconveniences and miseries arising from it, less and fewer
than they would be without this passion. It is as manifest,

that the indulgence of it is, with regard to society, a painful means of obtaining these ends. Considered in itself, it is very undesirable, and what society must very much wish to be without. It is in every instance absolutely an evil in itself; because it implies producing misery; and, consequently, must never be indulged or gratified for itself, by any one who considers mankind as a community or family, and himself as a member of it.

Let us now take this in another view. Every natural appetite, passion, and affection, may be gratified in particular instances, without being subservient to the particular chief end, for which these several principles were respectively implanted in our nature. And if neither this end, nor any other moral obligation, be contradicted, such gratification is innocent. Thus, I suppose, there are cases in which each of these principles, this one of resentment excepted, may innocently be gratified, without being subservient to what is the main end of it: that is, though it does not conduce to, yet it may be gratified without contradicting that end, or any other obligation. But the gratification of resentment, if it be not conducive to the end for which it was given us, must necessarily contradict, not only the general obligation to benevolence, but likewise that particular end itself. The end for which it was given is, to prevent or remedy injury; *i. e.* the misery occasioned by injury; *i. e.* misery itself: and the gratification of it consists in producing misery; *i. e.* in contradicting the end for which it was implanted in our nature.

This whole reasoning is built upon the difference there is between this passion and all others. No other principle, or passion, hath for its end the misery of our fellow-creatures. But malice and revenge meditates evil itself; and to do mischief, to be the author of misery, is the very thing which gratifies the passion: this is what it directly tends towards, as its proper design. Other vices eventually do mischief; this alone aims at it as an end.

Nothing can with reason be urged in justification of revenge, from the good effects which the indulgence of it were before mentioned* to have upon the affairs of the world; because, though it be a remarkable instance of the

* Ser. viii. p. 76.

wisdom of Providence, to bring good out of evil, yet vice is vice to him who is guilty of it. "But suppose these good effects are foreseen;" that is, suppose reason in a particular case leads a man the same way as passion : why then, to be sure, he should follow his reason in this as well as in all other cases. So that, turn the matter which way ever you will, no more can be allowed to this passion, than hath been already.*

As to that love of our enemies which is commanded; this supposes the general obligation to benevolence or good-will towards mankind; and this being supposed, that precept is no more than to forgive injuries; that is, to keep clear of those abuses before mentioned; because, that we have the habitual temper of benevolence is taken for granted.

Resentment is not inconsistent with good-will; for we often see both together in very high degrees, not only in parents towards their children, but in cases of friendship and dependence, where there is no natural relation. These contrary passions, though they may lessen, do not necessarily destroy each other. We may therefore love our enemy, and yet have resentment against him for his injurious behaviour towards us. But when this resentment entirely destroys our natural benevolence towards him, it is excessive, and becomes malice or revenge. The command to prevent its having this effect, *i. e.* to forgive injuries, is the same as to love our enemies; because that love is always supposed, unless destroyed by resentment. .

"But though mankind is the natural object of benevolence, yet may it not be lessened upon vice, *i. e.* injury?" Allowed : but if every degree of vice or injury must destroy that benevolence, then no man is the object of our love; for no man is without faults.

"But if lower instances of injury may lessen our benevolence, why may not higher, or the highest destroy it?" The answer is obvious. It is not man's being a social creature, much less his being a moral agent, from whence *alone* our obligations to good-will towards him arise. There is an obligation to it prior to either of these, arising from his being a sensible creature; that is, capable of happiness or misery. Now this obligation cannot be superseded by

* Ser. viii. p. 75.

his moral character. What justifies public execution is, not that the guilt or demerit of the criminal dispenses with the obligation of good-will; neither would this justify any severity; but, that his life is inconsistent with the quiet and happiness of the world: that is, a general and more enlarged obligation necessarily destroys a particular and more confined one of the same kind, inconsistent with it. Guilt or injury then does not dispense with or supersede the duty of love and good-will.

Neither does that peculiar regard to ourselves, which was before allowed to be natural* to mankind, dispense with it: because that can no way innocently heighten our resentment against those who have been injurious to ourselves in particular, any otherwise than as it heightens our sense of the injury or guilt; and guilt, though in the highest degree, does not, as hath been shown, dispense with or supersede the duty of love and good-will.

If all this be true, what can a man say, who will dispute the reasonableness, or the possibility, of obeying the divine precept we are now considering? Let him speak out, and it must be thus he will speak. "Mankind, *i. e.* a creature defective and faulty, is the proper object of good-will, whatever his faults are, when they respect others; but not when they respect me myself." That men should be *affected* in this manner, and *act* accordingly, is to be accounted for like other vices; but to *assert* that it *ought*, and *must* be thus, is self-partiality possessed of the very understanding.

Thus, love to our enemies, and those who have been injurious to us, is so far from being a *rant*, as it has been profanely called, that it is in truth the law of our nature, and what every one must see and own, who is not quite blinded with self-love.

From hence it is easy to see, what is the degree in which we are commanded to love our enemies, or those who have been injurious to us. It were well if it could be as easily reduced to practice. It cannot be imagined, that we are required to love them with any peculiar kind of affection. But suppose the person injured to have a due natural sense of the injury and no more; he ought to be affected towards

* Ser. viii. p. 73.

the injurious person in the same way any good men, unin-
terested in the case, would be; if they had the same just
sense, which we have supposed the injured person to have,
of the fault: after which there will yet remain real good-
will towards the offender.

Now, what is there in all this, which should be thought
impracticable? I am sure there is nothing in it unreasonable. It is indeed no more than that we should not indulge
a passion, which, if generally indulged, would propagate itself
so as almost to lay waste the world: that we should suppress that partial, that false self-love, which is the weakness
of our nature; that uneasiness and misery should not be
produced, without any good service to be served by it;
and that we should not be affected towards persons differently from what their nature and character require.

But since, to be convinced that any temper of mind and
course of behaviour is our duty, and the contrary vicious,
hath but a distant influence upon our temper and actions,
let me add some few reflections, which may have a more
direct tendency to subdue those vices in the heart, to beget
in us this right temper, and lead us to a right behaviour towards those who have offended us; which reflections, however, shall be such as will further show the obligations we
are under to it.

No one, I suppose, would choose to have an indignity
put upon him, or be injuriously treated. If, then, there be
any probability of a misunderstanding in the case, either
from our imagining we are injured when we are not, or representing the injury to ourselves as greater than it really
is, one would hope an intimation of this sort might be
kindly received, and that people would be glad to find the
injury not so great as they imagined. Therefore, without
knowing particulars, I take upon me to assure all persons
who think they have received indignities or injurious treatment, that they may depend upon it, as in a manner certain,
that the offence is not so great as they themselves imagine.
We are in such a peculiar situation, with respect to injuries
done to ourselves, that we can scarce any more see them as
they really are, than our eye can see itself. If we could
place ourselves at a due distance, *i. e.* be really unprejudiced,
we should frequently discern that to be in reality inadvertence and mistake in our enemy, which we now fancy we

F 5

see to be malice or scorn. From this proper point of view we should likewise, in all probability, see something of these latter in ourselves, and most certainly a great deal of the former. Thus the indignity of injury would almost infinitely lessen, and perhaps at last come out to be nothing at all. Self-love is a medium of a peculiar kind : in these cases it magnifies every thing which is amiss in others, at the same time that it lessens every thing amiss in ourselves.

Anger also, or hatred, may be considered as another false medium of viewing things, which always represents characters and actions much worse than they really are. Ill-will not only never speaks, but never thinks well, of the person towards whom it is exercised. Thus, in cases of offence and enmity, the whole character and behaviour is considered with an eye to that particular part which has offended us, and the whole man appears monstrous, without any thing right or human in him; whereas, the resentment should surely, at least, be confined to that particular part of the behaviour which gave offence, since the other parts of a man's life and character stand just the same as they did before.

In general, there are very few instances of enmity carried to any length, but inadvertency, misunderstanding, some real mistake of the case, on one side however, if not on both, has a great share in it.

If these things were attended to, these ill-humours could not be carried to any length amongst good men, and they would be exceedingly abated amongst all. And one would hope they might be attended to : for all that these cautions come to is really no more than desiring that things may be considered and judged of as they are in themselves, that we should have an eye to and beware of what would otherwise lead us into mistakes. So that to make allowances for inadvertence, misunderstanding, for the partialities of self-love, and the false light which anger sets things in— I say, to make allowances for these, is not to be spoken of as an instance of humbleness of mind, or meekness and moderation of temper, but as what common sense should suggest, to avoid judging wrong of a matter before us, though virtue and morals were out of the case. And therefore it as much belongs to ill men, who will indulge the vice I have been arguing against, as to good men who endeavour to subdue it in themselves. In a word, all these cautions concerning anger and self-love are no more than desiring a man, who was looking through a glass which either magnified or lessened, to take notice that the objects are not in themselves what they appear through that medium.

To all these things one might add, that resentment being out of the case, there is not, properly speaking, any such thing as direct ill-will in one man towards another. Therefore the first indignity or injury, if it be not owing to inadvertence or misunderstanding, may however be resolved into other particular passions or self-love: principles quite distinct from ill-will, and which we ought all to be disposed to excuse in others, from experiencing so much of them in ourselves. A great man of antiquity is reported to have said, that as he never was indulgent to any one fault in himself, he could not excuse those of others. This sentence could scarce with decency come out of the mouth of any human creature. But if we invert the former part, and put it thus—that he was indulgent to many faults in himself, as it is to be feared the best of us are, and yet was implacable, how monstrous would such an assertion appear? And this is the case in respect to every human creature, in proportion as he is without the forgiving spirit I have been recommending.

Further, Though injury, injustice, oppression, the baseness of ingratitude, are the natural objects of indignation, or, if you please, of resentment, as before explained, yet they are likewise the objects of compassion, as they are their own punishment, and without repentance will for ever be so. No one ever did a designed injury to another, but at the same time he did a much greater to himself. If therefore we could consider things justly, such an one is, according to the natural course of our affections, an object of compassion, as well as of displeasure: and to be affected really in this manner, I say really, in opposition to show and pretence, argues the true greatness of mind. We have an example of forgiveness in this way in its utmost perfection, and which indeed includes in it all that is good, in that prayer of our blessed Saviour on the cross—"Father, forgive them; for they know not what they do!"

But, *lastly*, The offences which we are all guilty of against God, and the injuries which men do to each other, are often mentioned together; and, making allowances for the infinite distance between the Majesty of heaven and a frail mortal, and likewise for this, that he cannot possibly be affected or moved as we are; offences committed by others against ourselves, and the manner in which we are apt to be affected with them, give a real occasion for calling to mind our own sins against God. Now, there is an apprehension and presentiment natural to mankind, that we ourselves shall one time or other be dealt with as we deal with others, and a peculiar acquiescence in and feeling of the equity and justice of this equal distribution. This natural notion of equity the Son of Sirach has put in the strongest way—"He that revengeth shall find vengeance from the Lord, and he will surely keep his sins in remembrance. Forgive thy neighbour the hurt he hath done unto thee, so shall thy sins also be forgiven when thou prayest. One man beareth hatred against another, and doth he seek pardon from the Lord? He showeth no mercy to a man which is like himself, and doth he ask forgiveness of his own sins?"* Let any one read our Saviour's parable of "the king who took account of his servants;"† and the equity and rightness of the sentence which was passed upon him who was unmerciful to his fellow-servant, will be felt. There is somewhat in human nature, which accords to and falls in with that method of determination. Let us then place before our eyes the time which is represented in the parable; that of our own death, or the final judgment. Suppose yourselves under the apprehensions of approaching death; that you were just going to appear, naked and without disguise, before the Judge of all the earth, to give an account of your behaviour towards your fellow-creatures, could any thing raise more dreadful apprehensions of that judgment than the reflection that you had been implacable and without mercy towards those who had offended you—without that forgiving spirit towards others, which, that it may now be exercised towards yourselves, is your only hope? And these natural apprehensions are authorised by our Saviour's application of the parable—"So likewise shall my heavenly Father do also unto you, if ye from your hearts forgive not every one his brother their trespasses." On the other hand, suppose a

* Eccles. xxviii. 1—4.   † Matt. xviii.

good man in the same circumstance, in the last part and close of life, conscious of many frailties, as the best are, but conscious too that he had been meek, forgiving, and merciful; that he had in simplicity of heart been ready to pass over offences against himself;—the having felt this good spirit will give him, not only a full view of the amiableness of it, but the surest hope that he shall meet with it in his Judge. This likewise is confirmed by his own declaration : " If ye forgive men their trespasses, your heavenly Father will likewise forgive you." And that we might have a constant sense of it upon our mind, the condition is expressed in our daily prayer. A forgiving spirit is therefore absolutely necessary, as ever we hope for pardon of our own sins, as ever we hope for peace of mind in our dying moments, or for the divine mercy at that day when we shall most stand in need of it.

SERMON X.

UPON SELF-DECEIT.

---

2 SAMUEL xii. 7.

And Nathan said to David, Thou art the man.

THESE words are the application of Nathan's parable to
David, upon occasion of his adultery with Bathsheba, and
the murder of Uriah her husband. The parable, which is
related in the most beautiful simplicity, is this :* "There
were two men in one city; the one rich and the other poor.
The rich man had exceeding many flocks and herds; but
the poor man had nothing, save one little ewe-lamb, which
he had bought and nourished up; and it grew up together
with him and with his children: it did eat of his own meat,
and drank of his own cup, and lay in his bosom, and was
unto him as a daughter. And there came a traveller unto
the rich man, and he spared to take of his own flock, and of
his own herd, to dress for the wayfaring man that was
come unto him, but took the poor man's lamb, and dressed
it for the man that was come to him. And David's anger
was greatly kindled against the man, and he said to Nathan,
As the Lord liveth, the man that hath done this thing shall
surely die. And he shall restore the lamb fourfold, because
he did this thing, and because he had no pity." David
passes sentence, not only that there should be a fourfold
restitution made, but he proceeds to the rigour of justice,
"The man that hath done this thing shall die." And this

* Verse 1.

judgment is pronounced with the utmost indignation against
such an act of inhumanity : " As the Lord liveth, he shall
surely die : and his anger was greatly kindled against the
man." And the prophet answered, " Thou art the man."
He had been guilty of much greater inhumanity, with the
utmost deliberation, thought, and contrivance. Near a year
must have passed, between the time of the commission of
his crimes and the time of the prophet's coming to him;
and it does not appear from the story, that he had in all this
while the least remorse or contrition.

There is not any thing, relating to men and characters,
more surprising and unaccountable than this partiality to
themselves, which is observable in many; as there is nothing
of more melancholy reflection, respecting morality, virtue,
and religion. Hence it is that many men seem perfect
strangers to their own characters. They think, and reason,
and judge quite differently upon any matter relating to
themselves, from what they do in cases of others where
they are not interested. Hence it is one hears people ex-
posing follies, which they themselves are eminent for ; and
talking with great severity against particular vices, which, if
all the world be not mistaken, they themselves are notori-
ously guilty of. This self-ignorance and self-partiality may
be in all different degrees. It is a lower degree of it, which
David himself refers to in these words, " Who can tell how
oft he offendeth ? O cleanse thou me from my secret faults."
This is the ground of that advice of Elihu to Job : " Surely
it is meet to be said unto God,—That which I see not
teach thou me; if I have done iniquity, I will do no more."
And Solomon saw this thing in a very strong light when he
said, " He that trusteth his own heart is a fool." This likewise was the reason why that precept, " Know thyself,"
was so frequently inculcated by the philosophers of old.
For if it were not for that partial and fond regard to ourselves, it would certainly be no great difficulty to know our
own character, what passes within the bent and bias of our
mind; much less would there be any difficulty in judging
rightly of our own actions. But from this partiality it frequently comes to pass, that the observation of many men's
being themselves last of all acquainted with what falls out in
their own families, may be applied to a nearer home, to·
what passes within their own breasts.

There is plainly, in the generality of mankind, an absence of doubt or distrust, in a very great measure, as to their moral character and behaviour; and likewise a disposition to take for granted, that all is right and well with them in these respects. The former is owing to their not reflecting, not exercising their judgment upon themselves; the latter, to self-love. I am not speaking of that extravagance, which is sometimes to be met with; instances of persons declaring in words at length, that they never were in the wrong, nor had ever any diffidence of the justness of their conduct, in their whole lives: no, these people are too far gone to have any thing said to them. The thing before us is indeed of this kind, but in a lower degree, and confined to the moral character; somewhat of which we almost all of us have, without reflecting upon it. Now, consider how long, and how grossly, a person of the best understanding might be imposed upon by one of whom he had not any suspicion, and in whom he placed an entire confidence; especially if there were friendship and real kindness in the case: surely this holds even stronger with respect to that self we are all so fond of. Hence arises in men a disregard of reproof and instruction, rules of conduct and moral discipline, which occasionally come in their way: a disregard, I say, of these, not in every respect, but in this single one, namely, as what may be of service to them in particular towards mending their own hearts and tempers, and making them better men. It never in earnest comes into their thoughts, whether such admonitions may not relate, and be of service to themselves; and this quite distinct from a positive persuasion to the contrary, a persuasion from reflection that they are innocent and blameless in those respects. Thus we may invert the observation which is somewhere made upon Brutus, that he never read but in order to make himself a better man. It scarce comes into the thoughts of the generality of mankind, that this use is to be made of moral reflections which they meet with; that this use, I say, is to be made of them by themselves, for every body observes and wonders that it is not done by others.

Further, there are instances of persons having so fixed and steady an eye upon their own interest, whatever they place it in, and the interest of those whom they consider as themselves, as in a manner to regard nothing else; their

views are almost confined to this alone. Now, we cannot
be acquainted with, or in any propriety of speech be said
to know any thing but what we attend to. If, therefore,
they attend only to one side, they really will not, cannot see
or know what is to be alleged on the other. Though a man
hath the best eyes in the world, he cannot see any way but
that which he turns them. Thus these persons, without
passing over the least, the most minute thing which can
possibly be urged in favour of themselves, shall overlook
entirely the plainest and most obvious things on the other
side. And whilst they are under the power of this temper,
thought, and consideration upon the matter before them,
has scarce any tendency to set them right; because they
are engaged; and their deliberation concerning an action
to be done, or reflection upon it afterwards, is not to see
whether it be right, but to find out reasons to justify or
palliate it; palliate it, not to others, but to themselves.

In some there is to be observed a general ignorance of
themselves, and wrong way of thinking and judging in
every thing relating to themselves; their fortune, reputation, every thing in which self can come in; and this perhaps attended with the rightest judgment in all other
matters. In others, this partiality is not so general, has
not taken hold of the whole man, but is confined to some
particular favourite passion, interest, or pursuit: suppose
ambition, covetousness, or any other. And these persons
may probably judge and determine what is perfectly just
and proper, even in things in which they themselves are
concerned, if these things have no relation to their particular favourite passion or pursuit. Hence arises that amazing
incongruity; and seeming inconsistency of character, from
whence slight observers take it for granted, that the whole
is hypocritical and false; not being able otherwise to reconcile the several parts; whereas, in truth, there is real
honesty, so far as it goes. There is such a thing as men's
being honest to such a degree, and in such respects, but no
further. And this, as it is true, so it is absolutely necessary to be taken notice of, and allowed them; such general
and undistinguishing censure of their whole character, as
designing and false, being one main thing which confirms
them in their self-deceit. They know that the whole cen-

sure is not true, and so take it for granted that no part of it is.

But .to go on with the explanation of the thing itself: vice in general consists in having an unreasonable and too great regard to ourselves, in comparison of others. Robbery or murder is never from the love of injustice or cruelty, but to gratify some other passion, to gain some supposed advantage: and it is false selfishness alone, whether cool or passionate, which makes a man resolutely pursue that end, be it ever so much to the injury of another. But whereas, in common and ordinary wickedness, this unreasonableness, this partiality and selfishness, relates only, or chiefly, to the temper and passions; in the characters we are now considering, it reaches to the understanding, and influences the very judgment.* And, besides that general want of distrust and diffidence concerning our own character, there are, you see, two things, which may thus prejudice and darken the understanding itself; that over-fondness for ourselves, which we are all so liable to; and also being under the power of any particular passion or appetite, or engaged in any particular pursuit. And these, especially the last of the two, may be in so great a degree as to influence our judgment, even of other persons and their behaviour. Thus a man, whose temper is formed to

* That peculiar regard for ourselves which frequently produces this partiality of judgment in our own favour, may have a quite contrary effect, and occasion the utmost diffidence and distrust of ourselves; were it only, as it may set us upon a more frequent and strict survey and review of our own character and behaviour. This search or recollection itself implies somewhat of diffidence; and the discoveries we make, what is brought to our view, may possibly increase it. Good-will to another may either blind our judgment, so as to make us overlook his faults; or it may put us upon exercising that judgment with greater strictness, to see whether he is so faultless and perfect as we wish him. If that peculiar regard to ourselves leads us to examine our own character with this greater severity, in order really to improve and grow better, it is the most commendable turn of mind possible, and can scarce be to excess. But if, as every thing hath its counterfeit, we are so much employed about ourselves, in order to disguise what is amiss, and to make a better appearance; or if our attention to ourselves has chiefly this effect, it is liable to run up into the greatest weakness and excess, and is, like all other excesses, its own disappointment; for scarce any show themselves to advantage, who are over solicitous of doing so.

ambition or covetousness, shall even approve of them sometimes in others.

This seems to be in a good measure the account of self-
partiality and self-deceit, when traced up to its original.
Whether it be, or be not, thought satisfactory, that there is
such a thing is manifest ; and that it is the occasion of a
great part of the unreasonable behaviour of men towards
each other ; that by means of it they palliate their vices
and follies to themselves ; and that it prevents their applying to themselves those reproofs and instructions which
they meet with either in Scripture or in moral and religious
discourses, though exactly suitable to the state of their own
mind, and the course of their behaviour.   There is one
thing further to be added here, that the temper we distinguish by hardness of heart with respect to others, joined
with this self-partiality, will carry a man almost any lengths
of wickedness, in the way of oppression, hard usage of
others, and even to plain injustice, without his having, from
what appears, any real sense at all of it.   This, indeed, was
not the general character of David ; for he plainly gave
scope to the affections of compassion and good-will, as well
as to his passions of another kind.

But as some occasions and circumstances lie more open
to this self-deceit, and give it greater scope and opportunities than others, these require to be particularly mentioned.

It is to be observed, then, that as there are express determinate acts of wickedness, such as murder, adultery, theft ;
so, on the other hand, there are numberless cases in which
the vice and wickedness cannot be exactly defined, but
consists in a certain general temper and course of action,
or in the neglect of some duty, suppose charity or any
other, whose bounds and degrees are not fixed.   This is
the very province of self-deceit and self-partiality ; here it
governs without check or control.   " For what commandment is there broken ? Is there a transgression where there
is no law ? a vice which cannot be defined ?"

Whoever will consider the whole commerce of human
life, will see that a great part, perhaps the greatest part, of
the intercourse amongst mankind, cannot be reduced to
fixed determinate rules.   Yet in these cases there is a right
and a wrong : a merciful, a liberal, a kind and compassionate behaviour, which surely is our duty ; and an unmerciful

contracted spirit, a hard and oppressive course of behaviour, which is most certainly immoral and vicious. But
who can define precisely wherein that contracted spirit and
hard usage of others consist, as murder and theft may be
defined? There is not a word in our language which expresses more detestable wickedness than *oppression;* yet
the nature of this vice cannot be so exactly stated, nor the
bounds of it so determinately marked, as that we shall be
able to say, in all instances, where rigid right and justice
ends and oppression begins. In these cases there is great
latitude left for every one to determine for, and consequently to deceive himself. It is chiefly in these cases that
self-deceit comes in ; as every one must see that there is
much larger scope for it here than in express, single, determinate acts of wickedness. However, it comes in with respect to the *circumstances* attending the most gross and
determinate acts of wickedness. Of this, the story of
David, now before us, affords the most astonishing instance.
It is really prodigious to see a man, before so remarkable
for virtue and piety, going on deliberately from adultery to
murder, with the same cool contrivance, and, from what
appears, with as little disturbance, as a man would endeavour to prevent the ill consequences of a mistake he
had made in any common matter. The total insensibility
of mind, with respect to those horrid crimes, after the commission of them, manifestly shows that he did some way or
other delude himself; and this could not be with respect to
the crimes themselves, they were so manifestly of the
grossest kind. What the particular circumstances were
with which he extenuated them, and quieted and deceived
himself, is not related.

Having thus explained the nature of internal hypocrisy
and self-deceit, and remarked the occasions upon which it
exerts itself, there are several things further to be observed
concerning it : that all of the sources to which it was
traced up, are sometimes observable together in one and
the same person ; but that one of them is more remarkable,
and to a higher degree in some, 'and others of them are so
in others ; that, in general, it is a complicated thing, and
may be in all different degrees and kinds : that the temper
itself is essentially in its own nature vicious and immoral.

It is unfairness, it is dishonesty, it is falseness of heart, and is, therefore, so far from extenuating guilt, that it is itself the greatest of all guilt in proportion to the degree it prevails; for it is a corruption of the whole moral character in its principle.   Our understanding, and sense of good and evil, is the light and guide of life : " If, therefore, this light that is in thee be darkness, how great is that darkness ?"* For this reason our Saviour puts an *evil eye* as the direct opposite to a *single eye;* the absence of that simplicity which these last words imply being itself evil and vicious. And whilst men are under the power of this temper, in proportion still to the degree they are so, they are fortified on every side against conviction ; and when they hear the vice and folly of what is in truth their own course of life exposed in the justest and strongest manner, they will often assent to it, and even carry the matter further; persuading themselves, one does not know how, but some way or other persuading themselves, that they are out of the case, and that it hath no relation to them.   Yet, notwithstanding this, there *frequently appears* a suspicion that all is not right as it should be : and perhaps there is *always* at bottom somewhat of this sort.   There are, doubtless, many instances of the ambitious, the revengeful, the covetous, and those whom, with too great indulgence, we only call the men of pleasure, who will not allow themselves to think how guilty they are, who explain and argue away their guilt to themselves; and though they do really impose upon themselves in some measure, yet there are none of them but have, if not a proper knowledge, yet at least an implicit suspicion, where the weakness lies, and what part of their behaviour they have reason to wish unknown or forgotten for ever.   Truth, and real good sense, and thorough integrity, carry along with them a peculiar consciousness of their own genuineness : there is a feeling belonging to them which does not accompany their counterfeits, error, folly, half-honesty, partial and slight regards to virtue and right, so far only as they are consistent with that course of gratification which men happen to be set upon. And, if this be the case, it is much the same as if we should suppose a man to have had a general view of some

* Matt. vi. 23.

scene, enough to satisfy him that it was very disagreeable,
and then to shut his eyes, that he might not have a particular or distinct view of its several deformities. It is as easy
to close the eyes of the mind as those of the body: and
the former is more frequently done with wilfulness, and
yet not attended to, than the latter; the actions of the
mind being more quick and transient than those of the
senses. This may be further illustrated by another thing
observable in ordinary life. It is not uncommon for persons who run out their fortunes, entirely to neglect looking
into the state of their affairs, and this from a general
knowledge that the condition of them is bad. These extravagant people are perpetually ruined before they themselves expected it; and they tell you for an excuse, and
tell you truly, that they did not think they were so much in
debt, or that their expenses so far exceeded their income.
And yet no one will take this for an excuse, who is sensible
that their ignorance of their particular circumstances was
owing to their general knowledge of them; that is, their
general knowledge that matters were not well with them,
prevented their looking into particulars. There is somewhat of the like kind with this in respect to morals, virtue,
and religion. Men find that the survey of themselves,
their own heart and temper, their own life and behaviour,
doth not afford them satisfaction; things are not as they
should be, therefore they turn away, will not go over particulars, or look deeper, lest they should find more amiss.
For who would choose to be put out of humour with himself? No one, surely, if it were not in order to mend, and
to be more thoroughly and better pleased with himself for
the future.

If this sincere self-enjoyment and home-satisfaction be
thought desirable, and worth some pains and diligence, the
following reflections will, I suppose, deserve your attention,
as what may be of service and assistance to all who are in
any measure honestly disposed, for avoiding that fatal self-
deceit, and towards getting acquainted with themselves.

The *first* is, that those who have never had any suspicion
of, who have never made allowances for this weakness in
themselves, who have never (if I may be allowed such a
manner of speaking) caught themselves in it, may almost
take it for granted that they have been very much misled

2

by it. For consider: nothing is more manifest, than that
affection and passion of all kinds influence the judgment.
Now, as we have naturally a greater regard to ourselves
than to others, as the private affection is more prevalent
than the public, the former will have proportionally a
greater influence upon the judgment, upon our way of considering things. People are not backward in owning this
partiality of judgments, in cases of friendship and natural
relation. The reason is obvious why it is not so readily
acknowledged, when the interest which misleads us is more
confined, confined to ourselves: but we all take notice of
it in each other in these cases. There is not any observation more common, than that there is no judging of a matter from hearing only one side. This is not founded upon
supposition, at least it is not always, of a formed design
in the relater to deceive: for it holds in cases where he ex-
pects that the whole will be told over again by the other
side. But the supposition, which this observation is founded
upon, is the very thing now before us; namely, that men
are exceedingly prone to deceive themselves, and judge too
favourably in every respect, where themselves, and their
own interest, are concerned. Thus, though we have not
the least reason to suspect that such an interested person
hath any intention to deceive us, yet we of course make
great allowances for his having deceived himself. If this
be general, almost universal, it is prodigious that every man
can think himself an exception, and that he is free from
this self-partiality. The direct contrary is the truth.
Every man may take for granted that he has a great deal
of it, till, from the strictest observation upon himself, he
finds particular reason to think otherwise.

Secondly, There is one easy and almost sure way to
avoid being misled by this self-partiality, and to get acquainted with our real character: to have regard to the
suspicious part of it, and keep a steady eye over ourselves
in that respect. Suppose then a man fully satisfied with
himself, and his own behaviour; such an one, if you please,
as the Pharisee in the gospel, or a better man—well, but
allowing this good opinion you have of yourself to be true,
yet every one is liable to be misrepresented. Suppose then
an enemy were to set about defaming you, what part of
your character would he single out? What particular scan-

dal, think you, would he be most likely to fix upon you?
And what would the world be most ready to believe?
There is scarce a man living but could, from the most
transient superficial view of himself, answer this question.
What is that ill thing, that faulty behaviour, which I am
apprehensive an enemy, who was thoroughly acquainted
with me, would be most likely to lay to my charge, and
which the world would be most apt to believe? It is indeed
possible that a man may not be guilty in that respect. All
that I say is, let him in plainness and honesty fix upon that
part of his character for a particular survey and reflection;
and by this he will come to be acquainted, whether he be
guilty or innocent in that respect, and how far he is one or
the other.

Thirdly, It would very much prevent our being misled
by this self-partiality, to reduce that practical rule of our
Saviour, "Whatsoever ye would that men should do to
you, do ye even so to them," to our judgment and way of
thinking. This rule, you see, consists of two parts. One
is, to substitute another for yourself, when you take a survey of any part of your behaviour, or consider what is proper and fit and reasonable for you to do upon any occasion:
the other part is, that you substitute yourself in the room
of another; consider yourself as the person affected by
such a behaviour, or towards whom such an action is
done; and then you would not only see, but likewise feel
the reasonableness or unreasonableness of such an action
or behaviour. But, alas! the rule itself may be dishonestly applied: there are persons who have not impartiality
enough with respect to themselves, nor regard enough for
others, to be able to make a just application of it. This
just application, if men would honestly make it, is, in effect,
all that I have been recommending; it is the whole thing,
the direct contrary to that inward dishonesty as respecting
our intercourse with our fellow-creatures. And even the
bearing this rule in their thoughts may be of some service:
the attempt thus to apply it, is an attempt towards being
fair and impartial, and may chance unawares to show them
to themselves, to show them the truth of the case they are
considering.

Upon the whole it is manifest, that there is such a thing
as this self-partiality and self-deceit: that in some persons

it is to a degree which would be thought incredible, were
not the instances before our eyes; of which the behaviour
of David is perhaps the highest possible one, in a single
particular case; for there is not the least appearance that
it reached his general character: that we are almost all of
us influenced by it in some degree, and in some respects:
that therefore, every one ought to have an eye to, and
beware of it. And all that I have further to add upon this
subject is, that either there is a difference between right
and wrong, or there is not: religion is true, or it is not.
If it be not, there is no reason for any concern about it:
but if it be true, it requires real fairness of mind and
honesty of heart. And if people will be wicked, they had
better of the two be so from the common vicious passions
without such refinements, than from this deep and calm
source of delusion; which undermines the whole principle of
good; darkens the light, that "candle of the Lord within,"
which is to direct our steps; and corrupts conscience,
which is the guide of life.

SERMON XI.

UPON THE LOVE OF OUR NEIGHBOUR.

PREACHED ON ADVENT SUNDAY.

ROMANS xiii. 9.

*And if there be any other commandment, it is briefly compre-
hended in this saying, namely, Thou shalt love thy neighbour
as thyself.*

IT is commonly observed, that there is a disposition in
men to complain of the viciousness and corruption of the
age in which they live, as greater than that of former ones;
which is usually followed with this further observation, that
mankind has been in that respect much the same in all
times. Now, to determine whether this last be not contradicted by the accounts of history; thus much can scarce be
doubted, that vice and folly takes different turns, and some
particular kinds of it are more open and avowed in some
ages than in others; and, I suppose, it may be spoken of
as very much the distinction of the present, to profess a
contracted spirit, and greater regards to self-interest, than
appears to have been done formerly. Upon this account it
seems worth while to inquire, whether private interest is
likely to be promoted in proportion to the degree in which
self-love engrosses us, and prevails over all other principles;
" or whether the contracted affection may not possibly be so
prevalent as to disappoint itself, and even contradict its
own end, private good?"

And, since, further, there is generally thought to be some
peculiar kind of contrariety between self-love and the love
of our neighbour—between the pursuit of public and of
private good; insomuch, that when you are recommending
one of these, you are supposed to be speaking against the
other; and from hence arises a secret prejudice against, and
frequently open scorn of, all talk of public spirit and real
good-will to our fellow-creatures; it will be necessary to
"inquire what respect benevolence hath to self-love, and
the pursuit of private interest to the pursuit of public?"
Or whether there be any thing of that peculiar inconsistence
and contrariety between them, over and above what there
is between self-love and other passions and particular affections, and their respective pursuits?

These inquiries, it is hoped, may be favourably attended
to; for there shall be all possible concessions made to the
favourite passion, which hath so much allowed to it, and
whose cause is so universally pleaded; it shall be treated
with the utmost tenderness and concern for its interests.

In order to this, as well as to determine the fore-mentioned questions, it will be necessary to consider the nature,
the object, and end of that self-love, as distinguished from
other principles or affections in the mind, and their respective objects.

Every man hath a general desire of his own happiness;
and likewise a variety of particular affections, passions, and
appetites, to particular external objects. The former proceeds from, or is, self-love, and seems inseparable from all
sensible creatures, who can reflect upon themselves and
their own interest or happiness, so as to have that interest
an object to their minds: what is to be said of the latter is,
that they proceed from, or together make up, that particular nature, according to which man is made. The object
the former pursues is somewhat internal, our own happiness, enjoyment, satisfaction; whether we have, or have not,
a distinct particular perception what it is, or wherein it
consists: the objects of the latter are this or that particular external thing, which the affections tend towards, and of
which it hath always a particular idea or perception. The
principle we call self-love never seeks any thing external
for the sake of the thing, but only as a means of happiness or
good: particular affections rest in the external things them-

selves. One belongs to a man as a reasonable creature reflecting upon his own interest or happiness; the other, though quite distinct from reason, are as much a part of human nature.

That all particular appetites and passions are towards *external things themselves*, distinct from the *pleasure arising from them*, is manifested from hence, that there could not be this pleasure, were it not for that prior suitableness between the object and the passion: there could be no enjoyment or delight for one thing more than another, from eating food more than from swallowing a stone, if there were not an affection or appetite to one thing more than another.

Every particular affection, even the love of our neighbour, is as really our own affection, as self-love: and the pleasure arising from its gratification is as much my own pleasure, as the pleasure self-love would have from knowing I myself should be happy some time hence, would be my own pleasure. And if, because every particular affection is a man's own, and the pleasure arising from its gratification his own pleasure, or pleasure to himself, such particular affection must be called self-love; according to this way of speaking, no creature whatever can possibly act but merely from self-love; and every action and every affection whatever is to be resolved up into this one principle. But then this is not the language of mankind: or, if it were, we should want words to express the difference between the principle of an action, proceeding from cool consideration that it will be to my own advantage; and an action, suppose of revenge, or of friendship, by which a man runs upon certain ruin, to do evil or good to another. It is manifest the principles of these actions are totally different, and so want different words to be distinguished by: all that they agree in is, that they both proceed from, and are done to gratify an inclination in a man's self. But the principle or inclination in one case is self-love; in the other, hatred, or love of another. There is then a distinction between the cool principle of self-love, or general desire of our own happiness, as one part of our nature, and one principle of action; and the particular affections towards particular external objects, as another part of our nature, and another principle of action. How much soever, therefore, is to be allowed to self-love, yet it cannot be allowed to be the whole of our inward constitution; because, you see, there are other parts or principles which come into it.

Further, private happiness or good is all which self-love can make us desire, or be concerned about. In having this consists its gratification; it is an affection to ourselves—a regard to our own interest, happiness, and private good: and in the proportion a man hath this, he is interested, or a lover of himself. Let this be kept in mind, because there is commonly, as I shall presently have occasion to observe, another sense put upon these words. On the other hand, particular affections tend towards particular external things; these are their objects; having these is their end; in this consists their gratification: no matter whether it be, or be not, upon the whole, our interest or happiness. An action, done from the former of these principles, is called an interested action. An action, proceeding from any of the latter, has its denomination of passionate, ambitious, friendly, revengeful, or any other, from the particular appetite or affection from which it proceeds. Thus self-love, as one part of human nature, and the several particular principles as the other part, are themselves, their objects and ends, stated and shown.

From hence it will be easy to see how far, and in what ways, each of these can contribute and be subservient to the private good of the individual. Happiness does not consist in self-love. The desire of happiness is no more the thing itself, than the desire of riches is the possession or enjoyment of them. People may love themselves with the most entire and unbounded affection, and yet be extremely miserable. Neither can self-love any way help them out, but by setting them on work to get rid of the causes of their misery, to gain or make use of those objects which are by nature adapted to afford satisfaction. Happiness or satisfaction consists only in the enjoyment of those objects which are by nature suited to our several particular appetites, passions, and affections. So that if self-love wholly engrosses us, and leaves no room for any other principle, there can be absolutely no such thing at all as happiness or enjoyment of any kind whatever; since happiness consists in the gratification of particular passions, which supposes the having of them. Self-love then does not constitute *this* or *that* to be

our interest or good; but our interest or good being constituted by nature and supposed self-love, only puts us upon
obtaining and securing it. Therefore, if it be possible that
self-love may prevail and exert itself in a degree or manner
which is not subservient to this end, then it will not follow
that our interest will be promoted in proportion to the degree in which that principle engrosses us, and prevails over
others. Nay, further, the private and contracted affection,
when it is not subservient to this end, private good, may,
for any thing that appears, have a direct contrary tendency
and effect. And if we will consider the matter, we shall see
that it often really has. Disengagement is absolutely necessary to enjoyment; and a person may have so steady
and fixed an eye upon his own interest, whatever he places
in it, as may hinder him from attending to many gratifications within his reach, which others have their minds free
and open to. Over-fondness for a child is not generally
thought to be for its advantage; and, if there be any guess
to be made from appearances, surely that character we call
selfish is not the most promising for happiness. Such a
temper may plainly be, and exert itself in a degree and
manner which may give unnecessary and useless solicitude
and anxiety, in a degree and manner which may prevent
obtaining the means and materials of enjoyment, as well as
the making use of them. Immoderate self-love does very
ill consult its own interest; and how much soever a paradox it may appear, it is certainly true, that, even from self-
love, we should endeavour to get over all inordinate regard
to, and consideration of, ourselves. Every one of our passions and affections hath its natural stint and bound, which
may easily be exceeded; whereas our enjoyments can
possibly be but in a determinate measure and degree.
Therefore such excess of the affection, since it cannot procure any enjoyment, must in all cases be useless, but is
generally attended with inconveniences, and often is downright pain and misery. This holds as much with regard to
self-love as to all other affections. The natural degree of
it, so far as it sets us on work to gain and make use of the
materials of satisfaction, may be to our real advantage : but
beyond or besides this, it is in several respects an inconvenience and disadvantage. Thus, it appears, that private
interest is so far from being likely to be promoted in pro-

portion to the degree in which self-love engrosses us, and
prevails over all other principles, that *the contracted affection may be so prevalent, as to disappoint itself, and even .
contradict its own end, private good.*

" But who, except the most sordidly covetous, ever
thought there was any rivalship between the love of greatness, honour, power, or between sensual appetites, and
self-love ?   No, there is a perfect harmony between them.
It is by means of these particular appetites and affections
that self-love is gratified in enjoyment, happiness, and satisfaction.   The competition and rivalship is between self-love
and the love of our neighbour.   That affection which leads
us out of ourselves, makes us regardless of our own interest,
and substitute that of another in its stead."   Whether then
there be any peculiar competition and contrariety in this
case, shall now be considered.

Self-love and interestedness was stated to consist in or be
an affection to ourselves, a regard to our own private good :
it is, therefore, distinct from benevolence, which is an
affection to the good of our fellow-creatures.   But that benevolence is distinct from, that is, not the same thing with
self-love, is no reason for its being looked upon with any
peculiar suspicion, because every principle whatever, by
means of which self-love is gratified, is distinct from it.
And all things, which are distinct from each other, are
equally so.   A man has an affection or aversion to another :
that one of these tends to, and is gratified by doing good,
that the other tends to, and is gratified by doing harm, does
not in the least alter the respect which either one or the
other of these inward feelings has to self-love.   We use
the word *property* so as to exclude any other persons having
an interest in that, of which we say a particular man has the
property : and we often use the word *selfish* so as to exclude
in the same manner all regards to the good of others.   But
the cases are not parallel : for, though that exclusion is
really part of the idea of property ; yet such positive exclusion, or bringing this peculiar disregard to the good of others
into the idea of self-love, is in reality adding to the idea, or
changing it from what it was before stated to consist in,
namely, in an affection to ourselves.*   This being the

* Page 105.

whole idea of self-love, it can no otherwise exclude good-will or love of others, than merely by not including it, no otherwise than it excludes love of arts, or reputation, or of any thing else.   Neither, on the other hand, does benevo-lence, any more than love of arts or of reputation, exclude self-love.   Love of our neighbour, then, has just the same respect to, is no more distant from self-love, than hatred of our neighbour, or than love and hatred of any thing else. Thus the principles, from which men rush upon certain ruin for the destruction of an enemy, and for the preservation of a friend, have the same respect to the private affection, are equally interested, or equally disinterested : and it is of no avail, whether they are said to be one or the other.   There-fore, to those who are shocked to hear virtue spoken of as disinterested, it may be allowed, that it is indeed absurd to speak thus of it ; unless hatred, several particular instances of vice, and all the common affections and aversions in mankind, are acknowledged to be disinterested too.   Is there any less inconsistence between the love of inanimate things, or of creatures merely sensitive, and self-love, than between self-love, and the love of our neighbour ?   Is desire of, and delight in the happiness of another any more a diminution of self-love, than desire of and delight in the esteem of another ? They are both equally desire of and delight in somewhat external to ourselves : either both or neither are so.   The object of self-love is expressed in the term self : and every appetite of sense, and every particular affection of the heart, are equally interested or disinterested, because the objects of them all are equally self or somewhat else. Whatever ridicule, therefore, the mention of a disinterested principle or action may be supposed to lie open to, must, upon the matter being thus stated, relate to ambition, and every appetite and particular affection, as much as to bene-volence.   And indeed all the ridicule, and all the grave perplexity, of which this subject hath had its full share, is merely from words.   The most intelligible way of speaking of it seems to be this : that self-love, and the actions done in consequence of it, (for these will presently appear to be the same as to this question,) are interested ; that particu-lar affections towards external objects, and the actions done in consequence of those affections, are not so.   But every one is at liberty to use words as he pleases.   All that is here insisted upon is, that ambition, revenge, benevolence, all particular passions whatever, and the actions they produce, are equally interested or disinterested.

Thus it appears, that there is no peculiar contrariety between self-love and benevolence; no greater competition between these, than between any other particular affections and self-love. This relates to the affections themselves. Let us now see whether there be any peculiar contrariety between the respective courses of life which these affections lead to; whether there be any greater competition between the pursuit of private and of public good, than between any other particular pursuits and that of private good.

There seems no other reason to suspect that there is any such peculiar contrariety, but only that the course of action which benevolence leads to, has a more direct tendency to promote the good of others, than that course of action which love of reputation, suppose, or any other particular affection, leads to. But that any affection tends to the happiness of another, does not hinder its tending to one's own happiness too. That others enjoy the benefit of the air and the light of the sun, does not hinder, but that these are as much one's own private advantage now, as they would be if we had the property of them exclusive of all others. So a pursuit which tends to promote the good of another, yet may have as great tendency to promote private interest, as a pursuit which does not tend to the good of another at all, or which is mischievous to him. All particular affections whatever, resentment, benevolence, love of arts, equally lead to a course of action for their own gratification, *i. e.* the gratification of ourselves: and the gratification of each gives delight: so far, then, it is manifest, they have all the same respect to private interest. Now, take into consideration further, concerning these three pursuits, that the end of the first is the harm; of the second, the good of another; of the last, somewhat indifferent: and is there any necessity, that these additional considerations should alter the respect, which we before saw these three pursuits had to private interest; or render any one of them less conducive to it than any other? Thus, one man's affection is to honour, as his end; in order to obtain which, he thinks no pains too great. Suppose another, with such a singularity of mind, as to have the

same affection to public good, as his end, which he endeavours with the same labour to obtain. In case of success,
surely the man of benevolence hath as great enjoyment as
the man of ambition ; they both equally having the end
their affections, in the same degree, tended to : but in case
of disappointment, the benevolent man has clearly the
advantage ; since endeavouring to do good, considered as a
virtuous pursuit, is gratified by its own consciousness, *i. e.*
is in a degree its own reward.

And as to these two, or benevolence and any other particular passions whatever, considered in a further view, as
forming a general temper, which more or less disposes us
for enjoyment of all the common blessings of life, distinct
from their own gratification : is benevolence less the temper of tranquillity and freedom, than ambition or covetousness ? Does the benevolent man appear less easy with
himself, from his love to his neighbour ? Does he less
relish his being ? Is there any peculiar gloom seated on
his face ? Is his mind less open to entertainment, to any
particular gratification ? Nothing is more manifest, than
that being in good humour, which is benevolence whilst it
lasts, is itself the temper of satisfaction and enjoyment.

Suppose then a man sitting down to consider, how he
might become most easy to himself, and attain the greatest
pleasure he could ; all that which is his real natural happiness : this can only consist in the enjoyment of those
objects, which are by nature adapted to our several faculties. These particular enjoyments make up the sum total
of our happiness ; and they are supposed to arise from
riches, honours, and the gratification of sensual appetites.
Be it so : yet none profess themselves so completely happy
in these enjoyments, but that there is room left in the
mind for others, if they were presented to them. Nay,
these, as much as they engage us, are not thought so high,
but that human nature is capable even of greater. Now
there have been persons in all ages, who have professed
that they found satisfaction in the exercise of charity, in the
love of their neighbour, in endeavouring to promote the
happiness of all they had to do with, and in the pursuit of
what is just, and right, and good, as the general bent of
their mind, and end of their life ; and that doing an action
of baseness or cruelty, would be as great violence to *their*

self, as much breaking in upon their nature, as any external
force. Persons of this character would add, if they might
be heard, that they consider themselves as acting in the
view of an infinite Being, who is in a much higher sense
the object of reverence and of love, than all the world
besides; and, therefore, they could have no more enjoyment from a wicked action done under his eye, than the
persons to whom they are making their apology could, if all
mankind were the spectators of it; and that the satisfaction
of approving themselves to his unerring judgment, to whom
they thus refer all their actions, is a more continued settled
satisfaction than any this world can afford; as also that they
have, no less than others, a mind free and open to all the
common innocent gratifications of it such as they are.
And, if we go no further, does there appear any absurdity
in this? Will any one take upon him to say, that a man
cannot find his account in this general course of life, as
much as in the most unbounded ambition, or the excesses
of pleasure? Or that such a person has not consulted so
well for himself, for the satisfaction and peace of his own
mind, as the ambitious or dissolute man? And though the
consideration, that God himself will in the end justify their
taste, and support their cause, is not formally to be insisted
upon here; yet thus much comes in, that all enjoyments
whatever are much more clear and unmixed, from the
assurance that they will end well. Is it certain then that
there is nothing in these pretensions to happiness? especially when there are not wanting persons, who have supported themselves with satisfactions of this kind in sickness,
poverty, disgrace, and in the very pangs of death; whereas,
it is manifest all other enjoyments fail in these circumstances. This surely looks suspicious of having somewhat
in it. Self-love, methinks, should be alarmed. May she
not possibly pass over greater pleasures, than those she is
so wholly taken up with?

The short of the matter is no more than this. Happiness consists in the gratification of certain affections, appetites, passions, with objects which are by nature adapted to
them. Self-love may indeed set us on work to gratify
these: but happiness or enjoyment has no immediate connexion with self-love, but arises from such gratification
alone. Love of our neighbour is one of those affections.

This, considered as a virtuous principle, is gratified by a consciousness of endeavouring to promote the good of others : but considered as a natural affection, its gratification consists in the actual accomplishment of this endeavour. Now, indulgence or gratification of this affection, whether in that consciousness, or this accomplishment, has the same respect to interest, as indulgence of any other affection ; they equally proceed from, or do not proceed from self-love ; they equally include, or equally exclude, this principle. Thus it appears, that " benevolence and the pursuit of public good have at least as great respect to self-love and the pursuit of private good, as any other particular passions, and their respective pursuits."

Neither is covetousness, whether as a temper or pursuit, any exception to this. For if by covetousness is meant the desire and pursuit of riches for their own sake, without any regard to, or consideration of the uses of them ; this hath as little to do with self-love, as benevolence hath. But by this word is usually meant, not such madness and total distraction of mind, but immoderate affection to, and pursuit of riches as possessions, in order to some further end ; namely, satisfaction, interest, or good. This, therefore, is not a particular affection, or particular pursuit, but it is the general principle of self-love, and the general pursuit of our own interest ; for which reason, the word *selfish* is by every one appropriated to this temper and pursuit. Now, as it is ridiculous to assert, that self-love and the love of our neighbour are the same ; so neither is it asserted, that following these different affections hath the same tendency and respect to our own interest. The comparison is not between self-love and the love of our neighbour ; between pursuit of our own interest, and the interest of others ; but between the several particular affections in human nature towards external objects, as one part of the comparison ; and the one particular affection to the good of our neighbour, as the one part of it : and it has been shown, that all these have the same respect to self-love and private interest.

There is indeed frequently an inconsistence, or interfering between self-love or private interest, and the several particular appetites, passions, affections, or the pursuits they lead to. But this competition or interfering is merely accidental ; and happens much oftener between pride,

8

revenge, sensual gratifications, and private interest, than
between private interest and benevolence. For nothing is
more common, than to see men give themselves up to a
passion or an affection to their known prejudice and ruin,
and in direct contradiction to manifest and real interest,
and the loudest calls of self-love : whereas the seeming
competitions and interfering between benevolence and private interest, relate much more to the materials or means
of enjoyment, than to enjoyment itself. There is often an
interfering in the former, where there is none in the latter.
Thus, as to riches : so much money as a man gives away,
so much less will remain in his possession. Here is a real
interfering. But though a man cannot possibly give without lessening his fortune, yet there are multitudes might
give without lessening their own enjoyment; because they
may have more than they can turn to any real use or advantage to themselves. Thus, the more thought and time
any one employs about the interests and good of others, he
must necessarily have less to attend his own ; but he may
have so ready and large a supply of his own wants, that
such thought might be really useless to himself, though of
great service and assistance to others.

The general mistake, that there is some greater inconsistence between endeavouring to promote the good of
another and self-interest, than between self-interest and
pursuing any thing else, seems, as hath already been hinted,
to arise from our notions of property ; and to be carried on
by this property's being supposed to be itself our happiness
or good. People are so very much taken up with this one
subject, that they seem from it to have formed a general
way of thinking, which they apply to other things that they
have nothing to do with. Hence, in a confused and slight
way, it might well be taken for granted, that another's
having no interest in an affection, (*i. e.* his good not being
the object of it) renders, as one may speak, the proprietor's
interest in it greater ; and that if another had an interest in
it, this would render his less, or occasion that such affection
could not be so friendly to self-love, or conducive to private
good, as an affection or pursuit which has not a regard to the
good of another. This, I say, might be taken for granted,
whilst it was not attended to, that the object of every particular affection is equally somewhat external to ourselves :

and whether it be the good of another person, or whether it
be any other external thing, makes no alteration with regard
to its being one's own affection, and the gratification of it
one's own private enjoyment.   And so far as it is taken for
granted, that barely having the means and materials of
enjoyment is what constitutes interest and happiness; that
our interest and good consists in possessions themselves, in
having the property of riches, houses, lands, gardens, not in
the enjoyment of them; so far it will even more strongly be
taken for granted, in the way already explained, that an affection's conducing to the good of another, must even
necessarily occasion it to conduce less to private good, if
not to be positively detrimental to it.   For, if property and
happiness are one and the same thing, as by increasing the
property of another, you lessen your own property, so by
promoting the happiness of another, you must lessen your
own happiness.   But whatever occasioned the mistake, I
hope it has been fully proved to be one; as it has been
proved, that there is no peculiar rivalship or competition
between self-love and benevolence ; that as there may be a
competition between these two, so there may also between
any particular affection whatever and self-love; that every
particular affection, benevolence among the rest, is subservient to self-love, by being the instrument of private enjoyment; and that in one respect benevolence contributes more
to private interest, *i. e.* enjoyment or satisfaction, than any
other of the particular common affections, as it is in a degree its own gratification.

And to all these things may be added, that religion, from
whence arises our strongest obligation to benevolence, is so
far from disowning the principle of self-love, that it often
addresses itself to that very principle, and always to the
mind in that state when reason presides ; and there can no
access be had to the understanding, but by convincing men,
that the course of life we would persuade them to is not
contrary to their interest.   It may be allowed, without any
prejudice to the cause of virtue and religion, that our ideas
of happiness and misery are, of all our ideas, the nearest
and most important to us ; that they will, nay, if you please,
that they ought to prevail over those of order, and beauty,
and harmony, and proportion, if there should ever be, as it
is impossible there ever should be, any inconsistency be-

tween them : though these last, too, as expressing the fitness of actions, are real as truth itself. Let it be allowed,
though virtue or moral rectitude does indeed consist in
affection to and pursuit of what is right and good, as such :
yet that, when we sit down in a cool hour, we can neither
justify to ourselves this or any other pursuit, till we are
convinced that it will be for our happiness, or, at least, not
contrary to it.

Common reason and humanity will have some influence
upon mankind, whatever becomes of speculations : but, so
far as the interests of virtue depend upon the theory of it
being secured from open scorn, so far its very being in the
world depends upon its appearing to have no contrariety to
private interest and self-love. The foregoing observations,
therefore, it is hoped, may have gained a little ground in
favour of the precept before us, the particular explanation of
which shall be the subject of the next discourse.

I will conclude, at present, with observing the peculiar
obligation which we are under to virtue and religion, as
enforced in the verses following the text, in the epistle for
the day, from our Saviour's coming into the world. " The
night is far spent, the day is at hand ; let us, therefore, cast
off the works of darkness, and let us put on the armour of
light," &c. The meaning and force of which exhortation is,
that Christianity lays us under new obligations to a good
life, as by it the will of God is more clearly revealed, and as
it affords additional motives to the practice of it, over and
above those which arise out of the nature of virtue and vice;
I might add, as our Saviour has set us a perfect example of
goodness in our own nature. Now, love and charity is
plainly the thing in which he had placed his religion ; in
which, therefore, as we have any pretence to the name of
Christians, we must place ours. He hath at once enjoined
it upon us by way of command, with peculiar force : and by
his example, as having undertaken the work of our salvation, out of pure love and good-will to mankind. The endeavour to set home this example upon our minds, is a very
proper employment of this season, which is bringing on the
festival of his birth ; which, as it may teach us many excellent lessons of humility, resignation and obedience to the
will of God ; so there is none it recommends with greater

authority, force, and advantage, than this of love and charity; since it was "for us men, and for our salvation, that
he came down from heaven, and was incarnate, and was
made man;" that he might teach us our duty, and more
especially that he might enforce the practice of it, reform
mankind, and finally bring us to that " eternal salvation, of
which he is the Author to all those that obey him."

SERMON XII.

UPON THE LOVE OF OUR NEIGHBOUR.

ROMANS xiii. 9.

And if there be any other commandment, it is briefly comprehended in this saying, namely, Thou shalt love thy neighbour as thyself.

HAVING already removed the prejudices against public spirit, or the love of our neighbour, on the side of private interest and self-love; I proceed to the particular explanation of the precept before us, by showing "who is our neighbour: in what sense we are required to love him as ourselves: the influence such love would have upon our behaviour in life." And lastly, "How this commandment comprehends in it all others."

I. The objects and due extent of this affection will be understood by attending to the nature of it, and to the nature and circumstances of mankind in this world. The love of our neighbour is the same with charity, benevolence, or good-will. It is an affection to the good and happiness of our fellow-creatures. This implies in it a disposition to produce happiness: and this is the simple notion of goodness, which appears so amiable wherever we meet with it. From hence it is easy to see, that the perfection of goodness consists in love to the whole universe. This is the perfection of Almighty God.

But as man is so much limited in his capacity, as so small a part of the creation comes under his notice and influence, and as we are not used to consider things in so general a way; it is not to be thought of, that the universe should

be the object of benevolence to such creatures as we are.
Thus, in that precept of our Saviour's, "Be ye perfect, even
as your Father which is in heaven is perfect,"* the perfection of the Divine goodness is proposed to our imitation, as
it is promiscuous, and extends to the evil as well as the good;
not as it is absolutely universal, imitation of it in this respect being plainly beyond us.   The object is too vast.
For this reason moral writers also have substituted a less
general object for our benevolence, mankind.   But this
likewise is an object too general, and very much out of our
view.   Therefore, persons more practical have, instead of
mankind, put our country; and made the principle of virtue, of human virtue, to consist in the entire uniform love
for our country: and this is what we call a public spirit;
which in men of public stations is the character of a patriot.
But this is speaking to the upper part of the world.   Kingdoms and governments are large; and the sphere of action
of far the greatest part of mankind is much narrower than
the governments they live under: or, however, common
men do not consider their actions as affecting the whole
community, of which they are members.   There plainly is
wanting a less general and nearer object of benevolence for
the bulk of men than that of their country.   Therefore the
Scripture, not being a book of theory and speculation, but
a plain rule of life for mankind, has, with the utmost possible
propriety, put the principle of virtue upon the love of our
neighbour; which is that part of the universe, that part of
mankind, that part of our country, which comes under our
immediate notice, acquaintance, and influence, and with
which we have to do.

This is plainly the true account or reason, why our
Saviour places the principle of virtue in the love of our
neighbour; and the account itself shows who are comprehended under that relation.

II. Let us now consider in what sense we are commanded to love our neighbour as ourselves.

This precept, in its first delivery by our Saviour, is thus
introduced: "Thou shalt love the Lord thy God with all
thine heart, with all thy soul, and with all thy strength;
and thy neighbour as thyself."   These very different man-

* Matt. v. 48.

ners of expression do not lead our thoughts to the same
measure or degree of love, common to both objects; but
to one peculiar to each.   Supposing, then, which is to be
supposed, a distinct meaning and propriety in the words,
"as thyself;" the precept we are considering will admit
of any of these senses; that we bear the same kind of
affection to our neighbour, as we do to ourselves; or, that
the love we bear to our neighbour should have some certain
proportion or other to self-love : or, lastly, that it should
bear the particular proportion of equality, that it be in the
same degree.

First, The precept may be understood as requiring only
that we have the same kind of affection to our fellow-creatures, as to ourselves.   That, as every man has the principle
of self-love, which disposes him to avoid misery, and consult his own happiness : so we should cultivate the affection
of good-will to our neighbour, and that it should influence
us to have the same kind of regard to him.   This, at least,
must be commanded; and this will not only prevent our
being injurious to him, but will also put us upon promoting
his good.   There are blessings in life, which we share in
common with others; peace, plenty, freedom, healthful seasons.   But real benevolence to our fellow-creatures would
give us the notion of a common interest in a stricter sense :
for in the degree we love another, his interest, his joys,
and sorrows, are our own.   It is from self-love that we
form the notion of private good, and consider it as our own :
love of our neighbour will teach us thus to appropriate to
ourselves his good and welfare : to consider ourselves as
having a real share in his happiness.   Thus the principle of
benevolence would be an advocate within our own breasts,
to take care of the interests of our fellow-creatures, in all
the interferings and competitions which cannot but be, from
the imperfections of our nature, and the state we are in.
It would, likewise, in some measure, lessen that interfering;
and hinder men from forming so strong a notion of private
good, exclusive of the good of others, as we commonly do.
Thus, as the private affection makes us in a peculiar manner
sensible of humanity, justice, or injustice, when exercised
towards ourselves; love of our neighbour would give us
the same kind of sensibility in his behalf.   This would be
the greater security of our uniform obedience to that most

equitable rule : "Whatsoever ye would that men should do unto you, do ye even so unto them."

All this is indeed no more than that we should have a real love to our neighbour ; but then, which is to be observed, the words, *as thyself*, express this in the most distinct manner, and determine the precept to relate to the affection itself. The advantage which this principle of benevolence has over other remote considerations is, that it is itself the tempter of virtue ; and likewise that it is the chief, nay, the only effectual security of our performing the several offices of kindness we owe to our fellow-creatures. When, from distant considerations, men resolve upon any thing to which they have no liking, or, perhaps, an averseness, they are perpetually finding out evasions and excuses ; which need never be wanting, if people look for them : and they equivocate with themselves in the plainest cases in the world. This may be in respect to single determinate acts of virtue : but it comes in much more, where the obligation is to a general course of behaviour ; and most of all, if it be such as cannot be reduced to fixed determinate rules. This observation may account for the diversity of the expression in that known passage of the prophet Micah, "To do justly, and to love mercy." A man's heart must be formed to humanity and benevolence, he must love mercy, otherwise he will not act mercifully in any settled course of behaviour. A consideration of the future sanctions of religion is our only security of persevering in our duty, in cases of great temptations ; so to get our heart and temper formed to a love and liking of what is good, is absolutely necessary in order to our behaving rightly in the familiar and daily intercourses amongst mankind.

Secondly, The precept before us may be understood to require, that we love our neighbour in some certain proportion or other, according as we love ourselves. And indeed a man's character cannot be determined by the love he bears to his neighbour, considered absolutely : but the proportion which this bears to self-love, whether it be attended to or not, is the chief thing which forms the character and influences the actions. For, as the form of the body is a composition of various parts ; so likewise our inward structure is not simple or uniform, but a composition of various passions, appetites, affections, together with rationality ;

including in this last both the discernment of what is right, and a disposition to regulate ourselves by it. There is greater variety of parts in what we call a character, than there are features in a face : and the morality of that is no more determined by one part, than the beauty or deformity of this is by one single feature : each is to be judged of by all the parts or features not taken singly, but together. In the inward frame the various passions, appetites, affections, stand in different respects to each other. The principles in our mind may be contradictory, or checks and allays only, or incentives and assistants to each other. And principles, which in their nature have no kind of contrariety or affinity, may yet accidentally be each other's allays or incentives.

From hence it comes to pass, that though we were able to look into the inward contexture of the heart, and see with the greatest exactness in what degree any one principle is in a particular man ; we could not from thence determine how far that principle would go towards forming the character, or what influence it would have upon the actions, unless we could likewise discern what other principles prevailed in him, and see the proportion which that one bears to the others. Thus, though two men should have the affection of compassion in the same degree exactly, yet one may have the principle of resentment, or of ambition, so strong in him as to prevail over that of compassion, and prevent its having any influence upon his actions ; so that he may deserve the character of a hard or cruel man : whereas the other, having compassion in just the same degree only, yet having resentment or ambition in a lower degree, his compassion may prevail over them, so as to influence his actions, and to denominate his temper compassionate. So that, how strange soever it may appear to people who do not attend to the thing, yet it is quite manifest, that when we say one man is more resenting or compassionate than another, this does not necessarily imply that one has the principle of resentment or of compassion stronger than the other. For if the proportion which resentment or compassion bears to other inward principles, is greater in one than in the other ; this is itself sufficient to denominate one more resenting or compassionate than the other.

Further, the whole system, as I may speak, of affections

(including rationality) which constitute the heart, as this
word is used in Scripture and on moral subjects, are each and
all of them stronger in some than in others. Now the proportion which the two general affections, benevolence and self-
love, bear to each other, according to this interpretation of
the text, denominates men's character as to virtue. Suppose
then one man to have the principle of benevolence in a
higher degree than another : it will not follow, from hence,
that his general temper, or character, or actions, will be
more benevolent than the other's. For he may have self-
love in such a degree as quite to prevail over benevolence ;
so that it may have no influence at all upon his actions :
whereas benevolence in the other person, though in a lower
degree, may yet be the strongest principle in his heart ; and
strong enough to be the guide of his actions, so as to denominate him a good and virtuous man. The case is here as
in scales : it is not one weight considered in itself, which
determines whether the scale shall ascend or descend : but
this depends upon the proportion which that one weight
hath to the other.

It being thus manifest, that the influence which benevolence has upon our actions, and how far it goes towards
forming our character, is not determined by the degree
itself of this principle in our mind, but by the proportion it
has to self-love and other principles ; a comparison also
being made in the text between self-love and the love of
our neighbour : these joint considerations afforded sufficient
occasion for treating here of that proportion : it plainly is
implied in the precept, though it should be questioned
whether it be the exact meaning of the words " as thyself."

Love of our neighbour, then, must bear some proportion
to self-love : and virtue, to be sure, consists in the due
proportion. What this due proportion is, whether as a
principle in the mind, or as exerted in actions, can be
judged of only from our nature and condition in this world.
Of the degree in which affections and the principles of action, considered in themselves, prevail, we have no measure : let us then proceed to the course of behaviour, the
actions they produce.

Both our nature and condition require that each particular man should make particular provision for himself ; and
the inquiry, what proportion benevolence should have to

self-love, when brought down to practice, will be what is a
competent care and provision for ourselves? And how certain soever it be, that each man must determine this for
himself; and how ridiculous soever it would be, for any
to attempt to determine it for another: yet it is to be observed that the proportion is real: and that a competent
provision has a bound; and that it cannot be all which we
can possibly get and keep within our grasp, without legal
injustice.   Mankind almost universally bring in vanity,
supplies for what is called a life of pleasure, covetousness,
or imaginary notions of superiority over others, to determine this question: but every one who desires to act
a proper part in society, would do well to consider how far
any of them come in to determine it, in the way of moral
consideration.   All that can be said is, supposing what, as
the world goes, is so much to be supposed that it is scarce
to be mentioned, that persons do not neglect what they
really owe to themselves; the more of their care and thought,
and of their fortune, they employ in doing good to their
fellow creatures, the nearer they come up to the law of perfection, "Thou shalt love thy neighbour as thyself."

  Thirdly, If the words, "as thyself," were to be understood of an equality of affection, it would not be attended
with those consequences, which perhaps may be thought to
follow from it.   Suppose a person to have the same settled
regard to others as to himself; that in every deliberate
scheme or pursuit he took their interest into the account in
the same degree as his own, so far as an equality of affection would produce this; yet he would, in fact, and ought
to be, much more taken up and employed about himself,
and his own concerns, than about others and their interests.
For, besides the one common affection towards himself and
his neighbour, he would have several other particular affections, passions, appetites, which he could not possibly feel
in common both for himself and others: now these sensations themselves very much employ us, and have perhaps
as great influence as self-love.   So far indeed as self-love,
and cool reflection upon what is for our interest, would set
us on work to gain a supply of our own several wants;
so far the love of our neighbour would make us do the
same for him: but the degree in which we are put upon
seeking and making use of the means of gratification, by

the feeling of those affections, appetites, and passions, must necessarily be peculiar to ourselves.

That there are particular passions, (suppose shame, resentment,) which men seem to have, and feel in common both for themselves and others, makes no alteration in respect to those passions and appetites which cannot possibly be thus felt in common. From hence (and perhaps more things of the like kind might be mentioned) it follows, that though there were an equality of affection to both, yet regards to ourselves would be more prevalent than attention to the concerns of others.

And from moral considerations it ought to be so, supposing still the equality of affection commanded: because we are in a peculiar manner, as I may speak, intrusted with ourselves; and, therefore, care of our own interest, as well as of our conduct, particularly belongs to us.

To these things must be added, that moral obligations can extend no further than to natural possibilities. Now, we have a perception of our own interests, like consciousness of our own existence, which we always carry about with us; and which, in its continuation, kind, and degree, seems impossible to be felt in respect to the interests of others.

From all these things it fully appears, that though we were to love our neighbour in the same degree as we love ourselves, so far as this is possible; yet the care of ourselves, of the individual, would not be neglected; the apprehended danger of which seems to be the only objection against understanding the precept in this strict sense.

III. The general temper of mind which the due love of our neighbour would form us to, and the influence it would have upon our behaviour in life, is now to be considered.

The temper and behaviour of charity is explained at large, in that known passage of St. Paul: " Charity suffereth long, and is kind; charity envieth not, doth not behave itself unseemly, seeketh not her own, thinketh no evil, beareth all things, believeth all things, hopeth all things."* As to the meaning of the expressions, " seeketh not her own, thinketh no evil, believeth all things;" however those expressions may be explained away, this meekness, and, in

* 1 Cor. xiii.

some degree, easiness of temper, readiness to forego our right for the sake of peace, as well as in the way of compassion, freedom from mistrust, and disposition to believe well of our neighbour; this general temper, I say, accompanies, and is plainly the effect of love and good-will.   And, though such is the world in which we live, that experience and knowledge of it not only may, but must beget in us greater regard to ourselves, and doubtfulness of the characters of others, than is natural to mankind, yet these ought not to be carried further than the nature and course of things make necessary.   It is still true, even in the present state of things, bad as it is, that a real good man had rather be deceived, than be suspicious; had rather forego his known right, than run the venture of doing even a hard thing. This is the general temper of that charity, of which the apostle asserts, that if he had it not, giving his "body to be burned would avail him nothing;" and which he says, "shall never fail."

The happy influence of this temper extends to every different relation and circumstance in human life. It plainly renders a man better, more to be desired, as to all the respects and relations we can stand in to each other. The benevolent man is disposed to make use of all external advantages in such a manner as shall contribute to the good of others, as well as to his own satisfaction. His own satisfaction consists in this. He will be easy and kind to his dependents, compassionate to the poor and distressed, friendly to all with whom he has to do. This includes the good neighbour, parent, master, magistrate: and such a behaviour would plainly make dependence, inferiority, and even servitude, easy. So that a good or charitable man, of superior rank in wisdom, fortune, authority, is a common blessing to the place he lives in: happiness grows under his influence. This good principle in inferiors would discover itself in paying respect, gratitude, obedience as due. It were, therefore, methinks, one just way of trying one's own character, to ask ourselves, Am I in reality a better master or servant, a better friend, a better neighbour, than such and such persons; whom, perhaps, I may think not to deserve the character of virtue and religion so much as myself?

And as to the spirit of party, which unhappily prevails

H

amongst mankind, whatever are the distinctions which serve
for a supply to it, some or other of which have obtained in
all ages and countries; one who is thus friendly to his kind,
will immediately make due allowances for it, as what cannot
but be amongst such creatures as men, in such a world as
this. And as wrath and fury and overbearing upon these
occasions proceed, as I may speak, from men's feeling only
on their own side; so a common feeling, for others as well
as for ourselves, would render us sensible to this truth,
which it is strange can have so little influence; that we ourselves differ from others, just as much as they do from us.
I put the matter in this way, because it can scarce be expected that the generality of men should see, that those
things which are made the occasions of dissension and fo-
menting the party-spirit, are really nothing at all: but it
may be expected from all people, how much soever they are
in earnest about their respective peculiarities, that humanity,
and common good-will to their fellow-creatures, should
moderate and restrain that wretched spirit.

This good temper of charity likewise would prevent strife
and enmity arising from other occasions: it would prevent
our giving just cause of offence, and our taking it without
cause. And in cases of real injury, a good man will make
all the allowances which are to be made; and, without
any attempts of retaliation, he will only consult his own and
other men's security for the future, against injustice and
wrong.

IV. I proceed to consider lastly, what is affirmed of the
precept now explained, that it comprehends in it all others;
i. e. that to love our neighbour as ourselves includes in it all
virtues.

Now, the way in which every maxim of conduct, or
general speculative assertion, when it is to be explained at
large, should be treated, is, to show what are the particular
truths which were designed to be comprehended under such
a general observation, how far it is strictly true; and then
the limitations, restrictions, and exceptions, if there be exceptions, with which it is to be understood. But it is only
the former of these, namely, how far the assertion in the
text holds, and the ground of pre-eminence assigned to the
precept of it, which in strictness comes into our present
consideration.

However, in almost every thing that is said, there is somewhat to be understood beyond what is explicitly laid down, and which we of course supply; somewhat, I mean which would not be commonly called a restriction or limitation. Thus, when benevolence is said to be the sum of virtue, it is not spoken of as a blind propension, but as a principle in reasonable creatures, and so to be directed by their reason: for reason and reflection come into our notion of a moral agent. And that will lead us to consider distant consequences, as well as the immediate tendency of an action: it will teach us, that the care of some persons, suppose children and families, is particularly committed to our charge by nature and Providence; as also, that there are other circumstances, suppose friendship or former obligations, which require that we do good to some, preferably to others. Reason, considered merely as subservient to benevolence, as assisting to produce the greatest good, will teach us to have particular regard to these relations and circumstances; because it is plainly for the good of the world that they should be regarded. And as there are numberless cases, in which, notwithstanding appearances, we are not competent judges, whether a particular action will upon the whole do good or harm; reason in the same way will teach us to be cautious how we act in these cases of uncertainty. It will suggest to our consideration, which is the safer side; how liable we are to be led wrong by passion and private interest; and what regard is due to laws, and the judgment of mankind. All these things must come into consideration, were it only in order to determine which way of acting is likely to produce the greatest good. Thus, upon supposition that it were in the strictest sense true, without limitation, that benevolence includes in it all virtues; yet reason must come in as its guide and director, in order to attain its own end, the end of benevolence, the greatest public good. Reason then being thus included, let us now consider the truth of the assertion itself.

First, It is manifest that nothing can be of consequence to mankind or any creature, but happiness. This then is all which any person can, in strictness of speaking, be said to have a right to. We can, therefore, owe no man any thing, but only to further and promote his happiness, according to our abilities. And, therefore, a disposition and endeavour to do good to all with whom we have to do, in the degree and manner which the different relations we stand in to them require, is a discharge of all the obligations we are under to them.

As human nature is not one simple uniform thing, but a composition of various parts, body, spirit, appetites, particular passions, and affections; for each of which reasonable self-love would lead men to have due regard, and make suitable provision: so society consists of various parts, to which we stand in different respects and relations; and just benevolence would as surely lead us to have due regard to each of these, and behave as the respective relations require. Reasonable good-will, and right behaviour towards our fellow-creatures, are in a manner the same: only that the former expresseth the principle as it is in the mind; the latter, the principle as it were become external, *i. e.* exerted in actions.

And so far as temperance, sobriety, and moderation in sensual pleasures, and the contrary vices, have any respect to our fellow-creatures, any influences upon their quiet, welfare, and happiness; as they always have a real, and often a near influence upon it; so far it is manifest those virtues may be produced by the love of our neighbour, and that the contrary vices would be prevented by it. Indeed, if men's regard to themselves will not restrain them from excess, it may be thought little probable, that their love to others will be sufficient: but the reason is, that their love to others is not, any more than the regard to themselves, just, and in its due degree. There are, however, manifest instances of persons kept sober and temperate from regard to their affairs, and the welfare of those who depend upon them. And it is obvious to every one, that habitual excess, a dissolute course of life, implies a general neglect of the duties we owe towards our friends, our families, and our country.

From hence it is manifest, that the common virtues, and the common vices of mankind, may be traced up to benevolence, or the want of it. And this entitles the precept, "Thou shalt love thy neighbour as thyself," to the pre-eminence given to it; and is a justification of the apostle's

assertion, that all other commandments are comprehended
in it; whatever cautions and restrictions* there are, which
might require to be considered, if we were to state particularly and at length, what is virtue and right behaviour in
mankind. But,

Secondly, It might be added, that in a higher and more
general way of consideration, leaving out the particular nature of creatures, and the particular circumstances in which
they are placed, benevolence seems in the strictest sense to
include in it all that is good and worthy; all that is good,
which we have any distinct particular notion of.   We have
no clear conception of any positive moral attribute in the
Supreme Being, but what may be resolved up into goodness.
And, if we consider a reasonable creature, or moral agent,
without regard to the particular relations and circumstances

* For instance : as we are not competent judges what is, upon the
whole, for the good of the world, there may be other immediate ends
appointed us to pursue, besides that one of doing good, or producing
happiness.   Though the good of the creation be the only end of the
Author of it, yet he may have laid us under particular obligations,
which we may discern and feel ourselves under, quite distinct from a
perception that the observance or violation of them is for the happiness or misery of our fellow-creatures. And this is, in fact, the case.
For there are certain dispositions of mind, and certain actions, which
are in themselves approved or disapproved by mankind, abstracted
from the consideration of their tendency to the happiness or misery
of the world; approved or disapproved by reflection, by that principle
within, which is the guide of life, the judge of right and wrong.
Numberless instances of this kind might be mentioned.   There are
pieces of treachery, which in themselves appear base and detestable to
every one.   There are actions which, perhaps, can scarce have any
other general name given them than indecencies, which yet are odious
and shocking to human nature.   There is such a thing as meanness,
a little mind, which, as it is quite distinct from incapacity, so it raises
a dislike and disapprobation quite different from that contempt which
men are too apt to have of mere folly.   On the other hand, what we
call greatness of mind is the object of another sort of approbation
than superior understanding. Fidelity, honour, strict justice, are themselves approved in the highest degree, abstracted from the consideration of their tendency. Now, whether it be thought that each of these
are connected with benevolence in our nature, and so may be considered as the same thing with it ; or whether some of them be thought
an inferior kind of virtues and vices, somewhat like natural beauties
and deformities ; or, lastly, plain exceptions to the general rule ; thus
much, however, is certain, that the things now instanced in, and numberless others, are approved or disapproved by mankind in general, in
quite another view than as conducive to the happiness or misery of
the world.

in which he is placed, we cannot conceive any thing else to come in towards determining whether he is to be ranked in a higher or lower class of virtuous beings, but the higher or lower degree in which that principle, and what is manifestly connected with it, prevail in him.

That which we more strictly call piety, or the love of God, and which is an essential part of a right temper, some may perhaps imagine no way connected with benevolence; yet, surely, they must be connected, if there be indeed in being an object infinitely good. Human nature is so constituted, that every good affection implies the love of itself; *i. e.* becomes the object of a new affection in the same person. Thus, to be righteous, implies in it the love of righteousness; to be benevolent, the love of benevolence; to be good, the love of goodness; whether this righteousness, benevolence, or goodness, be viewed as in our own mind, or in another's: and the love of God, as a Being perfectly good, is the love of perfect goodness, contemplated in a being or person. Thus morality and religion, virtue and piety, will at last necessarily coincide, run up into one and the same point, and love will be in all senses *the end of the commandment.*

O Almighty God, inspire us with this divine principle; kill in us all the seeds of envy and ill-will; and help us, by cultivating within ourselves the love of our neighbour, to improve in the love of thee. Thou hast placed us in various kindreds, friendships, and relations, as the school of discipline for our affections: help us, by the due exercise of them, to improve to perfection, till all partial affection be lost in that entire, universal one, and thou, O God, shalt be all in all!

SERMON XIII. XIV.

UPON THE LOVE OF GOD.

MATTHEW xxii. 37.

Thou shalt love the Lord thy God with all thy heart, and with all thy soul, and with all thy mind.

EVERY body knows, you therefore need only just be put in mind, that there is such a thing as having so great horror of one extreme as to run insensibly and of course into the contrary; and that a doctrine's having been a shelter for enthusiasm, or made to serve the purposes of superstition, is no proof of the falsity of it: truth or right being somewhat real in itself, and so not to be judged of by its liableness to abuse, or by its supposed distance from, or nearness to, error. It may be sufficient to have mentioned this in general, without taking notice of the particular extravagances which have been vented under the pretence or endeavour of explaining the love of God; or how manifestly we are got into the contrary extreme, under the notion of a reasonable religion; so very reasonable as to have nothing to do with the heart and affections, if these words signify any thing, but the faculty by which we discern speculative truth.

By the love of God, I would understand all those regards, all those affections of mind, which are due immediately to him from such a creature as man, and which rest in him as their end. As this does not include servile fear, so neither will any other regards, how reasonable soever, which respect any thing out of, or besides, the perfection of

the Divine nature, come into consideration here. But all
fear is not excluded, because his displeasure is itself the
natural proper object of fear. Reverence, ambition of his
love and approbation, delight in the hope or consciousness
of it, come likewise into this definition of the love of God;
because he is the natural object of all those affections or
movements of mind, as really as he is the object of the
affection, which is in the strictest sense called love; and all
of them equally rest in him, as their end; and they may
all be understood to be implied in these words of our
Saviour, without putting any force upon them; for he is
speaking of the love of God and our neighbour as containing the whole of piety and virtue.

It is plain that the nature of man is so constituted as to
feel certain affections upon the sight or contemplation of
certain objects. Now, the very notion of affection implies
resting in its object as an end. And the particular affection to good characters, reverence and moral love of them,
is natural to all those who have any degree of real goodness
in themselves. This will be illustrated by the description
of a perfect character in a creature, and by considering the
manner in which a good man, in his presence, would be
affected towards such a character. He would of course
feel the affections of love, reverence, desire of his approbation, delight in the hope or consciousness of it. And surely
all this is applicable, and may be brought up to, that Being
who is infinitely more than an adequate object of all those
affections; whom we are commanded to " love with all our
heart, with all our soul, and with all our mind." And of these
regards towards Almighty God, some are more particularly
suitable to and becoming so imperfect a creature as man, in
this mortal state we are passing through; and some of them,
and perhaps other exercises of the mind, will be the employment and happiness of good men in a state of perfection.

This is a general view of what the following discourse
will contain. And it is manifest the subject is a real one:
there is nothing in it enthusiastical or unreasonable. And
if it be indeed at all a subject, it is one of the utmost
importance.

As mankind have a faculty by which they discern speculative truth, so we have various affections towards external
objects. Understanding and temper, reason and affection,

are as distinct ideas as reason and hunger; and, one would think, could no more be confounded. It is by reason that we get the ideas of several objects of our affections: but in these cases reason and affection are no more the same than sight of a particular object, and the pleasure or uneasiness consequent thereupon are the same. Now, as reason tends to and rests in the discernment of truth, the object of it—so the very nature of affection consists in tending towards, and resting in, its objects as an end. We do indeed often, in common language, say, that things are loved, desired, esteemed, not for themselves, but for somewhat further, somewhat out of and beyond them: yet, in these cases, whoever will attend, will see that these things are not in reality the objects of the affections, *i. e.* are not loved, desired, esteemed, but the somewhat further and beyond them. If we have no affections which rest in what are called their objects, then what is called affection, love, desire, hope in human nature, is only an uneasiness in being at rest—an unquiet disposition to action, progress, pursuit, without end or meaning. But if there be any such thing as delight in the company of one person, rather than of another, whether in the way of friendship, or mirth and entertainment, it is all one, if it be without respect to fortune, honour, or increasing our stores of knowledge, or any thing beyond the present time: here is an instance of an affection absolutely resting in its object as its end, and being gratified in the same way as the appetite of hunger is satisfied with food. Yet nothing is more common than to hear it asked, What advantage a man hath in such a course, suppose of study, particular friendships, or in any other? nothing, I say, is more common than to hear such a question put in a way which supposes no gain, advantage, or interest, but as a means to somewhat further: and if so, then there is no such a thing at all as real interest, gain, or advantage. This is the same absurdity with respect to life, as an infinite series of effects without a cause is in speculation. The gain, advantage, or interest, consists in the delight itself, arising from such a faculty's having its object: neither is there any such thing as happiness or enjoyment, but what arises from hence. The pleasures of hope and of reflection are not exceptions: the former being only this happiness anticipated—the latter the same

happiness enjoyed over again after its time. And even the
general expectation of future happiness can afford satisfaction only as it is a present object to the principle of self-
love.

It was doubtless intended that life should be very much
a pursuit to the gross of mankind. But this is carried so
much farther than is reasonable, that what gives immediate
satisfaction, *i. e.* our present interest, is scarce considered as
our interest at all. It is inventions, which have only a
remote tendency towards enjoyment, perhaps but a remote
tendency towards gaining the means only of enjoyment,
which are chiefly spoken of as useful to the world. And
though this way of thinking were just, with respect to the
imperfect state we are now in, where we know so little of
satisfaction without satiety, yet it must be guarded against
when we are considering the happiness of a state of perfection—which happiness being enjoyment, and not hope, must
necessarily consist in this, that our affections have their
objects, and rest in those objects as an end, *i. e.* be satisfied
with them. This will further appear in the sequel of this
discourse.

Of the several affections, or inward sensations, which
particular objects excite in man, there are some, the having
of which implies the love of them, when they are reflected
upon.* This cannot be said of all our affections, principles,
and motives of action. It were ridiculous to assert that a
man, upon reflection, hath the same kind of approbation of
the appetite of hunger, or the passion of fear, as he hath
good-will to his fellow-creatures. To be a just, a good, a
righteous man, plainly carries with it a peculiar affection to,
or love of justice, goodness, righteousness, when these
principles are the objects of contemplation. Now if a man
approves of or hath an affection to any principle, in and
for itself, incidental things allowed for, it will be the same
whether he views it in his own mind or in another—in himself or in his neighbour. This is the account of our

---

* St. Austin observes, *Amor ipse ordinate amandus est, quo bene
amatur quod amandum est, ut sit in nobis virtus qua vivitur bene, i. e.*
The affection which we rightly have for what is lovely, must ordinate
justly, in due manner, and proportion, become the object of a new
affection, or be itself beloved, in order to our being endued with that
virtue which is the principle of a good life. Civ. Dei. l. 15, c. 22.

approbation of our moral love and affection to good characters, which cannot but be in those who have any degrees of real goodness in themselves, and who discern and take notice of the same principle in others.

From observation of what passes within ourselves, our own actions, and the behaviour of others, the mind may carry on its reflections as far as it pleases—much beyond what we experience in ourselves or discern in our fellow-creatures. It may go on, and consider goodness as become an uniform continued principle of action, as conducted by reason, and forming a temper and character absolutely good and perfect, which is in a higher sense excellent, and proportionably the object of love and approbation.

Let us then suppose a creature perfect according to his created nature : let his form be human, and his capacities no more than equal to those of the chief of men : goodness shall be his proper character, with wisdom to direct it, and power, within some certain determined sphere of action, to exert it : but goodness must be the simple actuating principle within him; this being the moral quality which is amiable, or the immediate object of love, as distinct from other affections of approbation. Here then is a finite object for our mind to tend towards, to exercise itself upon : a creature, perfect according to his capacity, fixed, steady, equally unmoved by weak pity, or more weak fury and resentment, forming the justest scheme of conduct; going on undisturbed in the execution of it, through the several methods of severity and reward, towards his end—namely, the general happiness of all with whom he hath to do, as in itself right and valuable. This character, though uniform in itself, in its principle, yet exerting itself in different ways, or considered in different views, may, by its appearing variety, move different affections. Thus, the severity of justice would not affect us in the same way, as an act of mercy : the adventitious qualities of wisdom and power may be considered in themselves; and even the strength of mind which this immoveable goodness supposes, may likewise be viewed as an object of contemplation, distinct from the goodness itself. Superior excellence of any kind, as well as superior wisdom and power, is the object of awe and reverence to all creatures, whatever their moral character be; but so far as creatures of the lowest rank were good, so far the view of this character, as simply good, must appear amiable to them, be the object of, or beget love. Further, suppose we were conscious that this superior person so far approved of us, that we had nothing servilely to fear from him; that he was really our friend, and kind and good to us in particular, as he had occasionally intercourse with us, we must be other creatures than we are, or we could not but feel the same kind of satisfaction and enjoyment (whatever would be the degree of it) from this higher acquaintance and friendship, as we feel from common ones; the intercourse being real, and the persons equally present in both cases. We should have a more ardent desire to be approved by his better judgment, and a satisfaction in that approbation, of the same sort with what would be felt in respect to common persons, or be wrought in us by their presence.

Let us now raise the character, and suppose this creature, for we are still going on with the supposition of a creature, our proper guardian and governor; that we were in a progress of being towards somewhat further; and that this scheme of government was too vast for our capacities to comprehend; remembering still that he is perfectly good, and our friend as well as our governor. Wisdom, power, goodness, accidentally viewed any where, would inspire reverence, awe, love. And as these affections would be raised in higher or lower degrees, in proportion as we had occasionally more or less intercourse with the creature endued with those qualities, so this further consideration and knowledge, that he was our proper guardian and governor, would much more bring these objects and qualities home to ourselves; teach us they had a greater respect to us in particular; that we had a higher interest in that wisdom, and power, and goodness. We should, with joy, gratitude, reverence, love, trust, and dependence, appropriate the character, as what we had a right in, and make our boast in such our relation to it. And the conclusion of the whole would be, that we should refer ourselves implicitly to him, and cast ourselves entirely upon him. As the whole attention of life should be to obey his commands, so the highest enjoyment of it must arise from the contemplation of his character, and our relation to it, from a consciousness of his favour and approbation, and from the exercise of those affections towards him, which could not but be raised from his presence. A being who hath these attributes, who stands in this relation, and is thus sensibly present to the mind, must necessarily be the object of these affections. There is as real a correspondence between them, as between the lowest appetite of sense and its object.

That this Being is not a creature, but the Almighty God; that he is of infinite power, and wisdom, and goodness, does not render him less the object of reverence and love, than he would be, if he had those attributes only in a limited degree. The Being who made us, and upon whom we entirely depend, is the object of some regards. He hath given us certain affections of mind, which correspond to wisdom, power, goodness; i. e. which are raised upon view of those qualities. If, then, he be really wise, powerful, good, he is the natural object of those affections, which he hath endued us with, and which correspond to those attributes. That he is infinite in power, perfect in wisdom and goodness, makes no alteration; but only that he is the object of those affections raised to the highest pitch. He is not indeed to be discerned by any of our senses: " I go forward, but he is not there; and backward, but I cannot perceive him : on the left hand, where he doth work, but I cannot behold him : he hideth himself on the right hand that I cannot see him. Oh, that I knew where I might find him ! that I might come even to his seat."* But is he then afar off ? Does he not fill heaven and earth with his presence ? The presence of our fellow-creatures affects our senses, and our senses give us the knowledge of their presence ; which hath different kinds of influence upon us ; love, joy, sorrow, restraint, encouragement, reverence. However, this influence is not immediately from our senses, but from that knowledge. Thus, suppose a person neither to see nor hear another, not to know by any of his senses, but yet certainly to know that another was with him ; this knowledge might, and in many cases would, have one or more of the effects before mentioned. It is therefore not only reasonable, but also natural, to be affected with a presence, though it be not the object of our senses : whether it be, or be not, is merely an accidental circumstance, which needs not come

* Job xxiii.

into consideration ; it is the certainty that he is with us, and we with him, which hath the influence. We consider persons then as present, not only when they are within reach of our senses, but also when we are assured by any other means, that they are within such a nearness ; nay, if they are not, we can recall them to our mind, and be moved towards them as present. And must he, who is so much more intimately connected with us, that "in him we live, and move, and have our being," be thought too distant to be the object of our affections? We own and feel the force of amiable and worthy qualities of our fellow-creatures ; and can we be insensible to the contemplation of perfect goodness? Do we reverence the shadows of greatness here below? are we solicitous about honour, and esteem, and the opinion of the world? and shall we not feel the same with respect to him, whose are wisdom and power in their original; who "is the God of judgment, by whom actions are weighed?" Thus, love, reverence, desire of esteem, every faculty, every affection, tends towards, and is employed about its respective object in common cases : and must the exercise of them be suspended with regard to him alone, who is an object, an infinitely more than adequate object, to our most exalted faculties; him " of whom, and through whom, and to whom are all things ?"

As we cannot remove from this earth, or change our general business on it, so neither can we alter our real nature. Therefore, no exercise of the mind can be recommended, but only the exercise of those faculties you are conscious of. Religion does not demand new affections, but only claims the direction of those you already have, those affections you daily feel ; though unhappily confined to objects, not altogether unsuitable, but altogether unequal to them. We only represent to you the higher, the adequate objects of those very faculties and affections. Let the man of ambition go on still to consider disgrace as the greatest evil ; honour as his chief good. But disgrace, in whose estimation? Honour, in whose judgment? This is the only question. If shame, and delight in esteem, be spoken of as real, as any settled ground of pain or pleasure, both these must be in proportion to the supposed wisdom and worth of him by whom we are contemned or esteemed. Must it then be thought enthusiastical to speak of a sensibility of this sort, which shall have respect to an unerring judgment—to infinite wisdom ; when we are assured this unerring judgment, this infinite wisdom, does observe upon our actions ?

It is the same with respect to the love of God in the strictest and most confined sense. We only offer and represent the highest object of an affection, supposed already in your mind. Some degree of goodness must be previously supposed : this always implies the love of itself, an affection to goodness : the highest, the adequate object of this affection, is perfect goodness ; which, therefore, we are to " love with all our heart, with all our soul, and with all our strength." " Must we then, forgetting our own interest, as it were go out of ourselves, and love God for his own sake ?" No more forget your own interest, no more go out of yourselves, than when ye prefer one place, one prospect, the conversation of one man to that of another. Does not every affection necessarily imply, that the object of it be itself loved ? If it be not, it is not the object of the affection. You may and ought, if you can, but it is a great mistake to think you can love, or fear, or hate any thing, from consideration that such love, or fear, or hatred, may be a means of obtaining good or avoiding evil. But the question, whether we ought to love God for his sake or for our own, being a mere mistake in language ; the real question, which this is mistaken for, will, I suppose, be answered by observing, that the goodness of God already exercised towards us, our present dependence upon him, and our expectation of future benefits, ought, and have a natural tendency, to beget in us the affection of gratitude and greater love towards him, than the same goodness exercised towards others : were it only for this reason, that every affection is moved in proportion to the sense we have of the object of it : and we cannot but have a more lively sense of goodness, when exercised towards ourselves, than when exercised towards others. I added expectation of future benefits, because the ground of that expectation is present goodness.

Thus, Almighty God is the natural object of the several affections,—love, reverence, fear, desire of approbation. For though he is simply One, yet we cannot but consider him in partial and different views. He is in himself one

uniform Being, and for ever the same, without " variable-
ness or shadow of turning :" but his infinite greatness, his
goodness, his wisdom, are different objects to our mind.
To which is to be added, that from the changes in our own
characters, together with his unchangeableness, we cannot
but consider ourselves as more or less the objects of his
approbation, and really be so.　For if he approves what is
good, he cannot, merely from the unchangeableness of his
nature, approve what is evil.　Hence must arise more various movements of mind, more different kinds of affections.
And this greater variety also is just and reasonable in such
creatures as we are, though it respects a Being, simply one,
good, and perfect.　As some of these affections are most
particularly suitable to so imperfect a creature as man, in
this mortal state we are passing through ; so there may be
other exercises of mind, or some of these in higher degrees,
our employment and happiness in a state of perfection.

SERMON XIV.

CONSIDER then our ignorance, the imperfection of our
nature, our virtue, and our condition in this world, with
respect to an infinitely good and just Being, our Creator
and Governor, and you will see what religious affections of
mind are most particularly suitable to this mortal state we
are passing through.

Though we are not affected with any thing so strongly
as what we discern with our senses ; and though our nature
and condition require, that we be much taken up about
sensible things ; yet our reason convinces us that God is
present with us, and we see and feel the effects of his goodness : he is, therefore, the object of some regards.　The
imperfection of our virtue, joined with the consideration of
his absolute rectitude or holiness, will scarce permit that
perfection of love, which entirely casts out all fear : yet
goodness is the object of love to all creatures who have any

degree of it themselves; and consciousness of a real en-/ deavour to approve ourselves to him, joined with the consideration of his goodness, as it quite excludes servile dread and horror, so it is plainly a reasonable ground for hope of his favour. Neither fear, nor hope, nor love then are excluded; and one or another of these will prevail, according to the different views we have of God; and ought to prevail, according to the changes we find in our own character. There is a temper of mind made up of, or which follows from all three, fear, hope, love; namely, resignation to the divine will, which is the general temper belonging to this state, which ought to be the habitual frame of our mind and heart, and to be exercised at proper seasons more distinctly, in acts of devotion.

Resignation to the will of God is the whole of piety: it includes in it all that is good; and is a source of the most settled quiet and composure of mind. There is the general principle of submission in our nature. Man is not so constituted as to desire things, and be uneasy in the want of them, in proportion to their known value: many other considerations come in to determine the degrees of desire; particularly, whether the advantage we take a view of, be within the sphere of our rank. Who ever felt uneasiness upon observing any of the advantages brute creatures have over us? And yet it is plain they have several. It is the same with respect to advantages belonging to creatures of a superior order. Thus, though we see a thing to be highly valuable; yet, that it does not belong to our condition of being, is sufficient to suspend our desires after it, to make us rest satisfied without such advantage. Now, there is just the same reason for quiet resignation in the want of every thing equally unattainable, and out of our reach in particular, though others of our species be possessed of it. All this may be applied to the whole of life; to positive inconveniences as well as wants; not indeed to the sensations of pain and sorrow, but to all the uneasinesses of reflection, murmuring, and discontent. Thus is human nature formed to compliance, yielding submission of temper. We find the principles of it within us, and every one exercises it towards some objects or other; *i. e.* feels it with regard to some persons, and some circumstances. Now, this is an excellent foundation of a reasonable and religious resignation. Nature

teaches and inclines us to take up with our lot : the consideration, that the course of things is unalterable, hath a
tendency to quiet the mind under it, to beget a submission
of temper to it.   But when we can add, that this unalterable course is appointed and continued by infinite wisdom
and goodness ; how absolute should be our submission, how
entire our trust and dependence !

This would reconcile us to our condition; prevent all the
supernumerary troubles arising from imagination, distant
fears, impatience; all uneasiness, except that which necessarily arises from the calamities themselves we may be under.
How many of our cares should we by this means be dis-
burdened of!   Cares not properly our own, how apt soever
they may be to intrude upon us, and we to admit them; the
anxieties of expectation, solicitude about success and disappointment, which in truth are none of our concern.   How
open to every gratification would that mind be, which was
clear of these incumbrances !

Our resignation to the will of God may be said to be perfect, when our will is lost and resolved up into his; when
we rest in his will as our end, as being itself most just, and
right, and good.   And where is the impossibility of such
an affection to what is just, and right, and good, such a
loyalty of heart to the Governor of the universe, as shall
prevail over all sinister indirect desires of our own? Neither
is this at bottom any thing more than faith, and honesty,
and fairness of mind : in a more enlarged sense, indeed,
than those words are commonly used.   And as, in common
cases, fear and hope and other passions are raised in us by
their respective objects; so this submission of heart, and
soul, and mind, this religious resignation, would be as
naturally produced by our having just conceptions of
Almighty God, and a real sense of his presence with us.
In how long a degree soever this temper usually prevails
amongst men, yet it is a temper right in itself : it is what
we owe to our Creator ; it is particularly suitable to our
mortal condition, and what we should endeavour after for
our own sakes in our passage through such a world as this;
where is nothing upon which we can rest or depend ; nothing but what we are liable to be deceived and disappointed
in.   Thus we might " acquaint ourselves with God, and be
at peace." This is piety and religion in the strictest sense,

considered as a habit of mind: an habitual sense of God's presence with us; being affected towards him, as present, in the manner his superior nature requires from such a creature as man: this is to walk with God.

Little more need be said of devotion or religious worship, than that it is this temper exerted into act. The nature of it consists in the actual exercise of those affections towards God, which are supposed habitual in good men. He is always equally present with us: but we are so much taken up with sensible things, that " lo, he goeth by us, and we see him not: he passeth on also, but we perceive him not."* Devotion is retirement, from the world he has made, to him alone : it is to withdraw from the avocations of sense, to employ our attention wholly upon him as upon an object actually present, to yield yourselves up to the influence of the Divine presence, and to give full scope to the affections of gratitude, love, reverence, trust, and independence; of which infinite power, wisdom, and goodness, is the natural and only adequate object. We may apply to the whole of the devotion those words of the Son of Sirach: " When you glorify the Lord, exalt him as much as you can ; for even yet will he far exceed : and when you exalt him, put forth all your strength, and be not weary: for you can never go far enough." Our most raised affections of every kind cannot but fall short and be disproportionate, when an infinite Being is the object of them. This is the highest exercise and employment of mind, that a creature is capable of. As this divine service and worship is itself absolutely due to God, so also is it necessary in order to a further end ; to keep alive upon our minds a sense of his authority, a sense that, in our ordinary behaviour amongst men, we act under him as our Governor and Judge.

Thus you see the temper of mind respecting God, which is particularly suitable to a state of imperfection; to creatures in a progress of being towards somewhat further.

Suppose, now, this something further attained : that we were arrived at it: what a perception will it be, to see, and know, and feel, that our trust was not vain, our dependence not groundless ? That the issue, event, and consum-

* Job ix. 11.

mation, came out such as fully to justify and answer that
resignation ? If the obscure view of the Divine perfection,
which we have in this world, ought in just consequence to
beget an entire resignation ; what will this resignation be
exalted into, " when we shall see face to face, and know as
we are known ?" If we cannot form any distinct notion of
that perfection of the love of God, which casts out all fear;
of that enjoyment of him, which will be the happiness of
good men hereafter: the consideration of our wants and capacities of happiness, and that he will be an adequate
supply to them, must serve us instead of such distinct
conception of the particular happiness itself.

Let us then suppose a man entirely disengaged from business and pleasure, sitting down alone and at leisure, to
reflect upon himself and his own condition of being. He
would immediately feel that he was by no means complete
of himself, but totally insufficient for his own happiness.
One may venture to affirm, that every man hath felt this,
whether he hath again reflected upon it or not. It is feeling this deficiency, that they are unsatisfied with themselves,
which makes men look out for assistance from abroad ;
and which has given rise to various kinds of amusements,
altogether needless any otherwise than as they serve to fill
up the blank spaces of time, and so hinder their feeling
this deficiency, and being uneasy with themselves. Now, if
these external things we take up with were really an adequate supply to this deficiency of human nature, if by their
means our capacities and desires were all satisfied and filled
up ; then it might be truly said, that we had found out the
proper happiness of man ; and so might sit down satisfied,
and be at rest in the enjoyment of it. But if it appears
that the amusements, which men usually pass their time
in, are so far from coming up to, or answering our notions
and desires of happiness or good, that they are really no
more than what they are commonly called, somewhat to
pass away the time ; i. e. somewhat which serves to turn
us aside from, and prevent our attending to this our internal poverty and want ; if they serve only, or chiefly, to
suspend, instead of satisfying our conceptions and desires of
happiness ; if the want remains, and we have found out
little more than barely the means of making it less sensible : then we are still to seek for somewhat to be an

adequate supply to it. It is plain that there is a capacity in the nature of man, which neither riches, nor honours, nor sensual gratifications, nor any thing in this world, can perfectly fill up, or satisfy; there is a deeper and more essential want than any of these things can be the supply of. Yet surely there is a possibility of somewhat, which may fill up all our capacities of happiness; somewhat, in which our souls may find rest; somewhat which may be to us that satisfactory good we are inquiring after. But it cannot be any thing which is valuable only as it tends to some further end. Those, therefore, who have got this world so much into their hearts, as not to be able to consider happiness as consisting in any thing but property and possessions, which are only valuable as the means to somewhat else, cannot have the least glimpse of the subject before us; which is the end not the means; the thing itself, not somewhat in order to it. But if you can lay aside that general, confused, undeterminate notion of happiness, as consisting in such possessions: and fix in your thoughts, that it really can consist in nothing but in a faculty's having its proper object: you will clearly see, that in the coolest way of consideration, without either the heat of fanciful enthusiasm, or the warmth of real devotion, nothing is more certain than that an infinite Being may himself be, if he pleases, the supply to all the capacities of our nature. All the common enjoyments of life are from the faculties he hath endued us with, and the objects he hath made suitable to them. He may himself be to us infinitely more than all these: he may be to us all that we want. As our understanding can contemplate itself, and our affections be exercised upon themselves by reflection, so may each be employed in the same manner upon any other mind: and since the Supreme Mind, the Author and Cause of all things, is the highest possible object to himself, he may be an adequate supply to all the faculties of our souls; a subject to our understanding, and an object to our affections.

Consider, then: when we shall have put off this mortal body, when we shall be divested of sensual appetites, and those possessions which are now the means of gratification shall be of no avail; when this restless scene of business and vain pleasures, which now diverts us from ourselves, shall be all over: we, our proper self, shall still remain: we

shall still continue the same creatures we are, with wants
to be supplied, and capacities of happiness. We must
have faculties of perception, though not sensitive ones;
and pleasure or uneasiness from our perceptions, as now
we have.

There are certain ideas, which we express by the words,
order, harmony, proportion, beauty, the furthest removed
from any thing sensual. Now, what is there in those intellectual images, forms of ideas, which begets that approbation, love, delight, and even rapture, which is seen in
some persons' faces upon having those objects present
to their minds? "Mere enthusiasm!"—Be it what it will:
there are objects, works of nature, and of art, which all
mankind have delight from, quite distinct from their affording gratification to sensual appetites; and from quite another
view of them, than as being for their interest and further
advantage. The faculties from which we are capable of
these pleasures, and the pleasures themselves, are as natural, and as much to be accounted for, as any sensual appetite whatever, and the pleasure from its gratification.
Words, to be sure, are wanting upon this subject: to say
that every thing of grace and beauty throughout the whole
of nature, every thing excellent and amiable, shared in differently lower degrees by the whole creation, meet in the
Author and Cause of all things; this is an adequate, and
perhaps improper way of speaking of the Divine nature:
but it is manifest, that absolute rectitude, the perfection of
being, must be in all senses, and in every respect, the
highest object to the mind.

In this world it is only the effects of wisdom, and power,
and greatness which we discern: it is not impossible, that
hereafter the qualities themselves in the Supreme Being
may be the immediate object of contemplation. What
amazing wonders are opened to view by late improvements?
What an object is the universe to a creature, if there be a
creature who can comprehend its system? But it must be
an infinitely higher exercise of the understanding, to view
the scheme of it in that Mind which projected it, before its
foundations were laid. And surely we have meaning to
the words, when we speak of going further, and viewing,
not only this system in his mind, but the wisdom and intelligence itself from whence it proceeded. The same may

2

be said of power. But since wisdom and power are not God, (he is a wise, a powerful Being,) the Divine nature may therefore be a further object to the understanding. It is nothing to observe that our senses give us but an imperfect knowledge of things: effects themselves, if we knew them thoroughly, would give us but imperfect notions of wisdom and power; much less of his being in whom they reside. I am not speaking of any fanciful notion of seeing all things in God, but only representing to you, how much a higher object to the understanding an infinite Being himself is, than the things which he has made; and this is no more than saying, that the Creator is superior to the works of his hands.

This may be illustrated by a low example. Suppose a machine, the sight of which would raise, and discoveries in its contrivance gratify, our curiosity; the real delight, in this case, would arise from its being the effect of skill and contrivance. The skill in the mind of the artificer would be a higher object, if we had any senses or ways to discern it. For, observe, the contemplation of that principle, faculty, or power, which produced any effect, must be a higher exercise of the understanding than the contemplation of the effect itself. The cause must be a higher object to the mind than the effect.

But whoever considers distinctly what the delight of knowledge is, will see reason to be satisfied that it cannot be the chief good of man: all this, as it is applicable, so it was mentioned with regard to the attribute of goodness. I say, goodness. Our being and all our enjoyments are the effects of it: just men bear its resemblance: but how little do we know of the original, of what it is in itself? Recall what was before observed concerning the affection to moral characters; which, in how low a degree soever, yet is plainly natural to man, and the most excellent part of his nature: suppose this improved, as it may be improved, to any degree whatever, "in the spirits of just men made perfect:" and then suppose that they had a real view of that "righteousness, which is an everlasting righteousness:" of the conformity of the Divine will to the law of truth, in which the moral attributes of God consist; of that goodness in the sovereign mind, which gave birth to the universe; add, what will be true of all good men hereafter, a con-

sciousness of having an interest in what they are contem·
plating; suppose them able to say, "This God is our God
for ever and ever:" would they be any longer to seek for
what was their chief happiness, their final good? Could the
utmost stretch of their capacities look further? Would not
infinite perfect goodness be their very end, the last end and
object of their affections; beyond which they could neither
have, nor desire; beyond which they could not form a wish
or thought?

Consider wherein that presence of a friend consists
which has often so strong an effect, as wholly to possess the
mind, and entirely suspend all other affections and regards
and which itself affords the highest satisfaction and enjoy·
ment. He is within reach of the senses. Now, as our
capacities of perception improve, we shall have, perhaps by
some faculty entirely new, a perception of God's presence
with us, in a nearer and stricter way; since it is certain he
is more intimately present with us than any thing else can
be. Proof of the existence and presence of any being, is
quite different from the immediate perception, the consciousness of it. What then will be the joy of heart, which
his presence, and "the light of his countenance," who is the
life of the universe, will inspire good men with, when they
shall have a sensation, that he is the sustainer of their being;
that they exist in him; when they shall feel his influence to
cheer, and enliven, and support their frame, in a manner of
which we have now no conception? He will be, in a literal
sense, "their strength and their portion for ever."

When we speak of things so much above our comprehension, as the employment and happiness of a future state,
doubtless it behoves us to speak with all modesty and distrust of ourselves. But the Scripture represents the happiness of that state, under the notions of "seeing God,
seeing him as he is, knowing as we are known, and seeing
face to face." These words are not general or undetermined, but express a particular determinate happiness.
And I will be bold to say, that nothing can account for, or
come up to these expressions but only this, that God himself will be an object to our faculties; that he himself will
be our happiness, as distinguished from the enjoyments of
the present state, which seem to arise, not immediately from
him, but from the objects he has adapted to give us delight.

3

To conclude : let us suppose a person tired with care and sorrow, and the repetition of vain delights which fill up the round of life ; sensible that every thing here below, in its best estate, is altogether vanity. Suppose him to feel that deficiency of human nature, before taken notice of ; and to be convinced that God alone was the adequate supply to it. What could be more applicable to a good man, in this state of mind, or better express his present wants and distant hopes, his passage through this world as a progress towards a state of perfection, than the following passages in the devotions of the royal prophet ? They are plainly, in a higher and more proper sense, more applicable to this than they could be to any thing else. "I have seen an end of all perfection. Whom have I in heaven but thee ? and there is none upon earth that I desire in com- parison of thee. My flesh and my heart faileth : but God is the strength of my heart, and my portion for ever. Like as the hart desireth the water-brooks, so longeth my soul after thee. O God. My soul is athirst for God ; yea, even for the living God ; when shall I come to appear before him ? how excellent is thy loving kindness, O God ! And the children of men shall put their trust under the shadow of thy wings. They shall be satisfied with the plenteous- ness of thy house : and thou shalt give them drink of thy pleasures, as out of the river. For with thee is the well of life : and in thy light shall we see light. Blessed is the man whom thou choosest, and receivest unto thee : he shall dwell in thy court, and shall be satisfied with the pleasures of thy house, even of the holy temple. Blessed is the people, O Lord, that can rejoice in thee : they shall walk in the light of thy countenance. Their delight shall be daily in thy name ; and in thy righteousness shall they make their boast. For thou art the glory of their strength ; and in thy loving kindness they shall be exalted. As for me, I will behold thy presence in righteousness ; and when I awake up after thy likeness, I shall be satisfied with it. Thou shalt show me the path of life ; in thy presence is the fulness of joy, and at thy right hand there is pleasure for evermore."

I

SERMON XV.

UPON THE IGNORANCE OF MAN.

ECCLES. viii. 16, 17.

*When I applied mine heart to know wisdom, and to see
the business that is done upon the earth; then I beheld
all the work of God, that a man cannot find out the
work that is done under the sun; because though a man
labour to seek it out, yet he shall not find it; yea, further,
though a wise man think to know it, yet shall he not be
able to find it.*

THE writings of Solomon are very much taken up with
reflections upon human nature and human life; to which
he hath added, in this book, reflections upon the constitution of things. And it is not improbable, that the little
satisfaction, and the great difficulties he met with in his
researches into the general constitution of nature, might be
the occasion of his confining himself, so much as he hath
done, to life and conduct. However, upon that joint review, he expresses great ignorance of the works of God,
and the method of his providence in the government of the
world; great labour and weariness in the search and
observation he had employed himself about; and great disappointment, pain, and even vexation of mind, upon that
which he had remarked of the appearance of things, and
of what was going forward upon this earth. This whole
review and inspection, and the result of it, sorrow, perplexity,
a sense of his necessary ignorance, suggests various reflections to his mind. But, notwithstanding all this ignorance

and dissatisfaction, there is somewhat upon which he assuredly rests and depends : somewhat which is the conclusion of the whole matter, and the only concern of man. Following this his method and train of reflection, let us consider,

I. The assertion of the text, the ignorance of man ; that the wisest and most knowing cannot comprehend the ways and works of God : and then,

II. What are the just consequences of this observation and knowledge of our own ignorance, and the reflections which it leads us to.

I. The wisest and most knowing cannot comprehend the works of God, the methods and designs of his providence in the creation and government of the world.

Creation is absolutely and entirely out of our depth, and beyond the extent of our utmost reach. And yet, it is as certain that God made the world, as it is certain that effects must have a cause. It is indeed in general no more than effects, that the most knowing are acquainted with : for as to causes, they are as entirely in the dark as the most ignorant. What are the laws by which matter acts upon matter, but certain effects ; which some, having observed to be frequently repeated, have reduced to general rules ? The real nature and essence of beings likewise is what we are altogether ignorant of. All these things are so entirely out of our reach, that we have not the least glimpse of them. And we know little more of ourselves, than we do of the world about us : how we were made, how our being is continued and preserved, what the faculties of our minds are, and upon what the power of exercising them depends. "I am fearfully and wonderfully made : marvellous are thy works, and that my soul knoweth right well." Our own nature, and the objects we are surrounded with, serve to raise our curiosity ; but we are quite out of a condition of satisfying it. Every secret which is disclosed, every discovery which is made, every new effect which is brought to view, serves to convince us of numberless more which remain concealed, and which we had before no suspicion of. And what if we were acquainted with the whole creation, in the same way, and as thoroughly as we are with any single object in it ? What would all this natural knowledge amount to ? It

must be a low curiosity indeed which such superficial
knowledge would satisfy. On the contrary, would it not
serve to convince us of our ignorance still, and to raise our
desire of knowing the nature of things themselves; the
author, the cause, and the end of them?

As to the government of the world: though from consideration of the final causes which cóme within our knowledge; of characters, personal merit and demérit; of the favour
and disapprobation, which respectively are due and belong to
the righteous and the wicked, and which, therefore, must
necessarily be in a mind which sees things as they really
are; though, I say, from hence we may know somewhat
concerning the designs of Providence in the government of
the world, enough to enforce upon us religion and the practice of virtue; yet, since the monarchy of the universe is a
dominion unlimited in extent, and everlasting in duration,
the general system of it must necessarily be quite beyond
our comprehension. And, since there appears such a subordination and reference of the several parts to each other,
as to constitute it properly one administration or government, we cannot have a thorough knowledge of any part,
without knowing the whole. This surely should convince
us, that we are much less competent judges of the very
small part which comes under our notice in this world, than
we are apt to imagine. "No heart can think upon these
things worthily: and who is able to conceive his way? It
is a tempest which no man can see: for the most part of
his works are hid. Who can declare the works of his justice? For his covenant is afar off, and the trial of all
things is in the end;" *i. e.* the dealings of God with the
children of men are not yet completed, and cannot be judged
of by that part which is before us. "So that a man cannot
say, This is worse than that: for in time they shall be well
approved. Thy faithfulness, O Lord, reacheth unto the
clouds: thy righteousness standeth like the strong mountains: thy judgments are like the great deep. He hath made
every thing beautiful in his time: also he hath set the
world in their heart; so that no man can find out the work
that God maketh from the beginning to the end." And
thus St. Paul concludes a long argument upon the various
dispensations of Providence: "O the depth of the riches

both of the wisdom and knowledge of God! How un-
searchable are his judgments, and his ways past finding
out! For who hath known the mind of the Lord?"

Thus, the scheme of Providence, the ways and works of
God, are too vast, of too large extent for our capacities.
There is, as I may speak, such an expanse of power, and
wisdom, and goodness, in the formation and government of
the world, as is too much for us to take in or comprehend.
Power, and wisdom, and goodness, are manifest to us in all
those works of God which come within our view: but
there are likewise infinite stores of each poured forth
throughout the immensity of the creation; no part of which
can be thoroughly understood, without taking in its reference and respect to the whole: and this is what we
have not faculties for.

And as the works of God, and his scheme of government, are above our capacities thoroughly to comprehend;
so there possibly may be reasons which originally made it
fit that many things should be concealed from us, which
we have perhaps natural capacities of understanding; many
things concerning the designs, methods, and ends of divine
Providence in the government of the world. There is no
manner of absurdity in supposing a veil on purpose drawn
over some scenes of infinite power, wisdom, and goodness,
the sight of which might some way or other strike us too
strongly; or that better ends are designed and served by
their being concealed, than could be by their being exposed
to our knowledge. The Almighty may cast clouds and
darkness round about him, for reasons and purposes of
which we have not the least glimpse or conception.

However, it is surely reasonable, and what might have
been expected, that creatures in some stage of their being,
suppose in the infancy of it, should be placed in a state of
discipline and improvement, where their patience and submission is to be tried by afflictions, where temptations are
to be resisted, and difficulties gone through in the discharge
of their duty. Now, if the greatest pleasures and pains
of the present life may be overcome and suspended, as they
manifestly may, by hope and fear, and other passions and
affections; then the evidence of religion, and the sense of
the consequences of virtue and vice, might have been such,
as entirely in all cases to prevail over those afflictions, diffi-

culties and temptations; prevail over them so, as to render them absolutely none at all. But the very notion itself now mentioned, of a state of discipline and improvement, necessarily excludes such sensible evidence and conviction of religion, and of the consequences of virtue and vice. Religion consists in submission and resignation to the Divine will. Our condition in this world is a school of exercise for this temper: and our ignorance, the shallowness of our reason, the temptations, difficulties, afflictions, which we are exposed to, all equally contribute to make it so. The general observation may be carried on; and whoever will attend to the thing will plainly see, that less sensible evidence with less difficulty in practice, is the same as more sensible evidence, with greater difficulty in practice. Therefore, difficulties in speculation as much come into the notion of a state of discipline, as difficulties in practice: and so the same reason or account is to be given of both. Thus, though it is indeed absurd to talk of the greater merit of assent, upon little or no evidence, than upon demonstration; yet the strict discharge of our duty, with less sensible evidence, does imply in it a better character, than the same diligence in the discharge of it upon more sensible evidence. This fully accounts for and explains that assertion of our Saviour, "Blessed are they that have not seen, and yet have believed;"* have become Christians and obeyed the gospel, upon less sensible evidence, than that which Thomas, to whom he is speaking, insisted upon.

But after all, the same account is to be given, why we were placed in these circumstances of ignorance, as why nature has not furnished us with wings: namely, that we were designed to be inhabitants of this earth. I am afraid we think too highly of ourselves: of our rank in the creation, and of what is due to us. What sphere of action, what business is assigned to man, that he has not capacities and knowledge fully equal to? It is manifest he has reason, and knowledge, and faculties, superior to the business of the present world: faculties which appear superfluous, if we do not take in the respect which they have to somewhat further, and beyond it. If to acquire knowledge were our proper end, we should indeed be but poorly provided: but if somewhat else be our business and duty, we

* John xx. 29.

may, notwithstanding our ignorance, be well enough furnished for it; and the observation of our ignorance may be of assistance to us in the discharge of it.

II. Let us, then, consider what are the consequences of this knowledge and observation of our own ignorance, and the reflection it leads us to.

First, We may learn from it, with what temper of mind a man ought to inquire into the subject of religion; namely, with expectation of finding difficulties, and with a disposition to take up and rest satisfied with any evidence whatever which is real.

He should beforehand expect things mysterious, and such as he will not be able thoroughly to comprehend, or go to the bottom of. To expect a distinct comprehensive view of the whole subject, clear of difficulties and objections, is to forget our nature and condition; neither of which admit of such knowledge with respect to any science whatever. And to inquire with this expectation, is not to inquire as a man, but as one of another order of creatures.

Due sense of the general ignorance of man would also beget in us a disposition to take up and rest satisfied with any evidence whatever which is real. I mention this as the contrary to a disposition, of which there are not wanting instances, to find fault with and reject evidence because it is not such as was desired. If a man were to walk by twilight, must he not follow his eyes as much as if it were broad day and clear sunshine? Or, if he were obliged to take a journey by night, would he not "give heed to any light shining in the darkness, till the day should break and the day-star arise?" It would not be altogether unnatural for him to reflect how much better it were to have daylight: he might, perhaps, have great curiosity to see the country round about him; he might lament that the darkness concealed many extended prospects from his eyes, and wish for the sun to draw away the veil: but how ridiculous would it be to reject with scorn and disdain the guidance and direction which that lesser light might afford him, because it was not the sun itself! If the make and constitution of man, the circumstances he is placed in, or the reason of things, affords the least hint or intimation that virtue is the law he is born under, scepticism itself should lead him to the most strict and inviolable practice of it; that he may

not make a dreadful experiment of leaving the course of
life marked out for him by nature, whatever that nature be,
and entering paths of his own, of which he can know
neither the dangers nor the end. For, though no danger be
seen, yet darkness, ignorance, and blindness are no manner of security.

Secondly, Our ignorance is the proper answer to many
things which are called objections against religion ; particularly to those which arise from the appearances of evil
and irregularity in the constitution of nature and the
government of the world. In all other cases it is thought
necessary to be thoroughly acquainted with the whole of a
scheme, even one of so narrow a compass as those which
are formed by men, in order to judge of the goodness or
badness of it : and the most slight and superficial view of
any human contrivance comes abundantly nearer to a
thorough knowledge of it than that part which we know of
the government of the world does to the general scheme
and system of it ; to the whole set of laws by which it is
governed. From our ignorance of the constitution of things,
and the scheme of Providence in the government of the
world ; from the reference the several parts have to each
other, and to the whole ; and from our not being able to
see the end and the whole ; it follows that however perfect things are, they must even necessarily appear to us
otherwise, less perfect than they are.*

* Suppose some very complicated piece of work, some system or
constitution, formed for some general end, to which each of the parts
had a reference. The perfection or justness of this work or constitution would consist in the reference and respect which the several
parts have to the general design. This reference of parts to the
general design may be infinitely various, both in degree and kind.
Thus, one part may only contribute and be subservient to another ;
this to a third ; and so on through a long series, the last part of which
alone may contribute immediately and directly to the general design.
Or a part may have this distant reference to the general design, and
may also contribute immediately to it. For instance : if the general
design or end for which the complicated frame of nature was brought
into being, is happiness, whatever affords present satisfaction, and
likewise tends to carry on the course of things, hath this double
respect to the general design. Now, suppose a spectator of that
work or constitution was in a great measure ignorant of such various
reference to the general end, whatever that end be, and that upon a
very slight and partial view which he had of the work, several things
appeared to his eye as disproportionate and wrong, others just and

Thirdly, Since the constitution of nature, and the methods and designs of Providence in the government of the world, are above our comprehension, we should acquiesce in, and rest satisfied with our ignorance, turn our thoughts from that which is above and beyond us, and apply ourselves to that which is level to our capacities, and which is our real business and concern. Knowledge is not our proper happiness. Whoever will in the least attend to the thing, will see that it is the gaining, not the having of it, which is the entertainment of the mind. Indeed, if the proper happiness of man consisted in knowledge, considered as a possession or treasure, men who are possessed of the largest share would have a very ill time of it, as they would be infinitely more sensible than others of their poverty in this respect. Thus, "He who increases knowledge would" eminently " increase sorrow." Men of deep research and curious inquiry should just be put in mind, not to mistake what they are doing. If their discoveries serve the cause of virtue and religion, in the way of proof, motive to practice, or assistance in it ; or if they tend to render life less unhappy, and promote its satisfactions ; then they are most usefully employed : but bringing things to light, alone and of itself, is of no manner of use, any otherwise than as an entertainment or diversion. Neither is this at all amiss, if it does not take up the time which should be employed in better works. But it is evident that there is another mark set up for us to aim at ; another end appointed us to direct our lives to : an end which the most knowing may fail of,

beautiful : what would he gather from these appearances ? He would immediately conclude there was a probability, if he could see the whole reference of the parts appearing wrong to the general design, that this would destroy the appearance of wrongness and disproportion : but there is no probability that the reference would destroy the particular right appearances, though that reference might show the things already appearing just, to be so likewise in a higher degree or another manner. There is a probability that the right appearances were intended : there is no probability that the wrong appearances were. We cannot suspect irregularity and disorder to be designed. The pillars of a building appear beautiful ; but their being likewise its support, does not destroy that beauty : there still remains a reason to believe that the architect intended the beautiful appearance, after we have found out the reference, support. It would be reasonable for a man of himself to think thus upon the first piece of architecture he ever saw.

and the most ignorant arrive at. " The secret things belong unto the Lord our God ; but those things which are
revealed belong unto us, and to our children for ever, that
we may do all the words of this law."   Which reflection of
Moses, put in general terms, is, that the only knowledge
which is of any avail to us is that which teaches us our duty,
or assists us in the discharge of it.   The economy of the
universe, the course of nature, almighty power exerted in
the creation and government of the world, is out of our
reach.   What would be the consequence, if we could really
get an insight into these things, is very uncertain ; whether
it would assist us in, or divert us from, what we have to do
in this present state.   If, then, there be a sphere of knowledge, of contemplation and employment, level to our capacities, and of the utmost importance to us, we ought
surely to apply ourselves with all diligence to this our proper business, and esteem every thing else nothing, nothing
as to us, in comparison of it.   Thus Job, discoursing of
natural knowledge, how much it is above us, and of wisdom
in general, says, " God understandeth the way thereof, and
he knoweth the place thereof.   And unto man he said,
Behold, the fear of the Lord, this is wisdom, and to depart
from evil is understanding."   Other orders of creatures
may perhaps be let into the secret counsels of heaven, and
have the designs and methods of Providence, in the creation
and government of the world, communicated to them ; but
this does not belong to our rank or condition.   " The fear
of the Lord, and to depart from evil," is the only wisdom
which man should aspire after, as his work and business.
The same is said, and with the same connexion and con-
text, in the conclusion of the book of Ecclesiastes.   Our
ignorance, and the little we can know of other things, affords a reason why we should not perplex ourselves about
them ; but no way invalidates that which is the " conclusion
of the whole matter, Fear God, and keep his commandments : for this is the whole concern of man."   So that
Socrates was not the first who endeavoured to draw men
off from labouring after, and laying stress upon, other
knowledge, in comparison of that which related to morals.
Our province is virtue and religion, life and manners : the
science of improving the temper, and making the heart better.   This is the field assigned us to cultivate ; how much

it has lain neglected is indeed astonishing. Virtue is demonstrably the happiness of man ; it consists in good actions,
proceeding from a good principle, temper, or heart. Overt
acts are entirely in our power. What remains is, that we
learn to keep our heart; to govern and regulate our passions, mind, affections : that so we may be free from the
impotencies of fear, envy, malice, covetousness, ambition ;
that we may be clear of these, considered as vices seated
in the heart, considered as constituting a general wrong
temper ; from which general wrong frame of mind, all the
mistaken pursuits, and far the greatest part of the unhappiness of life, proceed. He who should find out one rule to
assist us in this work, would deserve infinitely better of
mankind than all the improvers of other knowledge put
together.

Lastly. Let us adore that infinite wisdom, and power,
and goodness, which is above our comprehension. " To
whom hath the root of wisdom been revealed ? Or who
hath known her wise counsels ? There is one wise, and
greatly to be feared ; the Lord sitting upon his throne. He
created her, and saw her, and numbered her, and poured
her out upon all his works." If it be thought a considerable thing to be acquainted with a few, a very few, of the
effects of infinite power and wisdom, the situation, bigness,
and revolution of some of the heavenly bodies, what sentiments should our minds be filled with concerning him who
appointed to each its place, and measure, and sphere of
motion, all which are kept with the most uniform constancy ?
Who " stretched out the heavens, and telleth the number of the stars, and calleth them all by their names.
Who laid the foundations of the earth, who comprehendeth
the dust of it in a measure, and weigheth the mountains in
scales, and the hills in a balance." And when we have
recounted all the appearances which come within our view,
we must add, " Lo, these are parts of his ways; but how
little a portion is heard of him ? Canst thou by searching
find out God? Canst thou find out the Almighty unto
perfection ? It is as high as heaven ; what canst thou do ?
Deeper than hell ; what canst thou know ?"

The conclusion is, that in all lowliness of mind we set
lightly by ourselves : that we form our temper to an

implicit submission to the Divine Majesty ; beget within ourselves an absolute resignation to all the methods of his providence, in his dealings with the children of men : that, in the deepest humility of our souls, we prostrate ourselves before him, and join in that celestial song, " Great and marvellous are thy works, Lord God Almighty! Just and true are thy ways, thou King of saints ! Who shall not fear thee, O Lord, and glorify thy name ?"

SIX SERMONS,

PREACHED UPON PUBLIC OCCASIONS.

SERMON I.

PREACHED BEFORE THE INCORPORATED SOCIETY FOR THE PROPA-
GATION OF THE GOSPEL IN FOREIGN PARTS,

At their Anniversary Meeting in the Parish Church of St. Mary-le-Bow.

On Friday, February 16, 1738-9.

MATTHEW xxiv. 14.

*And this gospel of the kingdom shall be preached in all the
world, for a witness unto all nations.*

THE general doctrine of religion, that all things are
under the direction of one righteous Governor, having been
established by repeated revelations in the first ages of the
world, was left with the bulk of mankind, to be honestly
preserved pure and entire, or carelessly forgotten, or wilfully
corrupted. And though reason, almost intuitively, bare
witness to the truth of this moral system of nature, yet it
soon appeared, that "they did not like to retain God in
their knowledge," * as to any purposes of real piety. Natural
religion became gradually more and more darkened with
superstition, little understood, less regarded in practice; and

* Rom. i. 28.

the face of it scarce discernible at all, in the religious es-
tablishments of the most learned, polite nations. And how
much soever could have been done towards the revival of it
by the light of reason, yet this light could not have discovered what so nearly concerned us, that important part in
the scheme of this world which regards a Mediator; nor
how far the settled constitution of its government admitted
repentance to be accepted for remission of sins, after the
obscure intimations of these things, from tradition, were
corrupted or forgotten. One people, indeed, had clearer
notices of them, together with the genuine scheme of natural
religion preserved in the primitive and subsequent revelations committed to their trust; and were designed to be a
witness of God, and a providence to the nations around
them: but this people also had corrupted themselves and
their religion to the highest degree that was consistent with
keeping up the form of it.

In this state of things, when Infinite Wisdom saw proper,
the general doctrine of religion was authoritatively repub-
lished in its purity; and the particular dispensation of Providence, which this world is under, manifested to all men,
even " the dispensation of the grace of God towards us,"[*]
as sinful, lost creatures, to be recovered by repentance
through a Mediator, who was " to make reconciliation for
iniquity, and to bring in everlasting righteousness,"[†] and at
length established that new state of things foretold by the
prophet Daniel, under the character of " a kingdom, which
the God of heaven would set up, and which should never
be destroyed."[‡] This, including a more distinct account of
the instituted means whereby Christ the Mediator would
" gather together in one, the children of God that were
scattered abroad,"[§] and conduct them to " the place he is
gone to prepare for them;"[||] is the gospel of the kingdom,
which he here foretells, and elsewhere commands, should
" be preached in all the world, for a witness unto all nations.
and it first began to be spoken by the Lord, and was confirmed unto us by them that heard him; God also bearing
them witness, both with signs and wonders, and with
divers miracles, and gifts of the Holy Ghost, according to

---

* Eph. iii. 2.   † Dan. ix. 24.   ‡ Dan. ii. 44.
§ John xi. 52. || John xiv. 2, 3.

his own will:"* by which means it was spread very widely among the nations of the world, and became a witness unto them.

When thus much was accomplished, as there is a wonderful uniformity in the conduct of Providence, Christianity was left with Christians, to be transmitted down pure and genuine, or to be corrupted and sunk; in like manner as the religion of nature had been left with mankind in general. There was however this difference, that by an institution of external religion fitted for all men, (consisting in a common form of Christian worship, together with a standing ministry of instruction and discipline,) it pleased God to unite Christians in communities or visible Churches, and all along to preserve them, over a great part of the world; and thus perpetuate a general publication of the gospel. For these communities, which together make up the Catholic visible church, are, *First*, The repositories of the written oracles of God: and in every age have preserved and published them in every country, where the profession of Christianity has obtained. Hence it has come to pass, and it is a thing very much to be observed in the appointment of Providence, that even such of these communities as, in a long succession of years, have corrupted Christianity the most, have yet continually carried, together with their corruptions, the confutation of them; for they have everywhere preserved the pure original standard of it, the Scripture, to which recourse might have been had, both by the deceivers, and the deceived, in every successive age. *Secondly*, any particular church, in whatever place established, is like " a city that is set on a hill, which cannot be hid,"† inviting all who pass by to enter into it. All persons to whom any notices of it come, have, in Scripture language, the " kingdom of God come nigh unto them." They are reminded of that religion which natural conscience attests the truth of; and they may, if they will, be instructed in it more distinctly, and likewise in the gracious means whereby sinful creatures may obtain eternal life; that chief and final good, which all men, in proportion to their understanding and integrity, even in all ages and countries of the heathen world, were ever in pursuit of. And, *lastly*, Out of these churches

* Heb. ii. 3, 4. † Matt. v. 14.

have all along gone forth persons, who have preached the gospel in remote places with greater or less good effect : for the establishment of any profession of Christianity, how-ever corrupt, I call a good effect, whilst accompanied with a continued publication of the Scripture, notwithstanding it may for some time lie quite neglected.

From these things, it may be worth observing, by the way, appears the weakness of all pleas for neglecting the public service of the church. For though a man prays with as much devotion and less interruption at home, and reads better sermons there, yet that will by no means excuse the neglect of his appointed part in keeping up the profession of Christianity amongst mankind. And this neglect, were it universal, must be the dissolution of the whole visible church, *i. e.* of all Christian communities ; and so must pre-vent those good purposes which were intended to be an-swered by them ; and which they have, all along, answered over the world. For we see, that by their means the event foretold in the text, which began in the preaching of Christ and the apostles, has been carried on, more or less, ever since, and is still carrying on ; these being the providential means of its progress. And it is, I suppose, the completion of this event which St. John had a representation of under the figure of " an angel flying in the midst of heaven, hav-ing the everlasting gospel to preach unto them that dwell on the earth, and to every nation, and kindred, and tongue, and people."*

Our Lord adds in the text, that this should be " for a witness unto them ;" for an evidence of their duty, and an admonition to perform it. But what would be the effect, or success of the general preaching of the gospel, is not here mentioned. And therefore the prophecy of the text is not parallel to those others in Scripture, which seemed to foretell the glorious establishment of Christianity in the last days ; nor does it appear that they are coincident, otherwise than as the former of these events must be supposed pre-paratory to the latter. Nay, it is not said here, that God " willeth all men should be saved, and come unto the know-ledge of the truth,"† though this is the language of Scrip-ture elsewhere. The text declares no more, than that it was

* Rev. xiv. 6.   † Tim. ii. 4.

the appointment of God, in his righteous government over the world, that "the gospel of the kingdom should be preached for a witness unto it."

The visible constitution and course of nature, the moral law written in our hearts, the positive institutions of religion, and even any memorial of it, are all spoken of in Scripture under this, or the like denomination : so are the prophets, apostles, and our Lord himself. They are all witnesses, for the most part unregarded witnesses, in behalf of God, to mankind. They inform us of his being and providence, and of the particular dispensation of religion which we are under : and continually remind us of them ; and they are equally witnesses of these things, whether we regard them or not. Thus after a declaration that Ezekiel should be sent with a divine message to the children of Israel, it is added, " and they, whether they will hear, or whether they will forbear, (for they are a rebellious house) yet shall know that there hath been a prophet among them."* And our Lord directs the seventy disciples, upon their departure from any city which refused to receive them, to declare, "notwithstanding, be ye sure of this, that the kingdom of God is come nigh unto you."† The thing intended in both these passages is, that which is expressed in the text by the word "witness." And all of them together evidently suggest thus much, that the purposes of Providence are carried on, by the preaching of the gospel, to those who reject it as well as to those who embrace it. It is indeed true, "God willeth that all men should be saved," yet, from the unalterable constitution of his government, the salvation of every man cannot but depend upon his behaviour, and, therefore, cannot but depend upon himself ; and is necessarily his own concern, in a sense in which it cannot be another's. All this the Scripture declares in a manner the most forcible and alarming : " Can a man be profitable unto God, as he that is wise may be profitable unto himself? Is it any pleasure to the Almighty that thou art righteous? or is it gain to him that thou makest thy ways perfect?‡ If thou be wise thou shalt be wise for thyself : but if thou scornest, thou alone shalt bear it.§ He that heareth, let

* Ezek. ii. 5, 7. † Luke x. 11.
‡ Job xxii. 2, 3. § Prov. ix. 12.

him hear : and he that forbeareth let him forbear."* And
again, " he that hath ears to hear let him hear : but if any
man be ignorant, *i. e.* wilfully, let him be ignorant."† To
the same purpose are those awful words of the angel, in
the person of him to whom " all judgment is committed.‡
He that is unjust, let him be unjust still : and he that is
filthy, let him be filthy still : and he that is righteous, let
him be righteous still : and he that is holy, let him be holy still.
And. behold, I come quickly ; and my reward is with me, to
give every man according as his work shall be."§ The
righteous government of the world must be carried on ; and
of necessity, men shall remain the subjects of it, by being
examples of its mercy, or of its justice. " Life and death
are set before them, and whether they like shall be given
unto them."‖ They are to make their choice, and abide
by it ; but whichsoever their choice be, the gospel is equally
a witness to them ; and the purposes of Providence are answered by this witness of the gospel.

From the foregoing view of things we should be reminded, that the same reasons which make it our duty to instruct the ignorant in the relation which the light of nature
shows they stand in to God their Maker, and in the obligations of obedience ; resignation, and love to him which
arise out of that relation, make it our duty likewise to instruct them in all those other relations which revelation informs us of, and in the obligations of duty which arise out
of them. And the reasons for instructing men in both
these, are of the very same kind as for communicating any
useful knowledge whatever. God if he had so pleased
could indeed miraculously have revealed every religious
truth which concerns mankind, to every individual man ;
and so he could have every common truth ; and thus have
superseded all use of human teaching in either. Yet, he
has not done this : but has appointed, that men should be
instructed by the assistance of their fellow creatures in
both. Further : though all knowledge from reason is as
really from God, as revelation is, yet this last is a distinguished favour to us, and naturally strikes us with the
greatest awe, and carries in it an assurance, that those things

* Ezek. iii. 27.   † 1 Cor. xiv. 38.   ‡ John v. 22.
§ Rev. xxii. 11, 12.   ‖ Eccles. xv. 17.

which we are informed of by it, are of the utmost importance to us to be informed of. Revelation, therefore, as it demands to be received with a regard and reverence peculiar to itself, so it lays us under obligations, of a like peculiar sort, to communicate the light of it. Further still : it being an indispensable law of the gospel, that Christians should unite in religious communities, and these being intended for* repositories of the written " oracles of God," for standing memorials of religion to unthinking men, and for the propagation of it in the world ; Christianity is very particularly to be considered as a trust deposited with us in behalf of others, in behalf of mankind, as well as for our own instruction. No one has a right to be called a Christian, who doth not do somewhat in his station towards the discharge of this trust ; who doth not, for instance, assist in keeping up the profession of Christianity where he lives. And it is an obligation but little more remote, to assist in doing it in our factories abroad ; and in the colonies to which we are related, by their being peopled from our own mother country, and subjects, indeed very necessary ones, to the same government with ourselves ; and nearer yet is the obligation upon such persons, in particular, as have the intercourse of an advantageous commerce with them.

Of these our colonies, the slaves ought to be considered as inferior members, and therefore to be treated as members of them, and not merely as cattle or goods, the property of their masters. Nor can the highest property possible to be acquired in these servants, cancel the obligation to take care of their religious instruction. Despicable as they may appear in our eyes, they are the creatures of God, and of the race of mankind, for whom Christ died : and it is inexcusable to keep them in ignorance of the end for which they were made, and the means whereby they may become partakers of the general redemption. On the contrary, if the necessity of the case requires that they may be treated with the very utmost rigour that humanity will at all permit, as they certainly are ; and, for our advantage, made as miserable as they well can be in the present world ; this surely heightens our obligation to put them into as advantageous a situation as we are able, with regard to another.

* Page 164.

The like charity we owe to the natives; owe to them in a much stricter sense than we are apt to consider, were it only from neighbourhood and our having gotten possessions in their country. For incidental circumstances of this kind appropriate all the general obligations of charity to particular persons, and make such and such instances of it the duty of one man rather than another. We are most strictly bound to consider these poor uninformed creatures, as being in all respects of one family with ourselves, the family of mankind; and instruct them in our " common salvation;"* that they may not pass through this stage of their being like brute beasts, but be put into a capacity of moral improvements, how low soever they must remain as to others, and so into a capacity of qualifying themselves for a higher state of life hereafter.

All our affairs should be carried on in the fear of God, in subserviency to his honour, and the good of mankind. And thus navigation and commerce should be consecrated to the service of religion, by being made the means of propagating it in every country with which we have any intercourse. And the more widely we endeavour to spread its light and influence, as the fore-mentioned circumstances, and others of the like kind, open and direct our way, the more faithful shall we be judged in the discharge of that trust† which is committed to us as Christians, when our Lord shall require an account of it.

And it may be some encouragement to cheerful perseverance in these endeavours, to observe, not only that they are our duty, but also that they seem the means of carrying on a great scheme of Providence, which shall certainly be accomplished. For " the everlasting gospel shall be preached to every nation :‡ and the kingdoms of this world shall become the kingdoms of our Lord, and of his Christ."§

However, we ought not to be discouraged in this good work, though its future success were less clearly foretold; and though its effect now in reforming mankind, appeared to be as little as our adversaries pretend. They indeed, and perhaps some others, seem to require more than either

---

* Jude 3.   † Page 125.
‡ Rev. xiv. 6.   § Rev. xi. 15.

experience or scripture give ground to hope for, in the present course of the world. But the bare establishment of Christianity in any place, even the external form and profession of it, is a very important and valuable effect. It is a serious call upon men to attend to the natural, and the revealed doctrine of religion. It is a standing publication of the gospel, and renders it a witness to them; and by this means the purposes of Providence are carrying on, with regard to remote ages, as well as to the present. " Cast thy bread upon the waters : for thou shall find it after many days. In the morning sow thy seed, and in the evening withhold not thine hand; for thou knowest not whether shall prosper, either this or that, or whether they both shall be alike good."* We can look but a very little way into the connexions and consequences of things : our duty is to spread the incorruptible seed as widely as we can, and leave it to " God to give the increase."† Yet thus much we may be almost assured of, that the gospel, wherever it is planted, will have its genuine effect upon some few; upon more, perhaps, than are taken notice of in the hurry of the world. There are, at least, a few persons in every country and successive age, scattered up and down, and mixed among the rest of mankind; who, not being corrupted past amendment, but having within them the principles of recovery, will be brought to a moral and religious sense of things, by the establishment of Christianity where they live ; and then will be influenced by the peculiar doctrines of it, in proportion to the integrity of their minds, and to the clearness, purity, and evidence, with which it is offered them. Of these our Lord speaks in the parable of the sower, "as understanding the word, and bearing fruit, and bringing forth, some an hundred fold, some sixty, some thirty."‡ One might add, that these persons, in proportion to their influence, do at present better the state of things ; better it even in the civil sense, by giving some check to that avowed profligateness, which is a contradiction to all order and government, and, if not checked, must be the subversion of it.

These important purposes, which are certainly to be expected from the good work before us, may serve to show

* Eccles. xi. 1, 6.   † 1 Cor. iii. 6.   ‡ Matt. xiii. 23.

how little weight there is in that objection against it, from
the want of those miraculous assistances with which the first
preachers of Christianity proved its truth.   The plain state
of the case is, that the gospel, though it be not in the same
degree a witness to all who have made it known to them ;
yet in some degree is so to all.   Miracles, to the spectators
of them, are intuitive proofs of its truth : but the bare
preaching of it is a serious admonition to all who hear it, to
attend to the notices which God has given of himself by the
light of nature ; and, if Christianity be preached with its
proper evidence, to submit to its peculiar discipline and laws :
if not, to inquire honestly after its evidence in proportion to
their capacities.   And there are persons of small capacities
for inquiry and examination, who yet are wrought upon by it
to "deny ungodliness and worldly lusts, and live soberly,
righteously, and godly in this present world,"* in expectation
of a future judgment by Jesus Christ.   Nor can any Christian who understands his religion object that these persons
are Christians without evidence ; for he cannot be ignorant
who has declared, that "if any man will do his will, he shall
know of the doctrine, whether it be of God."†   And, since
the whole end of Christianity is to influence the heart and
actions, were an unbeliever to object in that manner, he
should be asked, whether he would think it to the purpose
to object against persons of like capacities, that they are
prudent without evidence, when, as is often the case, they
are observed to manage their worldly affairs with discretion.

The design before us being therefore in general unexcep-
tionably good, it were much to be wished, that serious men
of all denominations would join in it.   And let me add,
that the foregoing view of things affords distinct reasons
why they should.   For, first, by so doing, they assist in a
work of the most useful importance, that of spreading over
the world the Scripture itself, as a divine revelation ; and
it cannot be spread under this character, for a continuance,
in any country, unless Christian churches be supported there,
but will always, more or less, so long as such churches
subsist : and therefore, their subsistence ought to be provided for.   In the next place, they should remember, that
if Christianity is to be propagated at all, which they

* Tit. ii. 12, 13.   † John vii. 17.

acknowledge it should, it must be in some particular form of profession. And though they think ours liable to objections, yet it is possible they themselves may be mistaken; and whether they are or no, the very nature of society requires some compliance with others. And whilst, together with our particular form of Christianity, the confessed standard of Christian religion, the Scripture, is spread; and especially whilst every one is freely allowed to study it, and worship God according to his conscience; the evident tendency is, that genuine Christianity will be understood and prevail. Upon the whole, therefore, these persons would do well to consider how far they can with reason satisfy themselves in neglecting what is certainly right, on account of what is doubtful whether it be wrong; and when the right is of so much greater consequence one way, than the supposed wrong can be on the other.

To conclude: atheistical immorality and profaneness, surely, is not better in itself, nor less contrary to the design of revelation, than superstition. Nor is superstition the distinguishing vice of the present age, either at home or abroad. But if our colonies abroad are left without a public religion, and the means of instruction, what can be expected, but that from living in a continual forgetfulness of God, they will at length cease to believe in him, and so sink into stupid atheism? And there is too apparent danger of the like horrible depravity at home, without the like excuse for it. Indeed amongst creatures naturally formed for religion, yet so much under the powers of imagination, so apt to deceive themselves, and so liable to be deceived by others, as men are, superstition is an evil which can never be out of sight. But even against this, true religion is a great security, and the only one. True religion takes up that place in the mind which superstition would usurp, and so leaves little room for it; and likewise lays us under the strongest obligations to oppose it. On the contrary, the danger of superstition cannot but be increased by the prevalence of irreligion, and by its general prevalence the evil will be unavoidable. For the common people wanting a religion, will of course take up with almost any superstition which is thrown in their way; and, in process of time, amidst the infinite vicissitudes of the political world, the leaders of parties will certainly be able to serve them-

selves of that superstition, whatever it be, which is getting
ground; and will not fail to carry it on to the utmost length
their occasions require. The general nature of the thing
shows this, and history and fact confirm it. But what
brings the observation home to ourselves is, that the great
superstition of which this nation, in particular, has reason
to be afraid, is imminent; and the ways in which we may
very supposably be overwhelmed by it, obvious. It is,
therefore, wonderful, those people, who seem to think there
is but one evil in life, that of superstition, should not see
that atheism and profaneness must be the introduction of it.
So that, in every view of things, and upon all accounts,
irreligion is at present our chief danger. Now the several
religious associations among us, in which many good men
have of late united, appear to be providentially adapted to
this present state of the world. And as all good men are
equally concerned in promoting the end of them, to do it
more effectually, they ought to unite in promoting it; which
yet is scarce practicable upon any new models, and quite
impossible upon such as every one would think unexceptionable. They ought therefore to come into those already
formed to their hands, and even take advantage of any
occasion of union, to add mutual force to each other's
endeavours in furthering their common end, however they
may differ as to the best means, or any thing else subordinate to it. Indeed there are well-disposed persons, who
much want to be admonished, how dangerous a thing it is to
discountenance what is good, because it is not better, and
hinder what they approve, by raising prejudices against
some under-part of it. Nor can they assist in rectifying
what they think capable of amendment, in the manner of
carrying on these designs, unless they will join in the designs
themselves, which they must acknowledge to be good and
necessary ones. For what can be called good and necessary by Christians, if it be not so to support Christianity
where it must otherwise sink, and propagate it where it
must otherwise be unknown; to restrain abandoned, bare-
faced vice, by making useful examples, at least of shame,
perhaps of repentance; and to take care of the education of
such children, as otherwise must be even educated in wickedness, and trained up to destruction? Yet good men, separately, can do nothing proportionable to what is wanting

in any of these ways; but their common, united endeavours, may do a great deal in all of them.

And besides the particular purposes which these several religious associations serve, the more general ones, which they all serve, ought not to be passed over. Every thing of this kind is, in some degree, a safeguard to religion—an obstacle, more or less, in the way of those who want to have it extirpated out of the world. Such societies also contribute more especially towards keeping up the face of Christianity among ourselves; and by their obtaining here, the gospel is rendered more and more a witness to us.

And if it were duly attended to, and had its genuine influence upon our minds, there would be no need of persuasions to impart the blessing; nor would the means of doing it be wanting. Indeed, the present income of this Society, which depends upon voluntary contributions, with the most frugal management of it, can in no wise sufficiently answer the bare purposes of our charter; but the nation, or even this opulent city itself, has it in its power to do so very much more, that I fear the mention of it may be thought too severe a reproof, since so little is done. But if the gospel had its proper influence upon the Christian world in general, as it is the centre of trade and the seat of learning, a very few ages, in all probability, would settle Christianity in every country, without miraculous assistances. For scarce any thing else, I am persuaded, would be wanting to effect this, but laying it before men in its divine simplicity, together with an exemplification of it in the lives of Christian nations. " The unlearned and unbelievers, falling down on their faces, would worship God, and report that God is in us of a truth."*

* 1 Cor. xiv. 24, 25.

K

SERMON II.

PREACHED BEFORE THE RIGHT HON. THE LORD MAYOR, THE COURT
OF ALDERMEN, THE SHERIFFS, AND THE GOVERNORS OF THE
SEVERAL HOSPITALS OF THE CITY OF LONDON,

At the Parish Church of St. Bridget, on Monday in Easter-Week, 1740.

PROVERBS xxii. 2.

*The rich and poor meet together: the Lord is the maker
of them all.*

THE constitution of things being such, that the labour of
one man, or the united labour of several, is sufficient to
procure more necessaries than he or they stand in need of,
which it may be supposed was in some degree the case,
even in the first ages; this immediately gave room for
riches to arise in the world, and for men's acquiring them
by honest means—by diligence, frugality, and prudent management. Thus some would very soon acquire greater
plenty of necessaries than they had occasion for, and others,
by contrary means, or by cross accidents, would be in want
of them. And he who should supply their wants, would
have the property in a proportionable labour of their hands,
which he would scarce fail to make use of instead of his
own, perhaps, together with them, to provide future necessaries in greater plenty. Riches then were first bestowed
upon the world, as they are still continued in it, by the
blessing of God upon the industry of men, in the use of
their understanding and strength. Riches themselves have

always this source; though the possession of them is conveyed to particular persons by different channels. Yet still, " the hand of the diligent maketh rich,"* and, other circumstances being equal, in proportion to its diligence.

But to return to the first rich man; whom we left in possession of dependents, and plenty of necessaries for himself and them. A family would not be long in this state, before conveniences, somewhat ornamental, and for entertainment, would be wanted, looked for, and found out. And, by degrees, these secondary wants, and inventions for the supply of them, the fruits of leisure and ease, came to employ much of men's time and leisure. Hence a new species of riches came into the world, consisting of things which it might have done well enough without, yet thought desirable, as affording pleasure to the imagination, or the senses. And these went on increasing, till, at length, the superfluities of life took in a vast larger compass of things than the necessaries of it. Thus luxury made its inroad, and all the numerous train of evils its attendants; of which poverty, as bad an one as we may account it, is far from being the worst. Indeed the hands of the generality must be employed, and a very few of them would now be sufficient to provide the world with necessaries; and therefore the rest of them must be employed about what may be called superfluities; which could not be, if these superfluities were not made use of. Yet the desire of such things insensibly becomes immoderate, and the use of them almost, of course, degenerates into luxury; which, in every age, has been the dissipation of riches, and in every sense, the ruin of those who were possessed of them; and therefore cannot be too much guarded against by all opulent cities. And as men sink into luxury, as much from fashion as direct inclination, the richer sort together may easily restrain this vice, in almost what degree they please; and a few of the chief of them may contribute a great deal towards the restraining it.

It is to be observed further, concerning the progress of riches, that had they continued to consist only in the possession of the things themselves which were necessary, and of the things themselves which were, upon their own

* Prov. x. 4.

K 2

account, otherwise desirable; this, in several respects, must
have greatly embarrassed trade and commerce, and have set
bounds to the increase of riches in all hands, as well as
confined them in the hands of a few.   But, in process of
time, it was agreed to substitute somewhat more lasting and
portable, which should pass every where, in commerce, for
real natural riches: as sounds had before, in language, been
substituted for thoughts.   And this general agreement, (by
what means soever it became general,) that money should
answer all things, together with some other improvements,
gave full scope for riches to increase in the hands of particular persons, and likewise to circulate into more hands.
Now this, though it was not the first origin of covetousness, yet it gives greater scope, encouragement, and temptation to covetousness, than it had before.   And there is
moreover the appearance, that this artificial kind of riches,
money, has begot an artificial kind of passion for them;
both which follies well-disposed persons must, by all means,
endeavour to keep clear of.   For, indeed, "the love of riches
is the root of all evil;"* though riches themselves may be
made instrumental in promoting every thing that is good.

The improvement of trade and commerce has made
another change, just hinted at, and I think, a very happy
one, in the state of the world, as it has enlarged the middle
rank of people; many of which are, in good measure, free
from the vices of the highest and the lowest part of mankind.   Now these persons must remember, that whether, in
common language, they do, or do not, pass under the denomination of rich, yet they really are so, with regard to
the indigent and necessitous; and that, considering the great
numbers which make up this middle rank among us, and
how much they mix with the poor, they are able to contribute very largely to their relief, and have in all respects a
very great influence over them.

You have heard now the origin and progress of what
this great city so much abounds with, riches: as far as
I had occasion to speak of these things.   For this brief account of them has been laid before you for the sake of the
good admonitions it afforded.   Nor will the admonitions be
thought foreign to the charities, which we are endeavouring

* 1 Tim. vi. 10.

to promote. For these must necessarily be less, and the occasions for them greater, in proportion as industry should
abate, or luxury increase. And the temper of covetousness
is, we all know, directly contrary to that of charity, and
eats out the very heart of it. Then, lastly, there are good
sort of people, who really want to be told, that they are included in the admonitions to be given to the rich, though
they do see others richer than themselves.

The ranks of rich and poor being thus formed, they
meet together : they continue to make up one society. The
mutual want which they still have of each other, still
unites them inseparably. But they meet upon a footing of
great inequality. For, as Solomon expresses it in brief,
and with much force, " the rich ruleth over the poor." *
And thus their general intercourse, with the superiority on
one hand, and dependence on the other, are in no sort accidental, but arise necessarily from a settled providential
disposition of things, for their common good. Here, then,
is a real standing relation between the rich and the poor.
And the former must take care to perform the duties
belonging to their part of it ; for these chiefly the present
occasion leads me to speak to, from regard to Him who
placed them in that relation to the poor, from whence
those duties arise, and who " is the Maker of them all."

What these duties are, will easily be seen, and the obligations to them strongly enforced, by a little further reflection upon both these ranks, and the natural situation which
they are in with respect to each other.

The lower rank of mankind go on, for the most part, in
some track of living, into which they got by direction or
example ; and to this their understanding and discourse, as
well as labour, are greatly confined. Their opinions of
persons and things they take upon trust : their behaviour
has very little in it original, or of home-growth ; very little
which may not be traced up to the influence of others, and
less which is not capable of being changed by such influence. Then, as God has made plentiful provision for all
his creatures, the wants of all, even of the poorest, might
be supplied, so far as it is fit they should, by a proper distribution of it. This being the condition of the lower part

* Prov. xxii. 7.

of mankind, consider now what influence, as well as power, their superiors must, from the nature of the case, have over them. For they can instil instruction, and recommend it in a peculiar manner by their example, and enforce it still further with favour and discouragement of various kinds. And experience shows, that they do direct and change the course of the world as they please. Not only the civil welfare, but the morals and religion of their fellow-creatures, greatly depend upon them ; much more indeed than they would, if the common people were not wanting to their duty. All this is evidently true of superiors in general ; superiors in riches, authority, and understanding, taken together: And need I say how much of this whole superiority goes along with riches? It is no small part of it which arises out of riches themselves. In all governments, particularly in our own, a good share of civil authority accompanies them. Superior or natural understanding may, or may not; but when it does not, yet riches afford great opportunities for improvement, and may command information : which things together are equivalent to natural superiority of understanding.

But I am sure you will not think I have been reminding you of these advantages of riches, in order to beget in you that complacency and trust in them, which you find the Scripture every where warning you against. No : the importance of riches, this their power and influence, affords the most serious admonition in the world to those who are possessed of them. For it shows, how very blameable even their carelessness in the use of that power and influence must be : since it must be blameable in a degree proportionate to the importance of what they are thus careless about.

But it is not only true, that the rich have the power of doing a great deal of good, and must be highly blameable for neglecting to do it; but it is moreover true, that this power is given them by way of trust, in order to their keeping down that vice and misery, with which the lower people would otherwise be quite over-run. For without instruction and good influence, they, of course, grow rude and vicious, and reduce themselves to the utmost distresses, often to very terrible ones, without deserving much blame. And to these must be added their unavoidable distresses, which yet admit

of relief.   This their case plainly requires that some natural
provision should be made for it: as the case of children
does, who, if left to their own ways, would almost infallibly
ruin themselves.   Accordingly, Providence has made provision for this case of the poor; not only by forming their
minds peculiarly apt to be influenced by their superiors, and
giving those superior abilities to direct and relieve them,
but also by putting the latter under the care and protection
of the former; for this is plainly done, by means of that
intercourse of various kinds between them, which, in the
natural course of things, is unavoidably necessary.   In the
primitive ages of the world, the manner in which "the rich
and poor met together," was in families.   Rich men had
the poor for their servants; not only a few for the offices
about their persons, and for the care of what we now call
domestic affairs, but great numbers also for the keeping of
their cattle, the tillage of their fields, for working up their
wool into furniture and vestments of necessary use, as well
as ornament, and for preparing them those many things at
home, which now pass through a multitude of unknown
poor hands successively, and are by them prepared, at a
distance, for the use of the rich.   The instruction of these
large families, and the oversight of their morals and religion,
plainly belonged to the heads of them.   And that obvious
humanity, which every one feels, must have induced them
to be kind to all whom they found under their roof, in
sickness and in old age.   In this state of the world, the
relation between the rich and the poor could not but be
universally seen and acknowledgèd.   Now indeed it is less
in sight, by means of artificial methods of carrying on business, which yet are not blameable.   But the relation still
subsists, and the obligations arising out of it; and cannot
but remain the same, whilst the rich have the same want of
the poor, and make the same use of them, though not so
immediately under their eye: and whilst the instruction,
and manners, and good or bad state of the poor, really depend in so great a degree upon the rich, as all these things
evidently do; partly in their capacity of magistrates, but
very much also in their private capacity.   In short, He
who has distributed men into these different ranks, and at
the same time united them into one society, in such sort as
men are united, has, by this constitution of things, formally

put the poor under the superintendency and patronage of
the rich. The rich then are charged, by natural providence, as much as by revealed appointment, with the care
of the poor : not to maintain them idle; which, were it
possible they could be so maintained, would produce greater
mischiefs than those which charity is to prevent ; but to take
care, that they maintain themselves by their labour, or,
in case they cannot, then to relieve them; to restrain
their vices, and form their minds to virtue and religion.
This is a trust; yet it is not a burden, but a privilege,
annexed to riches. And if every one discharged his share
of the trust faithfully, whatever be his share of it, the
world would be quite another place from what it is. But
that cannot be, till covetousness, debauchery, and every
vice, be unknown among the rich. Then, and not before,
will the manners of the poor be, in all respects, what
they ought to be, and their distresses find the full relief
which they ought to find. And, as far as things of this
sort can be calculated, in proportion to the right behaviour
of persons whom God has placed in the former of these
ranks, will be the right behaviour and good condition of
those who are cast into the latter. Every one of ability,
then, is to be persuaded to do somewhat towards this,
keeping up a sense of virtue and religion among the poor,
and relieving their wants; each as much as he can be persuaded to. Since the generality will not part with their
vices, it were greatly to be wished they would bethink
themselves, and do what good they are able, so far only as
is consistent with them. A vicious rich man cannot pass
through life without doing an incredible deal of mischief,
were it only by his example and influence ; besides neglecting the most important obligations, which arise from his
superior fortune. Yet still, the fewer of them he neglects,
and the less mischief he does, the less share of the vices
and miseries of his inferiors will lie at his door ; the less will
be his guilt and punishment. But conscientious persons of
this rank must revolve again and again in their minds, how
great the trust is which God has annexed to it. They
must each of them consider impartially, what is his own
particular share of that trust, which is determined by his
situation, character, and fortune together; and then set
himself to be as useful as he can, in those particular ways

which he finds thus marked out for him. This is exactly the precept of St. Peter: "As every man hath received the gift, even so minister the same one to another, as good stewards of the manifold grace of God."* And as rich men, by a right direction of their greater capacity, may entitle themselves to a greater reward; so, by a wrong direction of it, or even by great negligence, they may become "partakers of other men's sins,"† and chargeable with other men's miseries. For if there be at all any measures of proportion, any sort of regularity and order in the administration of things, it is self-evident, that "unto whomsoever much is given, of him shall be much required: and to whom much is committed, of him shall more be demanded."‡

But still it is to be remembered, that every man's behaviour is his own concern, for every one must give an account of his own works; and that the lower people are very greatly to blame in yielding to any ill influence, particularly following the ill example of their superiors; though these are more to blame in setting them such an example. For, as our Lord declares, in the words immediately preceding those just mentioned, "That servant which knew his Lord's will, and prepared not himself, neither did according to his will, shall be beaten with many stripes. But he that knew not, and did commit things worthy of stripes, shall be beaten with few stripes."§ Vice is itself of ill-desert, and therefore shall be punished in all; though its ill-desert is greater or less, and so shall be its punishment, in proportion to men's knowledge of God and religion; but it is in the most literal sense true, that "he who knew not his Lord's will, and committed things worthy of stripes, shall be beaten, though with few stripes." For it being the discernment that such and such actions are evil, which renders them vicious in him who does them, ignorance of other things, though it may lessen, yet it cannot remit the punishment of such actions in a just administration, because it cannot destroy the guilt of them; much less can corrupt deference and regard to the example of superiors, in matters of plain duty and sin, have this effect. Indeed the

* 1 Pet. iv. 10.   † 1 Tim. v. 22.
‡ Luke xii. 48.   § Luke xii. 47, 48.

lowest people know very well, that such ill example affords
no reason why they should do ill; but they hope it will be
an excuse for them, and thus deceive themselves to their
ruin; which is a forcible reason why their superiors should
not lay this snare in their way.

All this approves itself to our natural understanding,
though it is by means of Christianity chiefly, that it is thus
enforced upon our consciences. And Christianity, as it is
more than a dispensation of goodness, in the general notion
of goodness, even a dispensation of forgiveness, of mercy,
and favour on God's part, does in a peculiar manner
heighten our obligations to charity among ourselves. "In
this was manifested the love of God towards us,—that he
sent his Son to be the propitiation for our sins. Beloved,
if God so loved us, we ought also to love one another."*
With what unanswerable force is that question of our Lord
to be applied to every branch of this duty, "Shouldest not
thou also have had compassion on thy fellow-servant, even
as I had pity on thee?"† And can there be a stronger
inducement to endeavour the reformation of the world, and
bring it to a sense of virtue and religion, than the assurance
given us, "that he which converteth a sinner from the
error of his way," and, in like manner, he also who pre-
venteth a person's being corrupted, by taking care of his
education, "shall save a soul from death, and hide a multitude of sins?"‡

These things lead us to the following observations on the
several charities, which are the occasion of these annual
solemnities.

1. What we have to bestow in charity being a trust,
we cannot discharge it faithfully, without taking some care
to satisfy ourselves in some degree, that we bestow it upon
the proper objects of charity. One hears persons complain-
ing, that it is difficult to distinguish who are such: yet often
seeming to forget, that this is the reason for using their best
endeavours to do it. And others make a custom of giving
to idle vagabonds; a kind of charity, very improperly so
called, which one really wonders people can allow themselves in, merely to be relieved from importunity, or at best

* 1 John iv. 9, 10, 11.   † Matt. xviii. 33.
‡ James v. 20.

5

to gratify a false good-nature. For they cannot but know
that it is, at least, very doubtful whether what they thus
give will not immediately be spent in riot and debauchery.
Or suppose it be not, yet still they know they do a great
deal of certain mischief, by encouraging this shameful trade
of begging in the streets, and all the disorders which
accompany it. By the charities towards which I now ask
your assistance, as they are always open, so every one may
contribute to them with full assurance that he bestows upon
proper objects, and, in general, that he does vastly more
good, than by equal sums given separately to particular
persons. For that these charities really have these advantages, has been fully made out by some who have gone before me in the duty I am discharging, and by the reports
annually published at this time.*

Let us thank God for these charities in behalf of the
poor, and also on our own behalf, as they give us such clear
opportunities of doing good. Indeed, without them, vice
and misery, of which there is still so much, would abound
so much more in this populous city as to render it scarce
an inhabitable place.

2. Amongst the peculiar advantages of public charities
above private ones, is also to be mentioned, that they are
examples of great influence. They serve for perpetual
memorials of what I have been observing, of the relation
which subsists between the rich and the poor, and the duties
which arise out of it. They are standing admonitions to all
within sight or hearing of them, to " go and do likewise."†
Educating poor children in virtue and religion, relieving
the sick, and correcting offenders in order to their amendment, are, in themselves, some of the very best of good
works. These charities would indeed be the glory of your
city, though their influence were confined to it. But important as they are in themselves, their importance still increases by their being examples to the rest of the nation;
which, in process of time, of course copies after the me-
tropolis. It has, indeed, already imitated every one of
these charities; for, of late, the most difficult and expensive
of them, hospitals for the sick and wounded, have been
established : some within your sight, others in remote parts

---

* Here the report was read.   † Luke x. 37.

of the kingdom. You will give me leave to mention particularly, that in its second trading city,* which is conducted with such disinterested fidelity and prudence as I dare
venture to compare with yours. Again, there are particular persons very blameably inactive and careless, yet not
without good dispositions, who, by these charities, are reminded of their duty, and " provoked to love and to good
works."† And let me add, though one is sorry any should
want so slight a reason for contributing to the most excellent designs, yet if any are supposed to do so merely of
course, because they see others do it, still they help to support these monuments of charity, which are a continued
admonition to the rich, and relief to the poor : and herein
all good men rejoice, as St. Paul speaks of himself in a like
case, " yea, and will rejoice."‡

3. As all human schemes admit of improvement, all
public charities, methinks, should be considered as standing
open to proposals for it ; that the whole plan of them, in all
its parts, may be brought to as great perfection as is possible. Now, it should seem that employing some share of
the children's time in easy labour, suitable to their age,
which is done in some of our charity-schools, might be done
in most others of them with very good effect, as it is in all
those of a neighbouring kingdom. Then, as the only purposes of punishments, less than capital, are to reform the
offenders themselves, and warn the innocent by their example, every thing which should contribute to make this kind
of punishments answer these purposes better than it does,
would be a great improvement. And whether it be not a
thing practicable, and what would contribute somewhat

* As it is of very particular benefit to those who ought always to
be looked upon with particular favour by us, I mean our seamen, so
likewise it is of very extensive benefit to the large tracts of country
west and north of it. Then the medical waters near the city render
it a still more proper situation for an infirmary ; and so likewise
does its neighbourhood to the Bath Hospital : for it may well be
supposed that some poor objects will be sent thither, in hopes of relief from the Bath-waters, whose case may afterwards be found to require the assistance of physic or surgery ; and, on the other hand,
that some may be sent to our infirmary for help from those arts,
whose case may be found to require the Bath-waters. So that, if I am
not greatly partial, the Bristol infirmary as much deserves encouragement, as any charitable foundation in the kingdom.

† Heb. x. 24.   ‡ Phil. i. 18.

towards it, to exclude utterly all sorts of revel mirth from places where offenders are confined, to separate the young from the old, and force them both in solitude, with labour and low diet, to make the experiment how far their natural strength of mind can support them under guilt, and shame, and poverty: this may deserve consideration. Then again, some religious instruction, particularly adapted to their condition, would as properly accompany those punishments which are intended to reform, as it does capital ones. God forbid that I should be understood to discourage the provision which is made for it in this latter case : I heartily wish it were better than it is, especially since it may well be supposed, as the state of religion is at present among us, that some condemned malefactors may have never had the doctrine of the gospel enforced upon their consciences. But since it must be acknowledged of greater consequence, in a religious, as well as civil respect, how persons live than how they die, it cannot but be even more incumbent on us to endeavour, in all ways, to reclaim those offenders who are to return again into the world, than those who are to be removed out of it; and the only effectual means of reclaiming them is, to instil into them a principle of religion. If persons of authority and influence would take things of this and a like kind under their consideration, they might perhaps still improve those charities, which are already, I truly believe, under a better management than any other of so large a compass in the world. But,

4. With regard to the two particular branches of them last mentioned, I would observe, that our laws and whole constitution, civil and ecclesiastical, go more upon supposition of an equality amongst mankind than the constitution and laws of any other countries. Now, this plainly requires that more particular regard should be had to the education of the lower people here than in places where they are born slaves of power, and to be made slaves of superstition. It is, I suppose, acknowledged that they have greater liberty here than they have any where else in the world ; but unless care be taken for giving them some inward principle, to prevent their abusing this greater liberty, which is their birthright, can we expect it will prove a blessing to them? Or will they not, in all probability, become more dissolute, or more wild, and extravagant,

whatever wrong turn they happen to take, than people of
the same rank in other countries?

5. Let me again remind you of the additional reason
which persons of fortune have to take particular care of
their whole behaviour, that it be in all respects good and
exemplary, upon account of the influence which it will
have upon the manners of their inferiors. And pray observe how strictly this is connected with the occasion of our
present meeting; how much your good behaviour in private
life will contribute to promote the good design of all these
charities, and how much the contrary would tend to defeat
it, and even to produce the evils which they are intended
to prevent or to remedy. Whatever care be taken in the
education of these poor children at school, there is always
danger of their being corrupted when they come from it;
and this danger is greater in proportion to the greater
wickedness of the age they have to pass through. But if,
upon their coming abroad into the world, they find the
principles of virtue and religion recommended by the example of their superiors, and vice and irreligion really discountenanced, this will confirm them in the good principles
in which they have been brought up, and give the best
ground to hope they will never depart from them. And
the like is to be said of offenders, who may have had a
sense of virtue and religion wrought in them under the
discipline of labour and confinement. Again; dissolute and
debauched persons of fortune greatly increase the general
corruption of manners; and this is what increases want and
misery of all kinds. So that they may contribute largely to
any or all of these charities, and yet undo but a very small
part of the mischief which they do, by their example, as
well as in other ways. But still the mischief which they do,
suppose by their example, is an additional reason why they
should contribute to them; even in justice to particular persons, in whose ruin they may have an unknown share of
guilt, or, however, in justice to society in general; for
which they will deserve commendation, how blameable
soever they are for the other. And, indeed, amidst the
dark prospect before us, from that profligateness of manners
and scorn of religion which so generally abound, this good
spirit of charity to the poor discovering itself in so great a
degree, upon these occasions, and likewise in the late neces-

sitous time, even amongst persons far from being blameless
in other respects ; this cannot but afford hopes, that we are
not given over by Providence, and also that they themselves will at length consider, and not go on coutributing,
by the example of their vices, to the introduction of that
distress, which they so commendably relieve by their liberality.

To conclude : let our charity towards men be exalted into
piety towards God, from the serious consideration, that we
are all his creatures, a consideration which enforces that
duty upon our consciences, as we have any regard to him.
This kind of adjuration, and a most solemn one it is, one
often hears profaned by a very unworthy sort of people,
when they ask relief for God's sake. But surely the principle itself, which contains in it every thing great, and just,
and good, is grievously forgotten among us. To relieve
the poor for God's sake, is to do it in conformity to the
order of nature, and to his will, and his example, who is the
Author and Governor of it ; and in thankful remembrance,
that all we have is from his bounty. It is to do it, in his
behalf, and as to him. For " he that hath pity upon the
poor, lendeth unto the Lord."* And our Saviour has declared, that he will take as given to himself, what is given
in a well-chosen charity.† *Lastly*, It is to do it under a
sense of the account which will be required of what is committed to our trust, when the rich and poor, who meet here
upon terms of so great inequality, shall meet hereafter upon
a level, before him who " is the Maker of them all."

* Prov. xix. 17.   † Matt. xxv. 40.

SERMON III.

PREACHED BEFORE THE HOUSE OF LORDS, IN THE ABBEY
CHURCH OF WESTMINSTER.

On Friday, 30th January, 1740-41,

*Being the day appointed to be observed as the day of the Martyrdom
of King Charles I.*

---

1 Peter ii. 16.

*And not using your liberty for a cloak of maliciousness,
but as the servants of God.*

An history so full of important and interesting events, as
that which this day recalls annually to our thoughts, cannot
but afford them very different subjects for their most serious
and useful employment. But there seems none which it
more naturally leads us to consider than that of hypocrisy,
as it sets before us so many examples of it; or which will
yield us more practical instruction, as these examples so
forcibly admonish us, not only to be upon our guard against
the pernicious effects of this vice in others, but also to
watch over our own hearts, against every thing of the like
kind in ourselves; for hypocrisy, in the moral and religious
consideration of things, is of much larger extent than every
one may imagine.

In common language, which is formed upon the common
intercourses amongst men, hypocrisy signifies little more
than their pretending what they do not really mean, in
order to delude one another. But, in Scripture, which

treats chiefly of our behaviour towards God and our own consciences, it signifies not only the endeavour to delude our fellow-creatures, but likewise insincerity towards Him, and towards ourselves. And, therefore, according to the whole analogy of Scriptural language, " to use liberty as a cloak of maliciousness,"* must be understood to mean, not only endeavouring to impose upon others, by indulging . wayward passions, or carrying on indirect designs, under pretences of it; but also excusing and palliating such things to ourselves ; serving ourselves of such pretences to quiet our own minds in any thing which is wrong.

* The hypocrisy laid to the charge of the Pharisees and Sadducees, in Matt. xvi. at the beginning, and in Luke xii. 54, is determinately this, that their vicious passions blinded them so as to prevent their discerning the evidence of our Saviour's mission ; though no more understanding was necessary to discern it, than what they had, and made use of in common matters. Here they are called hypocrites, merely upon account of their insincerity towards God and their own consciences, and not at all upon account of any insincerity towards men. This last, indeed, is included in that general hypocrisy, which, throughout the gospels, is represented as their distinguished character ; but the former is as much included. For they were not men, who, without any belief at all of religion, put on the appearance of it only in order to deceive the world ; on the contrary, they believed their religion, and were zealous in it. But their religion, which they believed, and were zealous in, was, in its nature, hypocritical : for it was the form, not the reality ; it allowed them in immoral practices ; and, indeed, was itself in some respects immoral, as they indulged their pride, and uncharitableness, under the notion of zeal for it. See Jer. ix. 6. Psal. lxxviii. 36. Job viii. 13, and Matt. xv. 7—14, and xxiii. 13, 16, 19, 24, 26, where *hypocrite* and *blind* are used promiscuously. Again, the Scripture speaks of the " deceitfulness of sin ;" and its deceiving those who are guilty of it ; Heb. iii. 13. Eph. iv. 22. Rom. vii. 11 : of men's acting as if they could " deceive and mock God ;" Isa. xxix. 15. Acts v. 3. Gal. vi. 7 : of their " blinding their own eyes ;" Matt. xiii. 15. Acts xxviii. 27 ; and "deceiving themselves," which is quite a different thing from being deceived, 1 Cor. iii. 18. 1 John i. 8. Gal. vi. 3. James i. 22, 26. Many more coincident passages might be mentioned ; but I will add only one. In 2 Thess. ii. 11, it is foretold, that by means of some *force*, some energy of delusion, men should believe *the lie* which is there treated of : this *force of delusion* is not any thing without them, but somewhat within them, which it is expressly said, they should bring upon themselves, " by not receiving the love of the truth, but having pleasure in unrighteousness." Answering to all this is that very remarkable passage of our Lord, Matt. vi. 22, 23. Luke xi. 34, 35, and that admonition, repeated fourteen times in the New Testament, " he that hath ears to hear, let him hear." And the ground of this whole

Liberty, in the writings of the New Testament, for the most part signifies, being delivered from the bondage of the ceremonial law, or of sin and the devil, which St. Paul calls "the glorious liberty of the children of God."* This last is a progressive state: and the perfection of it, whether attainable in this world or not, consists in that "perfect love"† which St. John speaks of; and which as it implies an entire coincidence of our wills with the will of God, must be a state of the most absolute freedom, in the most literal and proper sense. But whatever St. Peter distinctly meant by this word *liberty*, the text gives occasion to consider any kind of it, which is liable to the abuse he here warns us against. However, it appears that he meant to comprehend that liberty, were it more or less, which they to whom he was writing, enjoyed under civil government; for of civil government he is speaking just before and afterwards :‡ "Submit yourselves to every ordinance of man for the Lord's sake; whether it be to the king, as supreme; or unto governors, as unto them that are sent by him. For so is the will of God, that with well-doing," of which dutiful behaviour towards authority is a very material instance, "ye may put to silence the ignorance of foolish men : as free," perhaps in distinction from the servile state of which he speaks afterwards,§ "and not using your liberty for a cloak of maliciousness," of any thing wrong, for so the word signifies; and therefore comprehends petulance, affectation of popularity, with any other like frivolous turn of

manner of considering things; for it is not to be spoken of as only a peculiar kind of phraseology, but it is a most accurate and strictly just manner of considering characters and moral conduct; the ground of it, I say, is, that when persons will not be influenced by such evidence in religion as they act upon in the daily course of life, or when their notions of religion (and I might add of virtue) are, in any sort, reconcileable with what is vicious, it is some faulty negligence, or prejudice, which thus deludes them; in very different ways, perhaps, and very different degrees. But when any one is thus deluded through his own fault, in whatever way or degree it is, he deludes himself. And this is as properly hypocrisy towards himself, as deluding the world is hypocrisy towards the world : and he who is guilty of it, acts as if he could deceive and mock God; and, therefore, is an hypocrite towards him, in as strict and literal a sense as the nature of the subject will admit.

* Rom. viii. 21.   † 1 John iv. 18.
‡ 1 Peter ii. 13.   § Verse 16.

mind, as well as the more hateful and dangerous passions, such as malice, or ambition : for all of which *liberty* may equally be " used as a cloak." The apostle adds, " but as the servants of God ; as free—but as his servants," who requires a dutiful submission to " every ordinance of man," to magistracy ; and to whom we are accountable for our manner of using the liberty we enjoy under it, as well as for all other parts of our behaviour. " Not using your liberty as a cloak of maliciousness, but as the servants of God."

Here are three things offered to our consideration :

First, A general supposition, that what is wrong cannot be avowed in its proper colours, but stands in need of some *cloak* to be thrown over it : *Secondly*, A particular one, that there is danger, some singular danger, of liberty's being made use of for this purpose : *Lastly*, An admonition not to make this ill use of our liberty, " but" to use it " as the servants of God."

I. Here is a general supposition, that what is wrong cannot be avowed in its proper colours, but stands in need of some *cloak* to be thrown over it. God has constituted our nature, and the nature of society, after such a manner, that, generally speaking, men cannot encourage or support themselves in wickedness, upon the footing of there being no difference between right and wrong, or by a direct avowal of wrong, but by disguising it, and endeavouring to spread over it some colours of right. And they do this in every capacity and every respect, in which there is a right or a wrong. They do it, not only as social creatures under civil government, but also as moral agents under the government of God : in one case, to make a proper figure in the world, and delude their fellow-creatures ; in the other, to keep peace within themselves, and delude their own consciences. And the delusion in both cases being voluntary, is, in Scripture, called by one name, and spoken against in the same manner ; though, doubtless, they are much more explicit with themselves, and more distinctly conscious of what they are about in one case than in the other.

The fundamental laws of all governments are virtuous ones, prohibiting treachery, injustice, cruelty ; and the law of reputation enforces those civil laws, by rendering these vices every where infamous, and the contrary virtues honourable, and of good report. Thus far the constitution of society is visibly moral; and hence it is, that men cannot live in it without taking care to cover those vices when they have them, and make some profession of the opposite virtues, fidelity, justice, kind regard to others, when they have them not: but especially is this necessary, in order to disguise and colour over indirect purposes, which require the concurrence of several persons.

Now, all false pretences of this kind are to be called hypocritical, as being contrary to simplicity; though not always designed, properly speaking, to beget a false belief. For it is to be observed, that they are often made without any formal intention to have them believed, or to have it thought that there is any reality under these pretences. Many examples occur of verbal professions of fidelity, justice, public regards, in cases where there could be no imagination of their being believed. And what other account can be given of these merely verbal professions, but that they were thought the proper language for the public ear; and made in business, for the very same kind of reasons as civility is kept up in conversation.

These false professions of virtue, which men have in all ages found it necessary to make their appearance with abroad, must have been originally taken up in order to deceive, in the proper sense: then they became habitual, and often intended merely by way of form; yet often still, to serve their original purpose of deceiving.

There is doubtless among mankind a great deal of this hypocrisy towards each other; but not so much as may sometimes be supposed. For part which has, at first sight, this appearance, is in reality that other hypocrisy beforementioned; that self-deceit of which the Scripture so remarkably takes notice. There are indeed persons, who live " without God in the world;" * and some appear so hardened, as to keep no measures with themselves. But as very ill men may have a real and strong sense of virtue and religion, in proportion as this is the case with any, they cannot be easy within themselves but by deluding their consciences. And though they should, in great measure, get

* Eph. ii. 12.

over their religion, yet this will not do. For as long as they carry about with them any such sense of things as makes them condemn what is wrong in others, they could not but condemn the same in themselves, and dislike and be disgusted with their own character and conduct, if they would consider them distinctly, and in a full light. But this sometimes they carelessly neglect to do, and sometimes carefully avoid doing. And as " the integrity of the upright guides him,"* guides even a man's judgment, so wickedness may distort it to such a degree, as that he may " call evil good, and good evil: put darkness for light, and light for darkness;"† and " think wickedly, that God is such an one as himself."‡ Even the better sort of men are, in some degree, liable to disguise and palliate their failings to themselves; but perhaps there are few men, who go on calmly in a course of very bad things, without somewhat of the kind now described in a very high degree. They try appearances upon themselves as well as upon the world, and with at least as much success; and choose to manage so as to make their own minds easy with their faults, which can scarce be without management, rather than to mend them.

But whether from men's deluding themselves, or from their intending to delude the world, it is evident, scarce any thing wrong in public has ever been accomplished, or even attempted, but under false colours; either by pretending one thing, which was right, to be designed, when it was really another thing, which was wrong; or, if that which was wrong was avowed, by endeavouring to give it some appearance of right. For tyranny, and faction so friendly to it, and which is indeed tyranny out of power, and unjust wars, and persecution, by which the earth has been laid waste; all this has all along been carried on with pretences of truth, right, general good. So it is, men cannot find in their heart to join in such things, without such honest words to be the bond of the union, though they know among themselves, that they are only words, and often though they know that every body else knows it too.

These observations might be exemplified by numerous instances in the history which led to them: and without

---

* Prov. xi. 3.   † Isa. v. 20.   ‡ Psal. l. 21.

them, it is impossible to understand in any sort the general character of the chief actors in it, who were engaged in the black design of subverting the constitution of their country. This they completed with the most enormous act of mere power, in defiance of all laws of God and man, and in express contradiction to the real design and public votes of that assembly, whose commission, they professed, was their only warrant for any thing they did throughout the whole rebellion.   Yet, with unheard-of hypocrisy towards men, towards God, and their own consciences, for without such a complication of it, their conduct is inexplicable ; even this action, which so little admitted of any cloak, was, we know, contrived and carried into execution, under pretences of authority, religion, liberty, and by profaning the forms of justice in an arraignment and trial, like to what is used in regular legal procedures.   No age, indeed, can show an example of hypocrisy parallel to this.   But the history of all ages, and all countries, will show what has been really going forward over the face of the earth, to be very different from what has been always pretended ; and that virtue has been every where professed much more than it has been any where practised : nor could society, from the very nature of its constitution, subsist without some general public profession of it.   Thus, the face and appearance which the world has in all times put on, for the ease and ornament of life, and in pursuit of further ends, is the justest satire upon what has in all times been carrying on under it; and ill men are destined, by the condition of their being as social creatures, always to bear about with them, and in different degrees, to profess, that law of virtue, by which they shall finally be judged and condemned.

II.   As fair pretences of one sort or other, have thus always been made use of by mankind to colour over indirect and wrong designs from the world, and to palliate and excuse them to their own minds, liberty, in common with all other good things, is liable to be made this use of, and is also liable to it in a way more peculiar to itself ; which was the second thing to be considered.

In the history which this day refers us to, we find our constitution in church and state destroyed under pretences not only of religion, but of securing liberty, and carrying it to a greater height.   The destruction of the former was with zeal of such a kind as would not have been warrantable, though it had been employed in the destruction of heathenism. And the confusions, the persecuting spirit, and incredible fanaticism, which grew up upon its ruins, cannot but teach sober-minded men to reverence so mild and reasonable an establishment, now it is restored for the preservation of Christianity, and keeping up a sense of it amongst us, and for the instruction and guide of the ignorant; nay, were it only for guarding religion from such extravagances: especially as these important purposes are served by it, without bearing hard in the least upon any.

And the concurrent course of things, which brought on the ruin of our civil constitution, and what followed upon it, are no less instructive. The opposition, by legal and parliamentary methods, to prerogatives unknown to the constitution, was doubtless formed upon the justest fears in behalf of it. But new distrusts arose: new causes were given for them; these were most unreasonably aggravated. The better part gradually gave way to the more violent; and the better part themselves seem to have insisted upon impracticable securities against that one danger to liberty of which they had too great cause to be apprehensive; and wonderfully overlooked all other dangers to it, which yet were, and ever will be many and great. Thus they joined in the current measures, till they were utterly unable to stop the mischiefs, to which, with too much distrust on one side, and too little on the other, they had contributed. Never was a more remarkable example of the wise man's observation, that " the beginning of strife is as when one letteth out water."* For this opposition, thus began, surely without intent of proceeding to violence; yet, as it went on like an overflowing stream in its progress, it collected all sorts of impurities, and grew more outrageous as it grew more corrupted, till at length it bore down every thing good before it. This naturally brought an arbitrary power in one shape, which was odious to every body, and which could not be accommodated to the forms of our constitution; and put us in the utmost danger of having it entailed upon us under another, which might. For at the king's return, such was the just indignation of the public at what

* Prov. xvii. 14.

it had seen, and fear of feeling again what it had felt from the popular side; such the depression and compliance, not only of the more guilty, but also of those who, with better meaning, had gone on with them; (and a great deal too far many of this character had gone;) and such the undistinguishing distrust the people had of them all, that the chief securities of our liberties seem to have been, their not being attempted at that time.

But though persons contributed to all this mischief and danger with different degrees of guilt, none could contribute to them with innocence, who at all knew what they were about. Indeed, the destruction of a free constitution of government, though men see or fancy many defects in it, and whatever they design or pretend, ought not to be thought of without horror. For the design is in itself unjust, since it is romantic to suppose it legal; it cannot be prosecuted without the most wicked means, nor accomplished but with the present ruin of liberty, religious as well as civil; for it must be the ruin of its present security. Whereas the restoration of it must depend upon a thousand future contingencies, the integrity, understanding, power, of the persons into whose hands anarchy and confusion should throw things; and who they will be, the history before us may surely serve to show no human foresight can determine; even though such a terrible crisis were to happen in an age, not distinguished for the want of principle and public spirit, and when nothing particular were to be apprehended from abroad. It would be partiality to say, that no constitution of government can possibly be imagined more perfect than our own; and ingenuous youth may be warmed with the idea of one against which nothing can be objected. But it is the strongest objection against attempting to put in practice the most perfect theory, that it is impracticable or too dangerous to be attempted. And whoever will thoroughly consider, in what degree mankind are really influenced by reason, and in what degree by custom, may, I think, be convinced, that the state of human affairs does not even admit of an equivalent, for the mischief of setting things afloat, and the danger of parting with those securities of liberty, which arise from regulations of long prescription and ancient usage; especially at a time when the directors are so very numerous, and the obedient so

few. Reasonable men, therefore, will look upon the general
plan of our constitution, transmitted down to us by our ancestors, as sacred; and content themselves with calmly
doing what their station requires towards rectifying the
particular things which they think amiss, and supplying the
particular things which they think deficient in it, so far as
is practicable without endangering the whole.

But liberty is in many other dangers from itself, besides
those which arise from formed designs of destroying it,
under hypocritical pretences, or romantic schemes of re-
storing it upon a more perfect plan. It is particularly liable to become excessive, and to degenerate insensibly into
licentiousness; in the same manner as liberality, for example, is apt to degenerate into extravagance. And as men
cloak their extravagance to themselves under the notion of
liberality, and to the world under the name of it, so licentiousness passes under the name and notion of liberty.
Now it is to be observed, that there is, in some respects or
other, a very peculiar contrariety between those vices which
consist in excess, and the virtues of which they are said to
be the excess, and the resemblance, and whose names they
affect to bear; the excess of any thing being always to its
hurt, and tending to its destruction. In this manner licentiousness is, in its very nature, a present infringement upon
liberty, and dangerous to it for the future. Yet it is treated
by many persons with peculiar indulgence under this very
notion, as being an excess of liberty. And an excess of
liberty it is to the licentious themselves: but what is it to
those who suffer by them, and who do not think that amends
is at all made them by having it left in their power to retaliate safely? When by popular insurrections, or defama-
tory libels, or in any like way, the needy and the turbulent
securely injure quiet people in their fortune or good name,
so far quiet people are no more free than if a single tyrant
used them thus. A particular man may be licentious without being less free; but a community cannot, since the
licentiousness of one will unavoidably break in upon the
liberty of another. Civil liberty, the liberty of a community, is a severe and a restrained thing; implies in the notion of it, authority, settled subordinations, subjection, and
obedience; and is altogether as much hurt by too little of
this kind as by too much of it. And the love of liberty,

when it is indeed the love of liberty which carries us to
withstand tyranny, will as much carry us to reverence
authority and support it; for the most obvious reason, that
one is as necessary to the very being of liberty, as the
other is destructive of it. And therefore the love of liberty,
which does not produce this effect—the love of liberty,
which is not a real principle of dutiful behaviour towards
authority—is as hypocritical as the religion which is not
productive of a good life. Licentiousness is, in truth, such
an excess of liberty, as is of the same nature with tyranny.
For, what is the difference between them, but that one is
lawless power exercised under pretence of authority, or by
persons invested with it; the other, lawless power exercised
under pretence of liberty, or without any pretence at all?
A people, then, must always be less free, in proportion as
they are more licentious; licentiousness being not only different from liberty, but directly contrary to it—a direct
breach upon it.

It is moreover of a growing nature, and of speedy growth
too; and, with the culture which it has amongst us, needs
no great length of time to get to such a height as no legal
government will be able to restrain, or subsist under;
which is the condition the historian describes, in saying,
they could neither bear their vices, nor the remedies of
them.* I said legal government; for, in the present state
of the world, there is no danger of our becoming savages.
Had licentiousness finished its work, and destroyed our constitution, power would not be wanting, from one quarter or
another, sufficient to subdue us, and keep us in subjection.
But government, as distinguished from mere power, free
government, necessarily implies reverence in the subjects of
it, for authority, or power regulated by laws, and a habit
of submission to the subordinations in civil life, throughout
its several ranks; nor is a people capable of liberty without
somewhat of this kind. But it must be observed, and less
surely cannot be observed, this reverence and submission
will, at best, be very precarious, if it be not founded upon
a sense of authority being God's ordinance, and the subordinations in life a providential appointment of things. Now,
let it be considered, for surely it is not duly considered,

* Nec vitia nostra, nec remedia pati possumus. Liv. l. i. c. l.

what is really the short amount of those representations
which persons of superior rank give, and encourage to be
given of each other, and which are spread over the nation?
Is it not somewhat, in itself and in its circumstances, beyond any thing in any other age or country of the world?
And what effect must the continuance of this extravagant
licentiousness in them, not to mention other kinds of it,
have upon the people in those respects just mentioned?
Must it not necessarily tend to wear out of their minds all
reverence for authority, and respect for superiors of every
sort; and, joined with the irreligious principles we find so
industriously propagated, to introduce a total profligateness
amongst them; since, let them be as bad as they will, it is
scarce possible they can be so bad as they are instructed
they may be, or worse than they are told their superiors
are?   And is there no danger that all this, to mention only
one supposable course of it, may raise somewhat like that
levelling spirit, upon atheistical principles, which in the last
age prevailed upon enthusiastic ones? not to speak of the
possibility, that different sorts of people may unite in it,
upon these contrary principles.   And may not this spirit,
together with a concurrence of ill humours, and of persons
who hope to find their account in confusion, soon prevail to
such a degree, as will require more of the good old principles of loyalty and of religion to withstand it, than appear
to be left amongst us?

What legal remedies can be provided against these mischiefs, or whether any at all, are considerations the farthest
from my thoughts.   No government can be free, which is
not administered by general stated laws; and these cannot
comprehend every case, which wants to be provided
against; nor can new ones be made for every particular
case, as it arises: and more particular laws, as well as more
general ones, admit of infinite evasions: and legal government forbids any but legal methods of redress, which cannot but be liable to the same sort of imperfections, besides
the additional one of delay: and whilst redress is delayed,
however unavoidably, wrong subsists.   Then there are very
bad things, which human authority can scarce provide
against at all, but by methods dangerous to liberty; nor
fully but by such as would be fatal to it.   Thees things
show, that liberty, in the very nature of it, absolutely re-

quires, and even supposes, that people be able to govern themselves in those respects in which they are free; otherwise their wickedness will be in proportion to their liberty, and this greatest of blessings will become a curse.

III. These things show likewise, that there is but one adequate remedy to the fore-mentioned evils, even that which the apostle prescribes in the last words of the text, to consider ourselves " as the servants of God," who enjoins dutiful submission to civil authority as his ordinance: and to whom we are accountable for the use we make of the liberty which we enjoy under it. Since men cannot live out of society, nor in it, without government, government is plainly a divine appointment; and consequently submission to it, a most evident duty of the law of nature. And we all know in how forcible a manner it is put upon our consciences in Scripture. Nor can this obligation be denied formally upon any principles, but such as subvert all other obligations. Yet many amongst us seem not to consider it as any obligation at all. This doubtless is, in a great measure, owing to dissoluteness and corruption of manners; but I think it is partly owing to their having reduced it to nothing in theory; whereas this obligation ought to be put upon the same footing with all other general ones, which are not absolute and without exception: and our submission is due in all cases, but those which we really discern to be exceptions to this general rule. And they who are perpetually displaying the exceptions, though they do not indeed contradict the meaning of any particular text of Scripture, which surely intended to make no alteration in men's civil rights, yet they go against the general tenor of Scripture. For the Scripture, throughout the whole of it, commands submission; supposing men apt enough of themselves to make the exceptions, and not to need being continually reminded of them. Now if we are really under any obligations of duty at all to magistrates, honour and respect, in our behaviour towards them, must doubtless be their due. And they who refuse to pay them this small and easy regard, who "despise dominion, and speak evil of dignities,"* should seriously ask themselves, what restrains them from any other instance whatever of undutifulness?

* Jude 8.

And if it be principle, why not from this? Indeed, free
government supposes, that the conduct of affairs may be
inquired into, and spoken of with freedom.   Yet surely this
should be done with decency, for the sake of liberty itself:
for its honour, and its security.   But be it done as it will,
it is a very different thing from libelling, and endeavouring
to vilify the persons of such as are in authority.   It will be
hard to find an instance, in which a serious man could
calmly satisfy himself in doing this.   It is in no case
necessary, and, in every case, of very pernicious tendency.
But the immorality of it increases, in proportion to the integrity and superior rank of the persons thus treated.   It is
therefore in the highest degree immoral, when it extends to
the supreme authority in the person of a prince, from
whom our liberties are in no imaginable danger, whatever
they may be from ourselves; and whose mild, and strictly
legal government, could not but make any virtuous people
happy.

A free government, which the good providence of God
has preserved to us through innumerable dangers, is an
invaluable blessing.   And our ingratitude to him, in abusing of it, must be great in proportion to the greatness of
the blessing, and the providential deliverances by which it
has been preserved to us.   Yet the crime of abusing this
blessing receives further aggravation from hence, that such
abuse always is to the reproach, and tends to the ruin of it.
The abuse of liberty has directly overturned many free
governments, as well as our own, on the popular side; and
has, in various ways, contributed to the ruin of many which
have been overturned on the side of authority.   Heavy,
therefore, must be their guilt, who shall be found to have
given such advantages against it, as well as theirs who have
taken them.

Lastly, The consideration that we are the servants of
God, reminds us, that we are accountable to him for our
behaviour in those respects, in which it is out of the reach
of all human authority, and is the strongest enforcement of
sincerity; as "all things are naked, and open, unto the
eyes of him with whom we have to do."*   Artificial behaviour might perhaps avail much towards quieting our

* Heb. iv. 13.

consciences, and making our part good in the short competitions of this world; but what will it avail us, considered
as under the government of God?   Under his government
"there is no darkness, nor shadow of death, where the
workers of iniquity may hide themselves."* He has indeed
instituted civil government over the face of the earth, " for
the punishment of evil-doers, and for the praise," the apostle
does not say the rewarding, but "for the praise of them
that do well."† Yet as the worst answer these ends in
some measure, the best can do it very imperfectly. Civil
government can by no means take cognizance of every
work, which is good or evil: many things are done in
secret; the authors unknown to it, and often the things
themselves: then it cannot so much consider actions, under the view of their being morally good or evil, as under
the view of their being mischievous, or beneficial to society;
nor can it in any wise execute judgment in rewarding what
is good, as it can, and ought, and does, in punishing what
is evil.   But "God shall bring every work into judgment,
with every secret thing, whether it be good, or whether it
be evil."‡

* Job xxxiv. 22.   † 1 Pet. ii. 14.   ‡ Eccles. xii. 14.

SERMON IV.

PREACHED IN THE PARISH CHURCH OF CHRIST-CHURCH, LONDON,

On Thursday, May 9, 1745;

Being the time of the Yearly Meeting of the Children educated in the Charity Schools, in and about the Cities of London and Westminster.

PROVERBS xxii. 6.

Train up a child in the way he should go; and when he is old he will not depart from it.

HUMAN creatures, from the constitution of their nature, and the circumstances in which they are placed, cannot but acquire habits during their childhood, by the impressions which are given them, and their own customary actions. And long before they arrive at mature age, these habits form a general settled character. And the observation of the text, that the most early habits are usually the most lasting, is likewise every one's observation. Now, whenever children are left to themselves, and to the guides and companions which they choose, or by hazard light upon, we find by experience, that the first impressions they take, and course of action they get into, are very bad: and so, consequently, must be their habits, and character, and future behaviour. Thus, if they are not trained up in the way they "should go," they will certainly be trained up the way they should not go; and, in all probability, will persevere in it, and become miserable themselves, and mischievous to society; which, in event, is worse upon account of both,

than if they had been exposed to perish in their infancy.
On the other hand, the ingenuous docility of children before they have been deceived, their distrust of themselves,
and natural deference to grown people, whom they find
here settled in a world where they themselves are strangers,
and to whom they have recourse for advice as readily as
for protection; which deference is still greater towards
those who are placed over them: these things give the
justest grounds to expect, that they may receive such impressions, and be influenced to such a course of behaviour,
as will produce lasting good habits; and, together with the
dangers before mentioned, are as truly a natural demand
upon us to "train them up in the way they should go," as
their bodily wants are a demand to provide them bodily
nourishment. Brute creatures are appointed to do no more
than this last for their offspring; nature forming them, by
instincts, to the particular manner of life appointed them,
from which they never deviate. But this is so far from
being the case of men, that, on the contrary, considering
communities collectively, every successive generation is
left, in the ordinary course of Providence, to be formed by
the preceding one; and becomes good or bad, though not
without its own merit or demerit, as this trust is discharged
or violated, chiefly in the management of youth.

We ought, doubtless, to instruct and admonish grown
persons, to restrain them from what is evil, and encourage
them in what is good, as we are able; but this care of
youth, abstracted from all consideration of the parental affection: I say, this care of youth, which is the general notion of education, becomes a distinct subject and a distinct
duty, from the particular danger of their ruin, if left to
themselves, and the particular reason we have to expect
they will do well, if due care be taken of them. And from
hence it follows, that children have as much right to some
proper education, as to have their lives preserved; and
that, when this is not given them by their parents, the care
of it devolves upon all persons, it becomes the duty of all
who are capable of contributing to it, and whose help is
wanted.

These trite, but most important things, implied indeed in
the text, being thus premised as briefly as I could express
them, I proceed to consider distinctly, the general manner

in which the duty of education is there laid before us; which will further show its extent, and further obviate the idle objections which have been made against it. And all this together will naturally lead us to consider the occasion and necessity of schools for the education of poor children, and in what light the objections against them are to be regarded.

Solomon might probably intend the text for a particular admonition, to educate children in a manner suitable to their respective ranks and future employments: but certainly he intended it for a general admonition, to educate them in virtue and religion, and good conduct of themselves in their temporal concerns. And all this together, in which they are to be educated, he calls " the way they should go," *i. e.* he mentions it not as a matter of speculation, but of practice. And conformably to this description of the things in which children are to be educated, he describes education itself: for he calls it " training them up;" which is a very different thing from merely teaching them some truths necessary to be known or believed. It is endeavouring to form such truths into practical principles in the mind, so as to render them of habitual good influence upon the temper and actions, in all the various occurrences of life. And this is not done by bare instruction; but by that, together with admonishing them frequently, as occasion offers: restraining them from what is evil, and exercising them in what is good. Thus the precept of the apostle concerning this matter is, to " bring up children in the nurture and admonition of the Lord:"* as it were by way of distinction from acquainting them merely with the principles of Christianity, as you would with any common theory. Though education were nothing more than informing children of some truths of importance to them, relating to religion and common life, yet there would be great reason for it, notwithstanding the frivolous objections concerning the danger of giving them prejudices. But when we consider, that such information itself is really the least part of it, and that it consists in endeavouring to put them into right dispositions of mind, and right habits of living, in every relation and

* Eph. vi. 4.
L 5

every capacity ; this consideration shows such objections to
be quite absurd; since it shows them to be objections
against doing a thing of the utmost importance at the natural opportunity of our doing it, childhood and youth; and
which is indeed, properly speaking, our only one. For
when they are grown up to maturity, they are out of our
hands, and must be left to themselves. The natural authority on one side ceases, and the deference on the other.
God forbid, that it should be impossible for men to recollect themselves, and reform at an advanced age ; but it is
in no sort in the power of others to gain upon them ; to
turn them away from what is wrong, and enforce upon
them what is right, at that season of their lives, in the manner we might have done in their childhood.

Doubtless, religion requires instruction, for it is founded
in knowledge and belief of some truths ; and so is common
prudence in the management of our temporal affairs : yet
neither of them consists in the knowledge or belief even of
these fundamental truths; but in our being brought, by
such knowledge or belief, to a correspondent temper and
behaviour. Religion, as it stood under the Old Testament,
is perpetually styled, " the fear of God ;" under the New,
" faith in Christ." But as that fear of God does not signify
literally being afraid of him, but having a good heart, and
leading a good life, in consequence of such fear, so this
faith in Christ does not signify literally believing in him, in
the sense that word is used in common language, but becoming his real disciples, in consequence of such belief.

Our religion being then thus practical, consisting in a
frame of mind and course of behaviour suitable to the dispensation we are under, and which will bring us to our
final good ; children ought, by education, to be habituated
to this course of behaviour, and formed into this frame of
mind. And it must ever be remembered, that if no care
be taken to do it, they will grow up in a direct contrary
behaviour, and be hardened in direct contrary habits ; they
will more and more corrupt themselves, and spoil their proper nature; they will alienate themselves farther from God;
and not only neglect, but " trample under foot," the means
which he, in his infinite mercy, has appointed for our recovery. And upon the whole, the same reasons which

3

show, that they ought to be instructed and exercised in
what will render them useful to society, secure them from
the present evils they are in danger of incurring, and procure them that satisfaction which lies within the reach of
human prudence ; show likewise, that they ought to be instructed and exercised in what is suitable to the highest relations in which we stand, and the most important capacity
in which we can be considered ; in that temper of mind and
course of behaviour, which will secure them from their
chief evil, and bring them to their chief good : besides
that, religion is the principal security of men's acting a
right part in society, and even in respect to their own temporal happiness, all things duly considered.

It is true, indeed, children may be taught superstition
under the notion of religion; and it is true also, that, under
the notion of prudence, they may be educated in great mistakes as to the nature of real interest and good, respecting
the present world. But this is no more a reason for not
educating them according to the best of our judgment, than
our knowing how very liable we all are to err in other
cases, is a reason why we should not, in those other cases,
act according to the best of our judgment.

It being then of the greatest importance, that children
should be thus educated, the providing schools to give this
education to such of them as would not otherwise have it,
has the appearance, at least at first sight, of deserving a
place amongst the very best of good works. One would be
backward, methinks, in entertaining prejudices against it :
and very forward, if one had any, to lay them aside, upon
being shown that they were groundless. Let us consider
the whole state of the case. For though this will lead us
some little compass, yet I choose to do it : and the rather,
because there are people who speak of charity-schools as a
new-invented scheme, and therefore to be looked upon with
I know not what suspicion. Whereas it will appear, that
the scheme of charity-schools, even the part of it which is
most looked upon in this light, teaching the children letters
and accounts, is no otherwise new, than as the occasion for
it is so.

Formerly, not only the education of poor children, but
also their maintenance, with that of the other poor, were
left to voluntary charities. But great changes of different

sorts happening over the nation, and charity becoming more
cold, or the poor more numerous, it was found necessary to
make some legal provision for them. This might, much
more properly than charity-schools, be called a new scheme.
For, without question, the education of poor children was
all along taken care of, by voluntary charities, more or
less: but obliging us by law to maintain the poor, was new
in the reign of Queen Elizabeth. Yet, because a change
of circumstances made it necessary, its novelty was no
reason against it. Now, in that legal provision for the
maintenance of the poor, poor children must doubtless have
had a part in common with grown people. But this could
never be sufficient for children, because their case always
requires more than mere maintenance; it requires that
they be educated in some proper manner. Wherever there
are poor who want to be maintained by charity, there must
be poor children, who, besides this, want to be educated by
charity. And whenever there began to be need of *legal*
provision for the *maintenance* of the poor, there must immediately have been need also of some *particular* legal
provision in behalf of poor children for their *education;*
this not being included in what we call their maintenance.
And many, whose parents are able to maintain them, and
do so, may yet be utterly neglected as to their education.
But possibly it might not at first be attended to, that the
case of poor children was thus a case by itself, which required its own particular provision. Certainly it would
not appear, to the generality, so urgent an one as the want
of food and raiment. And it might be necessary, that a
burden so entirely new as that of a poor-tax was at the time
I am speaking of, should be as light as possible. Thus the
legal provision for the poor was first settled, without any
particular consideration of that additional want in the case
of children; as it still remains with scarce any alteration in
this respect. In the mean time, as the poor still increased,
or charity still lessened, many poor children were left exposed, not to perish for want of food, but to grow up in
society, and learn every thing that is evil, and nothing that
is good in it; and when they were grown up, greatly at a loss
in what honest way to provide for themselves, if they could be
supposed inclined to it. And larger numbers, whose case was
not so bad as this, yet were very far from having due care

taken of their education. And the evil went on increasing, till it was grown to such a degree, as to be quite out of the compass of separate charities to remedy. At length some excellent persons, who were united in a Society* for carrying on almost every good work, took into consideration the neglected case I have been representing; and first of all, as I understand it, set up charity-schools: or, however, promoted them, as far as their abilities and influence could extend. Their design was not in any sort to remove poor children out of the rank in which they were born, but, keeping them in it, to give them the assistance which their circumstances plainly called for; by educating them in the principles of religion, as well as civil life; and likewise making some sort of provision for their maintenance: under which last I include clothing them, giving them such learning, if it is to be called by that name, as may qualify them for some common employment, and placing them out to it as they grow up. These two general designs coincide, in many respects, and cannot be separated. For teaching the children to read, though I have ranked it under the latter, equally belongs to both: and without some advantages of the latter sort, poor people would not send their children to our charity-schools; nor could the poorest of all be admitted into any schools, without some charitable provision of clothing. And care is taken, that it be such as cannot but be a restraint upon the children. And if this, or any part of their education, gives them any little vanity, as has been poorly objected, whilst they are children, it is scarce possible but that it will have even a quite contrary effect when they are grown up, and ever after remind them of their rank. Yet still we find it is apprehended, that what they here learn may set them above it.

But why should people be so extremely apprehensive of the danger, that poor persons will make a perverse use of every the least advantage, even the being able to read, whilst they do not appear at all apprehensive of the like danger for themselves or their own children, in respect of riches or power, how much soever; though the danger of perverting these advantages is surely as great, and the perversion itself of much greater and worse consequence. And by what

* Society for Promoting Christian Knowledge.

odd reverse of things has it happened, that such as pretend
to be distinguished for the love of liberty, should be the
only persons who plead for keeping down the poor, as one
may speak ; for keeping them more inferior in this respect,
and, which must be the consequence in other respects,
than they were in times past ? For, till within a century or
two, all ranks were nearly upon a level as to the learning in
question.   The art of printing appears to have been providentially reserved till these latter ages, and then providentially brought into use, as what was to be instrumental for
the future in carrying on the appointed course of things.
The alterations which this art has even already made in the
face of the world, are not inconsiderable.   By means of it,
whether immediately or remotely, the methods of carrying
on business are, in several respects, improved, "knowledge
has been increased,"* and some sort of literature is become
general.   And if this be a blessing, we ought to let the
poor, in their degree, share it with us.   The present state
of things, and course of Providence, plainly leads us to do
so.   And if we do not, it is certain, how little soever it be
attended to, that they will be upon a greater disadvantage,
on many accounts, especially in populous places, than they
were in the dark ages : for they will be more ignorant,
comparatively with the people about them, than they were
then : and the ordinary affairs of the world are now put in
a way which requires that they should have some knowledge
of letters, which was not the case then.   And therefore, to
bring up the poor in their former ignorance, now this
knowledge is so much more common and wanted, would
be, not to keep them in the same, but to put them into a
lower condition of life than what they were in formerly.
Nor let people of rank flatter themselves, that ignorance
will keep their inferiors more dutiful and in greater subjection to them : for surely there must be danger, that it will
have a contrary effect, under a free government such as
ours, and in a dissolute age.   Indeed, the principles and
manners of the poor, as to virtue and religion, will always
be greatly influenced, as they always have been, by the example of their superiors, if that would mend the matter.
And this influence will, I suppose, be greater, if they are

* Daniel xii. 4.

kept more inferior than formerly in all knowledge and improvement. But unless their superiors of the present age, superiors, I mean, of the middle, as well as higher ranks in society, are greater examples of public spirit, of dutiful submission to authority, human and divine, of moderation in diversions, and proper care of their families and domestic affairs; unless, I say, superiors of the present age are greater examples of decency, virtue, and religion, than those of former times; for what reason in the world is it desirable, that their example should have this greater influence over the poor? On the contrary, why should not the poor, by being taught to read, be put into a capacity of making some improvement in moral and religious knowledge, and confirming themselves in those good principles, which will be a great security for their following the example of their superiors, if it be good, and some sort of preservative against their following it, if it be bad? And serious persons will farther observe very singular reasons for this amongst us; from the discontinuance of that religious intercourse, between pastors and people in private, which remains in Protestant churches abroad, as well as in the church of Rome; and from our small public care and provision for keeping up a sense of religion in the lower rank, except by distributing religious books. For in this way they have been assisted; and any well-disposed person may do much good amongst them, and at a very trifling expense, since the worthy society before mentioned has so greatly lessened the price of such books. But this pious charity is an additional reason why the poor should be taught to read, that they may be in a capacity of receiving the benefit of it. Vain indeed would be the hope, that any thing in this world can be fully secured from abuse. For as it is the general scheme of divine Providence to bring good out of evil; so the wickedness of men will, if it be possible, bring evil out of good. But upon the whole, incapacity and ignorance must be favourable to error and vice; and knowledge and improvement contribute, in due time, to the destruction of impiety as well as superstition, and to the general prevalence of true religion. But some of these observations may perhaps be thought too remote from the present occasion. It is more obviously to the purpose of it to observe, that reading, writing, and accounts, are useful, and whatever

cause it is owing to, would really now be wanted in the
very lowest stations : and that the trustees of our charity-
schools are fully convinced of the great fitness of joining to
instruction easy labour, of some sort or other, as fast as it
is practicable; which they have already been able to do in
some of them.

Then as to placing out the poor children, as soon as they
are arrived at a fit age for it, this must be approved by every
one, as it is putting them in a way of industry under domestic government, at a time of life, in some respects, more
dangerous than even childhood.   And it is a known thing,
that care is taken to do it in a manner which does not set
them above their rank ; though it is not possible always to
do it exactly as one would wish.   Yet I hope it may be
observed without offence, if any of them happen to be of a
very weakly constitution, or of a very distinguished capacity,
there can be no impropriety in placing these in employments
adapted to their particular cases ; though such as would be
very improper for the generality.

But the principal design of this charity is to educate poor
children in such a manner, as has a tendency to make them
good, and useful, and contented, whatever their particular
station be.   The care of this is greatly neglected by the
poor ; nor truly is it more regarded by the rich, considering
what might be expected from them.   And if it were as
practicable to provide charity-schools, which should supply
this shameful neglect in the rich, as it is to supply the like,
though more excusable, neglect in the poor, I should think
certainly, that both ought to be done for the same reasons.
And most people, I hope, will think so too, if they attend to
the thing I am speaking of ; which is the moral and religious part of education ; which is equally necessary for all
ranks, and grievously wanting in all.   Yet in this respect
the poor must be greatly upon a disadvantage, from the
nature of the case ; as will appear to any one who will consider it.

For if poor children are not sent to school, several years
of their childhood, of course, pass away in idleness and loi-
tering.   This has a tendency to give them, perhaps a feeble
listlessness, perhaps a headstrong profligateness of mind ;
certainly an indisposition to proper application as they grow
up, and an aversion afterwards, not only to the restraints of

religion, but to those which any particular calling, and even the nature of society require. Whereas children kept to stated orders, and who, many hours of the day, are in employment, are by this means habituated, both to submit to those who are placed over them, and to govern themselves; and they are also by this means prepared for industry in any way of life in which they may be placed. And all this holds, abstracted from the consideration of their being taught to read : without which, however, it will be impracticable to employ their time; not to repeat the unanswerable reasons for it before mentioned. Now, several poor people cannot, others will not, be at the expense of sending their children to school. And let me add, that such as can and are willing, yet if it be very inconvenient to them, ought to be eased of it, and the burden of children made as light as may be to their poor parents.

Consider next the manner in which the children of the poor, who have vicious parents, are brought up in comparison with other children whose parents are of the same character. The children of dissolute men of fortune may have the happiness of not seeing much of their parents. And this, even though they are educated at home, is often the case, by means of a customary distance between them, which cannot be kept amongst the poor. Nor is it impossible that a rich man of this character, desiring to have his children better than himself, may provide them such an education as may make them so, without his having any restraint or trouble in the matter. And the education which children of better rank must have for their improvement in the common accomplishments belonging to it, is of course, as yet, for the most part, attended with some sort of religious education. But the poor, as they cannot provide persons to educate their children; so, from the way in which they live together in poor families, a child must be an eye and ear-witness of the worst part of his parent's talk and behaviour. And it cannot but be expected, that his own will be formed upon it. For, as example in general has very great influence upon all persons, especially children, the example of their parents is of authority with them, when there is nothing to balance it on the other side. Now, take in the supposition that these parents are dissolute, profligate people; then, over and above giving their children no sort

of good instruction, and a very bad example, there are
more crimes than one, in which it may be feared they will
directly instruct and encourage them ; besides letting them
ramble abroad wherever they will, by which, of course,
they learn the very same principles and manners they do at
home. And from all these things together, such poor children will have their characters formed to vice, by those
whose business it is to restrain them from it. They will be
disciplined and trained up in it. This surely is a case which
ought to have some public provision made for it. If it cannot have an adequate one, yet such an one as it can; unless
it be thought so rare as not to deserve our attention. But,
in reality, though there should be no more parents of this
character amongst the poor in proportion, than amongst the
rich, the case which I have been putting will be far from
being uncommon. Now, notwithstanding the danger to
which the children of such wretched parents cannot but be
exposed, from what they see at home : yet by instilling
into them the principles of virtue and religion at school, and
placing them soon out in sober families, there is ground to
hope they may avoid those ill courses, and escape that ruin
into which, without this care, they would almost certainly
run. I need not add how much greater ground there is to
expect, that those of the children who have religious parents will do well. For such parents, besides setting their
children a good example, will likewise repeat and enforce
upon them at home the good instructions they receive at
school.

After all, we find the world continues very corrupt.
And it would be miraculous indeed, if charity-schools alone
should make it otherwise ; or if they should make even all
who are brought up in them, proof against its corruptions. The truth is, every method that can be made use of
to prevent or reform the bad manners of the age, will appear
to be of less effect, in proportion to the greater occasion there
is for it ; as cultivation, though the most proper that can
be, will produce less fruit, or of a worse sort, in a bad climate than in a good one. And thus the character of the
common people, with whom these children are to live in the
ordinary intercourse of business and company when they
came out into the world, may more or less defeat the good
effects of their education. And so likewise may the charac-

ter of men of rank, under whose influence they are to live. But whatever danger may be apprehended from either or both of these, it can be no reason why we should not endeavour, by the likeliest methods we can, to better the world, or keep it from growing worse. The good tendency of the method before us is unquestionable. And I think myself obliged to add, that upon a comparison of parishes where charity-schools have been for a considerable time established, with neighbouring ones in like situations, which have had none, the good effects of them, as I am very credibly informed, are most manifest. Notwithstanding, I freely own, that it is extremely difficult to make the necessary comparison in this case, and form a judgment upon them. And a multitude of circumstances must come in to determine, from appearances only, concerning the positive good which is produced by this charity, and the evil which is prevented by it; which last is full as material as the former, and can scarce be estimated at all. But surely there can be no doubt whether it be useful or not to educate children in order, virtue, and religion.

However, suppose, which is yet far from being the case, but suppose it should seem, that this undertaking did not answer the expense and trouble of it, in the civil or political way of considering things, what is this to persons who profess to be engaged in it, not only upon mere civil views, but upon moral and Christian ones? We are to do our endeavours to promote virtue and religion amongst men, and leave the success to God: the designs of his providence are answered by these endeavours, "whether they will hear, or whether they will forbear:" i. e. whatever be the success of them: and the least success in such endeavours is a great and valuable effect.*

From these foregoing observations, duly considered, it will appear, that the objections which have been made against charity-schools, are to be regarded in the same light with those which are made against any other necessary things: for instance, against providing for the sick and the aged poor. Objections in this latter case could be considered no otherwise than merely as warnings of some in-

* See the Sermon before the Society for the Propagation of the Gospel.

convenience which might accompany such charity, and might, more or less, be guarded against, the charity itself being still kept up; or as proposals for placing it upon some better footing. For though amidst the disorder and imperfection in all human things, these objections were not obviated, they could not, however, possibly be understood as reasons for discontinuing such charity; because, thus understood, there would be reasons for leaving necessitous people to perish. Well disposed persons, therefore, will take care that they be not deluded with objections against this before us, any more than against other necessary charities, as though such objections were reasons for suppressing them, or not contributing to their support, unless we can procure an alteration of that to which we object. There can be no possible reasons for leaving poor children in that imminent danger of ruin, in which many of these must be left, were it not for this charity. Therefore objections against it cannot, from the nature of the case, amount to more than reasons for endeavouring, whether with or without success, to put it upon a right and unexceptionable footing, in the particular respects objected against. And if this be the intention of the objectors, the managers of it have shown themselves remarkably ready to second them; for they have shown even a docility in receiving admonitions of any thing thought amiss in it, and proposals for rendering it more complete. And under the influence of this good spirit, the management of it is really improving: particularly in greater endeavours to introduce manufactures into these schools, and in more particular care to place the children out to employments in which they are most wanted, and may be most serviceable, and which are most suitable to their ranks. But if there be anything in the management of them, which some particular persons think should be altered, and others are of a contrary opinion, these things must be referred to the judgment of the public, and the determination of the public complied with. Such compliance is an essential principle of all charitable associations, for without it they could not subsist at all; and by charitable associations, multitudes are put in mind to do good, who otherwise would not have thought of it; and infinitely more good may be done than possibly can by the separate endeavours of the same number of charitable persons.

Now, he who refuses to help forward the good work before us, because it is not conducted exactly in his own way, breaks in upon that general principle of union, which those who are friends to the indigent and distressed part of our fellow-creatures, will be very cautious how they do in any case ; but more especially will they beware how they break in upon that necessary principle in a case of so great importance as is the present.   For the public is as much interested in the education of poor children, as in the preservation of their lives.

This last, I observed, is legally provided for. The former is left amongst other works of charity, neglected by many who care for none of these things, and to be carried on by such only as think it their concern to be doing good. Some of you are able, and in a situation to assist in it in an eminent degree, by being trustees, and overlooking the management of these schools ; or in different ways countenancing and recommending them, as well as by contributing to their maintenance ; others can assist only in this latter way.   In what manner and degree then it belongs to you, and to me, and to any particular person, to help it forward, let us all consider seriously, not for one another, but each of us for himself.

And may the blessing of Almighty God accompany this work of Charity, which he has put into the hearts of his servants, in behalf of these poor children ; that being now "trained up in the way they should go, when they are old they may not depart from it." May he, of his mercy, keep them safe against the innumerable dangers of this bad world, through which they are to pass, and preserve them unto his heavenly kingdom.

SERMON V.

PREACHED BEFORE THE HOUSE OF LORDS, IN THE ABBEY CHURCH
OF WESTMINSTER,

On Thursday, June 11, 1747 :

Being the Anniversary of his Majesty's Happy Accession to the Throne.

---

1 TIMOTHY ii. 1, 2.

*I exhort, that first of all, supplications, prayers, interces-
sions, and giving of thanks, be made for all men : for
kings, and for all that are in authority ; that we may
lead a quiet and peaceable life, in all godliness and
honesty.*

IT is impossible to describe the general end which Providence has appointed us to aim at, in our passage through
the present world, in more expressive words than these very
plain ones of the apostle, " to lead a quiet and peaceable
life, in all godliness and honesty." " A quiet and peaceable life," by way of distinction, surely, from eager tumul-
tuary pursuits in our private capacity, as well as in opposition both to our making insurrections in the state, and to
our suffering oppression from it. " To lead a quiet and
peaceable life, in all godliness and honesty," is the whole that
we have any reason to be concerned for. To this the constitution of our nature carries us: and our external condition
is adapted to it.

Now, in aid to this general appointment of Providence,
civil government has been instituted over the world, both

by the light of nature and by revelation, to instruct men in
the duties of fidelity, justice, and regard to common good,
and enforce the practice of these virtues, without which
there could have been no peace or quiet amongst mankind;
and to preserve, in different ways, a sense of religion, as
well as virtue, and of God's authority over us.   For if we
could suppose men to have lived out of government, they
must have run wild, and all knowledge of divine things must
have been lost from among them.   But by means of their
uniting under it, they have been preserved in some tolerable
security from the fraud and violence of each other; order,
a sense of virtue, and the practice of it, has been, in some
measure, kept up; and religion, more or less pure, has been
all along spread and propagated. So that I make no scruple
to affirm, that civil government has been, in all ages, a
standing publication of the law of nature, and an enforcement of it; though never in its perfection, for the most part
greatly corrupted, and, I suppose, always so in some degree.

And, considering that civil government is that part of
God's government over the world, which he exercises by
the instrumentality of men, wherein that which is oppression, injustice, cruelty, as coming from them, is, under his
direction, necessary discipline, and just punishment; considering, that " all power is of God,"* all authority is properly
of divine appointment; men's very living under magistracy
might naturally have led them to the contemplation of
authority in its source and origin; the one supreme, absolute
authority of Almighty God, by which he " doth according
to his will in the army of heaven, and among the inhabitants
of the earth;"† which he now exerts, visibly and invisibly,
by different instruments, in different forms of administration,
different methods of discipline and punishment; and which
he will continue to exert hereafter, not only over mankind,
when this mortal life shall be ended, but throughout his universal kingdom; till, by having rendered to all according to
all their works, he shall have completely executed that just
scheme of government, which he has already begun to
execute in this world, by their hands whom he has appointed
for the present " punishment of evil doers, and for the praise
of them that do well."‡

* Rom. xiii. 1.   † Dan. iv. 35.   ‡ 1 Pet. ii. 14.

And though that perfection of justice cannot in any sort take place in this world, even under the very best governments : yet, under the worst, men have been enabled to lead much more quiet and peaceable lives, as well as to attend to and keep up a sense of religion, much more than they could possibly have done without any government at all.   But a free Christian government is adapted to answer these purposes in a higher degree, in proportion to its just liberty, and the purity of its religious establishment.   And as we enjoy these advantages, civil and religious, in a very eminent degree, under a good prince, and those he has placed in authority over us, we are eminently obliged to offer up supplications and thanksgivings in their behalf : to pay them all that duty which these prayers imply ; and " to lead," as those advantages enable, and have a tendency to dispose us to do, " quiet and peaceable lives, in all godliness and honesty."

Of the former of these advantages, our free constitution of civil government, we seem to have a very high value. And if we would keep clear from abuses of it, it could not be overvalued, otherwise than as every thing may, when considered as respecting this world only.   We seem, I say, sufficiently sensible of the value of our civil liberty.   It is our daily boast, and we are in the highest degree jealous of it.   Would to God we were somewhat more judicious in our jealousy of it, so as to guard against its chief enemy, one might say, the only enemy of it we have at present to fear, I mean licentiousness : which has undermined so many free governments, and without whose treacherous help no free government, perhaps, ever was undermined.   This licentiousness, indeed, is not only dangerous to liberty, but it is actually a present infringement of it in many instances. But I must not turn this good day into a day of reproach. Dropping, then, the encroachments which are made upon our liberty, peace, and quiet, by licentiousness, we are certainly a freer nation than any other we have an account of ; and as free, it seems, as the very nature of government will permit.   Every man is equally under the protection of the laws ; may have equal justice against the most rich and powerful ; and securely enjoy all the common blessings of life, with which the industry of his ancestors, or his own, has furnished him.   In some other countries the upper part of the world is free; but in Great Britain the whole body of the people is free. For we have at length, to the distinguished honour of those who began, and have more particularly laboured in it, emancipated our northern provinces from most of their legal remains of slavery; for voluntary slavery cannot be abolished, at least not directly, by law. I take leave to speak of this long-desired work as done; since it wants only his concurrence, who, as we have found by many years' experience, considers the good of his people as his own. And I cannot but look upon these acts of the legislature, in a further view, as instances of regard to posterity, and declarations of its readiness to put every subject upon an equal footing of security and freedom, if any of them are not so, in any other respects, which come into its view; and as a precedent and example for doing it.

Liberty, which is the very genius of our civil constitution, and runs through every branch of it, extends its influence to the ecclesiastical part of it. A religious establishment, without a toleration of such as think they cannot, in conscience, conform to it, is itself a general tyranny; because it claims absolute authority over conscience, and would soon beget particular kinds of tyranny of the worst sort, tyranny over the mind, and various superstitions, after the way should be paved for them, as it soon must, by ignorance. On the other hand, a constitution of civil government without any religious establishment, is a chimerical project, of which there is no example; and which, leaving the generality without guide and instruction, must leave religion to be sunk and forgotten amongst them; and, at the same time, give full scope to superstition and the gloom of enthusiasm; which last, especially, ought surely to be diverted and checked, as far as it can be done without force. Now, a reasonable establishment provides instruction for the ignorant, withdraws them, not in the way of force, but of guidance, from running after those kinds of conceits. It doubtless has a tendency, likewise, to keep up a sense of real religion, and real Christianity, in a nation; and is, moreover, necessary for the encouragement of learning: some parts of which the Scripture revelation absolutely requires should be cultivated.

It is to be remarked, further, that the value of any particular religious establishment is not to be estimated merely by what it is in itself, but also by what it is in comparison

M

with those of other nations; a comparison which will sufficiently teach us, not to expect perfection in human things. And what is still more material, the value of our own ought to be very much heightened in our esteem, by considering what it is a security from; I mean that great corruption of Christianity, popery, which is ever hard at work to bring us again under its yoke. Whoever will consider the popish claims to the disposal of the whole earth, as of divine right; to dispense with the most sacred engagements; the claims to supreme absolute authority in religion; in short, the general claims which the canonists express by the words, plenitude of power;—whoever, I say, will consider popery as it is professed at Rome, may see that it is manifest open usurpation of all human and divine authority. But even in those Roman catholic countries where these monstrous claims are not admitted, and the civil power does, in many respects, restrain the papal, yet persecution is professed, as it is absolutely enjoined, by what is acknowledged to be their highest authority, a general council, so called, with the pope at the head of it; and is practised in all of them, I think, without exception, where it can be done safely. Thus they go on to substitute force instead of argument; and external profession made by force instead of reasonable conviction. And thus corruptions of the grossest sort have been in vogue for many generations, in many parts of Christendom, and are so still, even where popery obtains in its least absurd form; and their antiquity and wide extent are insisted upon as proofs of their truth;—a kind of proof which, at best, can be only presumptive, but which loses all its little weight, in proportion as the long and large prevalence of such corruptions has been obtained by force.

Indeed, it is said in the book of Job, that the worship of "the sun and moon was an iniquity to be punished by the judge."* And this, though it is not so much as a precept, much less a general one, is, I think, the only passage of Scripture which can, with any colour, be alleged in favour of persecution of any sort; for what the Jews did, and what they were commanded to do, under their theocracy, are both quite out of the case. But, whenever that book was written, the scene of it is laid at a time when idolatry was in its

* Job xxxi. 26—28.

infancy, an acknowledged novelty, essentially destructive of
true religion, arising, perhaps, from mere wantonness of
imagination.   In these circumstances, this greatest of evils,
which afterwards laid waste true religion over the face of the
earth, might have been suppressed at once, without danger of
mistake or abuse. And one might go on to add, that if those
to whom the care of this belonged, instead of serving themselves
of prevailing superstitions, had in all ages and countries
opposed them in their rise, and adhered faithfully to that
primitive religion, which was received " of old, since man
was placed upon earth,"* there could not possibly have been
any such difference of opinion concerning the Almighty
Governor of the world, as could have given any pretence for
tolerating the idolatries which overspread it.   On the contrary, his universal monarchy must have been universally
recognized, and the general laws of it more ascertained and
known, than the municipal ones of any particular country
can be. In such a state of religion, as it could not but have
been acknowledged by all mankind, that immorality of every
sort was disloyalty to him, " the high and lofty One that
inhabiteth eternity, whose name is Holy ;"† so it could not
but have been manifest, that idolatry, in those determinate
instances of it, was plain rebellion against him ; and, therefore, might have been punished as an offence of the highest
kind, against the supreme authority in nature.   But this is
in no sort applicable to the present state of religion in the
world.   For if the principle of punishing idolatry were now
admitted amongst the several different parties in religion,
the weakest in every place would run a great risk of being
convicted of it ; or, however, heresy and schism would soon
be found crimes of the same nature, and equally deserving
punishment.   Thus the spirit of persecution would range
without any stop or control, but what should arise from its
want of power.   But our religious establishment disclaims
all principles of this kind, and desires not to keep persons
in its communion, or gain proselytes to it, by any other
methods than the Christian ones of argument and conviction.
    These hints may serve to remind us of the value we ought
to set upon our constitution in church and state, the advantages of which are the proper subjects of our commemoration

* Job xx. 4.   † Isaiah lvii. 15.

on this day, as his Majesty has shown himself, not in words but in the whole course of his reign, the guardian and protector of both. And the blessings of his reign are not only rendered more sensible, but are really heightened, by its securing us from that pretender to his crown, whom we had almost forgot, till our late danger renewed our apprehensions; who, we know, is a professed enemy to our church, and grown old in resentments, and maxims of government, directly contrary to our civil constitution; nay, his very claim is founded in principles destructive of it. Our deliverance, and our security, from this danger, with all the other blessings of the king's government, are so many reasons for " supplications, prayers, intercessions, and giving of thanks," to which we are exhorted, as well as for all other dutiful behaviour towards it; and should also remind us to take care and make due improvement of those blessings, " by leading," in the enjoyment of them, " quiet and peaceable lives, in all godliness and honesty."

The Jewish church offered sacrifices even for heathen princes, to whom they were in subjection; and the primitive Christian church, the Christian sacrifices of supplications and prayers, for the prosperity of the emperor and the state; though they were falsely accused of being enemies to both, because they would not join in their idolatries. In conformity to these examples of the church of God in all ages, prayers for the king, and those in authority under him, are part of the daily service of our own. And for the day of his inauguration a particular service is appointed, which we are here assembled in the house of God to celebrate. This is the first duty we owe to kings, and those who are in authority under them, that we make prayers and thanksgivings for them. And in it is comprehended, what yet may be considered as another, paying them honour and reverence. Praying for them is itself an instance and expression of this, as it gives them a part in our highest solemnities. It also reminds us of that further honour and reverence which we are to pay them, as occasions offer, throughout the whole course of our behaviour. " Fear God, honour the king,"* are apostolic precepts; and " despising government, and speaking evil of dignities,"† apostolic descriptions of such

* 1 Pet. ii. 17.   † 2 Pet. ii. 9, 10.

as " are reserved unto the day of judgment to be punished."
And if these evil speeches are so highly criminal, it cannot
be a thing very innocent to make a custom of entertaining
ourselves with them.

Further, if we are to pray "that we may," that it may
be permitted us "to lead a quiet and peaceable life," we
ought surely to live so, when, by means of a mild equal
government, it is permitted us; and be very thankful, first
to God, and then to those whom he makes the instruments
of so great good to us, and pay them all obedience and
duty; though every thing be not conducted according to our
judgment, nor every person in employment whom we may
think deserving of it. Indeed, opposition, in a legal regular
way, to measures which a person thinks wrong, cannot but
be allowed in a free government. It is in itself just, and
also keeps up the spirit of liberty. But opposition, from indirect motives, to measures which he sees to be necessary,
is itself immoral: it keeps up the spirit of licentiousness;
is the greatest reproach of liberty, and in many ways
most dangerous to it; and has been a principal means of
overturning free governments. It is well, too, if the
legal subjection to the government we live under, which
may accompany such behaviour, be not the reverse of
" Christian subjection; subjection for wrath only," and "not
for conscience sake."* And one who wishes well to his
country will beware how he inflames the common people
against measures, whether right or wrong, which they are
not judges of. For no one can foresee how far such dis-
affection will extend; but every one sees, that it diminishes
the reverence which is certainly owing to authority. Our
due regards to these things are indeed instances of our
loyalty, but they are in reality as much instances of our
patriotism too. Happy the people who live under a prince
the justice of whose government renders them coincident!

Lastly, As, by the good providence of God, we were
born under a free government, and are members of a pure
reformed church, both of which he has wonderfully preserved through infinite dangers: if we do not take heed to
live like Christians, nor to govern ourselves with decency
in those respects in which we are free, we shall be a dis-

* Rom. xiii. 5.

honour to both. Both are most justly to be valued: but
they may be valued in the wrong place. It is no more a
recommendation of civil, than it is of natural liberty,* that
it must put us into a capacity of behaving ill. Let us then
value our civil constitution, not because it leaves us the
power of acting as mere humour and passion carries us, in
those respects in which governments less free lay men under
restraints: but for its equal laws, by which the great are
disabled from oppressing those below them. Let us trans-
fer, each of us, the equity of this our civil constitution to
our own personal character; and be sure to be as much
afraid of subjection to mere arbitrary will and pleasure in
ourselves, as to the arbitrary will of others. For the tyranny of our own lawless passions is the nearest and most
dangerous of all tyrannies.

Then as to the other part of our constitution, let us value
it, not because it leaves us at liberty to have as little religion
as we please, without being accountable to human judica-
tories; but because it affords us the means and assistance
to worship God according to his word; because it exhibits
to our view, and enforces upon our conscience, genuine
Christianity, free from the superstitions with which it is de-
filed in other countries. These superstitions naturally tend
to abate its force: our profession of it, in its purity, is a
particular call upon us to yield ourselves up to its full influence; "to be pure in heart;"† "to be holy in all manner of conversation."‡ Much of the form of godliness is
laid aside amongst us: this itself should admonish us to attend more to the "power thereof."§ We have discarded
many burdensome ceremonies: let us be the more careful
to cultivate inward religion. We have thrown off a multitude of superstitious practices, which were called good
works: let us the more abound in all moral virtues, these
being unquestionably such. Thus our lives will justify and
recommend the Reformation; and we shall "adorn the doctrine of God our Saviour in all things."‖

* Natural liberty as opposed to necessity, or fate.
† Matt. v. 8.   ‡ 1 Pet. i. 15.   § 2 Tim. iii. 5.   ‖ Tit. ii. 10.

SERMON VI.

PREACHED BEFORE HIS GRACE CHARLES, DUKE OF RICHMOND,
PRESIDENT, AND THE GOVERNORS OF THE
LONDON INFIRMARY,

*For the Relief of Sick and Diseased Persons, especially Manufac-
turers, and Seamen in Merchant Service, &c.*

At the Parish Church of St. Lawrence-Jewry, on Thursday,
March 31, 1748.

---

1 PETER iv. 8.

*And above all things, have fervent charity among yourselves;
for charity shall cover the multitude of sins.*

As we owe our being, and all our faculties, and the very
opportunities of exerting them, to Almighty God, and are
plainly his, and not our own, we are admonished, even
though we should " have done all those things which are
commanded us, to say, we are unprofitable servants."* And
with much deeper humility must we make this acknowledgment when we consider in how " many things we have
all offended."† But still the behaviour of such creatures
as men, highly criminal in some respects, may yet in others
be such as to render them the proper objects of mercy, and,
our Saviour does not decline saying, "thought worthy of
it."‡ And conformably to our natural sense of things, the
Scripture is very express, that mercy, forgiveness, and in

---

* Luke xvii. 10.   † James iii. 2.   ‡ Luke xx. 35.

general, charity to our fellow-creatures, has this efficacy in a very high degree.

Several copious and remote reasons have been alleged, why such pre-eminence is given to this grace or virtue: some of great importance, and none of them perhaps without its weight. But the proper one seems to be very short and obvious, that by fervent charity, with a course of beneficence proceeding from it, a person may make amends for the good he has blameably omitted, and the injuries he has done, so far, as that society would have no demand upon him for such his misbehaviour; nor consequently would justice have any in behalf of society, whatever it might have upon other accounts. Thus, by fervent charity, he may even merit forgiveness of men: and this seems to afford a very singular reason, why it may be graciously granted him by God: a very singular reason, the Christian covenant of pardon always supposed, why divine justice should permit, and divine mercy appoint, that such his charity should be allowed to "cover a multitude of sins."

And this reason leads me to observe, what Scripture, and the whole nature of the thing shows, that the charity here meant, must be such hearty love to our fellow-creatures, as produceth a settled endeavour to promote, according to the best of our judgment, their real lasting good, both present and future: and not that easiness of temper, which, with peculiar propriety, is expressed by the word good-humour, and is a sort of benevolent instinct left to itself, without the direction of our judgment. For this kind of good-humour is so far from making the amends before-mentioned, that, though it be agreeable in conversation, it is often most mischievous in every other intercourse of life; and always puts men out of a capacity of doing the good they might, if they could withstand importunity, and the sight of distress, when the case requires they should be withstood; many instances of which case daily occur, both in public and private. Nor is it to be supposed, that we can any more promote the lasting good of our fellow-creatures, by acting from mere kind inclinations, without considering what are the proper means of promoting it, than that we can attain our own personal good, by a thoughtless pursuit of every thing which pleases us. For the love of our neighbour, as much as self-love, the social affections, as much as the private ones, from their very nature, require to be under the direction of our judgment. Yet it is to be remembered, that it does in no sort become such a creature as man to harden himself against the distresses of his neighbour, except where it is really necessary; and that even well-disposed persons may run into great perplexities, and great mistakes too, by being over-solicitous in distinguishing what are the most proper occasions for their charity, or who the greatest objects of it. And therefore as, on the one side, we are obliged to take some care not to squander that which, one may say, belongs to the poor, as we shall do, unless we competently satisfy ourselves beforehand, that what we put to our account of charity will answer some good purpose: so, on the other side, when we are competently satisfied of this, in any particular instance before us, we ought by no means to neglect such present opportunity of doing good, under the notion of making further inquiries; for of these delays there will be no end.

Having thus briefly laid before you the ground of that singular efficacy, which the text ascribes to charity in general—obviated the objection against its having this efficacy—and distinguished the virtue itself from its counterfeits—let us now proceed to observe the genuineness and excellency of the particular charity, which we are here met together to promote.

Medicine, and every other relief, " under the calamity of bodily diseases and casualties," no less than the daily necessaries of life, are natural provisions, which God has made for our present indigent state, and which he has granted in common to the children of men, whether they be poor or rich; to the rich, by inheritance or acquisition; and by their hands to the disabled poor.

Nor can there be any doubt, but that public infirmaries are the most effectual means of administering such relief; besides that they are attended with incidental advantages of great importance; both which things have been fully shown, and excellently enforced, in the annual sermons upon this and the like occasions.

But, indeed, public infirmaries are not only the best, they are the only possible means by which the poor, especially in this city, can be provided, in any competent measure, with

M 5

the several kinds of assistance which bodily diseases and
casualties require. Not to mention poor foreigners, it is
obvious no other provision can be made for poor strangers
out of the country, when they are overtaken by these calamities, as they often must be, whilst they are occasionally
attending their affairs in this centre of business. But even
the poor who are settled here, are in a manner strangers to
the people amongst whom they live; and, were it not for
this provision, must unavoidably be neglected, in the hurry
and concourse around them, and be left unobserved to lan-
guish in sickness, and suffer extremely, much more than
they could in less populous places, where every one is known
to every one, and any great distress presently becomes the
common talk; and where also poor families are often under the particular protection of some or other of their rich
neighbours, in a very different way from what is commonly
the case here. Observations of this kind show, that there
is a peculiar occasion, and even a necessity, in such a city
as this, for public infirmaries, to which easy admittance may
be had; and here in ours no security is required, nor any
sort of gratification allowed; and that they ought to be
multiplied, or enlarged, proportionably to the increase of
our inhabitants: for to this the increase of the poor will always bear proportion: though less in ages of sobriety and
diligence, and greater in ages of profusion and debauchery.

Now, though nothing to be called an objection in the
way of argument can be alleged against thus providing for
poor sick people, in the properest, indeed the only way in
which they can be provided for; yet persons of too severe
tempers can, even upon this occasion, talk in a manner,
which, contrary surely to their intention, has a very malig-
nant influence upon the spirit of charity—talk of the ill-de-
serts of the poor, the good uses they might make of being
left to suffer more than they do, under distresses which they
bring upon themselves, or however might, by diligence and
frugality, provide against; and the idle uses they may make
of knowing beforehand, that they shall be relieved in case of
those distresses. Indeed, there is such a thing as a prejudice against them, arising from their very state of poverty,
which ought greatly to be guarded against; a kind of prejudice, to which perhaps most of us, upon some occasions,
and in some degree, may inattentively be liable, but which

pride and interest may easily work up to a settled hatred of them; the utter reverse of that amiable part of the character of Job, that "he was a father to the poor."* But it is undoubtedly fit, that such of them as are good and industrious should have the satisfaction of knowing beforehand, that they shall be relieved under diseases and casualties : and those, it is most obvious, ought to be relieved preferably to others. But these others, who are not of that good character, might possibly have the apprehension of those calamities, in so great a degree as would be very mischievous, and of no service, if they thought they must be left to perish under them. And though their idleness and extravagance are very inexcusable, and ought by all reasonable methods to be restrained ; and they are highly to be blamed for not making some provision against age and supposable disasters, when it is in their power; yet it is not to be desired, that the anxieties of avarice should be added to the natural inconveniences of poverty.

It is said, that our common fault towards the poor is not harshness, but too great lenity and indulgence. · And if allowing them in debauchery, idleness, and open beggary ; in drunkenness, profane cursing and swearing in our streets, nay, in our houses of correction : if this be lenity, there is doubtless a great deal too much of it. And such lenity towards the poor is very consistent with the most cruel neglects of them, in the extreme misery to which those vices reduce them. Now, though this last certainly is not our general fault, yet it cannot be said, every one is free from it. For this reason, and that nothing which has so much as the shadow of an objection against our public charities, may be entirely passed over, you will give me leave to consider a little the supposed case above mentioned, though possibly some may think it unnecessary, that of persons reduced to poverty and distress by their own faults.

Instances of this there certainly are. But it ought to be very distinctly observed, that in judging which are such, we are liable to be mistaken ; and more liable to it, in judging to what degree those are faulty, who really are so in some degree. However, we should always look with mildness upon the behaviour of the poor ; and be sure not to expect

* Job xxix. 16.

more from them than can be expected, in a moderate way of considering things. We should be forward, not only to admit and encourage the good deserts of such as do well, but likewise, as to those of them who do not, be ever ready to make due allowances for their bad education, or, which is the same, their having had none; for what may be owing to the ill example of their superiors, as well as companions, and for temptations of all kinds. And remember always, that be men's vices what they will, they have not forfeited their claim to relief under necessities, till they have forfeited their lives to justice.

" Our heavenly Father is kind to the unthankful and the evil ; and sendeth his rain on the just and on the unjust."* And, in imitation of him, our Saviour expressly requires, that our beneficence be promiscuous. But we have, moreover, the Divine example for relieving those distresses, which are brought upon persons by their own faults ; and that is exactly the case we are considering. Indeed the general dispensation of Christianity is an example of this ; for its general design is to save us from our sins, and the punishments which would have been the just consequence of them. But, the Divine example, in the daily course of nature, is a more obvious and sensible one. And though the natural miseries which are foreseen to be annexed to a vicious course of life are providentially intended to prevent it, in the same manner as civil penalties are intended to prevent civil crimes ; yet those miseries, those natural penalties, admit of, and receive natural reliefs, no less than any other miseries which could not have been foreseen or prevented. Charitable providence then, thus manifested in the course of nature, which is the example of our heavenly Father, most evidently leads us to relieve, not only such distresses as were unavoidable, but also such as people by their own faults have brought upon themselves. The case is, that we cannot judge in what degree it was intended they should suffer, by considering what, in the natural course of things, would be the whole bad consequences of their faults, if those consequences were not prevented when nature has provided means to prevent great part of them. We cannot, for instance, estimate what degree of present

* Matt. v. 45.   Luke vi. 35.

sufferings God has annexed to drunkenness, by considering the diseases which follow from this vice, as they would be if they admitted of no reliefs or remedies; but by considering the remaining misery of those diseases, after the application of such remedies as nature has provided. For as it is certain on the one side, that those diseases are providential corrections of intemperance, it is as certain on the other, that the remedies are providential mitigations of those corrections; and altogether as much providential, when administered by the good hand of charity in the case of our neighbour, as when administered by self-love in our own. Thus the pain, and danger, and other distresses of sickness and poverty remaining, after all the charitable relief which can be procured; and the many uneasy circumstances which cannot but accompany that relief, though distributed with all supposable humanity; these are the natural corrections of idleness and debauchery, supposing these vices brought on those miseries. And very severe corrections they are; and they ought not to be increased by withholding that relief, or by harshness in the distribution of it. Corrections of all kinds, even the most necessary ones, may easily exceed their proper bound; and when they do so, they become mischievous; and mischievous in the measure they exceed it. And the natural corrections which we have been speaking of, would be excessive, if the natural mitigations provided for them were not administered.

Then persons, who are so scrupulously apprehensive of every thing, which can possibly, in the most indirect manner, encourage idleness and vice, (which, by the way, any thing may accidentally do,) ought to turn their thoughts to the moral and religious tendency of infirmaries. The religious manner in which they are carried on, has itself a direct tendency to bring the subject of religion into the consideration of those whom they relieve; and, in some degree, to recommend it to their love and practice, as it is productive of so much good to them, as restored ease and health, and a capacity of resuming their several employments. It is to virtue and religion, they may mildly be admonished, that they are indebted for their relief. And this, amongst other admonitions of their spiritual guide, and the quiet and order of their house, out of the way of bad examples, together with a regular course of devotion, which it were greatly to be wished might be daily; these means it is to be hoped, with the common grace of God, may enforce deeply upon their consciences those serious considerations, to which a state of affliction naturally renders the mind attentive ; and that they will return, as from a religious retreat, to their several employments in the world, with lasting impressions of piety in their hearts. By such united advantages, which these poor creatures can in no sort have any other way, very remarkable reformations have been wrought. Persons of the strictest characters, therefore, would give a more satisfactory proof, not to the world, but to their own consciences, of their desire to suppress vice and idleness, by setting themselves to cultivate the religious part of the institutions of infirmaries, which, I think, would admit of great improvements, than by allowing themselves to talk in a manner which tends to discountenance either the institution itself, or any particular branch of it.

Admitting, then, the usefulness and necessity of these kinds of charity, which, indeed, cannot be denied; yet every thing has its bounds. And, in the spirit of severity beforementioned, it is imagined that people are enough disposed, (such, it seems, is the present term,) to contribute largely to them. And some, whether from dislike of the charities themselves, or from mere profligateness think, " these formal recommendations of them at church every year might very well be spared."

But surely it is desirable, that a customary way should be kept open for removing prejudices, as they may arise, against these institutions; for rectifying any misrepresentations which may, at any time, be made of them; and informing the public of any new emergencies ; as well as for repeatedly enforcing the known obligations of charity, and the excellency of this particular kind of it. Then sermons, you know, amongst Protestants, always of course accompany those more solemn appearances in the House of God : nor will these latter be kept up without the other. Now public devotions should ever attend, and consecrate public charities. And it would be a sad presage of the decay of these charities, if ever they should cease to be professedly carried on in the fear of God, and upon the principles of religion. It may be added, that real charitable persons will approve of these frequent exhortations to charity, even

though they should be conscious that they do not themselves stand in need of them, upon account of such as do.
And such can possibly have no right to complain of being
too often admonished of their duty, till they are pleased to
practise it. It is true, indeed, we have the satisfaction of
seeing a spirit of beneficence prevail, in a very commendable degree, amongst all ranks of people, and in a very distinguished manner in some persons among the highest;
yet it is evident, too many of all ranks are very deficient in
it, who are of great ability, and of whom much might be
expected. Though every thing, therefore, were done in
behalf of the poor which is wanted, yet these persons ought
repeatedly to be told, how highly blameable they are for
letting it be done without them; and done by persons of
whom great numbers must have much less ability than
they.

But whoever can really think, that the necessities of the
disabled poor are sufficiently provided for already, must be
strangely prejudiced. If one were to send you to themselves to be better informed, you would readily answer,
that their demands would be very extravagant; that persons
are not to be their own judges in claims of justice, much
less in those of charity. You, then—I am speaking to the
hard people above-mentioned—you are to judge what provision is to be made for the necessitous, so far as it depends
upon your contributions. But ought you not to remember,
that you are interested, that you are parties in the affair, as
well as they? For is not the giver as really so, as the
receiver? And as there is danger that the receiver will
err one way, is there not danger that the giver may err the
other; since it is not matter of arbitrary choice, which has
no rule, but matter of real equity, to be considered as in
the presence of God, what provision shall be made for the
poor? And therefore, though you are yourselves the only
judges what you will do in their behalf, for the case admits
no other; yet, let me tell you, you will not be impartial,
you will not be equitable judges, until you have guarded
against the influence which interest is apt to have upon
your judgment, and cultivated within you the spirit of
charity to balance it. Then you will see the various remaining necessities which call for relief. But that there
are many such, must be evident at first sight to the most

careless observer, were it only from hence, that both this and the other hospitals are often obliged to reject poor objects which offer, even for want of room, or wards to contain them.

Notwithstanding many persons have need of these admonitions, yet there is a good spirit of beneficence, as I observed, pretty generally prevailing.   And I must congratulate you upon the great success it has given to the particular good work before us; great, I think, beyond all example, for the time it has subsisted.   Nor would it be unsuitable to the present occasion, to recount the particulars of this success.   For the necessary accommodations which have been provided, and the numbers who have been relieved, in so short a time, cannot but give high reputation to the London Infirmary.   And the reputation of any particular charity, like credit in trade, is so much real advantage, without the inconveniences to which that is sometimes liable. It will bring in contributions for its support; and men of character, as they shall be wanted, to assist in the management of it; men of skill in the profession, men of conduct in business, to perpetuate, improve, and bring it to perfection.   So that you, the contributors to this charity, and more especially those of you by whose immediate care and economy it is in so high repute, are encouraged to go on with "your labour of love,"* not only by the present good, which you see is here done, but likewise by the prospect of what will probably be done, by your means in future times, when this Infirmary shall become, as I hope it will, no less renowned, than the city in which it is established.

But to see how far it is from being yet complete, for want of contributions, one need only look upon the settled rules of the house for admission of patients.   See there the limitations which necessity prescribes, as to the persons to be admitted.   Read but that one order, though others might be mentioned, that "none who are judged to be in an asthmatic, consumptive, or dying condition, be admitted on any account whatsoever."   Harsh as these words sound, they proceed out of the mouth of charity herself.   Charity pronounces it to be better, that poor creatures, who might receive much ease and relief, should be denied it, if their case

* Heb. vi. 10.

does not admit of recovery, rather than that others, whose case does admit of it, be left to perish. But it shocks humanity to hear such an alternative mentioned; and to think that there should be a necessity, as there is at present, for such restrictions, in one of the most beneficent and best managed schemes in the world. May more numerous or larger contributions, at length open a door to such as these; that what renders their case in the highest degree compassionable, their languishing under incurable diseases, may no longer exclude them from the house of mercy!

But, besides the persons to whom I have been now more particularly speaking, there are others, who do not cast about for excuses for not contributing to the relief of the necessitous, perhaps are rather disposed to relieve them, who yet are not so careful as they ought to be, to put themselves into a capacity of doing it. For we are as really accountable for not doing the good which we might have in our power to do, if we would manage our affairs with prudence, as we are for not doing the good which is in our power now at present. And hence arise the obligations of economy upon people in the highest, as well as in the lower stations of life, in order to enable themselves to do that good, which, without economy, both of them must be incapable of; even though, without it, they could answer the strict demands of justice, which yet we find neither of them can. "A good man showeth favour, and lendeth; and," to enable himself to do so, "he will guide his affairs with discretion."* For want of this, many a one has reduced his family to the necessity of asking relief from those public charities to which he might have left them in a condition of largely contributing.

As economy is the duty of all persons without exception, frugality and diligence are duties which particularly belong to the middle, as well as lower ranks of men; and more particularly still, to persons in trade and commerce, whatever their fortunes be. For trade and commerce cannot otherwise be carried on, but is plainly inconsistent with idleness and profusion; though indeed, were it only from regard to propriety, and to avoid being absurd, every one should conform his behaviour to what his situation in life

* Psal. cxii. 5.

requires, without which the order of society must be broken in upon. And considering how inherited riches, and a life of leisure, are often employed, the generality of mankind have cause to be thankful, that their station exempts them from so great temptations; that engages them in a sober care of their expenses, and in a course of application to business: especially as these virtues, moreover, tend to give them, what is an excellent ground-work for all others, a staved equality of temper and command of their passions. But when a man is diligent and frugal, in order to have it in his power to do good; when he is more industrious, or more sparing, perhaps, than his circumstances necessarily require, that he may " have to give to him that needeth ;"* when he "labours in order to support the weak ;"† such care of his affairs is itself charity, and the actual beneficence which it enables him to practise, is additional charity.

You will easily see, why I insist thus upon these things, because I would particularly recommend the good work before us to all ranks of people in this great city. And I think I have reason to do so, from the consideration, that it very particularly belongs to them to promote it. The gospel, indeed, teaches us to look upon every one in distress as our neighbour, yet neighbourhood, in the literal sense, and likewise several other circumstances, are providential recommendations of such and such charities, and excitements to them; without which the necessitous would suffer much more than they do at present. For our general disposition to beneficence would not be sufficiently directed, and, in other respects, would be very ineffectual, if it were not called forth into action by some or other of those providential circumstances, which form particular relations between the rich and the poor, and are, of course, regarded by every one in some degree. But, though many persons among you, both in the way of contributions, and in other ways no less useful, have done even more than was to be expected, yet I must be allowed to say, that I do not think the relation the inhabitants of this city bear to the persons for whom our Infirmary was principally designed, is sufficiently attended to by the generality; which may be owing to its

* Eph. iv. 28.   † Acts xx. 35.

late establishment. It is, you know, designed principally for " diseased manufacturers, seamen in merchant service, and their wives and children;" and poor manufacturers comprehend all who are employed in any labour whatever, belonging to trade and commerce. The description of these objects shows their relation, and a very near one it is to you, my neighbours, the inhabitants of this city. If any of your domestic servants were disabled by sickness, there is none of you but would think himself bound to do somewhat for their relief. Now these seamen and manufacturers are employed in your immediate business. They are servants of merchants, and other principal traders; as much your servants as if they lived under your roof; though, by their not doing so the relation is less in sight. And supposing they do not all depend upon traders of lower rank, in exactly the same manner, yet many of them do; and they have all connexions with you, which give them a claim to your charity preferable to strangers. They are indeed servants of the public; and so are all industrious poor people, as well as they. But that does not hinder the latter from being more immediately yours. And as their being servants to the public is a general recommendation of this charity to all other persons, so their being more immediately yours, is surely a particular recommendation of it to you. Notwithstanding all this, I will not take upon me to say that every one of you is blameable who does not contribute to your Infirmary, for yours it is in a peculiar sense; but I will say, that those of you who do, are highly commendable. I will say more, that you promote a very excellent work, which your particular station is a providential call upon you to promote. And there can be no stronger reason than this for doing any thing, except the one reason, that it would be criminal to omit it.

These considerations, methinks, might induce every trader of higher rank in this city, to become a subscriber to the Infirmary which is named from it; and others of you, to contribute somewhat yearly to it, in the way in which smaller contributions are given. This would be a most proper offering, out of your increase, to him whose " blessing maketh rich."* Let it be more or less, " every man

* Prov. x. 22.

according as he purposeth in his heart; not grudgingly, or
of necessity, for God loveth a cheerful giver."*

The large benefactions of some persons of ability may be
necessary in the first establishment of a public charity, and
are greatly useful afterwards in maintaining it: but the expenses of this before us, in the extent and degree of perfection to which one would hope it might be brought, cannot
be effectually supported, any more than the expenses of
civil government, without the contribution of great numbers.   You have already the assistance of persons of the
highest rank and fortune, of which the list of our governors
and the present appearance are illustrious examples.   And
their assistance would be far from lessening, by a general
contribution to it amongst yourselves. On the contrary, the
general contribution to it amongst yourselves, which I have
been proposing, would give it still higher repute, and more
invite such persons to continue their assistance, and accept
the honour of being in its direction.   For the greatest persons receive honour from taking the direction of a good
work, as they likewise give honour to it.   And by these
concurrent endeavours, our Infirmary might at length be
brought to answer, in some competent measure, to the
occasions of our city.

Blessed are they who employ their riches in promoting so
excellent a design.   The temporal advantages of them are
far from coming up, in enjoyment, to what they promise at
a distance.   But the distinguished privilege, the prerogative of riches is, that they increase our power of doing good.
This is their proper use.   In proportion as men make this
use of them, they imitate Almighty God : and co-operate
together with him in promoting the happiness of the world ;
and may expect the most favourable judgment which their
case will admit of, at the last day, upon the general repeated maxim of the gospel, that we shall then be treated ourselves as we now treat others.   They have moreover the
prayers of all good men, those of them particularly whom
they have befriended ; and, by such exercise of charity,
they improve within themselves the temper of it, which is
the very temper of heaven.   Consider, next, the peculiar
force with which this branch of charity, alms-giving, is

* 2 Cor. ix. 7.

recommended to us in these words, "He that hath pity upon the poor, lendeth unto the Lord;"* and in these of our Saviour, "Verily, I say unto you, in as much as ye have done it," relieved the sick and needy, "unto one of the least of these, my brethren, ye have done it unto me."† Beware you do not explain away these passages of Scripture, under the notion that they have been made to serve superstitious purposes; but ponder them fairly in your heart, and you will feel them to be of irresistible weight. Lastly, let us remember, in how many instances we have all left undone those things which we ought to have done, and done those things which we ought not to have done. Now, whoever has a serious sense of this, will most earnestly desire to supply the good, which he was obliged to have done, but has not, and undo the evil which he has done, or neglected to prevent; and when that is impracticable, to make amends, in some other way, for his offences—I *can* mean only to our fellow-creatures. To make amends, in some way or other, to a particular person, against whom we have offended, either by positive injury, or by neglect, is an express condition of our obtaining forgiveness of God, when it is in our power to make it. And, when it is not, surely the next best thing is, to make amends to society by fervent charity, in a course of doing good: which riches, as I observed, put very much within our power.

How unhappy a choice, then, do those rich men make, who sacrifice all these high prerogatives of their state to the wretched purposes of dissoluteness and vanity, or to the sordid itch of heaping up, to no purpose at all; whilst, in the mean time, they stand charged with the important trust, in which they are thus unfaithful, and of which a strict account remains to be given.

* Prov. xix. 17.   † Matt. xxv. 40.

A CHARGE

DELIVERED TO THE CLERGY,

At the Primary Visitation of the Diocese of Durham, in the Year 1751.

WITH NOTES,

CONTAINING A DEFENCE OF THE CHARGE AGAINST THE
OBJECTIONS OF AN ANONYMOUS WRITER,[*]

BY THE EDITOR.

It is impossible for me, my brethren, upon our first meeting of this kind, to forbear lamenting with you the general decay of religion in this nation, which is now observed by every one, and has been for some time the complaint of all serious persons. The influence of it is more and more wearing out of the minds of men, even of those who do not pretend to enter into speculations upon the subject; but the number of those who do, and who profess themselves unbelievers, increases, and with their numbers their zeal. Zeal! it is natural to ask—for what? Why, truly, *for*

---

[*] The publication of Bishop Butler's Charge, in the year 1751, was followed by a Pamphlet, printed in 1752, entitled, *A Serious Inquiry into the Use and Importance of External Religion, occasioned by some Passages in the Right Reverend the Lord Bishop of Durham's Charge to the Clergy of that Diocese, &c., humbly addressed to his Lordship.* This Pamphlet has been reprinted in a miscellaneous work: such parts of it, as seemed most worthy of observation, the reader will find in the Notes subjoined to those passages of the Charge, to which the Pamphlet refers.

nothing, but *against* every thing that is good and sacred amongst us.

Indeed, whatever efforts are made against our religion, no Christian can possibly despair of it. For he, who has *all power in heaven and earth*, has promised that *he will be with us to the end of the world*. Nor can the present decline of it be any stumbling-block to such as are considerate; since he himself has so strongly expressed what is as remarkably predicted in other passages of Scripture, the great defection from his religion which should be in the latter days, by that prophetic question, *When the Son of Man cometh, shall he find faith upon the earth?* How near this time is, God only knows; but this kind of Scripture signs of it is too apparent. For as different ages have been distinguished by different sorts of particular errors and vices, the deplorable distinction of ours is, an avowed scorn of religion in some, and a growing disregard to it in the generality.

As to the professed enemies of religion, I know not how often they may come in your way; but often enough I fear, in the way of some at least among you, to require consideration, what is the proper behaviour towards them. One would, to be sure, avoid great familiarities with these persons, especially if they affect to be licentious and profane in their common talk. Yet, if you fall into their company, treat them with the regards which belong to their rank; for so we must people who are vicious in any other respect. We should study what St. James, with wonderful elegance and expressiveness, calls *meekness of wisdom*, in our behaviour towards all men, but more especially towards these men; not so much as being what we owe to them, but to ourselves and our religion; that we may *adorn the doctrine of God our Saviour*, in our carriage towards those who labour to vilify it.

For discourse with them; the caution commonly given, not to attempt answering objections which we have not considered, is certainly just. Nor need any one, in a particular case, be ashamed frankly to acknowledge his ignorance, provided it be not general. And though it were, to talk of what he is not acquainted with, is a dangerous method of endeavouring to conceal it. But a considerate person, however qualified he be to defend his religion, and

answer the objections he hears made against it, may sometimes see cause to decline that office. Sceptical and profane men are extremely apt to bring up this subject at
meetings of entertainment, and such as are of the freer
sort; innocent ones, I mean, otherwise I should not suppose you would be present at them. Now religion is by far
too serious a matter to be the hackney subject upon these
occasions. And by preventing its being made so, you will
better secure the reverence which is due to it, than by entering into its defence. Every one observes, that men's
having examples of vice often before their eyes, familiarizes
it to the mind, and has a tendency to take off that just abhorrence of it which the innocent at first felt, even though
it should not alter their *judgment* of vice, or make them
really *believe* it to be less evil or dangerous. In like manner, the hearing religion often disputed about in light familiar conversation, has a tendency to lessen that sacred regard to it, which a good man would endeavour always to
keep up, both in himself and others. But this is not all:
people are too apt, inconsiderately, to take for granted, that
things are really questionable, because they hear them often
disputed. This, indeed, is so far from being a consequence,
that we know demonstrated truths have been disputed, and
even matters of fact, the objects of our senses. But were
it a consequence—were the evidence of religion no more
than doubtful, then it ought not to be concluded false any
more than true, nor denied any more than affirmed; for
suspense would be the reasonable state of mind with regard
to it. And then it ought in all reason, considering its infinite importance, to have nearly the same influence upon
practice, as if it were thoroughly believed. For would it
not be madness for a man to forsake a safe road, and prefer
to it one in which he acknowledges there is an even chance
he should lose his life, though there were an even chance
likewise of his getting safe through it? Yet there are people absurd enough to take the supposed doubtfulness of religion for the same thing as a proof of its falsehood, after
they have concluded it doubtful from hearing it often called
in question. This shows how infinitely unreasonable sceptical men are, with regard to religion: and that they really
lay aside their reason upon this subject, as much as the
most extravagant enthusiasts. But, further, cavilling and

objecting upon any subject, is much easier than clearing up difficulties; and this last part will always be put upon the defenders of religion. Now, a man may be fully convinced of the truth of a matter, and upon the strongest reasons, and yet not be able to answer all the difficulties which may be raised upon it.

Then, again, the general evidence of religion is complex and various. It consists of a long series of things, one preparatory to and confirming another, from the very beginning of the world to the present time. And it is easy to see how impossible it must be, in a cursory conversation, to unite all this into one argument, and represent it as it ought: and could it be done, how utterly indisposed people would be to attend to it—I say, in a cursory conversation : whereas, unconnected objections are thrown out in a few words, and are easily apprehended, without more attention than is usual in common talk. So that, notwithstanding we have the best cause in the world, and though a man were very capable of defending it, yet I know not why he should be forward to undertake it upon so great a disadvantage, and to so little good effect, as it must be done amidst the gaiety and carelessness of common conversation.

But then it will be necessary to be very particularly upon your guard, that you may not *seem*, by way of compliance, to join in with any levity of discourse respecting religion. Nor would one let any pretended argument against it pass entirely without notice ; nor any gross ribaldry upon it, without expressing our thorough disapprobation. This last may sometimes be done by silence ; for silence sometimes is very expressive ; as was that of our blessed Saviour before the Sanhedrim, and before Pilate. Or it may be done by observing mildly, that religion deserves another sort of treatment, or a more thorough consideration, than such a time, or such circumstances, admit. However, as it is absolutely necessary that we take care, by diligent reading and study, to be always prepared, to be *ready always to give an answer to every man that asketh a reason of the hope that is in us;* so there may be occasions when it will highly become us to do it. And then we must take care to do it in the spirit which the apostle requires, *with meekness and fear :** *meekness* towards those

* 1 Pet. iii. 15.

N

who give occasions for entering into the defence of our religion ; and with *fear*, not of them, but of God ; with that reverential fear, which the nature of religion requires, and which is so far from being inconsistent with, that it will inspire proper courage towards men. Now, this reverential fear will lead us to insist strongly upon the infinite greatness of God's scheme of government, both in extent and duration, together with the wise connexion of its parts, and the impossibility of accounting fully for the several parts, without seeing the whole plan of Providence to which they relate ; which is beyond the utmost stretch of our understanding. And to all this must be added, the necessary deficiency of human language, when things divine are the subject of it. These observations are a proper full answer to many objections, and very material with regard to all.

But your standing business, and which requires constant attention, is with the body of the people ; to revive in them the spirit of religion, which is so much declining. And it may seem, that whatever reason there be for caution as to entering into any argumentative defence of religion *in common conversation*, yet that it is necessary to do this *from the pulpit*, in order to guard the people against being corrupted, however, in some places. But then surely it should be done in a manner as little controversial as possible. For though such as are capable of seeing the force of objections, are capable also of seeing the force of the answers which are given to them, yet the truth is, the people will not competently attend to either. But it is easy to see which they will attend to most. And to hear religion treated of, as what many deny, and which has much said against it as well as for it : this cannot but have a tendency to give them ill impressions at any time : and seems particularly improper for all persons at a time of devotion ; even for such as are arrived at the most settled state of piety :—I say, at a time of devotion, when we are assembled to yield ourselves up to the full influence of the Divine Presence, and to call forth into actual exercise every pious affection of heart. For it is to be repeated, that the heart and course of affections may be disturbed, when there is no alteration of judgment. Now, the evidence of religion may be laid before men without any air of controversy. The proof of the being of God, from final causes, or the design and wisdom which appears

in every part of nature, together with the law of virtue
written upon our hearts;* the proof of Christianity, from
miracles, and the accomplishment of prophecies; and the
confirmation which the natural and civil history of the
world gives to the Scripture account of things : these evidences of religion might properly be insisted on, in a way
to affect and influence the heart, though there were no
professed unbelievers in the world ; and therefore may be
insisted on, without taking much notice that there are such.
And even *their* particular objections may be obviated without a formal mention of them. Besides, as to religion in
general, it is a practical thing, and no otherwise a matter of
speculation, than common prudence in the management of
our worldly affairs is so. And if one were endeavouring to
bring a plain man to be more careful with regard to this
last, it would be thought a strange method of doing it, to
perplex him with stating formally the several objections
which men of gaiety or speculation have made against pru-

* The law of virtue written upon our hearts.]—The author of the
Inquiry, mentioned above, informs, in his Postscript, that "the certain
consequence of referring mankind to a *law of nature, or virtue, written
upon their hearts*, is their having recourse to *their own sense of things*
on all occasions ; which being, in a great majority no better than fa-
mily-superstition, party-prejudice, or self-interested artifice, (perhaps
a compound of all,) will be too apt to overrule the plain precepts of
the gospel." And he declares, he has " no better opinion of the *clearness, certainty, uniformity, universality*, &c. of this law, than" he has
" of the *importance of external religion*." What then must we say
to St. Paul, who not only asserts in the strongest terms, the reality
of such a law, but speaks of its obligation as extending to all mankind ? blaming some among the Gentiles as *without excuse*, for not
adverting to and obeying it ; and commending others for *doing by
nature* (in contradistinction to revelation) *the things contained in the
law*, thus *showing the work of the law written in their hearts*. If, because " natural religion is liable to be mistaken, it is high time to have
done with it in the pulpit ;" how comes it that the same apostle refers
the Philippians to the study of this religion, to *whatsoever things are
true, honest, just, lovely, and of good report ?* And yet, without such a
study, our knowledge of the moral law must always remain imperfect;
for a complete system of morality is certainly nowhere to be found
in the Old or New Testament.* When a Christian minister is enforcing the duties or doctrines of revealed religion, he may perhaps do
well to tell his people he has " *no other* proof of the original truth, obligations, present benefits, and future rewards of religion, to lay before them, than what is contained in the Scriptures." But what if his
purpose be to inculcate some moral virtue ? Will it not be useful here,
[* See the second of Dr. Balguy's Charges.]

dence, and the advantages which they pleasantly tell us folly
has over it; though one could answer those objections ever
so fully.

Nor does the want of religion, in the generality of the
common people, appear owing to a speculative disbelief, or
denial of it, but chiefly to thoughtlessness, and the common
temptations of life. Your chief business, therefore, is to
endeavour to beget a practical sense of it upon their hearts,
as what they acknowledge their belief of, and profess they
ought to conform themselves to. And that is to be done,
by keeping up, as well as we are able, the form and face of
religion with decency and reverence, and in such a degree
as to bring the thoughts of religion often to their minds;*

besides observing that the practice of that virtue is enjoined by a divine command, to recommend it still further to his hearers, by showing that it approves itself to our inward sense and perception, and accords with the native sentiments and suggestions of our minds? Me-
taphysicians may say what they will of our feelings of this sort, being
all illusive, liable to be perverted by education and habit, and judged
of by men's *own sense of things*: they, whose understandings are yet
unspoiled by philosophy and vain deceit, will be little disposed to listen
to such assertions. Nor are there wanting arguments which prove,
and, as should seem, to the satisfaction of every reasonable inquirer,
that the great and leading principles of moral duties have in all ages
been the same; that such virtues as benevolence, justice, compassion,
gratitude, accidental obstacles removed, and when the precise meaning of the words has been once explained, are instinctively known
and approved by all men; and that our approbation of these is as much
a part of our nature implanted in us by God, and as little liable to
caprice and fashion, as the sense of seeing, given us also by him, by
which all bodies appear to us in an erect, and not an inverted position.* Mr. Locke's authority has been generally looked up to as decisive on such questions; and his sentiments have been embraced implicitly, and without examination. That great and good man, however,
is not to be charged with the pernicious consequences which others
have drawn from his opinions: consequences which have been carried
to such a length, as to destroy all moral difference of human actions;
making virtue and vice altogether arbitrary; *calling evil good, and
good evil; putting darkness for light, and light for darkness; putting
bitter for sweet, and sweet for bitter.*

[* See the third of Bishop Hurd's Sermons, vol. i.]

* By keeping up the form and face of religion—in such a *degree,*
as to bring the thoughts of religion *often* to their minds.]—To this it
is said by our *Inquirer*, that "the clergy of the Church of England
have no way of keeping up the *form* and *face* of religion any *oftener,*
or in *any other degree,* than is directed by the prescribed order of the
church." As if the whole duty of a parish priest consisted in reading,

and then endeavouring to make this form more and more subservient to promote the reality and power of it. The form of religion may indeed be, where there is little of the thing itself; but the thing itself cannot be preserved amongst mankind without the form.* And this form frequently occurring in some instance or other of it, will be a frequent admonition† to bad men to repent, and to good

prayers, and a sermon on Sundays, and performing the occasional offices appointed in the Liturgy! One would think the writer who made this objection had never read more of the charge than the *four pages* he has particularly selected for the subject of his animadversions. Had he looked farther, he would have found other methods recommended to the clergy, of introducing a sense of religion into the minds of their parishioners, which occur *much oftener* than the times allotted for the public services of the church: such as family prayers; acknowledging the divine bounty at our meals; personal applications from ministers of parishes to individuals under their care, on particular occasions and circumstances: as at the time of confirmation, at first receiving the holy communion, on recovery from sickness, and the like; none of which are prescribed in our established ritual, any more than those others so ludicrously mentioned by this writer, "bowing to the east, turning the face to that quarter in repeating the creeds, dipping the finger in water, and therewith crossing the child's forehead in baptism."

* The thing itself cannot be preserved amongst mankind without the form.]—The Quakers reject all forms, even the two of Christ's own institution; will it be said, that "these men have no religion preserved among them?" It will neither be said nor insinuated. The Quakers, though they have not the *form*, are careful to keep up the *face* of religion; as appears, not only from the custom of assembling themselves for the purposes of public worship on the Lord's day, but from their silent meetings on other days of the week. And that they are equally sensible of the importance of maintaining the influence of religion on their minds, is manifest from the practice of what they call *inward prayer*, in conformity to the direction of Scripture to *pray continually;* "Which," saith Robert Barclay, "cannot be understood of *outward* prayer, because it were impossible that men should be always upon their knees, expressing the *words* of prayer; which would hinder them from the exercise of those duties no less positively commanded."—*Apology for the Quakers*, Prop. xi. *of Worship.*

† This form *frequently* occurring in some instance or other of it, will be a *frequent* admonition, &c.]—Here it has been objected, that "the *number, variety*, and *frequent* occurrence of forms in religion, are too apt to be considered by *the generality* as *commutations* for their vices, as something *substituted* in lieu of repentance, and as loads and incumbrances upon true Christian edification." This way of arguing against the use of a thing from the abuse of it, instead of arguing from the nature of the thing itself, is the master sophism that pervades the whole performance we are here examining. What reasonable man ever denied that the pomp of outward worship has been sometimes

men to grow better; and also be the means of their doing so.

That which men have accounted religion in the several countries of the world, generally speaking, has had a great and conspicuous part in all public appearances, and the face of it been kept up with great reverence throughout all ranks, from the highest to the lowest; not only upon occasional solemnities, but also in the daily course of behaviour. In the heathen world, their superstition was the chief subject of statuary, sculpture, painting, and poetry. It mixed itself with business, civil forms, diversions, domestic entertainments, and every part of common life. The Mahometans are obliged to short devotions five times between morning and evening. In Roman Catholic countries, people cannot pass a day without having religion recalled to their thoughts, by some or other memorial of it; by some ceremony, or public religious form, occurring in their way;*

mistaken for inward piety? that positive institutions, when rested in as ends, instead of being applied as means, are hurtful to the interests of true religion? Not Bishop Butler certainly, who blames the observances of the Papists on this account, some of them as being " in themselves wrong and superstitious;" and others, as being " made subservient to the purposes of superstitition," and for this reason "abolished by our reformers." In the mean while, it will still be true, that bodily worship is by no means to be discarded, as unuseful in exciting spiritual devotion; on the contrary, that they mutually assist and strengthen each other; and that a mere mental intercourse with God, and a religious service purely intellectual, is altogether unsuitable to such a creature as man, during his present state on earth.

* In Roman Catholic countries, people cannot pass a day without having *religion* recalled to their thoughts—by some ceremony, or public *religious* form, occurring in their way.]—" What in the former period, (when speaking of the Heathen world,) was called *superstition,* becomes in this, (when speaking of Roman Catholics,) *Religion, and Religious forms;* which the Papists pretending to connect with Christianity, and the Charge giving no hint that this is no more than a pretence, a plain reader must needs take this as spoken of the means and memorials of true religion, and will accordingly consider these as recommended to his practice and imitation." If a plain reader, at first view of the passage alluded to, should inadvertently fall into such a mistake, he would find that mistake immediately corrected by the very next sentence that follows, where the religion of the Roman Catholics, and their superstition, are distinguished from each other in express words. But the terms in question are used with the strictest propriety. The design of the Bishop, in this part of his Charge, is to consider religion, not under the notion of its being true, but as it affects the senses and imaginations of the multitude. For

besides their frequent holidays, the short prayers they are
daily called to, and the occasional devotions enjoined by
confessors. By these means their superstition sinks deep
into the minds of the people, and their religion also into the
minds of such among them as are serious and well-disposed.
Our reformers, considering that some of these observances
were in themselves wrong and superstitious, and others of
them made subservient to the purposes of superstition,
abolished them, reduced the form of religion to great simplicity, and enjoined no more particular rules, nor left any
thing more of what was external in religion, than was, in a
manner, necessary to preserve a sense of religion itself upon
the minds of the people. But a great part of this is neglected by the generality amongst us; for instance, the
service of the church, not only upon common days, but
also upon saints' days; and several other things might be
mentioned. Thus they have no customary admonition, no
public call to recollect the thoughts of God and religion
from one Sunday to another.

It was far otherwise under the law. "These words,"
says Moses to the children of Israel, "which I command
thee, shall be in thine heart: and thou shalt teach them
diligently unto thy children, and shalt talk of them when
thou sittest in thine house, and when thou walkest by the

so the paragraph begins: " That which men *have accounted* religion
in the several countries of the world, (whether the religion be true or
false is beside his present argument,) generally speaking, has had a
great and conspicuous part in all public appearances." This position
he illustrates by three examples, the Heathen, the Mahometan, and
the Roman Catholic religions. The two first of these, having little or
nothing of true religion belonging to them, may well enough be characterised under the common name of superstition: the last contains
a mixture of both: which, therefore, the Bishop, like a good writer,
as well as a just reasoner, is careful to distinguish. In Roman
Catholic countries, a man can hardly travel a mile without passing a
crucifix erected on the road side: he may either stop to worship the
image represented on the cross, or he may simply be reminded by it
of his own relation to Christ crucified: thus by one and the same outward sign, "religion may be recalled to his thoughts," or superstition
may take possession of his mind. In the celebration of the Eucha-
rist, the elements of bread and wine are regarded by a Papist as the
very body and blood of Christ; to a Protestant, they appear only as
symbols and memorials of that body and blood; what in one is an act
of rational devotion, becomes in the other an instance of the grossest
superstition, if not idolatry.

way, and when thou liest down, and when thou risest up."*
And as they were commanded this, so it is obvious how
much the constitution of that law was adapted to effect it,
and keep religion ever in view. And without somewhat of
this nature, piety will grow languid even among the better

* *And when thou risest up.*]—Allowing that "what Moses in this
passage wanted to have effected was obedience to the *moral* law,"
nothing, sure, could be of greater use in securing that obedience than
the practice here enjoined. Our *Inquirer*, however, is of a different
opinion, and "very much questions whether his Lordship could have
fallen upon any passage in the Old Testament, which relates at all to
his subject, that would have been less favourable to his argument."
Who shall decide, &c. ?—The Bishop goes on, "As they (the Jews)
were commanded this, so it is obvious how much the constitution of
their law was adapted to effect it, and keep religion ever in view."
Upon which the *Inquirer* remarks, "It was then very ill, or at least
very unwisely done, to abrogate that law, whose constitution was
adapted to so excellent a purpose." Let us first see what may be
offered in defence of the Bishop, and then consider what is to be
said in answer to his opponent. The purpose for which the Mosaic
constitution was established was this: to preserve, amidst a world
universally addicted to polytheism and idolatry, the great doctrine
of the Unity of the Divine Nature, *till the seed should come to whom
the promise was made.* As a means to this end, the Israelites were
not only to be kept separate from every other nation ; but the better to insure such separation, they were to be constantly employed
in a multifarious ritual, which left them neither time nor opportunity
for deviating into the superstitious observances of their Pagan neighbours. And this, I suppose, may suffice for vindicating the Bishop's
assertion, that "the constitution of the Jewish law was adapted
to keep religion ever in view." But the Jewish law was not only
adapted to this end ; we are next to observe, that the end itself was
actually gained. For though it be too notorious to be denied, that
the Jews did not always confine their religious homage to the God of
Israel, but polluted the service, due to him alone, with foreign worship ; yet, even in their worst defection, it should be remembered,
they never totally rejected the true Jehovah ; and after their return
from captivity, they were so thoroughly cured of all remaining pro-
pensity to the idolatrous rites of heathenism, as never again to violate
their allegiance to the God of their fathers. It appears then, that in
consequence of the Jewish separation, the principle of the Unity was
in fact preserved inviolate among that people till the coming of Christ.
When the Mosaic constitution had thus attained its end, and mankind
were now prepared for the reception of a *better covenant*, the law ex-
pired of course ; the partition wall that had divided the Jew from the
Gentile was taken down, and all distinction between them lost, under
the common name of Christians. And this may suffice to show, in
opposition to our *Inquirer*, that it was both very *well* and very *wisely*
done to abrogate a law, when the purpose for which the law had been
enacted was accomplished.

sort of men ; and the worst will go on quietly in an abandoned
course, with fewer interruptions from within than they would
have were religious reflections forced oftener upon their
minds,* and consequently with less probability of their amendment.   Indeed, in most ages of the church, the care of reasonable men has been, as there has been for the most part occasion,
to draw the people off from laying too great weight upon external things, upon formal acts of piety.   But the state of matters
is quite changed now with us.   These things are neglected
to a degree, which is, and cannot but be attended with, a decay
of all that is good.   It is highly seasonable now to instruct
the people in the importance of external religion.†

And doubtless under this head must come into consideration, a proper regard to the structures which are conse-

* Were religious reflections *forced* oftener upon their minds.]—
"According to the Bishop's doctrine, then," says the *Inquirer*, "it
should be not only good policy, but wholesome discipline, to *force*
men in *England* to come to church, and in *France* to go to mass."
And again, "If externals have this virtue to *enforce* religious reflections, it must be right to *compel* those who are indisposed to such reflections, to attend these memorials."   Yes ; granting that the sense
of the passage in the Charge is not shamefully perverted, and that we
are to understand the Bishop here to speak of *external* force and com-
pulsion.   Whereas by "religious reflections *forced*," is plainly meant
no more than religious reflections oftener *thrown in men's way, brought*
more frequently *into their thoughts*, so as to produce an habitual recollection that they are always in the Divine presence.

† To instruct the people in the importance of external religion.]—
"The importance of external religion," the *Inquirer* remarks, "is the
grand engine of the Papists, which they play with the greatest effect
upon our common people, who are always soonest taken and ensnared
by *form* and *show ;* and, so far as we concur with them in the principle, we are doing their work ; since, if externals, as such, are important, the plain natural consequence is, *the more of them the better.*"
He had the same reflections once before : " If true religion cannot be
preserved among them without *forms*, the consequence must be, that
the *Romish* religion, having—*more frequent* occurrences of forms,
is better than other religions, which have *fewer* of these—occurrences."   To this argument I reply, *Nego consequentiam.*   There may
be too much of form in religion, as well as too little ; the one leads to
enthusiasm, the other degenerates into superstition ; one is puritanism,
the other popery ; whereas, the rational worship of God is equally
removed from either extreme.   Did the *Inquirer* never hear of the
possibility of having too much of a good thing ?   Or does he suppose,
with the late historian of Great Britain, that all religion is divided
into two species, the superstitious and the fanatical ; and that whatever is not one of these, must of necessity be the other ?

crated to the service of God. In the present turn of the age, one may observe a wonderful frugality in every thing which has respect to religion, and extravagance in every thing else. But amidst the appearances of opulence and improvement in all common things, which are now seen in most places, it would be hard to find a reason why these monuments of ancient piety should not be preserved in their original beauty and magnificence. But in the least opulent places they must be preserved in becoming repair; and every thing relating to the divine service be, however, decent and clean; otherwise we shall vilify the face of religion whilst we keep it up. All this is indeed principally the duty of others. Yours is to press strongly upon them what is their duty in this respect, and admonish them of it often, if they are negligent.

But then you must be sure to take care and not neglect that part of the sacred fabric which belongs to you to maintain in repair and decency. Such neglect would be great impiety in you, and of most pernicious example to others. Nor could you, with any success, or any propriety, urge upon them their duty in a regard in which you yourselves should be openly neglectful of it.

Bishop Fleetwood has observed,* that "unless the good public spirit of building, repairing, and adorning churches, prevails a great deal more among us, and be more encouraged, a hundred years will bring to the ground a huge number of our churches." This excellent prelate made this observation forty years ago; and no one, I believe, will imagine, that the good spirit he has recommended prevails more at present than it did then.

But if these appendages of the divine service are to be regarded, doubtless the divine service itself is more to be regarded; and the conscientious attendance upon it ought often to be inculcated upon the people, as a plain precept of the gospel, as the means of grace, and what has peculiar promises annexed to it. But external acts of piety and devotion, and the frequent returns of them, are moreover necessary to keep up a sense of religion, which the affairs of the world will otherwise wear out of men's hearts. And the frequent returns, whether of public devotions, or of any

* Charge to the Clergy of St. Asaph, 1710.

thing else, to introduce religion into men's serious thoughts, will have an influence upon them, in proportion as they are susceptible of religion, and not given over to a reprobate mind.   For this reason, besides others, the service of the church ought to be celebrated as often as you can have a congregation to attend it.

But, since the body of the people, especially in country places, cannot be brought to attend it oftener than one day in a week ; and since this is in no sort enough to keep up in them a due sense of religion ; it were greatly to be wished they could be persuaded to any thing which might, in some measure, supply the want of more frequent public devotions, or serve the like purposes.   Family prayers, regularly kept up in every house, would have a great good effect.

Secret prayer, as expressly as it is commanded by our Saviour, and as evidently as it is implied in the notion of piety, will yet, I fear, be grievously forgotten by the generality, till they can be brought to fix for themselves certain times of the day for it : since this is not done to their hands, as it was in the Jewish church, by custom or authority. Indeed, custom, as well as the manifest propriety of the thing, and examples of good men in Scripture, justify us in insisting, that none omit their prayers, morning or evening, who have not thrown off all regards to piety.   But secret prayer comprehends, not only devotions before men begin and after they have ended the business of the day, but such also as may be performed while they are employed in it, or even in company.   And truly, if besides our more set devotions, morning and evening, all of us would fix upon certain times of the day, so that the return of the hour should remind us to say short prayers, or exercise our thoughts in a way equivalent to this ; perhaps there are few persons in so high and habitual a state of piety, as not to find the benefit of it.   If it took up no more than a minute or two, or even less time than that, it would serve the end I am proposing ; it would be a recollection, that we are in the Divine presence, and contribute to our "being in the fear of the Lord all the day long."

A duty of the like kind, and serving to the same purpose, is the particular acknowledgment of God when we are partaking of his bounty at our meals.   The neglect of this is

*

said to have been scandalous to a proverb in the heathen world ;* but it is without shame laid aside at the tables of the highest and the lowest ranks among us.

And as parents should be admonished, and it should be pressed upon their consciences, to teach their children their prayers and catechism, it being what they are obliged to upon all accounts ; so it is proper to be mentioned here, as a means by which they will bring the principles of Christianity often to their own minds, instead of laying aside all thoughts of it from week's-end to week's-end.

General exhortations to piety, abstracted from the particular circumstances of it, are of great use to such as are already got into a religious course of life, but such as are not, though they be touched with them, yet when they go away from church, they scarce know where to begin, or how to set about what they are exhorted to. And it is with respect to religion, as in the common affairs of life, in which many things of great consequence intended, are yet never done at all, because they may be done at any time, and in any manner ; which would not be, were some determinate time and manner voluntarily fixed upon for the doing of them. Particular rules and directions then, concerning the times and circumstances of performing acknowledged duties, bring religion nearer to practice ; and such as are really proper, and cannot well be mistaken, and are easily observed,—such particular rules in religion, prudently recommended, would have an influence upon the people.

All this, indeed, may be called *form ;* as every thing external in religion may be merely so. And, therefore, whilst we endeavour in these, and other like instances, to keep up the *form* of godliness† amongst those who are our care, and over whom we have any influence, we must endeavour also that this form be made more and more subservient to promote the power of it.‡ Admonish them to take heed that they mean what they say in their prayers, that their thoughts and intentions go along with their words, that they really in their hearts exert and exercise before God the

* Cudworth on the Lord's Supper, p. 8.   Casaub. in Athenæum, l. i. c. xi. p. 22.   Duport. Præl. in Theophrastum Ed. Needham, c. ix. p. 335, &c.
    † 2 Tim. iii. 5.   ‡ Ibid.

affections they express with their mouth. Teach them, not that external religion is nothing, for this is not true in any sense; it being scarce possible, but that it will lay some sort of restraint upon a man's morals: and it is moreover of good effect with respect to the world about him. But teach them, that regard to one duty will in no sort atone for the neglect of any other. Endeavour to raise in their hearts such a sense of God as shall be an habitual, ready principle of reverence, love, gratitude, hope, trust, resignation, and obedience. Exhort them to make use of every circumstance which brings the subject of religion at all before them; to turn their hearts habitually to him; to recollect seriously the thoughts of his presence, "in whom they live, and move, and have their being;" and, by a short act of their mind, devote themselves to his service. If, for instance, persons would accustom themselves to be thus admonished by the very sight of a church, could it be called superstition? Enforce upon them the necessity of making religion their principal concern, as what is the express condition of the Gospel covenant, and what the very nature of the thing requires. Explain to them the terms of that covenant of mercy, founded in the incarnation, sacrifice, intercession of Christ, together with the promised assistance of the Holy Ghost, not to supersede our own endeavours, but to render them effectual. The greater festivals of the church being instituted for commemorating the several parts of the Gospel history, of course lead you to explain these its several doctrines, and show the Christian practice which arises out of them. And the more occasional solemnities of religion, as well as these festivals, will often afford you the fairest opportunities of enforcing all these things in familiar conversation. Indeed, all affectation of talking piously is quite nauseous; and though there be nothing of this, yet men will easily be disgusted at the too great frequency or length of these occasional admonitions. But a word of God and religion dropped sometimes in conversation, gently, and without any thing severe, or forbidding, in the manner of it; this is not unacceptable. It leaves an impression, is repeated again by the hearers, and often remembered by plain well-disposed persons longer than one would think. Particular circumstances, too, which render men more apt to receive instruction, should be laid hold of

to talk seriously to their consciences. For instance, after
a man's recovery from a dangerous sickness, how proper is
it to advise him to recollect and ever bear in mind, what
were his hopes, or fears, his wishes, or resolutions, when
under the apprehension of death ; in order to bring him to
repentance, or confirm him in a course of piety, according
as his life and character has been. So likewise the terrible
accidents which often happen from riot and debauchery,
and indeed almost every vice, are occasions providentially
thrown in your way, to discourse against these vices in common conversation, as well as from the pulpit, upon any such
accidents happening in your parish, or in a neighbouring
one. Occasions and circumstances of the like kind to some
or other of these occur often, and ought, if I may so speak,
to be catched at, as opportunities of conveying instruction,
both public and private, with great force and advantage.

Public instruction is also absolutely necessary, and can in
no sort be dispensed with. But, as it is common to all who
are present, many persons strangely neglect to appropriate
what they hear to themselves, to their own heart and life.
Now, the only remedy for this in our power is a particular
personal application. And a personal application makes a
very different impression from a common general one.
It were, therefore, greatly to be wished that every man
should have the principles of Christianity, and his own particular duty, enforced upon his conscience, in a manner
suited to his capacity in private. And, besides the occasional opportunities of doing this, some of which have been
intimated, there are stated opportunities of doing it. Such,
for instance, is confirmation ; and the usual age for confirmation is that time of life, from which youth must become more and more their own masters, when they are
often leaving their father's house, going out into the wide
world, and all its numerous temptations ; against which
they particularly want to be fortified, by having strong
and lively impressions of religion made upon their minds.
Now, the 61st canon expressly requires, that every minister that hath care of souls shall use his best endeavour
to prepare and make able—as many as he can, to be confirmed ; which cannot be done as it ought, without such
personal application to each candidate in particular as I am
recommending. Another opportunity for doing this is

when any one of your parishioners signifies his name, as intending for the first time to be partaker of the communion. The Rubric requires, that all persons, whenever they intend to receive, shall signify their names beforehand to the minister; which, if it be not insisted upon in all cases, ought absolutely to be insisted upon for the first time. Now, this even lays it in your way to discourse with them in private upon the nature and benefits of this sacrament, and enforce upon them the importance and necessity of religion. However, I do not mean to put this upon the same footing with catechising youth, and preparing them for confirmation; these being indispensable obligations, and expressly commanded by our canons. This private intercourse with your parishioners, preparatory to their first communion, let it, if you please, be considered as a voluntary service to religion on your part, and a voluntary instance of docility on theirs. I will only add, as to this practice, that it is regularly kept up by some persons, and particularly by one, whose exemplary behaviour in every part of the pastoral office is enforced upon you by his station of authority and influence in (this part* especially of) the diocese.

I am very sensible, my brethren, that some of these things, in places where they are greatly wanted, are impracticable, from the largeness of parishes, suppose. And where there is no impediment of this sort, yet the performance of them will depend upon others, as well as upon you. People cannot be admonished or instructed in private, unless they will permit it. And little will you be able to do in forming the minds of children to a sense of religion, if their parents will not assist you in it; and yet much less, if they will frustrate your endeavours by their bad example, and giving encouragement to their children to be dissolute. The like is to be said also of your influence in reforming the common people in general, in proportion as their superiors act in like manner to such parents; and whilst they, the lower people, I mean, must have such numerous temptations to drunkenness and riot every where placed in their way. And it is cruel usage we often meet with, in being censured for not doing what we cannot do,

* The Archdeaconry of Northumberland.

without what we cannot have, the concurrence of our cen-
surers.   Doubtless, very much reproach which now lights
upon the clergy, will be found to fall elsewhere, if due allowances were made for things of this kind.   But then, we,
my brethren, must take care and not make more than due
allowances for them.   If others deal uncharitably with us,
we must deal impartially with ourselves, as in a matter of
conscience, in determining what good is in our power to
do; and not let indolence keep us from setting about what
really is in our power; nor any heat of temper create
obstacles in the prosecution of it, or render insuperable
such as we find, when perhaps gentleness and patience
would prevent, or overcome them.

Indeed, all this diligence to which I have been exhorting
you and myself, for God forbid I should not consider myself as included in all the general admonitions you receive
from me; all this diligence in these things does indeed suppose, that we *give ourselves wholly to them.*   It supposes,
not only that we have a real sense of religion upon our own
minds, but also that to promote the practice of it in others
is habitually uppermost in our thought and intention, as the
business of our lives.   And this, my brethren, is the business of our lives, in every sense and upon every account.
It is the general business of all Christians as they have opportunity; it is our particular business.   It is so, as we
have devoted ourselves to it by the most solemn engagements; as, according to our Lord's appointment, we "live
of the Gospel;"* and as the preservation and advancement
of religion, in such and such districts, are, in some respects,
our appropriated trust.

By being faithful in the discharge of this our trust,
by thus "taking heed to the ministry we have received
in the Lord, that we fulfil it,"† we shall do our part toward
reviving a practical sense of religion amongst the people
committed to our care.   And this will be the securest bar-
rier against the efforts of infidelity; a great source of which
plainly is, the endeavour to get rid of religious restraints.
But whatever be our success with regard to others, we
shall have the approbation of our consciences, and may rest
assured, that as to ourselves at least, "our labour is not in
vain in the Lord."‡

---

* 1 Cor. ix. 14.   † Col. iv. 17.   ‡ 1 Cor. xv. 58.

CORRESPONDENCE

DR. BUTLER AND DR. CLARKE.

THE FIRST LETTER.*

REVEREND SIR,

I SUPPOSE you will wonder at the present trouble, from one who is a perfect stranger to you, though you are not so to him ; but I hope the occasion will excuse my boldness. I have made it, sir, my business, ever since I thought myself capable of such sort of reasoning, to prove to myself the being and attributes of God. And being sensible that it is a matter of the last consequence, I endeavoured after a demonstrative proof ; not only more fully to satisfy my own mind, but also in order to defend the great truths of natural religion, and those of the Christian revelation which follow from them, against all opposers ; but must own, with concern, that hitherto I have been unsuccessful ; and though I have got very probable arguments, yet I can go but a very little way with demonstration in the proof of those things. When first your book on those subjects (which by all, whom I have discoursed with, is so justly esteemed) was recommended to me, I was in great hopes

---

* The following correspondence may, with the utmost propriety, be introduced into this edition of Dr. Butler's works, as the letters to Clarke were written by Butler, then a student at a dissenting academy in *Tewkesbury*. Though not generally known, Butler was the person who signed himself, *A Gentleman in Gloucestershire.*

of having all my inquiries answered. But since in some
places, either through my not understanding your meaning,
or what else I know not, even that has failed me; I almost
despair of ever arriving to such a satisfaction as I aim at,
unless by the method I now use. You cannot but know,
sir, that of two different expressions of the same thing,
though equally clear to some persons, yet to others, one of
them sometimes is very obscure, though the other be perfectly intelligible. Perhaps this may be my case here; and
could I see those of your arguments of which I doubt, differently proposed, possibly I might yield a ready assent to
them. This, sir, I cannot but think a sufficient excuse for
the present trouble; it being such an one as I hope may
prevail for an answer, with one who seems to aim at nothing
more than that good work of instructing others.

In your demonstration of the being and attributes of
God, Prop. VI.* [Edit. 2d. p. 69, and 70.] you propose to
prove the infinity or omnipresence of the self-existing Being.
The former part of the proof seems highly probable;
but the latter part, which seems to aim at demonstration, is
not to me convincing. The latter part of the paragraph is,
if I mistake not, an entire argument of itself, which runs
thus: "To suppose a finite being to be self-existing, is to
say, that it is a contradiction for that being not to exist, the
absence of which may yet be conceived without a contradiction; which is the greatest absurdity in the world." The
sense of these words, "the absence of which," seems plainly
to be determined by the following sentence, to mean its
absence from any particular place. Which sentence is to
prove it to be an absurdity; and is this: "For if a being
can, without a contradiction, be absent from one place, it
may, without a contradiction, be absent from another place,
and from all places." Now, supposing this, to be a consequence, all that it proves is, that if a being can, without a
contradiction, be absent from one place at one time, it may,
without a contradiction, be absent from another place, and
so from all places, at different times. (For I cannot see
that if a being can be absent from one place at one time,
therefore it may, without a contradiction, be absent from

* Page 45. edit. 4th; p. 41. edit. 6th; p. 43. edit. 7th; p. 44.
edit. 8th.

all places at the same time, *i. e.* may cease to exist.) Now if it proves no more than this, I cannot see that it reduces the supposition to any absurdity. Suppose I could demonstrate, that any particular man should live a thousand years; this man might, without a contradiction, be absent from one, and from all places, at different times; but it would not from thence follow, that he might be absent from all places at the same time, *i. e.* that he might cease to exist. No; this would be a contradiction, because I am supposed to have demonstrated that he should live a thousand years. It would be exactly the same, if, instead of a thousand years, I should say, for ever; and the proof seems the same, whether it be applied to a self-existent or a dependent being.

What else I have to offer is in relation to your proof that the self-existent Being must of necessity be but one. Which proof is as follows, in Prop. VII.* [Edit. 2d. p. 74.] "To suppose two or more different natures existing of themselves, necessarily and independent from each other, implies this plain contradiction; that each of them being independent from the other, they may either of them be supposed to exist alone; so that it will be no contradiction to imagine the other not to exist, and consequently, neither of them will be necessarily existing." The supposition indeed implies, that since each of these beings is independent from the other, they may either of them exist alone, *i. e.* without any relation to, or dependence on, the other; but where is the third idea, to connect this proposition and the following one, viz. so that it will be no contradiction to imagine the other not to exist? Were this a consequence of the former proposition, I allow it would be demonstration, by the first corollary of Prop. III.† [2d Edit. p. 26.] But since these two propositions [they may either of them be supposed to exist alone], and [so that it will be no contradiction to imagine the other not to exist], are very widely different; since likewise it is no immediate consequence, that because either may be supposed to exist independent from

* Page 48. edit. 4th; p. 44. edit. 6th; p. 46. edit. 7th; p. 47. edit. 8th.

† Page 16, 17. Edits. 4th, 6th, 7th, and 8th.

the other, therefore the other may be supposed not to exist
at all; how is what was proposed, proved? That the propositions are different, I think is plain; and whether there
be an immediate connexion, every body that reads your
book must judge for themselves. I must say, for my own
part, the absurdity does not appear at first sight any more
than the absurdity of saying, that the angles below the base
in the isosceles triangle are unequal; which, though it is
absolutely false, yet I suppose no one will lay down the
contrary for an axiom; because, though it is true, yet there
is need of a proof to make it appear so.

Perhaps it may be answered, that I have not rightly explained the words, to exist alone; and that they do not
mean only, to exist independent from the other; but that,
existing alone, means that nothing exists with it. Whether
this or the other was meant, I cannot determine; but,
whichever it was, what I have said will hold. For if this
last be the sense of those words, [They either of them may
be supposed to exist alone,] it indeed implies that it will
be no contradiction to suppose the other not to exist; but
then I ask, how come these two propositions to be connected;
that, to suppose two different natures existing of themselves
necessarily and independent from each other, implies that
each of them may be supposed to exist alone in this sense?
Which is exactly the same as I said before, only applied to
different sentences. So that, if existing alone be understood
as I first took it, I allow it is implied in the supposition;
but cannot see that the consequence is, that it will be no
contradiction to suppose the other not to exist. But if the
words, existing alone, are meant in the latter sense, I grant,
that if either of them may be supposed thus to exist alone,
it will be no contradiction to suppose the other not to exist:
but then I cannot see, that to suppose two different natures
existing, of themselves, necessarily and independent from
each other, implies that either of them may be supposed to
exist alone in this sense of the words; but only, that either
of them may be supposed to exist without having any relation to the other, and that there will be no need of the
existence of the one in order to the existence of the other.
But though upon this account, were there no other principle of its existence, it might cease to exist; yet on the

account of the necessity of its own nature, which is quite distinct from the other, it is an absolute absurdity to suppose it not to exist.

Thus, sir, I have proposed my doubts, with the reasons of them: in which, if I have wrested your words to another sense than you designed them, or in any respect argued unfairly, I assure you it was without design. So I hope you will impute it to mistake. And, if it will not be too great a trouble, let me once more beg the favour of a line from you, by which you will lay me under a particular obligation to be, what, with the rest of the world, I now am,

Reverend SIR,

Your most obliged Servant, &c.

November 4th, 1713.

THE ANSWER TO THE FIRST LETTER.

SIR,

DID men, who publish controversial papers, accustom themselves to write with that candour and ingenuity with which you propose your difficulties, I am persuaded almost all disputes might be very amicably terminated, either by men's coming at last to agree in opinion, or, at least, finding reason to suffer each other friendly to differ.

Your two objections are very ingenious, and urged with great strength and acuteness. Yet I am not without hopes of being able to give you satisfaction in both of them. To your first, therefore, I answer: whatever may, without a contradiction, be absent from any one place at any one time; may, also, without a contradiction, be absent from all places at all times. For, whatever is absolutely necessary at all, is absolutely necessary in every part of space, and in every point of duration. Whatever can at any time be conceived possible to be absent from any one part of space, may for the same reason, [viz. the implying no contradiction in the nature of things,] be conceived possible to be absent from every other part of space at the same time; either by ceasing to be, or by supposing it never to have begun to be. Your instance about demonstrating a man to live 1000 years, is what (I think) led you into the mistake; and is a good instance to lead you out of it again. You may suppose a man shall live 1000 years, or God may reveal and promise he shall live 1000 years; and upon that supposition, it shall not be possible for the man to be absent from all places in any part of that time. Very true: but why shall it not be possible? Only because it is contrary to the supposition, or to the promise of God; but not contrary to the absolute nature of things; which would be the case, if the man existed necessarily, as every part of space does. In supposing you could demonstrate, a man should live 1000 years, or one year; you make an impossible and contradictory supposition. For though you may know certainly, (by revelation suppose,) that he will live so long; yet this is only the certainty of a thing true in fact, not in itself necessary: and demonstration is applicable to nothing but what is necessary in itself, necessary in all places and at all times equally.

To your second difficulty, I answer: what exists necessarily, not only must so exist alone, as to be independent of any thing else; but, (being self-sufficient,) may also so exist alone, as that every thing else may possibly (or without any contradiction in the nature of things) be supposed not to exist at all: and consequently, (since that which may possibly be supposed not to exist at all, is not necessarily existent,) no other thing can be necessarily existent. Whatever is necessarily existing, there is need of its existence in order to the supposal of the existence of any other thing; so that nothing can possibly be supposed to exist, without presupposing and including antecedently the existence of that which is necessary. For instance: the supposal of the existence of any thing whatever, includes necessarily a presupposition of the existence of space and time; and if any thing could exist without space or time, it would follow that space and time were not necessarily existing. Therefore, the supposing anything possibly to exist alone, so as not necessarily to include the presupposal of some other thing, proves demonstrably, that that other thing is not necessarily existing; because, whatever has necessity of existence, cannot possibly in any conception whatsoever, be supposed away. There cannot possibly be any notion of the existence of any thing, there cannot possibly be any notion of existence at all, but what shall necessarily pre-include the notion of that which has necessary existence. And, consequently, the two propositions which you judged independent, are really necessarily connected, These sorts of things are indeed very difficult to express, and not easy to be conceived but by very attentive minds : but to such as can and will attend, nothing (I think) is more demonstrably convictive.

If any thing still sticks with you in this, or any other part of my books, I shall be very willing to be informed of it : who am,

SIR,

Your assured Friend and Servant,

S. C.

November 10, 1713.

P. S.—Many readers, I observe, have misunderstood my second general proposition ; as if the words [some one unchangeable and independent Being,] meant [one only—Being.] Whereas the true meaning, and all that the argument there requires, is, [some one at least.] That there can be but one, is the thing proved afterwards in the seventh proposition.

THE SECOND LETTER.

REVEREND SIR,

I HAVE often thought that the chief occasions of men's differing so much in their opinions, were, either their not understanding each other, or else, that instead of ingenuously searching after truth, they have made it their business to find out arguments for the proof of what they have once asserted. However, it is certain there may be other reasons for persons not agreeing in their opinions : and where it is so, I cannot but think with you, that they will find reason to suffer each other to differ friendly; every man having a way of thinking, in some respects, peculiarly his own.

I am sorry I must tell you, your answers to my objections are not satisfactory. The reasons why I think them not so, are as follows :—

You say, " Whatever is absolutely necessary at all, is absolutely necessary in every part of space, and in every point of duration." Were this evident, it would certainly prove what you bring it for; viz. " that whatever may, without a contradiction, be absent from one place at one time, may also be absent from all places at all times." But I do not conceive, that the idea of ubiquity is contained in the idea of self-existence, or directly follows from it; any otherwise than as, whatever exists, must exist somewhere. You add, " Whatever can at any time be conceived possibly to be absent from any one part of space, may for the same reason [viz. the implying no contradiction in the nature of things,] be conceived possibly to be absent from every other part of space, at the same time." Now I cannot see, that I can make these two suppositions for the same reason, or upon the same account. The reason why I conceive this being may be absent from one place, is because it doth not contradict the former proof, [drawn from the nature of things,] in which I proved only that it must necessarily exist. But the other supposition, viz. that I can conceive it possible to be absent from every part of space at one and the same time, directly contradicts the proof that it must exist somewhere; and so is an express contradiction. Unless it be said, that as, when we have proved the three angles of a triangle equal to two right ones, that relation of the quality of its angles to two right ones, will be wherever a triangle exists; so, when we have proved the necessary existence of a being, this being must exist every where. But there is a great difference between these two things: the one being the proof of a certain relation, upon supposition of such a being's existence with such particular properties; and consequently, wherever this being and these properties exist, this relation must exist too. But from the proof of the necessary existence of a being, it is no evident consequence that it exists every where. My using the word demonstration, instead of proof, which leaves no room for doubt, was through negligence, for I never heard of strict demonstration of matter of fact.

In your answer to my second difficulty, you say; "Whatsoever is necessarily existing, there is need of its existence, in order to the supposal of the existence of any other thing." All the consequences you draw from this proposition, I see proved demonstrably; and consequently, that the two propositions I thought independent, are closely connected. But how, or upon what account, is there need of the existence of whatever is necessarily existing, in order to the existence of any other thing? Is it as there is need of space and duration, in order to the existence of any thing; or is it needful only as the cause of the existence of all other things? If the former be said, as your instance seems to intimate, I answer, Space and duration are very abstruse in their natures, and, I think, cannot properly be called things, but are considered rather as affections which belong, and in the order of our thoughts are antecedently necessary, to the existence of all things. And I can no more conceive how a necessarily existing being can, on the same account or in the same manner as space and duration are, be needful in order to the existence of any other being, than I can conceive extension attributed to a thought: that idea no more belonging to a thing existing, than extension belongs to thought, but if the latter be said, that there is need of the existence of whatever is a necessary being, in order to the existence of any other thing; only as this necessary being must be the cause of the existence of all other things: I think this is plainly begging the question; for it supposes that there is no other being exists, but what is casual, and so not necessary. And on what other account, or in what other manner than one of these two, there can be need of ths existence of a necessary being in order to the existence of any thing else, I cannot conceive.

Thus, sir, you see I entirely agree with you in all the consequences you have drawn from your suppositions, but cannot see the truth of the suppositions themselves.

I have aimed at nothing in my style but only to be intelligible: being sensible that it is very difficult (as you observe) to express one's self on these sorts of subjects, especially for one who is altogether unaccustomed to write upon them.

o

I have nothing at present more to add, but my sincerest thanks for your trouble in answering my letter, and for your professed readiness to be acquainted with any other difficulty that I may meet with in any of your writings. I am willing to interpret this, as somewhat like a promise of an answer to what I have now written, if there be any thing in it which deserves one. I am,

Reverend Sir,

Your most obliged humble Servant.

November 23, 1713.

THE ANSWER TO THE SECOND LETTER.

Sir,

It seems to me, that the reason why you do not apprehend ubiquity to be necessarily connected with self-existence, is because, in the order of your ideas, you first conceive a being, (a finite being, suppose,) and then conceive self-existence to be a property of that being; as the angles are properties of a triangle, when a triangle exists: whereas, on the contrary, necessity of existence, not being a property consequent upon the supposition of the things existing, but antecedently the cause or ground of that existence, it is evident this necessity, being not limited to any antecedent subject, as angles are to a triangle, but being itself original, absolute and (in order of nature) antecedent to all existence, cannot but be every where, for the same reason that it is any where. By applying this reasoning to the instance of space, you will find, that by consequence it belongs truly to that substance, whereof space is a property,* as duration also is. What you say about a necessary being existing somewhere, supposes it to be finite; and being finite, supposes some cause which determined that such a certain quantity of that being should exist, neither more or less; and that cause must either be a voluntary cause; or else such a necessary cause, the quantity of whose power must

* Or, mode of existence.

be determined and limited by some other cause. But in original absolute necessity, antecedent (in order of nature) to the existence of any thing, nothing of all this can have place; but the necessity is necessarily every where alike.

Concerning the second difficulty, I answer, That which exists necessarily, is needful to the existence of any other thing; not considered now as a cause, (for that indeed is begging the question,) but as a *sine qua non*; in the sense as space is necessary to every thing, and nothing can possibly be conceived to exist, without thereby presupposing space: which, therefore, I apprehend to be a property or mode of the self-existent substance; and that, by being evidently necessary itself it proves that the substance, of which it is a mode, must also be necessary: necessary both in itself, and needful to the existence of any thing else whatsoever. Extension, indeed, does not belong to thought, because thought is not a being; but there is need of extension to the existence of every being, to a being which has or has not thought, or any other quality whatsoever.

I am, Sir,

Your real Friend and Servant.

London, November 28, 1713.

THE THIRD LETTER.

Reverend Sir,

I DON'T very well understand your meaning when you say that you think, in the order of my ideas, I first conceive a being (finite suppose) to exist, and then conceive self-existence to be a property of that being. If you mean, that I first suppose a finite being to exist I know not why; affirming necessity of existence to be only a consequent of its existence; and that, when I have supposed it finite, I very safely conclude it is not infinite; I am utterly at a loss, upon what expressions in my letter this conjecture can be founded. But if you mean, that I first of all prove a being to exist from eternity, and then, from the reasons of things, prove that such a being must be eternally necessary; I freely own it.   Neither do I conceive it to be irregular or absurd; for there is a great difference between the order in which things exist, and the order in which I prove to myself that they exist.   Neither do I think my saying a necessary being exists somewhere, supposes it to be finite; it only supposes that this being exists in space, without determining whether here, or there, or every where.

To my second objection, you say, That which exists necessarily, is needful to the existence of any other thing, as a *sine qua non*; in the sense space is necessary to every thing: which is proved (you say) by this consideration, that space is a property of the self-existent substance; and being both necessary in itself, and needful to the existence of every thing else; consequently the substance, of which it is a property, must be so too.   Space, I own, is in one sense a property of the self-existent substance; but, in the same sense, it is also a property of all other substances. The only difference is in respect to the quantity.   And since every part of space, as well as the whole, is necessary; every substance consequently must be self-existent, because it hath this self-existent property; which, since you will not admit for true, if it directly follows from your arguments, they cannot be conclusive.

What you say under the first head, proves (I think) to a very great probability, though not to me with the evidence of demonstration; but your arguments under the second, I am not able to see the force of.

I am so far from being pleased that I can form objections to your arguments, that, besides the satisfaction it would have given me in my own mind, I should have thought it an honour to have entered into your reasonings, and seen the force of them.   I cannot desire to trespass any more upon your better employed time: so shall only add my hearty thanks for your trouble on my account, and that I am, with the greatest respect,

Reverend Sir,
Your most obliged humble Servant.

December 5, 1713.

THE ANSWER TO THE THIRD LETTER.

SIR,

THOUGH, when I turn my thoughts every way, I fully persuade myself there is no defect in the argument itself; yet in my manner of expression I am satisfied there must be some want of clearness, when there remains any difficulty to a person of your abilities and sagacity. I did not mean that your saying a necessary Being exists somewhere, does necessarily suppose it to be finite ; but that the manner of expression is apt to excite in the mind an idea of a finite being, at the same time that you are thinking of a necessary Being, without accurately attending to the nature of that necessity by which it exists. Necessity absolute, and antecedent (in order of nature) to the existence of any subject, has nothing to limit it ; but, if it operates at all, (as it must needs do,) it must operate (if I may so speak) every where and at all times alike. Determination of a particular quantity, or particular time or place of existence of any thing, cannot arise but from somewhat external to the thing itself. For example : why there should exist just such a small determinate quantity of matter, neither more or less, interspersed in the immense vacuities of space, no reason can be given. Nor can there be any thing in nature, which could have determined a thing so indifferent in itself, as is the measure of that quantity, but only the will of an intelligent and free agent. To suppose matter or any other substance necessarily existing in a finite determinate quantity ; in an inch-cube, for instance, or in any certain number of cube-inches, and no more, is exactly the same absurdity, as supposing it to exist necessarily, and yet for a finite duration only ; which every one sees to be a plain contradiction. The argument is likewise the same in the question about the original of motion. Motion cannot be necessarily existing ; because, it being evident that all determinations of motion are equally possible in themselves, the original determination of the motion of any particular body this way rather than the contrary way, could not be necessary in itself, but was either caused by the will of an intelligent and free agent, or else was an effect produced and determined without any cause at all, which is an express contradiction; as I have shown in my demonstration of the being and attributes of God, p. 14 [Edit. 4th and 5th;] p. 12 [Edit. 6th, 7th, and 8th.]

To the second head of argument I answer,—space is a property [or mode] of the self-existent substance, but not of any other substances. All other substances are in space, and are penetrated by it; but the self-existent substance is not in space, nor penetrated by it, but is itself (if I may so speak) the substratum of space, the ground of the existence of space and duration itself. Which [space and duration] being evidently necessary, and yet themselves not substances, but properties or modes, show evidently that the substance, without which these modes could not subsist, is itself much more (if that were possible) necessary. And as space and duration are needful (i. e. *sine qua non*) to the existence of every thing else; so, consequently, is the substance, to which these modes belong in that peculiar manner which I before mentioned.

I am, Sir,

Your affectionate Friend and Servant.

December 10, 1713.

THE FOURTH LETTER.

Reverend Sir,

WHATEVER is the occasion of my not seeing the force of your reasonings, I cannot impute it to (what you do) the want of clearness in your expression. I am too well acquainted with myself, to think my not understanding an argument a sufficient reason to conclude that it is either improperly expressed, or not conclusive; unless I can clearly show the defect of it. It is with the greatest satisfaction I must tell you, that the more I reflect on your first argument, the more I am convinced of the truth of it; and it now seems to me altogether unreasonable to suppose absolute necessity can have any relation to one part of space more than another; and if so, an absolutely necessary Being must exist every where.

I wish I was as well satisfied in respect to the other. You say,—All substances, except the self-existent one, are in space, and are penetrated by it. All substances, doubtless, whether body or spirit, exist in space: but when I say that a spirit exists in space, were I put upon telling my meaning, I know not how I could do it any other way than by saying, such a particular quantity of space terminates the capacity of acting in finite spirits at one and the same time, so that they cannot act beyond that determined quantity. Not but that I think there is somewhat in the manner of existence of spirits in respect of space, that more directly answers to the manner of the existence of body; but what that is, or of the manner of their existence, I cannot possibly form an idea. And it seems (if possible) much more difficult to determine what relation the self-existent Being hath to space. To say he exists in space, after the same manner that other substances do, (somewhat like which I too rashly asserted in my last,) perhaps would be placing the Creator too much on a level with the creature; or however, it is not plainly and evidently true: and to say the self-existent substance is the substratum of space, in the common sense of the word, is scarce intelligible, or at least is not evident. Now, though there may be a hundred relations distinct from either of these, yet how should we come by ideas of them, I cannot conceive. We may indeed have ideas to the words, and not altogether depart from the common sense of them, when we say the self-existent substance is the substratum of space, or the ground of its existence: but I see no reason to think it true; because space seems to me to be as absolutely self-existent, as it is possible anything can be: so that, make what other supposition you please, yet we cannot help supposing immense space; because there must be either an infinity of being, or (if you will allow the expression) an infinite vacuity of being. Perhaps it may be objected to this, that though space is really necessary, yet the reason of its being necessary, is its being a property of the self-existent substance; and that it being so evidently necessary, and its dependence on the self-existent substance not so evident, we are ready to conclude it absolutely self-existent, as well as necessary; and

that this is the reason why the idea of space forces itself
on our minds, antecedent to, and exclusive of (as to the
ground of its existence) all other things. Now this, though
it is really an objection, yet it is no direct answer to what
I have said; because it supposes the only thing to be
proved, viz. that the reason why space is necessary, is its
being a property of a self-existent substance. And supposing
it not to be evident, that space is absolutely self-existent;
yet, while it is doubtful, we cannot argue as though the
contrary were certain, and we were sure that space was only
a property of the self-existent substance. But now, if space
be not absolutely independent, I do not see what we can
conclude is so; for it is manifestly necessary itself, as well
as antecedently needful to the existence of all other things,
not excepting (as I think) even the self-existent substance.

All your consequences I see follow demonstrably from
your supposition; and, were that evident, I believe it would
serve to prove several other things as well as what you
bring it for. Upon which account, I should be extremely
pleased to see it proved by any one. For, as I design the
search after truth as the business of my life, I shall not be
ashamed to learn from any person; though at the same
time I cannot but be sensible, that instruction from some
men, is like the gift of a prince, it reflects an honour on the
person on whom it lays an obligation.

I am, Reverend SIR,

Your obliged Servant,

December 16, 1713.

THE ANSWER TO THE FOURTH LETTER.

SIR,

MY being out of town most part of the month of January,
and some other accidental avocations, hindered me from
answering your letter sooner. The sum of the difficulties
it contains is (I think) this: that it is difficult to determine what relation the self-existent substance has to space:
that to say it is the substratum of space, in the common
sense of the word, is scarce intelligible, or at least is not

evident : that space seems to be as absolutely self-existent, as it is possible any thing can be : and that, its being a property of the self-existent substance, is supposing the thing that was to be proved. This is entering indeed into the very bottom of the matter; and I will endeavour to give you as brief and clear an answer as I can.

That the self-existent substance is the substratum of space, or space a property of the self-existent substance, are not perhaps very proper expressions; nor is it easy to find such. But what I mean is this : the idea of space (as also of time or duration) is an abstract or partial idea ; an idea of a certain quality or relation, which we evidently see to be necessarily existing; and yet which (not being itself a substance) at the same time necessarily presupposes a substance, without which it could not exist; which substance consequently must be itself (much more, if possible) necessarily existing. I know not how to explain this so well, as by the following similitude : a blind man, when he tries to frame to himself the idea of body, his idea is nothing but that of hardness. A man that had eyes, but no power of motion, or sense of feeling at all, when he tried to frame to himself the idea of body, his idea would be nothing but that of colour. Now as, in these cases, hardness is not body; and colour is not body; but yet, to the understanding of these persons, those properties necessarily infer the being of a substance, of which substance itself the persons have no idea : so space, to us, is not itself substance, but it necessarily infers the being of a substance, which affects none of our present senses ; and being itself necessary, it follows that the substance, which it infers, is (much more) necessary.

I am, SIR,

Your affectionate Friend and Servant.

January 29, 1714.

THE FIFTH LETTER.

REVEREND SIR,

You have very comprehensively expressed, in six or seven lines, all the difficulties of my letter, which I should have endeavoured to have made shorter, had I not been afraid an

improper impression might possibly occasion a mistake of
my meaning. I am very glad the debate is come into so
narrow a compass; for I think now it entirely turns upon
this, whether our ideas of space and duration are partial, so
as to presuppose the existence of some other thing. Your
similitude of the blind man is very apt to explain your
meaning, (which I think I fully understand,) but does not
seem to come entirely up to the matter. For, what is the
reason that the blind man concludes there must be somewhat external, to give him that idea of hardness? It is
because he supposes it impossible for him to be thus affected,
unless there were some cause of it; which cause, should it
be removed, the effect would immediately cease too; and he
would no more have the idea of hardness, but by remembrance. Now, to apply this to the instance of space and
duration: since a man, from his having these ideas, very
justly concludes that there must be somewhat external,
which is the cause of them; consequently, should this cause
(whatever it is) be taken away, his ideas would be so too:
therefore, if what is supposed to be the cause be removed,
and yet the idea remains, that supposed cause cannot be the
real one. Now, granting the self-existent substance to be
the substratum of these ideas, could we make the supposition of its ceasing to be, yet space and duration would still
remain unaltered: which seems to show that the self-
existent substance is not the substratum of space and duration. Nor would it be an answer to the difficulty, to say,
that every property of the self-existent substance is as
necessary as the substance itself; since that will only hold,
while the substance itself exists: for there is implied in
the idea of a property, an impossibility of subsisting without
its substratum. I grant, the supposition is absurd: but
how otherwise can we know whether any thing be a property of such a substance, but by examining whether it
would cease to be, if its supposed substance should do so?
Notwithstanding what I have now said, I cannot say that I
believe your argument not conclusive; for I must own my
ignorance, that I am really at a loss about the nature of space
and duration. But did it plainly appear that they were
properties of a substance, we should have an easy way with
the atheists: for it would at once prove demonstrably an
eternal necessary self-existent Being; that there is but one

such; and that he is needful in order to the existence of all other things. Which makes me think, that though it may be true, yet it is not obvious to every capacity; otherwise it would have been generally used, as a fundamental argument, to prove the being of God.

I must add one thing more: that your argument for the omnipresence of God seemed always to me very probable. But being very desirous to have it appear demonstratively conclusive, I was sometimes forced to say what was not altogether my opinion. Not that I did this for the sake of disputing (for, besides the particular disagreeableness of this to my own temper, I should surely have chosen another person to have trifled with;) but I did it to set off the objection to advantage, that it might be more fully answered. I heartily wish you as fair treatment from your opponents in print, as I have had from you: though, I must own, I cannot see, in those that I have read, that unprejudiced search after truth, which I would have hoped for.

I am, Reverend Sir,
Your most humble Servant,

February 3, 1714.

THE ANSWER TO THE FIFTH LETTER.

Sir,

In a multitude of business, I mislaid your last letter; and could not answer it, till it came again to my hands by chance. We seem to have pushed the matter in question between us as far as it will go; and upon the whole I cannot but take notice, I have very seldom met with persons so reasonable and unprejudiced as yourself, in such debates as these.

I think all I need say in answer to the reasoning in your letter is, that your granting the absurdity of the supposition you were endeavouring to make, is consequently granting the necessary truth of my argument. If* space and dura-

* Ut partium temporis ordo est immutabilis, sic etiam ordo partium spatii. Moveantur hæc de locis suis, et movebuntur (ut ita dicam) de seipsis.—NEWTON, *Princip. Mathemat. Schol. ad definit.* 8.

tion necessarily remain, even after they are supposed to be
taken away, and be not (as it is plain they are not) themselves substances ; then the* substance on whose existence
they depend, will necessarily remain likewise, even after it
is supposed to be taken away ; which shows that supposition
to be impossible and contradictory.

As to your observation at the end of your letter, that the
argument I have insisted on, if it were obvious to every capacity, should have more frequently been used as a fundamental argument for the proof of the being of God ; the
true cause why it has been seldom urged, is, I think, this :
that the universal prevalency of Cartes's absurd notions
(teaching that matter† is necessarily infinite and necessarily eternal, and ascribing all things to mere mechanic laws
of motion, exclusive of final causes, and of all will, and intelligence, and divine Providence from the government of
the world) hath incredibly blinded the eyes of common
reason, and prevented men from discerning him in whom
they live, and move, and have their being. The like has
happened in some other instances. How universally have
men for many ages believed that eternity is no duration at
all, and infinity no amplitude? Something of the like
kind has happened in the matter of transubstantiation, and
(I think) in the scholastic notion of the Trinity, &c.

I am, SIR,

Your affectionate Friend and Servant.

April 8, 1714.

* Deus non est æternitas vel infinitas, sed æternus et infinitus ;
non est duratio vel spatium, sed durat et adest. Durat semper, et
adest ubique ; et existendo semper et ubique, durationem et spatium, æternitatem et infinitatem, constituit. Cum unaquæque ; spatii
particula, sit semper ; et unumquodque ; durationis indivisibile mo-
mentum, ubique ; certe rerum omnium fabricator ac Dominus, non
erit nunquam nusquam. Omni præsens est, non per virtutem solam,
sed etiam per substantiam ; nam virtus sine substantia subsistere non
potest. In ipso continentur et moventur universa, &c.—NEWTON,
Princip. Mathemat. Schol. general. sub finem.

† Pluto implicare contradictionem, ut mundus (meaning the material world) sit finitus.—CARTES, *Epist.* 69. *Partis Primæ.*

THE END.

W. Tyler, Printer, Bolt Court, London.

Printed in the United States
113276LV00003B/7/A